The Magic Kingdom

BOOKS BY STEVEN WATTS

The Republic Reborn:
War and the Making of Liberal America, 1790–1820

The Romance of Real Life:
Charles Brockden Brown and the Origins of American Culture

The Magic Kingdom:
Walt Disney and the American Way of Life

The
Magic Kingdom

Walt Disney and the
American Way of Life

Steven Watts

HOUGHTON MIFFLIN COMPANY | BOSTON | NEW YORK
1997

For the Croatian Princess

For information about permission to reproduce selections from this book, write to Permissions, Houghton Mifflin Company, 215 Park Avenue South, New York, New York 10003.

Library of Congress Cataloging-in-Publication Data
Watts, Steven, date.
  The Magic Kingdon : Walt Disney and the American way of
life / Steven Watts.
      p.   cm.
  Includes bibliographical references and index.
  ISBN 0-395-83587-9
  1. Disney, Walt, 1901–1966. 2. Animators — United States —
Biography. I. Title.
NC1766.U52D5927   1997
791.43′092 — dc21   97-18301 CIP [B]

Printed in the United States of America

Book design by Lisa Diercks

QUM 10 9 8 7 6 5 4 3 2 1

"We just try to make a good picture. And then the professors come along and tell us what we do."

— Walt Disney, *Time*, 1937

"But how does a human being react to a stimulus? He's lost the sense of play he once had and he inhibits physical expression. He's the victim of a civilization whose ideal is the unbotherable, poker-faced man and the attractive, unruffled woman. Even the gestures get to be calculated. They call it poise. The spontaneity of the animals — you find it in small children, but it's gradually trained out of them."

— Walt Disney, *Saturday Evening Post*, 1954

"Of all the activists of public diversion, Uncle Walt was the one most precisely in the American mainstream — in taste and morality, attitudes and opinions, prides and prejudices. The revealing clue is his familiar (and utterly sincere) statement that he never made a picture he didn't want his family to see. His competitors made pictures they thought, or guessed, the public wanted to see. Disney operated through maximum *identification* with John Doe; the others seek to discover what John Doe is like in order to cater to him."

— John Bright, *The Nation*, 1967

Acknowledgments

WALT DISNEY HAS BEEN a presence in my life for as long as I can remember, and writing about him seems like the most natural thing in the world. My boyhood in the rural Midwest in the 1950s and early 1960s was saturated with his creations and productions. My attendance at a showing of *Pinocchio* with my great-aunt, an elderly schoolteacher who loved the movies, and one of my younger brothers created a vivid memory of Monstro the whale gobbling up bad little boys. My fascination with Davy Crockett inspired my father to make me a modified version of the famous coonskin hat, using a squirrel pelt with the tail hanging down the back, and a crude Kentucky long rifle cut silhouette-style out of a board. For a boy tromping around in the woods, they were good enough. On many late afternoons I was ritually mesmerized by *The Mickey Mouse Club,* eagerly ingesting the global documentaries and boisterously laughing at cartoons, obediently internalizing Jimmie Dodd's aphorisms, and ogling Annette Funicello for reasons that were compelling yet still rather mysterious. The first color television show I ever saw, with the entire extended family gathered at my grandparents' house for the proud debut of this miracle machine, was *Walt Disney's Wonderful World of Color.*

Even much later, when cultural revolution had inspired in me a bushy beard, shoulder-length hair, threadbare clothes, radical political sloganeering, and rock-and-roll musicianship, a trip to Disney World produced a state of fascination bordering on euphoria. Rather ironically, the attractions, the atmosphere, and the people in this tightly managed amusement park created a magical, sparkling atmosphere for someone distraught over the bitter social divisions, bourgeois stuffiness, and coldhearted power politics of the early 1970s. When I went to raucous showings of *Fantasia* and *Alice in Wonderland* with large groups of college friends who had been, shall we say, suitably prepared for a fantasy experience, my reaction only intensified. Several years later, professional training as a cultural historian led me to a deeper, soberer consideration of this popular entertainer's influence. Walt Disney's curious status in modern America — beloved popular figure and object of intellectual disdain, manipulator of a massive culture-industry machine and reassuring avuncular presence — seemed to cry out for explanation. These personal and public, emotional and intellectual influences have converged to produce this book.

It would never have been completed without the help of many people. First of all, the staff of the Walt Disney Archives at the Disney Studio in Burbank, California, has earned my heartfelt thanks. This facility is the mother lode of source material for the student of Disney, and over the course of many, many research trips during the last five years, I received valuable help in numerous ways from David R. Smith, Robert Tieman, Becky Cline, Collette Espino, and Adina Lerner. They graciously responded to my endless requests for materials, patiently answered a flood of questions, no matter how naive or uninformed, and provided road maps and directions to a country boy struggling to navigate the Los Angeles freeway system. Dave and Robert also combed through the entire manuscript, correcting factual errors and misspellings and suggesting a variety of revisions and rethinkings. I very much appreciate the entire staff's cooperation and hard work. Even though they "fired" me on numerous occasions for outbursts of orneriness or incompetence, everyone at the Disney Archives has become my valued friend.

Many employees of the Disney Studio, both past and present, kindly granted interviews and shared with me their perceptions of incidents, issues, and personalities in the history of this entertainment enterprise. This group includes the late Bill Cottrell, Marc and Alice Davis, Peter Ellenshaw, John Hench, Ollie Johnston, David Iwerks, Donald Iwerks, Fess Parker, Frank Thomas, and the late Robert Weinstein. Nolie Walsh Fishman talked to me at some length about the personality and career of her ex-husband, Bill Walsh. Van Arsdale France forwarded his memoir of a long career at Disneyland, along with a couple of notes of encouragement. Among the Disney family, Diane Disney Miller conversed with me at some length on several occasions, although we never quite sat down for a formal interview. She also kindly arranged a meeting with her mother, Lillian Disney, with whom I conducted a delightful interview on a pleasant summer afternoon at the Disney home in Holmby Hills. Roy E. Disney spent a couple of hours talking with me about his father, Roy O. Disney, and commenting on a variety of issues involving the studio and the family. Talking at length with these firsthand observers helped me gain a much greater feel for Walt Disney and his studio, and it has added considerable richness to the book.

I am grateful to the historians and scholars who looked over various segments of the manuscript and offered suggestions, criticisms, and encouragement: Jean Agnew, Joyce Appleby, John Bullion, Ken Cmiel, David Cochran, Bob Collins, Noralee Frankel, J. P. Healey, Jackson Lears, George Lipsitz, Robert Newman, David Roediger, Joan Rubin, Cecelia Tichi, Steve Weinberg, and Robert Westbrook. My colleague Jonathan Sperber helped me focus my ideas during many stimulating conversations on the second floor of Read Hall. I owe a special debt to Lary May, an expert on twentieth-century culture and the movies, whose close examination of my argument and evidence produced many shrewd and helpful observations. My old friend and officemate from graduate school, Susan Curtis, also read the entire manuscript with care, articulated a perspective shaped by her own skilled interpretations of American cultural history, and sternly took me to task on a number of points, many of which demanded rethinking and revision. She has my gratitude.

Several specialists in the history of the Disney enterprise gave me invaluable assistance. Paul Anderson, editor of *Persistence of Vision,* a delightful and highly informative journal of Disney history, read the manuscript with a keen eye and forwarded a great deal of valuable commentary. In addition, he provided full access to his considerable collection of written and oral sources on the history of the Disney Studio and helped me track down a number of elusive items. John Canemaker, author of several excellent books on Disney and animation, not only commented expertly on the manuscript but shared research materials and offered encouragement and insights in a number of conversations. J. B. Kaufman and Michael Barrier, also specialists on Disney animation, provided information and research leads early in my work. A Disneyphile supreme, Stan Deneroff, shared his insights on the history of Disney animation and orchestrated many evenings of good conversation and entertainment on my trips west.

At the University of Missouri and in the city of Columbia, a number of colleagues, students, and friends assisted in various ways. The University of Missouri Research Board generously granted support by reducing my teaching load during one semester and tendering travel funds for several trips to the Disney Studio. Richard Bienvenu helped solve computer mysteries on several occasions. Sarah Kidd, Mary Milligan, and Joanie Higham efficiently transcribed taped interviews with Disney staffers. Mary Ann Fitzwilson, Angie Hemphill, and Jenna Higgins helped me with research tasks. Kathleen Wells-Morgan exchanged memories with me of a Disney-tinged childhood. Dan Viets, in addition to showing great enthusiasm for the project, provided valuable research materials on Marceline and Walt Disney's Missouri connection. Frank Fillo solved a sticky technological problem, while John Heyl and Mary Hartigan lent me the use of their fax machine as the project was getting off the ground. My bandmates in Big Muddy offered many opportunities to flee the discipline of the writing desk and sharpen my chops on the

Gibson 335, while old friends and foes at Brewer Fieldhouse helped me sustain the illusion of basketball prowess.

On a more personal note, my mother and father, Kenneth and Mary Watts, hosted many a comfortable stopover in Phoenix as I flew to the West Coast, providing support and good Mexican food. In southern California, my brother and his family — Tim, Christy, Matt, Kelly, Adam, and Samantha Watts — opened their house to me on many weekends and offered companionship, trips to the San Diego Zoo and to see the Los Angeles Lakers, and a chance to watch some of my nephews and nieces grow up.

Ronald Goldfarb, my agent, encouraged this effort from the beginning, negotiated skillfully on two separate occasions, and helped me understand that more than two hundred and fifty academics are allowed to read an author's book. At Houghton Mifflin Company, Liz Duvall skillfully line edited the manuscript, while Steve Fraser deserves some kind of award. He patiently critiqued the manuscript as it dribbled in over deadline, protested only a little when its size simply squashed the original agreement about a word limit, endured my whining and screeching as he released hot air from the prose, and pointed out how to pound a mass of writing into a book. He is the prototype of a talented editor, and I am deeply indebted to him.

Greatest thanks go to my wife, Patti Sokolich Watts, who has endured goodnaturedly the Disney invasion of our household for several years. She has listened to my ideas, offered some of her own, read and commented on the manuscript, and only occasionally looked troubled at the sight of a grown man getting worked up about Donald Duck and Mickey Mouse. Along with our herd of canine, feline, and equine companions, she has made the farm on Creasy Springs Road our own private version of the magic kingdom.

Contents

IV. Disney and the American Century

Illustrations

A patriotic Disney poster from the 1940s *(Copyright © Disney Enterprises, Inc., courtesy of the Disney Archives)*

following page 334:

Walt tinkering with his miniature steam train *(Copyright © Disney Enterprises, Inc., courtesy of the Disney Archives)*

Lillian, Walt, Diane, and Sharon, 1949 *(AP/Wide World Photos)*

An ad for *Cinderella* merchandise, 1950 *(Author's collection)*

Walt and CBS vice president Adrian Murphy, 1951 *(UPI/Corbis-Bettmann)*

Walt holding up a stagecoach at the Burbank studio, 1954 *(UPI/Corbis-Bettmann)*

An aerial view of Disneyland, summer 1955 *(AP/Wide World Photos)*

Walt testifying before the House Un-American Activities Committee in 1947 *(UPI/Corbis-Bettmann)*

An announcement from the Motion Picture Alliance for the Preservation of American Ideals *(Reprinted from Walt Disney's FBI file)*

Fess Parker talking to two young admirers, 1956 *(Fess Parker collection)*

Bill Walsh admiring the view in Paris in 1961 *(Author's collection)*

The shah of Iran and the empress Farah enjoying the Matterhorn ride, 1962 *(UPI/Corbis-Bettmann)*

The December 31, 1962, cover of *Newsweek* *(Copyright © 1962, Newsweek)*

Walt and WED staff members surveying balloons designed for the 1964 World's Fair *(Copyright © Paul Fusco, Look)*

Walt and engineers with the Audio-Animatronic figure of Abraham Lincoln, 1964 *(Copyright © Paul Fusco, Look)*

John Hench beside the WEDway system test track, 1961 *(Roger Broggie collection)*

Walt beside a map of the EPCOT project in Florida, 1966 *(Copyright © Disney Enterprises, Inc., courtesy of the Disney Archives)*

Introduction

A FEW YEARS AGO, I accompanied my wife on an evening's visit to her cousin's house. This young woman met us at the door with her little boy, a cute tyke with a thatch of red hair who was full of curiosity and energy. He was trying to learn to talk, so we sat on the floor playing with him for a while and encouraging his verbal efforts. Right at the cusp of speech, he would look at us determinedly, screw up his face, and totter around, waving his arms as he tried to articulate a hilarious babble of sounds into words. But he couldn't quite manage the feat beyond the two, predictably, he had down cold: "mommy" and "eat." After a time, his mother slipped a video into the VCR as the adults settled back for a little conversation. I kept one eye on him, however. To my astonishment, as a cartoon flashed onto the screen, he said a single word, as clear as a bell: "Disney."

In a nutshell, that little incident frames the subject of this book. How and when did Walt Disney become such a powerful, pervasive presence in our culture that he exists at the level of language itself? What explains this entertainer's enormous popularity and enduring impact on generations of modern Americans, young and old alike? Why has "Disney" become so influential that, not only in this case but in countless others, it is something to be imbibed along with mother's milk?

Answering these questions is no simple matter. Part of the difficulty lies in the sheer scope of the man and his work. Walt Disney has been, arguably, the most influential American of the twentieth century. Beginning in the late 1920s and with accelerating speed over subsequent decades, the multifaceted Disney enterprise flooded the United States and indeed much of the globe with short cartoons, feature-length animations, live-action films, comic books, records, nature documentaries, television shows, colossal theme parks, and consumer merchandise. From Chile to China, California to

Cannes, tens of millions of people who never heard of Franklin D. Roosevelt or William Faulkner or Martin Luther King, Jr., could identify Mickey Mouse or Donald Duck in an instant. Like Coca-Cola and baseball, this leisure empire presided over by an avuncular gentleman with a warm chuckle, a small mustache, and a large imagination became a universal symbol of the United States.

Moreover, Walt Disney himself has become encrusted in myths that diverge sharply. On the one hand, his disciples venerate Saint Walt as a beloved purveyor of innocent imagination, uplifting fantasy, and moral instruction. On the other hand, his denouncers bitterly decry Huckster Walt as an artistic fraud, an imperialist, a cynical manipulator of commercial formulas, and a saccharine sentimentalist. Such divisions have muddied the waters and made detached assessment of his significance extremely difficult. He did little to clarify the situation — he simply denied that his work had any broader meaning.

But this legendary entertainer in fact did much more than he knew. First of all, Walt Disney operated not only as an entertainer but as a historical mediator. His creations helped Americans come to terms with the unsettling transformations of the twentieth century. This role was unintentional but decisive. Disney entertainment projects were consistently nourished by connections to mainstream American culture — its aesthetics, political ideology, social structures, economic framework, moral principles — as it took shape from the late 1920s through the late 1960s. The socioeconomic trauma of the Great Depression, for instance, provided much of the grist for the Disney mill in its first great burst of popularity, in the 1930s. Two decades later, the aspirations and anxieties of the Cold War helped fuel a second great expansion of the studio's work.

Second, Disney's creative work marked a clear arc as it blazed across the American cultural sky in the middle decades of the century. In its early stages, studio productions often carried a charge of social criticism. Although immersed in fantasy and sentimentalism, Disney's animated films often playfully provoked, pricked, and probed the conventional. They stood both inside and outside the cultural mythos of modern America, accepting its essential values while gently satirizing its weaknesses or excesses. Not coincidentally, this critical instinct flourished alongside the daring aesthetics of the "golden age" of the Disney Studio. Over the next twenty years, however, critiques of the social order gradually gave way to a powerful preservationist impulse. By the 1950s, the studio's work lost its edge even as it gained huge new popularity. Moving completely inside the mainsteam culture, Disney now defined American traditions, built a cultural embankment around them, and assumed a defensive position. Yet here too it mirrored mainstream America. A move from criticism to consolidation largely defined the culture of the United States as it encountered the upheaval of economic depression and global warfare before facing the tense confrontations of the postwar era.

These two themes are embedded in the Disney story. In part, the unfolding of Walt's own life, from its humble beginnings in the Midwest through his meteoric rise as an entertainment magnate in southern California, reflected his historical role in modern America. The man, his character, his beliefs and values, his activities, his family ties and friendships, reveal much about the special relationship he maintained with an enormous audience of ordinary Americans. But the man cannot be separated from his enterprise. The achievements of "Disney," we must remember, were not the achievements of one man alone, no matter how brilliant or forceful, but of a complex organization enlisting dozens, eventually thousands, of extremely talented people. Thus we must supplement Walt's own story with that of the evolution of the Disney Studio, its artistic and business endeavors, and the activities of those who played key roles in its development.

We cannot understand the full significance of Disney, moreover, only by looking at the movies he made, the products he developed, and the characters he created. The consumption of these entertainment products — the way they were received, understood, and interpreted by his audience — is equally revealing. This is a tricky business, of course, because the reactions of ordinary moviegoers and amusement-park patrons are not recorded and are nearly impossible to analyze. But we can gain some sense of his reception in reactions to and discussions of Disney in myriad public venues. For decades, a host of film reviewers and art critics, journalists and authors of letters-to-the-editor, politicians and advertisers, advice writers and intellectuals have grappled with the meaning of Disney. Examining their work takes us at least a few steps closer to understanding not only what Disney made but what was made of Disney.

What follows is something of a hybrid genre: part biography and part cultural analysis, an anatomy of Disney's productions as well as an anatomy of their consumption. It suggests that in a host of important ways, Walt Disney played a key role in defining the American way of life in the modern era. His story is in many respects the story of America's mainstream values and their development in the twentieth century. This fascinating tale began in the Midwest in the early 1900s.

Part I

The Road to Hollywood

1

Disney and the Rural Romance

N 1956 WALT DISNEY RETURNED to his past. The creator of Mickey Mouse, *Snow White and the Seven Dwarfs*, television's *Disneyland* show, and a fabulous amusement park, now one of the most famous people in the world, went back to Marceline, Missouri, the tiny town of some 2500 residents where he had lived as a boy. The city fathers had built a park with a swimming pool and named it after their well-known native son. They had invited Disney to the festivities, scarcely believing that he would take time to attend. To their surprise, however, he agreed, and he showed up on July 4 with several members of his family and staff in tow, including his brother Roy, the Disney Studio business manager. The visit was full of reminiscences. Viewing the local landmarks, talking with townspeople, and visiting his parents' old farm, Disney waxed nostalgic about Marceline. "I feel so sorry for people who live in cities all their lives and . . . don't have a little home town," he told a crowd at the park dedication. "I'm glad my dad picked out a little town where he could have a farm, because those years that we spent here have been memorable years."[1]

There was more to this event, however, than met the eye. Disney's celebration of Marceline and the accompanying injunction that everyone should have small-town roots rang true to his character and his sentiments. But it didn't quite ring true to the facts. Walt Disney had not been born in Marceline. In fact, he lived there for only three and a half years, from age four until he was eight. He had not even set foot in Marceline for over forty-five years, spending the vast majority of his life in those same big cities — Chicago, Kansas City, Los Angeles — whose inhabitants he claimed to pity. Disney's memory, in other words, took a back seat to his need for mythmaking. His love for this village was genuine, but like much else about this fascinating and elusive man, it was touched by ambiguity.

I. Between the Country and the City

Marceline was typical of many midwestern towns. Perched among the gently rolling hills of Linn County in north-central Missouri, it lay surrounded by expanses of prairie that gave way to occasional patches of oak, hickory, sycamore, and scrub cedar. Incorporated in 1888 as a creature of the Santa Fe Railroad, it had sprung up along the new line connecting Chicago and Kansas City, as the Santa Fe Land, Town, and Improvement Company first bought up land and then platted and sold lots to create a new terminal point. Within six months the population numbered about 2500, and local real estate speculation ran wild. Typically, Marceline saw an overnight explosion of frame houses accompanied by the more gradual construction of supporting institutions — several saloons, a post office, two banks, a small theater, the office of a local newspaper, and a sprinkling of small retail shops. Hard on their heels came the churches, inevitable in the pious Midwest; seven denominations appeared within two years of the town's founding. By the early twentieth century, however, the boom days had faded. As the population leveled off and economic growth receded, the town settled into a provincial routine that was equal parts stability and simplicity, community and confinement.[2]

Marceline, in other words, did not seem the sort of place to inspire a sense of magic and fantasy. But it did precisely that to Walt Disney. As a matter of fact, this rather unremarkable town held a key to the boundless creativity that fueled the enormous Disney cultural enterprise. The Disney family moved there in 1906, when Walt was four years old. Although they stayed only a few years while his father tried his hand at farming, this period had an impact on the young boy's psyche and values that lingered for a lifetime. As an adult, he often talked about his love of rural life and spun tales about his Marceline days. Such sentiments were not only for public consumption. In late middle age, rich and famous as a Hollywood filmmaker, Disney built a small barn behind his house near Beverly Hills to serve as a workshop. It was an exact replica of the one he remembered from the Marceline farm.[3]

Friends and family also testified to this influence. Disney's wife, Lillian, once discussed Marceline's hold on her husband: "I don't know why Marceline was so important to him. He didn't live there very long . . . But there was something about the farm that was very important to him. He worked hard but he enjoyed the work. He liked the animals and he liked being close to the soil. Work can be relaxing on a farm, even though it's hard. He always said that apples never tasted so good as when they were picked off the trees on the farm." An artist at the Disney Studio once glimpsed the same emotional current in his boss. Residing on a tiny farm outside Los Angeles in the late 1930s, he was happy to receive a visit from Walt and his family one Saturday afternoon. The two Disney girls hugged the baby farm animals, and their world-famous father snapped a couple of photographs before commenting "Boy, I envy you." As the astonished employee's jaw dropped, Disney continued, "Yeah, boy, someday I'd like to live on a ranch and have animals myself." He gazed off and said, "When I was a kid, we lived on a farm and we had all kinds of animals. I'd like to have that again."[4]

Reaching beyond Walt's personal life, Marceline's rural images also had a profound influence on his work. It became something of a standing joke at the studio, for example, that Walt had a great fondness for outhouse humor. An interviewer once asked a group of story men and animation directors about this, and after several muffled guffaws and an exchange of glances, one of them diplomatically described his sense of humor as "rural." He explained, "The sort of things that tickled Walt were outhouse gags, goosing gags, bedpans and johnnypots, thinly disguised farts, and cow's udders." Disney readily confessed to this. As he once noted, "I know in the early cartoons I used to feature a little outhouse and I know darn well I got that here in Marceline . . . We got a lot of laughs with that outhouse. But, of course, as we got a little more money to work with, why, we got a little more refined about it. The outhouse had to go."[5]

Memories of Marceline, however, had a deeper influence. Many of the Disney Studio's famous animated shorts from the late 1920s through the 1940s, including both the Mickey Mouse cartoons and the more adventurous Silly Symphonies, revolved around rural motifs and small-town adventures. *Steamboat Willie* (1928), for instance, the groundbreaking sound cartoon that made stars of both Mickey and Walt, featured a Twain-like riverboat setting and gags and comedic situations associated with farm animals. *The Country Cousin* (1936) drew its humor from the misadventures of a rural rube from Podunk who went to visit his tuxedo-clad cousin, Monty the city mouse. Even with the studio's gradual move to live-action films in the 1950s and 1960s, the rural influence remained strong. A trio of small-town films set in the early twentieth century, for instance, were so close to Walt Disney's heart that they moved him to tears. Both *Pollyanna* (1960) and *Those Calloways* (1965) elicited a strong reaction from him, and director David Swift and producer Winston Hibler were shocked to see him cry unashamedly when he previewed the rough-cut versions of these films. *So Dear to My Heart* (1949), a deeply nostalgic movie set on a midwestern farm in 1903, struck him even harder. "*So Dear* was especially close to me," he once admitted to a reporter. "Why, that's the life my brother and I grew up with as kids out in Missouri. The great racehorse Dan Patch [a figure in the film] was a hero to us. We had Dan Patch's grandson on my father's farm."[6]

Thus Marceline inspired a whole state of mind, a love affair with small-town America. A pair of nagging questions, however, remain unanswered: What exactly made the town such a reservoir of inspiration for Disney's imagination, especially since his actual contact with it was so limited? And, perhaps even more important, why did American audiences respond so enthusiastically, even rapturously, to this personal vision? The complex answers to these questions lie in history, particularly in the broad transformations that were remaking the United States in the early decades of the twentieth century.

During Disney's youth, in fact, small-town America was beginning a period of rapid decline. As historians have made clear, in the decades from 1880 to 1920 the United States saw a series of sweeping shifts that took it far in the direction of a modern urban industrial society. Galloping industrial growth, mushrooming corporations, the late-century flood of immigrants from southern and eastern Europe, and an explosion of urban growth irrevocably transformed the socioeconomic landscape. This array of far-reaching changes prompted a momentous cultural shift. By the turn of the century, Victorian culture, with its values of self-control, domesticity, and a stern work ethic, was giving way to a consumer culture based on a code of material abundance, leisure, and self-fulfillment. In the early 1900s, a new vision of America was becoming clearer and clearer. In an atmosphere of growing material abundance, the ideas that human instincts should be sated rather than restrained, that leisure had a place above old-fashioned attachments to productivity, that the external projections of human personality were more important than the internal restraints of character, emerged as threads of a new national culture.[7]

Disney's small-town America, the source of his golden memories, was in fact beginning to vanish even as he experienced it. At some level he sensed this acutely, because the stable years he spent in Marceline were a brief respite from the geographic mobility and emotional turmoil that characterized the great bulk of his childhood. Hence an irony: Walt Disney insisted on the value of deep roots in rural community precisely because his own roots ran so shallow. The desperation of his grasp for this ideal stability only revealed the ephemeral nature of its object. Disney's obsession with small-town America simply highlighted the larger pattern of dislocation and urban flux that actually colored his early life. His popular audience, many of its members also suffering from the dislocations of historical change, likewise yearned for the stability and comfort of a way of life that was vanishing.

In later years, Walt liked to portray himself as a self-effacing farmboy from the Midwest. Ward Kimball, a leading Disney animator and one of Walt's few close friends, noted that his boss was "very preoccupied with his own history" and set many of his pictures in "the Gay Nineties or the early 1900s — because that was when he was a kid." Indeed, it seems clear that Disney mythologized his past and presented it to the public. But the process was more tangled than anyone, especially he himself, ever realized. Its complexity began to form in his earliest childhood years.[8]

II. Son of the Midwest

Walt Disney, whose working-class parents struggled to make a living, spent much of his boyhood on the move. He was born on December 5, 1901, in Chicago, Illinois. His first name honored the preacher of the local Congregational church, of which his parents were devoted members, while his middle name, Elias, came from his father, a carpenter and occasional lay preacher. Only a handful of photographs have survived from his infancy, but one depicts the nine-month-old Walt seated on a wicker fan-back chair in a frilly white baby gown and slippers, looking curiously out at the camera. His older brother Roy remembered pushing him along the street in a baby carriage and buying him small toys with his odd-job earnings. Elias Disney worked as a small-time contractor, building houses throughout the city. His wife, Flora, helped her husband by drawing construction plans and keeping the books while managing a bustling household of five children. She had designed the family's modest two-story house at 1249 Tripp Avenue in northwestern Chicago, and Elias had built it.[9]

By the time Walt was nearly five years old, his parents had grown increasingly wary of life in the big city. Elias, especially, had become uneasy. In part it was a matter of crime, noise, and overcrowding, which disturbed his hopes of tranquillity and advancement for his children. But it was also a case of Elias's notorious wanderlust. Since young manhood he had roamed the country, searching for success in a variety of jobs: railroad machinist and carpenter in Colorado, farmer in Kansas, hotel proprietor and orange-grove owner and mail carrier in Florida. By the time of his retirement, he would have moved at least five more times throughout the Midwest and on the West Coast. His decade and a half in Chicago was a record for staying put, and he began searching for a new location for his family and a new path to success.

Early in 1906, Elias decided to turn again to farming. His brother, Robert, owned several hundred acres near Marceline, and several other relatives lived nearby, so Elias purchased the farm of a recently deceased Civil War veteran and in April the Disney family settled into a small, one-story white house set on forty-five acres of land. It was a multiuse farm, with both crops and livestock, and Elias and his three older sons — Herbert, Ray, and Roy — began the backbreaking labor of planting corn, wheat, and sorghum and raising hogs, cattle, and horses. The work of the traditional farm wife, with its constant round of cooking and baking, preserving food, washing clothes, gardening, and churning butter, proved no less taxing for Flora.

Walt, too young to do much useful work, had the run of the place. He romped in the surrounding fields and woods and encountered birds and wildlife of all kinds. The boy loved to splash in local creeks and play in the farm orchard, and he grew especially fond of watching the Santa Fe trains as they passed on the tracks a short distance from his house. He often had the companionship of a small Maltese terrier — "He was my pal," he said some fifty years later — or a small pig named Skinny he raised with a baby bottle. Both pets followed him everywhere. In later years, Walt loved to tell stories of his heroic hog-riding exploits during these years: apparently he would jump on the back of his father's sows and ride them around the barnyard until they dumped him off in the nearby pond. He also began school, attending Marceline's Park School, where he learned the rudiments of reading, writing, arithmetic, and geography.

This carefree, even idyllic time was not destined to last. Elias's farming endeavor floundered within a few short years, and the failure could be traced to a number of sources. Angered by their father's moral strictness, demands for unrelenting labor, and tightfistedness, Herbert and Ray left the farm after a couple of years to make their own way, returning to Chicago and later going to Kansas City. Moreover, Elias was simply not a very good farmer. Refusing to use fertilizers, he managed to produce only small harvests, and he was unable to tailor his crops to the market. Illness proved to be the final straw. In the winter of 1909–10, he caught typhoid fever, then fell victim to pneumonia and was unable to do any farmwork at all. In early 1910 he was forced to sell his farm at auction — he barely got back what he paid for it — along with all of his livestock and equipment. This event was heartbreaking for the younger Disneys, especially Walt, who saw his familiar rural world disappear on the auctioneer's block.

This time Elias Disney headed to Kansas City, and the family settled there in the late spring of 1910, after the younger children finished school in Marceline. Opportunity seemed bright there; at the eastern edge of the Great Plains wheat belt, Kansas City was emerging as a major livestock trading center and beginning a period of rapid growth. Because of his age and relatively poor health, Elias was unable to pursue strenuous physical labor, but he was able to purchase an extensive newspaper distributorship, delivering the *Times* in the morning and the *Star* in the evening and on Sundays to some seven hundred subscribers.

For eight-year-old Walt, this was the start of a difficult era. While Elias managed the operation, his two younger sons did the lion's share of the actual work. Roy and Walt rose every morning around three-thirty and picked up the newspapers in bulk around four-thirty. They spent the next several hours folding and delivering them on foot and by hand; their father forbade them to throw the papers from bicycles and insisted that they place them on subscribers' porches or behind their screen doors. Rainstorms in the spring and blizzards in the winter added to the burden, and, of course, the boys attended a full day of school after this work. Roy followed the example of his older brothers and left home in 1912, but Walt was stuck. He endured this bone-wearying schedule for six years.

Living in Kansas City, however, brought more than work to the boy. A bright and creative, if not particularly scholarly, student, Walt attended Benton Grammar School. He had demonstrated a flair for drawing since his Marceline days and now began to attend art classes for children at the Kansas City Art Institute. He supplemented this talent with a new interest in performing and entertainment. Something of a natural ham, he became close friends with a classmate named Walt Pfeiffer, and the "Two Walts" formed a youthful partnership, specializing in performing comedy skits and crude vaudeville routines for friends and at a small local theater.

Young Disney graduated from Benton School in June 1917 with a vague hope of combining his interests in drawing and comedy in an interesting new field: cartoons. Once again, however, his father's lust for mobility and success disrupted the family. As the newspaper distributorship was providing only a minimal living in Kansas City, Elias chanced upon a business opportunity back in Chicago. An acquaintance approached him with an offer to invest in the O-Zell jelly factory, where, in return for his entire life savings, he could become part owner and head of construction. Elias leaped at the chance and moved his family back to the banks of Lake Michigan in late spring 1917.

This time, however, Walt gained his first breath of freedom. He remained behind for the summer to work on the Santa Fe Railroad out of Kansas City. It was one of the happiest periods of his life. Gaining a position as a "news butcher" with the Van Noyes Interstate News Company, he sold newspapers, popcorn, peanuts, fruit, cold drinks, and other snacks to passengers. He worked runs out of Kansas City into half a dozen states, and he loved it. Talking with grizzled old railroad veterans — engineers, firemen, baggage-men — and wearing an impressive blue uniform with gold buttons, he fell prey to the romance of the railroad. He visited dozens of new towns, stayed overnight in boarding houses, and had a number of minor adventures. It mattered little that he made practically no money. It was with considerable reluctance that he left this summertime adventure to join his family in Chicago, and he did so with a new sense of independence and a feel for life's possibilities.

When Walt entered Chicago's McKinley High School, in the fall of 1917, he combined his new sense of self-reliance with his old creative urge in a renewed enthusiasm for drawing. He drew cartoons for the *Voice*, McKinley's student newspaper, attended classes several nights a week at the Chicago Institute of Art, and made the acquaintance of cartoonists for the Chicago *Herald* and *Tribune*. He also began attending vaudeville shows to assemble a file of the best jokes and gags. In order to assuage his father's suspicions about the entertainment world, he worked a number of jobs to contribute to the household income: handyman and night watchman at the jelly factory, gateman for Chicago's elevated railway line, delivery boy for the post office. By fall of 1918, however, a new adventure loomed on the horizon.

Walt had been intensely jealous when Roy had enlisted in the navy and gone off to fight in World War I. Eager to get out of high school and into uniform, the younger brother first planned to cross the border and enroll in the Canadian army, which was accepting younger recruits than the U.S. Army. When that ploy failed, he began to explore the possibility of joining the Red Cross Ambulance Corps. He learned that while the outfit accepted volunteer drivers aged seventeen and above, it also required passports and parental signatures of approval. Sixteen-year-old Walt implored his parents to sign, but his father refused because he was opposed to the war and already had three sons in the armed forces. Flora was more supportive. She believed that Walt would simply run off if they refused, so she forged Elias's name on the passport application while her son moved his birthdate back a year. After this deception, the young man was accepted into the American Ambulance Corps and embarked on a great adventure.

Walt Disney was never in physical danger during his World War I service. Indeed, the armistice had been signed and the fighting was over before he left a harbor in Connecticut for France. Nonetheless, the young midwesterner experienced an entirely new world during his ten months in Europe. His official duties consisted of driving Red Cross supply trucks and ambulances, doing rudimentary repair work on these machines, and providing a taxi service for army officers. He spent some time in Paris and served at an evacuation hospital and then a Red Cross canteen in the French countryside. Eventually he became something of a guide for visiting dignitaries and chauffeured several guests through parts of France and the Rhine Valley in Germany.

Throughout his tour of duty, young Disney avidly pursued cartooning. He sent drawings to his high school newspaper and submitted cartoons to the leading humor magazines, *Life* and *Judge* (they were rejected). He drew posters for the Red Cross and sketches for his friends, and he decorated several vehicles with figures of various kinds. Walt also pursued some new forms of recreation that his straitlaced parents would have frowned upon — drinking, smoking, and card playing — and at some point he purchased a German shepherd puppy. Yet he remained the dutiful son in many respects, avoiding the sexual temptations of Frenchwomen and sending a portion of his salary every month to his mother for safekeeping. When the last American troops left and the American Ambulance Corps was disbanded in September 1919, he booked passage home.

Walt Disney had left home a boy and returned a young man. Arriving in Chicago taller and heavier, and with considerably more worldly experience, he immediately felt constrained. High school seemed impossibly juvenile after a stint in Europe, and his father's offer of a job at the jelly factory was scarcely more appealing. Walt had determined to make his way as an artist, in one fashion or another, and a few weeks in Chicago convinced him that opportunity lay elsewhere. He made one of the truly significant decisions of his life — to return to Kansas City and seek his fortune as a cartoonist.

The facts of Walt Disney's youth are fairly well known, but their significance remains more elusive. On the surface, his early years presented little that was particularly noteworthy. The events of his youth were fairly typical for a midwestern boy in the early 1900s, and seemingly they could have happened to anyone and given rise to any number of adult careers. Beneath the surface, however, several trends offer keys to his sensibility.

Childhood had seen the emergence of several basic personality traits. Even as a youngster, Walt Disney impressed friends and family with his mischievous curiosity and fun-loving nature. His younger sister Ruth, for instance, noted that her brother had had an engaging personality as a boy and "was always thinking of ideas." As a matter of fact, she confessed, even later in life "Walt always seemed like a kid to me." Restless creativity and a hankering for the spotlight were apparent even in grammar school. A classmate remembered when Walt, a sixth-grader, went to school on Lincoln's birthday dressed in a suit, a homemade stovepipe hat, and a fake beard and recited the Gettysburg Address from memory. The principal was so impressed that he hauled Walt around to every class in the school for a repeat performance. At home, the boy was a committed prankster. Once he dressed in his mother's clothes, went around to the front door pretending to be a neighbor, and engaged Flora in conversation before she realized who it was. Another time he discovered a small rubber bladder that could be inflated with a straw to make things rise, and he startled his mother one afternoon by making her pots seem to rise of their own accord from the kitchen table. When he came home from Europe, he tried to convince his parents that the Rock of Gibraltar had been adorned with a giant lighted Prudential Insurance sign. The gag-filled, merry cartoons of Mickey Mouse and Donald Duck were but a short step from such boyish escapades.[10]

Those cartoons also drew on another youthful source: Walt Disney's early blending of art and entrepreneurship. He demonstrated a talent for drawing at an early age. In Marceline, for example, he sketched Dr. Sherwood's prize horse and was overjoyed to receive a quarter in return. Not long after that he infuriated his parents by painting pictures on the side of their farmhouse with roofing tar (he thought it would wash off). His brother Roy recalled that their aunt Maggie, who was enamored of Walt from the time he was a little boy, kept him supplied with pencils and Big Chief Indian tablets of paper. A bit later, in Kansas City, when Walt was around nine years old, he drew a flip book of crude animation for his sister when she had the measles. Another time he stayed up all night making an elaborate drawing of the human circulatory system for a class assignment, and it was so good that his teacher thought he had traced it.

At the same time, the boy's talent and his commercial sense began to merge. His friend Walt Pfeiffer clearly remembered several examples of this: young Disney drawing illustrations for the Benton School newspaper, drawing advertising cartoons for a local barber in return for free haircuts, earning money by peddling hand-drawn advertisements to local merchants. During Disney's days in the ambulance corps in France, this instinct became more highly developed. He painted decorations on his comrades' jackets for ten francs a job. He also developed a commercial concern with a friend remembered only as "the Georgia cracker." Shrewdly observing the market for war artifacts, the two got their hands on a supply of German army helmets, and after the cracker put a bullet hole in each one, Disney painted them with phony camouflage. Banging the helmets with rocks and rubbing them in dirt to complete the deception, the partners made a tidy profit from these "genuine" relics of the war.[11]

Yet Disney's entrepreneurial sense also adhered to a rather complex work ethic that clearly arose from a childhood of hard labor. Curiously, although he was consistently described as a workaholic in his adult life, he evolved in his early days a pronounced aversion to *physical* labor. This is not to say that he was lazy. Far from it, as his abundance of youthful jobs certainly demonstrated. His sister once recounted a story of how Walt was turned down for a summer job at the post office because of his age; he went home and subtly penciled age lines on his face, borrowed his father's overcoat and hat, and went back and got the job. The determination to succeed was certainly not the problem.[12]

But in a series of interviews in the mid-1950s, Disney recalled at great length the pain he suffered during his years of newspaper deliveries. He described falling asleep in the early morning hours behind stacks of newspapers and being so cold in the winter that he would cry when no one was around. Indeed, he claimed to have a recurring nightmare rooted in this trauma. As he told an interviewer, he still dreamed "that I have missed customers on my [newspaper] route . . . And I wake up and think, gosh, I've got to hurry and get back . . . It's the darnedest thing." Because of this regimen, Disney said, "I never had any real play time." In fact, when he got married, in 1925, he told his bride that lawn work and gardening were out of the question, because "I just did too much of it as a kid, and I just didn't want to do it." Even as a young man he made it clear that creative work, rather than the grind of physical effort, would pave his way to success.[13]

Young Disney carried into adulthood two other attitudes that shaped his course in important ways. First, he rejected the extreme piety of his parents. Flora and particularly Elias were rather strict Congregationalists, and faithful churchgoing was the rule in the Disney family. Walt rebelled, not by turning to disbelief but by relaxing his whole attitude toward religion. His daughter Diane explained how he would drop her and her sister at the Christian Science Sunday school and pick them up later, saying, "He had an intensely religious youth. He'd been brought up in a strictly regimented church atmosphere. His father was a deacon at one time. Reading this and knowing this now, I can understand why he had such a free attitude towards our religion. He wanted us to have religion. He definitely believed in God. Very definitely. But I think he'd had it [with organized religion] as a child."[14]

Second, Disney learned to detest the burden of poverty. Thinking back to his family's struggle for economic survival in Kansas City, he remembered going door-to-door with a pushcart, helping his mother peddle country butter in various neighborhoods to help meet expenses. "But it was embarrassing at times," he said, "because I went to school with the kids that lived there, you know? They were kind of . . . wealthy children." Much later, a friend at the Disney Studio noted that his boss "had this craving for ice cream sodas and candy bars because as a kid he couldn't afford them." Walt had colorful jars of candy all over his studio office and constantly offered some to visitors. At home, he built a huge soda fountain in his club room, complete with all the attachments and extras. According to a friend, "He'd get behind the fountain like a soda jerk and fix these huge goopy things for his guests, ice cream sodas and the biggest banana splits you ever saw. He loved doing that. He loved having that soda fountain because as a kid he couldn't spend money for ice cream. His youth was scratching for pennies and nickels and tossing whatever he earned into the kitty at home."[15]

Disney's ten months in France, he was fond of telling friends, constituted "a lifetime of experience" that was valuable beyond reckoning. In fact, his whole notion of education flowed from this episode. "I think I got a greater education by [serving in the ambulance corps] than you can ever jam into anybody by going through this methodical business of going to school every day," he speculated. "You can't force people to be scholars . . . There's other ways that people get educated." Military experience, he argued, had provided maturity and worldly wisdom at a young age and taught him to "line right up on an objective. And I went for it. And I've never had any regrets." For this extremely creative man who never graduated from high school, childhood had shaped a certain viewpoint: the world was a series of obstacles, and education meant taking classes in the school of hard knocks. Practicality and experience beat out abstraction any day.[16]

Yet all of these factors — the creative and lighthearted personality, the commercial bent, the intense desire to succeed, the rebellion against organized religion and poverty, the faith in practical education — were overshadowed by a dim but nagging awareness of flux and dislocation. The Disney family's recurring moves from city to countryside to city, lack of community roots, and constant straining for respectability and success, which always fell a bit short, fed Walt's sense of disruption and loss. The adult Disney seems to have locked away much of this painful emotional baggage, determined to mythologize his early life as the opening chapters of an American success story where good triumphed over evil and progress overcame adversity. Certainly no disciple of self-awareness, he avoided exploring his own sense of deprivation. But one can see evidence of it quite clearly in his attitudes toward a few emotionally charged topics.

The subject of family was one such matter. Disney carried out of boyhood a great fondness for a big family full of warmth and happiness, a feeling largely shaped by his own family's lack of such qualities. Walt Pfeiffer provided valuable evidence on this count. He remembered that his boyhood friend loved to spend time in the Pfeiffer household, as this big German clan engaged in evening rounds of singing, joke telling, and general gaiety. Mr. Pfeiffer, an official of the United Leatherworkers Union who delighted in the theater and vaudeville, encouraged the Two Walts in their fledgling entertainment careers. When an angry Elias Disney came looking for his son one day, fearing that he was involved in some kind of trouble, Mr. Pfeiffer "had to give him a talking-to and tell him that [Walt] was always welcome at our house and he was one of the family and we always looked on him as that." And Mrs. Pfeiffer was like a "second mother" to the boy. In later years, Diane Disney Miller reported a similar relationship between her father and his wife's "big happy family. He loved being with them," she noted. "They had the warmth that I think his family lacked." Walt's sister Ruth told of his habit of saying, "I want to have ten kids and let them do whatever they want." Like other relics of a settled community, the notion of a large, tight-knit family proved especially attractive to a boy who sorely missed it in his own early experience.[17]

In a more curious and complex way, young Walt Disney also translated his boyhood sense of loss into a wary view of women. On the one hand, he associated women with security in a particularly intense fashion. His mother, for instance, always served as a kind of emotional bulwark against the demands and punishments of his very strict father. As Walt noted later, "My mother was the one with the humor . . . We could even conspire with my mother to get around my dad, you know? . . . Mother would just put him down in his place. She'd say, 'Now Elias, now Elias, you stop that! Now Elias, you're going too far!'" In a 1940 letter to one of his favorite teachers in Kansas City, Miss Daisy Beck, he reminisced in a similar vein. He had a vivid memory of marching into school on winter mornings, nearly frozen from delivering newspapers, and seeing "you and Miss Shrewsbury standing over the radiators while the heat billowed out your skirts," he wrote. "It looked very comfortable to me on those cold mornings — and sometimes I wished that I might have worn skirts myself!" While in grammar school, he took the rather peculiar action of being the only boy in his class to sign up for a domestic science class rather than manual training. But his reasons soon became clear. "He was happy as could be in there," even though many of his classmates made fun of him, his sister later recalled, "because the girls were all making over him something terrible."[18]

These experiences of female security, however, gave way to resentment when the adolescent Walt saw his ideal violated. In the summer of 1917 he ran into a pretty classmate named Josephine while working on the Santa Fe Railroad. But when he said hello, "she looked at me and looked the other way out the window." The girl "was a little snit," he concluded. That same summer a man on the train gave him the address of a place to stay on a stopover in Pueblo, Colorado, but when Walt arrived and sat down for refreshment, he noticed a number of couples acting in a rather lascivious manner. "Well, I was pretty naive, but I soon caught on to where in the hell I was, you see?" he recalled of this venture into a bordello. "Then I got out of there as fast as I could drink the beer."[19]

Apparently having limited interest in girls throughout his adolescence, Walt experienced genuine disillusionment during his Red Cross duty. When they disembarked in France, the contingent of young ambulance drivers was indoctrinated about the dangers of picking up venereal disease. "Those horrible color slides" made a strong impact on Disney, and prompted him to say even forty years later, "That's when you begin to hate women." After his service ended, a final incident really soured his attitude. He had corresponded with a girl from his high school throughout his European service and he went back to Chicago loaded with "French blouses and perfume" for her. Then he found out she had been married for three months. He angrily gave all the gifts to his sister-in-law and decided that "I was through with women."[20]

Once again, however, Disney's brief stay in the Missouri countryside gave the strongest testimony to his dismay over the flux and contingency of his youth. As his daughter once stated flatly, "He idealized and romanticized this period on the farm in Marceline." Disney cherished memories of community characters to whom he had grown close — Erastus Taylor, a grizzled Civil War veteran full of stories; Doc Sherwood, a retired physician who wore a black Prince Albert coat and plucked his beard rather than shaving

— and family members whose presence enlivened the household. Years later, he still chuckled over a visit from urban cousins, whom the family cow chased up a tree. He told stories about how he and his brother were hired to wash a hearse in town, and Roy did all the work while "I played dead inside the hearse all day." He described with great affection Elias's brother, Uncle Ed, who went from one relative to another because he was "touched in the head," a man-child who "never grew up" but who delighted his nephew with a whimsical sense of fun and play. "I loved Uncle Ed, you know?" Walt would say simply many years later. He clearly felt a sense of belonging in Marceline, of stability and rootedness and place.[21]

This became even clearer when Disney waxed nostalgic about the shared rituals of country life. Sorghum threshing in the fall, for instance, had made a particularly strong impression. Local farmers gathered with their wagons and their families beside a large steam thresher. The men worked the machinery while their wives cooked an enormous meal, and in Walt's words, "everything was done in a [spirit of] community help." Hog-butchering day brought the same kind of cooperation and fellowship, and the boy loved it. But his sense of belonging was shattered when his family moved — perhaps the source of his most profound feelings of loss.[22]

Like hordes of his fellow Americans, Walt Disney was very ambivalent about the sweeping social changes that took place during his childhood. He became powerfully attuned to the notion of history as progress, a theme that helped him flourish as a creative entertainer, but a nostalgic attraction to nineteenth-century rural traditions pulled with almost equal force. This complex, ambivalent engagement with modern America first found expression in Walt's simmering confrontation with his father.

III. Elias Disney: "What Can It Be Used For?"

January 1, 1938, was the fiftieth wedding anniversary of Elias and Flora Disney, and they gathered at the Hollywood home of their famous son Walt along with the rest of their children — Ray, Herbert, Roy, and Ruth. Walt, ever the showman and historian, tape-recorded much of the event. Conducting a mock interview with his parents, he joked that his notoriously strict father "always enjoyed a good time" and inquired playfully, "Don't you want to make whoopee on your golden wedding anniversary?" The slightly nonplussed Elias replied, "Oh, we don't want to go to any extremes a-tall" as Flora added, "He don't know how to make whoopee." Walt then asked his mother about fifty years of life with the old man, adding, "I think he was kind of ornery at times, wasn't he, huh?" In such an atmosphere of good-humored kidding, the family's affection radiated from the day's celebration.[23]

But things had not always been that way, particularly between Walt and his father. Elias, a man of stern temperament, had clashed with all of his sons in their younger days, and his relationship with his youngest boy had been especially difficult. Their confrontations were partly a matter of divergent personalities, but also partly a matter of historical and cultural change. The dour, demanding father simply talked a different language from his vivacious, creative son.

Elias Disney's life had been a frustrated search for business success, full of restless movement and misadventures. Born in Ontario in 1859, he had come to the United States as a teenager with his parents and spent much of his adult life moving through a number of jobs. He married Flora Call in 1888, and five children arrived between 1889 and 1903. For Elias, two characteristics particularly colored life — his morality and his politics. He had been raised very strictly, probably in the Congregational church, and his parents had brooked no self-indulgence. Roy Disney recalled a story that his father once told about his boyhood love for fiddle-playing. Because Elias's parents didn't approve, he had gone off into the woods and practiced and then sneaked into the local dance hall to play with other local musicians. At some point his parents got wind of this, however, and went to the dance hall themselves. "They found their son playing the fiddle, and Grandma went up and grabbed it away from him and busted it all to hell over his head, took him by the ear, and marched him home," Roy related. "The devil was in the fiddle, to their notion. Dancing was just evil." However mortified Elias must have been by this incident, he nonetheless carried many of the same attitudes into his own adulthood.[24]

As a father, Elias developed his own stern Protestant morality. In many ways, his creed reflected the cluster of values — self-control, hard work, thrift, determined striving for material success and moral virtue — so characteristic of nineteenth-century culture. He built a reputation for his tight ways with money. A Marceline neighbor later recalled that when he was in the Disney home, he noticed "how plainly they lived. They had none of the frills of life." Stories of obsessive thrift abounded. His children remembered how Elias would instruct Flora to "go easy on the butter" on their bread to save money. (Their mother became a heroine to her children by buttering the bread and handing it to them butter side down so her husband wouldn't notice.) Elias refused to ride the streetcars in Kansas City when he could walk for free. When he visited California to build a house for one of his nephews, he was proud of staying there for three months and spending only one dollar, even though he saw much of the state. He took advantage of free rides and free meals from real estate developers, who offered such perks to prospective buyers of property. Walt was especially fond of telling how his father carried a little coin purse in Kansas City. "He had a quarter. And my mother would have to go into his pocketbook every so often and take the quarter out and put a new one in," Walt said with a chuckle. "I'm not kidding you, it was turning green."[25]

But Elias's frugality was not always a laughing matter. This issue caused such friction with his sons that it triggered the departure of his two oldest boys. Ray and Herbert, angered by their father's attempts to impound money they earned by working for their uncle, simply abandoned the farm and struck out on their own. In Kansas City, his two remaining sons faced a similar situation. Elias was unwilling to pay them for their work distributing newspapers, considering it to be a family obligation. When Roy left home to pursue his own career and Elias had to hire several boys to deliver papers, he still refused to compensate Walt. In Walt's words, "He said that it was part of my job. I was part of the family. He said, 'I clothe you and feed you and things.' So he wouldn't pay me." The embittered boy ended up ordering extra papers to deliver on his own time to earn some spending money. When Walt returned from his ambulance service in France and asked for the money he had sent home as savings so he could start up a small commercial art business in Kansas City, Elias allowed Flora to send only part of the amount, believing that Walt was wasting his money on such a venture.[26]

To this rigid dogma of hard work, thrift, and simplicity Elias added a corollary — the necessity of self-denial. In good Victorian fashion, he personally testified to the virtues of self-control and demanded it in his family. "My dad never drank whiskey or smoked or used any swear words . . . and [he was] very slow to catch on to a gag or a joke," Walt once told a reporter. This self-denying temperament extended to Elias's language in slightly comical fashion. Remembering his father's attempts to curb a passionate temper, Roy reported that he became a great mock cusser. Sputtering and fuming in frustration, Elias would let fly with "consarnit, Great Scott, land o' living, land o' Goshen, all those corny old expressions." Friends of the family reaffirmed this impression; one recalled that Elias, opposed to anything that smacked of frivolity, "was kind of churchy, as we called it in those days . . . Everybody was no good [in his eyes] because they drank or something, or led a fast life."[27]

In the fluid world of the early twentieth century, where social institutions and moral values were in a state of transition, however, Elias's worldview was becoming increasingly antiquated. It even encouraged certain self-destructive tendencies. Walt came to believe that his father was deceived in his various business ventures, for instance, because "he thought everyone was as honest as he was." Elias's hidebound moralism led him to refuse to use fertilizer on his crops, since "putting fertilizer on plants was just the same as giving whiskey to a man — he felt better for a little while, but then he was worse off than he was before." Such attitudes produced a kind of naiveté about the world, a characteristic that stayed with Elias until late in life. With some amusement, Roy once related that his elderly father, seeking to buy a small rooming house in Portland, never noticed that many of the rooms were rented several times each night. When Roy went up to check the books and okay the purchase, he saw immediately that Elias had nearly managed to buy a whorehouse.[28]

Not surprisingly, Elias's severe attitudes gave rise to a child-rearing philosophy of "spare the rod and spoil the child." He ran his household with an iron fist and did not shrink from imposing his authority by physical punishment. Old-fashioned to the core, he disciplined all his children, particularly his youngest son. Young Walt, with his flair for art and his attraction to vaudeville, seemed to flout Elias's moral code. A long series of confrontations resulted. The father disapproved of the son's propensity for drawing, and when Walt returned from France determined to be a cartoonist, Elias bitterly opposed the move. The boy's instinct for showmanship grated even more. As Walt Pfeiffer recalled, "Old Elias didn't like anything that had anything to do with entertainment." When the Two Walts performed at local theaters, young Disney would sneak out of his bedroom window and join his friend "so that his dad wouldn't know it, 'cause we were kind of afraid of him." Sometimes things would get nasty. According to a family member, Walt once took Roy's blue serge suit without permission to perform a Charlie Chaplin routine at a local theater. When Elias found out, he was furious. As a cousin said, "Elias was very strict with Walt, and he administered frequent beatings."[29]

Elias's forbidding moral vision also illuminated his politics, but with a curious twist. He was a lifelong socialist. If cultural and religious life demanded self-denial and piety, this ascetic reformer believed, political and social life demanded virtuous civic conduct as well. In the words of his daughter Ruth, Elias's idealism led him to embrace "the philosophy of socialism — which seemed to him then to be a fair way for people to live." In the 1890s he had been an enthusiastic supporter of the Democratic reformer William Jennings Bryan, but then he transferred his loyalty to the socialist Eugene V. Debs. He subscribed to the socialist newspaper *The Appeal to Reason* and became notorious for his willingness to talk politics. Apparently he would talk with anyone about socialism, and even brought an assortment of "strange characters" and "tramps" to his house to feed them and convert them to his political religion. When Flora finally refused to allow this invasion of her dinner table, he fed them out on the steps. In fact, Walt remembered socialism as one of the earliest inspirations for his drawing. As he noted many years later, after looking at his father's socialist publications "I got so I could draw capital and labor pretty good — the big, fat capitalist with the money, maybe with his foot on the neck of the laboring man with the little cap on his head."[30]

Walt's encounter with his father's rigid moral and political principles triggered a highly ambivalent response. Full of love and resentment in equal proportions, eager both to please and to escape Elias, the sensitive boy developed a deep-seated tension over paternal authority. In almost a literal sense, it haunted him. In his recurring adult nightmare of forgetting to deliver some of the newspapers on his Kansas City route, his dad would "be waiting up at that corner" to punish him for his laxness. Ward Kimball, a Disney Studio animator and close friend, felt that his boss never got over his father's strictness, which in Kimball's view negatively "influenced Walt's relation to other people." Yet Diane Miller recalled that her father talked of Elias "constantly" and often with great affection. He "loved his dad. He thought he was tough . . . But he loved that old man."[31]

This complex confrontation with Elias and his world surfaced again and again in Walt's psyche. Throughout his life he was eager to discuss his father. On the one hand, his comments were filled with affection and admiration for the old man's virtues — the commitment to his family's welfare, the gritty work ethic, the respect for education and good citizenship. On the other hand, however, resentment of the elder Disney's authoritarianism would bubble out with little prompting. Walt often told how Elias tried to force him to learn the fiddle so he would always be able to earn some money as a musician. The boy had no talent for it; he had trouble with holding his right arm in the correct position for bowing. But the father insisted, and "he used to slap the hell out of me to get that elbow down." When Walt helped with the carpentry as the family added space to their house, Elias frequently exploded. Walt recalled this episode some forty years later: "My dad was an impatient person. But he knew what he wanted to do and he expected you to know just what he wanted to do . . . [and if I faltered] he'd get mad, you see. And he'd start after me. And my dad was the kind of guy who'd pick up anything near him . . . He'd pick up a saw and try to hit you with the broad side of the saw. He'd pick up a hammer, you know, and hit you with the handle." The boy finally had enough of such treatment and walked off the construction job in anger.[32]

Elias's physical intimidation seems to have left deep scars on his son's emotional makeup. His "violent temper" eventually led to a liberating confrontation. After accusing Walt of insolence when he was about fourteen, Elias ordered him to the basement for "a good whipping." As they descended, however, Roy whispered to Walt that he didn't have to take it anymore. So when Walt saw Elias prepare to strike him, he grabbed the older man's wrists and refused to let go. Unable to break his grip, Elias finally started to cry. This was a turning point, and Elias never touched Walt in anger again. Even this traumatic incident, however, raised mixed feelings in the youngest Disney boy. He admitted that "I worshipped him . . . And he meant well every time he did anything like that." The long series of arguments, punishments, and finally physical confrontations produced in Walt not bitter condemnation but anguished confusion: "My dad . . . wanted his children to get fully educated. He was fighting for 'em and everything. He was a good dad. He thought of nothing but his family . . . [But] he had this violent temper

. . . It was hard to sit down and have a family talk with him, sit down and have a friendly talk . . . [because] he was always bothered."[33]

Over the long term, Walt consciously pulled away from much of his father's cultural and political morality. His stern upbringing, for instance, caused him to relax in his own child-rearing practices. "It was a thing I never forgot. You just can't do that with children," he noted of his father's domineering ways. "I never discounted the intelligence in my kids . . . I talk to my kids . . . You know, people don't realize sometimes that a child has a lot of good reasoning, you know?" Elias's ways also shaped Walt's view of money. In contrast to his father's notorious tightness, he developed a more carefree attitude; money was simply something to use for more important ends. While Elias was reluctant to spend a nickel, Walt once revealed with a chuckle, "The funny thing is, I didn't inherit any of that thrift."[34]

For his part, Elias never really understood his son or the nature of his fabulous success in the entertainment world. In 1932, while being interviewed at his small home in Portland, he was asked to comment on the skyrocketing fame of Walt Disney and his creation Mickey Mouse. Obviously a bit perplexed, Elias could provide only a stock answer from the tradition of the work ethic. "Walt has always been a good boy and has worked hard for the success he has attained," he said solemnly. An even better gauge of the cultural canyon separating father and son occurred in 1939, when Walt was building his state-of-the-art studio in Burbank and took Elias for a tour of the construction site. As they walked around the facility and surveyed the unfinished buildings, they carried on an awkward conversation. The filmmaker was a bit confused by the old man's repeated question, "Walter, what can it be *used* for?"

> I couldn't quite grasp what he was after and suddenly it dawned on me. He meant if we failed how could we liquidate . . . how could we get our money back out of it, see? So I said, 'Now this would make a perfect hospital.' The rest of the tour I didn't talk about a studio; I talked about a hospital . . . how they could put operating rooms above . . . the wide corridors . . . [and] we could put bathrooms in between [the many rooms]. I went through the whole darn studio and explained the thing to him as a hospital. He was happy.[35]

It should not be surprising that for the no-nonsense, utilitarian Elias, a hospital was far more attractive than an animated film studio. A creature of the nineteenth century, he perceived an institution to repair human breakdown as a reflection of common sense, while mass entertainment and consumer indulgence appeared frivolous. With his deeply ingrained commitment to self-denying individualism, nose-to-the-grindstone producerism, and virtuous politics, Elias Disney never made his peace with the corporate, bureaucratic, consumer society of twentieth-century America.

IV. Back to the Future

Elias Disney died a rather lonely old man. His wife succumbed to a terrible accident in 1938 — a new gas furnace malfunctioned, sending deadly fumes throughout the Los Angeles house given to them by their two moviemaking sons — and he never recovered. "He was just lost without her. It was the darnedest thing. After she died, I never felt so sorry for anybody in my life as I did my dad," Walt once noted. "I used to take my kids over to see him every Sunday. There was nothing, he was just lost. It was a very sad thing." When Elias himself died, in 1941, Walt received the telegram while he was in South America on an extended business trip. After a moment of hesitation, he decided not to return for the funeral. This provided perhaps one last sign of his lingering sense of alienation. But a host of other actions disclosed his equally strong sense of obligation to his father.[36]

In the mid-1950s, Walt Disney rebuilt the world of his father at his amusement park, Disneyland. With Main Street, USA, the 1890s-style thoroughfare along which visitors must pass to enter other sections of the park, he paid homage to turn-of-the-century America. In a 1959 publication, he explicitly noted its emotional and historical roots:

> Many of us fondly remember our "small home town" and its friendly way of life at the turn of the century. To me, this era represents an important part of our heritage, and thus we have endeavored to recapture those years on Main Street, U.S.A. at Disneyland. Here is the America of 1890–1910, at the crossroads of an era, where the gas lamp is gradually being replaced by the electric lamp, the plodding, horse-drawn streetcar is giving way to the chugging "horseless carriage." America was in transition: the discoveries of the late 19th century were beginning to affect our way of life. Main Street represents the typical small town in the early 1900s — the heartline of America.

Not surprisingly, Disneyland's "typical" small-town street was nearly a replica, although highly idealized, of Marceline's main street, as photographs of the latter make clear.[37]

Walt underlined this personal connection with another flourish. Walking down Main Street, USA, the visitor can look up to the left and see neatly stenciled on a second-story store window the words "Elias Disney, Contractor. Est. 1895." At Walt's direction, this little sign displays to all passers-by his link with the past. By choosing "contractor" from among his father's many professions, and by placing it in a setting far more stable than any that had existed in real life, Walt once again revealed his yearning for rootedness.

Ambiguity, however, rather than straightforward nostalgia, colored Walt Disney's attitude toward the past. It is curious that the buildings on Main Street, USA are not life-size but on a smaller scale. The official reason for this lay in a shrewd assessment of human nature: smaller buildings would establish an intimate sense of comfort and security, thus helping to lure people deeper into the folds of the Disney fantasy. As Walt once explained, "We had every brick and shingle and gas lamp made five-eighths true size. This cost more, but made the street a toy, and the imagination can play more freely with a toy."[38]

But the smaller buildings probably held another layer of meaning for him, one he was less able to articulate. He seemed to be striving, almost literally, to knock his father's world down to size. He reconstructed that world as a childhood experience to be savored like other innocent memories, but it was one that ultimately must be transcended. Walt succeeded in miniaturizing the world of his father, thereby taming the moral demands that had so traumatized him in his younger days. As he once observed, in a revealing choice of language, Main Street, USA appealed because "people like to think their world is somehow more grown up than Papa's was."[39]

Standing midway between the country and the city, both emotionally and historically trapped between the demands of his father's moral code and the attractive new creed of consumer America, Disney spent much of his life struggling with his conflicting feelings about his personal history. Like other influential architects of modern America who used their money to clutch at a vision of the past — Henry Ford and Dearborn Village, for instance, or John D. Rockefeller and Williamsburg, Virginia — Disney came to cherish the traditional values and structures that he had helped to destroy.

Ultimately, his profound ambivalence about cultural and social change became a key to his success. Like him, many Americans harbored feelings that were part enthusiasm, part fear, and part anguished accommodation. Throughout Disney's creative life, his genius lay in a strong, if only half-conscious, feel for this abiding tension. The Hollywood master of enchantment, with his heart firmly planted in the rural Midwest, reflected the fears and fantasies of a people facing the unfamiliar. He felt the same things they did. And they loved him for it.

2

Young Man Disney and Mickey Mouse

THE PHOTOGRAPHS bespeak an innocent time of life. Several young men, all around twenty years of age and colleagues in a fledgling film company, mug for the camera, frolicking and striking heroic poses. Dressed smartly in the fashion of the early 1920s, they sport longish slicked-back hair and wear knickers and colorful long stockings or flannel trousers and vests, topped by jaunty caps or fedoras set at a rakish angle. Although frozen in time by the camera, the poses radiate lightheartedness and the faces convey the cocky arrogance of youth.

In one snapshot, this group stages an action scene on top of a building. One young man stares intently through the lens of the camera, another grips the director's megaphone and spurs on the action with upraised fist, and two actors grapple in a supposed life-and-death struggle at the edge of a precipice. In another photo, they assemble on a steep rock formation in the city park. Smirking and clowning, they peer out over the landscape as a disheveled figure appears from behind them with a crazed look and an upraised hatchet. In yet another photo, they smile proudly as they lounge in and around a shiny Model T. Outfitted as an advertisement for their film company, the car is about to depart in a city parade. Their leader, a thin, intense, confident young man with sharp features and dark hair, sits proudly in the back seat.[1]

Walt gathered around him in Kansas City a remarkable collection of young men. Talented, ambitious, and hardworking, they labored together for a time in a commercial art studio before joining Disney in an independent enterprise. As they explored the new field of animation, their work came to rival the efforts emerging from the studios of New York City. These young pioneers were united by a spirit of intense creativity and boisterous male bonding.

Beneath the surface, however, a strong undercurrent of competitive tension pulled events in unexpected directions. First of all, the images of innocence masked Disney's driving ambition. For those who knew him well, this quality was evident even in his young manhood. For all his proclivity for easygoing horseplay, a desire for success gnawed at him and drove him relentlessly, motivating his personal relationships as well as his professional decisions.

In addition, the innocent photographs from the Kansas City days could not predict the fact that within a few years, everyone in them would abandon Walt Disney, leaving the struggling Disney Studio for the enticements of another entertainment entrepreneur. These young men eventually became some of the leading cartoon producers in Hollywood, and by 1930 the gang had disbanded completely, with no small amount of hard feeling involved.

The fluid, even treacherous quality of Disney's career in the 1920s — the tense competitiveness, the organizational flux, the search for amusement formulas — reflected the transformations of early twentieth-century America. The story began to unfold in the post–World War I bustle of Kansas City.

I. The Little Engine That Could

In late autumn 1919, shortly after his return from France, Walt Disney flew the family nest in Chicago for good, hoping to find employment as a newspaper cartoonist in Kansas City. He reunited with his brother Roy, who had returned from the war to find work at a local bank, and took up residence once again at the old Disney house on Bellefontaine Street. For a short time he pounded the pavement looking for a newspaper job, but both the Kansas City *Star* and the *Journal* turned him down. Discouragement began to overwhelm his boyish enthusiasm.[2]

At Roy's suggestion, Walt took a slightly different tack. He applied for work at the Pesmen-Rubin Commercial Art Studio after a job opening came to his attention. He was accepted for a temporary position, and he eagerly began working on a variety of assignments, designing letterheads, contributing humorous texts, and making sketches and layouts for advertisements. Working for a wide range of clients, including farm supply companies and department stores, he grew especially fond of drawing newspaper advertisements and program covers for the Newman Theater. Even more important, he made the acquaintance of a young artist of Dutch extraction with the rather odd name of Ubbe Iwwerks (later he shortened it to simply Ub Iwerks). Although their relationship saw several ups and downs, they became lifelong colleagues.

Within a few weeks, after the Christmas rush subsided, both Disney and Iwerks were laid off. They floundered for a bit but then made the bold decision to go into business for themselves. With the energetic Walt taking the lead and the quiet, intense Ub following in his wake, the two eighteen-year-olds established Iwerks-Disney Commercial Artists in January 1920 (the original name was Disney-Iwerks, but they decided that sounded like an optical company). Disney focused on cartooning and salesmanship while Iwerks concentrated on lettering and drawing. Excited to be independent entrepreneurs, they drummed up a small amount of business, but unfortunately made an even smaller amount of money. The enterprise lasted only a month.

In early February the two young men came across an advertisement for a job at the Kansas City Film Ad Company. With uncertain prospects and dwindling resources, they found the possibility of a steady income alluring. So Walt, with Ub's encouragement, applied for the position and was hired. After several weeks, he convinced the company of his friend's merits and Iwerks joined up as well. The company produced crudely animated one-minute advertising films to be shown at movie theaters before the main feature. Disney jumped into his work with typical enthusiasm. Dissatisfied with the techniques of his employers — standard operating procedure was to use paper cutouts of figures, whose joints would be moved and photographed against a background to make them "move" — he began to explore the drawing process of more sophisticated New York productions. He checked out books on animation and motion from the public library and began to compile a file of tracings and photostats. As his drawin became more realistic, he began to invent gags and story twists that enlivened his work.

He also went much further. After talking his employer into lending him a stop-action camera, he set up a rough studio in his garage and began to experiment with his own animated films. Often laboring late into the night after his workday, he gradually completed several cartoons, which he peddled to local theaters under the heading Newman Laugh-O-Grams. Their popularity made him a darling of A. Vern Cauger, the owner of the Film Ad Company, and something of a celebrity around Kansas City. But after his suggestion to develop a series of animated shorts was rejected by Cauger, who wanted to stay with the lucrative advertising emphasis, Disney decided to break out on his own.

In May 1922 the ambitious young commercial artist left his promising career at the Film Ad Company to establish Laugh-O-Gram Films. With

$15,000 in backing from a number of local investors, he incorporated the business, purchased office and animation equipment, and began to assemble a staff. Ub Iwerks joined him, as did several young artists from the Film Ad Company — Hugh Harman, Walker Harman, Rudolf Ising, and Carmen "Max" Maxwell — and it was this group that was featured in those playful photographs from the early 1920s. These energetic young men, along with a salesman, a secretary, an inker and painter, and a business manager, occupied a five-room suite on the second floor of a building in downtown Kansas City.

Laugh-O-Gram Films compensated for inexperience with enthusiasm. Under Disney's direction, the company tackled a number of projects: a series of animated fairy-tale shorts for Pictorial Clubs, a distribution company, some newsreel footage for Universal and Pathé, and various filmed advertisements. Occasionally they supplemented the company income with moving baby pictures, song illustrations, and an occasional live-action film of a local parade. Walt and his associates barged around Kansas City in a spirit of jocularity, camaraderie, and creativity. Determined to work and eager to play, they did both constantly and with great energy. Not surprisingly, however, their meager profits began to put a damper on the fun and games. Many weeks the employees received only half their wages, because the company was low on funds. Although they bore it with good grace for a time, but late 1922 many of them drifted away to earn a steadier income.

In early 1923, Disney hit on an idea that he hoped would revive the floundering enterprise. Combining his interests in animation and live-action films, he proposed to create an entertainment hybrid by placing a human figure in a cartoon setting. Thus were born the Alice comedies, which featured a cute, inquisitive little girl (played initially by six-year-old Virginia Davis) acting against an animated background and romping with an animated menagerie of characters. After receiving encouragement from a New York distributor, Disney began producing the first in the series, *Alice's Wonderland*. Dwindling resources and mounting expenses, however, converged to undermine the project. Reduced to living in his office and eating beans out of a can, Disney completely exhausted his funds as his staff deserted him. With his options rapidly shrinking, he reluctantly decided to get out of both animation and Kansas City. After notifying his creditors of pending bankruptcy and consulting with his brother Roy, he made a decisive move. In July 1923 he left for Hollywood.

After several days of train travel — even though he was nearly penniless, he scraped together enough money to travel first class — Disney arrived in Los Angeles, determined to make it as a director of live-action movies. He found lodging with an uncle, Robert Disney, and immediately began haunting the major movie studios, looking for work. Concocting a few white lies that inflated his status in the film world, he gained access to various studio lots and hung around hoping to make connections. Roy, who was also in Los Angeles, recuperating from tuberculosis in a veterans' hospital, tried to be encouraging. But nothing materialized. Walt was reluctant to get back into cartoons, believing that New York animation techniques had left him far behind, but finally, broke and depressed, he concluded that he had no choice.

He decided to revive the Alice comedies project and use it as a launching board. He reestablished contact with his New York distributor, Margaret Winkler, by sending her a letter on impressive new stationery emblazoned with the heading *Walt Disney, Cartoonist*. He wrote,

> This is to inform you that I am no longer connected with the Laugh-O-Gram Films, Inc., of Kansas City, Mo., and that I am establishing a studio in Los Angeles for the purpose of producing the new and novel series of cartoons I have previously written you about.
>
> The making of these new cartoons necessitates being located in a production center that I may engage trained talent for my casts, and be within reach of the right facilities for producing.
>
> I am taking with me a select number of my former staff and will in a very short time be producing at regular intervals . . .

Except for the claims about the staff, the studio, and the production schedule, Disney was completely accurate in this report.[3]

With typical confidence, however, the young man pulled off this brazen ploy. Impressed with the brief sample that he had sent along, which was all he had salvaged from the Kansas City project, Winkler sent back a telegram ordering six of these cartoons. A jubilant Walt rushed to the veterans' hospital and convinced Roy to become his business manager. He then dashed to his uncle Robert and convinced him to lend $500. Disney was in business, and in October 1923 the newborn, shaky Disney Brothers Studio signed a contract with Winkler for the Alice films, along with an option for two more series.

Over the next year Disney climbed back to his feet. For $10 a month he rented a storefront on Kingswell Avenue in Los Angeles where he set up a tiny three-room studio. Under a window sign proclaiming DISNEY BROS. STUDIO, he hired two animators to relieve him of drawing duties — one of them was a Californian named Ham Hamilton, and the other was Ub Iwerks — as he immersed himself in direction, production, and story development. Within a couple of months the studio hired a cameraman and a janitor and rented a vacant lot three blocks away that allowed for outdoor shooting. All of this resulted in a steady flow of films with titles like *Alice and the Wild West Show*, *Alice Cans the Cannibals*, *Alice Chops the Suey*, and *Alice Foils the Pirates*.

The initial contract called for one Alice cartoon per month. By late 1924, however, Margaret Winkler's husband, Charles Mintz, had taken over the distribution company, and he negotiated a second agreement with Disney Brothers, which speeded up the schedule to one film every three weeks. With money arriving steadily and production demand escalating, Walt decided to bring in four more of his old Kansas City colleagues — Hugh and Walker Harman, Rudolf Ising, and Friz Freleng — to assist with the animation. By the summer of 1925 the staff numbered a dozen and was still growing. The fledgling studio turned out twelve Alice shorts in 1924, eighteen in 1925, and twenty-six in 1926, and with prosperity it steadily outgrew its facilities. Having paid a deposit on a vacant lot at 2719 Hyperion Avenue, Disney Brothers began construction of a new studio, and the company moved in throughout the spring of 1926.[4]

By late in that year, however, Disney clearly had exhausted the creative possibilities of the Alice films. With Charles Mintz's encouragement and a request from his backer, Universal Pictures, the young producer began to develop a new, completely animated film series with a character named Oswald the Lucky Rabbit. It debuted in the spring of 1927 and, after a few problems were ironed out, became a great success. Oswald was a playful, attractive, and energetic character, and his films were bright, briskly paced, and full of humor. The cartoons quickly gathered a popular audience and even began to attract the attention of animators in New York. As Oswald cartoons such as *The Mechanical Cow, The Ol' Swimming 'Ole, Trolley Troubles,* and *Poor Papa* appeared, a steady flow of profits solidified the studio's financial situation. Walt was able to bulk up the creative staff with even more additions.

Then, in 1928, Disney confronted the first major crisis of his career. Early in the year, as the current Oswald contract expired, he traveled to New York to negotiate a new one with Mintz. Full of confidence, he asked for a modest increase in the price per cartoon, in light of the revenues that the series had piled up. Disney was stunned and confused when Mintz offered him *less!* Then the blow fell. Mintz told him to take it or leave it, because he himself had lured away most of Disney's staff, with the exception of Ub Iwerks. Moreover, Mintz said, the character of Oswald was the legal property of Universal Pictures, not Walt Disney. With the ultimatum came an offer: come with me and be paid a generous salary, or lose everything. Although shocked and disheartened, Disney never hesitated. He declined the offer, abandoned the Oswald character, and resigned himself to losing most of his staff. But on the train back to Los Angeles, he determined to find a new character and a fresh series somehow.

Arriving back at the studio in March, Walt held a number of secret, intense brainstorming sessions with Iwerks, the only loyalist from the Kansas City gang, and his brother Roy. The small group toyed with a number of new characters and tried to conceptualize a cartoon series that would save the studio. Within a few days, most of the other animators went to work for Mintz. Things looked bleak, but out of this desperate situation came a new character: Mickey Mouse. As he emerged from those frantic meetings, Mickey was little more than a reworked version of Oswald the Lucky Rabbit — the ears were shortened, the figure was made more rounded, and the character became more lovable.[5]

Once Mickey came to life, Disney moved quickly. Thinking of Charles Lindbergh's recent transatlantic flight, Walt and Ub worked up a short film for Mickey entitled *Plane Crazy,* and quickly followed it with a second cartoon called *The Gallopin' Gaucho.* Then came a truly daring move. Convinced that sound movies were here to stay — *The Jazz Singer,* with Al Jolson, had premiered in late 1927 — Walt decided to proceed with a Mickey film that would be synchronized to sound. *Steamboat Willie* was completed as a silent film, but its action was syncopated to songs "Steamboat Bill" and "Turkey in the Straw," as marks on the film cued the music, sound effects, and skimpy dialogue. With film in hand, Disney dashed off to New York in search of sound technology. On the way he visited with Carl Stalling, a musician and old friend in Kansas City, who quickly composed a formal score for the cartoon which he timed to the marks on the film.

Once in New York, Disney negotiated with RCA to record the soundtrack, but concluded that they wanted too much money for a very poor sound quality. He then hooked up with Pat Powers, a movie industry wheeler-dealer who had a system called Cinephone. They came to an agreement and arranged to hire a small orchestra and a number of sound-effects men to record the score for *Steamboat Willie.* After a false start at the first recording session, the orchestra leader followed the film marks closely, and he nailed the synchronization at the second session. A jubilant Walt wangled a two-week engagement for the film at New York's Colony Theatre, and it was an instant hit. Audiences loved it, favorable reviews began to appear in local newspapers, and the trade journals offered laudatory comments.

In a matter of days, film distribution companies began to call on Disney, trying to strike a deal. Every one offered a generous production advance to the studio but wanted to buy the cartoons outright in return. Determined to remain independent, Disney refused them all. Instead he turned once more to Pat Powers, who believed that the Mickey Mouse series was a way to promote his Cinephone sound system. Powers agreed to advance the Disney brothers enough money to make the films and distribute them nationally, and to take only 10 percent of the gross for his share. For his part, Disney agreed to rent, at a considerable fee, the Cinephone sound technology for a ten-year period.

With the deal struck, Disney roared into action. In early 1929 he expanded his studio once again, hiring a number of New York animators whom he had contacted while on the East Coast. A steady stream of Mickey

Mouse shorts began to appear within a matter of months. Films like *Mickey's Follies, Mickey's Choo Choo, The Jazz Fool,* and *The Plow Boy* garnered great popular acclaim and made Mickey Mouse a national fad by late in the year. At the same time the Disney Studio began to develop another cartoon series. At the suggestion of Carl Stalling, who had now joined the staff, it produced a number of short films based on musical themes. The Silly Symphonies, each of which stood independently, with no recurring characters, were more experimental in their techniques and structure than the Mickeys and full of free-flowing fantasy. *The Skeleton Dance* inaugurated these fascinating films, followed over the next couple of years by *Frolicking Fish, Monkey Melodies,* and *Arctic Antics.* Thus by the start of the new decade, with a popular character and armloads of innovation, Walt Disney had hit his stride as a popular entertainer, and a bright future seemed all but assured.

Then disaster struck once again, and from a completely unexpected quarter. In January 1930 Disney went to New York to consult with Pat Powers about some nagging financial problems in their arrangement: Powers's payments to the studio from the distribution of the shorts often arrived late, or not at all, and lagged behind the expected and reported sales figures. Walt was determined to renegotiate the arrangement. But when he confronted Powers and demanded an explanation, Powers calmly informed him that he had hired Ub Iwerks away, that Carl Stalling would follow Iwerks, and that Powers was prepared to set Iwerks up in an independent studio to do a new cartoon series. By enticing Disney's chief animator and close friend to leave, Powers believed he had gained the upper hand, so he proposed to take over the entire management of the Disney Studio, offering to pay Walt a very generous weekly salary.

Although shaken by the news of Iwerks's and Stalling's defection — they were the last of the old Kansas City group — Disney dug in his heels and turned Powers down flat. After huddling with Roy, he maneuvered for survival once again. First, the Disney Studio bought out the contract with Powers for a large cash settlement. Then the brothers arranged a new distribution deal with Columbia Pictures, which was eager to take advantage of Mickey Mouse's popularity. A short time later they reached an even better agreement with United Artists and the Bank of America. Finally, Walt channeled a new influx of talent into his Hollywood organization, much of it again from New York City, to replace Iwerks. Although seriously jolted by the Powers debacle, the Disney Studio lost its footing only temporarily. Quickly resuming production, it vaulted even higher and entered an era of enormous creativity and fame.

By the early 1930s, Walt Disney had fulfilled the American dream. The poor but ambitious innocent from the Midwest, full of ideas and eager to work, had headed west and struck gold in the hills of Hollywood. Mickey

Mouse had become famous, and the Silly Symphonies had begun taking animation into unexplored realms of creativity. Yet Disney's success cannot be understood as an isolated event. It unfolded as part and parcel of much larger cultural changes in the early twentieth century. Shaped by the rise of consumerism in the economic realm, bureaucracy in the social structure, and corporate liberalism in politics, an enormous historical transformation had reworked the meaning of entertainment and the definition of success. And it entangled Walt Disney in more ways than he ever fully understood.

II. Mice, Music, and Mass Culture

In the mid-1920s, Hollywood perched on the northern rim of Los Angeles, shining as a beacon to modern America. A sleepy suburb as late as 1910, it had attracted growing numbers of moviemakers over the next decade and a half, luring them with its bright, dry climate and gentle temperatures and its nearness to a variety of settings (ocean, desert, big city, small town) and diverse ethnic groups (Asians, Hispanics, Anglos). By the early 1920s a cluster of studios had sprung up among the gently rolling hills of Hollywood. Movies rapidly became the national pastime, and millions of people became entranced with a parade of cinematic celebrities and glamour. On the cutting edge of a new frontier, Hollywood seemed to embody new possibilities for success in modern America.[6]

The consolidation of the studio system stabilized and nourished the growth of the new movie capital. Beginning in the 1910s and building strength over the next several years, power was centralized in a few studios that dominated Hollywood production. The "Big Eight" — Paramount, Twentieth Century–Fox, MGM, Universal, Warner Brothers, Columbia, United Artists, and RKO — arose, under the leadership of dynamic businessmen, many of them Jewish immigrants. Located on a scattering of lots within a short distance of one another, these movie factories utilized new techniques of mass production, corporate consolidation, and financial centralization, as well as extensive subsidiary and distribution companies, to virtually control the market throughout the United States. By the late 1920s these giant conglomerates, directed by men like Adolph Zukor, Louis B. Mayer, Harry Cohn, and Jack Warner, dominated American movies and laid the groundwork for Hollywood's golden age. Like much of the rest of the country, Hollywood had fallen under the sway of corporate organization.[7]

The rise of Hollywood was also part of another sea-change in American life, namely the emergence of mass culture and its accompanying "leisure ethic." By the 1920s, a decades-long revolt against the genteel strictures of Victorianism had largely succeeded, and its triumph was particularly evident in the area of entertainment, where traditional distinctions between uplifting, didactic, bourgeois entertainment and bawdy, rough-hewn, working-class pastimes were steadily disappearing. The emergence of commercialized entertainment in the early 1900s — vaudeville, professional sports, amusement parks, urban music clubs, radio, phonograph records — helped blur class distinctions. The American love affair with the movie represented the apex of this new ethos.[8]

Walt Disney grasped the key characteristics of this new entertainment paradigm — leisure, laughter and tears, excitement and thrills, fantasy and self-fulfillment, consumption — and worked them into a unique, delightful new form. Mickey's antics embodied a carnival spirit of fun that tapped elements from popular music, vaudeville comedy, and dance, and playful social satire to feed the fantastic images that moved magically across the screen. This enchanting mélange strove for neither realism nor uplift, but for simple mass entertainment. Part of Mickey's appeal lay in his intrinsic cuteness and charm, of course, but much of it also flowed from a much broader source. Simply put, Disney had a visceral instinct for the rhythms and emotions of mass culture.

Early in the 1920s, Disney had begun to borrow themes and techniques from other mass entertainments to use in his animated series. Many of his early Alice comedies, for instance, bore a strong resemblance to the Our Gang comedies of Hal Roach, in terms of both the stories and the troupe of child actors. A bit later, critics noted the vaudeville overtones of many of his animated shorts. Articles praised the strong sense of rhythm and motion in Disney cartoons and described their creator as shaping modern fairy tales — "'Puss-in-Boots' adapted to a flapper jazz age." James William Fitzpatrick, writing in the New York *Motion Picture Herald,* captured the mass culture angle most clearly when he noted that Disney's short cartoons pleased a contemporary "universal audience . . . [consisting of] patrons of differing tastes."[9]

Walt himself made no secret of the foundation of his early productions. In a 1931 interview, he described his studio's mischievous attempts to model its animated villains on their live counterparts on the silver screen. In the Mickey Mouse films, the artists "make rough cat villains to resemble Wallace Beery and smooth, polished cat villains to look like Erich von Stroheim." He explained at some length that his cartoons were based on a certain reading of the American public. "We have found out that they want most to laugh," he reported. "We learned after hard lessons, too, that the public wants its heroes. Most of all we learned that the American public loves dance music." This unique blend of music, mischief, dance, comedy, and heroic melodrama remained central to the Disney appeal for a long time.[10]

Disney's debt to varied mass entertainment forms appeared clearly, for example, in films like *Blue Rhythm* (1931), where Mickey plays boisterous ragtime songs at the piano; the keys start jumping off the keyboard in excitement, Minnie slinks into view singing a raucous blues tune, and a full-fledged vaudeville song-and-dance routine unfolds. A host of Mickey Mouse films wandered down the same cultural path. As they appeared steadily in the late 1920s and early 1930s, these wildly popular shorts shared a number of traits: the technological dazzle of sound, highly rhythmic music, gag-filled slapstick comedy, and a carnival chaos that gleefully upended the natural and social order.

Comedy, of course, played an evident role in Mickey's various misadventures. The constant barrage of jokes, puns, ludicrous entanglements, and outrageous satire delighted audiences across the country. Several decades later, in describing the early days of his studio, Walt recalled how he and his artists threw barrels of gags into the films "because I was desperate. I mean, I didn't even like 'em then, but I had to get [a short movie] out every two weeks." "I used to work very hard on gag situations," he remembered, and "I set up a special group of fellows just to work on [those] situations." He and his staff would constantly bounce comedy ideas off one another, and on at least one occasion they borrowed inspiration from "an old burlesque routine."[11]

An irreverent slapstick humor flowered everywhere in the Mickey shorts from this period and attracted audiences with a wide variety of fantastic imagery, whimsy, and irreverence. *The Gallopin' Gaucho*, for instance, offered as its setting a tavern so rough that the side door had a sign reading FAMILY ENTRANCE. In *Plane Crazy*, Minnie leaps out of an airplane and floats to safety using her bloomers as a parachute. A few years later, Mickey engaged in a Keystone Kops routine at the conclusion of *Traffic Troubles* (1931), driving his jalopy at breakneck speed through a farmyard and crashing through a barn, only to emerge covered with feathers. *Mickey's Mechanical Man* (1933) follows the fate of Mickey's slightly miswired robot boxer, who goes berserk and pulverizes everything in sight whenever he hears a horn go off.

This array of comedic situations was punctuated by dance numbers. In something of a thematic omen, Minnie appeared as a seductive dancer in *The Gallopin' Gaucho*, and she was followed by a host of imitators. *Jungle Rhythm*, for example, a Mickey film of 1929, was largely a collection of synchronized dance routines that focused on a host of jungle animals, especially a pair of agile monkeys, as they gyrated rhythmically to the music of Mickey's squeezebox. *Mickey's Follies* (1929) offered both a comical dance line of ducks and Mickey tap-dancing on top of his piano. Even *The Castaway* (1931), a Robinson Crusoe–style tale of lonely abandonment, presented Mickey playing show tunes on a washed-up piano as a group of lively seals danced to the music.

Music joined comedy and dance as the entertainment trinity in the early Disney films. The introduction of sound in animation, of course, gave prominent roles to musical scores much more quickly than sophisticated dialogue. In the early films, characters' voices remained little more than distinctive monosyllabic noises, and their words were few and far between. But the music flourished. In fact, a large number of Mickey Mouse movies from these years actually took shape as musical variety shows. In *The Opry House* (1929), a "Big Vaudeville Show" structures the whole narrative as Mickey performs a hilarious parody of classical music on the piano, Minnie sings "Yankee Doodle Dandy," and an inept orchestra of farm animals gleefully mangles selections from *Carmen*. Mickey appears as the leader of a raucous animal band in *Mickey's Follies*, a roadshow that features the singing of the theme song "Minnie's Yoo Hoo." Music appeared over and over again as a major feature of nearly every early Mickey film — Mickey as a violinist in *Just Mickey*, Minnie playing the accordion in *Traffic Troubles*, a huge ape playing the piano with both hands and both *feet* in *The Castaway*.

In another typical departure from tradition, these movies abandoned the strict moralism of nineteenth-century courting traditions to embrace a wholesome but more liberated idea of romance. Mickey and Minnie, of course, revealed this trend most clearly. In *Plane Crazy*, the plot follows Mickey's romantic pursuit of Minnie as they ride in a car that has been reworked into an airplane. Three years later, *Traffic Troubles* also featured Mickey courting his love interest in his automobile, the symbol of America's loosening sexual mores in the 1920s. In *Touchdown Mickey*, as the football hero is hauled off the field atop the uprooted goalposts, he kisses his swooning sweetheart. In a host of such films, Victorian decorum and the appearance of moral virtue had faded before the excitement of youthful romance.

The extent to which Disney's early films were part of a larger cultural realignment in America was revealed in a letter from an irate reader of the Atlantic City *Press* in New Jersey, who wrote on January 21, 1931, under the name "A Child Lover." This angry viewer denounced "the present day lack of decency on both stage and screen" and insisted that mass entertainment was corrupting children by counteracting moral influences at home. As this indignant reader asked, how could youngsters remain virtuous when they "are constantly having presented before them on the screen such subjects as easy divorce and remarriage, indecency in dress, dancing and suggestiveness? Even in such should-be-innocent subjects as . . . Mickey Mouse comedies, they are beginning to inject these same undesirable qualities. To say nothing of the gross vulgarity and stupidity of so many of the short sketches so continuously being panned off on a long enduring public." It ended with an appeal to parents. Does it "pay parents to fatten the purses of [movie] producers," the writer asked earnestly, "in return for having the sense of moral values in their children confused and debauched?"[12]

Disney's reflections on the subject made for a fascinating contrast. In an article entitled "The Cartoon's Contribution to Children," he confessed that while "wholesome entertainment" was a prime objective of his cartoons, the

Disney artists felt no obsessive concern over morality in their creative work. When a new Mickey Mouse short appeared, "we will not have worried one bit as to whether the picture will make the children better men and women, or whether it will conform with the enlightened theories of child psychology . . . It is not our job to teach, implant morals, or improve anything except our pictures. If Mickey has a bit of practical philosophy to offer the younger generation, it is to keep on trying. That's what we do who make animated cartoons."[13]

Perhaps nothing better reflected the multidimensional mass cultural appeal of Disney's early films than *The Whoopee Party* (1932). This delightful Mickey Mouse movie opens with Disney's animal characters holding a party at a private home. The atmosphere is sedate and genteel at first, with polite conversation, refreshments, and quiet music predominating. As Mickey and his musician friends begin playing more upbeat music, however, the group begins to dance, gradually moving faster and faster. As the pace quickens, even inanimate objects in the house — living room furniture, plates and saucers, shirts and pillows, a bed and chest of drawers — come to life and start gyrating. The music gets louder and more frenzied, confetti and noise-makers appear, and the boisterous crowd begins shouting "Whoopee!" When the police appear to break up the gathering, they are drawn into the frivolity and begin dancing themselves. Amid the general gaiety, Mickey and Minnie kiss as the film ends.

By virtue of this lively combination of music, dance, comedy, and fun morality, Mickey Mouse, the jazz-age entertainer, became a celebrity. A 1931 *Publishers Weekly* article noted that

> on March 15, seven hundred and twenty Sunday newspapers carried a full-page story about him; the *Saturday Evening Post* has given him preferred position on the "Post Scripts" page; Gardner Rea had a full-page cartoon about him in last week's *Life;* he is president of the kiddies' club that meets every Saturday morning with three million members; he probably is featured in the lights over two thousand movie entrances this week, and his name is Mickey Mouse. He will be published as a book by the David McKay Company on May 1st.[14]

Mickey became a staple of popular magazines such as *Life,* which ran a cartoon on March 20, 1931, that pictured a group of wealthy, cosmopolitan theatergoers walking out of a theater looking very downcast; the caption read "No Mickey Mouse!" Yet highbrow journals of opinion like *The Nation* also joined the publicity parade, naming both Mickey Mouse and the Silly Symphonies to its "honor roll" of the best films of 1930.[15]

This publicity onslaught encouraged an abiding image of Mickey Mouse as a star. By the 1920s, of course, the Hollywood star had become a symbol of leisure and consumer spending in American society. Film actors and actresses did not rely on inherited wealth but worked their way to success by virtue of their talent, charisma, and sex appeal. Living in palatial homes, driving sports cars, enjoying the pleasures of fame and fortune, engaging in a carefree life of amusement, movie stars flourished by virtue of "the ability to entertain and make people happy."[16]

While avoiding any mention of opulence, Mickey Mouse's extensive publicity fit easily into this larger trend. A magazine article in 1930 celebrated the character's birthday by announcing that "what it takes some actors a lifetime to accomplish — Mickey has attained in two short years. For he is, undoubtedly, one of the foremost stars of the talking screen." A raft of articles in this period enshrined the lovable mouse in the pantheon of movie stardom alongside such film greats as Charlie Chaplin, Douglas Fairbanks, Mary Pickford, Gloria Swanson, John Gilbert, Lon Chaney, and Ronald Colman. Gusts of rhetoric blew through movieland, proclaiming that a brilliant new figure had "flashed across the firmament of sound pictures, which bids fair to outshine all stars for a long time to come." Pickford declared the mouse to be her favorite actor, while Marion Davies told interviewers that she wanted to "make motion picture with Mickey." A 1931 Columbia Pictures publicity flyer pictured a smiling Mickey standing between Chaplin and Fairbanks, with a hand on each man's shoulder, as all three "stars" waved at the viewer. The caption read, "'Ray for Charlie and Doug! — Mickey." As Hollywood columnist Louella O. Parsons summarized, "Mickey Mouse has a bigger screen following than nine tenths of the stars in Hollywood."[17]

In 1929, with the start of the Silly Symphony series, Walt extended the parameters of his mass entertainment venture even further. Apparently this collection of animated shorts originated with Carl Stalling, Disney's musical director and old friend from Kansas City. After the Mickey shorts were up and running and gaining great popularity, Stalling went to Disney with an idea for, in his own words, a "musical series . . . [featuring] inanimate figures like skeletons, trees, flowers, etc. coming to life and dancing and doing other animated actions fitted to music more or less in a humorous and rhythmic mood." Wilfred Jackson, one of the studio's early animators, remembered the series' origins somewhat differently. Stalling and Disney were constantly arguing, he recalled, over whether the action should be tailored to the music or vice versa. Both being stubborn men, after a time they tired of arguing and agreed to have two series: the Mickeys, where the action would predominate, and a series of shorts where the music would take precedence.[18]

Whatever their specific beginnings, the Silly Symphonies allowed Disney more experimentation and freer expression than the Mickey cartoons. Years later he recalled that Mickey's success, ironically, had created problems, because theaters and audiences wanted "everything to be the same," while he wanted new ideas and patterns. As he put it, "The whole idea of the Symphonies was to give me another street to work on, you know. Getting away from a set pattern of a character. Each Symphony, the idea would be a different story based on music with comedy and things." Eric Larson, another studio artist from this period, added that this series grew out of a desire to enhance the artistry in animation by putting "more poetry in the production."[19]

The Silly Symphonies ranged widely, from stories based on fairy tales and mythology, such as *Playful Pan* (1930), *King Neptune* (1932), and *Old King Cole* (1933), to impressionistic treatments of the cycle of nature, such as *Springtime* (1929), *Winter* (1930), *Summer* (1930), and *Autumn* (1930), to fantastic comedy scenarios, such as *Arctic Antics* (1930), *Cannibal Capers* (1930), *The Spider and the Fly* (1931), and *Egyptian Melodies* (1931). As numerous critics commented, they often surpassed the Mickey shorts in their imagination, musical entertainment, and emotional intensity. Writing in *McCall's, American Magazine*, or the Kansas City *Film Review*, reviewers praised the series for its compelling creativity. The noted film critic Gilbert Seldes, writing in *The New Yorker* in 1931, admitted that he considered the Silly Symphonies to be "by far the greater of Disney's products . . . Disney's imagination is freer to roam than it is in the more formal Mouse series." The New York *Herald Tribune* offered a more pretentious analysis, suggesting that "their shrewd and surprisingly Rabelaisian humor" held the secret to their enthusiastic reception.[20]

A pair of innovative Silly Symphony shorts exemplified the nature of the series. *The Skeleton Dance* (1929), the first of the group to appear, brewed a humorously macabre concoction that, in the words of the New York *Daily Mirror*, "makes you shiver and makes you laugh." It opens in a moonlit cemetery, where a fight between shrieking cats so disturbs the calm atmosphere that a skeleton emerges from its grave to frighten them off. Soon other skeletons arise to form a quartet, and they perform elaborate synchronized dance routines to a Carl Stalling composition that borrows heavily from Edvard Grieg's classical piece "March of the Dwarfs." A host of gags punctuate the film. At one point, for instance, a skeleton detaches his own leg bone to use as a mallet for playing the xylophone on another's rib cage. Another skeleton grabs a slow-footed cat, stretches its tail, and plays it like a stringed instrument. As dawn breaks, the clanking dancers hurry back to the peace of their graves.[21]

The Merry Dwarfs (1929), another early Silly Symphony, mined its humor and energy from a less grotesque, if equally fantastic, vein. Evoking a kind of magical Old World atmosphere, the film opens in a small village where tiny workmen with tall hats and long beards are cleaning sidewalks and buildings, fitting shoes on a centipede, and forging horseshoes for the grasshoppers they use as steeds. When a brass band marches down the street, a festival erupts. The dwarfs pull barrels along behind the musicians and use the spigots to squirt beer into each other's mouths. Others drink beer from steins and, retiring to a forest where flowers and mushrooms tower over them, dance in synchronization. Wrapping leaves around their stomachs like tutus, they leap and cavort about, merrily pulling one another's beards and squashing their hats. This gag-filled film reaches a climax when two dwarfs fall into a beer barrel, pop up intoxicated, and perform an eye-spinning dance as the entire scene begins to wave and swirl. They collapse into a grinning heap as the movie ends. The whole film was rather daring for the Prohibition era.

As one student of the early films has put it, Disney "kept an alert eye on what was afoot in vaudeville, daily comic strips, circus, live theater, and live action films; documentaries, newsreels, Laurel and Hardy, the Our Gang comedies, and — even more than Chaplin — Douglas Fairbanks and Harold Lloyd." In a newspaper piece, Walt admitted to being a dyed-in-the-wool movie fan from early boyhood because of the genre's diversity. This medium, in his words, encompassed "the finest stage personalities, the best in concert and opera stars, great vaudevillians, . . . laughter, excitement, drama, music, or anything we happen to feel in the mood for."[22]

Critics and audiences alike responded to Disney's films with commingled wonderment and warmth. Typical of the torrent of praise was Harold W. Cohen's article in the Pittsburgh *Post Gazette*. Lauding both that "mad and merry little rodent, Mickey Mouse" and "those vastly entertaining Silly Symphonies," Cohen observed that

> not until a couple of years ago were you ever permitted to see and hear a six-legged spider pounding out Schubert's "Liebestraum" on a baby-grand piano or a pelican rattling off the Anvil Chorus from "Il Trovatore" on the bony skeleton of a giraffe . . .
>
> Here is a woodpecker driving rivets into a building with his beak, a spider grasping each end of a pianola with three legs and bouncing over the keys with his back to produce Tchaikovsky or Mendelssohn, Mickey playing a xylophone solo on a set of false teeth . . . an insect doing a tap dance skipping across a flock of railroad ties, or an assembly of elephants and tigers cheering lustily as a group of alley cats engage in an orchestral encounter . . .
>
> Hard work, imagination, and a keen appreciation of audience psychology go into every one of these Mickey pictures and Silly Symphonies.[23]

For all of Disney's appeal, however, it would be a mistake to view him solely as a cultural innovator. In fact, his early work displayed considerable ambivalence about the values of modern American life. A persistently nostalgic element played around its edges. Occasionally that element would move to center stage, in a number of guises. Many of Disney's earliest shorts, for instance, were set in rural environments that evoked the nineteenth-century past. Taking place on farms or in small villages, these films melded the comedy, dance, and music of urban America with a host of more familiar, traditional images. Beginning with *Steamboat Willie,* a significant proportion of the early Disney animations featured some kind of strong rural association. From *Barnyard Battle* in 1929 to *Musical Farmer* and *Barnyard Olympics* in 1932, they drew much of their humor from comic juxtapositions of urban and rural stereotypes. In subtle ways, many of them also tended to glorify the individualist work ethic, as Mickey, in particular, struggled against the odds to find happiness and success.

Two films illustrate the mixed cultural imagery of Disney's early work well. *The Barn Dance* (1928) contrasts two suitors for Minnie's affections. The virtuous Mickey pulls up in front of her house in a horse-drawn wagon, while the villainous Pete arrives in an automobile. Minnie rides off with Pete, but when the car breaks down she happily climbs on Mickey's wagon. The rest of the film, with overtones of Victorian melodrama, takes place at an old-fashioned rural barn dance, as the straw-footed hero and the urbane bully compete for Minnie's affections by showing off their dancing skills. *The Jazz Fool* (1929) presents more complex fare. Appealing to a mass audience recently entranced by Al Jolson, the film features a traveling jazz show and focuses its energy on music and comedy. At the same time, however, the plot unfolds not in an urban theater but in the countryside. The roadshow meanders through several villages, with Mickey playing the pipe organ from a truck. Cows begin dancing to the infectious melodies, and drying laundry jumps off the line and joins in the fun. Like many other Disney movies from this period, *The Jazz Fool* tempers its modern entertainment elements with strong doses of nostalgia.

This traditionalist element found an institutional ally in the Mickey Mouse Clubs, initiated by the Disney Studio around 1930 to help corral the children's audience. An emphasis on the formation of self-control, respect for hierarchical authority, and firm, internalized moral guidelines found clear expression in the Mickey Mouse Club creed officially annunciated in studio publicity:

> I will be upright and fair in all my dealings with my playmates. I will be truthful. I will obey my father and mother and will always stand ready to help people older than myself. I will obey my teachers and strive for high marks in my studies. I will always respond promptly to the call of the Chief Mickey Mouse and observe all the laws of the club.

A similar moral orientation also surfaced in studio releases instructing club leaders to cultivate association with women's clubs, parent-teacher associations, and other groups that favored engaging "young people in the proper form of entertainment." As a 1931 magazine article phrased it, the Mickey Mouse Clubs specialized in showing "clean films, with a rather elaborate ritual of patriotism and good-fellowship before and after."[24]

By the late 1920s, Walt Disney was easing his audience from one cultural milieu to another by placing exciting new genres and forms within customary social settings and mapping them with older moral signposts. This unique blend of comforting tradition and challenging innovation was to become a key to Disney's enduring popularity. Yet the story of Walt Disney's early career contained another crucial element. The allure of leisure and consumerism was steadily eroding the moral foundations of Victorianism and summoning forth new traits conducive to individual coping and achievement. One result was the new model of success that began to take shape in the early 1900s. Based on notions of personality, positive thinking, and bureaucratic maneuver, it helped redefine the very notion of selfhood. The young midwesterner's climb to fame and fortune illustrated many of the tenets and difficulties of this new ideology.

3

The Entertainer
as Success Icon

I N 1920 WALT DISNEY made his first screen appearance, in a crude
Newman Laugh-O-Gram sample reel produced in the garage of his
Kansas City home. In three brief vignettes, this short, flashy film aimed
to entice a local theater owner with vibrant visual images. It did more than it
intended. Its opening scene shows young Walt striding into his office, sitting
down at a drawing board, lighting his pipe, and starting to animate. Drawing
rapidly and deftly, he quickly churns out a series of gag sketches on local life,
including a caricature of himself as a busy commercial artist. The scene
creates an image of a sharply dressed, dynamic, and industrious young
entrepreneur, the same persona that Disney was promoting intensely in real
life. At the earliest stage of his entertainment career, he was eagerly embracing the old American success story of the self-made man overcoming obstacles on the way to fame and fortune. In less than a decade, his hopes were
fulfilled. He seemed a Horatio Alger character come to life.[1]

This familiar rags-to-riches tale, however, offered an important twist. In
the early twentieth century, many of the old guidelines for success seemed
increasingly dated. A society characterized by mass markets, bureaucracy,
corporate consolidation, and a growing leisure ethic held little place for
old-fashioned Victorian ideas that demanded such stern qualities as upstanding character, hard work, self-control, and compulsive thrift. By the
1920s these traditional values were wilting in a heated new atmosphere

dominated by an emphasis on personality, teamwork, self-fulfillment, and consumer spending. In other words, the world of Elias Disney was receding quickly, and his son now lived in a society that demanded new standards and dicta of success.

I. Losing Friends and Influencing People

In *How to Win Friends and Influence People* (1936), Dale Carnegie codified a message of success that he had developed over the previous two decades as a lecturer and essayist. Proclaiming that the aspiring person must abandon the hidebound moralism and probity of the vanished Victorian age, Carnegie urged instead a modern code of gamesmanship in which one manipulated one's behavior according to the perception of others, directed a constant barrage of flattery at friends and acquaintances, constructed "winning images," and focused one's psychic energies. Carnegie was not alone. A host of similar figures — the "positive thinkers," as one historian has termed this popular cadre — burst on the cultural scene in early twentieth-century America. One of the most famous would be Dr. Norman Vincent Peale, the dynamic minister whose message of positive thinking made him a national celebrity by the 1940s. Preaching variations of "mind cure" and utilizing popular psychologies, these success ideologues promised wealth, status, and peace of mind. Their central message resonated loud and long: in a mass society of impersonal bureaucratic institutions, marshaling one's psychic resources to construct a vivid personality offered the key to success and happiness.[2]

Although there is no evidence that Disney read the work of such modern guides to success, he instinctively adopted many of their principles, at least in part. Eager to enter the world of moviemaking, he carefully gauged its requirements for admission and achievement. Gazing from afar, he realized that Hollywood, like the rest of corporate America, increasingly demanded not only hard work and ambition but a set of newer qualities as well: salesmanship, management skills, and personality. Quite unselfconsciously, he began to draw upon abilities later popularized by writers like Carnegie and to synthesize them with the principles of self-help that he had imbibed as a child of the Midwest.

Even in the earliest stages of his career, as he tried to get Laugh-O-Grams off the ground and then to build his first Hollywood studio, the aspiring filmmaker exuded an intense ambition. Walt's sister-in-law Edna Disney recalled that even as a teenager he would come to her house for dinner and talk for hours about what he wanted to do in the animation field. Carmen Maxwell, an associate in both Kansas City and Los Angeles, remembered that "Walt always said, even back then, that he would make it big." "The reason he was successful was because he set a goal and he just went after it," noted Friz Freleng, another early colleague. "You'd have to break your neck keeping up with him. If you could. But you couldn't surpass him."[3]

The inner fire that fueled this ambition can be glimpsed in an incident in 1925. Up to that point, Disney's animation company had been called the Disney Brothers Studio. But when the success of the Alice comedies allowed for expansion into the two-story facility on Hyperion Avenue, Walt bluntly informed his brother Roy of a significant change. Henceforth, he announced, their operation would be known as the Walt Disney Studio. Roy, although somewhat annoyed, had little taste for the spotlight anyway and silently acquiesced.[4]

Walt frequently took pride in his passionate work ethic as a young man. In 1933, for instance, a magazine writer summarized his recipe for success in these words: "Invent your own job; take such an interest in it that you eat, sleep, dream, walk, talk, and live nothing but your work until you succeed." Disney himself recalled that early in his Hollywood career, he often went back to the studio after dinner or an early show, accompanied by his wife, to work late into the night. As he toiled away, Lillian would lie down on the davenport in his office and drift off to sleep. "And suddenly I'd look at my watch and it'd be 1:30. I'd look at her, she'd be sound asleep, and I'd keep on working till I finished," Disney related with a chuckle. "So I'd go in and wake her up and she'd say 'What time is it?' and I'd say 10:30, and we'd go home and she'd go to bed and never know."[5]

Disney's brash egotism and gargantuan capacity for labor may have been dictated in part by necessity. In the world of movie and animation production in the early decades of the century, manipulation and treachery ruled the day. Remembering those days as a constant struggle for survival, Disney described an "out-and-out cutthroat business" for the unwary commercial artist, where an unscrupulous figure would be "putting a knife in your back and he'll be laughing and having a drink with you." One of his animators said that "everybody was conspiring against the other one . . . Everybody had ambition; everybody wanted to be a producer." In this volatile and dangerous atmosphere, creativity required an aggressive, focused temperament to triumph.[6]

Hence the young studio head pushed himself and his employees hard. He focused on two goals. First, experience gradually led him to the conclusion that independent control of his business was the only way to success. He doggedly declared his intention in the late 1920s: "I'm going to go independent. I'm going to own [my films]. And I stuck to it." Second, Disney came to believe that excellence in production values provided the best means to achieve independence. A perfectionist at heart, he insisted that his studio present ever more creative efforts. Ben Sharpsteen, an animator who remained at the studio for nearly forty years, recalled his very first conversation with Disney, in 1929: "Walt's conclusion, from his experience to

date in the business, was that he had determined never to be at the mercy of a distributor again. His whole salvation was in making a product that so excelled that the public would recognize it and enjoy it as the best of entertainment, and that they would more or less demand to see Disney pictures. It was an extremely ambitious statement to make . . . But Walt made a simple statement that you can lick them with 'product.'"[7]

Disney's relentless drive for success, however, gradually began to erode the goodwill of his colleagues. For years the old Kansas City gang shared an informal division of labor, a youthful disdain for poverty, and a boyish enthusiasm that led them to antics like making large fake cameras and posing as important New York moviemakers. Operating on a shoestring budget, they would recycle the transparent animation cels after they had been photographed, washing them clean over and over until too many scratches made them unusable. When no buses ran out to the Hyperion studio and they were too poor to afford cars, Roy Disney would pick up half a dozen animators on Sunset Boulevard and drive them to work. But this group, once noted for its camaraderie and friendly hijinks, became infected with sullen resentment against its ambitious chief. Slowly but surely, Disney's animators abandoned him.[8]

One of the first conflicts occurred with Hugh Harman and Rudolf Ising, two artists who had been with Disney since the Laugh-O-Gram days. Both became disgruntled, claiming that Disney had offered them partnerships in his studio so they would come to Los Angeles and then reneged after they arrived. Ising was fired by Disney in 1927 after falling asleep while he worked at the monotonous task of photographing animation cels. Harman stayed on but increasingly clashed with Disney, whom he came to regard as a tyrant.[9]

Friz Freleng, another young artist from Kansas City, went out to the Disney Studio in 1927 to work as an animator. But "Walt and I never got along at all . . . clash of personalities," he noted years later. "I guess I had the same kind of temperament he did, and it just didn't work." Not only did Disney tend to insult Freleng's work, but he allowed no room for individual creativity. In the artist's words, "I couldn't take it. You did what Disney wanted to do. You couldn't do what *you* wanted to do. It had to be just Disney, you had to think like Disney, do what Disney did, and I wasn't that kind of guy. I had to do my own thing." Discouraged after a series of run-ins, Freleng finally skipped work one day and went to a movie on Wilshire Boulevard. To his dismay, while riding along on top of a double-decker bus, he looked down and locked eyes with Walt Disney, who was driving behind in his Moon roadster. The next day, when Freleng arrived at work, his desk had been cleared out. After a shouting match with Disney, he picked up his paycheck and quit.[10]

The staff discord finally came to a head in early 1928. An emissary of

Charles Mintz's secretly approached Hugh Harman and offered to set up the whole group in an independent studio to produce Oswald the Lucky Rabbit films. Harman accepted with little hesitation, and Disney's entire staff, with the exception of Ub Iwerks, left him high and dry. Harman reported to at least one acquaintance that the artists had gone to work for Mintz because they could no longer tolerate Disney's highhanded ways. They were joined by Freleng and Ising, both of whom had left the studio months before. Harman and Ising, the senior members of the group, never felt that they had betrayed their old boss. "They felt they owed no special loyalty to him," one interviewer noted. "Walt, they say, was too obviously devoted to the advancement of Walt Disney to inspire such feelings."[11]

Years later, Walt recalled his early attitudes with mingled pride and ruefulness: "I used to be less tolerant in those days because there was more pressure of that payroll and getting that picture out, and I guess I was a pretty tough guy at times . . . I can look back and [realize] I used to get mad and blow my top, kind of a Donald Duck type of thing, you know?" His single-minded sense of purpose, however, combined with other characteristics conducive to achievement in modern America.[12]

Salesmanship may have ranked highest among Disney's attributes. Nearly every observer of the young studio chief in the 1920s and early 1930s commented, usually with admiration, on his remarkable capacity to sell his product and himself. Edna Disney described it this way: "Walt had a way of telling you about what he wanted to do and explaining it to you in a way that you fell right in line with him. You would go right along with him. You couldn't help it . . . Walt had very expressive big brown eyes. And he used his eyes a lot. He'd go on, and he'd use his hands and his eyes . . . [He] just had a way of making you believe it all." He used his powers of persuasion regularly: he talked Roy out of a Los Angeles veterans' hospital to help him launch his Alice series; he convinced Rudolf Ising first to lend him $500 and then to accept company stock in lieu of a payback; he got a loan of $2000 from Carl Stalling. Even though Disney often struggled when trying to explain what he wanted, Stalling once noted, "He inspired us . . . We wanted to help him."[13]

Part of this magnetic, motivating personality could be attributed to a kind of positive thinking that was becoming a cultural gospel among many. Adolph Kloepper, the business manager of Laugh-O-Gram Films, noted that even in that company's darkest days, its youthful leader never sounded one note of defeat. "He was always optimistic about his ability and about the value of his ideas and about the possibilities of cartoons," he said. "Never once did I hear him express anything except determination to go ahead, because he believed in himself and he believed in what he was trying to accomplish." Roy Disney observed that even when his brother was scrounging around Los Angeles trying to break into the movie business, he was always full of enthusiasm. "Tomorrow was always going to answer all his problems," Roy noted. "He had a persistency, an optimism, about him all the time, a drive." Walt's own reminiscences underlined these qualities. He was never afraid to push ahead, he once said, even when faced with the most daunting obstacles. Having a "good, hard failure when you're young" was positive, he argued, because it forced you to learn. He summarized his energetic attitude in simple terms. "Actually, I think everything that ever happened to me was a good turn," he insisted. "I've never really been unhappy."[14]

A particularly important part of Disney's positive thinking involved the projection of an image. From early in his career, he carefully shaped a persona linked to achievement and success. He admitted to enjoying his first taste of celebrity in Kansas City, with the Newman Laugh-O-Gram films, and he subsequently worked ceaselessly to cultivate his image as a poor boy destined to make good through hard work and talent. In a 1931 article on the origins of Mickey Mouse, for example, he stressed that while he had come to Hollywood with practically no money, he had "had plenty of energy and enterprise." In later years he consistently embroidered this theme to create an aura of personal struggle that was almost mythological: the penniless years in Kansas City when he wore threadbare clothing, ate beans out of a can, slept in his studio, and survived because of the assistance of kind souls who believed in his potential, then his post-bankruptcy struggle against the odds in Hollywood to get his films off the ground. These early travails and their vanquishment became central to Disney's self-image.[15]

Such tales of climbing upward would have mattered little if left in the realm of private storytelling. But they were not. Journalists quickly seized on Disney's self-made-man image and began to translate it into a public legend. For instance, 1931 articles in the *American Magazine* and *Movie Mirror* described Disney as a typical young American who succeeded because of "hard, heartbreaking work." Within a few years, the descriptions smoothly shoehorned him into the category of American success story. Douglas Churchill, writing in the *New York Times Magazine* in 1934, described him as "the Horatio Alger of the cinema" and sketched "the life story of the farm youth, later newsboy, who through industry, courage, and all the other Algerian virtues attained international recognition." That same year a long article in *Fortune* used similar language. "Enough has been written about Disney's life and hard times already," it asserted, "to stamp the bald, Algeresque outlines of his career as familiarly on the minds of many Americans as the career of Henry Ford or Abraham Lincoln."[16]

Such acclaim ultimately bridged two cultural worlds. Disney did indeed have his share of old-fashioned virtues in the Horatio Alger mold, but he blended them with the more modern tenets of writers such as Carnegie and Peale. This cultural juxtaposition intruded into Disney's oldest friendship, with Ub Iwerks. The development of their tense, complex relationship laid bare some of the larger complexities of modern mass culture and its demands for success. It suggested that while some individuals flourished in the organizational, image-laden world of modern America, others viewed it as an alien land.

II. Ub Iwerks: "He Couldn't Sell Himself"

In the late 1920s, as the Mickey Mouse and Silly Symphony series began to garner public acclaim, credit went almost solely to the head of the Walt Disney Studio. But in professional circles another story made the rounds. Among animators and filmmakers, Ub Iwerks quietly gained a reputation as the real creative force of the Disney operation. Shamus Culhane, then a young artist at the Fleischer cartoon studio in New York, recalled that the appearance of every new Disney movie reinforced the notion that Iwerks was "the best animator in the business." Grim Natwick, creator of the famous Betty Boop character for Fleischer, noted simply that "the rumor in the East was that the genius of the Disney Studio was Iwerks." Even Les Clark, who trained under Iwerks on the way to becoming one of Disney's famous "nine old men," described his teacher as "a genius. He was like Walt."[17]

In fact, Iwerks worked closely with Walt Disney for a decade in a number of roles — as fellow apprentice, first business partner, head animator — and his contributions to Disney's success were enormous. At the very least, he served as Walt's right-hand man on the creative side of things in much the same way as Roy served on the financial side. Moreover, Walt and Ub were close personal friends as well as colleagues. Meeting as adolescents, they grew up in the business together.

Thus it was quite a shock when, in January 1930, Iwerks left the Disney Studio. Apparently allying himself with a move to torpedo the enterprise, he accepted funds from a scheming show business figure to start his own studio. His old boss and friend, evincing no small amount of bitterness in the wake of this startling action, felt betrayed. In fact, the reasons for the split were more complex. They lay partly in the record of the men's personal relationship — competitive, emotionally charged, verging on love/hate — but they also were shaped by demands for success. In this context, Disney and Iwerks, though they would be tightly linked throughout most of their professional careers, stood at polar opposites.

Their contrasting styles had surfaced in the earliest days of their relationship, in Kansas City. Disney and Iwerks met in the autumn of 1919 as young artists working at the Pesmen-Rubin Commercial Art Studio, struck up a friendship, and, after being laid off, became steadfast comrades, both personally and professionally. They first tried to start a small studio, subsequently worked together at the Kansas City Film Ad Company, and then joined forces in Disney's Laugh-O-Gram company. In those days Iwerks had a reputation as a "fantastic lettering man," so much so that between jobs he once made money by lettering tombstones on paper as a form of advertising for prospective cemetery clients. At the Film Ad Company, he got his first taste of animation by doing advertisements for hats, shoes, and lingerie. At Laugh-O-Gram in 1922–23, he continued to expand his animation skills and did considerable work on *Alice's Wonderland*, Walt's innovative film featuring both live action and animated figures.[18]

In certain ways, however, Disney and Iwerks made for quite a contrast. Walt was bubbling over with creativity and personality, unafraid to take risks, and clearly ambitious. Similarly creative, Ub could not have created a more different personal impression. Early photographs reveal a serious young man with tousled hair, a small mustache, and a calm, almost quizzical look on his face. Rectitude marked his character and silence his demeanor. While Disney loved to be the life of the party with his sparkling wit and inspired hijinks, Iwerks usually stood shyly to the side. He would participate in the continuous round of horseplay among the energetic young men at the Film Ad Company, but he seldom instigated any pranks. More than anything else, he exuded a quiet seriousness, so intense that strangers could believe that he was angry.

While respecting Iwerks's artistic talent, Disney also saw his shy personality as an easy target for friendly abuse. Reminiscing in later years, he recalled that when customers called, Ub "would just sit there. 'Cause he wasn't the kind to talk and he couldn't give the old sales pitch . . . *I* was the salesman." Some evidence suggests that the tension between the men extended a bit further. Notoriously shy with women, Iwerks found dating to be an intimidating experience. One story holds that Disney once set him up with a woman that he had admired from afar and then hid and used a studio camera to film the awkward encounter secretly for the next-day amusement of their coworkers. Both the young lady and her escort were furious.[19]

But whatever their differences in temperament, when Disney went bankrupt and fled to Los Angeles in search of fresh opportunities, Iwerks was the first man he summoned after securing a contract for the Alice pictures. In a letter confirming that his old friend would fill "a job as artist-cartoonist," Disney wrote enthusiastically that he was "glad you have made up your mind to come out. Boy you will never regret it — this is the place for you — a real country to work and play in — no kidding — don't change your mind — remember what old Horace Greeley said, 'Go west, young man, go west.' P.S. I wouldn't live in K.C. now if you gave me the place — yep, you bet — Hooray for Hollywood!!"[20]

Iwerks flourished at the Disney Studio and soon became a vital creative presence. With his usual quiet intensity, he devoted himself to animation, and within weeks of his arrival he was doing the lion's share of the studio's drawing. Disney was so impressed with the quality and quantity of his work that he himself turned increasingly to scripts and gags and stopped drawing almost completely by 1924. Part of Iwerks's facility appeared in the sheer speed with which he could turn out the huge number of drawings that were needed to create movement as they were photographed one by one. "I'd heard that Bill Nolan, who was doing 'Krazy Kat,' had done five hundred or six hundred drawings a day, so I really extended myself" to beat that record, he confessed much later.[21]

Iwerks's talents extended far beyond mere volume, though. He developed a more fluid style of animation that emphasized movement and action of characters. Up to that point most animators had relied heavily on "model sheets," often tracing directly from them and then making small revisions to suggest minute increments of movement. While still pinning up the sheets on his drawing table for guidance, Iwerks abandoned tracing to draw rapid free-style sketches that stressed flow and flexibility. Friz Freleng asserted that Iwerks was the most skillful artist at the studio, "more advanced in the technique of animation than anybody else, more than Walt or myself, or Harman and Ising . . . [He] was a perfectionist in the mechanics of animation." Although his work lacked a feel for the individual personality of characters, a trait for which the Disney Studio became justly famous in the 1930s, he was able to capture action in animation, which Disney was demanding in this period. Freleng remembered once when he was struggling to animate a World War I tank that turned and headed off into the distance, getting smaller and smaller: "I couldn't draw the tank to start with. And I was sitting next to Ub Iwerks, and Ub said, 'Well, let me help you with this.' So he took the sheet of paper and he made a few perspective lines and he drew a tank, one view and then the next position and the next position. And it took him five minutes, and he had it all sketched in. He was really an expert at it. And that's how I learned a little bit about animation, from Ub Iwerks."[22]

Iwerks's contributions did not go unrecognized by Disney. During the 1920s the animator's salary was the highest in the studio, even higher than Walt's and Roy's. According to financial records from the period, he began at $40 a week in 1924 and received steady raises until he was making $120 a week in 1927, with the prospering of the Oswald series. In 1928, he began putting part of his salary back into the business — first $20 a week and then $35 — as part of an arrangement with the Disney brothers whereby he would eventually secure a 20 percent interest in the company. In effect, he was moving into a partnership with his old friends.[23]

Iwerks's elevated position at the Disney Studio became evident during the Mintz crisis of 1928. His loyalty and sense of commitment came through with flying colors. Working closely with Walt and Roy to save the studio,

Iwerks became a key player in perhaps the most crucial development in the history of the Disney enterprise.[24]

The creation of Mickey Mouse has achieved the status of a legend. In later years, Walt the storyteller liked to spin a tale of coming up with the concept on the train home from the Mintz debacle in New York and pitching the idea of Mortimer Mouse to his wife, who recommended the name change. Walt claimed the character was inspired by a pet mouse from his poverty-stricken Kansas City days. While there may be some validity to this story, the truth is more complex. It seems clear that regardless of who originated the idea, Walt and Ub created Mickey together in those first few days of frantic meetings back at the Hyperion studio. Working under great pressure, they came up with a cute, compelling new animated character. Disney provided the voice and the personality for the charming little creature, while Iwerks gave him form with his deft drawing.[25]

The creation of Mickey was never a controversy for Iwerks. In later years, in a couple of brief interviews, he simply noted that after Walt's return from New York City they were scrambling to come up with a new character — drawing sketches of dogs and cats and other animals, looking through magazines for inspiration, finally stumbling across an idea for a mouse. They made some sketches during brainstorming sessions, "cooked up a story sitting around," and Lillian Disney gave their new creation a name. Iwerks believed that Mickey was based on Douglas Fairbanks, and thus he drew him as "an adventurous character . . . winning, gallant, and swash-buckling." It is clear that Iwerks never believed that Mickey was "his" character or that somehow Disney had stolen him. Both David and Donald Iwerks, Ub's sons, insist that their father felt no resentment over Mickey, and they report hearing him say many times that "it was what Walt *did* with Mickey that was important, not who created him."[26]

After the 1928 staff shakeup, Iwerks assumed an even larger role in productions of the Disney Studio. The only real animator left after the walkout — new artists did not arrive until the following year — he drew the lion's share of the first five Mickey Mouse animated shorts: *Plane Crazy, The Gallopin' Gaucho, Steamboat Willie, The Barn Dance,* and *The Opry House.* Particularly elated with the studio's development of sound cartoons, which premiered with *Steamboat Willie,* Iwerks reported that "I've never been so thrilled in my life . . . [it was] real intoxication." He also contributed heavily to *The Skeleton Dance,* the first of the Silly Symphony series, animating the whole film except for the opening scene. Even Walt Disney recognized Iwerks's newfound fame. In New York City in early 1929, he wrote to his wife that "everyone praised Ub's art work . . . Tell Ub that the New York animators take off their hats to his animation and all of them know who we are." In fact, the early Mickey Mouse cartoons were credited onscreen as "A Walt Disney Comic by Ub Iwerks," and Iwerks's name, in boldface type, was larger than Disney's. Ben Sharpsteen, one of the New Yorkers who arrived in 1929, put the matter more succinctly. "If there ever was a right-hand man to Walt," he noted, "it was Ub."[27]

Iwerks's life seemed full and content. In 1926 he had married Mildred Henderson, another transplanted midwesterner, and the couple had two sons over the next few years. On firm ground financially and working at full creative capacity, he had a bright life at the Disney Studio during this period. He and the staff labored mightily with a growing volume of films, but the work was fulfilling and fun, and they reveled in the great popular response. Iwerks told others that making movies in the late 1920s was so much fun that the staff "hated to go home at night, and we couldn't wait to get to the office in the morning." The vibrant atmosphere, the innovative films, and the good fellowship of the staff invigorated everyone, and in his words, "our enthusiasm got onto the screen." Two of his trainees, Les Clark and Jack Cutting, remembered that his gentlemanly demeanor — he was "the only animator who would stop his own work and encourage others" — eased the strains of the workplace. Iwerks in turn credited Disney's habit of mixing casually with his artists for creating the congenial, productive studio atmosphere. From all indications, Iwerks could not have been happier with his professional situation.[28]

Thus the events of January 1930 stunned everyone connected with Walt Disney. The young head of the studio was in New York for a showdown with Pat Powers, his distributor, whom he believed to be withholding payments from the bookings of Mickey Mouse films. When Disney pressed to see the books, Powers refused and then played his trump card: he showed Disney a telegram confirming that Iwerks had agreed to a contract to produce animated films on his own at a salary of $300 a week. Disney couldn't believe that his old friend had left him, but a telephone call to Roy in Los Angeles confirmed the bad news.[29]

The reasons for Iwerks's departure could not be explained simply. Most directly, a series of clashes over the correct process of animation had driven a wedge between the two creative forces in the Disney Studio. Apparently Disney had begun making two demands that Iwerks found unacceptable. First, in the evenings Disney would return to the workplace, arrange the drawings on an exposure sheet, and time them for photographing according to his own taste. Having drawn the frames according to his own sense of how the action should flow, Iwerks objected and began to time them himself before his boss could get there. Second — this problem began to emerge during the production of *The Skeleton Dance* — Disney began to insist that Iwerks follow the most modern method of animation, in which the artist made only the most crucial drawings in a series and an "in-betweener" filled in the remaining sketches. Fearing that he would lose a feel for the flow of action, Iwerks preferred to animate "straight ahead," doing a rough version of every drawing and letting assistants fill in the details later. This "series of run-ins with Walt," as Iwerks later described them, contributed to a growing rift between the two.[30]

Beneath Iwerks's festering resentment over these issues, however, lay another motivation. Chafing under Disney's firm direction of his studio, the artist began to manifest a desire for independence. Lawrence E. Watkin, a writer who knew him well in later years, reported that Iwerks left in 1930 not only over disagreements with Walt but because "he wanted to see if he could make it on his own." David Iwerks similarly asserted that his father, having garnered confidence from praise that had come his way with the early Disney films, simply wanted to blaze his own path in the animation world.[31]

But the whole truth lay buried even deeper. Evidence suggests that Ub Iwerks harbored a subtle resentment of Walt Disney, which is to say that while he respected him enormously, wanted to please him, even loved him, he often didn't like him. Disney evinced a similar attitude toward Iwerks. He recognized his talent but saw it as limited to mere craftsmanship and encased in a weak personality. These mutual undercurrents of resentment were never obvious, because both men made a habit of treating each other with praise and respect. Yet contrary evidence seeped from the edges of their relationship. Iwerks and Disney had known each other too well and for too long for things to be simply as they appeared.

Tension between the two artists probably had its origins in their business partnership back in Kansas City. When Disney left the month-old Iwerks-Disney Commercial Artists to take a job at the Film Ad Company — Iwerks insisted that he seize the opportunity — the business folded quickly because of Iwerks's lack of business skills. He was forced to appeal to Disney, who got him a job at the Film Ad Company. Iwerks, even though more experienced, was hired for less than his more personable friend, and according to Disney, that "always bothered Iwerks." Throughout the rest of the 1920s, first at Laugh-O-Grams and then in the early Hollywood studio, Iwerks continued to work in Disney's shadow. Ironically, it was the success of the Disney Studio that seems to have wedged them apart. With the booming popularity of Mickey Mouse and the Silly Symphonies, Disney's hard-driving ego swelled. This seems to have grated on Iwerks. While sharing Disney's high standards of production excellence, he resented the notion that there was only one way — Disney's way — to achieve them.[32]

Of course, with his upright standards and stiff temperament, Iwerks refused to say anything bad about Disney. Even decades later he would flare up when anyone said anything that put Disney in a bad light. As David Iwerks emphatically noted, "I never heard Ub say anything negative about Walt — not a word, not once, ever." At the same time, Iwerks's praise for Disney had a detached, almost abstract quality. He certainly stood in awe of Disney as a professional, describing him as a brilliant administrator, a man with quick intelligence, a shrewd promoter and businessman, and a path-breaking entertainer. But one searches in vain for something else, something that one might expect from such a longstanding friendship: an affection for Walt as a human being. One of Iwerks's comments gave a clue of that, but the sentiment was clouded by wistfulness and nostalgia. "Walt was very close to his men in those early days," he once commented, explaining that the studio chief had expressed interest in his staff members as human beings, not just as professionals. "He would stop by the artists' offices and chat or visit, ask about their outside interests, and maybe make a few suggestions about their animation. The men loved it, and they all responded." The implication is clear: this had been characteristic of the old days, but when the studio took off and the stakes grew higher, Disney changed.[33]

From Disney's perspective, the growing success of his studio by 1930 diminished Iwerks. The popularity and fame that enlarged his own ambition made his head animator seem smaller: skilled in drawing but limited in vision, naive and straitlaced, a valuable but vulnerable figure. Disney increasingly saw Iwerks as someone whose talents needed to be mobilized, whose quietly stubborn instincts needed to be dominated for the greater advancement of the studio. In 1928, for instance, as he was peddling the new Mickey Mouse films with sound in New York, he wrote an injunction demanding the quick completion of a film: "Listen, Ub. Show some of your old SPEED. Work like hell BOY. It is our one BIG CHANCE to make a real killing. Forget a lot of the fancy curves and pretty looking drawings and devote your time to the ACTION. You can do it — I know you can . . . GIVE HER HELL . . . Don't tell me it can't be done. It has got to be done . . . So quit acting nervous and fidgety. Forget everything . . . [and] get that DAMN picture back here in time." This method of simultaneously motivating and browbeating artists, of course, became central to Disney's long-term managerial style. As another old hand at the studio once described Iwerks and Disney, "They were partners, but Walt was the boss."[34]

In many ways, Disney's angry but oddly triumphant reaction to Iwerks's departure summarized his attitude. When he found out about it, he couldn't believe it. "I just can't feel that he would do a thing like that," Disney said; "this boy had been loyal to us." But hurt quickly turned to animosity. He quickly told Powers that now "I wouldn't want him. If he feels that way I could never work with him." In two quick telegrams, he urged Roy to characterize Iwerks's defection as foolish when talking to the staff. Then his animosity ostensibly turned to pity. According to Ben Sharpsteen, Disney took a kind of satisfaction in predicting that Iwerks wouldn't make it on his own. His attitude became one of "mainly feeling sorry for Ub, as Ub was not a leader." At one point, commenting on Iwerks's introspective, easygoing personality, Disney remarked, "I sure feel sorry for Ub when he has any personnel problems." He echoed his brother's assessment: "We know how gullible and easily led Ub is."[35]

In a fashion, of course, this was Disney's way of reasserting his own superiority in the face of a galling rejection. His comments, however, proved prophetic. The Ub Iwerks Studio, with financial support from Pat Powers and a facility on Santa Monica Boulevard, got up and running in the spring of 1930. It developed three series of animated cartoons in the years through 1936: Flip the Frog focused on the adventures of a rambunctious amphibian, Willie Whopper followed the farfetched yarns of a young boy, while Comi-Colors featured a number of fables. But the Iwerks Studio never achieved great success, and it floundered after a few years.[36]

As Disney had predicted, Iwerks's disposition proved his undoing as a leader and manager. Shamus Culhane, a young animator who drove from New York City to go to work at the new studio, gave a striking evaluation of his boss: "He was a slight man with a pallid complexion, a toothbrush moustache, and dark hair . . . Ub had a nice smile, but he rarely used it. Normally he had a very still face, with a carefully controlled absence of expression. Iwerks was laconic to an incredible degree. Where two words would suffice, he used one." These staid, even forbidding personal qualities tended to stifle the construction of gags and jokes, which were the lifeblood of early animation. Iwerks simply detested managerial tasks, "so when Ub saw he had hired someone with supervisory ability, he put him to work running the studio" and disappeared. When his staff looked to their boss to pass judgment, Iwerks would usually say, "You fellows go ahead and do it the way you want."[37]

Iwerks could usually be found hard at work in the studio machine shop, cultivating a growing interest in the technical aspects of filmmaking. Back in the earliest days of the Disney Studio, he had cleverly improvised a couple of mechanical contraptions, attaching an old hand-crank camera to a motor drive that utilized a telegraph key for operation and reworking an old silent projector into a crude moviola for direct viewing of films. By the early 1930s, this mechanical bent had begun to dominate everything else. Iwerks vanished into the machine shop for weeks at a stretch, developing things like his prototype of a multiplane camera, a sophisticated device that allowed the photographer to track shots through layers of glass backgrounds. The Disney engineers were also developing such an instrument in the 1930s, but while their vertical model eventually cost some $50,000, the ingenious Iwerks built a horizontal prototype out of parts from an old Chevrolet that he had picked up for $350! Along with a machinist friend, Lee Richardson, he happily experimented on many other projects, such as a three-dimensional filming machine built into the back of an old Studebaker. With a machine shop at home that allowed for even more experimentation, Iwerks increasingly devoted attention to his real love: the solution of technical problems in film production.[38]

After the Iwerks Studio folded in 1936, its talented, taciturn leader spent a few years doing contract work as an animation director for Warner Brothers and Columbia Pictures. By 1940, however, he had tired of scrambling for professional survival and made an intriguing decision. In an ironic closing of the circle, he contacted Ben Sharpsteen, who hired him back to the Disney Studio after nearly an eleven-year absence. He was put to work in the Checking Department, which oversaw the animation drawings as they went through the process of ink and painting and then photography. Disney feigned disinterest when the subject of his return was first broached; "Don't come to me asking who you're going to hire or what you're going to pay him," he groused to Sharpsteen. But within a few weeks, Disney decided that Iwerks's talents were being wasted — "You couldn't go out and ever hope to hire a man who was as well schooled in optics as Ub; he's a genius" — so he put him in charge of the new multihead optical printer project. Iwerks successfully developed this device, which allowed for the sophisticated synthesis of live-action and animation film, to his boss's delight. Thus began the second stage of his long association with Disney.[39]

After his return to the fold, Iwerks had a long and distinguished career, from 1940 to 1971. He played the central role in developing a wide array of technical innovations, including the sodium camera for combining live-action and cartoon productions, a traveling matte process for color cinematography, and a Xerox process for reproducing animation drawings onto cels that eliminated the need for inking. He won two Academy Awards for such innovative work. In addition, he designed many technical effects, including Circle-Vision, for attractions at Disneyland in the 1950s. During most of this time, he worked as a development engineer reporting directly to Walt Disney.[40]

Iwerks and Disney displayed a rather peculiar relationship throughout these decades. There was no bitterness or animosity on either side, but rather an accommodation, an unspoken agreement to forget the past. They dealt with each other on a professional plane, avoiding the social ties that had bound them in earlier days. In his own quiet way, Iwerks pledged loyalty to the Disney Studio and offered praise for its director. According to Lawrence Watkin, Iwerks was "devoted to Walt Disney" and unwilling to brook any criticism of him. He respected Disney's old-fashioned inclination to make an individual decision — "Anyplace else they have committee meetings after committee meetings; they'll talk a project to death" — and his tendency to gamble on innovation, but most of all he appreciated the studio chief's willingness to leave him alone to follow his own instincts in experimenting with technical projects. Upon his return he chose an old, tiny office near the machine shop and spent his time, as he described it, trying to "prowl around" looking for problems to solve. "I'm my own boss," he liked to tell friends. Finally, although he never said so directly, Iwerks had a strong desire to please Disney with his work. David Iwerks remembers Walt once putting an arm around Ub's shoulder to demonstrate his pleasure at some technical achievement. Ub grinned.[41]

Disney, as usual, demonstrated a more complex attitude about his old colleague. He genuinely admired Iwerks's talents, once remarking to a friend that Ub was not only "one of the nicest guys that ever lived" but also a "natural engineering genius." He quickly added, however, that Iwerks had failed to make it on his own because "he was too retiring to push himself into the consciousness of others." This tone also flared in Disney's occasional annoyance with Iwerks's tinkering. Dave Hand, the studio's supervising director for many years, once told how Walt, watching through his office window as Ub puttered with the engine of his car, said disgustedly, "Look at that — wasting his time out there. He could get a mechanic for sixty-five cents an hour to do that kind of work!" Iwerks's limited ambition, his self-containment, and his desire for simple pleasures were things Disney could never understand.[42]

Disney, while paying homage to the traditional values of individual success, recognized that the gritty determination and sustained labor of Horatio Alger were no longer enough; skills in personality, inspiration, and salesmanship were also required. Iwerks, for all his artistic innovation and technological ability, remained wedded to an old-fashioned standard of productivity and tight-lipped self-control. Desiring neither great wealth nor fame, he was happiest when left alone to pursue his own interests. He had little interest, and proudly so, in manipulating images, products, and self to smooth the path to success in modern mass culture. The very things at which Walt excelled, and which modern consumer America increasingly demanded, he respected little. A highly skilled, even brilliant artist and technician, he could be a valued cog in a modern bureaucratic machine. But he could never be its leader.

Ultimately, Ub Iwerks represented the photographic negative of the Walt Disney success portrait, as distinct and defined as the finished picture but curiously black where it should be white, and requiring a light to illuminate it. The difference between these two very different men was underlined back in the 1920s when, one day when work was a little slow at the Film Ad Company, the boys decided to play poker. Disney declined to join them and remained at his desk working busily at some task. During a lull in the game, Iwerks strolled over to see what he was doing and discovered that he was practicing his signature. As Iwerks said, "I knew right then that with his ego, Walt was going to make it." For his part, Disney noted that Iwerks, while talented and hardworking, would only go so far, because "he couldn't sell himself." Both men, with their mingled admiration and disdain, told more about the shifting culture of their age than they ever knew.[43]

III. Positive Thinking and Mass Entertainment

In the early 1930s, Walt Disney, popular entertainer, was gradually becoming Walt Disney, modern American success icon. In his newspaper column, Dale Carnegie himself lionized this young filmmaker as an unknown who made himself into "one of the most famous men in America." According to Carnegie, Disney deserved admiration for his assertion that "merely making money doesn't appeal" while wholesale immersion in the joyful labor of a career was "the adventure of his existence." Years later, Norman Vincent Peale acclaimed the beloved entertainer as the embodiment of his philosophy of positive thinking. Disney, he wrote, "couldn't forget his dream, for it grabbed him and wouldn't let go. He just kept on believing in himself and working and dreaming." As Peale concluded, "In America motivated dreams can come true . . . When you get discouraged and feel like throwing in the sponge, just remember Walt Disney and Mickey Mouse."[44]

Disney polished the same image. In 1949 he contributed a brief inspirational piece to Peale's magazine, *Guideposts*. A decade later, *Wisdom* magazine devoted an entire issue to him, and he took advantage of the opportunity to summarize much of his personal and professional philosophy. The editor's introduction set the tone: "In truest American tradition, Walt Disney rose from virtual obscurity to become, through his beloved character creations, filmland's greatest success . . . By virtue of his unsurpassed imagination, native genius, determination, and resourcefulness, he has utilized all so effectively as to become a world renowned, self-made pioneer in creating highly entertaining, thoroughly delightful, colorful, and educative motion picture spectacles." Disney's own lengthy reflections on his career, his work, and his audience followed. Given the adulatory tone established at the outset, it is not surprising that his ruminations were sprinkled with glib aphorisms, internal inconsistencies, and questionable generalities. Hagiography does not lend itself to critical thought. At the same time, however, two themes consistently threaded through his commentary and wove it together. More than anything else, he believed, the lessons of his life had taught him, first, the meaning of achievement, and second, the value of entertainment.[45]

Echoing many of the principles he had followed since the 1920s, Disney described a vision mingling elements of tradition and innovation. The old-fashioned son of Elias Disney dutifully presented several standard Victorian prescriptions. Opportunity beckoned even in the mid-twentieth century, he insisted, and many avenues to success remained open to the industrious and creative. Adversity often threatened, but facing it strengthened character, because "once you've lived through the worst, you're never quite as vulnerable afterwards." The work ethic, of course, was the most powerful way to follow opportunity and overcome adversity. "People often ask me if I know the secret of success and if I could tell others how to make their dreams come true," he wrote. "My answer is, you do it by working . . . The way to get started is to quit talking and began doing."[46]

At the same time, however, Disney modified these hoary directives with fresh messages gleaned from the bureaucratic arena of modern America. Individual initiative, no matter how valuable, was no longer enough. The successful person relied on team effort as well, avoiding behavior of a "freakish or 'genius'" sort and immersing himself in "the common stream of social life." Success, Disney insisted, did not come with "selfish achievements, but rather with the things we do for the people we love and esteem, and whose regard we need." This emphasis on teamwork and other-directedness led him to muffle the harsh voice of Victorian repression and replace it with the soft sounds of self-fulfillment. One element — positive thinking — really glued this amalgam together. Of the qualities that pushed people to achievement, he asserted, "the greatest of these is confidence. When you believe a thing, believe it all over, implicitly and unquestionably."[47]

Disney's thoughts on his own success never wandered far from another topic in this article: the importance of mass entertainment. He attributed much of his spectacular rise to a humble goal. "I am interested in entertaining people," he noted simply, "in bringing pleasure, particularly laughter, to others, rather than being concerned with 'expressing' myself or obscure creative impressions." Finding no more worthwhile goal, he devoted his energy to fulfilling his "responsibility as a mass entertainer." The Disney entertainment formula was simple: in a brisk and attractive manner, present the clash of virtue and wickedness, satirize human frailties, and personalize themes. Such leisure, as Disney saw it, was particularly suited to the conditions and temper of modern consumer America. The movies were no mere abstraction, but rather, in his words, "closely related to the life and labors of millions of people. Entertainment such as our business provides has become a necessity, not a luxury."[48]

The imperatives of success and mass culture always directed Disney's path. From the earliest days of his career, he repeatedly confessed the great passions of his life: he was in love with his work and in love with the idea of entertaining a mass audience. His meteoric rise in the 1920s and early 1930s had made him a dynamic success story and a wildly popular entertainer for millions of American consumers. The next decade, however, would prove that Walt Disney was a great deal more.

Part II

The Disney Golden Age

4

Disney and the Depression: Sentimental Populism

ROY E. DISNEY, Walt's nephew, once asked Bill Peet, a longtime
Disney employee, how the studio managed to secure and keep so
many talented artists in the 1930s. The irascible old story man
gave him a mischievous look, narrowed his eyes, and growled a one-word
answer: "Poverty." Animator Marc Davis told a similar tale. He recalled that
like other young people with sketchpads and pencils, he was lucky to find
employment, art training, and meal tickets at the Disney Studio in the days
when "there was no place a young artist could go to work." Even Walt
Disney admitted that hard times had nourished his early success. While
having lunch with a group of his leading animators and reminiscing about
the old days, he looked around the table and remarked, "Gee, you know, if it
hadn't been for the Depression, I wouldn't have had any of these guys."[1]

Many of Disney's animated shorts contained interesting commentaries
on the influence of economic disaster in the 1930s. *Mickey's Orphans* (1931),
for instance, opened with a mysterious hooded feline figure leaving a basket
of kittens on the protagonist's porch. Similarly, *Mickey's Good Deed* (1932)
based its plot on the mouse's desperate sale of his beloved pet, Pluto, to raise
cash for a penniless mother and her children. *Moving Day* (1936) followed
the adventures of Disney's animated characters when they were evicted from
their home by the sheriff because of nonpayment of rent. While such films

put smiles on the faces of their audiences with gags and happy endings, the laughter often arrived through the tears of an unhappy situation.

These fragments of story and film lore recall something often forgotten — that Disney's spectacular ascendancy in the American entertainment field corresponded almost exactly to the unfolding of the Great Depression. Just as Mickey Mouse began to take off in 1929, the stock market crashed, triggering one of the greatest social and economic disasters in American history. Over the next few years, while millions of Americans lost their jobs and homes, stood in lines at soup kitchens, and suffered the private agonies of failure, Disney's animated films steadily attracted mass audiences, and a swelling volume of box office receipts filled the company's coffers.

Admittedly, Disney, his people, and his films seldom faced the Depression directly. Nonetheless, the prolonged trauma of the 1930s had a powerful impact on his entertainment enterprise. It silently affected themes and plots, inspired the construction of story backdrops and settings, nudged satire in certain directions, and shaped the personalities of Disney's growing pantheon of popular animated characters. Such influence tended to surface indirectly and circuitously.

More important, however, the Great Depression provoked a shadowy but potent political sensibility emphasizing the dignity of "the little guy," the nobility of his struggle for survival against powerful forces in a hostile world, and his embodiment of the intrinsic goodness of the American "folk." More visceral than programmatic, this broad cultural politics derived partly from pressing social circumstances and partly from crucial elements in Disney's own midwestern, rural, working-class past. Assuming a populist shape, it offered an important clue to his great appeal.

But the ideological sensibility of Disney's Depression-era films was easily lost in the hubbub of publicity that accompanied the spectacular rise of the company's fortunes. By the early 1930s, Mickey Mouse and the Silly Symphonies had carried the young producer to fame; a burst of innovative work over the next decade took him to heights that were truly dizzying.

I. Triumph Amid Travail

In 1932 Walt Disney established another benchmark in his work: color animation. He had been intrigued with this idea for some time, and when Technicolor developed a three-color system appropriate for cartoons, he negotiated an exclusive right for the use of this process. A new Silly Symphony, *Flowers and Trees,* caused a sensation when it premiered on July 30 at Grauman's Chinese Theater. The story of woodland plants dancing and romancing to the music by Mendelssohn and Schubert was attractive enough, but the entranced audience spent most of their time exclaiming over the real star of the show — the film's radiant colors. Booking requests soared, and at year's end Disney received the first Academy Award ever given to an animated film. (At the same ceremony he received a special award for the creation of Mickey Mouse.) *Flowers and Trees* proved to be the precursor of a decade of stunning successes.

The year after his breakthrough with color, *Three Little Pigs* became Disney's bestseller. With its cute porcine characters, compelling story, and hypnotic theme song — "Who's Afraid of the Big Bad Wolf?" — this little movie triggered a spectacular national craze. The next few years saw a continued outpouring of films, as a steady flow of Mickey Mouses and Silly Symphonies cemented the Disney appeal in the public imagination.

Producing between fifteen and eighteen short films a year from 1933 to 1941, the Disney Studio covered a widening expanse of entertainment ground. Some of the more notable efforts gave glimpses of the various directions in which these movies headed. *Orphans' Benefit* and *The Tortoise and the Hare* both appeared in 1934, for example, the former showcasing the familiar Mickey Mouse gang and the latter providing a humorous updating of the familiar fable. The reworked fairy tale became another Disney genre, with films such as *Wynken, Blynken and Nod* (1938) and *The Ugly Duckling* (1931). Other productions — *The Cookie Carnival* (1935) and *Merbabies* (1938), for instance — concocted otherworldly fantasies of remarkable imagination. The year 1935 saw the release of *The Band Concert,* the first Mickey Mouse film in color. This delightful story presents Mickey's band conjuring up a tornado with its energetic playing, all the while suffering the musical torments of a fife-playing Donald Duck. Many critics consider it to be Disney's masterpiece among his animated shorts.

Some films from the 1930s relied on themes and structures from Disney's earlier work. *The Country Cousin* (1936) presents a rural/urban dichotomy and a famous scene in which the rustic bumpkin falls into a glass of champagne. Others, such as *Mickey's Gala Premiere* (1933), *Who Killed Cock Robin?* (1935), *Mickey's Polo Team* (1936), and *Mother Goose Goes Hollywood* (1938), concerned the world of mass entertainment, caricaturing Mae West, Laurel and Hardy, Bing Crosby, the Marx Brothers, W. C. Fields, Katharine Hepburn, and other movie stars. A number of films concentrated on displays of technical virtuosity. *Clock Cleaners* (1937) featured fabulous, dizzying perspective shots from high atop urban skyscrapers, while the lyrical *The Old Mill* (also 1937) utilized for the first time a camera device that created the illusion of three-dimensionality. Other movies highlighted comedy and satire. *Ferdinand the Bull* (1938), for example, portrays a hilariously docile, flower-sniffing protagonist who refuses to fight; to complete the bargain, Walt Disney is caricatured as the fuming matador. The 1930s Disney Studio, in short, offered many films, many dimensions, and many delights.

Not surprisingly, the growing volume and variety of Disney films during this decade inspired a growing menagerie of animated characters. Drawn from the animal world but loaded with human characteristics, they included Mickey and Minnie Mouse, of course, as well as Ferdinand, the Big Bad Wolf, and the plodding, persistent Toby Tortoise. A host of others also materialized: Mickey's loyal but gullible dog, Pluto; the simpleminded, shiftless, and blissful Goofy; Horace Horsecollar and Clarabelle Cow, those enthusiastically silly bit players; the strutting, grandiloquent matriarch with the mock operatic voice, Clara Cluck; and Pegleg Pete, the stubble-bearded, dastardly heavy of many a movie plot. After a bit part in *The Wise Little Hen* (1934), an ornery, short-tempered fowl named Donald Duck gradually moved into prominence in films like *Donald's Better Self* (1938) and *The Autograph Hound* (1939). With a belligerent sense of self-esteem and a proclivity for spectacular temper tantrums, Donald became so popular that he threatened to supplant Mickey as the studio star. To American moviegoers, Disney's assortment of pencil-and-paintbrush creations became as familiar and real as their flesh-and-blood counterparts Clark Gable, Shirley Temple, Gary Cooper, and Greta Garbo.

Although not as big as enterprises such as Universal, Columbia, and RKO, Disney's independent operation had clearly entered the realm of big business by the early 1930s. Its profit margins began sweeping upward. The Disney Studio produced nearly twenty short pictures a year according to its distribution agreement with United Artists; each cost about $50,000 to make, and each had an expected profit of roughly $120,000, minus distribution costs, in its first two years of release. To this income were added funds from older films still in release, as well as money from the studio's growing merchandising operation. All told, by the mid-1930s, the Disney Studio was pulling in around $660,000 a year in profits, the great majority of which it plowed back into various projects. In 1937 the studio negotiated a distribution contract with RKO that was even more favorable in terms of advance money and costs. Thus the 1930s marked a period of remarkable corporate growth for Walt and his enterprise, allowing him to protect his vaunted independence by putting it on a firm financial foundation.[2]

The advent of a truly daring project added a special emotional charge to life at the studio. In 1934 Walt began contemplating something never before attempted — the production of a full-length animated motion picture — and he gradually nudged it toward realization over the next couple of years. It came to dominate both the time and the creative energy of the Disney Studio by 1936, and created among the staff a sense of being part of a pathbreaking enterprise.

The production of *Snow White and the Seven Dwarfs* prompted mounting publicity and generated a great deal of public anticipation. When it finally premiered on December 21, 1937, audiences loved the story, believed in the animated characters, hissed the wicked queen, cried over the apparent death of the young heroine, and stood to cheer at the movie's happy conclusion. The picture created a tidal wave of national publicity that engulfed the movie industry, surpassing even the reaction to *Three Little Pigs*. This outpouring of popular approval culminated at the Academy Awards ceremony in 1939, when Shirley Temple awarded a special Oscar for *Snow White* to a nervous Walt Disney. Appropriately enough, it consisted of one full-size statue and seven miniature ones.

The spectacular success of *Snow White* catapulted the Disney Studio into an exciting new phase. Animated shorts, long the mainstay of the studio's efforts, began a gradual decline in the face of a growing commitment to animated features. Following the trail blazed by *Snow White*, Disney pushed forward a quartet of full-length films over the next four years. Surviving far beyond their own time, they became familiar, beloved artifacts of American popular culture.

Pinocchio, a picture adapted from the late-nineteenth-century Italian tale by Carlo Collodi, began production a few weeks after *Snow White's* premiere. Disney was determined to surpass the achievement of his first feature, and he put his staff to work with his usual energy and determination. After six months, however, he halted the project. Believing that the film lacked personality and appeal, he directed an overhaul to enliven the script and strengthen a number of central characters. The movie's final version featured various settings — a picturesque Old World village, a traveling puppet show, the ocean bottom, the inside of a monstrous whale — which provided ample opportunity for animation pyrotechnics and special effects. Pinocchio endures a whole series of adventures full of scary thrills, pathos, lighthearted fantasy, and moral struggle before finally realizing his dream at the movie's end. Along the way he encounters a cast of colorful characters — the Blue Fairy, who looks after his quest, the wicked puppetmaster Stromboli, the woodcarver Geppetto, and especially his companion and conscience, Jiminy Cricket. Finally released in February 1940, *Pinocchio* was not quite as popular as *Snow White*, but many critics thought it was superior to its predecessor.

Fantasia, perhaps the greatest experiment of Disney's early career, was released in November 1940 after a slow and complex gestation period. Disney originally planned to regenerate the standing of Mickey Mouse, whose career had waned by the late 1930s, in a short film without dialogue, which would be set to *The Sorcerer's Apprentice*, a concert piece by French composer Paul Dukas. Leopold Stokowski, the famous conductor, volunteered the Philadelphia Orchestra to record the music for the project. As the film moved toward completion, however, creative energy gathered its own momentum. Disney and Stokowski began to plan a feature-length film of vignettes that would illustrate the music of a number of composers. Known as "the concert feature" during production, this movie slowly assumed the structure of a classical concert, complete with intermission, with a series of animated representations suggested by musical abstractions. Works by Bach, Tchaikovsky, Beethoven, Stravinsky, Ponchielli, Mussorgsky, and Schubert filled out the program. Disney engaged Deems Taylor, the famous musical commentator, to provide narration, and his engineers developed a special multiaural sound system to duplicate the rich texture of a classical orchestra. *Fantasia* was controversial from the beginning. A lengthy and ambitious film, it failed to draw the huge audiences of its predecessors, while delighting, confusing, or overwhelming those who did attend. Not surprisingly, the movie's innovations caused bitter divisions among both movie and music critics.

Dumbo, a short and simple film, surprised nearly everyone at the Disney Studio in the early 1940s. Having spent enormous amounts of cash on animated features in the previous few years, the studio needed an inexpensive moneymaker, and this proved to be it. An unpretentious little movie based on a children's story and made on a shoestring budget, it seemed to fall together with few of the complications or false starts of the other feature projects. The result delighted everyone who saw it. Following a very tight, uncluttered story line, the narrative focused on a baby circus elephant whose ears are so gigantic that he is cruelly called Dumbo. Forced to perform as a clown, he eventually discovers an amazing talent: his huge ears enable him to fly! This allows him to become the star performer of the circus and triumph over his tormentors. With a story that tugs at the heartstrings, cleverly constructed scenes, and sharp characterizations, *Dumbo* quickly became famous for its admirable simplicity and ample heart. Only a year and a half in the making before its release in October 1941, it was the cheapest feature Disney ever made.

The next feature-length project, *Bambi,* closed the door on a remarkable decade of filmmaking. Based on the book by Felix Salten, this long-simmering project was begun in 1937, nourished by a small core of animators while other pictures were completed, and finally released in August 1942. This movie returned to the animal kingdom, which Disney had frequented in his short films, but in more depth and complexity. Less concerned with humor than nearly any other Disney animated feature, *Bambi*'s gentle, understated story of a young deer's maturation dramatized the cycle of nature in the forest and depicted humans as threats. The film's minimal dialogue helped emphasize its dominant trait — a strongly naturalistic style that captured even the smallest details of life in the wild. In fact, this became something of an obsession during production, as animators drew from hundreds of specially commissioned wildlife photographs and a number of live deer actually kept at the studio as models. In the end, *Bambi* offered a bittersweet evocation of childhood and family and a defense of nature against human encroachment. With a strong financial and critical reception, it quickly became a classic.

By the early 1940s, the triumph of Walt Disney Productions seemed complete. Guided by the dynamic vision of its young leader, the company was financially secure as it happily churned out innovative and popular films. In the heart of the Depression, millions of happy consumers flocked to Disney films. Walt became a mainstay at the Academy Awards ceremonies, where he won thirteen Oscars between 1932 and 1941, and hundreds of newspaper and magazine stories kept him and his work constantly in the public eye.

Much of the reason for this enormous popularity lay in Disney's instinctive feel for mass entertainment; his films had clever plots, compelling characters, freewheeling humor, captivating music, and technical virtuosity, and they were plain fun. This was always one of Disney's strong suits. But a subtle cultural politics also flavored his films throughout the 1930s, lending them no small appeal. Going beyond the escapist element of mass entertainment, the films counteracted the widespread loss of hope and self-confidence in America. In 1933, Franklin D. Roosevelt had inspired the American people with his ringing declaration that "the only thing we have to fear is fear itself." Throughout this period, Walt Disney and his films mounted their own fantastic assault on fear.

II. Defending the Embattled Folk

The plot of Preston Sturges's popular film *Sullivan's Travels* (1941) centered on John L. Sullivan, an idealistic but rather dimwitted Hollywood director who determines to leave behind the silly comedic movies on which he has based his career and make a profound social statement by filming an authentic, searing drama — its melodramatic title would be *Oh Brother, Where Art Thou?* — about the suffering of common people during the Depression. Disguising himself to gather material, he prowls the underside of an American city as a poverty-stricken, unemployed vagrant. All the while, of course, he is carefully monitored by his large staff, which follows at a discreet distance. The director accidentally becomes a genuine outsider, however, when a series of mishaps sends him to prison and he is put to work on a chain gang. *Sullivan's Travels* reaches its climax in a remarkable scene: when the prisoners are herded into a black rural church for a few moments of entertainment, Sullivan is astonished to see this audience of America's downtrodden, parishioners and prisoners alike, erupt in waves of joyful, cathartic laughter at an unexpected sight — a Mickey Mouse cartoon. He learns a lesson, and after returning to Hollywood, he abandons the pretentious Great Depression Drama and rededicates himself to making comedies. In his chastened words, "There's a lot to be said for making people laugh. Did you know that's all some people have?"

Sullivan's Travels presents an accurate celluloid snapshot of Disney's special influence during the Great Depression, and its famous laughing scene highlights several important points — the resilience of ordinary people in the face of privation and degradation, the healing power of popular culture, and Walt Disney's special affinity for both that audience and the medium that reached them. Through his own work in the 1930s, the master of animated movies shaped a cultural politics that went far beyond the laughter evoked by Mickey Mouse cartoons.

This was no simple matter, because on the surface of things, Walt Disney's political sensibility seemed elusive, if not nonexistent. He issued no ideological manifestos, endorsed no political causes, engaged in no overt social analysis in his films. He expressed little apparent interest in politics, even in one of the most agitated, tumultuous periods in American history. One of his only political forays was printed in the small magazine *Overland Monthly*, when he tried to extend his analysis of Mickey Mouse's appeal in political directions, and it culminated in embarrassment. Mickey, he explained to readers, had become a favorite of international figures and groups ranging from "Mr. King George and Mrs. Queen Mary" to "Mr. Mussolini" to "Mr. F. Roosevelt and family" to the warring Chinese and Japanese. "Mr. A. Hitler, the Nazi old thing, says that Mickey's silly. Imagine that!" Disney concluded rather childishly. "Well, Mickey is going to save Mr. A. Hitler from drowning or something some day . . . Then won't Mr. A. Hitler be ashamed."[3]

Most of the time, Disney simply ignored politics and social issues. In a 1937 cover story for *Time*, for instance, he confessed that when "we tried consciously to put some social meaning" into one of the Silly Symphonies, the studio produced "a tremendous flop." He was puzzled about any political implications in his films. "We just try to make a good picture," he noted rather gruffly in the same interview. "And then the professors come along and tell us what we do."[4]

But Disney *did* articulate a political position, albeit unintentionally, and its core was neither Republican nor Democratic, Hooverian nor Rooseveltian, as a few critics have offhandedly implied. Instead, it consisted of an instinctive populism that had been shaped by the provincial Midwest. Disney consistently infused his films with an ideology that glorified the American people and assumed a strongly egalitarian cast. Like many other areas of his thinking, it was untutored and emotional rather than systematic and articulate. Generally, the dogged persistence of Mickey Mouse or the libidinous outbursts of Donald Duck reaffirmed the ordinary citizen's capacity to survive and conquer all adversity. This broad populist agenda was more implicitly cultural than overtly political, more visceral than doctrinaire. It defended the dignity of the average citizen and elevated the wisdom of the American folk in a period when both had suffered massive trauma.

Disney's populist persuasion can be traced to several ideological influences persisting from nineteenth-century America — the Populist revolt of the late 1800s, with its rural opposition to urban industrial society and "money power"; the influence of the Protestant work ethic; the residue of republicanism, with its values of civic obligation. This creed tended to adhere to several principles. Highly suspicious of the machinery of modern finance and its cash matrix, populists upheld an ethic of "producerism," which stressed the moral value and dignity of labor and insisted that property ownership and personal independence provided the key to citizenship. This impulse in American political culture, according to Richard Hofstadter's elegant description, attempted

> to hold on to some of the values of agrarian life, to save personal entrepreneurship and individual opportunity and the character type they engendered, and to maintain a homogenous Yankee civilization . . . [Populism promoted] the ideal of a life lived close to nature and the soil, the esteem for the primary contacts of country and village life, the cherished image of the independent and self-reliant man, even the desire (for all the snobberies and hatreds it inspired) to maintain an ethnically more homogenous nation.[5]

Disney did not stand alone in his cultural politics. Similar sentiments sprouted everywhere in the 1930s as "petty bourgeois populism," to use Christopher Lasch's phrase, enjoyed a widespread resurgence. It appeared, for instance, in the village sentimentality of popular illustrator Norman Rockwell and the democratic optimism of folksinger Woody Guthrie. It surfaced in politician Huey Long's "every man a king" rhetoric and in composer Aaron Copland's music, such as "Fanfare for the Common Man," *Appalachian Spring,* and *Rodeo.* It influenced the criticism of Van Wyck Brooks, whose *Makers and Finders* series exalted the democratic tradition of American letters. It flowered in the neorealism of "regionalist" painters such as Thomas Hart Benton, Grant Wood, and Steuart Curry, whose canvases depicted the workaday heroism of rural midwesterners. It influenced Archibald MacLeish's calls for poetry in the mold of public speech and Lewis Mumford's agenda for reintegrating industrial technology with the "culture of the folk." And, it has been pointed out, this revitalization of American popular tradition took place under the left-wing auspices of the Popular Front. Overall, in the words of one recent assessment, the neopopulist upsurge of the 1930s helped shape the major ideological trend of the period: "a growing self-consciousness of an American way," a "fascination with the folk and its culture, past and present . . . a kind of collective identification with all of America and its people."[6]

In Disney's case, personal experience unquestionably influenced his political bent. His youth in the Midwest gave him golden memories of rural village life. His father's socialist politics also exerted an influence. Walt remembered his father as "a great friend of the working man . . . I grew up believing a lot of that." Thus he carried into adulthood much of the baggage of turn-of-the-century midwestern populism.[7]

Ben Sharpsteen noted that while his boss realized that bankers were necessary to film production, he "never had any reverence for them." As a matter of fact, Disney was fond of playing the naive, rural bumpkin when financiers put pressure on him. He would inquire if the studio was paying its interest, and when assured that it was, he would ask innocently if that wasn't how banks stayed in business. In 1928, when he was struggling to negotiate a contract, he assured his brother Roy that "none of our profits [are] going to some leech sitting at a big mahogany desk telling us what to do." A short time later, he denounced the whole financial "game" as "the damndest mixed-up affair I have ever heard of" and offered a blunt evaluation of businessmen: "They are all a bunch of schemers and just full of tricks that would fool a greenhorn . . . [I feel] like a sheep amongst a pack of wolves."[8]

Throughout the 1930s, Disney supported Franklin D. Roosevelt as the presidential candidate most sympathetic to average Americans. He also cultivated a self-consciously folksy image among the Hollywood elite, sometimes appearing at parties in his own home dressed in denim overalls and plaid flannel shirts. In the words of Ward Kimball, an animator and close friend, "he took a delight in letting them know that he was a common man." Disney also had a genuine appreciation for manual craftsmanship and often told associates of his enormous respect for the studio carpenters and cabinetmakers. His public pronouncements consistently polished this populist image. "The public likes little fellows in comedy," he noted in 1930. "Everyone picks on them and sympathy is aroused. So when they finally triumph over the bigger characters, the public rejoices with them." Years later he echoed that sentiment, pointing out that in his films "bullies are routed or conquered by our good little people, human or animal." He also took every opportunity to reaffirm his allegiance to an ethic of producerism. "I'm not interested in money, except for what I can do with it to advance my work," he claimed in a 1933 interview. "Work is the real adventure in life. Money is merely a means to make more work possible."[9]

Disney's instinctive populism permeated his 1930s cartoon shorts. Any number of Mickey Mouse's animated adventures featured a "triumph of the little guy" theme. In *Barnyard Battle* (1929), for instance, Mickey leads a battalion of mouse troops to victory by outwitting an enemy force of cats who are much larger and meaner. In *Mickey's Garden* (1935), the protagonist and Pluto accidentally spray themselves with insecticide and magically shrink to bug size. Beset by giant insects bent on revenge in a jungle of towering garden plants, the tiny characters suffer several narrow escapes before finding safety at the film's end. In *The Worm Turns* (1936), Mickey mixes a courage-building potion that turns the hierarchy of the natural world upside down. A number of creatures imbibe the mixture, with hilarious results: a fly beats up a spider trying to catch him, a mouse clobbers a cat looking to eat him, and the cat in turn terrorizes Pluto when Pluto tries to chase him as usual. Finally, Pluto is captured by the mean-spirited dog-catcher, but he takes the potion and chases the public official off the property. Mickey the populist icon appeared nowhere more clearly, perhaps, than in *Brave Little Tailor* (1938). Accidentally entering the service of the king, Mickey, as a tiny but courageous tailor in a medieval village, uses his wits to subdue a marauding giant and win the acclaim of the populace. By this time, Mickey's role as "official giant killer" had become an accustomed one.

Other Mickey Mouse films illustrated related aspects of Disney's populist vision. Satirical treatment of the idle rich flavored *Mickey's Good Deed* (1932), where the mouse, desperate to raise money for a weeping, penniless mother cat, temporarily sells Pluto to a wealthy family and their spoiled brat of a son. The strength and solidarity of the working-class family is depicted in *Mickey's Orphans* (1931), in which Mickey and Minnie take in a basket of kittens left on their doorstep by an impoverished mother. A humorous denigration of the smooth city slicker was at the heart of *Mickey's Rival* (1936), where the smooth-talking, sharp-dressing Mortimer Mouse and his fancy car fall victim to hubris while Mickey, a humiliated bumpkin, wins Minnie's affections through his steadiness and bravery.

Mickey's against-the-odds traits did not escape critical notice. Trying to explain the mouse's popularity, newspaper reviewers argued that it was because "he is a human being beset by the world's woes and because he is perpetually triumphant." Mickey represented "the cosmic victory of the underdog, the might of the meek." L. H. Robbins, writing in the *New York Times Magazine*, elaborated on this theme, noting that "to the timid among us, Mickey represents mankind beset by grim circumstances and escaping whole and right-side-up through luck . . . To the aggressive and the predatory among us, on the other hand, he symbolizes cleverness and resource . . . He outsmarts even Behemoth."[10]

As the Depression gradually began to wane, Mickey was surpassed in popularity by another character, the irascible Donald Duck. This was not completely an accident. Perhaps appealing to a recovering sense of social confidence in America by the late 1930s, the quick-tempered Donald captured audience's affections with an assertive, even belligerent determination to secure his place in the scheme of things. Displaying temper tantrums that were truly works of art and a squawking, half-intelligible voice that could raise the dead, the duck burst into Disney's short films as a cocksure populist hero.

Of all the Mickey Mouse films from the 1930s, *Moving Day* (1936) may have captured Disney's populist sensibility most fully. When Mickey's gang falls six months behind in their rent, the brutish sheriff (once again played by a swaggering, obnoxious Pete) appears at their door to repossess the house and sell their belongings at auction. Amid gag-filled mishaps and misadventures, Mickey, Donald, and Goofy scramble to pack up their furniture and escape. With everything in a state of chaos — Donald gets stuck in a goldfish bowl, Goofy is thwarted in his attempts to load a piano — the sheriff returns and the tenants make a run for their old, beat-up truck. As the gloating law officer stands triumphant, however, a gas leak explodes and blows the tenants' furniture into the truck. Mickey and his friends gleefully drive away, leaving the evil sheriff sitting atop a pile of smoldering splinters with a FOR SALE sign collaring his neck. To a Depression-era audience, *Moving Day*'s satisfying humor came from its aggrieved protagonists' getting the last laugh over the oppressive voice of authority.

In many ways, the Silly Symphony series ran parallel to the Mickey Mouse films in shaping a populist genre. One of the early Silly Symphonies, for instance, *The Spider and the Fly* (1931), revolves around an outrageously comic battle between a large, devouring spider and a collection of flies who resist their fate. As the spider moves in to wreak havoc, the diminutive flies fight back in highly imaginative ways: horseflies serve as cavalry steeds for smaller flies, who mount them and wield straight pins as lances; dragonflies carry tiny pilots armed with bombs of black pepper; centipedes act as tanks for contingents of fly infantrymen; squads of flies carry lighted matches to incinerate the spiderweb. The spider flees from this collective counterattack. Numerous other films, such as *The Ugly Duckling* (1931), *Three Blind Mouseketeers* (1936), and *Ferdinand the Bull* (1938), detailed the struggles of marginalized figures who buck the system, overcome their ostracism, and finally triumph over inequities. In these Disney films the outsider always won.

Like many of the Mickey Mouse efforts, the Silly Symphonies tended to glorify the virtues of simple rural life in opposition to the indulgences and oppressions of the big city. One such film was *The Country Cousin* (1936), which featured a rube from the farm who visits his urban cousin, only to fall victim to temptation. He is so overwhelmed by the opulence of the city apartment that he runs amuck at a banquet, falls into a champagne glass, gets drunk, stumbles around knocking food and dishes off the table, and belligerently starts a brawl with the household cat. Sliding down the gutter pipe and barely avoiding the crush of urban commuters' feet, the country cousin beats a hasty retreat to the uncluttered pleasures of rural existence. *Who Killed Cock Robin?* (1935) burlesqued corrupt public authority. After the lovesick protagonist is shot with an arrow and seemingly murdered, much of the film's humor flows from its satirical treatment of the inept police and the malfunctioning court system. Finally, films such as *The Tortoise and the Hare* reinforced the "producerist" ethic. Recounting a race where the plodding "Toby Tortoise, Slow but Sure" emerges victorious over the flashy "Max

Hare, the Blue Streak," the tale reassured viewers that success would follow in the wake of steady, persistent work habits.

Another topic Disney dealt with in the 1930s was the machine age and its discontents. Films such as *Santa's Workshop* (1932), *Busy Beavers* (1931), and *Father Noah's Ark* (1933) offered benign, gag-filled depictions of industrial production. But other animated shorts presented a more biting assessment of modern technology. Appraising the machine age's assault on human dignity, such movies focused on average people's struggles to survive against its indignities. In *Mickey's Amateurs* (1937), Goofy performs as a one-man band with the aid of an automated, gas-powered contraption that goes haywire in the end, whirling into pieces as its various instruments squeal madly. The darkly sadistic movie *The Mad Doctor* (1933) focuses on the potential horror of science and technology as it exposes a crazy physician who performs medical experiments by using a power saw to gather body parts from victims. Most of the time Disney aimed for the satirical middle ground, using humor to suggest that the triumph of technology had sown seeds of discord. Donald Duck's *Modern Inventions* (1937), for example, a takeoff on Charlie Chaplin's famous film *Modern Times*, shows Donald entering the Museum of Modern Marvels, only to become its victim. A robot butler keeps reappearing to swipe his hat, he is tied up by a wrapping machine, an automated baby basket force-feeds and diapers him, and an automatic barber chair finally turns him upside-down and trims his tail-feathers while administering a shoeshine to his face and beak.

Disney's portrayal of the problems and possibilities of modern technology elicited considerable commentary, as many critics took note of and wrestled with the implications of these popular cultural statements. For many critics, it seemed that Disney sought to cushion the negative impact of the machine age. Robert Feild argued that while the industrial revolution had made machinery the great enemy of art, this cartoonist had begun to reconcile the two with his production techniques and narrative themes. The Disney Studio, he believed, worked to create happy, fantastic images from the art world "with all the energy of twentieth-century science behind them." Gilbert Seldes may have put it best. In his 1937 book *The Movies Come from America,* he described Disney as "the great satirist of the machine age. In him, without a doubt, the machine becomes human — just when humanity is afraid mankind will be turned into a machine. To an American familiar with the American habit of tinkering with mechanisms, Disney's attitude in this respect is not particularly surprising. An American is not a machine worshiper — he is far too familiar with the machine. But he likes machines, and one might say that machinery likes him." Thus Disney throughout this period played a powerful mediating role with regard to modern technology, transforming intimidating, even frightening specters of dehumanization into fascinating and laughable images. Machines, he seemed to suggest over and over, had the potential to become the servants of the folk.[11]

Disney's personal film statement, a little-known Silly Symphony entitled *The Golden Touch* (1935), elaborated his populist instincts. Apparently miffed by Hollywood whispering that he was merely a manager while others did the real creative work, he sequestered the studio's top two artists, Fred Moore and Norm Ferguson, and personally produced a film, without the usual story and animation conferences. The result was less than successful — even Disney admitted later that the cartoon bombed with audiences — but it resonated politically. Drawing on the old tale of King Midas, the movie features a fat, bald old king who disdains women and wine but worships gold. When he is magically granted "the golden touch" by an elf, he is first overjoyed, then horrified as everything he touches turns into the valuable metal. Growing hysterical, he finally offers all of his earthly possessions for some food. "My kingdom for a hamburger!" he cries out tearfully. When his wish is granted, everything he owns — his treasure, the royal castle, even his clothes — vanishes as a hamburger on a plate appears in front of him. Chomping down, he happily informs the audience that this delightful prize came complete "with onions!" Obviously aimed at a Depression audience — Disney said that he had tried to give it "social significance" — the movie concerned the evil of mere moneymaking, the danger of an individual's overreaching his moral grasp, the false happiness accruing to mere wealth. Reaffirming the modest pleasures of the common man, *The Golden Touch* gave at least a quick glimpse of Disney's populist self-image.

Regardless of the conscious intent or explicit ideology of his films, the implicit force of Disney's populism set critical Geiger counters chattering during the 1930s. Many observers took note of the political implications of Disney's work, most often commenting on its consistent defense of the underdog. "Mickey, kin to little David, always wins against every Goliath. Donald Duck, the choleric knight, fights courageously against a malevolent world," wrote one essayist. Edward G. Smith offered a more specific argument in a 1935 essay entitled "St. Francis of the Silver Screen," which portrayed Disney as a political antidote to a poisonous "age of dictators and tyrants" in which Mussolini, Hitler, and Stalin "stride the world like a colossus." This Hollywood filmmaker inspired an antiauthoritarian politics, Smith believed, by reaffirming the heroic resilience of common people, especially with characters like Mickey Mouse: "In his smallness is his appeal. His squeak sounds farther than the roar of the largest lion. In the rough and tumble of a hundred adventures Mickey is always victorious. The meek (even the timid) inherit the earth . . . [He] runs fast, as a mouse does run. But push him too hard; arouse his chivalry; bring him face to face with a glowering bully, and the mouse becomes an acrobatic and resourceful lion."[12]

Many critics not only discerned a populist message in Disney's films but praised them as an effective political and social assault on the Great Depression. Some emphasized the practical, as did a tongue-in-cheek newspaper article in noting that Disney had merchandised so many goods that "it may truthfully be said that Mickey has done his part in ending the depression by putting hundreds or even thousands of employees on the payroll." More typical were the editorials and articles that praised Disney films for reviving hope and laughter among the American people. "When the last plaintive moan of the depression has faded to a feeble whisper and the last tear is dried," one editorialist intoned, "it might well be in order to give some thanks to Mr. Walter Disney." Praising Disney's films for their hope and courage, the Des Moines *Register* insisted that they effectively combated the "malign forces" that had traumatized American society. As the review stirringly concluded, "it is about time that we realized that Walt Disney, creator of Mickey Mouse, is one of the great political forces of our time."[13]

Disney's various populist works and the reaction they elicited reached a high point in a single small film, which took America by storm in 1933. Its rollicking story, adorable characters, odious villain, and hypnotic theme song all contributed to a tidal wave of popularity and commentary. More than any other Disney production, it carried a heavy political charge. To the utter astonishment of its maker, the film became the most famous Silly Symphony ever made. And it blared a message that seemed to have everyone in the United States discussing its implications and singing of hope.

III. Who's Afraid of the Big, Bad Wolf?

There had never been anything quite like it in American popular culture. An eight-minute cartoon released in May 1933, *Three Little Pigs* mesmerized the American public. The film, with its valiant little porcine heroes vanquishing "the big, bad wolf," according to one newspaper, quickly became "nearly universal in its spread," as the president quoted it in an address, ministers preached sermons on it, and dozens of articles analyzed it. In the words of another publication, Disney's fable "has captured the conversation of the country and is delighting full theatres every day. Newspapers are using the Three Little Pigs in political cartoons; we see them dancing around a disgruntled Wolf, who always represents the scoundrel opposition party. Department stores are selling 'three little pigskin' gloves. At any turn of the dial, the radio is likely to pick up the theme song." The film seemed to cast a spell over the country. Children and adults alike constantly talked about it, while "writers on such unrelated subjects as politics, sports, and finance sprinkle their copy with references to the big, bad this and the big, bad that."[14]

In New York City, one theater showing the film hired a horse-drawn carriage with a top-hatted driver to roll through various parts of town carrying three large stuffed pigs in the back seat, while another placed large cutouts of the pigs on the front sidewalk, complete with beards that lengthened as the weeks of the engagement piled up. In Dallas, a minor riot broke out at the Majestic Theatre when it forgot to run *Three Little Pigs* as advertised. A mob of angry patrons gathered in the lobby, pushing and yelling at the theater staff, and eventually forced the management to cut the feature film (already showing for some ten minutes) to show the Disney cartoon. When it finally appeared on the screen, according to a newspaper report, "a deafening cheer" erupted. The International Livestock Exposition even got into the act. Its February 1934 Quality in Meats exhibit in Chicago featured the wolf peering hungrily through a window at life-size figures of the three little pigs modeled in pure lard.[15]

A rather clever and well-done number in the Silly Symphony series, *Three Little Pigs* in fact seemed little different from many other Disney creations. It had been the work of some of the studio's top animators, and the story was a simplified version of the old folktale in which a sober, industrious little pig saves his profligate brothers from a ravenous wolf. Yet the key question remains: why was this animated short so incredibly popular? What led the public to embrace it so enthusiastically?[16]

In part it was a fad, which swept through a commercial society with little rhyme or reason beyond novelty. Its appeal also can be traced to the film's hit song, "Who's Afraid of the Big, Bad Wolf?" written by Disney Studio composer Frank Churchill, which had a catchy melody. The song's popularity led to sheet-music publication, widespread radio play, and movement into the repertoire of popular orchestras around the country. In ballrooms and dance halls, bandleaders immediately filled the dance floors whenever they struck up with it. In the words of one, "he couldn't get a bigger reaction from the crowd if he had President Roosevelt up there on the stand leading the band in 'The Star-Spangled Banner.'" The song's immense popularity triggered a humorous piece in *The New Yorker* by Frank Sullivan, who reported on his train ride back to New York City after he had been out of the country for several months. He hears the conductor whistling a catchy tune, learns its name, but is surprised when "seventeen people in his car join in to sing the refrain." At Grand Central Station, he sees with growing alarm that the song has captured the city, as porters, yardmen, baggage men, ticket-sellers, and commuters hum the tune. Sullivan then becomes rather dazed as he hears his taxi driver singing "Who's afraid of the big, bad cop?" while a policeman "using his nightstick as a fife, pranced off in the manner of the Little Pig who built his house of straw." He finally snaps when he is greeted at home by his parents with the melodious refrain, "'Take off your things and have a drink, have a drink, have a drink. Take off your things and have a drink, have a drink with us.' I found myself replying, 'I don't mind if I have a shot, have a shot, have a shot. I don't mind if I have a shot, have a shot with youse'... And that, my friends, is why I am leaving tomorrow for Vladivostok, there to remain until this thing blows over, or reaches Vladivostok."[17]

Some observers offered the straightforward explanation that *Three Little Pigs* captured the public fancy because it took the artistic and narrative skill of Disney productions to a new level. A number of editorials and reviews suggested simply that people responded to Disney's skillful utilization of the "beast fable," to the film's seamless blend of drawing, music, story, humor, and dance, and to its rollicking family appeal. Along the same lines, some pointed to the emergence of personality in this film as a key to its appeal. As one newspaper stressed, for the first time a Silly Symphony provided "not one, but three gallant and charming heroes" that the public could embrace. Disney himself endorsed this view, telling a Hollywood columnist that *Three Little Pigs* had opened up the field of animation by instilling personality into the characters, making them distinct and believable rather than mere drawings.[18]

More curmudgeonly critics, however, took a less benevolent view. Annoyed that any such film should be so popular, they speculated that its adoring reception revealed some kind of public pathology. Some sniffed that Americans were "reveling in something akin to a second childhood . . . an unmistakable symptom of softening of the national brain." Others complained that Disney's film revealed a growing public weakness for happy endings. A writer for the Philadelphia *Record* suggested half seriously that the uproar over this brief film and its theme song had made Walt Disney a "public enemy." *Three Little Pigs* had intoxicated the American people, he groused, and the fact that it came hurtling out of every available radio, theater, newspaper, and dinner party conversation made it "the great national menace."[19]

For some, the problem was not Disney's film but the intelligentsia who embraced it. A "flood of highbrow opinion" had nearly ruined Mickey Mouse in earlier years, some observers complained, and now *Three Little Pigs* was providing a new excuse for pretentious theorizing. Gleason Pease, in a syndicated column from New York, rolled his eyes at farfetched explanations he had encountered: Marxists insisted that the three protagonists represented the proletariat, the bourgeoisie, and the capitalists; "sophisticates" babbled on about the vision of a great artist; psychologists lectured about the film's appeal to "the escape motive" and "infantilism." This discourse of "symbolisms, psychological stimuli, release of inhibitions, and other ponderous things," another essayist opined, led the eggheads, as usual, straight past the obvious. The amazing appeal of this little film, he concluded rather waspishly, had a simple explanation: "The little pigs are merely very, very funny and very, very cute."[20]

The great bulk of the discourse about *Three Little Pigs*, however, eschewed art, personality, and music to concentrate on politics. A great many observers — film critics, editorialists, contributors of letters to the editor — viewed the film as a populist parable, a blow against the Great Depression on behalf of long-suffering common citizens. The movie garnered such extensive acclaim, many believed, because it reaffirmed hope amid a terrifying social plague, endorsed the basic goodness of the American folk, and illustrated the final triumph of the little guy.[21]

Most evaluations converged on a number of points. First, they almost universally decoded the movie's symbolism as the Big, Bad Wolf representing the Depression and the Three Little Pigs representing average citizens desperately fighting for survival against its attempts to devour them. One critic argued that millions had embraced the movie because the "wolf in America is behind every corner, behind every counter, on the heels of every person. One moment he blows away to the auction block the home and property of a farmer ruined by the financial crisis. Another moment he blows out of his comfortable house a man who's worked many years for Ford, but who couldn't make his last payment. Frightening, frightening is the grey wolf of unemployment." But just as the wolf did not prevail in the movie, he would not prevail in America. As one newspaper typically described Disney's message, "The Big, Bad Wolf, or his like, always comes to grief and the pink and roguish Little Pigs always are triumphant . . . Who's afraid?"[22]

Second, *Three Little Pigs* was regarded as a stirring manifesto of hope and courage. Much like FDR's inaugural speech a few months before this little movie's release, the film struck many as saying "all you have to fear is fear itself." A raft of articles in 1933 suggested that it "chased away the depression blues" and cut through the socioeconomic gloom to "send fresh blood through our arteries, to enable us to hold up our heads and face whatever tomorrow may bring." The movie's trio of protagonists survived assault and "built a sturdier house from the ruins and gave the big, bad wolf hell," observed an article in the High Point, North Carolina, *Enterprise*. "And that is what America is at last giving the depression."[23]

Third, numerous observers believed that *Three Little Pigs* encouraged the solidarity of the American folk by showing that all could pull together to defeat a common, ferocious enemy. A letter to the editor in the Dayton, Ohio, *News*, for example, argued that the Depression had divided people — the tenant had been set against the landlord, the consumer against the merchant, the manufacturer against the farmer, and everyone against the bankers. But through this film, which sped "the return of the people's courage," such divisions had been bridged and "a great golden-headed nail was driven deep into the coffin of the depression." According to another writer, the movie preached "the brotherhood of man" as the wise little pig took in his fellow victims yet "did not stop to argue whether the two little pigs deserved to be saved; and having saved them he did not lecture them."[24]

Finally, some critics explicitly linked *Three Little Pigs* to the hopeful, enthusiastic "spirit of recovery" characterizing Franklin Roosevelt's New Deal. An editorial in the Warren, Pennsylvania, *Times-Mirror,* for instance, insisted that Walt Disney's new hit film was cut from the same cloth as FDR and his National Recovery Administration. The animated tale "symbolized this new American NRA spirit in some way — the American power to defy disaster, to laugh and sing in the face of danger and trouble," it noted. A striking full-page ad in the October 13, 1933, New York *Times* for Bloomingdale's compared certain aspects of America's pre-Depression economic behavior — overproduction, low wages, unfair competition, cheaply made products — to the flimsy sticks and straws with which the two foolish pigs built their houses. The advertisement then prominently displayed a drawing of the wise pig constructing his house of sturdy bricks marked "NRA" and urged Americans to get behind "the man in the White House." Another newspaper editorial held that Disney's film "has given the nation a Recovery theme song" and concluded, "By golly, who *is* afraid of this big bad depression? Build your economic structure of proven bricks upon a solid foundation and chortle defiance to the wolf's blasts."[25]

As for Disney himself, he appeared genuinely befuddled by the widespread political reading of *Three Little Pigs.* Initially he rejected the notion entirely. Replying to an interviewer's question about the pigs' popularity, he admitted, "I don't know. You've got me. I'd like to find out myself just why people liked them. Then I'd know better how to do it again. We're just feeling our way here." A few years later, in *Time*'s cover story of December 27, 1937, the filmmaker recalled how everyone at the Disney Studio had been puzzled at people's discovery of social meaning in the film. "It was just another story to us," he recalled, "and we were in there gagging it just like any other picture. After we heard all the shouting, we sat back and tried to analyze what made it good." (This naive reading fit perfectly with the modest, "aw, shucks" persona that Walt liked to project.)[26]

At the same time, however, Disney was nothing if not shrewd. As he perceived the drift of the popular reception to *Three Little Pigs,* he subtly began to incorporate a political flavor into his comments on the film. In a brief 1933 essay, for example, he described Depression-era social conditions in terms of "the wolf eating the Fuller Brush man at the door and good men sleeping three deep on the benches of Pershing Square." The following year, in an article in the *Christian Science Monitor,* he sympathetically described a newspaper cartoon that had labeled the trio of dancing pigs "Confidence, Recovery, and Hope" and the wolf as "Slump," with the latter, of course, "stealing away with his tail between his legs." He claimed surprise that "statesmen, clergymen, editors, and other exalted personages would find in the simple message [the pigs] bore many lessons relating to thrift, security, good government, and the relations of nations." Disney admitted, however, that the film had provided solace to many Americans while driving home a simple moral lesson: "Wisdom and courage are enough to defeat big, bad wolves of every description, and send them slinking away all huffed and puffed out."[27]

In other words, at a half-conscious level, both the film and its reception seemed to touch Disney's political instincts. *Three Little Pigs* may not have been intended as a populist fable, but everything about it reflected its creator's social values. The wise pig appeared as yet another version of Disney's populist hero — a hardworking common man, committed to producerism and thrift, demonstrating the solidarity of the folk as he took in his brothers and routed their common enemy. The two foolish pigs provided gentle satire with their laziness, carefree social habits, and weakness for sensual temptation. And the wolf, of course, symbolized those powerful forces that threatened any common citizen given to nonproductivity and foolish self-indulgence. In 1933, after nearly four years of economic disaster, the blustering, fanged predator could hardly be seen as anything *other* than a symbol of the Depression.

5

Disney and the Depression: Populist Parables

ROM 1937 TO 1942, the pioneering series of feature-length animated films from the Disney Studio garnered great popular and critical acclaim. *Snow White and the Seven Dwarfs*, *Pinocchio*, *Fantasia*, *Dumbo*, and *Bambi* became a central, even beloved, part of this filmmaker's legacy. In fact, these movies established the creative high-water mark of the early Disney Studio, presenting a complex integration of various entertainment and artistic elements. They also shared something else — a common ideological thrust. With varying degrees of intensity, they highlighted important aspects of Disney's Depression-era politics. In the process, the dynamic filmmaker himself became something of a folk hero to an adoring American audience.

I. The Triumph of the Little Guy

Snow White, Disney's great experiment in moviemaking, carried a subtle but potent political charge. Its sentimental story of the beautiful young princess who survives the assault of her wicked stepmother masked a number of social themes that Disney had consistently articulated in many of his earlier short films — the triumph of the underdog, the value of hard work, and the virtues of community among common people.

From the very outset, Snow White is presented to the audience as an outsider, a young woman toppled from high position and subdued by capricious forces over which she has no control. She first appears onscreen as an orphaned princess who has been reduced to performing the menial labor of a scullery maid in the queen's household. She becomes the victim of corrupt power when the queen flies into a jealous rage about her innocent beauty and sends the royal huntsman to kill her. As Snow White frantically flees, the forest seems to hold a collection of devouring monsters that reach out to grab her. Then she unexpectedly encounters a small community of fellow souls nestled deep in the woods.

The figures who steal the show in *Snow White*, of course, are the seven dwarfs who shelter the girl in the forest. The quirky personalities and curious appearance of these quaint little men delighted 1930s audiences and made them laugh, but their character also forms no small part of their appeal. They are hardworking miners who tramp off to their labors, pickaxes slung over their shoulders, singing "Heigh-ho, It's Off to Work We Go" and chanting in unison, "Dig, dig, dig" as they bend to their backbreaking task. Their producerist ethic is reinforced by Snow White and the collection of forest animals that accompany her. Joining forces to clean the dwarfs' cottage, they labor joyfully and cooperatively, singing "Whistle While You Work." When the dwarfs and Snow White agree to set up a common household, their spontaneous musical celebration provides a striking image of Disney's populist heritage. Evoking barn dances of the rural Midwest, the party displays a community of producers reveling in their virtue. As the dwarfs merrily sing and dance with their new housemate, the spectacle represents the triumph of (literally) the little guy.

Preliminary conferences at the Disney Studio for *Snow White* indicated that at least in part, the populist dimension of the film was no accident. Surviving meeting notes indicate that Disney, executive director Dave Hand, and a number of story men debated at length how the seven dwarfs should be depicted as they labored at their diamond mine. Ultimately, they decided to emphasize two points. First, they concluded that the fabulous riches of the diamond mine must be essentially meaningless to these small workers. Urging a gentle satire on work and wealth, Disney suggested appropriate gags — the miners find a doorknob in a big pile of diamonds and "look at it with interest, keep it and throw the jewels away"; Sleepy nonchalantly tosses a huge diamond to hit and unhook the switch handle on the train car. Much more important was their satisfaction in their work, the "pleasant, happy feeling . . . [from] the way they have always mined, just another day in their lives." Second, the story team decided that the dwarfs should make a mockery of a labor process dominated by efficiency, organization, and a time clock. While the bearded little men work hard, chanting "dig, dig, dig" while "pounding, sifting, mechanical sounds" can be heard in the background, they also fool their leader, Doc, by moving the clock's hands ahead to get off work a little early. Again, Disney himself urged that humor would result from the juxtaposition of an admission that "we don't know what we dig 'em for" with the "dig, dig, dig" chant. In this formulation, the work itself rather than the financial payoff was the true reward.[1]

The ideological dimension of *Snow White* can be seen in the political responses it prompted, an extreme example of which appeared in the left's embrace of the film. The *People's World*, for instance, described the film as "Walt Disney's contribution to Marxist theory," with the princess standing as a symbol of "human decency being persecuted by a capitalistic step-mother," the dwarfs representing "a miniature Communistic society," the vultures "Trotskyites," and the poison apple "Hearst editorials." Other com-mentators offered less strained assessments. Some stressed its machine age connotations, arguing that Disney once again was trying to humanize and soften the industrial world, as in the initial scene at the dwarfs' cottage, when Snow White and her "army of quadrupeds [were] transformed into cleaning elements" and scoured the house with enginelike efficiency. Others insisted that this film was Disney's most important political statement since *Three Little Pigs*, a charming story of virtue, kindness, and honest labor that offered "faith in life which gives us courage in the dark." Disney's magical film, wrote Frank Nugent in the New York *Times*, presented a "tonic for disillusion" among common people in a modern world beset by wars, crime, and economic strife. "More than 250,000 New Yorkers already have seen this picture, have smiled contentedly together, have been united for a time — and for a time thereafter — in a common bond of enchanted delight. It is good for men to smile that way together over something sweet and innocent and clean . . . If anything is true today, it is that one touch of Disney makes the whole world kin."[2]

Pinocchio, Disney's next full-length film, told another story well suited to an audience conditioned by the travails of the Depression. With marked populist overtones, it chronicled a quest for stability, self-definition, and humanity within a threatening social environment. The film focuses on a little wooden puppet created by the woodcarver Geppetto, who wishes that the toy could become a real little boy. The Blue Fairy partially grants the wish — she turns Pinocchio into a live creature, although he remains made of wood — but she tells him that if he is to become fully human, he must learn morality, virtue, and courage. Thus he takes center stage as the most extreme kind of outsider, someone who must struggle for his very life as he tries to become a virtuous, productive human being.

An eager but gullible creature, Pinocchio faces social temptations and suffers assaults on all sides. He runs across a prototype of the legen-dary confidence man, an unscrupulous commercial sharper named J. Worthington Foulfellow (or "Honest John"), who tempts him out of school and onto the stage. He falls into the clutches of Stromboli, the greedy puppetmaster, who threatens to chop him into firewood if he doesn't cooperate. He is enticed by Lampwick, a young ruffian who leads him astray with cigarettes, beer, and pool halls on Pleasure Island, where he is nearly captured and sold abroad. After a narrow escape, Pinocchio finally confronts Monstro, an underwater leviathan who literally devours both the puppet and Geppetto.

Throughout these adventures, Pinocchio proves susceptible because of his own weaknesses — a tendency to lie to get out of trouble, a frivolous nature that lures him to the stage, a proclivity for sensual indulgences that leads him astray on the island for donkey-boys. But tragedy is averted when he proves himself worthy by saving his "father," Geppetto, at the end. In other words, the movie details an innocent individual's series of encounters with a threatening, corrupt social order. Pinocchio survives this school of hard knocks only by learning the lessons of responsibility, morality, and self-reliance. Like Mickey Mouse, the plodding Tortoise, and the Ugly Duckling, Pinocchio is a little guy who endures numerous tribulations before eventually triumphing against the odds.

The story conferences that accompanied *Pinocchio*'s production previewed many of the film's populist themes. At one of the earliest, Disney made it clear how he wanted to "set the mood" by letting the camera roam around Geppetto's shop. "Start where he says, 'Once upon a time there lived — not a princess — not a prince — not a king — but a little old man named Geppetto,'" he instructed. "It's humble all the way through, you see — 'and he didn't live in a marble hall or a big palace on a hill; he lived in a little village, with a little old shop in a little old side street' — everything is little, little, old, old — very humble." Disney argued that this atmosphere should be reinforced with images of strong familial ties; Geppetto, his goldfish Cleo, his cat Figaro, and the wooden puppet should form "a little, happy family." At another point, Disney pushed for a conception of Pleasure Island as a trap for those given to laziness and self-indulgence. The boys who were enticed there, he mused, should be depicted as kids "allowed to do anything and have anything. And the idea is that when kids can do as they please, they grow up and turn into stupid asses." In yet another discussion, he urged his staff to sharpen the characterization of J. Worthington Foulfellow, the fox, portraying him as a greedy "slicker" who "talks of making money on Pino" by selling him to a puppetmaster and then proclaiming, "'We'll take him for everything he's got or my name isn't —!'"[3]

Critics routinely described *Pinocchio* as far superior to *Snow White* and the greatest animated film ever made, and many noted its subtle cultural politics. First, they highlighted the gallery of money-grubbing, tyrannical villains who hindered the little puppet's attempts to become fully human. Disney's depiction of these dangerous characters, in the words of *Time*, rejected cuddly sentimentalism in favor of "savage adult satire." Second, most reviewers of the film praised its social and moral lessons — that hard work, self-restraint, and family connectedness underlay achievement and security. They noted approvingly that Disney was "taking the reform school tendencies" out of his little protagonist while encouraging individuals to "follow the path of bravery, truthfulness, and unselfishness."[4]

What held the entire social message together, of course, was the voice of Jiminy Cricket, the most compelling character in the film. Appointed "the Lord High Keeper of the Knowledge of Right and Wrong," he served as the mouthpiece of conscience and community. He played the key role in this morality tale, as critics observed, by steadfastly and humorously projecting "that still, small voice that nobody listens to" and eventually helping Pinocchio to success.[5]

Fantasia, another of Disney's great experiments, strode across the ideological terrain at a more oblique angle. With the release of this innovative movie, Disney stumbled directly into a debate with serious political overtones: should "highbrow" culture be separated and protected from popular entertainment and mass audiences? As critic Bosley Crowther observed, Disney must have known he was walking into a storm, because while he had previously kept "his works on a fairly plebeian level, [now he] was blithely invading the precincts of an aristocratic art." Some found this refusal to pay "homage to sacred cows" refreshing, while others found it almost sacrilegious. But whatever the reaction, the controversial question of cultural elitism revealed the populist dimension of *Fantasia*.[6]

Disney's highly experimental concert feature of 1940 certainly caricatured or gently satirized stiff-necked, elitist elements of high culture. Mickey Mouse's antics in "The Sorcerer's Apprentice," the dancing mushrooms in "The Nutcracker Suite," the informal jam session during the concert's intermission, and the intoxicated bacchanal in "The Pastoral Symphony" all worked to deflate the dignity of classical music and bring it down to earth with a thud. No scene did this more effectively than "The Dance of the Hours," with its parody of classical ballet by a hilarious menagerie — gangly ostrich ballerinas, the lecherous Ben Ali Gator, and especially the prima donna, Hyacinth Hippo. Such mockery, however, was balanced by a kind of awestruck reverence that characterized the bulk of the Tchaikovsky, Stravinsky, Beethoven, and Schubert pieces. Thus *Fantasia* offered no clear embrace of social egalitarianism or gallery of populist protagonists like the other Disney features from this era.

More telling, however, was Disney's proclaimed intent to use *Fantasia* as a vehicle to bring high art to the people. He clearly explained his rationale for the movie at one point: "We say that the public — that is, the audience — would always recognize and appreciate quality. It was this faith in the discrimination of the average person that led us to make such a radically different type of entertainment as *Fantasia*. We simply figured that if ordinary folk like ourselves could find entertainment in these visualizations of so-called classical music, so would the average person." In an interview-based article at the time of *Fantasia*'s release, the New York *Post* reported his determination to use "his screen medium to bring 'good music' to the masses." Many of his coworkers at the studio chimed in, observing that their leader defined his own taste as "the average man music audience" and set it up as a sounding board for shaping the project. A statement printed in the film's program informed viewers that "the beauty and inspiration of music must not be restricted to a privileged few but made available to every man, woman, and child." After viewing the production, the statement continued, the average person should be "much less humble about his ability to under-stand good music."[7]

In fact, Disney's idealism embroiled him in a controversy when *Fantasia* premiered in New York City. After a number of music writers publicly condemned the film as a travesty of classical music standards, the film-maker's midwestern political impulses boiled over. Appearing as guest of honor at a National Board of Review luncheon, he gave an informal inter-view to newspaper reporters. In his comments, he blasted those critics who set themselves up as "little tin gods, who reserve the right to tell us what we must do." *Fantasia*, he made clear, was intended to wash over elitist cultural barriers and expand cultural opportunity for common people.[8]

Many critics of this unusual film lined up behind Disney's populist agenda. From New York to Los Angeles, film writers voiced their apprecia-tion of *Fantasia*'s attempt, even if flawed or occasionally flat, to democratize culture. They commended its attempts to reach out to common citizens and described the movie as an honest effort to capture "the response of a layman to the evocations of great music" or an exploration of "high-class music" that "the average movie goer will find . . . [to be] a vast delight." They praised Disney as a man "who dares to thumb his nose at the word precious, thereby doing a lot of people who have been scared to death of classical music and its cult standards a great favor." As one columnist noted approv-ingly, *Fantasia* "will enlist new music lovers among those who before loved only Mickey Mouse."[9]

Like Disney, many of these critics chastised the movie's opponents as snobbish defenders of cultural privilege. With a certain relish, they skewered the supercilious, who, in the words of one, enjoyed "looking down their noses" at *Fantasia*. The Brooklyn *Eagle*, for instance, mocked those "austere" commentators who "bow too low and scrape too deep at this holy Shangri-La where they keep entombed the sanctified memories of their Bach, Beethoven, and Tchaikovsky." Pare Lorenz, a critic and prominent film-maker in his own right, offered Disney firm support for the film. As he told readers of *McCall's*, "I advise you to disregard the howls from the music critics . . . you can dismiss the complaints of the little hierarchy of music men who try to make music a sacrosanct, mysterious, and obscure art. Disney has brought it out of the temple, put it in carpet slippers and an old sweater, and made it work to surround, and support, and synchronize a brilliantly drawn series of animated color sketches."[10]

The 1942 film *Bambi*, with its gentle story of a young deer coming of age in the forest, expended most of its emotional energy in an exploration of nature's cycles. At the same time, however, its ideological theme paralleled that in *Pinocchio:* the individual's quest for security, self-definition, and family coherence, this time within a threatening *natural* order. Here a young deer encounters danger on all sides — hunters and ferocious dogs, forest fires, older and more experienced bucks — before growing up to become the lord of the forest. Conceived near the end of the Depression, *Bambi* took shape as another tale of a vulnerable protagonist whose virtue and bravery led him to surmount all difficulties thrown at him.

Of all Disney's early feature animations, however, *Dumbo* packed the most powerful populist punch. With great emotion and tenderness, this unpretentious film followed a circus elephant's struggles to survive in a hostile environment. Born with outlandishly big ears, the innocent little creature is shackled with a pair of tribulations. First, he faces an intense social elitism that makes him an object of snobbish ridicule. His mother, Mrs. Jumbo, loves him dearly, of course, but a quartet of elephant matrons mercilessly mock him as a "freak." Dumbo, as these obnoxious pillars of respectability begin calling him, immediately becomes a social misfit and outcast. The situation only worsens when he is verbally and physically tormented by a gang of small boys, an event that drives his mother into a rage and results in her imprisonment. He thus becomes a lonely outsider, cut off from respectability within the circus community and isolated even from his mother's love.

Second, the unfortunate Dumbo is quickly enveloped in a milieu of commercial exploitation. After he accidentally wreaks havoc on the elephants' usual routine inside the big tent, the circus managers force him into a demeaning role in the clown act, where he must play an endangered "baby" at the top of a burning building. To the crowd's great amusement, he is forced to jump and plunge through the clown firemen's safety net into a vat of plaster. This ordeal reduces Dumbo to tears, but the mercenary clowns decide that his frantic plunge to earth is hysterically funny. After the show they celebrate the new comic potential of their act by getting drunk and singing "We're Gonna Hit the Big Boss for a Raise." Dumbo's humiliation, it seems, will financially benefit the very people who exploit him.

In typical Disney fashion, however, the underdog finds success through an alliance with other outsiders. Dumbo becomes closely attached to another little figure, Timothy the Mouse, who determines to make him the star of the circus somehow. Significantly, this tiny creature takes revenge on Dumbo's matronly oppressors by playing on elephants' fear of mice and sends them squealing and jumping in terror. After Dumbo and Timothy accidentally imbibe some fermented water and mysteriously end up in the top of a tree, they encounter the Black Crows. These African-American caricatures initially mock the hapless elephant and his small companion, but they quickly become true friends to this rather curious pair. Full of jocular puns and hipster humor, the sympathetic crows help them to realize that Dumbo's huge ears give him the ability to fly. Moreover, they present him with a magic feather that bolsters his confidence in taking to the air. Significantly, at the movie's end, when the soaring Dumbo has become the star of the circus, Timothy the Mouse proudly appears as his besuited manager, signing a big Hollywood contract while Dumbo leads the crows in close formation over the circus train. All of the outsiders have come together to share their triumph.

Dumbo not only tugged at the heartstrings but stirred a sense of justice. This little movie embodied Disney's social values, and its little hero epitomized his long list of populist protagonists from the 1930s: the virtuous, defenseless underdog who struggles against arbitrary forces, bucks up his courage, finds his way to productive work, and ultimately joins with other marginalized figures to overcome their oppressors. His story was a social and political allegory for Depression-era America.

Critical discussions of *Dumbo* frequently grasped its political implications. Bosley Crowther, writing in the New York *Times,* argued that this sentimental film portrays "a woe-begone mite, . . . [who] finally ascends to triumph over the other elephants." Others warmly endorsed this tale of "ostracism, disgrace, demotion, running away, and a final triumph" and appreciated its satirical treatment of little Dumbo's persecutors. Disney's "slyly caustic comments about the better-than-thous" and the callous, exploitive clowns earned sympathetic praise, as did his treatment of the ringmaster, who came across as "the Simon Legree of the sawdust ring." Finally, a number of essays remarked on the alliance of outsiders who eventually triumph at movie's end. Both the New York *Herald Tribune* and *Newsweek* emphasized that the story detailed the adventures of an outsider "ostracized as a figure of fun until a sympathetic mouse and some helpful crows" prod him to success.[11]

RKO's "campaign book" for *Dumbo,* distributed to all theaters showing the movie, highlighted the social function of the Five Black Crows. Describing these characters as "wisecracking birds who speak in a warm, rich Negro accent," the booklet stressed that their comedic talents were surpassed only by their sympathy. The group first laughs at "the shy hero of the picture, and . . . then, taking pity, teaches him a trick or two about flying." Since the film could be viewed as an attack on unthinking prejudice, what was more appropriate than to have the most persecuted group in America, African-Americans, teach the young elephant how to survive and soar?[12]

If reviews can be trusted as a social barometer, *Dumbo* struck a nerve among a population unnerved for a decade by the Depression. As the Minneapolis *Evening Times* pointed out, in this film Disney seemed to grasp the vulnerabilities and weaknesses that tormented Americans. He "strips off the masks under which hide our foibles, frailties, fears, and he gives us a true-view reflection of what we really look like . . . the face behind the mask." But the film promoted not only understanding, most commentaries seemed to say, but an optimistic belief that triumph awaited the persistent underdog. As *PM* concluded, *Dumbo* taught that "people are essentially good, [and] it preaches sympathy, not derision, for Nature's slip-ups."[13]

None of the classic Disney features from 1937 to 1942, any more than the host of Mickey Mouse films or Silly Symphonies that preceded them, explicitly advanced a political agenda. But Disney's social and ideological values nonetheless pervaded the structure, characters, and narrative of these films. Moreover, these values were not his alone. While it is always risky to generalize about a large organization full of diverse and talented people, it seems clear that a populist breeze wafted through the Disney Studio in the 1930s. In this stimulating atmosphere, where creative output marked the highest standard of value and Disney himself was first among equals, one intense, brooding, charismatic individual stood out. Many considered Bill Tytla to be the most talented artist in the organization, and as much as anyone, he embodied its egalitarian, producerist spirit.

II. Bill Tytla: "A Fellow-Feeling with All Creation"

Vladimir "Bill" Tytla made an impression on most people that was not easily forgotten. With a muscular build, a shock of black hair, shaggy eyebrows, and a sweeping mustache, he matched his powerful appearance with an equally powerful style of drawing. Moreover, he threw himself into his work with a passion that often startled his colleagues. Frank Thomas remembered dropping by Tytla's office during the making of *Pinocchio* to consult on a complex scene involving the menacing character Stromboli: "Well, Bill was pure emotion, a wonderful guy, and his eyes would light up, he would tell me what Stromboli was like, what a big guy he was and how he'd move. He starts coming at me like this and backing me up across the room. I backed into the scene cabinet, half tipped the thing over, and all the scenes started spilling out all over, and Bill never stops." Thomas made a hasty, stumbling retreat from the room, which made him the butt of some laughter as the story made the studio rounds, but his experience was not unique. Tytla's passionate temperament, in tandem with his enormous artistic talent, set many people back on their heels.[14]

Yet this complex, committed man adopted no arrogant posture of romantic genius. Insecure about his artistic abilities, he saw himself as a part of the Disney Studio's larger mission in the 1930s and early 1940s. Even more important, in crucial ways he shared the cultural politics of its leader. Like Walt Disney, he nurtured an acute sensitivity to the plight of the outsider, an affinity for outdoor life, a strong ethic of hardworking individualism, and a rough-hewn producerism that gave scant regard to money. Tytla created some of the most famous scenes in Disney's classic animated movies, and in so doing helped illustrate the instinctive populism that flourished at the studio.

In terms of background, Tytla could not have been more different from Walt Disney. He was born on October 25, 1904, in Yonkers, New York, to Ukrainian and Polish immigrants. As a boy he demonstrated a precocious talent for art, and by the time he was in high school, he had begun skipping classes — like Disney, he never graduated — to attend sessions at the Art Students' League in New York City. A teacher named Boardman Robinson took the youth under his wing and forced him to abandon flashy affectations and concentrate on fundamental drawing techniques. Tytla expressed a lifelong admiration for this forceful mentor as someone, in his words, "who looked like a man and talked like one and had a very fine, subtle sense of humor." Absences from school got Tytla into legal trouble with the truant officers, but his father explained to the court that he was going to art school, and an autographed sketch presented to the judge was enough to get the charges dismissed.[15]

By the late 1910s, the youthful artist was working at the Barré-Bowers animation studio in New York City along with several others who later ended up at the Disney Studio — Dick Huemer, Bert Gillett, Ben Sharpsteen, Ted Sears, and George Stalling. In 1921 Tytla was briefly employed at Paramount Pictures in New York drawing titles and balloon captions for films. He then moved on to a long-term relationship with the animation enterprise of the Terry brothers, first working at John Terry's Greenwich Village studio drawing Judge Rummy and Happy Hooligan, then animating Aesop's fables for Paul Terry's Terrytoons.

After several years, however, Tytla apparently grew bored with the artistic limitations of the Terry Studio productions. In 1929 he went to Europe to travel, broaden his perspectives, and study painting. He stayed on the continent for nearly eighteen months, anchoring himself in Paris but traveling to London, Nice, and Vienna. He studied sculpture, which later proved to be a profound influence on his weighty, solid drawing style at Disney, and painted a number of landscapes and still lifes that showed the influence of Cézanne. He also closely analyzed the work of Brueghel, a painter whom a friend described as Tytla's "idol."[16]

By 1930 Tytla had exhausted his energy and funds and returned to New

York to resume his Terrytoons animation. To a serious young man fresh from a series of exhilarating artistic encounters, however, such work seemed even more crudely commercial than before. Older animators who specialized in quick, hack drawings of simple characters pulled down the biggest salaries, and they derided the young art school types as, according to Tytla, "Homo Bolsheviks." Even though Tytla demanded and received a series of raises in recognition of his talent, he grew increasingly dissatisfied. He had become close friends with another young animator, Art Babbitt, who sat across the aisle at the Terry Studio, and the two shared an apartment in the Bronx. In 1932, however, Babbitt left New York for Los Angeles to work for the upcoming studio of Walt Disney. When he praised his friend back east, Disney, who had already heard about Tytla from other Terry Studio refugees, expressed an interest in hiring him. Babbitt began sending a steady stream of inviting letters and telegrams to Tytla, who used them mainly to get salary raises from Terry. Eventually he broke down and went to California to work for Disney, though.[17]

Within a short time of his arrival at the Hyperion facility in 1934, Tytla earned a glowing reputation as one of the studio's best draftsmen. In particular, the strength and muscularity of his drawing — it seemed to flow almost physically out of his body onto the sheet — gained him a legion of admirers. He worked on a number of animated shorts released in 1935, excelling especially in the whimsical *Cookie Carnival,* for which he drew a number of charming and fantastic characters, and *Cock o' the Walk,* for which he created the swaggering, macho, prizefighting rooster. Indeed, his feel for heavies and villains was clear even at this early date.[18]

Tytla also secured his personal life. During his first years in Hollywood, he shared a nice house in Tuxedo Terrace with Art Babbitt. The two well-paid bachelors led something of a carefree existence. Babbitt cultivated his image as a ladies' man, a fact that occasionally annoyed his more reticent housemate, who once complained to friends that he was scared to come home late at night because "I never knew when I would step on Babbitt's bare butt while he was romancing some young actress on the living room floor." Within two years, Tytla met and married a young actress and artist's model and settled down to become a family man.[19]

By 1936, Tytla had become one of the Disney Studio's top animators and was embarked on the work that would establish his towering reputation for several decades. Disney appointed him one of four supervising animators on the initial feature project, *Snow White,* and he played a pioneer role in this landmark undertaking by developing the personalities of the seven dwarfs. After that he drew the imposing, menacing character of Stromboli in *Pinocchio.* In *Dumbo* he animated the little elephant himself with enormous emotion and acute sensitivity. Then, in *Fantasia,* Tytla seemed to be everywhere: he drew the Sorcerer in "The Sorcerer's Apprentice," the Cossack dance in "The Nutcracker Suite," and, most famously, the horribly evil Chernobog in "Night on Bald Mountain."

In this outpouring of work over half a decade, Tytla's distinct creative style emerged. Its benchmark was a powerful sense of emotion. Frank Thomas, for instance, described Tytla as "working through and feeling, feeling, feeling, until the thing started to gel to him." An artist who was "just *all* emotion," he jumped into his various tasks by seeking the "pure feeling" that made the character live. In Thomas's estimation, Tytla achieved "more power in animation than anyone else . . . [and his work had] just this *pow,* this strength that no one else has ever been able to get." Art Babbitt recounted that Tytla studied Richard Boleslavsky's famous text *Acting: The First Six Lessons* for insights that could be adapted to animation, while Zack Schwartz, an art director at the Disney Studio, believed that Tytla's "tremendous power and sense of form" came from his training as a sculptor.[20]

But to anyone who ever actually observed him at his desk, Bill Tytla's work style also provided a window into his creativity. One colleague noted that "you felt little sparks of electricity coming off him all the time," while another reported that he geared up for animating a character by stalking around his desk emoting, so that people thought, "What's that guy doing? He's gone crazy." Grim Natwick provided the most colorful recollection of Tytla at work:

> Bill hovered over his drawing board like a giant vulture protecting a nest filled with golden eggs. He was an intense worker — eager, nervous, absorbed . . . As a rule he began by making dozens of tiny sketches — thumbnails, no more than an inch high. He sketched on large or small scraps of paper, on exposure sheets, on laundry tickets, anything he could reach first when the drawing fever seized him . . . He clipped them together in strips, thumbtacked them to his bulletin board . . . Then, finally, with model sheets placed in convenient places, he began his animation in earnest . . .
>
> Key drawings were whittled out with impassioned pencil thrusts that tore holes in the animation paper. He often started with red pencils. If a line displeased him, he made corrections with blue pencil, then recorrected with black, then with brown, then green. Finally the kaleidoscopic drawing . . . [was] retraced in black. To end up with one drawing that pleased him, Bill might dump a dozen "imperfect" drawings into his wastebasket.

Tytla was so idolized by many younger animators at Disney that after he left for the day, they would storm into his office and scramble to gather the discarded sketches from his trash.[21]

Yet Tytla's work conveyed more than unbridled emotion and raw power. He also demonstrated a talent for portraying, with insight and often tenderness, the plight of the little guy. This characterized his important work in *Snow White,* for instance, for which he helped develop the personalities of the dwarfs. According to his fellow animators, Tytla largely created Grumpy and contributed in a major way to the leader, Doc, and the cute, mute little Dopey. Perhaps his most famous sequence in the film is the remarkable washing scene, where the dwarfs throw a reluctant Grumpy into the wash-tub after he has resisted cleaning up for dinner. Tytla pulled off a tour de force by drawing a frantic, action-packed scene while managing to keep seven personalities, motivations, and reactions distinctly different. Another high point, Frank Thomas and Ollie Johnston recalled, lay in his rendering of Grumpy after Snow White kisses him on the head. "The audience literally could feel the warmth that surged through him," they wrote, as Grumpy "finally released his bottled-up feelings."[22]

In *Dumbo,* Tytla may have reached his most intense identification with the outsider. Along with John Lounsbery, he animated the quartet of gossipy female elephants who deride Mrs. Jumbo's big-eared baby, and those char-acters may have helped him prepare psychologically for his memorable portrayal of the victimized little elephant. Tytla's Dumbo appeared in some of the tenderest, most poignant scenes in the history of Disney animation. For instance, the artist's marvelous picture of Dumbo being bathed by his doting mother, scampering around, splashing, and playing in the water while his mother indulgently looks on, movingly captures the universal bond between parent and young child. A bit later in the film, Tytla brought a lump to several generations of filmgoers' throats in the trunk-touching scene, where little Dumbo can have contact with his imprisoned mother only by touching, gently hugging, and swinging on her trunk through the bars of her jail wagon. "I saw a chance to do a character without using any cheap theatrics," Tytla noted in a 1941 interview in *Time.* "Most of the expressions and mannerisms I got from my own kid. There's nothing theat-rical about a two-year-old kid. They're real and sincere . . . [and] I tried to put all those things in Dumbo." This artist, whom Art Babbitt described as a "very sensitive and sentimental man," seemed to have an instinctive feel for those who struggle against the odds.[23]

It seemed obvious to those who knew him that Tytla's volatile tempera-ment fed his art directly. His personality revealed inner turmoil: a straining passion, a complex mixture of incredible intensity and almost painful shy-ness, a lingering feeling of insecurity about his work and its worth, an almost physical yearning to express a flood of bottled-up creativity and empathy. Tytla struggled to pour himself into his drawings. Friends de-scribed how he "attacked difficult animation with the gusto of a champion boxer," noted the superstitious and brooding nature that led him to refuse to talk about his animation projects, and were flabbergasted at the insecurity of this man who believed that he would fail at every new project to which he was assigned. Tytla's wife described him as working best under a lot of self-induced pressure. "He was like Vesuvius," she once said. "No matter what he worked on, every time he would come home with a different assignment, he would say, 'Oh God! I don't know. I've never done an elephant before, I've never done a whale before. Jesus! How am I going to do a giant? And dwarfs?'"[24]

Tytla created many affecting scenes with innocent characters such as Dumbo and *Snow White*'s Grumpy, but he gained most of his reputation from depicting villains, the frightening heavies whom audiences jeered and hissed. He seemed to uncover what made these unsympathetic characters tick, displaying an acute sensitivity to those who *seem* to be powerful but in fact end up as losers after their anger or strength has played itself out. Chernobog, his mountainous devil figure in *Fantasia*, concludes a nocturnal orgy of otherworldly power by meekly retreating before the sunshine and the coming of day. Stromboli, the hulking, threatening puppeteer who entices Pinocchio into his show before betraying his trust and enslaving him for profit, comes to a similar end — after wielding a cleaver and roaring about his authority over the puppet, he loses out to the Blue Fairy, who releases Pinocchio. A fellow animator pointed to Tytla's childhood as the inspiration for this character, noting that this "son of Ukrainian immigrants was raised in New York City, where one can walk down the streets of Little Italy and see fifty Strombolis in an hour."[25]

Tytla worked on *Fantasia* at the height of his creative powers at the Disney Studio. He animated Yen Sid, the powerful magician in "The Sorcerer's Apprentice" sequence, and slyly gave him one of Walt Disney's marked characteristics: the raised eyebrow of disapproval trained on Mickey Mouse at the end was the same look Disney often gave to his staff. But the monumental portrait of Chernobog conveyed unforgettably the power and emotion of Tytla's artistic style. Assigned the difficult task of animating the massive evil presence from Mussorgsky's "Night on Bald Mountain," he drew on his ethnic heritage. "Ukrainian folklore is based on Chernobog," he once explained in an interview. "Mussorgsky used terms I could understand." Asked about his approach, he replied, "I imagined that I was as big as a mountain, and made of rock, and yet I was feeling and moving."[26]

With typical fervor, Tytla rejected the studio's model for the character, a film of Bela Lugosi melodramatically acting out the part. Instead he had animation director Wilfred Jackson take off his shirt, get in front of the camera, and try to capture the *movement* of this mythical dark god as the music blared in the background. Then he retired into seclusion to draw. A few days later, the animator Thornton "T." Hee went to Tytla's office to consult about something, and "opened the door to find the room in semi-darkness, with Bill intently curled over his board. The only light came from the glow of the fluorescent lamp under Bill's drawing, which was shining up in his face in an eerie way. As T. Hee waited at the door, he felt a tension and a mystical force at work. Strange things were going on. T. was so unnerved by this sight that he quickly backed out into the hall without ever saying anything to Bill." The result, of course, was what many consider to be the most powerful scene in the history of animation: a massive, snarling, blazing-eyed Chernobog unfolds himself from the side of a mountain and hurls ghouls and demons into a fiery pit before retiring at dawn.[27]

Outside of his drawing, one of Tytla's few direct expressions of his artistic philosophy came in his lectures at the Disney Art School. Transcripts from two of his talks in the late 1930s are revealing. Speaking plainly, and often struggling to find the right words, he laid out his aesthetic code. Animators, he insisted, must strive to create figures that were "simply drawn, but with a lot of knowledge and feeling." They should avoid the temptation to be cute or coy; "whether it is called form, force, or vitality, you must get it in your work, for that will be what you feel, and drawing is your means of expressing it." Tytla also disparaged flashy artistic techniques using slashing lines, dramatic smudges, and bombastic fireworks in favor of simple, clear drawing. "Today we are really on the verge of something that is new," he concluded. "It will take a lot of real drawing — not clever, slick, superficial, fine-looking stuff but real, solid, fine drawing . . . Those animators will have to be able to put across a certain sensation or emotion."[28]

These lectures revealed Tytla's intense producerism and sense of craft. For this gifted and passionate man, the new feature-length movies being put together at the Disney Studio offered "the experience of a lifetime." The work transcended everything, and he implored the young artists to immerse themselves in every aspect of their craft. Hard work lay at the core of achievement, and Tytla described how "it's almost a physical pain to rough out one character and space it a certain way, and try to get his attitude a certain way." While staying within the confines of caricature and avoiding excessive naturalism, the animator needed to crawl inside and somehow capture the essence of real people. For the seven dwarfs, for instance, the artist needed to convey "the feeling of various kinds of texture — of the flesh, the jowls, into the eyes, the mouth, the texture of the hair and of old cloth." For Tytla, such injunctions led to a final lesson. "We can't be mystical about our work, we cannot turn out the lights and have confessions," he concluded sternly. "This is a business." Like the head of the studio, Tytla had little truck with art that failed to grab a popular audience of ordinary people.[29]

Tytla's special relationship with Walt Disney was one of the fascinating dimensions of his career at the studio. They were kindred souls in their relentless creative impulse. They shared a love of outdoor activities, as Disney's well-known rural tastes were matched by Tytla's love of hunting and horses. For a while, they played together on Walt's polo team.[30]

Disney and Tytla developed a mutual admiration. The artist frequently confessed his great esteem for the studio head, praising him as a "great guy" and noting that he was "miles ahead of the competition in all fields." And Tytla "was one of the few people that Walt ever permitted himself to be fond of," according to another animator. Disney appreciated the artist's no-non-sense integrity, once growing tickled when the emotional Tytla implored him in a meeting about assignments "to give me something with some balls to it." They apparently enjoyed a gruff masculine camaraderie. As Tytla once reported, "Walt had trouble with the liquid *I*. He always called me Wee-yum . . . He'd say, 'Wee-yum, whaddya know?' And I'd answer, 'Nothing until somebody tells me.'" But at the same time, Disney shrewdly realized that he could drive Tytla to even greater achievement with some well-aimed barbs. For instance, he once previewed a scene from *Pinocchio* of which Tytla was particularly proud and offered the deflating comment that it was "a helluva scene . . . [and] if anybody else had animated it, I would have passed it. But I expected something different from Bill." In Tytla's words, his boss "sank a ship with that remark." Both crushed and provoked, the animator spent several days rethinking the entire scene, redrew it from a different perspective, and finally gained Disney's enthusiastic approval.[31]

In what would become a great irony of his career at Disney, Tytla's populist sensibility came to the fore in the infamous labor strike at the studio in 1941. This divisive episode welled up from the lower levels of the Disney operation. Part of a drive for unionization, it focused on wages and job security for secondary artists, technicians, and support staff. Disney angrily interpreted the strike as a betrayal of his regard for his workers, but Tytla, one of only two major animators who supported the strike, was ambivalent. He was a reluctant striker who honored the picket line, in his own words, "because my friends were on strike. I was sympathetic with their views, but I never wanted to do anything against Walt." His close friend Art Babbitt was a leader of the insurgents, and Tytla felt a particular sense of loyalty to him. But it was clear that he wanted to settle the thing and get back to what was really important — the work. He got caught in the middle, as the story of an accidental encounter with Disney reveals. Walking into a local greasy spoon for lunch, he found Disney sitting in a booth. After shaking hands somewhat awkwardly, the two began to talk about how "the strike was foolish and unnecessary," and they agreed to meet in Disney's office later in the day to work out a solution. Before that could happen, however, lawyers apparently advised Disney that since Tytla was not an officer of the union and represented nobody, a meeting might be legally dangerous. The meeting was canceled. Both men, it seems clear, wanted to surmount the difficulties and get back to work, but they were trapped by something much larger than themselves.[32]

Unfortunately, the strike signaled the beginning of the end of Tytla's brilliant career at the Disney Studio. Even though he returned to the lot in the autumn of 1941 after a settlement had been negotiated, things were never the same. Disney and his loyalists held him at arm's length, and he gradually lost the emotional, inspired creativity that had motivated his work in the late 1930s. In his wife's words, "There was too much tension and electricity in the air. With Will, everything was instinctive and intuitive, and now the vibes were all wrong."[33]

Although Tytla participated in several projects during the early years of World War II, he decided to leave the Disney Studio and return to the East Coast. He bought an old farm in the Connecticut countryside and commuted to New York, where he worked for Terrytoons and the Fleischer Studio for several years before drifting into television commercials and freelance work. He suffered several debilitating strokes in the 1960s, became blind in one eye, and died on December 29, 1969. Perhaps the most poignant feature of his late career was a gnawing sense that leaving the Disney Studio had been a mistake. As his wife explained, "Will regretted it to the end of his life, because he realized he would never have the opportunity to work anywhere the way he did there." A friend put it more simply: "The Disney Studio was to be forever his Shangri-La."[34]

In 1940, Tytla tried to describe to a reporter from the *Atlantic Monthly* his veneration for Disney animation. Asked why working at the Disney Studio was so special, he replied, in his usual halting fashion, "You know, you and I have seen some outfits that *had* it. They had *something*. The thing here is like that — you know, you can't help feeling that you're going to grab that goddam Holy Grail."[35]

As one of his fellow artists once observed, "Tytla shared with Disney an overwhelming empathy, a fellow-feeling with all creation that was almost Franciscan." Like the moody, innovative midwesterner in whose studio he created wonderful things, the passionate Russian was an idealistic, instinctive populist at heart.[36]

III. The Folk Hero

Not all observers were convinced of Disney's ideological appeal during the Great Depression. Newspaper columnist Westbrook Pegler, an ardent fan of the filmmaker's work, wrote in 1941, "I defy anyone to discern anywhere in this entertainment any trace of a message to the human race." In his view, Disney's movies simply "ignore evil all about and lift his fellow man for an hour or more into that happy realm which he personally created." However, in Pegler's search for the evident, he missed the obvious. The lack of an explicit political message lured him into thinking that Disney lacked this dimension entirely.[37]

Contrary to Pegler's defiance, many people had noticed for years the political implications of Disney's work and made him an icon of cultural populism. Within the studio, for instance, animator Shamus Culhane described him as "the ideal philosopher-capitalist, a towering figure in this shoddy machine age" whose films championed excellence and humanism. From without, countless critics chimed in with claims about the filmmaker's social impact. Disney was praised as someone who "satirizes the 'survival of the fittest' idea . . . and laissez faire tradition in economics that persist in our social thinking," or denounced as the leader of a group of "disproportionate populists" who bowed before the power of "popular taste." Herbert Russell, in a tongue-in-cheek essay called "L'Affaire Mickey Mouse," argued that Mickey had become an international hero for common people. All over the world, he observed, this animated figure "has captivated the masses . . . He promises them release for the time from worry and unhappiness, and speaks of a promised land where anything can, and does, happen . . . Does he believe that the broken and oppressed people, wallowing in despond, will then turn to the one person whom they can depend upon for happiness and demand that Mickey shall become Emperor of the World? Perhaps Mickey isn't so dumb as he looks. Maybe that is why he is winning the ordinary folk."[38]

From all this commentary, however, one fact lingers. The Disney of the 1930s was no outspoken, dogmatic political popularizer but rather an unselfconscious one, and probably more influential and powerful for it. The appeal of his sentimental populism was visceral. For a mass audience of Americans suffering social and economic privation during the Depression, but yearning for a resurgence of hope, laughter, and faith in themselves, the social vision of Mickey Mouse, *Three Little Pigs*, and *Dumbo* proved to be both cathartic and reaffirming. In these films, as well as many others, Walt Disney wielded a political influence of which most politicians could only dream.

6

The Entertainer as Artist: Sentimental Modernism

THE HARVARD ART HISTORIAN Robert D. Feild spent nearly a year at the Disney Studio, from June 1939 to May 1940. Given the run of the facility, he took copious notes as he poked his head in and out of every department, previewed ongoing work, analyzed production procedures and artistic processes, interviewed animators and technicians, and talked to Disney himself. The result was *The Art of Walt Disney* (1942), the first extensive assessment of Disney's creative achievements. Feild believed that Disney's films had pioneered a new type of creative expression, undermining the outworn assumption that "music, painting, sculpture, and architecture . . . alone are *art*." By combining many of these older forms and transporting them into "a timeless, spatially unlimited realm," Disney's animation represented "perhaps the most potent form of artistic expression ever devised." If this book could be believed, there was little doubt that the United States had produced a figure of major artistic significance in the twentieth century.[1]

Not everyone, however, believed it. Even before his book was published, Professor Feild's teaching appointment at Harvard University was terminated. The situation became something of a minor scandal. Details of the case were never released, but it seems clear that many of Feild's academic colleagues viewed his foray into the realm of popular art with considerable suspicion. Both *Time* and the *Harvard Crimson* reported that he was dismissed by "Harvard's conservative art department because of too much enthusiasm for modern art, particularly Disney's." His teaching was certainly not the problem. The Boston *Evening Globe* described him as one of the most popular, provocative teachers on campus and noted that "students have jammed his lecture courses." Moreover, after Feild was fired, a group of fine arts majors began a campaign that condemned the action and demanded his reinstatement. There was no official reaction from the Disney Studio beyond a brief, guarded statement that "Robert Feild is held in high esteem by our staff of over 300 practical artists . . . Harvard's loss will be someone's gain." But the spectacle of intellectuals ferociously debating the aesthetic merits of Mickey Mouse, Donald Duck, and the Three Little Pigs must have caused considerable amusement to the practical-minded Disney artists.[2]

This incident recalls an important fact easily forgotten — whatever the final verdict may be, Walt Disney's "art" was once a serious and controversial subject in American culture. His films from "the golden age" were analyzed by film writers and cultural critics all over the country. Some of the commentary was outlandishly favorable. One writer, for instance, described Disney as "the most significant figure in graphic art since Leonardo . . . [He] drives right to the foothills of the New Art of the Future." Another claimed that Disney's "genuine works of art . . . represent a saga which will mark this era as vividly as Hogarth's engravings stamped the eighteenth century." An equally enthusiastic essayist insisted that the Hollywood producer had given the world "the first genuinely American art since that of the indigenous Indian." Less frequently, writers saw Disney's movies as likable fluff that, while clever or fascinating, had little substance.[3]

Disney was aware of the debate over his artistic merits and aesthetic contributions, but he was never comfortable with it. He saw it as a temptation to take himself too seriously. "We were awfully surprised when this stuff began to come in, pleased, flattered. Then we began to believe it," he told an interviewer in 1938. A brief tendency to pander to the critics resulted, Disney continued, but then "we got wise to ourselves. What was our original purpose? Why, to make people laugh. To make good comedies. To entertain." Disney's innate suspicion of artiness, however, bypassed the fact that this critical discussion was no easy thing to comprehend. Swirling about at several different levels, it concerned aesthetics, standards, and the relationship between high art and popular art.[4]

More often than not, Disney shaped his aesthetics in vague, unintended, and even ambiguous ways. An enormously gifted entertainer in search of laughs, innovations, and sales, he stumbled into the arena of modernist art in the 1930s and began experimenting with its forms and techniques. His artistic heart, however, continued to beat to the rhythm of nineteenth-century sentimental realism. This Victorian sensibility continually grappled with an audacious modernism, but neither impulse completely triumphed. The result was an aesthetic and cultural hybrid that, like many other aspects of Disney's work, melded daringly innovative elements with tradition. It helped to ease his audience into a new cultural epoch.

I. "Fantastic Things Based upon the Real"

From nearly the beginning, the voice of art could be heard clearly from the ballyhoo surrounding Disney's ascending entertainment enterprise. Many critics and writers saw Mickey Mouse and the Silly Symphonies as more than mere cartoons. By early in the 1930s, commentators from all corners of the country and in every kind of publication had begun to grapple with the aesthetic agenda and impact of these movies. In particular, it became clear that artistic modernism was a crucial context for understanding Disney's work.

Modernism, of course, has been notoriously difficult to define. It has sparked intense debate among scholars and critics for many years, and critical consensus often seems to exist on only one point: modernism was a fin-de-siècle, transatlantic cultural movement that gradually came to dominate Western art and culture in the first few decades of the twentieth century. Beyond that, agreement quickly frays.[5]

Nonetheless, several defining impulses lend some coherence to the disparate elements of American modernism. First, this cultural movement emerged in the United States in direct opposition to the principles and sensibility of Victorianism. Inspired by the great European experimenters like Freud, Stravinsky, Picasso, and Joyce, American modernists began to challenge bourgeois culture by undermining several of its bulwarks — a moral creed based on repression and rationality, a system of intellectual inquiry based on formalism, a genteel tradition of narrative realism in arts and letters. Second, in a more positive sense, modernists sought to recombine aspects of human experience that had been strictly separated by the Victorians — human and animal, civilized and savage, reason and emotion, intellect and instinct, conscious and unconscious — in order to reconstruct the totality of human nature. By smashing through a brittle surface of rationality and genteel beauty, they hoped to recover the vitality that lay in instinctual motivation, a fluidity of perception, and a turbulent subjectivity. Third, modernists endorsed a wide-ranging aesthetic experimentation in the hopes of capturing the elusive "simultaneity of experience" that seemed to characterize modern life. Believing that literary realism, visual perspective, and the chromatic musical scale could not adequately represent the complexities and confusions of an advanced industrial world, modernist artists embraced stream-of-consciousness narrative, abstract painting, and atonal music. Adopting an aesthetic as well as moral relativism, they bor-

rowed from non-Western "primitive" cultures, adapted technological artifacts and industrial motifs, dipped into European and American folk culture, and in many cases tried to dismantle barriers between "high" and
"low" culture, all in the interests of revitalizing artistic expression.[6]

Much of this, of course, seems far removed from the world of popular
entertainment and the theaters full of laughing, cheering fans of Mickey
Mouse and Donald Duck. But the culture of modernism created much of
the atmosphere enfolding Walt Disney's pioneering work in animation.
Modernist impulses flowered everywhere in Disney's world of fantasy,
which constantly blurred the line between imagination and reality to produce a wondrous universe where animals spoke, plants and trees acted
consciously, and inanimate objects felt emotion. A preoccupation with the
dream state in Disney's early films triggered a fusion of intellect and emotion, superego and id as warm fairy tales encapsulated dark, nightmarish
visions. Throughout the films there occurred a consistent blending of "high"
and "low" cultural forms. This engagement with modernism may have
developed unintentionally, even unconsciously, but it became an important
part of the Disney appeal.

However, Disney's aesthetic loyalties were divided. By the mid-1930s, he
had begun seeking greater and greater realism in his studio's animation.
Increasingly he sought a sunny, naturalistic style rooted in Victorian culture.
For decades genre painting and magazine illustration had reinforced a public taste for genteel realism — a trend observable in the enormous popularity of artists such as Norman Rockwell. This tradition, with its Victorian
instinct for skirting evil and tragedy, obscured as much as it illuminated.
Northrop Frye, for example, has described it rather unkindly as "stupid
realism," or "a kind of sentimental idealism, an attempt to present a conven-
tionally attractive or impressive appearance as an actual or attainable reality." Here was a depiction of people, objects, and scenes in which dark or
messy dimensions of reality had been wiped away. But it held a strong
attraction for Walt Disney and many others.[7]

Disney's balancing of these varied elements ultimately produced an attractive aesthetic hybrid that can be described as "sentimental modernism."
He created an overarching framework in which visual verisimilitude and a
free-flowing modernist sensibility supported each other with a kind of tensile strength. Sentimental modernism had several key characteristics. First, it
blended the real and the unreal, naturalism and fantasy, and manipulated
each in an attempt to illuminate the other. Second, it secured nonlinear,
irrational, quasi-abstract modernist explorations comfortably on the cultural map by utilizing certain tropes from the Victorian past — an exaggerated sentimentality, clearly defined moralism, disarming cuteness — as familiar artistic signposts. Third, it willingly dug down through layers of

consciousness to engage the fluidity of experience and action, but always returned to embrace rationality. Fourth, it animated the world — literally — by ascribing intention, consciousness, and emotion to living and inanimate objects alike, but did so in such a way as to downplay the presence of evil and tragedy. Fifth and finally, it good-naturedly satirized the pretensions of high culture and sought to invigorate it with the vitality of popular cultural expression.

Disney's aesthetic paradigm thus offered a series of cultural compromises. The filmmaker and his artists tried to pursue artistic innovation without leaving their popular audience lost, confused, groping for meaning. Sentimental modernism, like much else with this Hollywood innovator, served as a mediating impulse — between modernism and realism, art and commerce, aesthetics and entertainment, elitism and populism.

In fact, and contrary to Disney's insistence that he desired to make only pure entertainment, a concern with aesthetics, albeit rather diffuse and nonsystematic, gradually moved near the top of the studio's agenda. As his films grew more sophisticated — the Silly Symphonies proved especially demanding in this area — they demanded conceptualization, composition, and drawing capabilities that went far beyond what was needed for the old "rubber hose," visual-gag style. So in 1931, Disney made an arrangement with the Chouinard Art Institute in Los Angeles and began to send his artists there for evening classes, with the studio picking up the tab. In November 1932, at the suggestion of Art Babbitt, he took the next step and set up the Disney Art School on the Hyperion studio lot. He hired Don Graham, an instructor at Chouinard, to hold classes two evenings a week where the animators could study life drawing, composition, action analysis, and quick sketch techniques. So many artists attended that Graham soon took on several assistants and expanded the program to five nights a week. Then, in 1934–35, Disney set up a rigorous training program that brought aspiring animators to the studio, screened them over the course of several weeks' study, and hired the most promising to work as in-betweeners and apprentices. In this way, he gradually created a process that rationalized production, controlled the flow of talent, and schooled artists in what was rapidly becoming known as "the Disney style" of animation.[8]

As for the animators, they viewed themselves as serious artists. Hardheaded realists about the marriage of commerce and art in their field, they avoided extremes in defining their mission. Disney animation, most of them believed, was neither a mystical, elevated process of artistic creation nor a money-grubbing process of entertainment. They saw themselves as engaged in serious work in a rich new medium that encouraged artistic expression while demanding audience appeal. Bill Tytla, of course, had received extensive formal training and approached his mission at the Disney Studio with great gravity. Other animators, like Marc Davis, Frank Thomas, and Ollie Johnston, all of whom arrived in the 1930s, also had trained in the arts and perceived their work as a serious endeavor. Even Walt Disney made his real feelings clear in an outburst that many remembered. When a staff member wondered aloud in a story meeting if they were taking advantage of the cartoon medium, Disney reacted with considerable passion. "It's not just a cartoon," he replied sharply. "We have new worlds to conquer here."[9]

To this end, in the 1930s Disney began bringing prominent artists through the studio for lectures and consultations. For instance, Jean Charlot, the renowned French-Mexican muralist and color lithographer, gave a series of presentations on artistic design. Rico Lebrun, a draftsman and muralist with a special interest in anatomical structure, stayed at the studio for several months as a special lecturer and teacher. Thomas Hart Benton, Salvador Dali, and Frank Lloyd Wright came through for briefer stays, while a host of lesser lights made one-time appearances. Disney also hired a pair of European-trained artists, Albert Hurter and Gustav Tenggren, as full-time, in-house employees to do inspirational sketches and work on styling various film projects. By keeping the animation staff in contact with trends in the contemporary art world, the Disney Studio tended to reinforce its engagement with modernism.[10]

At the same time, however, significant signs of a movement toward realism also began to appear. The development of the multiplane camera was only the most conspicuous. This device held stacked glass backgrounds through which the camera eye could move, thus projecting a three-dimensional image on the screen. Ben Sharpsteen, one of Disney's chief lieutenants, noted that as feature-length projects were being developed, the animators made widespread use of live-action film as guidelines for their drawing. Some even utilized the rotoscope, a machine that projects film onto glass so the animator can trace figures. There was a parallel movement toward highly sophisticated color schemes in the interest of realism. Frank Thomas, for example, pointed out that the figure of Jiminy Cricket in *Pinocchio* had twenty-seven different colors. "You can't even think of twenty-seven parts of him to paint, let alone different colors to paint them," he joked. "But [Walt] wanted the thing to look real — this was an era when he wanted things to be real. He wanted it to be round, solid, reaching for perfection." Other artists concurred. According to Marc Davis and Ken Anderson, Disney was growing "impatient with the restrictions of a cartoon. He strived for more and more realism, more naturalism in the features."[11]

In the films themselves, of course, fantasy remained the springboard for Disney's eclectic approach. As one popular magazine noted, a typical Disney film would "delve freely into idealism and fantasy, make possible the utterly grotesque and unbelievable, portray and people lovely exotic fairylands, create and bring to life any creature of the imagination, and appeal to the emotions unfettered by realities." Never explicitly articulated but nonetheless powerful, an attempt to return magic, wonder, and irrationality to the modern world was central to Disney's work.[12]

This impulse had a historical resonance. Social theorist Max Weber, analyzing the cultural forms and sensibilities of advanced industrial society, had grappled with it in the early 1900s. The growth of scientific inquiry, empiricism, and industrial technology in the modern West, he argued, had encouraged a rationalization of human experience that emphasized the systematic laws of nature, technical calculations, and control of the natural environment. One result of this trend had been the "disenchantment" of the modern world, as magic, impulse, and the supernatural had been banished from the realm of acceptable explanation and experience. In Weber's words, contemporary life unfolded in "a world robbed of gods . . . [where] men have ventured to rationalize the image of the world as being a cosmos governed by impersonal rules . . . Rational, empirical knowledge has consistently worked through to the disenchantment of the world." The highly industrialized world of twentieth-century America only intensified these traits, as burgeoning technology and growing crazes for movements such as "scientific management" and "domestic science" systematized and extended the model of efficient production, emotional control, regulation of behavior, and rational process.[13]

In such a culture, Disney's unfettered world of imagination proved to be playfully subversive. Appealing to long-repressed elements in human makeup, the filmmaker unconsciously sought to reenchant a modern world often devoid of play, fantasy, and magic. Undercutting rationalization and its efficient engineering of experience, Disney nurtured a vibrant antimodern impulse that invested many of his films from this era with great emotional energy.

In many ways, of course, such highfalutin aesthetic maneuvering was at best incidental, and at worst unintended or unconscious. Most of the time Walt Disney simply followed his instincts in utilizing humor, comedy, and music in pursuit of mass entertainment, and any explicit thoughts about art lay deep in the shadows. Moreover, his artistic ideas were hard to pinpoint outside his work, since he was not given to theorizing. Yet Disney's thoughts on this subject clearly appeared in an eight-page, single-spaced studio memo of December 23, 1935. Untutored in theory but shrewd and full of native wit, this outline for the studio's training program represented the closest thing to a statement of artistic purpose this seat-of-the-pants commercial entertainer ever produced.

Neither abstraction nor realism alone provided the goal for animation, Disney insisted, but rather a combination of the two. In his words, carica-

ture, or the exaggeration of certain traits or features of a person or a character, provided the best means for achieving this blend:

> The first duty of the cartoon is not to picture or duplicate real action or
> things as they actually happen, but to give a caricature of life and action
> . . . The point must be made clear to the men that our study of the actual
> is not so that we may be able to accomplish the actual, but so that we may
> have a basis upon which to go into the fantastic, the unreal, the imagina-
> tive — and yet to let it have a foundation of fact, in order that it may more
> richly possess sincerity and contact with the public . . . I definitely feel that
> we cannot do the fantastic things based on the real unless we first know
> the real.[14]

In turn, this concern with caricature led to the study of motivation and
an emphasis on personality. For Disney, animated cartoons certainly relied
on a strong sense of action rooted in visual comedy. But at a deeper level, he
believed, animation must explore the rhyme and reason for action, the
motivation that causes it. In Disney's words, most of the time "the driving
force behind the action is the mood, the personality, the attitude of the
character — or all three." To create characters whom audiences cared about,
and to create action that would be appreciated and believed, the artist must
dig deeply into motivation and explore "the feelings of those characters."
This emphasis on "personality animation" became the hallmark of Disney
animation and the basis for the breakthroughs that elevated it far above the
competition.[15]

Finally, Disney's thoughts in this memo revealed an inchoate but powerful impulse to reenchant the modern world. According to his instructions,
the animator must "picture on the screen things that have run through the
imagination of the audience, to bring to life dream fantasies and imaginative
fancies that we have all thought of during our lives." Central to comedy and
the art of animation was the necessity of touching a "subconscious association" within the audience by invoking situations they had "felt, or seen, or
dreamt." Along the same lines, Disney argued that skillful animation must
incorporate the rhythms and melodies of music. If his animators really
studied the subject, Disney insisted, there would be "a realization on their
part of how primitive music is, how natural it is for people to want to go to
music — a study of rhythm, the dance — the various rhythms that enter
into their lives every day — how rhythmical the body really is — how well
balanced the body really is. That, in itself, is music. In other words, it could
be music in the body." In such fashion, Disney indicated how he half consciously sought to use animation as a way to reacquaint a cynical, rationalized modern society with lost primitive and magical elements.[16]

II. Sentimental Loyalties, Modernist Instincts

The Silly Symphony entitled *The Spider and the Fly* opened on an intriguing, disorienting visual note. It pictured a group of tiny flies congregated on the ceiling of a room that, in rather startling fashion, appears on the screen upside-down. Then, in a bizarre maneuver, the upended room begins to revolve, indicating the fly's perspective as it swirls down from the ceiling. This brief touch of skewed perspective suggested the playful modernist sensibility of the 1930s Disney Studio, not only unfolding an imaginary war between victimized flies and a marauding spider but upending the viewer's point of view. Like many other films from this period, it indicated how an often mischievous, always complex sentimental modernism flowered in this decade of creative ferment.

Throughout the 1930s, Disney and his artists steadily developed the aesthetic elements that went into their groundbreaking animation. Documents like the "Studio Animation Handbook" (1936) made clear that the Disney style emphasized clarity, simplicity, and smooth motion. Several technical innovations also helped place Disney animation at the cutting edge. The storyboard was a succession of sketches fastened to a large bulletin board which clearly plotted the flow of a film in its initial stages, while the exposure sheet mapped the rhythm and frequency of the drawings. The pencil test, run through a special projector, provided a rough version of actual film segments that could then be evaluated and revised. Such instruments and techniques helped the Disney Studio push caricature to the forefront of its aesthetic agenda.[17]

But another element became even more crucial to the Disney project: the development of personality in animated characters. Even in the Alice films of the 1920s, according to animator Friz Freleng, Disney would tell the staff, "I want the characters to *be* somebody. I don't want them just to be a drawing." Freleng added, "That's the first thing he brought to cartoons that nobody else ever thought of — to bring characters on the screen that you really cared about." In a private letter of 1937, Disney wrote, "We have always endeavored to create the feeling that these little characters are live, individual personalities — not just animated drawings."[18]

This focus on personality led to a certain structuring of the animation framework at the studio. In the Story Department, under Disney's guidance, writers began to develop stories that relied less on broad physical humor and slapstick gags and more on plot and characters' emotional states. The convergence of story developments and new artistic elements created a pathbreaking style often termed "acting animation." In a larger sense, it also led to what animation director Ham Luske termed an "illusion of life." "Walt always felt that everything you put on the page should be able to step out of that page and talk to you," Eric Larson elaborated. "[He wanted] something that actually lives and not just moves around." Marc Davis concurred, noting that "everything that went into every picture was to bring something alive . . . I suppose you could bring a pushpin to life if you did it properly."[19]

This array of techniques became the practical foundation on which Disney's aesthetic was constructed, as became evident in the Mickey Mouse movies and the Silly Symphony series. The two series converged in many ways. Mickey, far from being just another stock cartoon character pumping the audience for laughs with slapstick, quickly became a whimsical, mischievous personality for whom audiences developed great sympathy. With his merry cavorting through an imaginative playland where physical laws had vanished along with emotional restraints, the mouse and his gang became lovable, provocative, subversive modernist imps in American popular culture. For their part, the Silly Symphonies leavened their experimentalism and seriousness with a fair share of memorable characters and physical gags. Both series borrowed artistic influences from everywhere. As Disney admitted in a 1935 interview, he and his staff combed through every conceivable source of artistic expression for pointers and ideas — the great masterpieces of painting, modern magazine illustrations, Hollywood movies, advertising, posters. "With each picture we produce we are experimenting," he pointed out. Perhaps more important, the Mickey Mouse films and Silly Symphonies, each in its own fashion, fed the swelling stream of sentimental modernism at the Disney Studio, blending the fantastic and the real, the irrational and the sentimental, magic and empiricism, highbrow and lowbrow culture.[20]

Disney's short films during the Depression years created fantastic milieus completely removed from the workaday reality of contemporary life that, although occasionally frightening, ultimately affirmed the power of happy endings and virtuous actions. The world of Mickey Mouse presented to audiences a slightly twisted reality populated by quasi-human creatures and magical properties. Many of the Silly Symphonies moved in the same aesthetic direction. If anything, their fragmented, fantastic worlds were even more outlandish and varied. *Water Babies* (1935) and *Merbabies* (1938), for instance, explored magical aquatic atmospheres where energetic cherubs, playful wild creatures, and exotic flora frolic away from peering human eyes.

A large number of Disney movies from this period revolved around a motif of altered consciousness — a modernist concern — in dreams, hallucinations, and stream-of-consciousness associations. Such efforts were legion, ranging from the benign *Thru the Mirror* (1936), which animated Lewis Carroll's *Through the Looking Glass,* to nightmarish films such as *The Mad Doctor* (1933), in which a dreaming Mickey is pursued by a lunatic physician bent on obtaining body parts for medical experimentation. Perhaps the most striking example is *Lullaby Land* (1933), a remarkable Silly Symphony that explored unconsciousness in a manner that was equal parts sentimentalism and surrealism. A baby and his toy dog are tucked into bed for the evening, and as sleep comes they go tumbling off into Lullaby Land, a magical place where nurturing bushes loaded with powder puffs and talcum care for the infant and bulging-eyed trees loaded with tiny rattles shake them for his amusement. The sound of marching anticipates a most unusual parade with enchanting participants: a formation of cups banging on their saucers with spoons like giant drums, baby bottles with long giraffelike rubber necks waddling on stumpy legs, a brush merrily using a comb as a mouth harp, a battalion of strutting, helmeted diaper pins leading a clothespinned diaper to bring up the rear. The baby and his gingham dog playfully leapfrog along behind the parade until they come to the Forbidden Garden, where signs read BABY STAY AWAY, KEEP OUT, DON'T ENTER, NO NO, GO BACK. They immediately enter, of course, and come face to face with an array of dangerous objects: sharp knives and forks, scissors, hot curling irons, corkscrews and can openers, tacks, and a fountain of black ink. Most tempting, however, is a tree bearing gold pocket watches surrounded by bushes from which hammers are growing. The gleeful infant promptly plucks a hammer and smashes the watches to bits, then spies a big box of matches into which he dives for further play. When he lights the matches, however, they come to life as frightening bogeymen and chase him out of the Forbidden Garden. As the baby and his toy dog hide behind a tree from which baby bottles dangle, a kindly old man with a long white beard steps out from behind a candy-cane bush and sprinkles them with sand, thus conveying them safely back to sleep in their cradle.

Disney's aesthetic sensibility also blended high and low cultural forms. Some of his 1930s films, particularly the Silly Symphonies, paid homage to traditional culture. *Flowers and Trees* (1932), for example, accompanied its magical story with the music of Mendelssohn, Rossini, and Schubert, while *King Neptune* (1932) and *The Goddess of Spring* (1934) used mythological stories. But more often Disney leavened the weight of artistic tradition with the light, vibrant energy of popular cultural forms. A recurring setting, especially in Mickey Mouse films, was a stage show, where a succession of acts poked fun at Victorian gentility. Such movies as *Orphan's Benefit* (1934) and *Mickey's Grand Opera* (1942) offered a galaxy of images that tickled the cultural funnybone: a voluptuous Clara Cluck pompously shrieking fowl versions of opera librettos; an explosively incoherent Donald Duck squawking a poetry reading until the audience boos; formally dressed farm animals posing grandiosely as classical musicians; Clarabelle Cow and Goofy making a mockery of formal dance with their solemn, lead-footed maneuvers.

Two films provide particularly telling examples of Disney's humorous attempt to mediate high and low culture. *Just Mickey* (1930), also called

Fiddlin' Around, features Mickey as a romantic concert violinist. Dramatically whipping around a head of preposterously long hair, striking dramatic poses, and contorting his face, he hurtles through a fast-paced number before shifting gears into a slow piece. Moved by his own histrionics to the point of weeping, the overwrought performer finally pauses to blow his nose. For an encore, he plays the William Tell Overture so vigorously that he breaks his violin in half. *Symphony Hour* (1942) follows the same path by casting Mickey as the director of an animal orchestra performing on the *Macaroni Symphony Hour*. Before the performance, however, stagehand Goofy accidentally drops all of the instruments down an elevator shaft, where they are crushed and mangled. When the musicians try to play them, weird and comical sounds make a farce of the proceedings. The sponsor of the show, Sylvester Macaroni, flies into a rage about this, only to be astonished when the crowd roars its approval of this hilarious farce and showers the stage with flowers. The film ends with Macaroni embracing Mickey.

Meanwhile, the drive for realism often pulled in another direction, away from modernism. With the advent of its art school, lecture series, and training programs, the Disney Studio encouraged the addition of detail, perspective, and solid draftsmanship to both characters and backgrounds, as did the use of the rotoscope and the multiplane camera. The studio's move toward realism surfaced early on in the lyrical nature films in the Silly Symphony series, *Springtime* (1929) and the 1930 trio of *Summer, Autumn,* and *Winter,* which sought to capture the physical features and moods of the four seasons with a minimum of gags. Disney's growing commitment to visual realism was joined by a reliance on sentimentalism in the shaping of action, motivation, and character. This Victorian ethos became a central aspect of the Disney product, as seen, for instance, in the modified drawing of Mickey Mouse himself. From the scrambling, slightly subversive scamp of the late 1920s, who consisted of little more than a series of circles with pipestem legs and arms, he became a rounded, huggable, emotive figure with enormously expressive eyes and sophisticated muscular dexterity.

The full richness of Disney's sentimental modernism was brilliantly displayed in an animated short called *Music Land*, which appeared in 1935, perhaps Disney's most productive and creative year for short cartoons. A Silly Symphony, this delightful eight-minute piece told a story set in the Land of Symphony and the Isle of Jazz, two antagonistic kingdoms separated by the Sea of Discord. The princess from the former realm falls in love with the prince from the latter, and when he secretly visits her, he is captured and imprisoned inside a giant metronome. Consequently, war breaks out, and in the midst of battle the two lovers escape and flee in a small boat. When their peril becomes evident, a ceasefire is called and harmonious relations are established for a happy ending.

On the one hand, this clever, fast-paced, pun-filled tale skipped down a modernist path. With great wit, it satirized the tension between popular and classical music, and in the medley of intertwined symphonic and jazz styles that closed the film, it ultimately suggested a fusion of high and low cultural forms. Moreover, the cartoon offered a mélange of fantastic modernist images: architecture composed of giant organ pipes and welded brass instruments, characters who appeared as musical instruments, a language consisting only of various reedy, brassy, and stringed voices. Even the climactic war scene consisted of mock-heroic barrages of jazz riff notes hurled from one island and blasts of the 1812 Overture from the other. On the other hand, however, *Music Land* offered a traditional love story based on *Romeo and Juliet*. The conventional happy ending featured the marriage of the prince and princess, the joining of the King of Jazz and the Queen of Symphony, and the construction of a Bridge of Harmony between their islands. As for the animation, the drawing was rather realistic, depicting saxophones and violins molded and shaped into human form. Overall, this fascinating cartoon wove together numerous threads to produce a typically Disneyesque cultural fabric.

Disney's aesthetic experimentation was not limited to his short films. If anything, it was intensified in the groundbreaking feature films that began to dominate the studio's production schedule. By the late 1930s, sentimental modernism was appearing in even brighter, more compelling fashion in Disney's first, legendary, full-length movies.

III. Modernist Fantasies, Sentimental Memories

Disney's first feature films elaborated the aesthetic vision shaped in the 1930s. The sentiment, fantasy, and realism that colored these remarkable movies combined with more adventurous modernist touches: *Snow White*'s magical and metaphorical settings, *Pinocchio*'s theme of divided consciousness, *Dumbo*'s surrealistic outburst in the famous "pink elephants on parade" scene, and *Bambi*'s impressionistic views of the countryside. Among Disney's classic animated features, however, one in particular stood out in its sentimental modernism.

Enormously ambitious in scope, *Fantasia* greatly extended Disney's grasp as it combined animation and classical music, cartoon humor and mythology, geological science and religious piety, whimsy and intellectual seriousness. It not only sought to bring art to the people, according to Disney's best populist impulse, but elevated his aesthetic view to new heights as he and his artists consciously stirred together a visual potpourri of naturalism and abstraction. Whatever one thought of the results, one thing was clear — the field of animation, and probably the entire film industry, had never seen anything quite like it.

As production moved into high gear in the late 1930s, Walt, conductor Leopold Stokowski, musicologist Deems Taylor, and the entire studio staff worked frantically. Disney artists, urged on by their leader, eschewed broad gags for subtle touches of humor and elaborate forms of fantasy. Disney rejected a funny focus for this film, instead directing his staff to "please avoid slapstick gags in the ordinary sense; work instead toward fantasy and business with an imaginative touch." In Ben Sharpsteen's words, *Fantasia* represented a "progressive evolution" in the Disney style as the studio moved toward "higher-grade pictures instead of these slapstick things."[21]

As the concert feature gradually took shape, a spirit of excitement and experimentation permeated the studio. Official memos described the project as a "musical fantasy offering an opportunity for a new type of entertainment" and added that it "offers a challenge to the best imaginations on the lot. Please *give*." The production offered special challenges because of its complete lack of dialogue and reliance on sophisticated and well-known music. The animators, as Ollie Johnston pointed out, were forced to shift their emphasis from personality to pantomime, as characters had to act convincingly without the benefit of any spoken lines. Bill Garity, the chief engineer, took the lead in developing one of Disney's pet ideas: a sophisticated audio system for reproducing *Fantasia*'s music through several channels and multiple speakers located throughout theaters. This "Fantasound" system, in Garity's assessment, epitomized his boss's creative reach in this film: "There isn't anything that can't be done, he says, and the amazing part of it is that he is right. We've done things . . . most of them Walt's ideas, that looked impossible at first."[22]

Fantasia's steady movement through the production process gave rise to humorous incidents as well as creative tension. The inception of the project saw the curious spectacle of Stokowski and Taylor being addressed as "Stokie" and "Deems" by the first-name-only Disney staff. The numerous music and story meetings were colored by the contrast between Stokowski's beautiful, elegant English and Disney's colloquial, profane speech. In a preliminary conference devoted to choosing appropriate musical selections, Disney inquired if any piece might support a depiction of the creation and early development of life on Earth. Stokowski immediately said, "Why, yes! There's the *Sacre!*" Disney looked skeptical and replied disbelievingly, "The Sock?"[23]

External pressures and expectations helped heighten the atmosphere. A string of high-powered figures in the arts and sciences — painters Thomas Hart Benton and Grant Wood, biologist Julian Huxley, choreographer George Balanchine, novelist Thomas Mann, Stravinsky himself — paraded through the studio for glimpses of this extraordinary project. Most of them found the undertaking to be a fascinating experiment, but Frank Lloyd Wright proved the exception. After viewing a reel of rough drawings for sections of the film, he turned to Disney and commented acerbically, "If I were you, I would go away for a while, and I would sort of purify my mind and change my way of thinking, because this is not it." The studio chief vented his anger later, bursting out, "What the hell does he know?"[24]

Eventually, however, the efforts of Disney and his collaborators produced a unique movie that took both the realistic naturalism and the fluid fantasy of the Disney style to new levels. Filled with creative ambiguity, it walked an aesthetic tightwire between modernism and sentimental realism. The film's modernist features became obvious in the opening, where Bach's Toccata and Fugue in D Minor inspired a series of nearly pure pictorial abstractions. Splashes of color and swirling, melting forms predominated, with only the barest hint of identifiable objects such as violin bows or rolling waves. This bold beginning was followed by a parade of delightful, often bizarre images that dug deep into the unconscious: the charm of the dancing mushrooms in "The Nutcracker Suite," the dark magic of the relentless marching brooms with their pails of water in "The Sorcerer's Apprentice," the hilarity of the dainty hippo ballerinas in "The Dance of the Hours." Many modernist elements were there — the abstractions, the mingling of unlikely images from high and low culture, the contact between intellect and imagination, the juxtaposition of seriousness and satire. And, of course, the objective of the film, described as "hearing the pictures and seeing the music," defined the fluid sense of consciousness and experience that characterized this artistic mode.[25]

These features captured the attention of many critics, who noted the film's appeal to "the psychic stream" of music listeners as it helped them "glide through the space of consciousness." Favorable reviews in the *Art Digest* and *Theatre Arts* praised the pictorial abstractions in the movie. Emily Genauer, in an intriguing essay in the New York *World-Telegram*, gave the clearest explication of the film's modernism:

> We have no need to talk again of the substance of abstract art — to point out the beauty of form and color per se . . . Along comes Disney with his visual accompaniment to the Bach Toccata and Fugue — the first number of *Fantasia* — and it's all miraculously clear. Here are comet-like shapes shooting across the screen, lines agitated into sensuously beautiful patterns, undulating surfaces, areas of color penetrating each other . . . The whole thing is a succession of beautifully colored abstractions . . . One or two of them recall Kandinsky especially. There were several closely related to the surrealist Miro. And the opening-night audience — many of whom, doubtless, raise up their hands in horror at abstract painting — loved it.[26]

Disney did his part to encourage the notion of *Fantasia* as a modernist experiment. In a 1940 luncheon speech, he said that one of the film's goals was to broaden "the field of abstraction," and in subsequent years he elaborated on this. In typical fashion, he snorted at talk about artistic profundity, claiming that *Fantasia's* opening segment had resulted from a series of brainstorming sessions where participants merely attempted to capture Bach's improvising spirit. "We were kind of, you know, noodling around . . . It was just a bunch of stuff thrown in there," he said, "splashes of color, movements, rolling action." But the evidence suggests a slightly different picture. Disney had expressed his interest in the abstract animation of Englishman Len Lye in the mid-1930s, and he brought Oscar Fischinger, a German artist and filmmaker who experimented in the same area, to the studio in 1938–39 to provide abstract sketches and ideas for the Bach segment. Moreover, as Disney admitted in a 1944 statement, the Effects Department had been "nursing along" various ideas for abstractions long before *Fantasia.*[27]

At the same time, however, *Fantasia* set off this abstract aesthetic melody with striking flourishes of sentiment and naturalism. Cropping up periodically, they helped shape the vision of the film. The *Rite of Spring* section, for instance, illustrated Stravinsky's famous piece with a dramatic, strikingly realistic recreation of the volcanoes, dinosaurs, earthquakes, and biological trauma accompanying the Earth's early evolution. In "The Nutcracker Suite," several lovely segments offered an array of "dewdrop fairies," "frost fairies," "milkweed ballerinas," and "dancing flowers" that transformed nature into an idealized wonderland of sentimental beauty. With Beethoven's Pastoral Symphony, Disney's animators flirted with sentimental realism in their fanciful depiction of mythological themes. The frolicking of flying horses, centaurs, unicorns, and fauns set the stage for depictions of Bacchus, Vulcan, Iris, and Zeus. The Elysian Fields, with Mount Olympus towering over them, provided the setting for this segment, and they appeared on-screen with a Brueghel-like realism.

The Stravinsky segment drew comment for its scientific naturalism. One observer described it as akin to "a weird, coloriferous newsreel taken by some visitor from Mars during the early days of this planet." Many critics saw "The Nutcracker Suite" as the sentimental heart of the film, with its dancing thistles and mushrooms giving way to "luminous sugar-plum fairies [who] glide like fireflies through a gossamer world, sprinkling dewdrops on sleeping flowers." Emily Genauer noted that the film was replete with "natural forms strikingly stylized . . . whimsical but realistic."[28]

The concluding section of *Fantasia* brilliantly highlighted the tensile structure of Disney's approach. Its counterpoint of two drastically different pieces of music — Mussorgsky's "Night on Bald Mountain" and Schubert's "Ave Maria" — dramatized the cosmic battle between good and evil, the sacred and the profane in the world. Unintentionally, it also dramatized the film's aesthetic balancing act. The segment begins with Chernobog, the

Black God of evil and death, magically appearing out of the mountain and gathering witches, demons, and vampires in a furious dance before flinging them into a fiery pit. This powerful, otherworldly vision, depicted with a surge of primal energy, then gives way to an almost cloying, medieval realism. With the dawning light and the tolling of churchbells, we see a fog-shrouded line of candle-carrying pilgrims advancing across a bridge and through a shadowy forest. As the group finally emerges into a bright, beautiful meadow, the film ends to the strains of "Ave Maria" and the camera moves skyward to focus on the brilliant sun. The aesthetic tension is resolved with a visual apotheosis.

Fantasia's aesthetic features inspired a lively critical debate. Many popular magazines and newspapers loved the film, effusively praising it as a "trailblazing" and "revolutionary" experience, "a symphony concert . . . [that] leaves its audience gasping." The National Board of Review, a watchdog organization for groups like the PTA, the Daughters of the American Revolution, and the Better Film Councils, for the first time in its twenty-six-year history devoted a session of its national convention to a showing of the new Disney film. A subsequent citation described it as "leading in a direction where all makers of screen entertainment are bound to follow." But the film also became embroiled in controversy as a stream of overheated critical opinion began oozing over the public landscape.[29]

A fundamental division quickly emerged in the reception of this movie. Film and art critics, for the most part, found merit in its attempt to combine various forms of artistic expression — pictorial representations, music, drama, dance. Some, in fact, compared it with the ballet, a genre that also fused many elements into what New York *Times* critic Olin Downes called "the modern art of the choreographic theater." Overall, a rough consensus took shape around the view that *Fantasia* constituted a daring departure in moviemaking and as such exhibited both profound flaws and rich potential. In the colorful words of one commentator, it was "a promising monstrosity . . . [that] in spite of shortcomings partly due to the exploring character of the whole, partly to fundamental errors, is a work of promise."[30]

At the same time, music critics, with few exceptions, expressed deep reservations about *Fantasia*. Most of them felt that Disney — and Stokowski — had fundamentally misused classical music. They complained that saddling great musical pieces with preconceived images robbed them of their integrity and thus demonstrated a fundamental disrespect for the masters of the musical art. On another plane, they angrily noted that most of the selections in *Fantasia* had been rearranged and given false excitement through overly dramatic renderings and excessively fast tempos. In the words of the New York *Sun*'s Oscar Thompson, the music was full of "fireworks, rockets, roman candles, and pinwheels . . . [and] it suggests only too colorfully the well-trimmed Christmas tree." Others complained that the animation overwhelmed appreciation of the music by drawing laughs from caricatures and gasps from dramatic renderings. Some music critics, such as Benjamin DeCasseres, condemned the film outright, describing it as an exercise that "almost nauseated me — literally." *Fantasia* was a clownish degradation, he wrote angrily, that succeeded in "bringing great music down to the level of jazz" while merrily perpetuating a "travesty on great art."[31]

On November 25, 1940, Dorothy Thompson published a long review of *Fantasia* entitled "Minority Report" in the New York *Herald Tribune,* and it set off a major imbroglio. Given the essay's extreme sentiments, it was little wonder. "I left the theater in a condition bordering on nervous breakdown. I felt as though I had been subjected to an assault," Thompson wrote. Disney's film, she asserted, was "a performance of Satanic defilement," "a remarkable nightmare," "brutal and brutalizing." As she went on, she ratcheted her anger several notches higher: "All I could think to say of the 'experience' as I staggered out was that it was 'Nazi.' The word did not arise out of an obsession. Nazism is the abuse of power, the perverted betrayal of the best instincts, the genius of a race turned into black magical destruction, and so is 'Fantasia.'" Disney and his concert film, Thompson accused, had launched an attack on "the civilized world" by providing a sick caricature of the "Decline of the West." Warming to her theme, she made two specific complaints. First, the film reflected a "sadistic, gloomy, fatalistic, pantheistic," antihumanist philosophy where "Nature is titanic; man is a moving lichen on the stone of time." Second, she insisted, Disney and Stokowski had concocted an assault on civilized culture that made a mockery of great classical composers. The degradation of the Beethoven segment alone should have been "sufficient to raise an army, if there is enough blood left in culture to defend itself," Thompson wrote angrily, before noting that she stormed out of the theater unwilling to witness the film's concluding degradation of Mussorgsky and Schubert.[32]

After the smoke cleared, the piece prompted considerable reaction. Howard Barnes, Thompson's colleague on the *Herald Tribune,* described her outburst in his column as "sheer, unadulterated hysteria" and dismissed the charges of "Nazism" as ludicrous. Carl E. Lindstrom, critic for the Hartford, Connecticut, *Times,* joined the counterattack. Thompson's wielding of "the Nazi cudgel is the most conscienceless thing that has occurred to music in many a year. It should be widely and deeply resented," he wrote. While flawed, Disney's concert feature showed great potential for combining different branches of art. Lindstrom believed that it certainly deserved better than Thompson's screed, which was "Philistinism pure and simple."[33]

In many ways, *Fantasia* thus played out as a provocative aesthetic experiment. Even with the storm of controversy it blew up, other problems — its tremendous production costs, its great length and unfamiliar format, constricted foreign markets because of the outbreak of war in Europe — converged to make it a box office disappointment. A lukewarm popular response led to a drastic cutting of the movie's length and rerelease, but this offered little help. In some ways, though, this audacious film represented the culmination of Disney's early career. More clearly than any other project of this period, *Fantasia* demonstrated the range and capacity of its creator's aesthetic vision. It also threw him into the middle of a critical debate for which he was totally unprepared.

7

Of Mice and Men:
Art Critics and Animators

I N 1933, an amusing little story on animation's leading star appeared in the movie magazine *Screenland*. Entitled "The Art of Mickey Mouse," it satirized a recent showing of Disney watercolors and drawings at the Kennedy Art Gallery on Fifth Avenue. The author reported that Mickey, having shed his trademark short buttoned pants and oversize shoes, now wore "a morning coat, striped trousers, a gleaming white vest, and pearl gray spats." He insisted on being called Michael, and holding a walking stick under one arm and gazing through a pair of spectacles, he commented on the paintings' similarity to the works of Daumier and Matisse. The elegant mouse lectured the reporter: "Please, no unseemly noises. Remember that you are in the presence of Art! . . . Once I was just a slapstick comedian — oh, those tiresome days! Now I am not only a respected Artist, but a subject of Art as well." The pretense vanished, of course, when Minnie showed up and announced a great party where an open cookie jar would be available. Mickey bolted for the door, calling out over his shoulder, "See you again soon. I want to talk to you about Neo-impressionism."[1]

The whimsical article offered a brief taste of a fascinating and well-publicized debate in American culture during the 1930s — what were the artistic merits of Walt Disney's work? This discussion consisted of not only playful articles in fan magazines but serious pieces in some of the leading newspapers and journals of opinion. Commentary appeared in publications ranging from *Variety* and *Woman's Home Companion* to the New York *Times, Art Digest,* and *The Nation.* This public preoccupation raised a number of issues and became a fascinating part of Disney's emergence in the 1930s as a major cultural figure.

I. Is Disney Art?

The grounds for the debate were established at the onset of the decade, when diverse commentators began to insist that the Mickey Mouse and Silly Symphony films were not just clever entertainment but a serious new art form. By the mid-1930s, assertions that Mickey was a "supreme artistic achievement" or that Disney movies had gone "almost too far beyond popular understanding" were commonplace. Newspaper columns claimed that "there are only two genuinely American forms of art: jazz and Walt Disney." The *Art Digest* insisted that "Walt Disney has invented a new art and a very profound one. The animated cartoon under his hand has developed into a fourth dimensional world where anything can and does happen — where laws of gravitation are suspended, where physical resistance becomes limitless and, beyond all that, the sensitive imagination of a great artist has created something very close to the work of a real genius."[2]

Many critics agreed that the animation producer was truly a great artist. Newspaper essays carried such titles as "Walt Disney, Artist," while Mark Van Doren termed him a "first-rate artist" who "lives somewhere near the human center and knows innumerable truths that cannot be taught." It was not uncommon to see Disney described as "Leonardo da Disney" or "a twentieth-century Michelangelo," while his bustling, productive studio was compared to that of Rembrandt. With hushed reverence, stories on the Disney operation reported the prominence given to serious drawing and painting. "The word Art, spelled with a capital 'A,' is taboo on the Disney lot, but constant study is given to works of the great masters," the Hollywood *Citizen-News* reported.[3]

Affirmations of Disney as artist, however, went beyond generic praise. Critics marshaled serious formulations, arguments, and observations to buttress their claims. Dorothy Grafly, for example, art critic for the Philadelphia *Record* and curator of the art collections at Drexel University, became one of Walt Disney's most thoughtful and friendly critics. Not only did she write favorably of his work, but in the mid-1930s she organized an exhibition of Disney drawings at the Philadelphia Art Alliance. Her enthusiasm was rooted in a clear perception of Disney's aesthetic significance.

In July 1933, Grafly contributed an important essay to the *American Magazine of Art.* Entitled "America's Youngest Art," it explored animation in the United States and awarded Disney the lead role in the development of this "folk art of a sophisticated century." She grounded animation in the theories of Cézanne and his followers, who had tried to produce on canvas a semblance of movement. For Grafly, however, Disney's greatest importance lay in his relationship to modernist painting. According to her, modern artists had become increasingly addicted to egocentric, incomprehensible expression and "grown a bit tipsy on too much self-revelation, introspection, and abstraction." Disney had counteracted this trend by "doing more to keep art alive in the hearts of men, women, and children than all the exhibitions attended throughout the season by a little coterie of intelligentsia." Moreover, in Grafly's opinion, Disney achieved this salutary result not by rejecting modernism but by accepting and reworking it:

> Quite as much as Picasso he distorts and renders the unreal, but from this unreality one derives a fine emotional participation that brings conviction. One has passed through a unique experience . . . Like other forms of radical art, [Disney's work] repudiates representation, but it aims to provoke the poignant reality of the unreal. It, too, goes back to the study of the primitive and the child in its basic realization that to both, a fairy tale is more real than actual experience.[4]

A host of critics picked up and embroidered similar motifs throughout the 1930s. In a 1933 *Pearson's Magazine* piece entitled "Poetry in Celluloid," for example, the author concluded that the Silly Symphonies comprised "the New Poetry — the poetry of motion, mirth and melody blended into one harmonious whole." In the future, the author concluded confidently, critics "will speak with due reverence of the poet Disney who created this new art form." One critic even went so far as to suggest a realization of composer Richard Wagner's dream of a "union of the arts," since Disney's animated films synthesized music, drama, comedy, drawing, and dialogue into a beautiful whole.[5]

For some critics, the transcendence of time and space drew special attention as a factor in Disney's art. Barnet G. Braver-Mann, an advocate of modernist aesthetics in film, suggested that Disney's animation went far beyond other kinds of theater and movies in its "fantastic treatment of time, form, space, gravity, or place." Muralist Jean Charlot pursued a similar theme in a famous 1939 essay for the *American Scholar* entitled "But Is It Art? A Disney Disquisition." As he pointed out, the crucial difference between painting and animation "lies in the fact that the element of time which is artificial to the former becomes one of the essentials of the latter." Claude Bragdon noted in *Scribner's* that Disney's animation realized the artist's dream of "making his drawings move and speak."[6]

Even the music in Disney's films came in for special critical praise. Jerome Kern, while visiting Hollywood to write a movie score, made the astounding statement that "Walt Disney has made the twentieth century's only important contribution to music . . . Disney has made use of music as a language."

Arturo Toscanini, director of the New York Philharmonic, reportedly leaped to his feet after a screening of *The Band Concert* and shouted his praise: "Surely it is impossible! It is magnificent!" A detailed analysis in *Stage* magazine described the Silly Symphonies as "a rare kind of art" wherein musical and pictorial elements came together as a seamless whole. With the music in "a Bach chorale or a Mozart symphony," the writer contended, "from the smoothness and precision of the lucid thing you hear, you are not aware of the formidable equipment of harmonics, counterpoint, and pure mathematics that its composer had to possess. So with *les oeuvres* Disney."[7]

A few voices, however, were less enthusiastic. Noted caricaturist Al Hirschfeld, for example, scathingly described Disney's work as a depiction of "gingerbread realities . . . [that] belongs in the oopsy-woopsy school of art practiced mostly by etchers who portray dogs with cute sayings." Thomas Burton, writing in the *Saturday Review,* offered an analysis that was only slightly kinder. Disney's "is the art of soft-focus caricature, of picturing animals and men as lovable and amusing people. His art is all good-natured curves," Burton said. "This gives him all his talents to be put into surface entertainment. There is no place for social bite, grand manner, art theory in his work." By the late 1930s, some critics had begun accusing Disney of betraying his artistic potential by embracing technology and pictorial realism. According to one, the wonderful elements making up the "new art form" of the early Disney pictures — "a mixture of poetic charm and naïveté of fable and opéra bouffe, blended into fantasies for all ages" — had given way to a mere fascination with "new technical devices."[8]

In a measured, thoughtful evaluation written in 1941, theater critic Christopher La Farge also voiced misgivings. Measuring Disney's films against a standard of art, he judged that they fell a bit short. The animated movies of the 1930s had come close to "artistic excellence," he argued, but certain shortcomings had kept them from passing "the difficult line that always lies between the popular success and the work of art." For La Farge, Disney's biggest problem lay in his unfortunate tendency to mimic "reality and human actions." By contrast, true art demanded "the quality of abstraction . . . the stripping of action and mood to its essential characteristics until the point is reached where all that remains is the concentrated essence. That is what all the great artists have succeeded in doing." While Disney achieved this on occasion, creating film passages where "the motion was magnificently abstracted into a convincing, fairy-story unreality," too often his movies settled for a banal imitation of human live-action films. If he ever decided to make movies that were not possible in any other medium, La Farge concluded, he would be well on his way to creating "an art form in its own right."[9]

Despite such evaluations, the official art world provided an unexpected affirmation of Disney's art. As early as December 1933, the Chicago Art

Institute mounted a display of Disney drawings. Other institutions, such as the Fogg Art Museum at Harvard University and the Los Angeles County Museum, followed suit, and by late in the decade a prominent San Francisco art dealer, Guthrie Courvoisier, had become a go-between for the Disney Studio and galleries in many cities. Probably the most notorious showing occurred in 1938, when the Metropolitan Museum of Art in New York decided to exhibit a watercolor from *Snow White*. Dozens of newspaper stories, most of them praising this recognition of "the people's choice," carried news of the exhibition all over the country. As might be expected, jokes also made the rounds. One columnist puckishly predicted that treatises would soon be appearing dividing Disney's work into early, middle, and late periods, while another called for the election of Donald Duck to the American Academy of Arts and Letters. Humorist H. I. Philips probably garnered the biggest laugh with this bit of doggerel:

> Corot's in a back seat,
> Rembrandt's eyes are wet;
> Romney looks astounded —
> Disney's in the 'Met'!
> Figures, landscapes, faces
> Consternation share —
> Statues reel and totter —
> Dopey now is there![10]

Universities also provided reinforcement for the notion of Disney animation as art. In 1933, the College Art Association helped arrange an exhibition of Disney drawings in New York. Five years later, Harvard, Yale, and the University of Southern California granted honorary degrees to Walt Disney and publicly praised his importance as an artist. The Yale statement described him as the "creator of a new language of art" and asserted that he had "the originality characteristic of genius." Harvard president James Bryant Conan chimed in, characterizing Disney as "a magician who has created a modern dwelling for the muses."[11]

One of the most important debates concerned the vexed question of elitism in American culture. As a raft of essays and articles made clear, a pronounced appropriation of Disney films by intellectuals had become evident even by the early 1930s. This occurred not only in America but among European cultural theorists as well. Philippe Lamour, a young French critic, argued that Mickey Mouse represented "a new mode of human expression" that conveyed "the inexpressible, the non-existent, the abstract — pure madness, and all under a most natural-seeming aspect, apparent to all beholders." A 1931 article entitled "Europe's Highbrows Hail 'Mickey Mouse'" reviewed the recent writing on Disney animation from other French intellectuals: Philippe Soupault in *L'Europe Nouvelle*, J. P. Gélas in *L'Action Française*, Jean Morienval in *Le Cinéopse*, and Arlette Jazarin in *Comoedia*. In a typical evaluation, one claimed that Disney's work represented "the freest, the most unlimited, the most extravagant flights of the imagination," while another opined that it united "evocative power of design with the impalpable movement of life, with speech and with music. Thus it becomes a complete art."[12]

In the mid-1930s, humorist James Thurber reacted to the vogue of Disney-as-artist with a droll essay recommending a Disney version of *The Odyssey*. "The right 'Odyssey' has yet to be done," he noted dryly, and a Disney production "can be, I am sure, a far, far greater thing than even his epic of the three little pigs." In the same vein, a story entitled "Madame Cluck, Prima Donna" provided a mock-serious analysis of this Disney character's contribution to the opera. Noting her appearance in films like *Mickey's Grand Opera,* the author pointed out that she was "built on the lines of a parker house roll" and her powerful, heaving shriek of a voice may have "knocked down a tenor or two." "Reared on cracked corn," the article said, Clara Cluck "has a voice like the still sweep of a Van Gogh countryside, interrupted by the morning announcement that an egg has been laid."[13]

A rash of essays also poked fun at intellectuals and their serious readings of an imaginary rodent wearing short pants. In their self-important hands, according to one article's mocking words, the mouse's "penchant for doing what he wanted and when he wanted became an outlet for shackled humanity . . . [as] Mickey 'releases our inhibited consciousness.'" In "That Awful Word 'Art,'" a critic complained that "the moment Mickey Mouse became the pet of the highbrows and was elected to his place among the Arts, he became threatened with extinction." A columnist in the Brooklyn *Eagle* attacked the intellectualizing of Disney and Mickey Mouse with equal vehemence: "My fervent prayer is that this recognition of the lofty-domed won't last. It would be just too bad if such a gorgeously amusing creation should go arty. Nothing can be quite so effective in squeezing the vitality out of a screen character as to have its creator take the comments of the highbrows to heart. The creators become conscious of a great mission to fulfill, and then they're lost." Such commentators pleaded with Disney to forget any thoughts of cosmic significance and universal verities and to continue putting fun, cleverness, and "devil-may-care gusto" into his films.[14]

Class resentment frequently added a sharper edge to this criticism. Some, hostile to the arrogance and condescension of intellectual elites, turned on Disney's highbrow patrons with a vengeance. Alva Johnston, for example, writing in *Woman's Home Companion,* sarcastically noted that Disney "was discovered by the mob before he was discovered by the art world . . . [as] the masses gave a lesson in art appreciation to the intelligentsia." Others insisted that the chatter of the salon meant nothing to plain Americans. While average theatergoers considered Disney to be an artist, according to one newspaper editorial, they "would not give a thought to the question of whether his product may be described as Art, with a capital 'A.'" When Disney himself received learned tomes on his work, a reporter observed, fear that his staff would become art-conscious made him "order the publication taken away so that no one in the studio can read it."[15]

To complicate matters, some critics chastised both the highbrows who denigrated Disney and the populist, antielitist crowd who venerated him. A writer in the Schenectady *Gazette,* for instance, heatedly contended that among certain snobbish critics, a belief prevailed that Disney's work did not deserve recognition as art simply because "his work appeals to the masses." From the opposite direction, writers such as the Los Angeles *Times's* Arthur Millier expressed grave reservations about "popular" determinations of artistic merit. In a 1940 review of a Disney film, he took sharp issue with "a notion, which has been much propagandized during [the last] decade, that 'the people' are the immediate and infallible judges of art and that what they don't take straight to their bosoms is spinach." Popular acceptance of superb work like Disney's was fine, he concluded, "but it's no criterion of judgment in art."[16]

The many-sided debate over Disney's work raised a related question — how should the commercial and entertainment values of Hollywood filmmaking be factored into thinking about Disney as an artist? At the Disney Studio itself, a firm grasp of market reality always guided the pursuit of artistic excellence. In the late 1930s, for instance, a hard-nosed lecture by Ken O'Connor, one of Disney's leading young artists and designers, met this issue head on. "The animated cartoon is a shotgun marriage between art and mechanics, with King Midas fingering the trigger," he told his listeners. Basic artistic principles had to be meshed with a number of practical requirements — mechanical capability, space requirements, salesmanship — to sustain "outlets of commercial art — they are used to sell, to instruct, and in our medium, we hope, to entertain."[17]

To some critics, however, it appeared that commercial and entertainment factors were crowding out aesthetic considerations. Leftist dialectician Harry Alan Potamkin, in a hostile 1932 analysis, chastised Disney's intellectual supporters as "cultists" for wildly inflating the importance of his modest artistic accomplishments. In fact, Potamkin asserted, "There is too much gag in the Disney film and not enough idea." Claude Bragdon noted that the filmmaker's work had become steadily commercialized, a "three-ring circus, with . . . thrills, stunts, surprises and races punctuated with destruction and disaster."[18]

From another angle, Disney's films seemed to raise important sociological questions regarding the nature of an art in modern industrial society. Animation, after all, involved hundreds of people in a complex process.

Artists and their assistants produced thousands of drawings in assembly-line fashion; the drawings were combined and timed with mathematical precision; quasi-industrial processes of inking, painting, and photography finished the job. The difficulty, many pointed out, came with trying to evaluate such production as "art" according to traditional standards. Some observers claimed that Disney animation's union of art and science represented a natural flowering of "marked artistic genius in this mechanical age." But others feared that it was moving inexorably toward "a formula which afforded easy repetition for mass production." For still others, Disney's movies seemed to be urging an escape from the modern, mechanical world altogether. Lawrence Gould, the well-known psychologist, argued that the celluloid antics of Mickey Mouse and Donald Duck embodied a collective desire to escape the pressures of modern life and return to childhood. Gould believed that the highly rationalized and efficiency-demanding "condition of our life today is too much for us, and as soon as the whistle blows or the clock strikes five, we go back as completely as we can to childhood as an escape from worldly worries."[19]

Among this great bulk of aesthetic commentary, a trio of writers offered particularly insightful analyses. One, a pioneering moviemaker in his own right as well as a critic and theorist of film, made a sweeping social, cultural, and aesthetic evaluation of Disney's pictures from halfway around the globe. The second, an outspoken defender of popular culture since the early 1920s, saw Disney as a fascinating reflection of American civilization, its vitality, and its people. The third, the author of the first comprehensive survey of the American motion picture, defined Walt Disney as the only true film artist yet produced in this country.

Around 1940, Sergei Eisenstein began a series of articles on figures he considered to be masters of the cinema: D. W. Griffith, Charlie Chaplin, and Walt Disney. The Russian filmmaker and theorist had pioneered the technique of montage in early silent movies like *Potemkin,* and in a host of subsequent films and writings he had gone on to achieve a towering influence in the development of motion pictures. He had visited Hollywood in 1930 to participate in a couple of film projects and visited the Disney Studio, coming away with an autographed picture. Eisenstein believed Disney to be a giant among American artists. He was drawn to the powerful "primitivism" that seemed to inspire Disney's movies, a quality that he described in terms of an ecstatic, prelogical, folkloric animism. Disney's universe, he believed, was literally an animated one in which all objects and creatures, both moving and immobile, had life. It was paradise regained, a state of absolute human freedom where one saw a "mythological personification of phenomena of nature" that reflected "man's early psyche." As Eisenstein put it, Disney "creates on the conceptual level of man not yet shackled by logic, reason, or experience." In the long string of animated movies in the 1930s, one saw "man brought back, as it were, to those pre-stages that were traced out by Darwin."[20]

This primitivism had profound, complex implications. On the one hand, Eisenstein believed that Disney's protean animism had emerged in part as a revolt against capitalist rationalization. Industrial America's "logic of stan-dardization" had created a prelogical antithesis, he argued, and the fantastic experiences of Mickey Mouse and the Silly Symphonies appealed to this revulsion against industrial monotony. In Eisenstein's impassioned phrases, Disney films held a profound appeal

> for those who are shackled by hours of work and regulated moments of rest, by a mathematical precision of time, whose lives are graphed by the cent and the dollar. Whose lives are divided up into little squares like a chess board . . . that divide up the soul, feelings, thoughts, just as the carcasses of pigs are dismembered by the conveyor belts of Chicago slaughter houses, and the separate pieces of cars are assembled into me-chanical organisms by Ford's conveyor belts. That's why Disney's films blaze with colour. Like the patterns in the clothes of people who have been deprived of the colours in nature. That's why the imagination in them is limitless, for Disney's films are a revolt against partitioning and legislat-ing, against spiritual stagnation and greyness.

To emotion-starved residents of a world where logic, efficiency, productivity, and order dominated, Disney's animated universe created a mirage of magic and joy.[21]

According to Eisenstein, however, Disney's essential primitivism also fed modernist aesthetics. His "joyful and beautiful art" merged the prelogical with the technological. In the best modernist tradition, Disney created a universe that pushed aside logic, protested the "metaphysical immobility" of genteel formalism, and experimented aesthetically in the interests of recov-ering the vitality and emotionality of life. According to Eisenstein's admir-ing description, "This man seems to know not only the magic of all techni-cal means, but also all the most secret strands of human thought, images, ideas, feelings . . . He creates somewhere in the realm of the very purest and most primal depths." The Russian's conclusion was clear and unequivocal: "The work of this master is the greatest contribution of the American people to art."[22]

Gilbert Seldes, a drama and film critic for the *Dial*, had made his reputa-tion in the early 1920s with the publication of *The Seven Lively Arts*, an approving analysis of American popular culture. In its pages were enthusias-tic endorsement of the imagination and vitality of jazz, cartoon strips, vaudeville, and the films of Mack Sennett and Charlie Chaplin. By the 1930s, Seldes had become one of America's leading film writers. He proclaimed himself a moderate in his criticism — respectful of both high art and popular entertainment, sympathetic to leftist demands for social awareness but protective of the movies' obligation to create compelling unreality, and especially concerned with what he saw as film's reflection of America's distinctive values of action, energy, and dynamism. Writing for a variety of influential journals, he championed films that appealed to average citizens through their construction of a unique cinematic reality. He saw the movies as a popular art that embodied American democracy. And Walt Disney became one of his paragons.[23]

In a number of essays and reviews, Seldes proclaimed Disney's artistry a creative force that represented "the perfection of the movie." Yet he also feared that a susceptibility to artiness — in his words, to the "sentimental raptures over a kind of sweetness and a mistaken, slightly highbrow approval of the classic quality of these pictures" — might nudge Disney down the wrong path. That would be tragic, according to the critic, because at its best Disney's work was "a lively art that also reaches greatness, a degree of perfection in its field which surpasses our best critical capacity to analyze and which succeeds at the same time in pleasing children and simple folk."[24]

Seldes contended that Disney was a revolutionary, both extending and ultimately undermining the rationalist ethos of modern society. On the one hand, Disney's highly sophisticated system of production had expanded the logic of modern industrial America into the realm of popular entertainment. In Seldes's words,

> Some forty years ago, when human beings became a little bit intractable in shops and factories, scientific management stepped in and "rationalized" industry by the simple process of substituting machines for men. The moment it became clear that machinery could do the work well, it was no longer necessary to make concessions to human beings . . . [Disney has shown that one can] hire people to make animated drawings, always obedient, perfectly under control, and doing the work better than the living players.

At the same time, however, Disney had created a magical world of "complete enchantment" that pulled in the opposite direction. As Seldes wrote in 1938, his films may not "restore to us our natural impulse to dance, but it may keep that impulse alive in human beings until the conditions of society make it as natural for a man to dance as it is for him to run — and not from a policeman with tear gas or an aviator dropping bombs." Movies were both "an industry and an art," Seldes noted, and Disney's work offered "proof that the movies, as an art, are pure gold."[25]

At the end of the Depression decade, a critical history of American movies appeared under the title *The Rise of American Film*. Its author was Lewis Jacobs, a young writer associated with the journal *Experimental Cin-*

ema in the 1920s and early 1930s, whose critical viewpoint combined high aesthetic seriousness with a bent toward left-wing social reform. Beginning with the early years of the twentieth century, Jacobs traced the development of motion picture companies, film genres, significant movies, and particular directors. Ultimately, however, only one figure — a youthful creator of animated films on the outskirts of the Hollywood establishment — earned his unabashed praise. In a chapter entitled "Walt Disney: Virtuoso," he paid homage to this "modern Aesop," whose films he considered to be "perhaps the finest expression of motion picture art in contemporary America." Disney brought to films, he wrote, "a personal touch, a zeal for quality, an appreciation of artistry, and a disdain that is almost a fear of the 'formula' picture."[26]

One of Disney's greatest strengths, according to Jacobs, lay in the singular way in which one saw "reflections of the real world in the fantastic realm of [his] characters." The "brutality of the modern world" in the unsettled 1930s, Jacobs argued, found its counterpart in the "ruthless conflict and violence" that permeated films like *Mickey's Polo Team* and *Who Killed Cock Robin?* Although Disney disdained blatant political or social moralizing, his movies nonetheless reflected an age that glorified physical might. "Mickey is almost pure physical force," the author pointed out. "Although he is kindhearted, he is all nerves and muscle; he bangs, knocks, punches, mutilates, annihilates every obstacle in the path of his desires." But the triumphant aggressiveness of this libidinous mouse should be no surprise, because while Disney dealt in myth, "the events that transpire in his cartoons have their basis in actuality."[27]

For Jacobs, the high point of Disney's art may have been a fascinating use of color and sound to create a unique version of reality. "He disdains dialogue, fabricating an unreal world of sounds in unheard-of combinations," Jacobs contended. "His color, too, is wild, fantastic, subtle, or merely literal, for it depends not upon the real colors of objects but upon the pigmentation dictated by his imagination." Such techniques reflected not only a fertile imagination but the sensibility of a true artist busily creating a new world to challenge and fascinate audiences. "Not bound to imitating nature," Jacobs wrote, "he distorts it as he likes: a piano is instantly turned into a grand-opera singer, a daisy into a chorus girl." According to the unwavering conclusion of *The Rise of American Film*, "Walt Disney, today, stands as the virtuoso of the film medium."[28]

Thus throughout the 1930s, discussion of Disney's artistry branched off in a dozen directions. Ultimately, however, it tended to converge on one point. Essays and articles returned again and again to the aesthetic urge at the heart of Disney's films. Gilbert Seldes called this quality "the magic in seeing the impossible happen," while Dorothy Grafly termed it "the poignant reality of the unreal." For Philip Lamour it was "the abstract, pure madness expressed in a most natural-seeming aspect," while Lewis Jacobs phrased it as "reflections of the real world in the fantastic." Although no writer used the explicit terminology, such comments in fact highlighted the sentimental modernism of Disney's aesthetic agenda. As the *Art Digest* noted in 1940, "Here was 'abstract' art that was great. The difference between Disney's lines and . . . the abstractions of our 'pewee Picassos' is that Disney's abstracts actually function — [they] have something significant to do and do it. Picasso's abstractions and the abstractions of Braque likewise are profoundly functional."[29]

Disney's aesthetic quest for sentimental modernism was partly intentional and partly accidental, partly a matter of production and partly one of reception. Perhaps most important, it was the result not just of one man's aesthetic instincts but of a creative, dedicated group of artists consisting of a broad mix of types and talents. In the front rank stood Norm Ferguson and Fred Moore, two tremendously gifted and widely respected young men. Coming from different backgrounds and offering different styles, they made a significant contribution to the artistic ethos of Disney's golden age films.

II. Norm Ferguson and Fred Moore: Acting Animation and Personality Animation

As the Disney Studio began its rise to prominence, its staff of artists grew quickly both in size and in sophistication. First a few, then dozens, and eventually hundreds of talented young artists began to stream into the Hyperion Avenue facility from all over the country, eager to have a hand in the animation breakthroughs that seemed to occur on almost a daily basis. Many of them fell by the wayside as their grasp exceeded their ability, but a few hung on and quickly rose through the ranks to prominence within the Disney organization. Fred Moore and Norman Ferguson were the first to achieve such artistic stardom.

Although never particularly close friends, these two animators had curiously intertwined careers at the studio. They had several characteristics in common — a lack of formal artistic training but a vibrant and instinctive creativity, the ability to take a pioneering role in the development of several techniques that became synonymous with the Disney style, an eagerness to share their insights with others — and they shared a sad demise at the institution they loved. Moore and Ferguson played important roles throughout the 1930s. Key artists on the wildly popular *Three Little Pigs*, they subsequently were chosen by Walt Disney to animate his personal film project, *The Golden Touch*, and then appointed as two of four animation directors for *Snow White*. Through their innovative work, they became aesthetic trailblazers for the studio during this intensely creative decade.

Norman Ferguson, or "Fergy," as he was universally known in the environs of Hyperion Avenue, arrived at the Disney Studio in 1929. Part of the exodus of animators from New York, he had worked for several years in the cartoon industry before being lured to Hollywood. His background was rather unusual. Trained as an accountant, he became an animation cameraman at the Terrytoons studio. One evening he stayed late to shoot a scene and discovered that some of the drawings were missing. Since no one else was around, he drew them himself — with such skill that he was offered a job as an animator. He rapidly climbed the ladder at Terrytoons and came to the West Coast with considerable skill and experience. At the Disney operation his talent quickly flowered.[30]

Ferguson worked on both the Silly Symphonies and Mickey Mouse shorts and successfully developed a number of characters — the villainous Peg Leg Pete in several films, the trio of vaudeville dancers in *Frolicking Fish* (1930), and the Big Bad Wolf in *Three Little Pigs*. Handpicked by Disney for *The Golden Touch*, he drew the central character, King Midas. His most notable accomplishment, however, was Pluto. He first drew the flop-eared character as a nameless bloodhound in *The Chain Gang* (1930) and subsequently made this lovable, loyal canine a central figure in the expanding Disney menagerie. In films like *Playful Pluto* (1934) and *Mickey's Elephant* (1936), Mickey's inquisitive, slow-thinking dog displayed a comic persona rooted in hilarious physical reactions rather than dialogue (he was, of course, a nonspeaking character).[31]

By the late 1930s, Ferguson had moved into the feature-length films that were dominating the studio's creative energy. Chosen as a supervising animator for *Snow White*, he oversaw a number of sequences and personally drew the evil witch, the first of the great Disney villains. He created J. Worthington Foulfellow and Gideon the Cat for *Pinocchio*, did much of the famous pink elephant scene in *Dumbo*, and served as animation supervisor for the "Dance of the Hours" segment in *Fantasia*. Shortly thereafter, Disney appointed him production supervisor (his second-in-command) for a two-month tour of Latin America, a project that inspired the films *Saludos Amigos* (1943) and *The Three Caballeros* (1945). Throughout this period of remarkable artistic ferment, according to Ferguson's colleague Dick Huemer, "Fergy . . . was *it*. Not only the best at Disney's but consequently the best in the world."[32]

Ferguson's animation technique had an enormous influence. Perhaps more than any other individual, he developed several elements that became benchmarks of the studio's style: an emphasis on fluid motion, a strong quality of pantomime that conveyed a character's thought processes without dialogue, and a concern with motivation, or "acting animation." His emphasis on movement jumped, almost literally, out of his drawing. Developing a unique rough style that amazed his colleagues, he created a scene by completing with incredible swiftness a series of crude sketches that emphasized motion. At first glance, these drawings were a whirl of lines in which the character was barely discernible, but like impressionist paintings they gradually took on shape, coherence, and especially movement. "Fergy did the roughest penciling of anybody I ever saw or heard of," Dick Huemer recalled, and another animator described how the New Yorker "made rough drawings that looked like the map of a freight yard, and turned them out at breakneck speed."[33]

According to Jack Kinney, "When Fergy animated, he did whatever he needed for the action . . . He exaggerated everything, and that gave his drawings more life. Soon everybody started drawing looser and thinking more about the action than about how clean the drawings were or how tight the in-betweens were. This opened up more freedom of movement." In the opinion of Ollie Johnston and Frank Thomas, this style also allowed for easier alterations and additions of new ideas right up to the last minute. Shamus Culhane probed a bit deeper, arguing that Ferguson's rapid, emotional drawing allowed him to "tap into the unconscious" because the characters almost seemed to be coming to life on their own and acting spontaneously. This inattention to detail also permitted a greater focus on timing, a quality essential for convincing comedy and action. As long as Fergy had a good assistant who could refine his rough masterpieces into finished drawings, he could put out a steady surge of crude vitality to keep the films moving.[34]

The Silly Symphony *Frolicking Fish* was one of the first films with Ferguson's fluid movement, and according to Wilfred Jackson, it was "a big step forward in Disney animation." Ferguson's dancing fish did not stop and start woodenly, but "when one part would hold, something else would move. So there was never a complete stop." Disney was so impressed by the continuous motion that he made the whole staff study Fergy's technique in this sequence.[35]

It was Pluto, however, who provided the opportunity for Ferguson to develop another crucial aspect of his technique, pantomime. In the words of Ben Sharpsteen, Fergy created a looseness in Pluto that exaggerated his physical actions and highlighted his mental processes. The artist would contrast slow scenes in which the viewer could almost see thoughts going through Pluto's head with fast-action episodes in which the dog would react with a kind of manic physicality. With Ferguson illustrating a full range of feelings, from "dumb curiosity to panic," story man Ted Sears noted, the "audience feels all of Pluto's sensations." Probably the most famous example is the flypaper scene in *Playful Pluto,* where the hapless dog steps on some sticky insect paper and goes through several inept maneuvers trying to extricate himself, only to become ever more hopelessly attached. The hilarity comes from seeing "the wheels going around in the character's head," Ward Kimball observed. Fellow artists concluded that Ferguson's "talents as a pantomimist bordered on genius," and some simply called him the "Charlie Chaplin of the animation business."[36]

Ultimately, Ferguson's emphasis on motion and pantomime combined to create what many called "acting animation," a staple of Disney films in this era. Instead of relying on slapstick, the comedy flowed naturally from characters' physical action and its connection to their emotions and thoughts. This artistic mode encouraged the studio's Story Department, pushing it to invent plot lines that went beyond gags and entered the realm of emotion and motivation. As Disney once said at a large staff gathering, "Fergy, you're a great actor . . . That's why your animation is so good, because you feel. You feel what those characters feel."[37]

Ferguson drew on his love for old vaudeville shows to hone a keen sense of timing, pantomime, and showmanship. Never taught the rules of drawing, he regularly broke them to gain fresh results. As one animator laughingly commented, "He doesn't know that you can't raise the eyebrows above the head circle, so he goes ahead and does it, and gets a great effect."[38]

Ferguson's acting animation gained considerable influence partly because of his knack for sharing his work with others. Jack Kinney noted that "he taught anyone that wanted to ask him a question," and T. Hee described how, during the making of feature films, Ferguson would review rough pencil tests of the animation and provide a flurry of suggestions to grateful artists. As Dick Huemer noted, "Fergy was one sweet little guy, that's how everyone felt about him." He delivered lectures to the animation staff that outlined his approach. In a 1936 talk, for instance, he argued, "Pluto's comedy value lies in using him as a heavy, cumbersome, awkward dog, and to avoid the effect of lightness. Whenever he is used running, jumping, or falling, it is well to bear in mind the fact that a heavy dog would naturally need more anticipation to his run or jump, and in the case of a fall his land would take more stretching and recovering than that of a lighter dog."[39]

Small of stature and presenting a wide-eyed, unflappable countenance to the world, he "never got over being a New Yorker," in the words of Bill Cottrell. With his Brooklyn accent, three-piece suit and tie, and a cigarette often dangling from his lips, Fergy constantly sparked his conversation with "Yeah, yeah, you know, you know." He also had lots of nervous energy, habitually shaking his foot as he sat at his desk drawing; in conversation, he habitually twisted a little curl of hair that hung down over his forehead. But Ferguson's amicable face and sweet nature could be deceiving. As fellow artist Jack Cutting once observed, his "wide-open, pale-blue eyes and fixed smile looked guileless and friendly, but every so often you got the feeling that his smile was a mask and that behind it he was observing and noting everything you were doing."[40]

Ferguson was noted for his extraordinary devotion to the studio and its leader. In 1937, he bought Disney's old house after the studio head moved up to a larger one, and a few years later he was one of Disney's strongest supporters during the protracted and bitter labor strike. Shamus Culhane once recalled hearing Fergy claim that "when he became too old to animate, he'd take a job in the Disney parking lot!"[41]

While Norm Ferguson made a strong impact with his action animation, the studio was equally influenced by Fred Moore. Walt Disney liked to relate how the eighteen-year-old Moore had strolled into his office in 1929, fresh out of high school and dressed "in an old sweater, baggy slacks, and tennis shoes," and asked for work as an artist. With considerable skepticism, Disney asked about his qualifications. In reply, the young man "took some sketches out of his back pocket . . . 'I like to draw,' he said." The handful of wrinkled drawings so impressed Disney that he hired the applicant on the spot. This incident foreshadowed the nature of Fred Moore's brilliant career at the studio — informal, successful, and seemingly effortless. Over the next several years Moore played a central role in shaping the art of Disney animation. Reworking Mickey Mouse into his modern form, playing a crucial role in making *Snow White,* and animating dozens of scenes and characters, he practically created the emphasis on personality that became the signature of Disney animation.[42]

From the early 1930s on, Freddy Moore pointed the Disney Studio in new directions. He moved to the heart of things and audaciously redesigned its star attraction, changing Mickey Mouse's physical appearance for short films like *Pluto's Judgment Day* (1935) and *Brave Little Tailor* (1938). Ollie Johnston and Frank Thomas, who trained under him, explained how earlier animators had drawn Mickey as a simple series of circles, a technique that made for considerable inflexibility in his actions and expressions. Moore gave Mickey a supple pear-shaped body that was much more suited to the "squashing and stretching" of movement, and added more realistic eyes (complete with pupils), which greatly enhanced his capacity for expression. The young artist was extremely nervous when he showed the result to Disney for the first time in a "sweatbox" session where rough work was previewed. Disney had the scene rerun several times while Moore stood there, fidgeting and worrying. According to an onlooker, "Not a word was exchanged; then Walt turned to Fred, one eyebrow down, and said, 'Now that's the way I want Mickey to be drawn from now on!'"[43]

After this significant achievement, Moore turned to work on a number of Silly Symphonies, his most notable being the trio of porcine protagonists in *Three Little Pigs.* He and Bill Tytla drew the delightful characters of the seven dwarfs; in *Pinocchio,* he created the mischievous street boy Lampwick; and he followed that with Timothy Mouse in *Dumbo. Fantasia* found him drawing Mickey in "The Sorcerer's Apprentice" and the centaurettes in the Pastoral Symphony segment. In the 1940s, Moore was busy with character animation in both the South American productions and postwar compilation films like *Make Mine Music* (1946) and *Fun and Fancy Free* (1947).

A carefree, charming spirit for whom fun seemed to be the main object in life, Moore was frequently the life of the party at the Disney Studio. Like Norm Ferguson, he was a short man, with a wave of dark auburn hair and a mischievous grin. He liked to sport fashionable, if casual, clothes and considered himself to be a natty dresser. He also possessed uncommon physical grace and athletic ability. Known as "the most coordinated guy in the studio," he excelled at gymnastics, horseshoe pitching, polo, and baseball, and he would regularly hit the ball out of the field in studio games. He was a natural at any activity involving physical timing. Reigning champion in the animators' sport of throwing pushpins against the wooden office doors, he could fling two from each hand at the same time, or throw them behind his back or over his shoulder, and make them stick. Whenever physical skill was required, whether it was juggling or imitating Charlie Chaplin's walk, "Fred would always end up in a good pose — just like his drawings. He could not seem to do anything awkward."[44]

Moore's temperament was more complex. He liked to appear cocky in a good-natured and innocent way. He would work himself up for a project by playfully demanding that his ego be stroked — "Tell me how good I am, fellows" — then tear through a scene in a few hours and "stand around and joke how all those outrageous compliments were true." He craved the stimulation of fun and laughter. Constantly involved in horseplay, he loved to share humor with others. When he discovered one afternoon that rewinding the *Snow White* film made the dwarfs' voices come out in a hysterical new language, he waited until the next morning to set up a big production for his friends so they could all collapse with laughter. He became famous among his colleagues for the slightly naughty, highly valued sketches of sexy young women that he knocked off in odd moments and distributed to friends. At the legendary two-day Lake Narconian party for the Disney staff after the completion of *Snow White,* he left the ballroom, drunk, and fell out of a second-story window; what he thought were bushes actually were the tops of trees.[45]

Yet Moore also possessed a darker side. He tended to go through cycles in his drawing, following buoyantly productive periods with weeks of restlessness and despair. When such problems occurred, he turned superstitious, questioning the suitability of the drawing paper, the weight of the pencils, even the shade of the lead. To Frank Thomas, it was the artistic temperament surfacing: "The flair, the feeling, the almost . . . undisciplined feeling.

The pure emotion would come out . . . and then his dissatisfaction, the torment." As fellow animator Marc Davis once put it, Moore was "the boy genius of the studio who never grew up." He himself realized this in some way, caricaturing himself in Disney characters like Lampwick, the street scamp in *Pinocchio* who loved pranks, and even more in Dopey, the beloved dwarf from *Snow White*. This silent, endearing little character, as Moore's friends realized immediately, "seemed to contain so much of Fred himself — innocent but with a touch of mischief, naive but with just enough worldliness."[46]

Walt Disney maintained an interesting relationship with his star animator. He had a tremendous regard for Moore's talent and didn't try to cramp his carefree style. When important guests would visit the studio, Disney fell into the habit of taking them to the animation offices and asking Moore to sketch a couple of things for their amusement. On his part, Moore regarded Disney with respect but never fear or awe, and talked to him casually and without inhibition. He occasionally chafed at Disney's perfectionism and his constant pressure for new achievements. "Why does Walt always try to get us to do things we can't do?" he once complained. "Why doesn't he just let us do the things we *can* do?"[47]

Moore had a close relationship with his fellow animators, one fueled not just by prankish camaraderie but by a willingness to share his talent and techniques. His generosity was legendary, and not only endeared him to his colleagues but helped to spread his influence. Although he usually fumbled while trying to explain his style of drawing, and he certainly never articulated any abstract theories about his aesthetics or techniques, he happily and deftly demonstrated his ideas with a pencil. "He was such a help to other guys," animator Larry Clemmons remembered. "Guys would come into his room and say, 'Fred, how would you do this?' Fred would say, 'Well, here!' and he'd show them. He didn't lecture, he just did it . . . Fred could communicate his ideas through drawings better than anyone around."[48]

Moore had taken only a few evening art classes at Chouinard Art School after high school, but he sketched constantly on any scrap of paper, and another animator said simply, "He drew as easily as breathing." The charm of his work was based on several underlying characteristics. First, he demonstrated a strong grasp of design; his drawings had "everything in the right place" and usually in perfect proportion. Second, he had a graceful and accurate control over his line, whether it was short and sharp or long and flowing. "His line was beautiful," Frank Thomas and Ollie Johnston noted; "it almost had a quality of shading." Third, he succeeded in funneling a powerful sense of emotion into his drawings. He did not believe in a long process of correcting but threw himself wholeheartedly into the initial creative effort. He felt — and in his case it was true — that a first drawing better captured the excitement, the spontaneity, the feeling that were so central to bringing life to animated characters. Finally, Moore instinctively heightened the innocent appeal of his characters by having them repeatedly look upward to make them appear "more wistful, more hopeful, more vulnerable," or by having Mickey's cheeks move along with his mouth as he spoke to enhance the sincerity of his words.[49]

Moore's various techniques eventually converged to form what Disney had called for in his 1935 memo: "personality animation." More than anyone else at the studio, Moore proved adept at capturing the poses, the expressions, the look in the eyes, the language of the body that conveyed the unique essence of a character. He was able to feel his way intuitively into the interior of his animated creations and draw them from the inside out. "We should always let [the audience] see the characters think," he often told his fellow artists, and he followed his own advice with unparalleled success.[50]

On a few occasions, Moore overcame his verbal awkwardness and tried to articulate some of the secrets of his God-given talent. For example, after playfully pondering his own mistakes over the years, he decided at one point that most errors were the result of forgetting a few basic principles. He made a list of pointers and hung it over his desk to remind him "never to make that mistake again." He shared these crucial "14 Points of Animation" with his colleagues:

> 1. Appeal in drawing 2. Staging 3. Most interesting way? (Would anyone other than your mother like to see it?) 4. Most entertaining way? 5. Are you in character? 6. Are you advancing the character? 7. Is this the simplest statement of the main idea of the scene? 8. Is the story point clear? 9. Are the secondary actions working with the main action? 10. Is the presentation best for the medium? 11. Does it have two-dimensional clarity? 12. Does it have three-dimensional solidity? 13. Does it have four-dimensional drawing? (Drag and follow through) 14. Are you trying to do something that shouldn't be attempted? (Like trying to show the top of Mickey's head).[51]

Sometime in the late 1930s, Moore also presented a talk to the staff, complete with illustrations, that detailed his handling of the studio's main character. Entitled "Analysis of Mickey Mouse," this lecture offered a thumbnail sketch of his approach to animation. Appropriately enough, he opened by describing Mickey's personality. The animator, he asserted, must convey the qualities of an "average young boy . . . living in a small town, clean-living, fun-loving, bashful around girls, polite and as clever as he must be for the particular story." Flexibility is required, however, for in some pictures Mickey "has a touch of Fred Astaire, in others of Charlie Chaplin, and some of Douglas Fairbanks." But in drawing Mickey, the animator should remember that his "positions of body while walking, running, talking, etc. should contain the young boy feeling."[52]

Beginning in the early 1940s, the fabulous careers of Norman Ferguson and Fred Moore began to wane. Both continued at the Disney Studio for several more years, but increasingly they were hindered by professional and personal problems. Ferguson's decline may have begun with a subtle friction with Disney that developed during the mid-1940s, which came to a head over the film *Saludos Amigos*. According to Jack Kinney, Disney began putting intense pressure on Ferguson to finish the film, and apparently the animation director snapped back one day, "Maybe if you'd let us alone, we could get the damn thing out!" Disney did not take kindly to such challenges to his authority. In addition, Ferguson seems to have been left behind by advancing techniques in the field. In Ward Kimball's opinion, this innovative animator had always "understood movement . . . [but] when we gradually moved into more disciplined styles of drawing, Ferguson was kind of left by the wayside because he was not a trained artist." Finally, he was victimized by health problems. He not only suffered from diabetes, a condition that grew worse over the years, but fell into drinking excessively. The quality of his work began to slip, he was absent more frequently, and the Disney Studio let him go in the early 1950s. A few years later, apparently brokenhearted over his severance, Ferguson died of a heart attack.[53]

Moore's demise, in contrast, seemed linked to one major cause: alcohol. His fun-loving, partying personality had always led him to do a fair amount of drinking, but by the 1940s a problem was evident, and soon it became severe. He began to slip in and out of the studio for drinking bouts — with typical flair, he found ingenious routes for escape, sneaking through the studio commissary and sliding down the laundry chute — while younger artists such as Kimball and Johnston tried to cover up his sloppiness by correcting his exposure sheets. But as his friends noticed, his drinking was at least partly related to the growing obsolescence of his drawing. By the 1940s a new generation of animators had been trained at the Disney Studio, and he was finding it difficult to keep up with their new techniques and strategies. Having always relied on a wealth of natural talent, he never really studied his craft, tried to refine his style, or improved on its subtleties and nuances. Thus his work increasingly began to look dated. In a way, Moore had become a prisoner of his own temperament. Having peaked early — Marc Davis once exclaimed, "My God, Fred Moore *was* Disney drawing! — he lacked the self-discipline to keep improving. As he once told Ollie Johnston, "I have reached everything I want, and I'm only twenty-four. Now what do I do?" Ward Kimball put his finger on the problem: "Fred was the man of the hour and couldn't handle it [when he no longer was] . . . He just expected to be the man of the hour forever." The troubled artist, released by the studio in the early 1950s, died a short time later when he fell and hit his head on a car in an alcohol-induced fog. He was forty-two years old.[54]

Despite the sad ends of their careers, Ferguson and Moore made crucial contributions to Disney's films. Ferguson's acting animation stamped the Disney style with vitality and vigor for several generations, while Moore's personality animation provided much of its enduring appeal. Moore also remained an inspiration on a more personal level. In the 1980s, Disney animator Glen Keane admitted that he so admired his predecessor's work that he would go to the studio morgue, fish out drawings that were four or five decades old, and actually trace over them to try and capture some of their feeling. "And so now," he explained, "I feel that Freddy Moore's hand was helping me to draw."[55]

III. *"I Don't Know Anything about Art"*

By the late 1930s, the clamor over the "art" of Walt Disney finally forced Disney to respond. In a sprinkling of stories, the popular studio head began to let his own thoughts on the aesthetic merits of his popular movies be known. He usually simply said, "Don't ask me anything about art. I don't know anything about it." But on occasion — particularly in two long pieces in the *New York Times Magazine* — he offered some lengthy ruminations. His remarks — homespun, shrewd, ambiguous — were vintage Disney.[56]

The most striking feature of those remarks, predictably, was his elaborate protest against being labeled an artist. Ruefully admitting that he couldn't draw very well, Disney also claimed that he knew very little about great artists or the history of painting. He explained, with typical self-effacement, that "we are not artists but only moving picture producers trying to offer entertainment . . . [and] if the public likes what we turn out we just hold up our thumbs and consider ourselves lucky." His great aim was simply to amuse audiences. If certain people wanted to call his work art and hang it in museums, that would be a great honor, but "it won't change our policies any. We'll still go on in our old blundering way."[57]

Yet Disney followed such denials with a rhetorical question that cleverly twisted things in a different direction. As he asked S. J. Woolf, one of the *New York Times Magazine* reporters, "How can anyone say what art is?" He offered a similar query to Frank Nugent, the other interviewer: "Art? You birds write about it, maybe you can tell me." Someone who paints strange and incoherent shapes on canvas or hews a monstrosity out of a block of marble is deemed an artist, he noted, while someone who makes a graceful, beautiful piece of furniture is considered a mere cabinetmaker. The only reasonable conclusion, as he phrased it, was that "what is art for the goose is not art for the gander." This position, of course, allowed him to undercut his earlier protest: if no one knows what art is, how can it really be denied that Disney animation measures up?[58]

He then suggested his own modest definition of art, one that kept his studio's animation clearly in the background: "For me there must be something more in a picture than the literal rendering of an object . . . A man must have something to say, he must see things in a new and individual way. He must be stirred by the play of light on flesh or by the glow of the sun on trees and he must be able to put some of the emotion he feels onto his canvas. If he succeeds in doing this, then he is an artist." Disney implied that his studio's work met this standard, and for support he turned to the Old Masters. Many great painters would have appreciated his animation, he suggested, because they "had a sense of humor and a gift for caricature." Leonardo, Van Gogh, and Delacroix, for example, with their varied concerns about experimental forms, light, and music, would have fit right in at the Disney Studio.[59]

Disney's commentary suggested that at some level, he *did* take his work seriously as art. In one of the interviews, for example, he compared animation favorably to painting, arguing that the latter medium was handicapped by its reliance on drawing. Animation, by contrast, added sound, movement, and "the assistance of a thousand and one technical tricks." In another interview, he pointedly described the caricature in his films as "the art of revealing the essence of an object or personality through exaggeration and emphasis." He also stressed the recent vintage of animation, arguing that in this young, immature medium "we are still feeling our way, learning through trial and error, but growing consistently." Animation might seem to be mere illustration, but "that doesn't mean we'll always be stuck with slapstick. We'll get something beautiful into it if we can, and I think we can." Disney clearly planted the idea that if his animated films fell short of artistic excellence, they were steadily approaching that goal.[60]

The *New York Times Magazine* clearly supported Disney's ambition. It quoted the favorable comments of the curator of the Metropolitan Museum of Art, who observed that a Disney print hanging in one of its galleries was "something that is incontestably art." Nugent also explained that while Disney's craftsmen seemed indifferent to the tradition of formal art, they had studied the work of Degas, Cézanne, Renoir, and Seurat and "feel they are creating a new art form." The Disney Studio, he pointed out, differed little from the workshops of great artists such as Rubens, Rembrandt, and Cranach, where the masters merely added details to work done mostly by their journeymen artists and then signed their name to it. This journalist concluded confidently of Disney's animation, "Next month, next year, or next century some authority may exhume it and read into it part of the art history of our time."[61]

Ultimately, Walt Disney emerged from the agitated debates over his films in the 1930s in a powerful position. More than anything else, he succeeded in establishing himself as an aesthetic mediator in American popular culture. Respectful of artistic tradition yet open to modernist experimentation, anxious to uplift and eager to amuse, and armed with a flexible definition of art and a self-effacing modesty, he stood amid a number of contrary forces and created a special brand of animation. It offered an aesthetic hybrid of sentimental modernism, blending art and profit, aesthetics and entertainment, and popular audiences ate it up. Its mediating qualities helped to define the essence of Disney's appeal in the 1930s, and they also served him well over the next several decades.

8

Disney and American Culture

DESPITE HIS halfhearted protestations of artlessness, Walt Disney emerged as a major figure in American culture during the 1930s. Audiences flocked to his lively and popular short films early in the decade and then to the pathbreaking feature-length movies. Disney's films and their "stars" were breathlessly followed in fan magazines and Hollywood gossip columns, while his career and the activities of his studio were charted in popular publications such as *Time* and *Ladies' Home Journal*. Highbrow journals of opinion like the *New Republic* and *Art Digest* debated the political implications and artistic merits of his work. And the economic impact of his enterprise was undeniable, as waves of Disney merchandise flooded the American landscape.

Throughout this period, Disney himself began to assume a multifaceted persona, while the image of his products, which combined mischievous fantasy, childlike innocence, emotional warmth, and human resilience, became the focal point of skillful promotional campaigns that sought to tie it to dreams of material abundance. Both the man and his enterprise emerged as reassuring symbols of the American way of life.

I. Consuming the Disney Image

In the decade after Mickey Mouse's first big splash, Walt Disney appeared before the public eye as much more than an engaging filmmaker. Through a variety of means — articles that painted glowing pictures of the man and his work, press releases and marketing strategies from the studio itself, serious debates on the impact and meaning of his films — a larger-than-life image grew in both size and complexity.

During these years, one of the most persistent versions depicted Disney as "the independent artist." By the time of *Three Little Pigs*, journalists were routinely describing him as an artistic soul who sought not only public approval but "to satisfy himself and his own ideals as earnestly as any poet in a garret." Comparisons to Charlie Chaplin popped up repeatedly. Filmmaker and critic Pare Lorenz, writing in *McCall's*, painted a typical portrait of Disney's single-minded integrity. The filmmaker, he wrote, "lives, eats, and sleeps his work, and there is no board of directors to tell him how to make pictures, nor what the public wants, nor what stars to use. He is completely divorced from Hollywood in fact as well as fancy . . . There is not a writer, a director, a musician, not an actor making movies in the country today who can claim half that independence."[1]

Nor was Disney averse to polishing this reputation. In an interview in the late 1930s, he noted that with a little pushing his studio could turn out feature films more rapidly. "But what's the use?" he concluded. "The quality might suffer and it wouldn't be worth it."[2]

On December 27, 1937, *Time* put Disney on its cover and ran a lengthy article entitled "Mouse and Man." While the story dealt with a number of themes, it mainly concerned Disney as an artist. In particular, it used Rembrandt and his studio as a metaphor to explain the nature of Disney and his work. Like Rembrandt, Disney sought "guaranteed independence" for his endeavors and was interested in profit largely because it allowed him "to buy better materials to make better pictures." This conception revealed Disney to be "an artist, simple of purpose, utterly unself-conscious, superlatively good at and satisfied in his work, a thoroughgoing professional, just gagging it up and letting the professors tell him what he's done."[3]

Another dimension of the Disney image pictured him as a "visionary genius." This figure was a man whose creative brilliance touched all who knew him, inspiring his staff to realize his artistic dreams while entrancing audiences with flights of imagination. He appeared as a fountain of free-flowing ideas, not only envisioning plots and personalities and humor but anticipating far-reaching trends in motion pictures like sound and color. Disney himself, in a 1941 interview with *The New Yorker*, described his role as that of "pollen man." According to the reporter, the studio chief dashed around like a bee carrying pollen, saying, "I've got to know whether an idea goes here,' dumping some pollen into the chair, 'or here,' hurrying to our side of the room and dumping the rest of the pollen on our knees." Such creative capacity and exuberance led to paeans like one in the New York *Herald Tribune:* "In a community ridden by phony pretentiousness, [Disney] is the one person working out here who can with any justification be referred to as a genius."[4]

An even broader interpretation sought to elevate Disney above movie entertainment entirely. Many observers insisted that Mickey Mouse and the Silly Symphonies displayed not just humor or art but a kind of modern mythology dispensed by a profound fabulist. Although occasionally compared to Hans Christian Andersen or Homer, Disney most often was called the modern Aesop. In 1937, for example, both *Cosmopolitan* and education professor Karl W. Bigelow of Columbia University described him as "the Aesop of the twentieth century." In this incarnation, he strode forward as a mythical storyteller for the modern age.[5]

A pronounced moral imagery also began to surround Disney. While few popular entertainers from Hollywood managed to secure a reputation for public virtue, the creator of Mickey Mouse certainly did. He gradually acquired an image as "Saint Francis of the Silver Screen," in the phrase of one mid-1930s article. Disney as moralist combined the roles of the educator, the child psychologist, and even the theologian. Experts on child-raising and psychology publicly lauded his films for their healthy impact on young viewers, while newspapers praised him for refusing to license his characters to advertise liquor or tobacco. Essayists in journals such as the *Christian Century* suggested that *Snow White* drew on the tales of the Bible — the young girl and her animal friends lived in Eden; the witch and her apple were another version of the serpent in the Garden; the queen and her mirror symbolized the sin of selfishness; the death and revival of Snow White were the triumph of love — and thus upheld moral values by "the retelling of truth as basic as sin and salvation." Overall, as one commentator put it, Disney was an

> educator of the soul. He brings the soul of man nearer to the soul of the whole universe. For his world of birds and flowers and funny little bunnies is no unrelated fiction. The loving eye of the artist has noted the intricacies of life, the dip of the wing, the frisk of the tail, the droop or flourish of a petal. We are brought close to glowing nature and see that it is a thing of beauty . . . He does all that St. Francis set out to do: to worship God in all His happy, glowing, stumbling creatures.

No mere maker of amusing films, this Walt Disney was a major purveyor of moral values.[6]

Perhaps the most influential Disney image from this era, however, by dint of the fact that it influenced all the others, was that of the populist hero.

Among the hundreds of essays and newspaper articles appearing after 1928, most contained significant mention of Disney's humility, simple taste, and hardworking temperament. Figures such as Dale Carnegie emphasized that diligent parents had instilled in young Walt strong values of industriousness and integrity during a rural childhood often marked by poverty. Disney's lack of formal education, his simple tastes in food, his "ready-made suits and shirts" and "medium-priced domestic car," and his disdain for Hollywood luxury elicited praise. The filmmaker's views on money became almost legendary. A rash of articles made clear that he valued profit only insofar as it made more creativity possible. In a nationally syndicated 1931 article entitled "Movieland's Most Popular Star," Dan Thomas summarized this image: "He is unassuming and modest . . . qualities seldom found among the successful or even near-successful in Hollywood, where success and fame seem to be all that count. During working hours it would be difficult to pick out Disney from the rest of his staff unless you knew him by sight. At the studio he's just one of the boys, never giving anyone the impression they are working for him — it's always 'with him.'"[7]

Here was a hardworking, unassuming, generous, and grateful man of the people with a special affinity for the ordinary Americans from whom he had sprung. As syndicated columnist Ernie Pyle phrased it in 1938, Disney was just "plain people, despite fame and fortune." Success had rewarded but not spoiled him.[8]

Disney's growing personal myth gained substantial reinforcement from another quarter — a shrewd, persistent selling of the image to the American public, which began to gear up with the first success of Mickey Mouse. As would be true throughout the studio's long history, fantasy never drifted far from materialism. The 1930s witnessed the development of an enormous merchandising and marketing program that presented an array of commercial products with the Disney stamp. This was the first campaign in a long-term invasion of the consumer market. In related fashion, journalistic coverage of Disney's business activities helped imprint his image as an impresario of consumption.

One of the best examples was the early Mickey Mouse Clubs. The famous televised *Mickey Mouse Club* of the 1950s has become a part of modern American folklore, of course, but few realize that the first version of the club appeared two decades earlier. In 1930, Harry Woodin, a Los Angeles theater owner, founded a club based on the popular Disney character. It proved so successful at luring youthful patrons to his moviehouse that Disney envisioned the possibilities of a national network of such organizations. Woodin joined the Disney Studio as the manager of the campaign, and within several months hundreds of Mickey Mouse Clubs had sprung up all over the United States. Devoted to attracting young moviegoers with discounted ticket prices and special activities, the clubs met at local theaters and were often subsidized by local newspapers and businesses.[9]

The Disney organization nurtured the local outlets in several ways. It offered the Mickey Mouse Idea, a traveling show that featured comedy, music, dancing, and clothing and other merchandise. It forwarded advertising packets plugging "the magnetic pulling power of the world-famous Mickey Mouse Clubs" and breathlessly promising "ACCESSORIES! TIE-UPS! A CAMPAIGN BOOK!" It also managed the national network in part through the publication of the *Official Bulletin of the Mickey Mouse Club,* a missive that appeared regularly from the Hyperion studio. In a number from October 1931, for example, Walt wrote an enthusiastic message describing members as part of "a gigantic family." This edition also contained news from a number of local clubs and described plans for a national convention. It ran ads for Mickey Mouse pencil boxes and listed a variety of elaborate plans for celebrating Mickey's third birthday party — club picnics, festivities involving local dignitaries and merchants, shows featuring club members, parties for those at local orphanages, and many others.[10]

This Disney campaign became such a popular phenomenon that national magazines eventually took notice. "Mickey Mouse Clubs have been formed in about five hundred American cities and some 500,000 boys and girls belong to them," announced *McCall's* in August 1932. "Buttons are sent to the members and there is an official yell." A 1932 piece in the *Motion Picture Herald* put the numbers even higher, reporting the existence of seven hundred clubs with a membership "on the way to the million mark." Other articles described how club members attended Disney showings at moviehouses where "a Chief Mickey Mouse and a Chief Minnie Mouse" led them in reciting "an official greeting, a theme song, and a creed." At the local level, clubs like the one in Milwaukee advertised twin goals in the newspaper — first, educational programs featuring "life in other lands, the wonders of industry, of research and of nature," and second, "entertainment . . . that will help your individual progress, [and] some that will be just plain enjoyment." Most local clubs also moved along under the impetus of corporate sponsorship, like the Wharton, Texas, unit, which acknowledged support from the local newspaper as well as "Scott Drug Co., John Roten Co., R. B. System, Coca-Cola Bottling Co., F. I. Moore, Dr. William J. Quirke, Joe Schwartz and the People's Cotton Oil Company."[11]

The growth of the Disney enterprise also gained support from a series of clever merchandising moves. Back in the 1920s, Disney had been introduced to commercial promotion by Universal Pictures, which had pushed Oswald the Lucky Rabbit by licensing a candy bar and a child's stencil set bearing his likeness. In the late 1920s and early 1930s, with the birth of Mickey Mouse, the Disney Studio began to bombard theater owners with suggestions for commercial "tie-ups." Working through the press sheets of its film distributor, Columbia Pictures, it suggested a host of arrangements — Mickey Mouse sweatshirts to be carried by local sporting goods stores, monogrammed rain slickers for high school and college students, window displays for local cheese merchants to play up the rodent angle. Disney also began to license his animated star to companies for commercial use. Dozens of manufacturers adopted the mouse to promote their goods, and Disney proudly acknowledged that Mickey Mouse, within three years of his first appearance, was represented on "jewelry, earthenware, dolls, soap, and candy . . . linen, children's frocks, and toys of all descriptions." Gilbert Seldes noted that at a national trade fair, "forty percent of all the novelties offered were inspired by Mickey Mouse."[12]

That was only the beginning. By the mid-1930s, a skyrocketing merchandising operation saw Mickey Mouse and other Disney characters licensed to seventy-five manufacturers in the United States, forty-five in England, twenty in Canada, six in France, and six in Spain and Portugal. According to the business journal *Buying and Selling,* merchandise bearing Disney likenesses sold in the amount of $20 million from mid-1933 to mid-1934, with the Disney company receiving commissions ranging from 2.5 percent to 10 percent. Clients included some of the giants of American industry — RCA Victor, General Foods, International Silver Company, National Dairy Products, Hickok Manufacturing, and Emerson Radio Corporation. By 1937, more than four hundred items bearing the Disney trademark had burst onto the American market, and ten years later the figures were simply stunning. By the mid-1940s, the Disney name was selling about $100 million worth of goods per year, with a profit to the studio of between $500,000 and $800,000. As one observer summed up, with only slight hyperbole, "No doubt about it, Mickey Mouse is the greatest thing in the history of merchandising."[13]

Two tales of corporate salvation demonstrated the power of the Disney appeal. In the mid-1930s, the Ingersoll-Waterbury Company, in severe financial straits, secured a license from Disney to produce a Mickey Mouse watch. Little did the company expect that this inexpensive timepiece would sweep the country, secure its maker's economic future, and become one of the great commercial fads of the 1930s. Around the same time, the Lionel Corporation, also hovering on the brink of bankruptcy, contracted with Disney to make an electric-train toy — a handcar with Mickey and Minnie pumping the handle. Sales promptly went through the roof, and the company's fortunes revived. No matter how spectacular such events were, however, the relentless march of legions of Mickey Mouse products proved even more impressive. In 1935, one look at Disney's commercial activity produced this lengthy, somewhat disquieting description:

Undeniably, and appallingly, it is Mickey Mouse's day. Shoppers carry Mickey Mouse satchels and briefcases bursting with Mickey Mouse soap, candy, playing-cards, bridge favors, hairbrushes, china-ware, alarm clocks and hot-water bottles, wrapped in Mickey Mouse paper, tied with Mickey Mouse ribbon and paid for out of Mickey Mouse purses with savings hoarded in Mickey Mouse banks.

At the lunch counter — Mickey Mouse table covers and napkins — they consume Mickey Mouse biscuits and dairy products while listening to Mickey Mouse music from Mickey Mouse phonographs and radios . . .

And the children live in a Mickey Mouse world. They wear Mickey Mouse caps, waists, socks, shoes, slippers, garters, mittens, aprons, bibs, and underthings . . . They play with Mickey Mouse velocipedes, footballs, baseballs, bats, catching gloves . . . paint sets, sewing sets, stamping sets . . . masks, blackboards, and balloons.

Until day is done, when they sup from Mickey Mouse cups, porringers, and baby plates and lie down to sleep in Mickey Mouse pajamas between Mickey Mouse crib sheets, to waken in the morning smiling at Mickey Mouse pictures on the nursery walls. In time, no doubt, there will be Mickey Mouse wallpaper for them.[14]

Probably the key move in this blitz of the market came in 1932, when Herman "Kay" Kamen reached an agreement with the studio to become director of Walt Disney Enterprises and, as one analyst put it, "Mickey Mouse's commercial godfather." This merchandising dynamo, head of the Kamen-Blair Company, had dazzled American business for a decade with his innovative department store promotions and advertising. A man of great charm, energy, and shrewdness, he stormed into action, and within a short time he had centralized the advertising, promotion, and packaging of Disney products in his New York office, opened a number of international branch offices, and reached agreement with several large manufacturing companies. He also negotiated into every licensing contract the stipulation that goods must be approved for quality by Disney before going on the market. For nearly two decades, until his accidental death in 1949, Kamen and his dynamic organization played a key role in making Disney products a staple of American consumer consciousness.[15]

In turn, however, Kamen's success wrought a subtle but significant change in Disney production. By the late 1930s, merchandising had become an intrinsic part of the moviemaking process. *Snow White* was the first film to have a complete merchandising campaign in place by the day the film opened. The release of *Pinocchio* followed the same strategy, with a nation-wide marketing campaign for movie-related goods splashed over newspapers and magazines throughout the United States. Stix, Baer, and Fuller, the huge department store in St. Louis, for instance, ran large newspaper ads for Jiminy Cricket and Pinocchio dolls and Pinocchio party favors, coin banks, ties, playing cards, soap, and games. In an Oregon newspaper, Stein's Snow White Bread Company advertised a Pinocchio circus game for anyone who filled out an application card with their local grocer, and in Virginia, the Richmond Dairy Company began to sell its cottage cheese in a series of ten-ounce Pinocchio glasses that featured different characters from the movie. A trade journal, *The Boy's Outfitter,* advertised a whole line of boys' clothes and furnishings based on "Walt Disney's *Pinocchio,*" which it proclaimed loudly as "THE MAGIC SIGN OF SALES AND PROFITS IN BOYS' WEAR!" In Washington, D.C., the Gillette Company promised free masks of Pinocchio characters with the purchase of Gillette blue blades, with the assurance that "Dad will enjoy smooth, clean, painless shaves with these keen double-edged blades. The children will have lots of fun with the masks."[16]

By the mid-1930s, Disney's economic activities became subject to increasing public attention. Yet another image — the entertainer as entrepreneur — was to become a key part of the Disney legacy. With titles such as "Mickey Mouse Goes into Business," "Mickey Mouse and the Bankers," and "Mickey Mouse, Salesman," articles uniformly praised the business acumen of the Disney operation in terms of salesmanship, clever merchandising, and market maneuvering. L. H. Robbins's "Mickey Mouse Emerges as an Economist," published in the *New York Times Magazine,* for instance, concluded that the Disney enterprise resembled a perpetual motion machine, because "the better the art of the Disney studio, the better the by-products sell, and the better they sell, the better the art again. It is something novel in business cycles; it never gets worse." As Robbins concluded, "The fresh cheering is for Mickey the Big Business Man, the world's super-salesman."[17]

The highly publicized success of the Disney merchandising effort testified to the fact that even during the Depression, the consumer market was becoming an ever more powerful influence in American life. From Mickey Mouse watches to Snow White birthday dresses, from Donald Duck Easter-egg dyeing kits to Three Little Pigs alarm clocks, Disney goods promised sales to merchants and happiness to consumers. No one understood this better than Earnest Elmo Calkins, a noted advertising expert. "I offer Mickey Mouse as a symbol of the unrealized power of advertising," he insisted in *Advertising and Selling.* The Disney "publicity machine," he contended, was marking a new stage in American business development.

> The usual course of events has been reversed. Ordinarily a manufacturer gives his product a name and mark and proceeds to make them known by advertising, but in these instances the trade mark is made known first, and then applied to the goods. The publicity that is swelling Walt Disney's

income cost him nothing. It was a free gift from the newspapers. But it has a tangible dollars and cents value far beyond its original aim and purpose . . . It suggests the spirit at least which should be put into all advertising to arouse the buying public and sell it things, the appeal to the imagination.[18]

The various images accruing to Walt Disney in this period — the independent and visionary artist, the humble populist hero, the modern fabulist and moralist, the successful entrepreneur of imagination — involved not just amusement but a whole constellation of social values, moral judgments, and economic imperatives. But the real heart of the Disney phenomenon — Walt's personal values and character traits — was seldom glimpsed by the public.

II. The Man Behind the Mouse

Walt Disney was no simple man. Even when he was a youthful, energetic animation producer in Hollywood, his personality had an elusive quality that could appear unsettling, especially to those who knew him well. Jack Kinney, for instance, a longtime animator and director at the studio, noted that "Walt went to great lengths to portray himself as a shy person, 'Uncle Walt,' a kindly, self-effacing farmboy from the Midwest," but at the same time he "could swear like a trooper and he had a terrific ego." Other friends sensed a tension in Disney between an instinctive emotional warmth and a cold calculation of self-interest. Seldom reacting with indifference, most acquaintances either loved and respected or resented and distrusted him, and many sustained all of these emotions at once. Thus the authentic Disney remained hard to corner. Yet some insights come from following the trail of his ambition, which was so powerful that it drove him to the verge of emotional and physical collapse.[19]

In 1931, as few people have realized, Walt Disney suffered what was commonly called a nervous breakdown. "I went all to pieces . . . I cracked up. I got very irritable," he told an interviewer over two decades later. "I got to a point that I couldn't talk on the telephone. I'd begin to cry and the least little thing, I'd just go that way . . . It used to be hard to sleep." Doctors recommended a regimen of exercise and relaxation, and Disney's condition subsequently improved. He became something of a health addict, engaging in sports such as boxing, golf, and horseback riding and advocating esoteric techniques like taking a morning glass of sauerkraut juice. In 1935 he suffered a recurrence of debilitating nerves, and at his brother Roy's suggestion he left the country with his family for a three-month vacation in Europe.[20]

Disney knew the true nature of his problem. As he admitted to Ernie Pyle as early as 1938, he had suffered "a couple of breakdowns from overwork." He was a driven man, and his relentless push for success had gradually overwhelmed his emotional constitution. He tried to relax and even took to preaching the dangers of overwork, but long hours of obsessive labor — he later described a steady regimen of "worry" and a routine of "pound, pound, pound" — formed the substance of his life in the 1930s. Work was at once his greatest strength and his greatest weakness. More than anything else, the nervous collapses served as an indication of his youthful personality: hard-driving, spinning with creativity, demanding, burdened with stress.[21]

Nothing showed this more clearly than an episode at the very outset of Disney's Hollywood career. In 1928 and 1929 he spent many weeks in New York, dealing with a succession of crises — the loss of Oswald the Rabbit, an attempt to secure an audio system, and the search for a distribution deal for the Mickey Mouse films. In this stressful context, he wrote a long series of letters to Roy, to Ub Iwerks, and to Lillian. This fascinating cache of missives, typed in the evenings on stationery from the Algonquin Hotel, fully displays Disney's farsightedness. Full of spelling errors, theatrical capital letters, bad grammar, and emotion, they nonetheless offer a clear view of the Disney enterprise's future. Sound movies, Disney wrote, were the wave of the future, and he planned to secure and install audio equipment in the Hyperion facility. Assuring Roy and Ub that "I am not pipe dreaming" but only looking to the future, he urged them to concentrate on coming up with "a few original ideas for our sound pictures." Perceiving that the time was right for sound cartoons, he overflowed with enthusiasm and creative ideas for new films.

> We could have a donkey sing a goofy Italian Opera. Have him sing it in a funny manner that could be more like a bunch of crazy sounds in time to the music. Also we could get some good stuff with a crazy jazz band playing a lot of crazy pieces . . . Pull the gag with the saxophone player pulling the chain and letting the spit out of the instrument into a bucket. A male quartet singing old time songs. Have them really sing. This would be a cinch to synchronize . . . We might broadcast a goofy burlesque prizefight for a finish. Have the gong, crowd cheering, the fighters getting socked and use a parrot for the announcer. I think this has possibilities.

As Disney exclaimed in a letter of February 1929, "Now is our chance to get a hold on the industry. So let's take advantage of the situation!"[22]

But Disney's prescient views on the future of films and entertainment receded before his awareness of a more immediate problem: the present situation as a struggle for survival. In highly emotional language, he pictured himself as operating in a hostile environment and engaged in a life-and-death contest with venality and incompetence. While this travail threatened to drive him to despair, ultimately it made him determined to succeed. On March 7, 1928, he reported that he was still "hanging around this Hell Hole waiting for something to happen . . . BUT I WILL FIGHT IT OUT ON

THIS LINE IF IT TAKES ALL SUMMER . . . It sure looks like a fight to the finish." A few months later, another letter acknowledged the fear of making a false step while he was "trying to see every side of the angles presented." Maneuvering among the motion picture studios, movie distributors, bankers, and sound technicians brought him little joy. Assessments like this one were far more frequent: "This DAMN TOWN is enough to give anybody the HEEBIE-JEEBIES!"[23]

Disney's tone typified his personality. The letters practically pulsated with energy as their author insisted, often with a vehemence that bordered on ferocity, on any and all means to enhance production from his studio. He implored Roy to gather any spare cash, to sell Walt's car, and to "slap a mortgage on everything we've got" to raise funds. The future depended on making the inaugural Mickey Mouse cartoons a success, and Walt begged his colleagues to use every ounce of energy in turning them out. As he wrote frantically to Ub on October 6, 1928, "Don't tell me it can't be done. It has got to be done. If you ever worked like HELL before in your life, do it now . . . So quit acting nervous and fidgety . . . Get that DAMN picture back here on time . . . If you fail it is going to put us in a hole. DON'T FAIL. It is not a matter of life and death. But DAMN near it."[24]

In typical fashion, however, Disney directed these frantic demands for speed, action, and production inward as well as outward. His letters radiated the self-imposed stress of the situation. Feeling the pressure to complete his films at this propitious moment, he succumbed to continuous nervous excitement. His agitated state of mind seeped out everywhere; "I am very nervous and upset," he confessed at one point, explaining that he was not sleeping well, had lost his appetite, and had dropped about ten pounds. While mounting frustrations brought despair, he also feared his opposite tendency to soar into exhilaration over a promising development, saying that "I have to keep myself down to earth for fear I may not accomplish as much if I let it get the best of me." The strain often seemed overwhelming, causing him to burst out, "I am anxious as hell to get everything going. I am homesick as HELL and don't want to stay in this damn town a minute longer than necessary." This atmosphere of intense pressure, which Disney partly created himself, was but a short step from his nervous collapse a few years later.[25]

Those who worked with Walt knew him best, and that was no accident. Even early in his career, he was so committed to the production of animated films that he appeared a confirmed workaholic. From a distance, family members such as his sister-in-law Edna Disney commented that they had "never seen anyone so interested in his work. He just sort of lived it." At the studio, that impression was even more striking. One of Walt's executive producers described how he never escaped the studio: "He never had his work off his mind, he never had time set aside for play. He was always preoccupied with the studio . . . There was no such thing as 'out of hours' with Walt." His work literally was his life. When he received a ticket for speeding, the incident became the basis for the short film *Traffic Troubles* (1931), and an overnight camping trip with the Bohemian Club became the inspiration for the comical snoring scene in *Snow White*. Disney regularly dropped in at the studio on Saturday and Sunday. His habit of snooping around in the offices of animators and story men, checking the storyboards for ideas and sketches, became legendary and prompted a long-standing joke: "Oh, no! Walt's going in for another remnant sale!"[26]

Disney's preoccupation with work, however, was no grim and ennervating obsession. He brought an intense enthusiasm and vision to his labors, and usually managed to infect his artists with those same qualities. His three-hour solo performance of the *Snow White* story on the Hyperion studio soundstage, done to inspire his assembled staff at the outset of this project, became legendary. Frank Thomas, awestruck by Disney's fervent emotional involvement in his early films, actually became convinced that Walt had "dreamed them when he was a boy . . . the characters were alive to him . . . And it wasn't just a matter of thinking about it, it was deep inside his imagination, these things were alive and real." Always excited about the start of a new project, Disney would corner anyone, anywhere, anytime, to describe the progress of things. Famous stories made the rounds, usually told with a shake of the head, of Walt blocking the doorway of a restaurant, enthusiastically telling a staff member his newest idea for a film, complete with animated gestures and leaping eyebrows, oblivious to all of the patrons staring, or Walt seeing a friend at a museum and excitedly acting out the plot of his latest movie. As Jack Kinney, a shrewd decoder of Disney's personality, once summed up, Walt was "a dreamer, but one who pursued his goals with clarity and an almost ferocious intensity."[27]

One quality perhaps more than any other proved effective in bringing those dreams to reality. To those who knew him best in the 1930s, Disney's salesmanship appeared to be one of his most striking characteristics. According to all observers, he could be a man of infectious charm and conviction, and he possessed an uncanny ability to communicate his beliefs and needs to others. Whether it was greeting studio visitors, selling the potential of his latest project to a group of bankers, or shaping the story and visuals of a film with his artists, Disney was usually irresistible and captivating. In particular, he employed two favorite techniques. Although he had a clear and potent idea of what he wanted done, he invariably used the word *we* instead of *I* in explaining some undertaking, thus disarming listeners and seeming to draw them into his confidence. According to Roy, he also practiced an eye-lock technique that tendered a psychological advantage. He "had an eye that would grab yours when he was telling you something and if you would waver and look around, he'd say, 'What's the matter, aren't you interested?'" Roy remembered. "Oh, he wouldn't let go of your eyes. He was so intent on everything he did, and that was his way of looking into you." But Walt's salesmanship was of a singular sort. He certainly had an interest in money — he told Hugh Harman in 1926 that if he had $10,000 he would quit the movie business and sell property on Sunset Strip, because "that's going to be the most valuable property in the world" — but that did not galvanize his imagination. Disney sold ideas and, even more important, himself. Ward Kimball understood this, once saying, "He was the world's best salesman because he believed in his product . . . It wasn't just a con job with him."[28]

As a workaholic and salesman, however, Disney displayed a self-confidence so complete that many came to see it as rampant egotism. Roy Disney, for example, told friends that when Disney Brothers Productions moved from its tiny storefront facility to the much larger Hyperion studio, Walt informed him that there would be a new sign: WALT DISNEY STUDIO, HOME OF MICKEY MOUSE AND SILLY SYMPHONIES. A reticent and secure man, Roy decided not to resist, and that was the end of it. In the mid-1930s, animator Ken Anderson had a similar experience. Disney stopped the young artist on the lot one day and congratulated him on his work. According to Anderson's account, "He said, 'Ken, I'm impressed by what you're doing . . . but I want you to know one thing . . . Well, there's one thing we're selling, just one, and that's the name "Walt Disney."' And he said, 'If you can buy that and be happy to work under the name Walt Disney, you're my man. But if you've got any ideas of selling "Ken Anderson," it's best for you to forget it right now.'"[29]

This powerful sense of self-promotion was interwoven with Walt's genuine, supreme confidence in his own judgment. Even in the earliest period of success, when the Mickey Mouse and Silly Symphony films were getting off the ground, he impressed his coworkers as "being absolutely sure of himself . . . he was positive about what he was going to do." Concentrating with an intensity so absolute that it shut everything else out, he made decisions about the content, pace, and style of his films with a single-mindedness that often skirted rudeness. Although he couldn't always explain it clearly, he knew what he wanted. In the words of animator Milt Kahl, "You couldn't push him around. I don't think anybody in the world could make him do anything he didn't want to do." Ward Kimball added that with any film project, "When Walt came in, it was his decision that made it good or bad. Regardless of how you thought it was." Nor did Disney brook many challenges to his judgments. In the late 1930s, sharing lunch with some of his staff at a local eatery, he needled director Wilfred Jackson about a recent short's being a "dud." Jackson, in a kidding mood, shot back that *The Golden*

Touch had been "even a worse stinker." According to another artist who was present, "Disney's response was a frozen glare at Jackson. The subject was dropped."[30]

Occasionally this powerful self-confidence would sour into surliness. Although Disney became worse in this regard in the 1940s, even as a young producer his penchant for intimidation and his ill-humor caused colleagues to exercise great caution. Jack Cutting admitted that while Disney could be charming when he wished, a preoccupation with work frequently made him "dour and indifferent toward people." Another artist complained about Disney's habit of putting people down publicly. "The worst thing about Walt was his way of bawling employees out in front of other employees. This was the thing you tried to avoid," he said. "Walt always told [an artist or story man] he was a dumb shit and didn't know his ass in front of everybody else. And this would deflate completely your pride and your ego and he knew it." But this habit of lashing out, many of the staff came to believe, masked insecurity. Feeling the pressure of success and the expectations of being labeled a genius, Disney occasionally cowed his subordinates as a way of convincing others, and himself, that he was truly master of the situation.[31]

At the opposite end of the emotional spectrum, however, Disney presented an array of genuinely endearing qualities in the 1930s. His enormous personal charm could melt the hardest heart, while his surliness barely covered a notorious sentimentality that could quickly reduce him to tears. Among themselves, Disney artists in the early days chuckled over their boss's softheartedness. They would push him to inject scarier, more powerful elements into the animated films, but he would always resist. According to one observer, he would demur with some embarrassment, saying, "'Awww . . . I don't know.' He wanted to see something funny. He wanted to be entertained." *Bambi*, probably the studio's most touching early feature movie, was among his favorites. According to Frank Thomas, Disney had tears in his eyes when he previewed some of the film's early scenes and commented, "Fellas, this is pure gold."[32]

A deep-seated informality also colored Disney's personality. A shirt-sleeves and first-name atmosphere prevailed at the Disney Studio, and it flowed from the highest level. According to everyone who worked for him, Disney was simply unconcerned with prestige, protocol, and shows of deference. Ward Kimball remembered with affection how he frequently dropped into the animators' offices to chat about a film, with not the slightest whiff of hierarchy clouding a genuine exchange of ideas. From the earliest days on Hyperion Avenue, he always insisted that even the lowliest employee call him Walt. He often ate lunch with studio artists, occasionally fraternized with them outside work hours, and enthusiastically participated in softball and volleyball games. "Walt was just one of the guys," according to Roy Williams, a story man who worked for Disney for over three decades. In fact, when Williams first applied for a job in 1929, he had a long conversation with a friendly office boy while waiting in an outer office. When it turned out that "this kid" was Walt Disney, Williams turned red with embarrassment, while the head of the studio just held some papers over his face "to keep me from seeing him smile."[33]

Of course, the informal boss could quickly give way to the moody, intense perfectionist who pored over every detail. A very quick study with a terrific memory, boundless energy, and an enormous capacity for absorbing new information, Disney could quickly become frustrated with those less gifted or less dedicated. The staff joked, with more than a tinge of resentment, that their boss stopped in the studio basement every day to don his "mood costume" for the day. "The seven faces of Walt," as they came to be known, were a familiar list of images: Simon Legree, the Bountiful Angel, Der Führer, Mr. Nice Guy, Ebenezer Scrooge, Mickey Mouse, and the Devil. Quickly grasping ideas, carrying them in new directions, and overflowing with sensitivity, intuition, and frustration, Disney "changed moods quickly" as he struggled to control the creative process. Jack Cutting, an employee since the late 1920s, probably described it most strikingly. Walt's personality, he once noted, was like "a drop of mercury rolling around on a slab of marble."[34]

An interesting gauge of this talented, volatile man appeared in his choice of heroes. The imposing General John J. Pershing first earned his veneration at the conclusion of World War I. Disney had long admired Charlie Chaplin, of course, and by the 1930s he developed a great esteem for Will Rogers and his homespun humor and midwestern mannerisms. Thomas Edison received plaudits for his acute sense of invention and experimentation and his ability to rise from humble origins. Disney's greatest hero, however, was Henry Ford, and in many ways it was a highly revealing choice.[35]

Elias Disney, like many leftists in the early twentieth century, had venerated Ford for his contributions to the common man, and his son, according to friends, followed in his footsteps. The two famous and popular figures shared many qualities. They admired each other's work for its groundbreaking influence on American life. Even more than Disney, the architect of the assembly line had transformed the landscape of modern America, by putting its people on wheels in his affordable, sturdily constructed Model T automobiles. Also like Disney, Ford had emerged from a nineteenth-century tradition of self-made success and entrepreneurship and harbored a nostalgic attitude toward the past. Both were determined to protect their independence and control over their enterprises. When they met face to face in Greenfield Village in the 1940s, Ford counseled Disney not to sell public stock in his company to avoid losing direction of its destiny. Finally, both the industrialist and the entertainer attempted to formulate a kind of humane, populist capitalism that would bring a quality product to the masses. Loners, moralists, and driven men, these two innovators had remarkably similar temperaments. Ford and Disney, according to a close friend of the latter, were the "last of the great rugged individualists. Maybe that was why they were impatient with people of lesser talent and impatient with themselves when they made mistakes."[36]

As Disney ascended in the 1930s, he demonstrated a distinct attitude toward the financial side of his work and a singular relationship with his audience, both of which crucially shaped the course of his enterprise. In both areas he expressed feelings that lay quite near to his heart.

A producerist view of money and a suspicion of big-city businessmen appeared clearly, for example, during his sojourn to New York in the late 1920s. In an anxious letter to his wife, he said, "I have certainly learned a lot about this game already. It is the damndest mixed-up affair I have ever heard of. It sure demands a shrewd and thoroughly trained mind to properly handle it. There are so many damned angles that continually come up . . . They are all a bunch of schemers and just full of tricks that would fool a greenhorn . . . I would be like a sheep amongst a pack of wolves." Other letters offered a litany of similar complaints about "crooks," "dirty work afoot," and losing out to "some leech sitting at a big mahogany desk telling us what to do." The only antidote for such poisonous chicanery, he believed, was "to lick them by the quality of our stuff," as he put it in a letter to Roy. He insisted that the honest and innovative productions of the Disney Studio — "every one of us will be earning our share and not carrying any dead timber" — would carry the day. As the field of animated sound films developed, Disney argued passionately, success would come to those who "work for quality and not quantity and quick money."[37]

Disney's disdain for bankers and the money culture became notorious among friends and acquaintances. Ben Sharpsteen, for instance, recalled that the studio's first full-fledged bookkeeper "nearly went crazy" as the enthusiastic studio head spent money like water in developing his projects. According to Sharpsteen, while Disney realized that bankers made it possible to make movies, "he never had any reverence for them." When pressed to the wall by his bankers to keep down expenses, he would snap, "I can't hire bookkeepers to draw pictures for me." Roy remembered his brother's views as less restrained. During the making of *Snow White*, he reported, Walt reacted to demands for financial restraint by angrily exclaiming that "bankers were just a bunch of goddam s.o.b.s." In the early 1940s, the Disney brothers had a meeting with Joe Rosenberg, their contact with the Bank of America, who was appealing for a cutback in production expenses. According to Roy, Walt finally burst out, "I'm disappointed in you, Joe. I thought you were a different kind of banker. But you turned out to be a regular goddamn banker. You'll loan a guy an umbrella on a sunshiny day, but when it rains you want it back." Roy's favorite story, however, came from the early 1930s. With the Depression causing enormous problems, Roy worried constantly about getting money, paying back loans, and meeting payrolls. But Walt offered little sympathy. "Quit worrying," he told Roy. "People aren't going to stop living just because the banks are closed. What the hell, we'll use anything — make potatoes the medium of exchange, we'll pay everybody in potatoes." With his imagination engaged elsewhere, Walt could never regard banks and finances as anything more than a necessary evil.[38]

Years later, Disney looked back over his early career and stated simply, "I've always been bored with making money. I've wanted to do things, I wanted to build things . . . What money meant to me was to do that, you see?" Clearly, in many ways he conformed to the model of the nineteenth-century entrepreneur for whom profit was but one part of a larger calculus of success, along with equally important factors such as personal achievement, moral progress, producerism, and character development.[39]

Equally striking was his empathy for his audience, those ordinary Americans who packed theaters all over the country in the 1930s to cheer his films. In a way, the situation was rather ironic. Few people claimed to know Disney really well — he had numerous casual friends and acquaintances, but he was a homebody, never a bonding sort — and he had no real bosom companions except Roy. But at the same time he demonstrated a remarkable feel for a collective abstraction — average Americans and their hopes, fears, and values. Disney never failed to amaze colleagues with his sense of the appropriate move to please audiences. Part of this skill was calculated. In the late 1920s, for instance, he attended as many movies as possible to observe audiences, because "he not only wanted to know what they thought of his pictures, but what they thought about other pictures." Within a few years, he developed the habit of taking the early print of an animated short film out to a theater in Glendale for a preview. After watching the audience's reaction, along with that of the artists he dragooned into going, he would analyze successful and unsuccessful sections alike, looking for patterns and reasons. In a 1933 article, he defined the "Mickey Mouse audience" with psychological insight. His films, he wrote, were aimed not at national, racial, political, or social groups but rather at "parts of people . . . that deathless, precious, ageless, absolutely primitive remnant of something in every world-wracked human being which makes us play with children's toys and laugh without self-consciousness at silly things . . . You know, the Mickey in us."[40]

But the greatest part of Disney's empathy came from pure instinct. An associate who observed him in action for some thirty years concluded that a master plan never existed and the studio head simply "drove by the seat of his pants all the time." Disney yearned to become a great entertainer, and he stuck to an endearing belief in the necessity of heroes, villains, and "a tear and a laugh" in his pictures. Even more, he maintained a determined innocence about his audience. In a radio talk in the late 1930s, he explained at some length his bedrock assumptions about human beings and the appeal of his films.

> Everybody in the world was once a child. We grow up. Our personalities change, but in every one of us something remains of our childhood . . . [that] knows nothing of sophistication and distinction. It's where all of us are simple and naive without prejudice and bias. We're friendly and trusting and it just seems that if your picture hits that spot in one person, it's going to hit that same spot in almost everybody. So, in planning a new picture, we don't think of grownups and we don't think of children, but just of that fine, clean, unspoiled spot down deep in every one of us that maybe the world has made us forget and that maybe our picture can help recall.[41]

Moreover, Disney maintained a scrupulous respect for ordinary people and their judgment, insisting that "the public is the gauge of taste. If it doesn't like what you've done, in nine cases out of ten you've done the wrong thing." In a philosophical mood, he revealed a bit of his thinking when he told Roy Williams, "When you're making pictures for an audience, you never play over their heads and you never play beneath them. You play right straight out at them." This respect for ordinary people — a desire to avoid condescending to or insulting the intelligence of his audience — helped create what Milt Kahl once described as "Walt's instinctive rapport with the public." Disney tried to face his audience, as he liked to say, as "Mr. Average Man," and he sustained a powerful sensitivity about what amused, moved, and entertained it. Millions of ordinary Americans responded with affection.[42]

Disney's instinctive empathy and respect for his audience seemed to galvanize his personal values in the 1930s and funnel them into the creative work he adored. The audience was central to everything — the nature of his work, the content of his films, and the vast approval they generated. He sought not only the happiness of consumers but their approval, and the emotional payoff from that quest — affection, fame, distinction — loomed much larger than wealth ever did in his personal calculations of worth. It was the engine that pushed Disney forward, and it helped make him a spokesman for the values of mainstream America in the mid-twentieth century.

A dramatic instance of Disney's increasingly prominent standing in American culture came in February 1938, when *Snow White and the Seven Dwarfs* opened in theaters around the United States. The film was an instant hit. The Disney Studio secured a stunning 15,000 booking contracts in its first few months of release, and the movie quickly established record-setting box office runs everywhere. More than 352,000 people saw it during a six-week engagement at Chicago's Palace Theater, for instance, breaking every record for both attendance and gross profit. Breathless reports of enthusiasm detailed unusual expressions of emotion, ranging from gales of laughter at the antics of the seven dwarfs to abundant tears when the seemingly dead young princess was mourned by her diminutive friends. In a New York theater, an awed film critic observed that the movie's conclusion brought "applause such as has never been heard from the average audience." A flood of favorable reviews added to *Snow White*'s aura. "Top ten" lists of movies from newspapers and journals included it without fail and often placed it at the very top. One reviewer, tongue planted firmly in his cheek, tried gamely to keep up with the adoration of the film. "If it were customary on this page to rate pictures by the common star or letter system," he wrote dryly, "'Snow White' would have to get six A's, 10 stars, eight bells, a dozen full moons, and three or four Haley's comets [sic]." By the summer of 1938, Disney and his spectacular achievement seemed to be on the lips of everyone in America.[43]

Snow White seemed to strike a fundamental chord among the millions of people who saw it, so much so that throughout 1938 and 1939, a number of articles probed the psychological dynamics of its appeal. Newspaper reviewers opined that the film "transports the care-worn adult back to the happy days of his childhood." In fact, a journalistic debate broke out over a psychologist's speech which claimed that *Snow White* offered only a pathetic "escape from reality" for people whose morale had been shattered by the Great Depression. Outraged rejoinders rushed to print. Many claimed that artistic endeavor by definition was transcendent, seeking "escape from the stern facts of concrete reality . . . to a larger reality." Others insisted that "a temporary opportunity to escape from unpleasant reality" constituted a normal, healthy response that allowed people to rest, gather their emotional resources, and attack their problems with new vigor.[44]

Snow White, of course, cemented Disney's cultural appeal with an array of commercial tie-ups and merchandising maneuvers. Anticipating the great appeal of the movie, Kay Kamen granted some seventy licenses to corporations for the production of a variety of goods with the Snow White stamp — clothing, food, toys, books, cutlery, phonograph records, and a host of others. Women's clothes became a particularly appealing item. Lucille Ball appeared in a series of fashion photographs wearing a "chapeau" patterned after those worn by the seven dwarfs, and *Women's Wear Daily* ran a special twenty-page section that highlighted movie-inspired clothing ranging from underwear and negligees to dresses and accessories. Large department stores in nearly every major city put together promotions of toys, books, and clothing in ground-level display windows. Companies were eager to get in on the action. In December 1937 the trade journal *Soap* carried a long piece insisting that the washing scenes in *Snow White* "represent a type of publicity for soap which money could never buy" and exhorting its readers to consider the possibilities of "Snow White Soap Flakes or Toilet Soap." The business journal *Dun's Review* concluded in April 1938 that this symbiotic process ("the picture promoted the sale of goods; the likenesses on the merchandise enhanced the popularity of the picture") had made *Snow White* a "dramatic example of a new force in merchandising."[45]

III. "Our American Culture"

On March 1, 1942, Walt Disney addressed an audience at the New York Metropolitan Opera by radio hookup from Los Angeles. Speaking during the intermission of a performance, he chose the topic "Our American Culture." The occasion provided a rare instance for Disney, the no-nonsense man of action, to stand back and reflect on the larger implications of his work and the context in which it existed. In one sense, the speech was full of patriotic platitudes. At the same time, however, it offered a concise portrait of his sensibility and his sense of the cultural meaning of his work.

A populist tenor pervaded the talk from the outset. After noting that "Dopey is as well qualified as I am to discuss culture in America," Disney examined the notion of culture itself. This was often seen, he said, as an elitist concept that was almost "un-American . . . Sort of snobbish and affected. As if it thought it was better than the next fellow." But he insisted that a more democratic situation actually existed in the modern United States, because for the most part, the materials of culture — books, newspapers and magazines, a public school system, radio and movies — were "available to rich and poor alike in great abundance." "Faith in the discrimination of the average person" drove his own work, he claimed, and that creed was reflected in his studio. His staff consisted of "ordinary folk" from "the average American home, with the average American advantages and upbringing," and they were determined to stay in touch with "the average audience."[46]

Disney also outlined his aesthetic loyalties. The fact that a popular cartoonist was lecturing at the Met suggested a modernist impulse of hierarchical mixing, of course, but he went on to launch a frontal attack on the gatekeeper mentality that often restricted cultural endeavor. "Convention and tradition can become tyrannical," he stated. "If we are to have a true and honest culture, we must be aware of the self-appointed tyrant who puts a fence around painting or art or music or literature and shouts, 'This is my preserve. Think as I do or keep out.'" According to him, a fluid sense of innovation and an expansive respect for personal artistry were required for a healthy culture. But as always, Disney hastened to add the tonic of sentiment to his aesthetic brew. Culture, he insisted, came from "selecting that which is fine and beautiful in life and throwing aside that which is mediocre and phony." As to identifying the good and the beautiful, he offered a familiar answer: "I believe that man recognizes it instinctively. I believe that you will find this spontaneous reaching out for the fine and the beautiful in all mankind."[47]

To this synthetic appeal — the sentimental modernist mixing the innovative and the beautiful, the populist evoking the virtue of ordinary people — Disney added a final dash of consumerism. Part of what enriched American culture, he pointed out, was those things "adding to our ease of life and leisure . . . [like] bathtubs and telephones, and automobiles and good roads and fine working conditions. And those other three million streamlined gadgets which make the average American home a miracle of comfort." From this mix of politics, aesthetics, and economics, Disney constructed his final entreaty. The essence of American culture, he concluded, lay in freedom — "freedom to believe what you choose and read, think and say . . . This spiritual and intellectual freedom which we Americans enjoy is our greatest cultural blessing." The ideals of "tolerance, democracy, and freedom" inspired people all over the world, and they should "make every American stand up and cheer for our American way of life." Disney the modernist, the populist, and the prophet of abundance appeared on the same stage, indistinguishable.[48]

In the broadest sense, Disney smoothed the jagged transition from the values of the Victorian age to those of a fledgling consumer America. In addition, he helped to dismantle barriers between highbrow and lowbrow cultural activity and to bridge the gulf that separated the realistic art of the nineteenth century from the modernism of the twentieth. Throughout, he negotiated the treacherous waters that lay between art and politics, synthesizing powerful impulses in subtle and soothing ways. Disney had a foot in the past and the present throughout the 1930s, and he helped Americans accommodate to a new age by appealing to older traditions while forging a new creed of leisure, self-fulfillment, and mass consumption. More than a mere cartoonist or entertainer, he managed to become, to use his own phrase, a spokesman for the American way of life. The role was enormously satisfying, and Walt Disney played it with gusto for many years.

9

The Fantasy Factory

I N 1941, at the height of his success, Walt Disney released a feature film that marked a significant departure from his earlier work. The movie, whimsically entitled *The Reluctant Dragon*, took a first, tentative step away from animation by mounting a foray into live-action films. Although a spate of animated segments spiced the plot, most of the action revolved around the escapades of Robert Benchley, one of America's favorite humorists. In addition, and perhaps even more strikingly, this project abandoned the traditional fantasy themes that had always driven Disney's work. Not a fairy princess or a personable puppet or a singing pig was in sight. Instead, *The Reluctant Dragon* turned in a more pragmatic direction for inspiration — toward the Disney operation itself.

The film offered a simple premise. Robert Benchley, believing that he had discovered a wonderful vehicle for a Walt Disney film in the children's story "The Reluctant Dragon," journeyed to the filmmaker's new studio in Burbank in hopes of selling the idea. Predictably, the bumbling humorist could never quite locate Walt and spent most of his time lost, stumbling from one department to another. He invaded an art class where novice animators were learning their craft. He accidentally entered a sound studio where sound effects were being added to a film, and another where a variety of hilarious cartoon voices were being recorded. He roamed into the animators' offices, where he was subjected to a lively synopsis of a new movie project. He wandered into the paint lab and observed the mixing of a rainbow of bright colors for application to the animation cels. When he finally found Walt, he discovered, to his dismay, that "The Reluctant Dragon" had already been filmed. The film played to Benchley's strength, offering numerous situations in which he could display his droll, self-deprecating wit. But it also fulfilled a deeper purpose — to give the American public a guided tour of the Disney Studio. The reasons for this move were not hard to discern.

The workings of the Disney Studio had become a source of great fascination for American moviegoers. Journalism had done its part to meet public demand throughout the 1930s, as the dozens of articles on Walt Disney, his movies, his art, and his image were accompanied by a steady procession of pieces on his organization. The studio's peculiar combination of industrial production and unfettered fantasy, its blending of cold-blooded profit and inspired art, added an air of mystery to its operation. Finally, its image as a sparkling oasis of creativity and fun in the hard-nosed film industry increased the desire for more information.

Articles like Paul Hollister's "Walt Disney: Genius at Work" fed this appetite. Appearing in a 1940 issue of the *Atlantic Monthly*, this essay purported to be about the man, but it devoted most of its energy to an analysis of his organization, his artists, and the way they did their work. Written shortly after the move from the Hyperion Avenue facility, the piece described Disney's new Burbank studio as "severely gay as a World's Fair model, as immaculate as a hospital, and as functional as a research scientist's dream laboratory." Hollister took readers on a step-by-step tour through the making of an animated film, sketching out the careful division of labor from the first story conferences and rough storyboard sketches through the recording of dialogue, animated drawing, inking and painting, addition of music and special effects, and final celluloid synthesis of all the elements. He also stressed the fact that the studio eschewed formality, rewarded merit, and stood as "the only factory on earth where practical jokes are a part of the production line." The spirit of this happy and productive place, in Hollister's evaluation, was one of "ruthless self-criticism, manic ingenuity, and precisionism."[1]

Such analyses usually painted a fairly reliable portrait of the Disney organization and often offered insightful glimpses of its spirit, but at the same time they smacked of superficiality. Journalists usually saw what they were supposed to see. Much of the inside story and behind-the-scenes activity at the studio eluded such image-making. Those actually working at the Disney Studio during its ascendency disclosed details about many facets of life inside the Mickey Mouse factory — the unique process by which these animated films were made, the organizational schemes that structured creative activity, the role of its famous chief in shaping the final product, and, of course, the galaxy of talented and colorful artists who worked for him.

The complex picture that emerges from this information — a blend of bureaucratic structure, creative lunacy, rationalized labor, and unusual personalities — provides important information. First, the rise of Disney and his studio cannot be understood by considering only the indicators of consumption: audiences, reviews, marketing, and ticket sales. Production, the precipitator of this cultural process, also played a crucial role. Second, despite the "Walt Disney Presents" that blared from the title of every film, this enterprise did not rely on just one man but involved dozens and eventually hundreds of creative artists and technical people.

I. A Factory or an Art Studio?

Expansion on all fronts became the normal course of events at the Disney Studio after Mickey Mouse captured the hearts of millions of American moviegoers. In the late 1920s the studio employed around two dozen people, but by 1934 its staff numbered nearly two hundred, in a variety of positions: animators and their assistants, inkers and painters, a twenty-four-piece orchestra, camera operators, and a wide variety of technicians. By 1940 the numbers had swelled even more dramatically; nearly twelve hundred people were working at the studio. The rapidly expanding staff brought in its wake an ever greater specialization of function. Animators, for instance, were divided not only into masters, assistants, in-betweeners, and clean-up artists but into those who drew characters and action and those who did layouts and backgrounds. By the end of the decade, to choose but one example, more than sixty people worked in the animated special effects section alone. Similar trends could be noted in most of the technical departments — story development, camera and photography, sound and voices, ink and paint, and many others.[2]

The expansion of the physical plant was almost as remarkable. The studio on Hyperion Avenue, which had served the operation since 1926, endured a steady process of additions. The construction of several small rooms and the movement of the building's walls outward prefaced a major addition in 1931, when a two-story animators' building and a soundstage went up at the rear of the lot. In half a decade, the studio grew from 1,600 square feet to around 20,000 square feet of working space. The next few years saw even more expansion — construction of another two-story animators' building, an ink-and-paint building, and a variety of labs and small bungalows to serve various departments, and eventually the purchase of apartment buildings and the rental of office space in adjacent areas. Even with all these additions, however, by the late 1930s the facility was bursting at the seams. After exploring several options, Disney finally decided to purchase fifty-one acres north of Hollywood, in Burbank, and he began planning the construction of a brand-new, state-of-the-art studio. This elaborate new production facility, which he planned down to the tiniest detail, became Walt's pride and joy.[3]

Physical growth was accompanied by a new cluster of images. Journalists often compared the studio to a slightly frenetic college campus where, in the words of one, "most of the artists, storymen, directors, and officials are young people who stroll through the grounds, many with books under their arms, tieless and hatless." On one occasion, even Disney himself noted that "our studio had become more like a school than a business." The image of a genial madhouse was another favorite. Harry Carr, writing in 1931, called it a playful "insane asylum," while Arthur Millier postulated in 1938 that the Disney operation was "a psychiatrist's heaven because none of the patients are dangerous." With musicians scurrying about humming pieces of melodies to themselves, artists making bizarre faces at themselves in mirrors as they chuckled and drew frantically, and grown people shrieking and howling animal noises on recording stages, the studio crawled with "inmates . . . contriving infinitesimal bits of lunacy." As Millier concluded, "It's a madhouse, that's what it is. And such a nice, refreshing one in this congenitally nutty world."[4]

Most frequently, however, two other images engaged the public imagination. First, there were numerous evocations of the Disney Studio as a "fun factory" (the concept placed equal emphasis on both words). For many Americans caught in the grip of the machine age, the Disney facility was an ideal representation of an industrial plant. Synthesizing artistic creation and efficient production, it promoted the idea that factories need not be degraded, dismal, and deplorable places. Many visitors were impressed by Disney's "smooth running piece of machinery," his "embodiment of systemization," as one of them called it. Without fail, however, they also noted the studio's integration of playful imagination with industrial efficiency. *Fortune*'s 1934 analysis of this special "myth maker's factory" probably offered the fullest analysis. The Disney Studio was "a factory, because the technical problems for producing [an animated film] . . . are solved with the utmost speed and efficiency which modern industrial methods will permit. But the result is no simple product like cigarettes or razor blades; it is myth . . . In Disney's studio a twentieth century miracle is achieved: by a system as truly of the machine age as Henry Ford's plant at Dearborn, true art is produced."[5]

A second image — that of the Disney Studio as a democratic, collective, creative paradise — also consistently found its way into print. While some observers found the place appalling — Frank Lloyd Wright denounced its ethos, snorting, "Democracy! That's not democracy, its mobocracy!" — most found it enchanting. In 1934, for instance, a long piece in the *Cinema*

Quarterly surveyed the extraordinary process by which a host of creative people melded their talents in order to fulfill a common vision. "Even in Soviet Russia, where group effort is paramount," noted the author, there was scarcely a comparable effort where "such heterogeneity of effort achieves so successfully homogeneity of accomplishment." A host of analyses followed the same track, describing the studio as "a completely democratic community," an organization that was "surely one of the most democratic in the annals of art," and an "easy-going Disneyan democracy." And of course Walt was accorded the greatest credit for this democratic, collective spirit of production. His quotations in newspaper stories — "We all work together, no one of us any more important than the other" — allowed an egalitarian spirit to shine through.[6]

The magical, effervescent atmosphere of the Disney Studio in the 1930s tended to obscure an underlying process of bureaucratization. In fact, the years from 1928 to 1941 saw an increasing rationalization in the production process that unfolded steadily over the long haul but lurched forward in the short term. In his own inimitable managerial style, Disney alternately promoted and undermined the growth of an efficient organization.

By the late 1930s, for instance, in-house publications began to attempt a clarification of the organization's structure. The *Organizational Manual*, printed on May 16, 1938, opened with a complex diagram that illustrated the functions and responsibilities of various departments of the Disney Studio. This flow chart, complete with boxes, arrows, and a number/letter grid so every employee could locate himself, defined work responsibilities and authority relationships as well as giving a clear picture of the studio's growing specialization. To drive the point home, the diagram and the index of names and titles were followed by nearly sixty pages of text that explained in great detail the "authority," "function," "responsibility," and "objective" of every job at the Disney Studio. As the booklet made clear on the opening page, "The objectives of this organization set-up are to facilitate the movement of work and to avoid waste . . . It is felt that these two objectives can be better accomplished through this centralized management and authority."[7]

Another 1938 booklet, *An Introduction to the Walt Disney Studio*, noted that the Disney artist must "adapt himself within a reasonable length of time to production requirements" or his value would be nil. Employees, it stated flatly, must accept the fact that salaries were based simply on the "ability to produce." A few years later, *The Ropes at Disney* (1943), another employee handbook, insisted that an explanation of "certain 'shoulds' and 'should nots' is necessary in an organization as complex as ours." The illustrated booklet went over employee policies, rules and regulations, and corporate expectations. Significantly, "Absence" was the first heading for discussion, and this section warned that "'absenteeism' has been officially drummed out of the Disney vocabulary . . . Unnecessary absence is a monkey wrench in the production machinery." Such publications, while careful to stress the informal atmosphere at the studio, nonetheless drove home the point that behind the friendly language and casual sensibility lay a concern with bureaucracy and efficiency.[8]

In May 1937, studio manager George Drake presented a lecture to youthful artists at the Chouinard Art Institute who were interested in coming to work for Disney. He stressed that the growth of the organization over the previous decade had made an artist's career less subject to personal whim and more a question of efficient, quality production. Career advancement depended on an objective assessment of contributions to the organization, not any one man's judgment. In Drake's words, "There is no personal element involved anymore . . . There used to be when the business was small and a one-man job, but now the business has developed to a stage where apprentices and men who are starting . . . must depend on their own ability and the quality of their own work to keep the job." Along the same lines, Drake urged the artists to avoid the pitfall of thinking that they were "just a little bit better than average" and would thus shoot to the top of the organization. It was filled with talented, creative people, and producers, directors, and supervising animators would decide if and when a man's work was worth more than the average and reward it fairly. But this happened only rarely, Drake noted, reiterating the cold facts of life: in terms of advancement, the "chances for a man in the studio depend on how high a price his work will bring."[9]

As the Disney operation was gearing up for its first feature-length project, Walt himself composed a lengthy "interoffice communication." This May 20, 1935, memo focused on a single topic — the need for greater work discipline. Disney discussed the problem of studio personnel visiting the work areas of others and disrupting their efforts. He stressed that while he did not wish to chain men to their desks for hours at a time, the need to stretch and relax should be met with a walk around the lot or a visit to the commissary, not an intrusive visit to another's workroom. His conclusion made it clear that he meant business:

> All that we expect a man to do is to keep his work at as high a quality as possible and put out enough of that quality work to earn his paycheck. No one could ask for less. We do expect you to assume your responsibilities. You know what your job is and what is to be done; and it is not my desire to force your cooperation. If you will not cooperate with me in [addressing] our problems for your own good and the good of the organization, you have no place in it.

As he described even more bluntly a couple of years later, animation was produced at the Disney Studio "much as an automobile goes through an assembly plant."[10]

Actually, the efficiency and order of the factory model had long fascinated Disney. Back in 1928, for example, as he struggled in New York to sell his Mickey Mouse films and secure the future of his operation, his numerous letters home had stressed the need for organization, rationalization, and efficiency in making animated movies. As he wrote to Roy Disney and Ub Iwerks, his frustrations over recording a satisfactory soundtrack for *Steamboat Willie* had convinced him of the need to control the whole process of production, from musical composition to synchronization technology to animation to sound effects. "The basis of a good organization," he concluded, lay in "systematizing everything."[11]

By the mid-1930s, Disney's commitment to efficient production openly embraced the factory model. In 1934 a reporter from *Fortune* noted that the studio chief was "childishly enchanted by factory methods," a fact that Disney consistently corroborated. In an article he contributed to the *Journal of the Society of Motion Picture Engineers*, he described studio growth around this time in revealing language:

> A greater degree of specialization was setting in. The plant was becoming more like a Ford factory, but our moving parts were more complex than cogs — [they were] human beings . . . who must be weighed and fitted into [their] proper place . . . Hundreds of young people were being trained and fitted into a machine for the manufacture of entertainment which had become bewilderingly complex. And this machine had been redesigned almost overnight from one for turning out short subjects into one aimed mainly at increased feature production.

A short time later, Disney described his "entertainment factory" as a place that mediated between the individualist impulse in art and assembly-line routine, with the result that by "sharing our ideas we multiply our powers of invention."[12]

Employees of the Disney Studio during its golden age were certainly sensitive to this emphasis on a division of labor and efficiency. Many of them commented at length on the bureaucracy and the specialization of function that colored the operation. Longtime animation director Jack Kinney, for instance, recalled that by the early 1930s Walt had "the assembly line running" at his studio. With some amusement, Dick Huemer noted that at this time the studio even attempted to assign everyone official numbers according to their years of service, an efficiency move that became the butt of jokes around the lot. For some, however, the situation was less amusing. Nancy Massie, who began working as an inker and painter in the late 1930s, explained how great pressures for speedy production were a fact of life. Her words conjured up images of demanding, efficiency-obsessed factory labor:

There were people who did nothing but time the inkers — you had five minutes to ink a Mickey Mouse cel and a little longer for certain characters in *Fantasia*. And charts were made of where you stood above and below the average.

One of the girls told us tricks to keep our speed up, like "Don't lift your head when you pick the paper cels off the shelves in front of you." It became a mechanical process . . . you'd ink the cel *fast*. They had people who would come along and pick up the tissue papers on the floor behind you and fill your inkwells. It was a six-day week, eight hours a day, with a fifteen-minute break in the afternoon, and lunch too, of course . . . I was ambitious. I could ink twenty-five cels an hour.[13]

The ethos of productive efficiency also fostered the notorious spirit of perfectionism that became nearly synonymous with the Disney name. A search for excellence colored the ambiance of the studio, and it made for a process of constructive criticism and revision. Hamilton Luske, one of Disney's key animation supervisors throughout this expansive era, captured the prevalent tone of things. His "General Outline of Animation Theory and Practice," published in the *Studio Animation Handbook,* stressed that a spirit of "cooperation and exchange of ideas" gave "the entire animation staff the opportunity to take advantage of every new method of achievement."[14]

Many members of the Disney staff confirmed the exhaustive scrutiny and revision that accompanied an animated film through production. The process was a long one: initial storyboard presentations plotted the direction of the movie; filmed "pencil tests" roughly delineated certain sections as they first came to life; action analysis seminars resulted in typed notes that were distributed the next day; at sweatbox sessions, nervous animators presented scenes on a moviola to Walt and the directors for their approval; the story men and animators held ongoing meetings. Overall, a vigorous spirit of critique fostered continuous refinements. As a journalist wrote in 1939 after a visit to the studio, "None of them, from Disney down to the littlest apprentice, ever is truly satisfied with his work . . . They snarl at criticism, but not for the usual reason in Hollywood: because they can't take it; but because they have already criticized themselves far more harshly than any outsider could."[15]

Yet for all of the growing bureaucratic efficiency, a contrary impulse — one might call it irrationalization — persisted tenaciously. This instinct, which Disney himself nourished, led to freewheeling improvisation, casual procedures, and personal connection rather than organizational discipline. In fact, it tended to undermine much of what the bureaucratic constructions had wrought. Several notable features revealed this tendency, none more dramatically than the striking informality of life on the Disney lot. In the early 1930s, for example, a journalist for *Pearson's Magazine* reported that the studio was "more like a home than a factory. From the moment you enter the reception room you are impressed by the atmosphere of good fellowship that reigns inside. Everybody wears a smile, and even the humblest employee addresses his chief as 'Walt.'" The first-name basis of proceedings at Disney became legendary, and the studio handbook officially told new employees that they were entering "a 'no-necktie, sweaters and slacks' organization. 'Businesslike informality' is an accepted Disney policy."[16]

Throughout the 1930s, Disney usually joined his employees for lunch at a modest restaurant near the Hyperion lot and sat at the animators' table. According to one of those present, he "never acted like the boss, though he always led the conversation." Moreover, the Disney Studio, at his insistence, never had a time clock, for he believed that it dampened employees' creativity as well as their enthusiasm for their work. Unlike animation studios on the East Coast, this Hollywood oasis also demanded no footage quotas from its artists. The emphasis, Disney insisted, should be on making revisions that would improve the final animated product, not on sheer volume of production.[17]

A casual atmosphere conducive to the creativity and comedy demanded by animated cartoons also prevailed. Work breaks were not only allowed, they were actually encouraged in order to promote fresh thinking and discourage burnout. According to a host of Disney employees, a constant round of horseplay, gags, and practical jokes punctuated the demanding routine. Goldfish mysteriously appeared in water coolers, stressed-out animators engaged in pushpin-throwing contests, story meetings turned into impromptu comedy shows, and Limburger cheese placed on the light bulbs under an animator's desk melted and ran onto the floor, to the great hilarity of all present. Walt consistently looked the other way, viewing such shenanigans as both a useful way to blow off steam in a highly stressful situation and a kind of psychological lubricant for the creative process.[18]

This ambiance extended to the variety of extracurricular activities that colored life at the Disney Studio. Staff members played casual sports nearly every day, for instance, and employees with a talent for music put together the Barnyard Band (later the Fire House Five Plus Two), which played regularly for studio dances. With Walt's encouragement, the *Mickey Mouse Melodeon*, officially the "house organ of the Disney Studio" and unofficially its gossip sheet, began publishing in November 1932. Consisting of tidbits of information contributed by employees, it was edited and distributed on mimeographed sheets by Walt's secretary, Carolyn Schaefer.[19]

Policy was also affected by the casual atmosphere. Studio procedure deemphasized a pecking order and encouraged inclusiveness in terms of participation and knowledge. As *An Introduction to the Walt Disney Studio* stated clearly, much of the studio's success "is due to Walt Disney's policy of complete dissemination of animation knowledge throughout the Studio. To stimulate growth it is imperative that every man in the Studio have access to all information about production. It can honestly be said that one man's knowledge is every man's knowledge in the Disney Studio."[20]

As numerous members of the staff testified, Disney also made it clear that quality production, not volume or cost cutting, headed the studio's agenda. Longtime employees insisted that Disney's success flowed from a determination to make the best possible films "no matter how much time it took or how much money it cost." Production supervisor Dave Hand, Walt's right-hand man throughout the 1930s, liked to tell a story about his chief's commitment to quality. Early in the decade, when Roy Disney chastised Walt in a meeting for cost overruns on a picture, Walt's eyebrow arched dangerously. He turned to his brother and "in an uncompromising, matter-of-fact, straight-from-the-shoulder answer, said quite simply, 'Roy, *we'll* make the pictures — *you* get the money.' That was that."[21]

Walt became notorious among the staff for undermining bureaucratic efficiency with a favorite tactic: making opposites work together. In the words of Frank Thomas, the studio head "had this philosophy that you will get better work if you put people together who have opposing views, because it will make each of them fight harder." Other artists agreed, noting that pitting people against each other in a creative situation appealed to Disney. He "loved that kind of conflict," according to one. "He thought rivalry was good, it made sparks, it stimulated people." Disney constantly shuffled people around from project to project, replacing and reassigning as his assessment of their talents evolved. He kept his staff off-balance and committed to pleasing him by combining harsh criticism with plum assignments. Dave Hand, for instance, reported that Disney regularly reacted to his directorial efforts with a stream of abuse: "You should never have become a director. You don't know what it's all about. You're hopeless. Anybody could have done a better job than you did." But then, often to the shock of observers, Disney would give Hand the plum assignments on new projects. In other words, Disney did not aim solely at smooth, efficient production. Instead, he sought creative ferment, achievement, and a praiseworthy result.[22]

Nonetheless, disgusted with the studio's haphazard production process, Disney would periodically get angry and bring in bureaucratic experts for advice. In Ben Sharpsteen's words, "Many times he hired outsiders [for consultation], and it was almost a joke. Walt would say 'We are all disorganized here. We don't know what we're doing.' And lo and behold, a corps of industrial engineers would show up with pencils and pads and end up with a production chart. And it was laughable because it didn't mean a thing." After praising the experts' efforts and committing their plans to paper, Disney would proceed either to ignore their advice entirely or to follow only the suggestions that he wanted to implement anyway. Viewing this situation from the inside, one animator reported that the result was both liberating and terrifying. In the words of Shamus Culhane, the casual atmosphere "only slightly alleviated our sense of strain and anxiety, because nobody was allowed to ease off from the pursuit of quality for an instant."[23]

One visitor to Disney's fantasy factory offered an impression felt by many: "You never know whether you're in a factory or an art studio." The most obvious result of this system was the delightful films that went flashing onto theater screens all over the country. But another consequence was not in the public view. The singular, stimulating, and often strange quality of life behind the walls of the Disney Studio offered abundant evidence of its unusual procedures and traditions.[24]

II. Whistle While You Work

The "golden age" Disney Studio, as nearly everyone agreed, was a very attractive place to work. Almost without fail, Disney employees believed they were part of something special, and many of them provided testaments to the magic of the Disney workplace.

Dave Hand, for instance, remembered this era for the incredible commitment and loyalty of the staff. "It would be hard to explain such cooperation in the inner workings of a normal commercial business," he noted years later, "but this 'business' did not fall into such a category." Mary Tebb, who worked at the other end of the studio spectrum for many years as an inker and painter, concurred fully. "That dedication was the greatest thing in the world — our dedication to Walt and the product, our unquestioning attitude," she remembered fondly. "No one ever said to Walt, 'Aw, that's too much work, I don't want to do it.' Oh no, you'd take it home and spend all night if you had to." Others simply described the experience in terms of being part of "one big happy family."[25]

For some, the sense of fulfillment fed a sense of belonging to a historic enterprise. Dick Huemer felt that, "like disciples who might have worked with Michelangelo, we were part of a thing that was maybe going to last." Many others used similar analogies from the world of high art. According to animator John Hubley, "Disney's studio was like a marvelous Renaissance craft hall. Young people were given a chance to study drawing, composition, animation, action. We studied old movies, layout, art direction. All of us were encouraged to take these free courses."[26]

Part of what made life at the Disney workshop so special was the continual creative stimulation. In one sense, of course, the production process by definition involved large numbers of highly imaginative people in invigorating labor. A "Can you top this?" atmosphere inevitably spiced this collaborative work. By habitually embarking on the new and untried in his film

Roy and Walt Disney visited Marceline, Missouri, where they had lived as children, in 1956. The locomotive was an attraction they donated to the city.

Flora and Elias Disney in 1913, when the family lived in Kansas City.

Lillian, Walt, Ruth, Roy, and Edna Disney in front of the storefront Disney Brothers Studio on Kingswell Avenue, 1925.

Walt and some of his staffers singing "Minnie's Yoo Hoo" in the studio, 1929. Standing, left to right: *Johnny Cannon, Walt, Bert Gillett, Ub Iwerks, Wilfred Jackson, Les Clark.* Sitting: *Carl Stalling, Jack King, Ben Sharpsteen.*

By 1931, a flood of licensed merchandise featured the studio's animated star, Mickey Mouse. Animator Norm Ferguson is seated in the lower right-hand corner, holding a Mickey Mouse doll.

The Walt Disney Studio on Hyperion Avenue during a construction project in the early 1930s. This is where the "golden age" films were made.

Walt and his staff often clowned around during storyboard meetings. This one was photographed for an article in Fortune *in 1934.*

The December 27, 1937, cover of Time *showed Walt holding figurines of the characters in the hit film* Snow White and the Seven Dwarfs, *which had just been released.*

Animator Fred Moore working on drawings of Jiminy Cricket for the film Pinocchio *in the late 1930s.*

Walt and one of his heroes, Charlie Chaplin, at the Santa Anita racetrack in 1939.

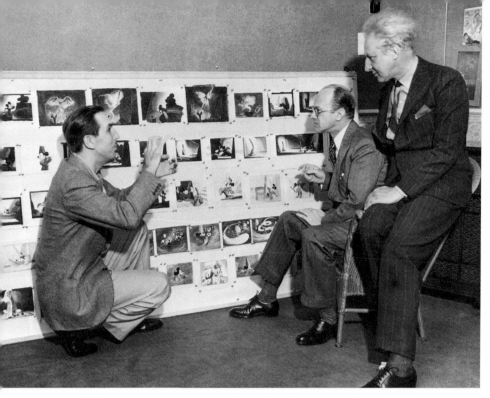

Walt, music authority Deems Taylor, and conductor Leopold Stokowski consulting about the storyboards for Fantasia, *1940.*

The leaders of the 1941 studio strike. Standing: George Bodle, Herb Sorrell, Fred Thompson, Bill Tytla, *and an unidentified man. Kneeling:* David Hilberman, Art Babbitt.

This flier from the Screen Cartoonists Guild was distributed during the strike.

Walt enjoying a barbecue in Argentina during his extended trip to South America in the fall of 1941.

During a visit to Washington, D.C., in 1942, Walt explained the storyboard sketches of The New Spirit *to Secretary of the Treasury Henry Morgenthau, Jr., and his assistants. The two men at the right are Disney artists Joe Grant and Dick Huemer.*

This patriotic poster from the 1940s features an array of Disney characters enlisting in the war effort.

projects, Disney lent an additional sense of adventure to this creative ferment. For that perfectionist as well as his employees, animation involved much more than production quotas and sales figures. It also involved a genuine search for fresh ideas and inventive thinking.

A continuous round of visiting artists provided a steady source of inspiration. In addition to Thomas Hart Benton, Aldous Huxley, and Rico Lebrun, Salvador Dali — who, somewhat surprisingly, seemed to be one of Disney's favorite artists — served as a consultant. Working on a couple of film projects that never came to fruition, the eccentric Spaniard also visited Disney's home. Diane, Walt's oldest daughter, distinctly remembered him riding on her father's steam-powered miniature train as it circled the house on a hot summer day, solemnly sitting in a black flannel overcoat and holding a walking stick, his waxed mustache glistening and a single red carnation in his lapel.[27]

But the landscape of daily life at the Disney Studio featured considerable excitement and fun as well as artistic illumination. A daily noontime softball game was a regular routine for many, including Walt, who would wolf down their brown-bag lunches, adjourn to a vacant lot, and engage in a fierce competition between the Marrieds and the Singles. According to one frequent participant, "Each game was hotly contested, with much yelling, kidding, griping, cheating, in an anything-to-win spirit, with a lot of laughs, which allowed all of us to forget our frustrations and the tough scenes lying back on our desks." In addition, many of the artists, in the prime of young manhood, played basketball, football, volleyball, horseshoes, or golf in the evenings or on weekends, and the games were often rough-and-tumble. Some even became involved in Walt's pet activity, polo, joining him for 6 A.M. practice sessions before going to work and then playing in organized matches against other southern California clubs.[28]

In the early days, when Prohibition was still in effect, many of Disney's employees would converge on a local speakeasy run by a saloonkeeper named Charlie Rivers to drink bootleg beer, relax, and compare notes. They remained loyal to this establishment throughout the 1930s, even after the sale of alcohol was legalized again. In fact, drinking, partying, and genial conversation became a regular part of the creative process as "inspirational" meetings often were convened at local watering holes. According to Jack Kinney, "Maybe more ideas were quenched than born in our frequent forays to favorite bars for liquid inspiration. But somehow the next day we'd pour out new ideas like the bartender had poured drinks the night before." Staff parties and dances were common, with the studio band providing the music. Receptionist Mary Flanagan became a favorite figure in studio social life when she turned an empty space in the new animation building into an unofficial commissary, selling gum, cigarettes, snacks, and coffee to grateful staff members. She enhanced her reputation even more through an activity that became an open secret, functioning as the studio bookie by handicapping the horses, collecting bets, and paying off the winners.[29]

The Disney Studio also saw its fair share of pranks and horseplay. As Ward Kimball later recalled "sheer desperation seemed to bring out a never-ending stream of humor." Jack Kinney told the famous story of how staff members once convinced a gullible associate that Walt was too busy to do the voice of Mickey Mouse on the radio and had expressed interest in him as a replacement. A mock audition was set up for this poor man in a studio, but his microphone was hooked up to the intercom as fellow workers looked on from the windows of adjoining buildings. Told that his falsetto Mickey voice lacked depth and vibrancy, the eager staffer was put through a series of ridiculous paces by the sound engineer, who asked him to jump up and down while speaking, then to grasp the microphone while he jumped, and finally, since his clothes were supposedly squeaking, to remove his shoes and socks and pants while jumping. As he cavorted and gyrated, observers laughed until tears rolled down their faces.[30]

Occasionally pranks took a bawdy form. Freddy Moore had long been famous among his peers for his sketches of beautiful, scantily clad young women. But during the final frenzied stages of production of *Snow White and the Seven Dwarfs*, restraint vanished and a flood of pornographic drawings came pouring out of the nooks and crannies of the Disney Studio. Working long overtime hours under intense deadline pressures, artists began to blow off steam by drawing outrageously lewd scenes of the saccharine young princess engaged in a mass orgy with the seven dwarfs. While these depraved cartoons made the rounds to the great hilarity of the staff, people were careful to keep them away from Walt, a notorious prude.[31]

Perhaps the most famous incident of studio debauchery, however, came during the infamous celebration following the completion of *Snow White*. After months of hard work, the film received huge critical and popular acclaim, and a grateful Walt arranged for a studiowide celebration at the Lake Norconian Club outside Los Angeles. After a variety of activities and sporting competitions during the day, the evening's festivities quickly degenerated into a libidinous bash. Imbibing booze in heroic portions, the exhausted but liberated staff cut loose, leaping fully clothed into the hotel swimming pool, falling drunkenly out of windows, hopping into bed with attractive coworkers. According to some accounts, when Walt arrived with his family to join the party, he was so shocked and outraged by the scene that he turned around and went home.[32]

Work pressures occasionally prompted peculiar behavior. Once, a flamboyant film narrator who had been dismissed for a breach of studio rules stopped outside Walt's office window and performed a full-scale, operatic rendition of "Someday My Prince Will Come" until he was sternly escorted from the premises by security guards amid thunderous applause from the staff. During the early stages of making *Bambi*, Rico Lebrun became obsessed with a dead fawn that had come into his possession. According to Frank Thomas and Ollie Johnston, Lebrun's enthusiasm for instructing the Disney artists in the finer points of animal anatomy prompted him to make a minute dissection of the carcass over most of a week. He first peeled back the skin, then looked at how the various joints worked, explored the muscular structure, and finally got down to the skeleton itself. Of course, by the time several nights had gone by, the stench was overwhelming. While the seemingly oblivious Lebrun bent over the rotting corpse to finish his labors, the nauseated animators stood on the far side of the room proclaiming as a group, "We can see just fine from back here!"[33]

Perhaps the most hilarious story about the golden age of the Disney Studio, however, came out of the Story Department. The conferences among that group, where nervous project directors presented their storyboard outlines to a critical audience of their colleagues, were tense affairs. Pointed criticism was inevitable, irreverence was typical, and ideas and concepts were kicked around, often with much laughter and shouting. A native New Yorker named Mike Myers debuted in front of this rough crowd in unforgettable fashion. As he arose, nerves on edge, to offer his first-ever storyboard presentation of a proposed Donald Duck short, he unconsciously lapsed into profanity-laden street vernacular to explain the plot. His presentation, according to one of his colleagues, went something like this:

> Well, we open on Donald Duck's house, it's early morning. The fuckin' sun's just peekin' over another fuckin' rooster, and boids start whistlin'. A cat yowls, Pluto wakes up an' starts chasin' the goddam cat, barking like a sonofabitch. All kinda noises are raisin' hell. Donald Duck leaps outta bed madder'n a goddam harnit. He trips over a pair of shoes and falls on his ass, then the fuckin' duck jumps to his feet and runs out the fuckin' door. He sees Pluto chasin' that goddam cat up a nearby fuckin' tree, raisin' hell with that fuckin' cat. Then the fuckin' duck runs on, swingin' a rake at the goddam dog. As the fuckin' duck takes a big swing at ol' Pluto, his fuckin' unnerwear catches ta a clothesline hung with red unnerwear, a goddam nightshirt, anna lotta socks and other fuckin' stuff, the fuckin' duck gets hisself all fucked up with the goddam clothes offa the fuckin' line an' he trips an' falls on his fuckin' ass again . . .

By this time, of course, the audience was howling, some of the veteran story men actually falling out of their chairs and rolling around on the floor in convulsions. Dave Hand, decidedly less amused, jumped to his feet and shouted over the uproar, "Mike, hold it! Walt won't stand still for you referring to Donald as 'that fuckin' duck'!" The completely nonplussed Myers could only reply, "Well, that's what he is, ain't he?"[34]

Walt himself became entangled in his fair share of comic episodes, which soon became part of studio lore. One time, for instance, he had his mustache singed off and his nose burned when an overeager Ken Anderson lit his cigarette with an overfilled lighter, which exploded into a small bonfire. According to the mortified employee, Disney "jumped clean out of his chair, holding his face, and said, 'What the goddamn hell are you trying to do, burn me up?' and he went sailing out of the room." Another time, shortly after the opening of the Burbank studio, Walt decided to spend the night on the sleeping couch in his office suite. After retiring, however, he discovered that the air-conditioning system automatically shut down at a set time, and the temperature inside began to skyrocket. When he tried to open a window, he found that all the windows had been sealed shut — at his own directive — to keep employees from altering the temperature. The only way he could obtain fresh air was by breaking the windowpanes with a chair![35]

Disney's idiosyncrasies as a producer also gave rise to several notorious maneuvers among his employees. It was common knowledge, for example, that he often snooped about the animators' offices in the evenings to get a fuller sense of how various projects were shaping up. As a result, artists made it a point before they headed home for the day to arrange their best work casually but carefully on the desk and storyboards, where the boss could see it. As many on the staff noticed, Disney also made a habit of saying, "Tighten it up and we'll take another look at it" when he viewed storyboards. Artists intentionally made crude, slightly sloppy versions of their cherished sketches and arranged them slightly out of kilter, with only one pushpin. After Walt's inevitable comment, they simply sharpened the lines, brightened the colors, and rehung the same drawings neatly, with four pins each. Their delighted boss would usually say, "Yeah, yeah, that's it — that's what I meant by tightening up your materials."[36]

Beneath Walt in the hierarchy of the Disney Studio, a whole cast of colorful characters brightened the nature of workaday life. Artistic giants like Bill Tytla, Fred Moore, and Norm Ferguson made an enormous impact with the power of their work and their unique, memorable personalities. They became objects of genuine admiration, emulation, and fondness for nearly everyone. In the same category stood Don Graham, head of the Disney Art School. Even the best animators admired this devoted, inspirational instructor, describing him as "extremely articulate" and "probably the greatest art teacher of our time." As one put it, "I learned more about animation from Don Graham than anyone else in the world . . . I'm just one of many who idolized the man." At the other extreme stood the petty tyrants of the studio. These included George Drake, the frustrated supervisor of the in-betweeners, who lorded it over these apprentice artists with a short fuse and a mean streak; Bert Gillett, a director whose success with *Three Little Pigs* went to his head, turning him into a finger-shaking, tantrum-throwing prima donna; and Clyde Geronomi, another director, whose abrasiveness with coworkers and crude behavior toward female employees eventually led many of the leading animators to refuse to work with him.[37]

Between the saints and the devils stood a contingent of striking characters who influenced the daily process of production in memorable ways during the 1930s. One of the most prominent was Dave Hand, a strong-willed, decisive, and ambitious man who joined the Disney operation as an animator in 1930, moved up to direct a number of shorts over the next several years, was appointed supervising director for the *Snow White* project, and became production manager for the entire studio. Hand made a forceful impression on the staff. Powerfully built, dark-haired, with a rugged face and a no-nonsense demeanor, he excelled at organizing projects and keeping things moving in a productive fashion. His relationship with Disney had a twofold quality. On the one hand, he devoted himself to bringing his boss's visions to life, and with great intensity he cajoled, prodded, and pushed everyone on the staff to that same end. On the other hand, he did not shrink from confronting his boss. Disney frequently found himself unable to articulate his desires, and just as frequently he changed his mind, and Hand would pressure him to make decisions, often during a heated argument. Disney told how his production manager would barge into his office "white with rage. He'd grip the edge of my desk until his knuckles turned white . . . I'd keep the desk between us." Disney appreciated this intensity, and Hand usually cooled down and said, "I can't function until I get mad!" He treated the animators and story men in the same way, demanding great effort while protecting them from meddling interruptions. As Hand once told a group of artists, "I'm not as creative as some of you, but I can make it work better than most of you." However, he eventually became disgruntled, and he left the studio in 1944 in a cloud of hard feelings. Some believed that he had grown bitter over unkept promises of advancement, but Hand would only admit to being increasingly annoyed at how Disney ignored his carefully wrought production structure.[38]

Albert Hurter symbolized how the unusual became ordinary at the Disney Studio. A tall, slender, almost gaunt man with a mustache and gentlemanly, quiet ways, Hurter played a unique artistic role: he sat at his desk, free from specific animation assignments, and made sketches for various projects in order to stimulate the other artists. Born in Switzerland and trained in France, he became the studio's resident reclusive genius. He joined the firm in 1932, and Disney immediately took a liking to him. The hundreds of drawings that began to pour off his sketchpad became the stuff of studio legend — fantastic, imaginative drawings, many of which had an innate fairy-tale, Old World quality to them. For example, his sketches inspired the quaint atmosphere of the dwarfs' cottage in *Snow White* and Geppetto's house in *Pinocchio,* as well as the mythological characters and Chernobog in

Fantasia. At the same time, many of them had a grotesque, surrealist quality — ambulating eyeballs, melons that came to life, creatures in the shape of human hands, pieces of crockery with human traits — which inspired wild flights of fantasy as they circulated about the studio. Much of Hurter's work was snatched up, kept, and displayed by his admiring colleagues. As one concluded, noting that Hurter effortlessly produced the "brilliant, beautiful stuff," there was "nobody like him, ever, *nobody!*"[39]

Hurter's artistic talent was matched by considerable personal eccentricity. Quiet and soft-spoken, he lived alone in a beat-up old rooming house in a rundown neighborhood in Los Angeles. He was devoted to stamp collecting and eventually amassed a world-class collection, but a suspicion of banks and his neighbors led him to carry his cash around in one of his shoes, which caused him to limp. Hurter was a loner who never married, never joined in studio social activities, and could be honest to the point of tactlessness. Once when a young apprentice asked for a frank evaluation of what was wrong with a drawing, he looked it over and solemnly replied, "There is nothing *right* with this." Extremely methodical, he inevitably arrived at the studio every morning at 6:30, smoked his beloved cigars and read the newspaper until he went to work at 8:00, and left promptly for home at 5:00. He would occasionally be glimpsed on weekends heading out to the desert to study landscapes and rock formations. A curious gentleman with a fertile imagination, he fell ill and died in 1941, leaving a large creative hole in the Disney operation.[40]

Another of the unforgettable characters of the golden age came with a name and an appearance that were equally outlandish — Thornton "T." Hee. This fun-loving artist was an all-round creative figure who worked as a story man, caricaturist, stylist, and director. He worked on short films like *Mother Goose Goes Hollywood* (1938), for which he contributed many caricatures of famous movie stars. His work in *Fantasia* was notable; he codirected the "Dance of the Hours" segment, full of delightful comedic characters such as Ben Ali Gator, Hyacinth Hippo, and the ostrich ballerinas. T. Hee's most famous contributions, however, came from his many delightful caricatures of studio personnel and his startling physical presence. A short, rotund man with a small mustache, wire-rimmed glasses, perpetually twinkling eyes, and highly developed sense of the outrageous, he loved to shock his colleagues with his appearance. He often came to the studio dressed in baggy burlap pants and shirts made for him by his wife, adorned with a brightly colored neckerchief and fancy Mexican huaraches and sporting long black hair that he cut himself. This startling image was enhanced by his considerable bulk — he weighed around 250 pounds — and his usual companion, story man Ed Penner, who liked to dress in mustard-colored pants, Hawaiian shirts, and East Indian moccasins. Garbed in such fashion, this pair made a hilarious story presentation for the *Mother Goose Goes Holly-*

wood project, Hee putting the crowd in stitches with his impersonation of Katharine Hepburn saying, "I've lost my sheep, really I have." T. Hee also possessed a knack for cracking up Walt. After Walt asked him whether he dyed his mustache, for example, he replied impertinently, "Yes sir, every morning, with chicken shit." And the studio chief loved him.[41]

The Voice Department also featured a pair of notable employees. Pinto Colvig, a former circus clown and original member of the Keystone Kops, came to the studio as a talented comedian and musician who played clarinet and ocarina as well as sang. Possessed of a flexible and expressive voice, he spoke for many Disney characters in short films, then achieved some fame as the voice of Goofy and then of Grumpy in *Snow White*. Clarence "Ducky" Nash was a vocal impressionist who specialized in animal voices and noises, and he came to Disney in 1934. His work included the voices of many of the animal characters in Disney films, but he gained his greatest fame as the squawking voice of that irascible cinematic fowl, Donald Duck.[42]

The Story Department stabled a collection of men whose imaginative, clever, and buoyant temperaments enlivened studio life as well as the plots of many a Disney film. Ted Sears, the head of this unit throughout the golden age, was a portly, sharp-dressing New Yorker always chomping on a cigar. An extremely clever man who was a committed practical jokester, he became famous for napping through story meetings and then waking up at the perfect moment to offer a great gag to solve a problem. The antics of Jack Kinney and Roy Williams, high school friends and fellow football players, became the talk of the studio. The former, a tall boisterous Irishman, and the latter, a balding, gruff man with a huge belly who much later became famous as one of the adult Mouseketeers on the Disney television series, collaborated on many projects, filmed and otherwise. They drove to work together in Williams's Ford roadster, which had a piece of railroad track welded to it as a "bumper" to push offending drivers off the road. Fondly insulting one another as "Fat Boy" and "Banana Nose," Williams and Kinney tossed off jokes effortlessly and specialized in horseplay, the exuberance of which sometimes led to smashed drawing boards and water coolers. In one of the most famous escapades in studio history, they joined forces against the hated George Drake. After enduring a particularly obnoxious temper tantrum, they grabbed the supervisor from each side and lifted him off the floor, firmly goosed him while he screamed like a banshee, carried him out of the building, and dumped him in the middle of Hyperion Avenue. They were sternly reprimanded, of course, but that scarcely mattered in light of the standing ovation they received from staff members who witnessed the incident.[43]

According to many accounts, Bill Peet, who started at the Disney Studio in 1937 and remained there for nearly thirty years, was the closest thing to Walt the studio ever produced. Also a native midwesterner, Peet, an artist and story man, had a knack for dreaming up "real, live characters that lived and breathed and thought and came from the heart." Over the years he developed a volatile, love-hate relationship with Walt. Argumentative and assertive, he was always ready to argue with his boss, and the fact that he was amazingly attuned to *Walt's* way of developing a story made it difficult for the studio chief to win those disagreements. Moreover, Peet, unlike many, was not afraid of Disney. A shrewd analyst of character, he propounded a theory of the "three Walts" — the dreamer, the realist, and the spoiler — and he quipped that you had to phone the front gate attendant each morning to see which one had showed up. He frequently joked that Walt, like all of the great despots in history, hated cats because he couldn't bend them to his will. For his part, Disney respected Peet's work enormously and occasionally dropped by his office just to talk. Probably because he sensed their underlying affinity, however, he grew resentful of Peet's talent and seldom lost a chance to put him in his place. Engaging in ruthless gamesmanship during story meetings, he would pick Peet's stories apart and demand wholesale changes and then, several days later, forgetting his qualms, force more changes that put things back in their original shape. Perhaps the most revealing comment about their relationship came from Walt himself. Someone once overheard him telling Peet, "You know, Bill, goddammit, if I had your talent, I wouldn't work for me."[44]

The complex studio structure, the abundant fun, and the fascinating personalities and creative shenanigans made for an electric, intense, and occasionally enchanted atmosphere at the Disney fantasy factory. But eventually this array of elements converged on the studio's central business — the making of animated movies. The process of production, with its characteristics and nuances, reveals much about the dynamic young entertainer and his organization.

10

The Engineering of Enchantment

WHEN Shamus Culhane first arrived for work at Disney's Hyperion Avenue studio in 1935, he could hardly believe his eyes. Used to crowded, dingy New York animation facilities, he was shocked to find everything cheerfully painted in "bright tints of raspberry, light blue, and gleaming white." He was equally startled to see that each animation team was ensconced in its own room, with "beautifully designed desks, upholstered chairs, cupboards for storing work in progress." And most amazing of all, each room had a moviola, a small projector for running and testing reels of animation. These were very expensive machines, and as Culhane noted, most studios had only one for their entire staff.[1]

Ward Kimball, who entered the Disney realm around the same time, had a strikingly different impression. Beginning work as a lowly in-betweener, he labored in the basement of one of the buildings along with dozens of others. With no air conditioning, the large room was so hot and damp that many of the in-betweeners would strip to the waist in the summertime. Sitting at small drawing tables in row after row and drawing like madmen to meet expectations, they looked like men on a slave ship, Kimball remembered.[2]

As these two recollections indicate, the Hyperion studio comprised a wide variety of physical circumstances and work conditions. Topnotch in certain ways — especially in its offerings to the stars among the animators and story men — the studio offered considerably less to those lower in the production hierarchy.

The new Burbank facility, of course, aimed to remedy all problems of space and comfort. With typical energy and commitment, Disney became involved with every aspect of its development, from designing animators' chairs to drawing up plans for underground utilities. He sought to build a kind of worker's paradise. The state-of-the-art facility overflowed with the most advanced kinds of amenities, aids, and equipment — air conditioning; sophisticated animation desks; spacious and well-landscaped grounds; buildings designed to capture natural light; separate buildings (connected by an underground tunnel) for the Inking and Painting, Camera, and Cutting Departments; a theater; individual soundstages for recording music, dialogue, and sound effects; a restaurant and a soda fountain for employees. While still plotting the construction, he would take groups of employees out to the site and talk excitedly about the studio, even though perplexed observers could see only "a treeless wasteland of nothing but tumbleweeds." When the Burbank compound was finally completed and the move from Hyperion Avenue took place, from the late fall of 1939 through the early spring of 1940, Disney and his staff capped a years-long evolution. Their refinement of an entertainment production process had made the Disney Studio the envy not only of Hollywood but of many throughout the United States.[3]

I. Producing the Fantastic

In many ways, the grand construction project in Burbank represented not just an upgrade of the studio's physical plant but an elaborate reflection of the Disney way of making movies. As it had evolved over the years, production increasingly involved many departments and intricate, interlocking activities. Walt provided a clear picture of how a Disney movie actually took shape in a piece entitled "Mickey Mouse Presents," which he contributed to a 1937 book of essays on Hollywood moviemaking. There he proudly described his studio units and their work: the Story Department, which initially plotted a tale; the director, who made an extensive blueprint of sections and scenes for the film; the Background Department, whose layout sketches related characters to setting; the animators, who developed characters and key action scenes in accordance with layout sheets and exposure sheets; the assistant animators, who contributed the "in-between" drawings while their assistants cleaned up rough sketches; the musical director, who scored appropriate music for various scenes; the effects animators, who added special visual touches; the inking and painting staff — all women — who traced the animators' pencil drawings onto cels and then added color;

the camera technicians, who shot the film a frame at a time; and the sound effects and dialogue experts, who added the final touches.[4]

As the intricate process of making films developed, the Disney Studio pioneered a series of innovations that became critical to its success. The storyboard, for example, a series of sketches pinned up on a cork board like a comic strip, allowed artists to envision an animated story as the camera would see it. The conference technique, where storyboards, artistic ideas, and character development were subject to intense critical analysis by a group, also began at the studio. Other production innovations included pencil tests and the Leica reel, both designed to iron out wrinkles before more expensive processes were involved. The former was a method of photographing and projecting crude pencil drawings, and the latter was a technique for projecting parts of an entire project — still sketches, rough animation, finished animation with backgrounds — that gave both director and artists an overall view of the film as it took shape. In terms of structure, the Disney Studio was the first animation operation to develop an extensive training program for its artists, bringing them up through the ranks as they studied anatomy, worked on the Disney style of caricature and personality, and attended action analysis classes where they watched slow-motion film and heard lectures from senior animators. In the late 1930s Disney established the Character Model Department, headed by Joe Grant. This special group of artists produced paintings, sketches, and small sculptures that served to shape the characters, style, and emotional texture of a film.[5]

More than any physical structure, technological development, or organizational technique, however, the institutional atmosphere at the Disney Studio fueled its success. A work culture devoted to industriousness, excellence, teamwork, and imagination held sway throughout the era, and staffers responded. As many studio artists testified, they threw themselves into their work because the organization gave them "all sorts of help no other studio in the world could ever give you" and guaranteed that a "Walt Disney presentation . . . stood for quality." The Disney Studio, as Dick Huemer once put it, poured much of its energy into "analyzing and reanalyzing . . . re-re-reanalyzing, discarding and starting all over again." This ethos of constant improvement inspired staffers to efforts that went far beyond the call of duty. Marc Davis, for instance, recalled that he and other aspiring animators in the 1930s would go to a local ballet studio in the evenings to try and capture the dancers' movements on their sketchpads, and on the weekends they would gather at zoos to sketch the animals and study their anatomy. In his words, "This was on our own time. We weren't told to do it, and yet we felt we needed it."[6]

The capabilities and values of the Disney organization appeared clearly with the making of *Snow White and the Seven Dwarfs*. The project began in

1934, when Walt summoned a group of artists and staffers to the Hyperion studio soundstage and gave a virtuoso solo performance for nearly three hours, acting out the parts of the main characters. Over the next few years, the staff followed up with a huge outlay of creative labor, putting in long hours month after month. Artist Grim Natwick, for instance, was assigned to animate the character of Snow White because of his experience drawing Betty Boop for Fleischer's Studio in New York. He was allowed two months of experimental drawing before he was asked to animate for the movie. He responded with almost two years of unstinting work and completed eighty-four scenes, nearly a tenth of the total footage in the movie. By late 1937, as the deadline loomed, Natwick was turning out an average of a thousand finished drawings a week. In similar fashion, the Special Effects Department worked frantically to develop new techniques for portraying atmospheric conditions such as fog and rain and quivering reflections in the water.[7]

The inkers and painters also made extraordinary contributions. Near the completion of the film, a problem cropped up: Snow White looked washed out, even anemic, on the actual film. Adding color to her cheeks only made her look clownish. The women in the Inking and Painting Department came up with a novel solution when one of them asked, "Walt, can we put a little rouge on her cheeks?" Pulling out their makeup compacts, they proceeded to dab rouge right onto the cels. When an astounded Disney wondered aloud whether they could put it precisely in the same spot time after time, one of them turned to him indignantly and said, "Well, of course we can! What do you think we've been doing all our lives?"[8]

The creation of *Bambi*, as surviving documents reveal, demonstrated how collaboration and a participatory ethic marked the making of a Disney film. A typical meeting on April 5, 1939, involved the head story man for the project, Perce Pearce, art instructor Don Graham, and visiting artist Rico Lebrun. Following a preview of several sections of the film, the men critiqued its various elements, discussing the issue of artistic style and debating the merits of caricature versus a more realistic depiction of animals and nature. They pondered questions of public reaction to drawing styles and explored the proper use of music to enhance certain visual features, arguing over the best method for conveying the smells and feel of a deep-forest atmosphere. At one point, Pearce summed up the dominant attitude of the Disney team. "It's a great experience," he noted of their filmmaking. "We are in the Stone Age of technique — a very early stage . . . Let's shoot as high as we can, considering the time element, and go after it." Lebrun summed up his admiration succinctly: "I have never found a more thoroughly self-critical bunch in my life."[9]

When a Disney film neared completion, it was screened in its rough version for a studio audience. As was typical during the 1930s, the group's reaction was closely monitored and recorded in detailed reports, which were studied closely. At the film's conclusion, questionnaires were distributed to gather reactions and suggestions, and then tabulated. Such treatment was given to *Bambi,* and the results were fascinating. An audience of about seventy staffers watched the rough film in October 1940 and then carefully responded to a set of questions about various sequences by checking boxes indicating a range of approval. Free-form written comments were also solicited, and the vast majority indicated serious attempts to evaluate and improve the film. Comments covered a wide range of topics:

> Most of the deer lines drag. Don't care a lot for the deer voices, delivery, and choice of lines. Felt a need for a greater voice difference between deer and smaller animals.

> Thumper is a scene stealer, be careful of him.

> In the [original] story, Man's relation to the animals and Nature was very strongly pushed. This, I feel, has been weakened . . . Nature is so much in evidence that Man doesn't seem to do a great deal but run around with a gun, and it is not convincing. The angle of man being forced to bow to Nature should be more strongly emphasized.

> Transition of seasons in relation to Bambi's growth was not very clear. Either he grew like hell or he had been some place else for quite a while.

> Because of the voice casting being so outstandingly good, Bambi's adolescent voice sounds incongruous and unconvincing. There's no evidence in his voice of Bambi's battle-won manhood after the fight over Faline. And when he becomes a full-fledged Prince of the Forest, there's no strength and confidence reflected in his voice.[10]

For all of its institutional complexity and energy, however, the production process at Hollywood's leading fantasy factory ultimately turned on a central axis: the judgments and guidance of Walt Disney. Throughout the 1930s and early 1940s, nearly every scene in every animated film that emerged from the studio carried the personal imprint, in one way or another, of its dynamic chief. Walt was a powerful, pervasive presence in the productive work of his studio, and no one who worked there doubted it for a second.

II. The Benign Dictator

During the 1930s, just after a preview of a Disney animated short at a local theater, the director of the film made a beeline for the exit. Dissatisfied with the result, he was determined to avoid his boss and the inevitable tongue-lashing that would be coming his way. He made it to his automobile but was delayed for a few minutes while other cars blocked his path. Then he saw an opening. He was darting from the parking lot into the street when he almost hit a pedestrian rushing along the sidewalk. It was Walt, who had come looking for him. While a string of blocked cars sat there honking, Walt angrily lectured the unhappy director about studio standards of excellence.[11]

Walt's wife, Lillian, liked to tell a rather different story about her husband. As the couple prepared to go to the Hyperion studio for the initial showing of the rough cut of *Snow White*, she apparently dallied a bit, fussing with her clothes and makeup. An impatient Walt urged her along, saying, "Hurry up, Lilly, or we won't get a seat!" His astonished wife could only reply, "At your own studio, your own showing, you won't get a seat?"[12]

These tales suggest something of Disney's combination of domination and naiveté, critical intensity and endearing innocence. They also reveal something of the complex reactions elicited from his employees. Staff members, experiencing their remarkable chief as almost a force of nature, approached him with varying combinations of respect, fear, affection, loyalty, awe, sycophancy, and dislike.

Ollie Johnston, a young artist who rose through the ranks to become a leading animator, probably put it best when he described Walt as a "benign dictator." Most employees agreed completely. In indisputable fashion, Walt ran the show and wielded power everywhere. In the words of a close associate, he was a "one-man studio" as he directed the creative planning for the great projects of this era and drove his staff relentlessly for ideas that would supplement his basic vision. Convinced that his own judgment about audiences and their tastes was superior, he shouldered a huge variety of tasks. He jettisoned his easygoing, casual style at story and animation meetings and adopted a posture that brooked little opposition. "What he said was final," animators agreed, and "he let you know when you wandered away from what he wanted." As Wilfred Jackson, a longtime film director, once observed, Walt "just about wore himself out trying to do every last thing."[13]

His management made a memorable impact. Those who spent even a little time around him quickly became accustomed to the Disney style: a total immersion in the creative process, volatile shifts of mood leading to warm encouragement or bitter criticism, a perfectionism that could be equally demanding and inspirational. His personal quirks and idiosyncrasies were legendary. Staffers listened for Disney's famous cough as a signal of his approach, and his body language in conferences served as a gauge of his state of mind — a slow tapping of the fingers usually indicated that he was mulling something over, fast tapping meant that he was growing impatient, and the famous arching eyebrow could signal everything from annoyance to surprise to intense interest.[14]

Disney also displayed a unique ability to handle talent. He had an almost intuitive sense of a person's particular creative strengths, even if they were latent, and he never hesitated to shunt people around until they found a useful niche. An artist or story man who was floundering in a given situation would often be moved to a completely different department, where, after the shock wore off, he would flourish. Director Ben Sharpsteen argued that this keen "ability to handle other people" was one of Disney's greatest strengths. Animator Eric Larson explained it in a slightly different way. Disney, he argued, had to manage a group of creative and assertive people, and he "had a way of taking those egos and making them work together as a team."[15]

Disney's ability to inspire his staff was apparent almost daily, and his employees never ceased to be amazed at it. One artist described how he typically "got me so enthused I couldn't wait to get back to my [drawing] board. He'd get you laughing and all excited about the personality of the character you were going to work with." Disney would go on regular tours of the facility, poking his head into everything, and with genuine interest ask even the lowliest technician or workman, "Hey, how's it coming? What have you got here?" The top animators reported similar experiences. In the words of one, "I don't know what intuitiveness he had, but you could have been laboring and struggling to come up with ideas and put them on boards . . . Walt would come in and he would see what you had and he would understand it, he would 'plus' it, he would leave you so inspired that you couldn't believe yourself. Just knowing he was around was a great thing."[16]

Disney's demanding, critical standards could be frustrating, but they also instilled a sense of pride in one's work that pervaded the studio. The artists and story men were thrilled when Disney regularly dismissed expense as an issue and urged them "to do better than [they] were capable of . . . He wanted sheer perfection." He would write and rewrite stories, revise animated scenes over and over, and work out his films "down to the last blink of the eye." Lillian observed that he frequently worked on scenes in the evenings, as he walked around the back yard making gestures, muttering to himself, laughing at ideas, and talking "to the sky, the birds, to anything." In staff meetings he would constantly interrupt presentations to question the efficacy of a gag, a character, or a situation. Typically he would raise his eyebrow, look intense, and stare at the presenter in an unnerving fashion. However, as one experienced Walt watcher noted, it was just his "tremendous powers of concentration at work, and I doubt he knew who he was looking at most of the time. But I'll never forget that piercing stare." Another artist remembered how Disney regularly phoned people over the weekend or late at night, bubbling over with enthusiasm for some new idea. Disney's theory of film production, he concluded, consisted of constantly "playing with the thing, working with it, evolving it, not just *boom* and that's it. It's the living with it, that's what he enjoyed."[17]

A spirit of innovation was another striking trait. Disney was always on the prowl for fresh concepts and encouraged his staff to come up with them, no matter how unusual or outlandish they might be. As T. Hee remembered, one of the filmmaker's strongest characteristics in the 1930s was his lack of reverence for traditional procedures in animation and an eagerness to find ways of doing things differently. Wilfred Jackson argued that the greatest strength of Disney's golden-age films was the "joyous, creative spirit" that came from his hands-on involvement, a quality that was gradually diluted in subsequent years.[18]

Disney excelled at a number of things, none more so than the job of story development. A naturally gregarious man, he loved talking (much more than listening, many noted), and he was "a great storyteller," according to Marc Davis. Gifted with a phenomenal memory, he retained enormous amounts of detailed information about humorous daily situations and funneled them into story ideas. As Milt Kahl once related, Disney would come into story conferences and "come up with ideas that — God! You'd wonder why somebody else didn't think of it. He did it and did it and did it . . . He was just a tremendously creative man and he'd start cooking. The funny thing about him, too, he could sell you something. He was such a g.d. good storyteller that it would sound great . . . He would come up with a great many ideas because he was cooking all the time; his brain was going all the time. He was like a fountain."[19]

In "Mickey Mouse Presents," Disney argued that an effective story man should carefully avoid several common pitfalls, including "wishful thinking," defined as the hope that a good long story would make a good short story, and "losing perspective," or seeing a film as a series of incidents rather than a unified whole. He also warned against harboring "pet ideas," special notions that were inappropriate to the story at hand, and indulging in excessive subtlety when direct and obvious situations and characters would prove far more appealing. Perhaps the greatest sin, however, lay in "forgetting the audience." Rushing past humorous spots, having too many complex matters going on at once, and veiling key plot clues all pointed to a lack of regard for the filmgoer's point of view, he believed. That could be deadly.[20]

Studio personnel spoke unanimously of Walt's tremendous acting ability. He later appeared in *The Reluctant Dragon* and hosted his television show, of course, but in this early period he remained rather shy about performing. His staff was shocked and delighted when once, quite unexpectedly, he appeared at a party in a Harpo Marx wig and joined in the presentation of a couple of skits. But in meeting after meeting, his artists agreed, Disney demonstrated "the instincts of an actor" as he uncannily mimicked the characters and conveyed the situations that needed to be animated. Artists eagerly anticipated his performances and went away thrilled and inspired by his characterizations. With his expressive hands, pliable face, intense eyes, and frantic eyebrows, he held his audience enthralled. In the words of Dick Huemer, "Walt would take stories and act them out at a meeting, and kill you laughing, they were so funny . . . You'd have the feeling of the whole thing. You'd know exactly what he wanted. We often wondered if Walt could have been a great actor or a comedian. The acting in them was what made his pictures so great."[21]

Ward Kimball and Marc Davis witnessed many of their boss's performances and concluded that when he got "carried away with a story or gag situation and start[ed] imitating something, he was just as great as Chaplin." For many animators, the big fear was that they would be unable to capture in drawing what they had just seen Disney act out. Moreover, his skill at pantomime fed the pervasive search for personality in the studio's films. While other animated movies from this era relied on comic episodes and outlandish gags, Disney humor flowed naturally out of character traits and quirks. "Without personality, the character may do funny or interesting things, but unless people are able to identify themselves with the character, its actions will seem unreal," Disney once said. "Without personality, a story cannot ring true to the audience."[22]

Most important, perhaps, Disney functioned brilliantly in the hard-to-define but central role of artistic visionary at his studio. Those who tried to define what he did kept coming back to the same words: "intuition," "instinct," a feel for the "essence of things," a "creative catalyst." Without theories or formulas, he grasped the crucial elements of a successful animated film and kept them in balance. An intensely sensitive man, he did not have the talent to draw a key idea himself, Frank Thomas once mused, but he could "communicate it to you . . . [with] all the personality, all the character, the timing. Walt made it all come to life so you could see it." He conjured up a clear vision of a film, inspired his story men and animators to get it on the screen, and kept the creative process moving with critical acumen and enthusiasm. The staff saw it again and again and never ceased to be amazed. Disney, as director Jack Cutting concluded simply, "made it all work."[23]

For all of his creative ability, however, Disney developed a number of bad managerial habits that caused no small amount of resentment, fear, and even bitterness among staffers. His egotism, for instance, could crowd out everyone else in a project. Even his greatest admirers occasionally grew sullen over the pressure to line up creatively behind him. According to Milt Kahl, working successfully with Disney usually meant agreeing with him, "so that the original ideas that you get . . . are pretty much along the lines he's already on." If an artist showed the slightest sign of rebellion or independence, commented another studio director, Disney "slapped him down so fast . . . [and] said, 'Look, nobody here is indispensable.'"[24]

Unfortunately, Disney also frequently engaged in what one studio staffer called "scare tactics" to keep the upper hand. This involved not only gruffness (which seemed an intrinsic part of his personality) but outright manipulation and insensitivity. As Jack Kinney noted, he would often pat a guy on the back one day and ignore him the next, thus keeping the employee in a state of confusion and emotional subservience. A man of strong opinions, Disney "could hold a grudge forever" when someone crossed him, added Kinney. Then, of course, there was his notorious practice of putting people down in public. Even animators like Ward Kimball and Ollie Johnston, who eventually were among his closest friends at the studio, dreaded "his way of bawling employees out in front of other employees." Often delivered with great sarcasm at staff meetings, Disney's jibes could create a humiliation that would linger for days or weeks. By cowing the staff in this way, he found it easier to bend them to his will.[25]

In later years, Disney admitted, "I've been a slave driver. Sometimes I feel like a dirty heel the way I pound, pound, pound." He expected excellence as a matter of course and seemed to forget that appreciation and approval could be very effective motivational tools. "His compliments were few and far between," said Kahl. "Most of the time, if he had something to say about [a project], it was critical. And if he liked it a lot, you didn't hear anything about it." Another artist noted a more frequent Disney tactic. "You knew you were pleasing Walt because he would tell someone else! You see, it was always secondhand," reported Kimball. These habits could make temperamental artists, except for the most secure or thick-skinned, feel unappreciated or resentful after their heroic efforts to produce good work.[26]

In extreme form, Disney's artistic vision could overwhelm his capacity for words. Often when he did not like something, he found it difficult to explain his objections or what he wanted as an alternative. The poor artist could only try to surmount his rhetorical confusion and discern the feeling that lay behind it. As Norm Ferguson liked to say, "Don't do what Walt says, do what Walt means." It led to even more confusion when Disney, working on instinct, forgot an earlier directive and demanded something else a few days later. And woe to the unfortunate employee who pointed out such inconsistency. Disney did not care for criticism of *his* ideas. When someone dared to disagree with his flow of creative thought, Jack Cutting observed, often the studio chief would "look like he had been hit in the face with a bucket of cold water — the eyebrow would go up and suddenly reality [rather than imagination] was the mood in the room."[27]

The ambiguous nature of Disney's managerial style appeared clearly in his relationship with two key groups, the directors and the animators. Film directors often became the targets of his ire. These vulnerable figures stood midway between their strong-willed chief and the artists who actually brought the movies to life, and as one of them put it bluntly, their main job was "getting on the screen what Walt visualized." They struggled to discern what their boss actually meant in his directives, because "he did not want some *other* thing done, no matter how much better you thought it might be." As Wilfred Jackson admitted ruefully, "I know I got roasted if it didn't suit him." Directors tended to become Disney's "whipping boys," as Ben Sharpsteen once put it, and Harry Tytle told of how he once made an animator's model for a film and Disney hated it; when Tytle replied gamely, "Well, at least you can give me an E for effort," his boss shot back, "I'll give you an S for shit."[28]

Animators, however, were a different matter. As Kimball put it, "Walt admired the animators, but he was always pissed off that he had to rely on them so much. That was the one job in the studio he couldn't do." Resentful of their special talent, he tended to play games with them. One moment he let it be known how much he admired a piece of work — always indirectly, of course — and the next he would bawl out the artist with such intensity that the targets of his wrath formed a "shit club," as they called it. Or he would tease them constantly about bringing in new talent. Or after the release of a highly successful film he would claim that "you guys worked too slow on that picture." While he subjected them to fierce criticism and occasional abuse, both he and they knew that the studio could not survive without skilled artists. Try as he might, Disney could not quite bend them to his will, so he handled them more carefully than other members of the staff.[29]

Ironically, for all the rationalized efficiency of his fantasy factory, Disney ultimately functioned as an old-fashioned, paternalistic owner. His intense personal involvement could be endearing, and it inspired devotion and affection among those who worked for him. "Somehow you would do anything to get a compliment from Walt," one artist explained. But his paternalism could inspire fear and inflict pain on those beneath him. Ollie Johnston, a close friend and associate, noted that many staffers recognized this fact and counseled him frankly, "Don't dance too close to the queen." Ken Anderson said that over the years Disney "did things that hurt me terribly. But by the same token, if a guy can hurt you that much, he can also make you love him that much."[30]

Disney's role in the process of film production may have been central, even domineering, but it did not nullify the complex bureaucracy that had grown up during the expansion of the 1930s. Many people occupied important niches in his organization, and their work contributed a great deal to the functioning of the whole. None did so more revealingly than an unimposing, stuffy, bespectacled man who oversaw much of its day-to-day operation. Standing close — perhaps too close — to Walt himself, he offered a fascinating perspective on the workings of the man and his operation.

III. Ben Sharpsteen: "Adapt to the Disney System"

Ben Sharpsteen knew one big thing about the Disney Studio, but he knew it very well. An employee for more than thirty years, one who rose through the ranks to become a key manager, he once explained the lesson he had learned as Disney began to build his organization. Sharpsteen recognized that the studio chief "was still the prime mover of production. He was still *the* spark plug. The whole movement of that organization was Walt Disney personally." Sharpsteen's appreciation of the need to maneuver in a complex organization under the strict control of one man became the key to his long, rewarding career at the fantasy factory. But it became a source of great pain as well.[31]

Sharpsteen was one of the Disney Studio success stories. After an early career in commercial art in northern California and on the East Coast, he had arrived in 1929 as part of an influx of animators, many from New York, as Disney sought to expand his operation. Laboring first as a director, later as a production supervisor, and eventually as the production manager for the entire studio, Sharpsteen stood between the boss and his staff of artists, writers, and technicians. Facing great pressures from both directions, he sought equilibrium as he struggled to protect his bureaucratic niche. He became the prototypical organization man during the 1930s and early 1940s.[32]

Sharpsteen worked for several years as an animator, but by his own admission he did not excel at this task. A hard worker, he drew various scenes and characters for 97 out of 116 Disney films released between 1929 and 1934, but he lacked the visual flair and the imagination to become an outstanding artist. As a result, Disney slowly pointed him in other directions. Sharpsteen began to act as a talent scout, scouring art schools and commercial art studios for artists whose work might enhance animated films. When Bert Gillett left in 1934, Disney suggested that Sharpsteen move into production, a role for which he proved well suited. Beginning with *Two Gun Mickey,* he directed some twenty short films before serving as sequence director or production supervisor for the new feature-length movies. Moreover, Disney put him in charge of the training program for novice animators. Throughout the 1940s and 1950s, Sharpsteen played a prominent role in studio production through involvement with a large number of projects: educational movies during World War II, the True-Life Adventures and People and Places series in the following decade, and films like *Cinderella* (1950) and *Alice in Wonderland* (1951). In the eyes of many, he stood right under Walt in the hierarchy.[33]

As a bureaucrat, Sharpsteen realized early on that Disney's vision of production depended equally on developing a sophisticated, skilled staff of artists, technicians, and craftsmen and on maintaining his own control over it. "Walt had long since realized that by himself, he could not animate, direct the efforts of other people, take care of the story work, and so forth. He knew that he would have to confine his efforts to supervising people, to getting stories and ideas together, to supervising the creative end of the business," the producer observed. "The only way that he could accomplish this objective was through a staff . . . [that would] work under his direction, to do as he would have it done . . . He was determined to have a team."[34]

As a director, Sharpsteen experienced firsthand the organizational imperatives of the Disney Studio. He described "walking a tightrope" to perform several delicate tasks: taking the story outline he was given and bringing it to life without losing any key elements, negotiating between the story men and animators (each of whom thought they alone were responsible for a film's success), and accommodating a demanding boss. Sharpsteen respected Disney's standards of excellence enormously and patiently endured countless grueling conference meetings and sweatbox sessions. At the same time, he observed close-up many of the managerial traits that created problems. Disney's tendency to be abrupt with his employees created resentments, and his notorious mood swings kept employees scrambling to adapt to spells where at one moment he was "terrifically optimistic and saw the world through rose-colored glasses" and at another full of "despondency . . . [where] you couldn't figure out what the devil was going wrong." Sharpsteen also felt the tension created by Disney's determination to stamp out any ego displays among his staff. Group effort was paramount in film production, he insisted, and he never failed to put in his place anyone who claimed to be a star at the studio.[35]

The Walt Disney Sharpsteen saw was hardly a paragon of industrial efficiency. "There was a note of comedy to Walt's attempts at organization," he noted. "There was one firm which came out with a work entitled *The Importance of Good Management* . . . [with] the 'ten commandments of good management.' But we laughed at that, because Walt consistently broke every one of those commandments." Although building a twentieth-century bureaucratic organization, Disney ran it with a personalized, nineteenth-century managerial style. This tendency gained force as it ran through Sharpsteen, who carried out Disney's orders, and filtered down to the staff he managed.[36]

Sharpsteen himself adopted what one observer called a "father-type role" toward the younger artists working under him. Eager to establish his authority, he could be demanding and domineering one moment and eager to dispense advice the next. This stern, self-disciplined man habitually called new artists into his office for a chat shortly after their arrival. He would first lecture them, in considerable detail, on the importance of following studio rules and procedures to keep their job and advance their career. On a kinder note, he would then counsel them to put some money in the bank, avoid flashy cars in favor of inexpensive but solid ones, and resist temptations to misbehave. As Bill Cottrell, Walt's brother-in-law and longtime employee, once noted, Sharpsteen "was good for the organization, even if a lot of the guys didn't like him."[37]

Some employees reacted by poking fun at Sharpsteen and his pedantic streak. Tolerating his stuffiness in public, they adopted a mocking attitude in private. According to Jack Kinney, for instance, the inevitable office romances that arose offered the perfect opportunity for ridiculing the straight-arrow image of the production manager. When artists and their girlfriends rented rooms for passionate trysts, it was a standing joke for the men to sign Ben Sharpsteen's name on the motel registers. As Kinney put it, the unfortunate bureaucrat became "the 'John Smith'" of the naughty boys in the Magic Kingdom."[38]

Of medium height with a strongly receding hairline and a small mustache, Sharpsteen wore wire-rimmed glasses and usually faced the world with a serious, even pinched expression on his face. With stiff mannerisms and a schoolmasterish style, he affected a rather hardnosed posture about the production process. Individuals had to adapt themselves to Disney standards and procedures or they would be gone, he liked to remind any artists who drifted toward creative self-indulgence. Sharpsteen also displayed few qualms about replacing employees who had worn out their value. The old-timers at the studio felt constant pressure from new, innovative artists who were eager to take their jobs, but he believed that such brutal competition was natural "all through life and not just at the Disney Studio."[39]

Some staffers respected Sharpsteen's intense work ethic and professionalism. Shamus Culhane, for instance, described him as a tough but fair director who spent hours going over his storyboard drawings, telling him "where the poses were usable, and [pointing out] the holes in the action where I was going to have to add my own interpretations . . . I left Sharpsteen's office with my head bursting with instructions." Jack Kinney, describing Sharpsteen's labors as "the whip, or supervising producer," on *Pinocchio*, noted simply, "Ben was very good at this. He was not a prima donna, just a darned good pusher." Bill Tytla, who had known Sharpsteen since their days as young animators in New York, always remembered his colleague's act of kindness in tearing out a page from a book on cartooning and giving it to him when he first arrived. According to the burly artist, "Some of the other men didn't like him — he was a hard taskmaster — but I always did."[40]

Many of Sharpsteen's colleagues, however, reacted less favorably. They sensed the insecurity lurking behind his stern facade, and this realization gave rise to resentment and eventually thinly disguised contempt. Such an attitude became especially prominent among the animators, many of whom saw Sharpsteen as a mediocrity who couldn't cut it as an artist and thus became a bureaucratic lackey who compensated by throwing his weight around. When Sharpsteen, not Disney himself, went before the staff in the late 1930s to announce that *Pinocchio* would follow *Snow White* as the next feature project, it caused a stir of animosity. Ken Anderson reacted typically, bursting out, "Who the hell are you to take Walt's place? You can't talk like Walt did." He explained, "We knew he was a big shot, that he was a manager . . . [but] that's the second team telling us what we were going to do next." Another artist commented dryly, "Ben is a son of a bitch — and I'm one of his best friends." The acid-tongued Bill Peet offered a devastating gibe that was repeated for years among the Disney artists: "He's okay. He just doesn't mean well."[41]

Sharpsteen's reputation gained a twist from his curious relationship with Disney. On the one hand, Sharpsteen was an adoring disciple who sought to carry out his master's every wish. He habitually lectured his coworkers on their boss's virtues, telling them that "they didn't appreciate Walt." On the other hand, he paid a very high price for that selfless devotion. As many noted, his loyalty and esteem seemed to flow out of his insecurity. Even his wife once privately admitted, "Ben realizes he is not talented, that he can't compete. He was fired off every job he had until Disney." Moreover, it was common knowledge that Sharpsteen was one of Disney's favorite targets for abuse, and that fact raised sympathy from even his harshest critics.[42]

Ward Kimball, for instance, observed the two men over many years and offered a shrewd assessment of their relationship. He himself was certainly no great friend of Sharpsteen's. This stern manager, he asserted, had "no talent" for drawing but demonstrated the "straw boss's talent for telling people what to do," so as the organization grew, Disney chose him as the man to carry out his orders. Sharpsteen recognized his own dependency, which made him a "prime insecure character" who then became "slightly sadistic with the new, young artists who were coming in. Somebody had to be a shit, you know," the colorful animator asserted. "Every business has them." But Sharpsteen was "more or less Walt's whipping boy for years," according to Kimball, and everyone knew it. "The verbal beatings and sleepless nights I know he had, because I talked to his wife, were a hell of a price to pay for getting his name up there on the screen."[43]

Many were struck by the way Disney frequently embarrassed his managerial assistant in public. Kimball recalled an incident that happened in the late 1930s, when Disney and the animation staff sat in the theater reviewing old, relatively crude Mickey Mouse films one evening so they could identify and study certain developments in technique. An early film that Sharpsteen had worked on, *Toreador Mickey*, appeared on the screen. "Walt spoke out so everybody could hear him in the auditorium, and said, 'Ha ha ha, Ben animated this stuff.' And then he paused and said, 'We call that the "rubber hose" school of animation,' which was a derogatory remark. There was another pause followed by, 'That was bad even in those days,' and everybody kinda laughs embarrassingly. Can you imagine how Ben felt, sitting there with new employees that were working for him and everything?"[44]

Sharpsteen's reaction to such episodes only underscored his insecurity. Realizing his emotional dependence on Disney for authority and his economic dependence on the studio for a job, he suffered such indignities silently. He vented his anger on subordinates, of course, but more often he internalized his discontent. Occasionally he wearily warned colleagues, "Don't ever get too close to Walt," or commiserated with others who felt the lash of Disney's anger, saying, "You'll get used to that." As he later admitted, "I never considered myself a sure thing at the studio . . . If I did not prove myself useful, I could be on the way out."[45]

Sharpsteen survived because he perceived the fundamentally paternalistic dynamic of the Disney organization and shaped his course accordingly: rely on the studio chief for support and protection and in return suffer the imposition of his authority, no matter how harsh. He demonstrated that the system was more important than anything or anyone, a lesson that had a profound personal impact. "Though Walt was very kind to me, there was never anybody who was indispensable at the studio," he once noted. "If I had never come to the Walt Disney Studio . . . [it] would not be one bit different. And that would apply to anybody."[46]

Sharpsteen revealed that even with a bureaucracy swelling rapidly in size and complexity, Walt maintained iron control over the studio's destiny. "He had to build an organization, but it was *his* judgment as to who was important in that organization," Sharpsteen said. "That was very important to him — that exquisite organization of talent where he could pull the strings and make this man do this and that man do that." And no one danced longer or more enthusiastically than Ben Sharpsteen. His long career at the studio — he lasted far longer than many more talented colleagues, from 1929 to 1959 — stood as mute testimony to that fact.[47]

Old habits die hard. When Sharpsteen retired, he left the Los Angeles area to live on a small ranch in northern California. A few years later, Disney dropped by for a visit. As he was shown around the place, he immediately fell into his customary ways and excitedly began to point out how this rural land could be developed. "Look," he told Sharpsteen, "we'll dam up the stream right here and then put a road over here!" The owner had to remind Disney gently that the land was not his. After Disney left, Sharpsteen shook his head and reflected on "what a really impossible person he had worked for all those years." Then he spotted the gift that the studio head had left sitting on a table for him. It was the Oscar the studio had received for a 1958 People and Places movie, *Ama Girls,* a film on which Sharpsteen had worked very hard. Deeply moved, the old studio manager knew that "it always embarrassed Walt to say thank you, so he took this silent, golden way." Thus even after his retirement, Ben Sharpsteen remained in Disney's grip.[48]

As Sharpsteen's experience suggests, Walt Disney's productive organization served as his greatest source of strength. It provided both the creative atmosphere in which his special brand of magical entertainment came to life and the institutional foundation upon which his enormous enterprise was built. Hundreds of artists, technicians, and managers toiled within this labyrinth to produce a Disney work, and they faced the historical ambiguities of an organization that tried to synthesize individual artistry and industrial technology, rationalized production and free-flowing creativity, corporate bureaucracy and old-fashioned paternalism. Many flourished, and some suffered. Sharpsteen once noted that no matter how talented the artist, "if he couldn't adapt himself to working under the Disney system, he was of no use to us."[49]

The "Disney system" eventually became a source of pain and disillusionment for a significant portion of the staff. The explosive growth of personnel, organization, and facilities in the 1930s contained the seeds of a crisis. The result was a bitter, escalating dispute that exploded in the early 1940s, bringing creative paralysis in its wake. Reeling badly from the impact of such unhappy events, both the fantasy factory and its leader did not recover for nearly a decade.

Part III

Trouble in Fantasyland

11

Animation and Its Discontents

IN JUNE 1941, *The Reluctant Dragon,* with its warm, sparkling portrayal of the Disney Studio, began to appear on movie screens throughout the United States. At the Burbank compound, according to this film, efficiency and creativity reigned side by side, youthful artists learned and exchanged ideas, and the wildest flights of imagination were combined with a dedicated work ethic. An array of gifted people merged their talents in a warm, magical atmosphere to bring Walt Disney's extraordinary visions to life. The situation could not have been more ironic.

At the very moment *The Reluctant Dragon* was released, the Disney Studio was being ripped apart by one of the bitterest labor strikes in the history of the film industry. The real-life scene at Burbank displayed not happy workers and creative magic but angry pickets, watchful police, and disenchanted strikebreakers. Hundreds of workers seeking union representation milled about the main gate on Buena Vista Street, chanting accusations of unfair labor practices and holding signs proclaiming ARE WE MICE OR MEN? and ONE GENIUS AND 700 DWARFS. Hundreds more crossed the picket line to continue work, and exchanges of insults between the two groups became a daily fact of life. There were minor physical clashes — pushing and shoving, spitting, pounding on cars that entered the lot — and Disney himself came close to getting into a fistfight with one of the strikers. The entire situation attracted an embarrassing amount of press attention. Always drawn to the sensational, especially when someone with Disney's pristine reputation was involved, reporters flocked to cover this outbreak of strife as they would to a minister accused of dipping his hand into the collection plate.

The Disney strike was a turning point in the studio's history. After over a decade of spectacular achievement, Disney and his high-flying enterprise began to bank into a long downward turn. In the tense atmosphere created by labor problems reinforced by wartime problems, the studio went into a tailspin that continued for much of the 1940s. The labor dispute was settled and Disney emerged from the ordeal emotionally and financially bloodied but unbroken, but things would never be the same. The travail made him a different man, his films different products, and his studio a different place.

I. The Strike

In February 1941, George Bodle, an attorney for the Screen Cartoonists Guild (SCG), filed charges with the National Labor Relations Board (NLRB) accusing Walt Disney Productions of unfair labor practices. This action precipitated several months of legal and political wrangling between the union and the studio management, which steadily worsened as no solution was reached. As a result, the SCG called a strike on May 28. It dragged on until September 15, when a negotiated resolution was finally reached with the help of the federal government.

The strike appeared to shock Disney and his management team, but it should have come as no great surprise. For several years two systemic problems had been a slow-burning fuse. First, long-term financial difficulties had mounted steadily in the aftermath of the unqualified success of *Snow White and the Seven Dwarfs*. The development of *Pinocchio* sponged up huge amounts of cash, but the film proved a marginal success at the box office. While the little film *Dumbo* later brought modest financial gains, both *Bambi* and *Fantasia* turned out to be large drains that garnered little profit. With the outbreak of war in Europe in the fall of 1939, foreign markets slammed shut, striking another blow. In this context, the large new production facility in Burbank, with its high operating costs, became an unexpected burden. As a result of this convergence of problems, the precarious financial health of the studio became the subject of much speculation. Rumors of staff layoffs and project cutbacks caused rumblings of discontent as well as outright fear.

In a broader context, the Hollywood film industry had been a familiar scene for labor agitation since the mid-1930s. The 1935 passage of the Wagner Act, the congressional statute offering government protection for labor organizing, had nourished the growth of unions in Hollywood, and almost every major group of workers in the movie industry had been organized by

1940. As part of this larger process, all of the big animation studios were beset by labor difficulties. The SCG, founded in 1936 and chartered a few years later as a local of the International Brotherhood of Painters, Decorators, and Paperhangers, focused its attention on the three major animation units. It won contracts with Metro-Goldwyn-Mayer and Schlesinger's and then turned to the Disney Studio.

To complicate matters further, the campaign to unionize the film industry was itself fraught with divisions. In 1926, an ongoing jurisdictional battle between two clusters of AFL unions — various craft unions on the one hand, and the International Alliance of Theatrical Stage Employees (IATSE) on the other — had produced the Studio Basic Agreement, a settlement that underwrote the dominance of the IATSE throughout the 1930s. By mid-decade, however, a growing number of labor groups had become convinced that the IATSE was corrupt and filled with racketeers and gangsters. These dissidents — a coalition of rebels from within the IATSE, outside CIO organizers eager to break the AFL stranglehold on Hollywood workers, and the Painters Union, led by Herb Sorrell — attempted to create an alternative labor organization but achieved only limited success. This more militant movement eventually became known as the Conference of Studio Unions (CSU), and Sorrell gradually emerged as its leading figure. The IATSE staunchly opposed the insurgents from the mid-1930s well into the following decade and denounced them as being riddled with Communist sympathizers. The Screen Cartoonists Guild, by allying itself with Sorrell's movement, thus became entangled in the larger labor feud in Hollywood.[1]

The long, complex struggle to unionize film workers, as well as the unsteady financial state of the Disney enterprise, provided a backdrop for the studio's labor difficulties. A cluster of specific problems within the studio proved far more immediate.

Disney's haphazard salary structure was one of the most serious causes of discontent. It was not so much that the staff was underpaid as that wages varied dramatically and erratically. Disney's animators, top story men, and key technicians received extremely generous salaries by Hollywood standards, but assistant animators, inkers and painters, and workers in the lower echelons did not. Moreover, the distribution of salaries struck many as being capricious and not consistently linked to genuine merit. Even Ward Kimball, one of Disney's best animators by the late 1930s and a friend and supporter to boot, described the situation with some bitterness. Two people would have done the same work for the same number of years, he noted angrily, and one would be making twice as much as the other. Merit raises seemed to come in the same arbitrary fashion, he added. Someone would be doing excellent work for some time and then "some sort of magic light would shine over the studio . . . and all of a sudden [he] might get a raise." But management would not standardize the rules, or even discuss the expectations, governing such raises. Perhaps the most galling episode for Kimball came in the late 1930s, when the studio brought in a flood of new animators from New York to help with the feature-length films. Not only were the newcomers awarded much higher salaries than the veterans, he recalled, but the veterans were expected to train them in Disney animation techniques.[2]

A pair of related controversies welled up around the wage system. First, the Disney Studio engaged in trial hirings, which created considerable bitterness. Apprentice animators would be admitted to the studio for several weeks of training, during which they were paid next to nothing, and then only a few would be chosen for regular employment. According to Ben Sharpsteen, even experienced artists would be judged by Disney as to whether they lived up to their potential. This protracted probation period "often dragged on for years, and it was not fair," Sharpsteen admitted, as it left employees hanging in limbo for long periods of time. Second, the famous Disney bonus system gradually created as much resentment as gratitude. Since the beginning, Disney had given bonuses to employees for contributing gags, story ideas, and extra creative efforts to projects. In the days of small-scale operation, this practice worked to encourage participation, bolster morale, and highlight the studio's commitment to quality productions. By 1941, however, with hundreds of employees working on a host of minor and major projects at the same time, the system began to founder. After the entire staff worked a frenzied schedule for months to complete *Snow White,* for instance, some were given large bonuses, some smaller amounts, and others none at all, with no explanation. Not surprisingly, a wave of discontent swept the studio. When the trade papers began announcing the huge grosses piled up by *Snow White,* bitterness only intensified. Complaints mounted as many concluded that favoritism and arbitrary judgments had corrupted the bonus system.[3]

Such practices gradually helped undermine the community ethic of the studio. In many ways, the enterprise had become the victim of its own success. Wage-related problems reflected nothing so much as its old-fashioned, nonrationalized, paternalistic origins. Informal bonuses and salaries shaped by daily contact with Disney were increasingly unsuited to the large-scale bureaucracy of the late 1930s and early 1940s, and the employment of hundreds of artists and craftspeople and dozens of directors and managers to produce several series of animated films made these practices not only obsolete but dangerous.

A generational rift among the artists also became a nagging source of internal strain. By 1941, a cadre of older artists had been ensconced in the system for at least a decade. Dedicated to its methods and proud of its creative traditions, these animators, directors, and assistants were convinced of the superiority of the Disney product and felt a strong sense of personal loyalty to the studio head. They were grateful for many years of fulfilling employment during the dark period of the Depression. In contrast, many of the younger artists who came to the studio during the great *Snow White* expansion had a different attitude. Many of them had gone from job to job to make ends meet during the Depression, and they often had more liberal political views. In fact, a considerable number had been caught up in the leftist culture of the Popular Front in California by 1940, and were influenced by militant labor organizers, the Democratic Federation for Political Unity, the *People's Daily World,* and, in certain cases, the Communist party. Bill Hurtz, a young animator who became one of the strike leaders, aptly described the split in the ranks: "The younger people were sufficiently independent and didn't have stars in their eyes about Walt, so that when the strike came at Disney's they were the leaders. They had knocked about during the Depression, and they had some kind of social consciousness. Whereas . . . [the typical older animator] who got his art education at Disney — and a very good one it was — tended to say, 'If it weren't for Walt, I wouldn't be where I am.'"[4]

The new Burbank studio proved to be a mixed blessing. While the employees appreciated this sophisticated, comfortable environment, many also felt strangely uncomfortable. Even among the most loyal employees there was a sense of being lost in a large, impersonal, bureaucratic atmosphere. Kimball, for example, complained that artists were not "factory workers. They're not putting fenders on Fords, or nuts on bolts, they're trying to do a good creative job." Ollie Johnston, another Disney loyalist, granted that while the Burbank studio was full of amenities, he preferred the Hyperion studio, which had "much more of a family feeling" since one "was in a room with a whole bunch of other guys and . . . could horse around a little bit and have a little bit of fun." In the new studio, he continued, you were isolated in a room with an assistant and placed in a wing with other artists working on the same project. Interacting with other artists meant going down the hall and getting through screens of secretaries or traversing several floors in a rather large building. The new arrangement corroded the old informality, intimacy, and camaraderie. In other words, it helped break down a sense of community.[5]

Finally, among the hundreds of new employees who never had personal contact with the studio head, Disney increasingly gained a reputation as a distant, cranky, self-interested, and even dictatorial figure. He had never been easy to work for, but in the early days his personal charm and passionate commitment to quality usually disarmed even the most disgruntled employee. Now a recurring complaint — lack of screen credits — became the catalyst for this larger issue. For years, since Ub Iwerks had left the studio, Disney animated films had carried only Walt's name, giving no screen credit to the many artists and craftspeople who participated in the process. *Snow White and the Seven Dwarfs* indicated a change in policy for feature films by carrying credits for many, but Disney still refused to run credits for the artists, musicians, and story men who worked on the studio's many short films. Among a talented group with healthy egos, public recognition probably meant as much as salary. Disney's apparent selfishness on this point caused a festering resentment that further infected labor relations.[6]

An array of problems thus made for fertile ground, which was eagerly plowed by union advocates. Since 1937, an independent animators' union had functioned at the Disney Studio, but its nature was highly suspect. Called the Federation of Screen Cartoonists, this organization had been encouraged by and received financial support from management. Moreover, it could only appeal to management for improved wages and working conditions, since it had no power of collective bargaining. The federation, in other words, was a classic company union. Dissatisfaction with its efforts mounted, and the fall of 1940 saw the beginnings of an organizing drive by the Screen Cartoonists Guild. By January 1941, it had gained enough support for the NLRB to recognize it as the bargaining unit for animators, story men, directors, and a wide variety of production workers. A few weeks later, the SCG filed charges with the NLRB accusing the studio of "yellow dog" contracts that forced employees to pay fines if they left the studio, annual blitzkriegs in which management forced out higher-paid artists so it could hire novices at cheaper wages, and company unionism. According to the statement accompanying these charges, "For some time effort has been made by the American Federation of Labor to negotiate fair wages and conditions for employees, and Mr. Disney stands today as the only unfair employer in motion pictures."[7]

The controversy escalated over the next few months. Disney resisted negotiation, arguing that a secret-ballot election was needed to see which of the organizations, the SCG or the company-backed federation, had the majority support of the staff. The SCG refused, insisting that the studio would intimidate employees to back the company union. Things built toward a confrontation as the NLRB inspected the studio in preparation for hearings on the complaint and then formally filed charges against it for supporting a company union. In response, the Federation of Screen Cartoonists dissolved itself, but it regrouped under a new name, the American Society of Screen Cartoonists, with the same officers. An outraged SCG immediately accused Disney of cynically refurbishing and foisting upon his employees "the same old company union in a new suit and with a new name." Maneuvering continued with no resolution until late May, when a studio action finally blew the lid off this overheated situation: Disney laid off two dozen union activists, including SCG president and senior animator Art Babbitt. With that, the SCG voted to strike.[8]

Hence on the morning of May 28, 1941, a remarkable scene unfolded at the Disney fantasy factory. As employees rolled up to the gate in their cars, they were greeted by a full-scale picket line of several hundred coworkers waving a forest of signs. Claims differed wildly about how many of the studio's 1200 employees went out (the best guess is that roughly one third struck), but whatever the numbers, a substantial division in the ranks was evident. Events quickly settled into the usual routine for labor disputes: demonstrators taking turns picketing during the day but gathering en masse at the gate at arrival and departure times, a handful of police guaranteeing order, strikers erecting a camp in a vacant field across the street from the gate, the footsore dissidents lining up for communal meals. AFL unions in southern California closed ranks with the strikers by agreeing to boycott Disney products.[9]

But the strike also had several unusual features. Disney artists were not run-of-the-mill industrial workers, of course, and comic inventiveness became the order of the day. Clever signs with carefully drawn images and snappy slogans abounded: a sketch of Jiminy Cricket with the caption "It's not cricket to pass a picket," Pluto saying "I'd rather be a dog than a scab," a caricature of a cross-eyed Walt with the caption "I can't see why they're unhappy." Congregating around the tiny hill on the vacant lot across from the gate, strikers listened to speeches for hours during the day and spent many evenings singing and dancing to the tunes supplied by members of the local musicians' union. Several colorful escapades lightened the usual round of picketing and speechmaking. In honor of the just-released *Reluctant Dragon*, a group of strikers formed a long dragon shape with a caricatured mask of Walt's face at its head, and the creature snaked around as the "Reluctant Disney" on the street. Another day, a group of shirtless, hooded male strikers paraded with a guillotine and a dummy made up to resemble Gunther Lessing, Disney's hated studio attorney. In a parody of the French Revolution, according to one observer, the gleeful dissidents "kept cutting Gunther Lessing's head off over and over."[10]

At first the atmosphere seemed relaxed, tolerant, even jovial. For the first few days of the standoff, the rival groups exchanged jokes and good-natured kidding as they met at the gate or talked through the fence surrounding the lot. But the situation soured as the confrontation dragged on with no settlement in sight. Confrontations replaced banter as tempers frayed and resentments flared. SCG supporters began to demonstrate not only at the studio but at theaters booking Disney films, and shocked moviegoers found themselves in the awkward position of crossing a picket line to see a movie.

The situation worsened. According to one animator who stayed inside, daily work became an ordeal as "every morning you would come in and everybody would be cussing at you from the picket line." Almost thirty-five years later, animator Jack Hannah described the strike as "like a civil war. Friends whom you had worked beside the day before were snarling and spitting on your car as you drove on the lot. It was a very emotional experience." Jack Kinney described the darkening atmosphere in more detail: "Cries of 'fink,' 'scab,' and other epithets were hurled against the nonstrikers, who retaliated by calling strikers 'Commies.' It was a mess . . . Long friendships between 'ins' and 'outs' were destroyed. The hostility was brutal. Strikers let air out of tires or took screwdrivers and scratched the cars as they drove through the gate. There were fights — even some shots were fired."[11]

According to a leader of the strikers, Walt hired about fifty private police to stand guard at the studio gate and rough up anyone who harassed strikebreakers. After several shoving incidents, the Burbank police ordered this force inside the studio fence to avoid further violence. But in July there was a physical clash at the Hollywood Roosevelt Hotel. When some 400 Disney loyalists met to form the Animated Cartoon Associates, yet another revamped company union, about 150 furious SCG members crashed the proceedings. A full-scale fistfight broke out at the entrance to the meeting room; the police were called in, but not before several black eyes, cracked lips, and bruised knuckles resulted.[12]

The heightening of physical tension was accompanied by an escalating war of words. *The Animator,* the official monthly bulletin of the SCG, carried a colorful account of how Disney attorneys Gunther Lessing and Howard Painter lost their tempers at an NLRB meeting and shouted that the SCG was a pack of "white-livered cowards." The SCG also began to publish a series of broadsides aimed at those who stayed on the job. With dramatic titles like "Help Us Put a Button on Mickey Mouse" and "Why We Are on Strike!" these documents defended the union decision to strike. In the words of one, "The Guild tried to cooperate — the Guild attempted to discuss its problems with the studio — it tried to meet with Walt — the officers of the studio remained deaf, dumb, and stubborn — there was no alternative — the Guild had to strike!" These missives described Disney as "the only anti-labor employer in the Hollywood motion picture industry today" and claimed that his primary motivation was simply "to break the strike." As one broadside claimed, "Disney's labor policy has been a combination of stall, stymie, and false promises."[13]

A broadside that appeared on July 28 offered a particularly revealing analysis of the social psychology of the dispute. It began with a heartfelt lament that the studio did not truly value the contributions of its employees. "The attitude of the company has been that the Studio is essential to the people who work in it," the broadside stated, "but that the people who work in it are in no way essential to the studio . . . that no one of us is necessary, no one is essential to Walt." The author revealed more when he explained how a sense of worth was crucial to animation artists: "The outstanding feature of our business is, unlike most productive businesses, its very *personal* nature . . . The men and women who turn out production are themselves the machines. That idea may not be appetizing to you individualists who like to consider yourselves artists and free souls, but it is nonetheless true . . . [and] essential in the production of a cooperative art form like ours." While wages and job security were certainly important to the strikers, the broadside concluded, the most vital issue was gaining "a feeling of importance, of being a necessary part of and contributing to the business." There was an emotional issue at the heart of the strike: employees had been drawn into the family feeling of the Disney operation, had accepted the benevolent paternalism of Walt, and then felt betrayed when they perceived a lack of regard from this father figure.[14]

A full-scale pamphlet war ensued as pro-Disney forces struck back. A group calling themselves the Committee of Twenty-One rushed into print a series of "exposés," as they called them, which attacked the SCG and its leadership. The membership of this cadre was uncertain, but it counter-attacked with great force. Posing an inflammatory opening question — "How do Communists gain control of Labor?" — it delineated how Communist organizers gained inroads into the legitimate union movement with brainwashing and emotional manipulation. The pamphlet then went after Herb Sorrell, detailing his activities as a member of the Communist party and a supporter of Communist causes. It ended with an appeal for every striker to ask the question, "Am I a loyal American or a dupe?"[15]

Subsequent missives described in detail a committed invasion of the entertainment industry by the Communist party and Sorrell, "a faithful devotee of Stalinism." They insisted that this struggle would end with either the Communists taking control of the motion picture industry or the movie producers kicking them out of every studio in Hollywood. Claiming to expose "the fifth columnists of our Democracy," the committee took direct aim at the agenda and tactics of the SCG: "We doubt if such a record of confused stupidity and addled egotism was ever before assembled. Your credulity and fears are mystifying. Your leadership *stinks.* Do not allow your American courage to be further DOPED with the paralyzing poisons of subversive RED SPIDERS . . . The freedoms of Democracy must not be misused by subversionists to destroy our democracy and our unions."[16]

Several years later, Sorrell scoffed at these accusations, insisting that the Disney dispute was simply part of a long-term campaign by AFL labor unions to organize the film industry. Several Communists were involved, he admitted, but he insisted that Disney's intransigence and his firing of the labor organizers had radicalized those figures. "I believe that Mr. Disney created more Communists with his substandard wage scales and the way he handled his people than has been since the union took over," he noted. "These artists are a temperamental kind of people who lean to anything that is crazy . . . we call them intellectuals. They have a lot of theory but no guts to go ahead with anything. And Mr. Disney had a lot of those people at the time."[17]

Other dissidents, such as Bill Melendez, defended the strike as a blow against the low wages paid to "the lower echelons," while David Hilberman argued that the revolt stemmed from Disney's arbitrary layoff policies and the fear and uncertainty coming from "no job security." Less strident critics of the studio, such as Shamus Culhane, pointed out that while Disney was certainly no villain, he "did not really understand the working conditions of the business . . . he just could not see that there was a need for an industry-wide organization."[18]

With equal fervor, Disney loyalists closed ranks behind their chief and his studio. Ben Sharpsteen contemptuously described the walkout as the work of "soreheads" who demanded recognition and advancement for mediocre work. In his opinion, a vocal minority of employees sought protection from the consequences of substandard performance, and the strike was their means of gaining unmerited tenure and recognition. "It was very difficult to apply union regulations to such an abstract thing as artistic talent," he concluded. Story man Roy Williams concurred, arguing that the employees who griped about wages "were the ones who didn't deserve much money. They would loaf or not be so good on the job, but those who worked hard and worked good got high pay — more than any other studio paid." Animators Marc Davis and Dick Huemer praised Disney for his benevolent, encouraging attitude and defended his right to be "hiring us to do what *he* wanted to do, not hiring us to do what *we* wanted to do." Roy Disney, never one to mince words, made a direct counterattack. The strike, he declared, came from the convergence of two factors: temperamental artists with "strong personalities" who wanted to run the show instead of Walt, and a film industry "in the throes of being taken over by the Commies."[19]

In midsummer, after several weeks of negotiations between the SCG and Disney management had brought no settlement, the studio procured the services of Willie Bioff, a noted Chicago labor racketeer associated with conservative elements in the AFL hierarchy, to circumvent the efforts of the SCG. Working through the offices of the IATSE and in cahoots with Disney managers, Bioff offered a settlement to the strikers in a famous meeting held at his ranch in southern California: reinstatement of striking employees without discrimination, recognition of the SCG, a closed shop, 50 percent retroactive pay for the time on strike, and an increased wage scale for those in the lower strata of jobs. The SCG angrily refused the offer.

In a full-page ad in *Variety,* the strikers vented their outrage about Bioff, a man they described as "a disgrace to organized labor." The SCG pointed out that he had served time after being convicted on a morals charge in Chicago and that he was now under federal indictment for income tax evasion and extortion of a half-million dollars from Hollywood film companies. Bioff, in their words, was "the most vicious racketeer in the history of the motion picture labor movement," and Disney should be ashamed of trying to "hand over the animated cartoon industry to this Chicago hoodlum." One cartoon in an SCG flyer showed Bioff dressed as a gangster, fedora pulled low over his eyes as he faced the world with a machine gun at the ready, while an angry Walt hid behind him shouting denunciations of the SCG. A broadside bitterly noted that Walt would join arms with a vicious labor hoodlum but refused to deal with his own employees or mediators from the federal government. "The studio was willing to sell us out to Bioff," the SCG concluded, but "we would rather go on working and fighting outside than to accept *any* contract that would have meant giving Bioff control over us."[20]

The Bioff maneuver, however, had a quick payoff for Disney management. Several AFL unions under the influence of Bioff and the more conservative IATSE — the Plasterers, Laboratory Workers, Utility Workers, Projectionists, Electrical Workers, and Studio Transportation Drivers unions — negotiated and signed contracts with the studio in early July. High-ranking representatives of the AFL and IATSE announced that the dispute was over, that any boycotts of Disney would be lifted, and that a back-to-work order was forthcoming. The SCG strikers vehemently resisted this move. Denying that their revolt had ended, they insisted that the Disney Studio had merely allied itself with the IATSE and Willie Bioff to scuttle their union. In a public announcement, the SCG stood firm, declaring that they had been "fully prepared for this strike-breaking move on the part of Willie Bioff" and that hundreds of Disney employees would remain on the picket line "until Disney recognizes our union and bargains with it as required by law." Thus the Disney strike became directly caught up in the larger struggle between two AFL factions.[21]

As these currents ebbed and flowed, making the dynamics of the situation increasingly murky, publicity attending the strike added uncomfortable external pressures. Journalists left a growing impression that the Disney operation was akin to an industrial plant, replete with the usual labor problems, rather than the innocent fun factory it purported to be. The Los Angeles *Times* and *Examiner,* the Hollywood *Citizen-News* and *Reporter,* and *Variety* regularly covered unfolding events in Burbank. The Willie Bioff episode particularly placed the studio in a bad light. With considerable distaste, newspaper stories described the studio's involvement with this "indicted AFL labor leader," calling it "another unpleasant chapter . . . [in] the story of the Chicago labor hoodlum muscling in on labor matters."[22]

Unpleasant publicity also surfaced nationally. Not surprisingly, the *Daily Worker* bitingly noted that Disney's "'call me Walt' gag has been successful in building up a superficial good fellowship . . . [but] good fellowship hasn't been accompanied by good wages." *Business Week,* at the other end of the political spectrum, carried a series of stories that focused on the studio's difficulties in defending its company union against SCG charges. *The Nation* simply noted that the strike was sounding the death knell for Disney's "paternalism." In rather arch phrases, it suggested that Disney must be squirming to see that the "wicked old fairy Organized Labor should be making trouble among his merry little Dwarfs. He must find it very exasperating that the vexatious question of the low wages he pays is continuously cropping up." Disney was not without his defenders, of course, and they praised him in the national press as a "friendly, democratic" fellow who had created a studio of "utilitarian perfection" for his employees. But Philip T. Hartung, writing in *Commonweal,* accurately captured the public's uneasiness over this whole affair. Gently chiding Disney for his stubbornness, he suggested that the strike had worn away some of the magic. "After all," he concluded, "this is USA's Hollywood, not England's coal mines; and we want to love the creator of Mickey Mouse and not have the reluctant Disney be the oppressing plant owner."[23]

The labor controversy was intensified by the personalities of the participants. The story of one — a senior animator who emerged as a central player — proved particularly revealing. A man of great talent and great ego, he strode forward as a public spokesman for the dissidents in the spring of 1941. In the process he became a touchstone for determining loyalty to or betrayal of Walt Disney.

II. Art Babbitt: "Walt Disney, You Should Be Ashamed of Yourself"

In 1978, at a gathering of the International Animated Film Society, Art Babbitt took center stage to hold forth on the strike that he had helped lead almost forty years before. Still burning with reformist fire, this old animator passionately denounced the labor policies of the Disney Studio, accusing the company of greed and strike-breaking tactics. He pled at great length the cause of the underpaid peons in the Disney operation, who had struggled with substandard wages. Ward Kimball, who was also in attendance, noted dryly that Babbitt, for all his sympathy for the downtrodden, had been "the only striker that had white-walled tires on his car."[24]

This comment reveals some of the controversy and contradictions that surrounded Art Babbitt's career at Disney. An outspoken, confident man, Babbitt had become a leading animator by the late 1930s. Elected president of the fledgling Screen Cartoonists Guild, he was dismissed for union activity on May 27, 1941, the act that precipitated the strike. Yet his genuine political idealism was marred by an overbearing self-righteousness that made him an object of resentment and contempt among many on the studio staff. Moreover, he displayed little understanding of his own ironic situation as the bitter critic but also a star of the Disney Studio who pulled down a very lucrative salary.

Babbitt came from a modest midwestern background similar to Walt Disney's. The oldest son in a large and impoverished family in Omaha, Nebraska, he had worked for years in various jobs to help his family survive while he dreamed of becoming a psychiatrist. A talent for drawing eventually led to a graphics job in an advertising agency and then to Paul Terry's Terrytoons studio in New York City. In 1932 he traveled to Hollywood and wangled an interview with Disney by hand-painting a huge letter (some fifteen by twenty feet) and sending it by special delivery. Disney was impressed, and after talking with the young artist, agreed to hire him as an assistant animator on a trial basis. Babbitt's talent quickly came to the fore and he steadily rose up through the hierarchy to become one of Disney's most valuable artists within a couple of years.[25]

By the mid-1930s, Babbitt was working on many of the projects that helped define Disney's golden age. In addition to working on Mickey Mouse shorts, he was selected as one of four animators who created the runaway hit film *Three Little Pigs*, and he went on to play a major role in *The Country Cousin*, the short that won an Academy Award. On the *Snow White* project, Babbitt helped develop and animate the lovable, silent little dwarf Dopey and the dark, dignified Wicked Queen. Shortly thereafter, he drew the lion's share of the character Geppetto in *Pinocchio* (years later he claimed this was the best work he ever did). He then became involved in *Fantasia*, for which he animated significant portions of the mushroom dance and various scenes from "The Nutcracker Suite" and the Beethoven Pastorale. For *Dumbo*, he helped animate the stork who delivered the baby elephant as well as several of the clown scenes. At least one indication of Babbitt's growing prestige at the studio was his appointment as a supervising animator on *Pinocchio*, *Fantasia*, and *Dumbo*.[26]

Throughout this era, Babbitt gained particular fame as the studio expert on Goofy. He was responsible for transforming this nebulous bit player into a star in the Disney galaxy of characters, partly by refining Goofy's physical characteristics but even more by empathetically translating his underlying psychology. In June 1934, Babbitt gave a talk entitled "Character Analysis of the Goof" to the assembled Disney artists, in which he shrewdly explained why Goofy moved and acted the way he did:

> Think of the Goof as a composite of an everlasting optimist, a gullible Good Samaritan, a halfwit . . . He can move fast if he has to, but would rather avoid any overexertion, so he takes what seems the easiest way. He is a philosopher of the barber shop variety . . . His brain being rather vapory, it is difficult for him to concentrate on any one subject . . . He is a

good-natured dumbbell who thinks he is pretty smart. He laughs at his own jokes because he can't understand any others . . . He talks to himself because it is easier for him to know what he is thinking if he hears it first.

The key to Goofy's personality, Babbitt once quipped, lay in the fact that he "thought very hard and very long about everything he did. And then he did it wrong!"[27]

Babbitt greatly admired the creative ethos of the Disney Studio. He was convinced that no other animation group went to such great lengths to analyze the characters and the story while painstakingly building films from storyboards to the completed product. Walt, he believed, set an example with his willingness to discard completed sections of movies if they didn't work, even though it might be quite costly. This created a warm, exciting atmosphere of creative integrity, and Babbitt reveled in the fact that Disney artists were "eager not only to learn new things for their own advantage, but they were eager to pass out information to anyone else."[28]

Babbitt's artistic accomplishments at the Disney Studio were exceeded only by his social reputation. Even among this large group of single, creative, and libidinous young men, he presented himself with such a confident flair that "you'd think he was the president of the company. His car was usually bigger than Walt's, which took a lot of nerve." Babbitt's lucrative salary — by 1935 he was getting $300 a week, or about $15,000 a year, at the height of the Depression — paid for two servants, a big house, two automobiles, and a good deal of entertainment. Slim, handsome, and gregarious, he became known as the foremost ladies' man on the lot. He ended up marrying Marge Belcher, the lithe young dancer who came to the studio to serve as a model for Snow White.[29]

Art Babbitt and Walt Disney developed a rather volatile relationship. Even at their first meeting in 1932, in Babbitt's words, "I knew I had a shrewd customer on my hands. There was electricity between us right from the very start . . . sort of a friendly antagonism where you feel each other out." Several minor clashes in succeeding years gradually created a strain. For instance, the romantic exploits of the sybaritic artist seemed to annoy his straitlaced boss. "I don't think Walt appreciated it at all," Babbitt recalled of his social reputation. And at the Hyperion studio, Disney decided at one point that the open doors between the animators' rooms were fostering too much socializing. He first tried locking them, but the artists unlocked them, so he had the studio carpenters nail them shut. When Babbitt discovered this, he stormed down to the carpenters' shop, grabbed a hammer, and angrily went to rip out the nails. At lunch that day, Disney said to a group of artists, "I just heard that Art Babbitt countered my orders and broke down the nailed doors. Who the hell does he think he is?" When someone replied quietly that Babbitt was a hell of a good animator, Disney's eyes narrowed and he growled, "He's not *that* good." But the doors remained open.[30]

Politics, however, drove the biggest wedge into their relationship. Over the course of the 1930s, Babbitt evolved into a leftist intellectual given to a preachy style of speechmaking that many found grating. "I talked loud and waved my arms a lot. I was indiscreet, I was not a politician. I said what I felt," he admitted later. Friends like Bill Hurtz described Babbitt as "a rebel — fiercely independent." But some coworkers found his politics to be mainly a matter of posturing and egotism, and they took to needling him at the end of the workday with the comment "See you at the demonstration."[31]

Nonetheless, Babbitt's political sensibility led him to resent several things about the Disney Studio. Like many employees, he was quite annoyed at Disney's habit of hogging all the credit, publicity, and Academy Awards for the collective work of the studio. As he stated later, "I want to give full credit to the genius of Walt Disney as far as his being an entrepreneur, a very forceful guy who was willing to risk everything for quality, who surrounded himself with the best people, who was a hell of an editor." But, he continued, the studio chief "was not a creator, he was not an artist." The Oscars in his office were for other people's "music or writing, animation or designing." Similarly, Babbitt bitterly resented the way Disney garnered praise for creating a studio art school where animators could work to develop their drawing skills. According to Babbitt, *he* had started the art classes as informal gatherings in his home, where a number of animators got together, hired a model, and compared notes as they struggled with life drawings. Only later did Disney move in, with the explanation, "Suppose it got in the newspapers that a bunch of Disney artists were drawing naked women in a private home." Disney gave the group permission to use the studio soundstage, and Babbitt claimed that he, not Disney, contacted Don Graham at the Chouinard Art Institute and persuaded him to come up to the Disney operation.[32]

Another issue was equally distressing to this idealistic, energetic animator — the low wages paid to assistant animators, in-betweeners, and inkers and painters. Babbitt had a major confrontation with Disney while *Fantasia* was being made. He asked for a raise for his assistant, Bill Hurtz, who had worked closely with him on many scenes yet was making roughly one tenth of his salary. When Babbitt requested a modest $2-a-week raise for Hurtz, he claimed, Disney replied, "Why don't you mind your own goddamned business? If he was worth it, he would be getting it." Babbitt rejoined that he would pay Hurtz out of his own pocket. Disney, infuriated, burst out, "The trouble with you is that you and your Communist friends live in a world so small you don't know what's going on around you!"[33]

In the late 1930s, Gunther Lessing, the studio attorney and Disney's labor adviser, enlisted Babbitt to become head of the Federation of Screen Cartoonists, the in-house organization at the studio. Naive in the ways of labor politics, the animator discovered only gradually that the federation was in fact "a company union that would keep regular unions from getting into the studio." As he began to grasp the situation, however, he attempted to act as a real union leader by going to management with a request for a raise of $2 a week for inkers and painters, who at that time worked for as little as $16 or $18 a week. Roy Disney refused to negotiate and warned Babbitt, "You keep your nose out of our business or we'll cut it off." Disillusionment set in, and within a short time Babbitt headed in a different direction.[34]

In the fall of 1940, the Screen Cartoonists Guild contacted Babbitt and asked for his support in their efforts to begin organizing the Disney Studio. He abandoned the federation and soon became one of the key organizers for this AFL crusade, holding social gatherings for Disney employees in his home, where he would sing the praises of the SCG and solicit new members. He also began to recruit on studio grounds whenever possible, a tactic that increasingly annoyed Disney and his management team. They warned Babbitt to desist from such activity and he refused, claiming protection from the Wagner Act. Tensions steadily mounted through the spring of 1941 as the SCG demanded collective bargaining power at the studio and appealed to the NLRB for recognition and support. In mid-February Babbitt began to play a leading role in pleading its case. The Disney Studio counterattacked in a highly personal way. On the day that Babbitt was to give a deposition before the labor board, he received quite a shock. As he later described the incident,

> Two detectives from the Burbank police station appeared in my office and arrested me, and the charge against me was carrying a concealed weapon. My weapon was so concealed that to this day they have not found it. I was taken to the Burbank jail . . . The chief of police in Burbank was the brother-in-law of the chief of studio security at Disney's. That's just a coincidence. The detectives picked me up at noon, took my fingerprints, the whole bit, and put me in the Burbank jail. I wasn't allowed to make any phone calls . . . At any rate, the girl who was the assistant chairman of the Disney unit of the Guild — I was the chairman — called the various jails . . . and finally she found out where I was in Burbank. All of a sudden I was released and taken to Disney's office, and Disney gave me a fatherly lecture to the effect that if I lived right and thought right everything would be marvelous.[35]

Finally, in late May, escalating tensions exploded and Babbitt was fired for union organizing on company time, along with thirteen other people. In dramatic fashion, two studio policemen came to his office with a letter of termination from Gunther Lessing. They allowed him to gather a few personal items and then escorted him out the gate as a crowd gathered to watch.

That night the Screen Cartoonists Guild held a meeting at the Roosevelt Hotel, and following a number of rousing speeches, including one by Babbitt, the group voted to go on strike the next morning.[36]

As chairman of the Disney SCG unit and one of only two senior animators who joined the strike — the other was Bill Tytla, who reluctantly walked out because of his long personal friendship with Babbitt, not for political reasons — Babbitt felt a sense of responsibility for seeing the strike through to success. He spent many hours organizing the picket line during the day and often spent his evenings going to other union meetings to solicit strike funds. He also convinced some southern California newspapers to pull Mickey Mouse and Donald Duck comic strips to put pressure on the studio. He helped oversee the construction of strike headquarters, with its tents and picnic tables, near a grove of eucalyptus trees across from the studio gate. Along with Herb Sorrell, he became a major voice in the long negotiating meetings with Roy Disney, Gunther Lessing, and Bill Garrity. After getting a tip from Sorrell, Babbitt even managed to secure a couple of burly union mechanics from Lockheed to help protect the sleeping strikers from hostile, drunken Disney loyalists who were threatening to wreck their tents in the middle of the night. Perhaps Babbitt's most impressive action, however, came when Willie Bioff entered the scene. Bioff's representatives picked up Babbitt one evening and took him for a ride to Bioff's house. Trying to pressure him into a settlement, the mobster offered him a $50-a-week raise to "go camping any time you please and stay as long as you like." Although Babbitt was scared to death, he refused, with the crack "Well, I'm sorry, Mr. Bioff, but I already have so much money I don't know how to spend it."[37]

As the strike stretched on through the summer, Babbitt's attacks on Disney grew more strident. The smoldering tension in their relationship burst into flame as the animator became increasingly disgusted with the studio chief's refusal to recognize the union, his delaying tactics, and his dalliance with Bioff. Babbitt contemptuously described Disney's worldview as "medieval" and his political ideology as that of a "caveman." He denounced the Disney brothers as crude "America Firsters" who believed that there was "a Communist behind every tree, every bush." Walt was a "benevolent dictator," Babbitt insisted. "You could never ask him for anything, [because] that was terrible," he noted angrily. "If he gave it to you, if it was like giving a beggar a quarter, that was all right . . . But he must be the one to give."[38]

After the strike was settled, in the fall of 1941, Disney adamantly refused to rehire Babbitt, and the matter went to court. But American involvement in World War II sidetracked the decision. Babbitt enlisted in the Marine Corps for the duration of the conflict, and when the war ended he won a victory in court and returned to his old job at the Disney Studio in late 1945, in his words, "to prove a point." It was a Pyrrhic victory. According to Jack Kinney,

"Art Babbitt and Walt hated each other's guts," and they passed one another in the hall of the animation building every day, glaring and refusing to speak. Babbitt, pointing to the terms of the court order, demanded that everything be exactly the way it had been before the strike: wall-to-wall carpeting, a corner office with a window, and a moviola for previewing animation work. For his part, Disney tried to make Babbitt's life miserable. He assigned the artist to a project never intended for production, encouraged other employees to give him the cold shoulder, and told anyone who worked with him, "If he gets in your way, you let me know." This tense situation lasted for a year, until Babbitt finally accepted a cash settlement in January 1947 and left the studio for good. He went on to a productive career over the next three decades as an animator for UPA, a director of commercials for Hanna-Barbera, and a consultant and teacher for a variety of animated film projects. To the end of his days, he harbored an intense dislike for his old boss. Walt Disney, he liked to tell people, displayed great talents, but the secret of his success lay in the fact that "he had the innate bad taste of the American people. He was audience-wise."[39]

Art Babbitt's prominent role in the Disney strike certainly brought him no small share of notoriety. Those who witnessed it never forgot the summer morning in 1941 when the studio chief drove slowly through the picket line around his studio, smiling and waving, and Babbitt grabbed a bullhorn and shouted, "Walt Disney, you should be ashamed of yourself." The assembled dissidents erupted in a loud chorus of boos. An angry Walt slammed on the brakes, jumped out of his automobile, and went for the animator with his fists up. Both men had to be restrained. Such passion caused great pain and grief to Babbitt, who carried to his grave a festering grudge against his old boss. It also affected Disney, who did not enjoy one of his finer moments during the strike. In turn shocked, hurt, enraged, and embittered, he struggled to understand and control a sustained crisis that nearly did him in.[40]

III. "The Toughest Period in My Whole Life"

Walt Disney had been suspicious of unions for a long time. Back in 1928, when he was in New York trying to record a sound film about Mickey Mouse, he had run up against barriers created by union work requirements. In a letter home to Roy and Ub, he described how he had been forced to hire a contractor, who then secured musicians (after taking a hefty percentage for himself) to make the experimental soundtrack for *Steamboat Willie*. "Boy, the unions are sure tough on movie recording," he wrote in frustration. "They are doing all they can to discourage the 'Sound Film' craze." Over the next decade, while the Disney Studio grew tremendously, he still saw no advantage in unionizing his workers. In fact, in the late 1930s the studio sponsored a series of seminars that denounced "industry-wide unionism" and suggested that Disney workers, as the elite in the animation industry, would be best served by the in-house organization.[41]

Unions simply ran against the grain of everything that Walt Disney was about. They violated his creative creed, which was linked to organizational flexibility and free-flowing innovation. They also seemed antithetical to his work ethic, with its moral center of self-made individualism and sturdy producerism. The success of the Disney enterprise, in the eyes of its founder, came from a mixture of his own inspired leadership and a rough-hewn democratic atmosphere that allowed his artists to flourish. The picture of self-sufficiency, protection, and participation, his organization did not need any outside guarantees of rights and conditions.

At first Disney could not bring himself to believe that his employees would organize and actually strike. When they did, he persisted in underestimating the strength of the movement. Finally, he proved incapable of understanding why nearly half of his employees were unhappy enough to revolt. His deeply engrained paternalism kept him from imagining any other model for organizing the work life of his studio, and his sense of self was so completely wrapped up in his work that any attack on it became an attack on him. Necessarily, then, the strike triggered an intensely personal reaction that was partly emotional and partly ideological. Never very successful at hiding his feelings, Disney expressed a deep hurt and bitterness as his work, and hence his life, seemed to unravel.

Early in 1941, Disney revealed his agitated state of mind. With unionizing efforts swirling in the background, he went before his employees to explain his position. As hundreds of them sat in the theater of the Burbank facility, he joked that everything he was about to say came from him and not some committee of managers and lawyers, and "that will probably account for some of the poor grammatical construction and the numerous two-syllable words." But the legal ramifications of the situation, he added, demanded that he read from a prepared statement and have his words recorded, to "insure not having things I did not say credited to me." He also carefully noted that the studio recognized the right of employees "to organize and to join in any labor organization of their own choosing." These precautionary statements prefaced a fascinating, lengthy explanation of Disney's worldview. Proud yet defensive, his soul-baring speech revealed the bedrock values that had supported his astounding success over the previous decade and a half but now blocked his understanding of a complex struggle within a modern bureaucratic institution.[42]

Disney began frankly. The studio had entered a period of financial crisis, he admitted, as the outbreak of war in Europe had closed markets, restricted production, and upset the credit schedule. But such problems, he argued, were not all that new. "In the twenty years I have spent in this business, I have weathered many storms," he stated. "It has been far from easy sailing. It has required a great deal of hard work, struggle, determination, confidence, faith, and above all, unselfishness." His belief that animation could be "one of the greatest mediums of fantasy and entertainment yet developed" had always pushed him onward. But now a pair of institutional behemoths had loomed up to block his path. First, the large banks that extended credit to the studio had panicked over the European crisis, clamped down on lending, and demanded curtailed production costs. Second, the federal government, with its corporate income tax rates, "leaves a company very little out of its profits for a company to expand with."[43]

He had resisted firing employees or lowering their salaries, he explained, because that would be unfair. He refused to sell out to a large, wealthy corporation because that would make him answerable to someone "with only one thought or interest — namely profits." The only way to avoid such draconian measures, he concluded, lay in increasing production and efficiency while lowering costs. But this course of action demanded loyalty from everyone. Rather defensively, he gave a detailed account of how he had scrimped and saved and mortgaged his own possessions over the years to build the studio while never missing a paycheck to his workers. Disney went through a long list of his actions on behalf of his employees — good wages, a spacious and accommodating new studio, a bonus system for meritorious work, compensated vacations and holidays, sick leave and medical benefits, and payment of overtime wages set by the government, even though such laws were meant for "the sweatshop factories, for the oppressed workers in the South, and definitely never intended for creative groups who are working and building for a future."[44]

Pleading with his employees to recognize that a strong, solid organization provided the best security for everyone, Disney tried to reassure them about its essential nature. He strenuously denied any desire for ironclad personal control, claiming, "I do not want this organization set up so that it would not function without me, merely to please my ego." He reaffirmed his distaste for hierarchy, asserting that promotion was based on finding individuals "who could be recognized as leaders not by the wearing of a badge, but by the respect of their fellow workers." Disavowing any personal greed, he claimed, "I have never been interested in personal gain or profit. This business and this studio have been my entire life." Finally, he proclaimed passionately, "It's my nature to be democratic. I want to be just a guy working in this plant . . . When I meet people in the hall I want to be able to speak to them, and have them speak back to me, and say hello with a smile. I can't work under any other conditions."[45]

Disney idealistically pictured himself in the garb of the 1930s populist — a determined foe of big bureaucracy, virtuous protecter of the little guy, and democratic defender of untrammeled creativity. Adding the final touches to this self-image, he concluded this remarkable speech with a ringing affirmation of self-reliant individualism and the work ethic. The solution to both the studio's financial crisis and the labor problem, he insisted, lay in

> *a good day's work.* Believe me, that will be a cure for all our problems. You can't deny that it is individual efficiency that leads to collective efficiency.
>
> My first recommendation to a lot of you is this: put your own house in order, put your own mind in order, and in doing so, if you find anything helpful, get that spirit of the Studio and pass it on to the other guy . . . If you're not progressing as you should, instead of grumbling and growling, do something about it. I would suggest that you talk to yourself first, complain to yourself first, be honest with yourself, and if you're at fault, give yourself a good kick in the fanny and do something about it . . . Too many people are inclined to self-pity.
>
> This business is ready to go ahead. If you want to go ahead with it, you've got to be ready for some hard work, you've got to strengthen yourself . . . and that strength comes from the individual strength of the employees. Don't forget this — it's the law of the universe that the strong shall survive and the weak must fall by the way, and I don't give a damn what idealistic plan is cooked up, nothing can change that.[46]

These heartfelt beliefs revealed much about Disney's state of mind, but they had little impact on the course of events. Many of his employees remained skeptical, and subsequent weeks of negotiation and maneuver succeeded only in bringing the Screen Cartoonists Guild and the studio to loggerheads. In late spring, with no solution in sight and rumors of a strike swirling around, the studio head again spoke to his assembled employees. This time frustration dominated his remarks. Disney asserted that the issue of a "free election" had emerged as the stumbling block, with him demanding a secret ballot among his employees to choose their bargaining unit and the SCG insisting that in such an election the Disney Studio would intimidate employees into voting for the company union. To Disney, the SCG position simply violated the principle of majority rule. In the words of Walter P. Spreckels, the studio's labor consultant and a former chair of the local NLRB, the SCG demanded to become "the sole collective bargaining agent *without* the holding of an election of any sort . . . This Walt refused to do then and has refused to do ever since." A frustrated Disney could only pledge to keep the studio open in the event of a walkout and to reject any settlement that involved retaliation against studio loyalists by fines, blacklists, or other threats.[47]

When the picket line actually materialized in late May, Disney's reaction swung wildly from one extreme to another. On the one hand, he appeared the picture of accommodation and good will, and perhaps even innocence. Around the second day of the strike, Ollie Johnston noted, he had just come through the picket line and he was "standing there with his hat on at a funny angle, and his coat over his arm, and kind of smiling at the guys out on the line, and he hollered something to one of them, all friendly, and said, 'Aw, they'll be back in a couple of days.'" Similarly, Marc Davis urged Disney to sit down and talk with the SCG business agent. Disney demurred, and "then he told me about a man in the early days in New York [Pat Powers] . . . who just stole him blind . . . 'God,' he said, 'you know this guy did these awful things to me and God, I just loved him.' He said, 'Marc, I don't want to meet this man, I might like him.'" But a different Disney appeared to other studio loyalists. Jack Kinney was called up to his office on the first day of the strike and was astonished at what he saw. Disney had hired a photographer to take pictures of the strikers, which he had then blown up to poster size and hung on the walls. "Walt walked around the room peering intently at each picture," Kinney recalled. "Pointing fingers, he said things like 'Damn, I didn't think *he* would go against me,' 'It figures,' 'What's his gripe?' or 'We can get along without him.' We got the uneasy feeling that he was filing his feelings away in his prodigious memory for some future revenge."[48]

Walt's difficulties in coming to terms with the unfolding dispute were intensified by the counsel he received. He was ill served by his advisers, particularly Gunther Lessing, whose role in the strike became a focus of controversy. A lawyer who liked to brag about his representation of the Mexican revolutionary Pancho Villa and his heirs, Lessing had become a fixture at the studio when he represented the Disney brothers in their legal wrangle with Pat Powers back in the late 1920s. Over the succeeding years, he became a force for political reaction at the studio. In the early 1930s, for instance, during socialist Upton Sinclair's run for the California governorship as a Democrat, he had called a meeting of the whole staff to warn them, according to one observer, "of the danger of a Commie revolution rolling through California if Sinclair got elected." A bit later, Lessing became the driving force behind and primary speaker at a series of anti-union seminars in 1940–41. One observer described his manner as "too slick, too facile, and too arrogant." With the strike, the attorney consistently urged Disney to stand tough against the dissidents, a tactic that succeeded only in reinforcing the image of the studio chief as an industrial boss. Lessing became widely disliked, even among Disney's supporters, for his scheming and heavy-handed tactics. When Ward Kimball heard that Art Babbitt had been jailed on the phony charge of carrying a concealed weapon, he noted that this "was one of the long list of deeds of chicanery that Gunther Lessing pulled." According to Kimball, "We all felt that Walt wanted to work it out and get on with the business . . . It was Gunther Lessing and his old-time cohorts that were feeding Walt a bunch of misinformation." For many on both sides of the picket line, the studio attorney appeared to be the primary source of their boss's inflexibility.[49]

Disney's attitude steadily hardened as the strike went on. Within a month of its beginning, few vestiges of the congenial Walt remained as his bitterness welled up in ever greater amounts. Perhaps the clearest indication of his state of mind came on July 2, when readers of trade papers like *Variety* and the *Hollywood Reporter* found a full-page statement from Walt Disney staring out at them. Addressed "To My Employees on Strike," it listed the studio's offer of reinstatement, recognition of the union, a closed shop, 50 percent retroactive pay for time on strike, increased wages, and paid vacation. But this was followed by a truly startling conclusion. "I believe that you have been misled and misinformed about the real issues underlying the strike at the studio," Disney wrote. "I am positively convinced that Communistic agitation, leadership, and activities have brought about this strike, and have persuaded you to reject this fair and equitable settlement." Obviously, such sentiments made it increasingly difficult for Disney to approach the middle ground and find a resolution to his studio's labor problems.[50]

Finally, after weeks of futile resistance, Disney was cornered into accepting a settlement. James F. Dewey and Stanley White, arbitrators from the Labor Department, negotiated a preliminary agreement on July 28 that recognized most of the union's demands: reinstatement of the strikers with pay and without discrimination, official job classifications and equalization of salaries, regular grievance procedures, paid vacations, severance pay, minimum guarantees of employment, and a closed union shop. Moreover, both sides concurred that a reduction of the workforce was necessitated by market conditions and agreed to negotiate an acceptable formula for layoffs. This final issue proved to be a major sticking point. On August 13 the Disney Studio unilaterally announced the layoff of 207 guild members and 49 nonstrikers, and the SCG immediately filed a protest with the Labor Department. The studio claimed financial cause, and another showdown loomed. On August 18, unable to reach an agreement, Walt Disney Productions closed down the studio completely for two weeks, and then extended the shutdown for another two weeks. The studio reopened only after James Dewey again arbitrated an acceptable formula for hiring and layoffs.[51]

Significantly, the negotiation process became easier when Walt stepped out of the picture. He left the country on August 17 on a goodwill tour of South America at the request of the State Department and Nelson Rockefeller, leaving Roy and the studio lawyers to work things out. Shortly before his departure, however, he unburdened himself in a lengthy, angry letter to Westbrook Pegler, a friend and prominent newspaper columnist. "To me, the entire situation is a catastrophe," he wrote. "The spirit that played such an important part in the building of the cartoon medium has been destroyed." The mainstream AFL unions, he insisted, had tried to resist the pressure to strike but had been overwhelmed by the SCG radicals. "I am convinced that this entire mess was Communistically inspired and led . . . Sorrell is dirty, sneaky, and as foul as they come and there is no doubt but he is a tool of the Communist group. I am positive that if we had been dealing with the organized, functioning union, this thing would have been settled a long time ago and to the satisfaction of all concerned."[52]

Perhaps the most revealing section of Disney's diatribe came in the form of an extended personal confession. The strike, he told Pegler, had opened his eyes to political reality in the United States. In his words,

> I was shocked into the realization that the Democracy which, as a kid in 1918, I went to fight for in France, was gone. To me, the real fight for Democracy is right here at home. Guts and not guns will win it . . . My eyes are open and I only hope that other people throughout the country, like myself, will be aroused to an understanding of what is happening to our government today . . . I have capitulated but, believe me, I'm not licked. I'm incensed . . . The dirty, foul means used against me in this fight cannot be easily forgotten. I was called a rat, a yellow-dog employer, and an exploiter of labor . . . My plant and methods were compared to a sweatshop and above all, I was accused of rolling in wealth. That hurt the most when the fact is that every damned thing I have is tied up in this business . . . I am thoroughly disgusted and would gladly quit and try to establish myself in another business if it were not for the loyal guys who believe in me — so, I guess I'm stuck with it . . . I have a case of the D.D.s — disillusionment and discouragement.

This was a far cry from Disney's optimistic, confident populism of the 1930s, and as many people would notice, it was an attitude that began to color the atmosphere of the post-strike Disney Studio.[53]

Disney never quite recovered from the controversy of 1941. According to Marc Davis, he began to distance himself from his staff and to cut back on the frills he had been so proud of at the Burbank studio. Frank Thomas, who saw less bitterness in Disney than others did, nonetheless admitted that "the great exuberance and fun" of the earlier studio had largely vanished.[54]

Many years later, Disney claimed that the strike "was probably the best thing that ever happened to me. It cleaned house . . . better than I could have ever done." The troublemakers and the agitators had shown their colors and gradually left the studio, and those who remained were "the backbone of my business." But such assurances rang hollow to those who witnessed the affair as a great tragedy. Jack Kinney, for instance, lamented that the post-strike studio "became a very hard-nosed place," while Shamus Culhane concluded that "the esprit de corps that made possible all the brilliant films of the 1930s was dead as a dodo."[55]

Socially, the strike had destroyed the image of a workers' paradise; time clocks arrived on the scene, along with bureaucratic controls coming from both union regulations and corporate rationalization. Creatively, the strike exploded the spirit of camaraderie, innovation, and participation that had inspired the wonderful creations of the 1930s. Financially, it blew a large hole in the studio's profits, as production, already curtailed by the growing world crisis, was further reduced.

Simply put, the Disney Studio changed irrevocably as a result of the strike, as an unidentified Disney artist eloquently put it in a letter to the editor of the Los Angeles *Times*. In his bitter words,

> The spirit is irretrievably gone . . . The "conditions" for which the strikers fought will be obtained; outside control, organization of robots, tribute money, endless boredom. You can't imagine what fun it was to work at Disney's . . . If you had an idea you could shout "Eureka" down the halls and get paid for your idea . . . Oh well, it was only a dream, anyway. The dream was shattered and organization, efficiency began making up the bed. It doesn't matter. We are not made of the stuff of dreams today. We are the masses, each cast from a single mold and set in allotted places, inseparable.

This writer, however, for all his genuine emotion, did not grasp the central irony of the situation — that Disney himself, by creating a large, complex bureaucratic organization, gradually had undermined the old-fashioned, virtuous, small-producer enterprise he so valued.[56]

Disney, of course, also failed to have this perception. Profoundly disillusioned, he was never quite the same after the strike. Many years later, he noted darkly that this incident was "the toughest period in my whole life." The coming of war only deepened the gloom enveloping Burbank.[57]

12

Disney and the Good War

I N THE FALL of 1941, after the strike was settled, many hoped that life
would return to some semblance of normality at the Disney Studio.
Such hopes proved short-lived. Only a few weeks later, the airplanes
of imperial Japan swooped down on Pearl Harbor. The day after the attack,
Walt Disney received an early morning call from his studio manager. "Walt,
the army is moving in on us," the man said. "They came up and said they
wanted to move in. I said I'd have to call you and they said, 'Call him,
but we're moving in anyway.'" With that, five hundred U.S. Army troops
marched into the Disney Studio. Part of the force stationed in the hills
around Los Angeles to protect aircraft factories, they repaired equipment in
the large soundstage, stored ammunition in the parking sheds, and posted
guards at all the entrances. They remained at the studio — the only Hollywood facility the army took over — for eight months. Thus the Disney
Studio began its encounter with the American government and the war.[1]

Disney and his staff enthusiastically enlisted in the war effort and produced a string of patriotic films. But these productions held limited popular
appeal and brought negligible profits. As a result, Disney began to revamp
his political orientation, molding the egalitarian, Depression-era populism
of his early films into a darker, more defensive form. Creativity was blunted,
profits disappeared, and the old spirit of joyful innovation nearly evaporated.

I. Mobilizing for Victory

Within a few weeks of the Pearl Harbor attack, the Disney fantasy factory had transformed itself into a wartime industrial plant. According to Carl Nater, who became studio coordinator for all wartime films, by mid-1942 over 93 percent of Disney production was connected to government contracts. The studio was deluged with projects, and animation teams began to crank out movies at an incredible rate. Before the war Disney's greatest annual output had totaled some 37,000 feet of film, but production now skyrocketed to over 200,000 feet per year. This not only dwarfed the wartime output of any other Hollywood studio, but it was done very inexpensively. The usual Disney animated movie cost between $200 and $250 per foot of completed film, but projects for the war effort were completed for around $4 per foot. Such achievements bolstered Nater's proud claim that the "home of Donald Duck has become not merely an essential war industry, but a bona fide 'war plant' operating under . . . plans as administered by the War Manpower Commission."[2]

This immersion in government work produced both a staggering volume and an incredible variety of films. With great energy and efficiency, the Disney operation began developing projects on a number of fronts. Most immediately, studio artists began a series of training films on aircraft identification for the Navy Department. These movies became part of the WEFT series, so named because of a military system emphasizing quick scanning of an aircraft's wings, engine, fuselage, and tail. (As the war went on, however, this system fell into disrepute, and the acronym WEFT was said to stand for "wrong every fucking time.") The Army Air Force, the Army Signal Corps, and the Air Transport Command also contracted with the studio for a flood of training films — *The Rules of the Nautical Road, Protection Against Chemical Warfare, Glider Training, High-Level Precision Bombing, Automotive Electricity for Military Vehicles, Dental Health, A Few Quick Facts about Venereal Disease, Ward Care of Psychotic Patients, Weather for the Navigator,* and *Operation of the C-1 Auto Pilot,* to name just a few. A few top-secret projects, such as a film on the maintenance and use of the new Norden bombsight and several briefing films on the Pacific islands marked for invasion by the Marine Corps, were subject to very tight security.[3]

In addition, the studio began a series of educational films for the government in the spring of 1942. *Food Will Win the War,* for example, was done for the Department of Agriculture as a celebration and encouragement of the American farmer's contribution to the war effort, while *Out of the Frying Pan into the Firing Line,* starring Minnie Mouse, showed American housewives how to save kitchen fat and grease for conversion into glycerine, a key ingredient in explosive shells. Disney also completed several educational films for the State Department and its coordinator of inter-American affairs.

Aimed at South America, with the intent of strengthening ties among nations of the Western Hemisphere, these movies dealt with health, environmental, and agricultural issues. *The Grain That Built a Hemisphere* charted the historical development of corn — it trumpeted that "corn is the symbol of a spirit that links the Americas in a common bond of union and solidarity" — and concluded with a paean to the grain's importance as a wartime commodity. *The Winged Scourge* showed how to combat malaria with scenes of the Seven Dwarfs cutting weeds, draining swampy areas, and spraying with oil and chemicals. Others, like *Insects as Carriers of Disease,* sought to explain how good health practices could deal with diseases spread by germs and parasites.[4]

This flood of films, however, reached only a small number of Americans. Most of Disney's popular influence during World War II came from a few short entertainment films that presented a lighthearted but patriotic look at life in the armed forces. A few featured Goofy and Pluto, but Donald Duck was the true wartime star in the Disney galaxy. Beginning with *Donald Gets Drafted,* he became a symbol of virtuous American military service. Entering the armed forces, he encountered petty frustrations that, as usual, prompted his famous outbursts of temper, but he always did his duty in the end. In films such as *Commando Duck, The Old Army Game, Sky Trooper,* and *Home Defense,* Donald Duck marched forward as Disney's representative.[5]

Several propaganda films showcased the Disney Studio's contribution to the war effort and polished its image in the public eye. Among these heavily satirical attacks on the Axis powers was *Reason and Emotion* (1943), a short film that analyzed the Nazi psyche by literally climbing inside someone's head. Two contrary impulses compete to sit in the driving seat of the brain: Reason, a soberly dressed, thinking, bespectacled character who counsels restraint and respect, and Emotion, dressed like a swarthy caveman, who promotes lust and anger. They first clash over the correct approach to a pretty girl, then Emotion cows Reason into accepting Nazi ideology. Finally, with a shifting image, they reach a correct balance in the head of an Allied fighter pilot. Another 1943 film, *Education for Death,* begins on a hilarious note as a young German boy learns the Nazi version of "Sleeping Beauty." Here an obese, lovesick Germania falls in love with a skinny Adolf Hitler, completely clad in outlandish armor, who then comically labors to lift the rotund maiden onto his horse. The movie quickly adopts a grim tone as the lad endures an indoctrination that teaches the superiority of the strong over the weak while burning books, breaking church windows, and pushing *Mein Kampf* over the Bible. It ends with images of rows of goosestepping Nazis slowly transforming into rows of graves.

Der Fuehrer's Face (1943) was the most successful of Disney's wartime films, winning an Academy Award. The film opens with Donald Duck dreaming he is working at a munitions factory in Nutziland, where he struggles unsuccessfully with the demands of an authoritarian state. The dream becomes a nightmare as he faces food shortages — breakfast consists of hard bread sprayed with the aroma of bacon and eggs, and a single coffee bean dipped into hot water on a string — and an accelerating assembly line where he scrambles to screw down bomb casings. Screaming "I can't stand it, I'm going nuts," Donald metaphorically explodes in a surrealistic scene where *he* becomes the object moving down the assembly line as the shell casings pound on him. He awakens, only to see the silhouette of a Nazi salute on the wall. He starts to shout "Heil Hitler!" and then realizes that it is a shadow from a miniature Statue of Liberty. He embraces the little statue and squawks with relief, "Am I glad to be a citizen of the United States!" A key factor in the film's success was its theme song, "Der Fuehrer's Face," a boisterous parody of German band music that featured a loud Bronx cheer in its chorus as a rotten tomato was thrown in Hitler's face.[6]

Disney's public image also gained luster from a unique little film made for the Treasury Department in the early weeks of the war. Entitled *The New Spirit,* it aimed at encouraging American citizens to support the war effort by paying their income taxes. Dick Huemer and Joe Grant worked frantically on an impossibly tight schedule in early 1942 and flew to Washington with the Disney brothers to present the project. But they ran into a problem when Treasury Secretary Henry Morgenthau and his advisers expressed their disappointment that Donald Duck was the star, not a special little character called Mr. Taxpayer. An angry Walt replied, "I've given you Donald Duck. At our studio, that's the equivalent of giving you Clark Gable out of the MGM stable." Morgenthau bowed to Disney's judgment, Donald remained, and the film was rushed to completion.

This was followed by a minor flap over funding. When the Treasury Department requested an $80,000 appropriation from Congress to pay for the film, some congressmen denounced the whole project as a convergence of government frivolity and private war profiteering. One exploded, "My God! Can you think of anything that would come nearer to making people hate to pay their income tax than the knowledge that $80,000 that should go for a bomber is to be spent for a moving picture to entertain people?" Congress refused to make the appropriation, even though a number of representatives rushed to the aid of the Disney Studio. The incident infuriated Disney, who defended himself in a letter to Senator Sheridan Downey of California. As he indignantly explained, not only did the government funding fail to cover production costs, but *The New Spirit* nosed out other Disney bookings and thereby cost the studio an additional $50,000. Underlining his own patriotism, he insisted that "we are not complaining. We are only trying to help." This incident was actually a tempest in a teacup, for Secretary Morgenthau had told the Disney party that the government did not really need enhanced tax revenues. Instead, he informed them, the film was intended "only for the purpose of keeping our people from squandering their spare cash, and thus creating artificial shortages in certain commodities, and so adversely affecting the economy."[7]

The New Spirit proved well worth the government's investment. This eight-minute film begins with a reluctant Donald Duck facing the prospect of income taxes. After the radio news reveals the dangers posed by Germany and Japan, however, Donald realizes that his patriotic duty lies in prompt payment, and he rushes to Washington to deliver his money in person. The film concludes with dramatic depictions of American factories turning out the machines of war and a Japanese battleship and a German submarine subsequently sinking to the bottom of the ocean. With its slogan "Taxes to Beat the Axis" and its striking images of Donald Duck with little American flags in place of his eyes, *The New Spirit* generated a positive popular response. Treasury Department agents who checked at theaters verified its enthusiastic reception and noted that "when Donald groaned at the mention of Income Tax, the audience groaned; when he decided to do his bit by paying it, they cheered." After the film's release, publicity also turned decidedly in Disney's favor. "This film, made for the Treasury Department, played to 26,000,000 people, 37% of whom, Gallup-polled, said it animated their willingness to pay taxes," said an article in *Time*. *Life* described it as "a first-rate job" that encouraged the prompt filing of tax returns, while *Look* ran a series of story sketches from the film that conveyed its basic message. Pieces in the *New York Times Magazine* and *This Week Magazine* called the film a "masterpiece" and praised it for showing "how Americans can play their part behind the front lines by paying this year's unprecedented taxes cheerfully."[8]

As a wartime industrial plant, the Disney Studio shed much of its whimsy and magic and bustled with serious work, military advisers, and a new concern with education. While the training films tended to be tedious and the tight military security an imposition, the studio also hummed with activity. As artist Lou Debney said, "There was a lot of excitement in the whole organization. It was not a case of business as usual." Jack Kinney concurred. "The joint was really jumping," he recalled, as crowded offices, rationing, identification cards, and air raid drills amplified the emotional intensity of life in the Disney compound.[9]

The wartime studio had its share of bizarre incidents. Ward Kimball recalled the evening when military personnel tested an extremely powerful new flare by firing one off the top of a studio building. It immediately lit up the entire grounds, and the group looked down to see "this couple banging away on the lawn, and the surprise on their faces . . . All of a sudden the sun comes up with no warning! And here is this guy with his pants down under a cork tree." Then there was the legendary occupation of Walt's office complex by Navy commander Raymond Farwell, a former university professor whose book, *The Rules of the Nautical Road*, had become the subject of a high-priority film project. Upon arriving at the studio as an adviser, Farwell took up Walt's generous offer to use his office suite for a few days until lodging in Burbank could be procured. Once he was in, however, it proved impossible to get him out. This "old codger," as one of the artists described him, simply made himself at home for several months. Farwell not only slept in Disney's bed but fixed all of his meals in the bedroom — he apparently made a habit of walking through busy staff meetings in Disney's office lugging a jar of pickles and dropping crumbs from an oversized sandwich — and washed out his clothes by hand in a bucket. Walt never found the courage to throw him out.[10]

An array of activities reflected aspects of wartime life at the studio. *Dispatch from Disney*, for example, an illustrated newsletter sent out from Burbank in 1943, attempted to bolster the morale of employees serving in the military. Leading off with letters from Walt and Roy, it included descriptions of film projects, satirical sketches of Hitler and Goering, a series of comic panels on the studio chief's hectic schedule entitled "A Day with Walt," profiles of several animators and story men, and, inserted, a series of sexy sketches by Disney artists called "Pin-Ups for Service Men." One article, "Laughter Knows How to Fight," summarized the studio's contribution to the war effort. "In this war, humor and fantasy have enlisted on the side of the United Nations," wrote Joe Grant and Dick Huemer. "They're fighting, and fighting hard . . . No other weapon of propaganda can ridicule the Axis, expose its absurdities, as deftly." By 1944, staffers also had put together a Disney camp show for servicemen stationed in the Los Angeles area. With a short animated film, musical numbers with singers and the studio band, a cancan routine, a comic skit, and demonstrations by artists, who quickly sketched cartoon characters on large easels, the show became a way for employees to participate in the war effort.[11]

Such activities did not go unnoticed. Writing under headlines that proclaimed "Mickey Mouse and Donald Duck Work for Victory" and "Walt Disney Goes to War," journalists heaped praise on the studio's film projects as an important contribution. Approving newspaper and magazine pieces quickly erased any lingering tarnish from the *New Spirit* controversy by stressing the nonprofit, public-spirited basis of Disney's wartime films. As one story informed readers, "Walt Disney Productions . . . [is] the only Hollywood studio which has converted itself 100 per cent to furthering the Nation's war effort." Others suggested that Disney was synonymous with the American resistance to authoritarianism. As a long 1942 article in *Life* concluded, the "peculiarly democratic" atmosphere of the Burbank studio was creating films that will "crusade for the kind of world where a free, popular art, using man's unlimited imagination, can flourish — where everyone has some chance to laugh and learn."[12]

For most observers, however, the studio's most important contribution lay simply in the effectiveness of its films, which aroused patriotic emotions, taught necessary skills to citizens, and melded serious purpose with humor. "Today Disney is the industry's prime realist," said an article in *Theatre Arts*. "The government in Washington looks to him more than it does to any other studio chief as a factor in building public morale, providing training and instruction to soldiers and sailors, and utilizing animated graphic art in expediting the intelligent mobilization of fighting men and civilians." J. P. McEvoy, writing in *This Week Magazine,* described Disney as "a propaganda genius for whom the Axis would give a dozen divisions." To all appearances, the wartime Disney Studio was full of creative and institutional vitality.[13]

Appearances, however, can be deceptive. For all the vigor projected by its flurry of production, the studio was barely staying afloat financially. And favorable publicity, while enhancing Disney's image as a patriot and an educator, brought little remuneration. The budget constraints, stifled creativity, and depleted ranks of artists were visible to anyone who peered behind the scenes. Having been traumatized by the strike of 1941, Disney generally experienced the next four years as another series of shocks to his worldview. A growing sense of frustration and disarray gradually became evident in both his personal life and his public productions.

II. Triumph and Disillusionment

During World War II, Walt Disney's most genuine burst of enthusiasm was for one of the most curious motion pictures in his studio's history. A war-related project that had no connection whatever to the federal government, this movie expressed Disney's evolving ideological position as it emphasized technological solutions to problems and appealed for American social and political unity.

Victory Through Air Power, released in 1943, was a full-length feature combining animation and live action that was based on the book of the same title by Major Alexander de Seversky. The author, a career military officer and aviation pioneer, had been arguing since the 1930s for a radical revamping of American military strategy to place greater reliance on long-range bombers and create a separate air force in the command structure. Seversky saw World War II as a great opportunity to put his theories into practice. Disney, claiming that Seversky's ideas reflected his own convictions, on May 4, 1942, wired to one of his staff members: "Am anxious contact Major Alexander Seversky by telephone and mail. Will you endeavor get this information to me earliest possible moment."[14]

By summer, the Disney Studio had secured film rights to Seversky's book and hired the author as a technical consultant. Disney even employed George Gallup to gauge the probable audience reaction to such an unusual production. The result of the project was a fascinating, uneven, didactic film that premiered in late summer 1943. The first sequence of *Victory Through Air Power* used animation to survey the history of aviation from the Wright brothers through World War I biplanes and modern aircraft in the 1930s, all with a decidedly comic flair. This was followed by a biographical segment on Seversky, which outlined the high points of his distinguished career: losing a leg as a fighter pilot for his native Russia during World War I, becoming an American citizen and working as a test pilot and aeronautical engineer for the military during the 1920s, coming up with a number of technical advances as an aircraft designer in the 1930s, winning the Bendix Trophy three times straight for setting air-speed records. Then Seversky, in live-action sequences, made his case for making long-range bombing the centerpiece of Allied strategy. This was interspersed with animated segments depicting historical events, maps, global geopolitical features, and future scenarios for the war. Particularly dramatic scenes showed the RAF protecting the withdrawal from Dunkirk and the airfights of the Battle of Britain; the Axis supply lines were shown as a gigantic Japanese octopus in the Pacific. The film culminated with two spectacular animated scenes: the bombing of German hydroelectric dams and a huge airborne attack on Tokyo, which reduced the city to rubble as the lifeless tentacles of the Japanese octopus released their hold on Pacific islands. The conclusion featured images of the U.S. flag and a triumphant eagle to strains of "America the Beautiful."[15]

The making of *Victory Through Air Power* prompted some of the more colorful episodes at the Disney Studio during this period. Seversky, a rather eccentric character, was at the center of many of them. A mysterious squeak on the tape, for instance, turned out to come from his artificial leg. Seversky, in the words of one acquaintance, "could be difficult to deal with, and some people thought he was a crank." His outspoken advocacy of his theories did not always sit well with other military figures on the lot. Navy commander John S. "Jimmy" Thatch, a fighter squadron commander who had returned from the Pacific theater to advise on Disney films, took great offense at Seversky's comparison of a carrier flight deck to a postage stamp. After seeing some of the storyboards for the film, Thatch issued a challenge: he would take on the author's enormous multigun bomber with his small fighter plane, using live ammunition, on one condition — that Seversky would promise to be in it![16]

An important film for Disney, *Victory Through Air Power* was wrought with controversy. Representatives from the Navy Department tried to discourage Disney, arguing that the project would scuttle their search for funds and resources, while a high-ranking officer in the air corps encouraged him to go ahead, because people didn't understand air power's growing centrality to the Allied military effort. In public interviews and statements, Disney admitted that the film was unusual but argued that "these are times for radical departures . . . I've tried to [make people laugh] in some sequences. But we believe that the basic ideas of this picture must be carried out before people are going to be able to laugh very much again." He insisted that his depiction of Seversky's ideas contributed to the war effort by advocating a strategy that pointed to a quicker victory and promised to save lives in the bargain. In private communication he disclosed an even stronger personal commitment, claiming that *Victory Through Air Power* would stir up discussion and get people "thinking and talking about the importance of real air power." While "many of the old diehards" held on to outdated ideas about military affairs, he wrote, "there is no doubt in my mind that air power is the weapon of victory, and the sooner we accept the plan for a great air offensive, the sooner we will win this war."[17]

Public reception of this film, however, proved enormously disappointing. *Victory Through Air Power* attracted only meager audiences and ended up losing money for the studio. In Carl Nater's blunt assessment, "The picture died at the box office." Many viewers found themselves confused, wondering if they were looking at entertainment or propaganda. Without sustained humor and a story, the film did not fit the mold of any Disney movie they had ever seen before. *Victory Through Air Power* seems to have prompted a reaction that was equal parts lukewarm patriotism, apathy, and bewilderment.[18]

Many reviews were rather negative. *The Daily Worker,* for instance, denounced the film's air power scheme as an "Arabian Nights fantasy" while suggesting that Seversky was an anti-Soviet reactionary whose ideas should be viewed with suspicion. James Agee, writing in *The Nation,* disapproved of the film's high-pressure salesmanship and added that its "machine-eat-machine" ethos masked the fact that "there were no suffering or dying civilians under all those proud promises of bombs." In another writer's view, the film's advocacy of mass bombing was "completely devoid of human values . . . [and] fails to give the impression of the loss of human life." Other critics insisted that the film's military strategy was dangerously naive, promising a "magical way of winning the war" that seemed to involve no loss or pain, and to some it offered a vision of such wholesale global destruction that one feared "that the world is actually coming to an end."[19]

Yet some critics lavished praise on *Victory Through Air Power.* Walter Wanger, in a patriotic paean in the *Saturday Review of Literature,* generally praised the project as an exhilarating, vigorous product of a studio completely immersed in the war effort. Others described the movie as a technical tour de force that offered a visionary picture of military strategy in a not-too-distant period. A gushing review in the New York *Mirror* even proclaimed it a masterpiece of idealistic propaganda, noting that it "set a new standard in impression and indoctrination. Its possibilities are limitless. It could have killed slavery, made or toppled Presidents."[20]

Most reviewers, however, were markedly ambivalent about this unorthodox film. Was it an exercise in education or entertainment? Or was it, as one essayist insisted, "a propaganda film, pure and simple"? Archer Winsten rated the movie "good" in the New York *Post*, but like many others he complained that the "humor, humanity, and imagination one expects from every Disney production are almost totally lacking in this very literal effort." *Life* worried that for all its fine history and entertainment, the film was guilty of "beguiling a fascinated public into the belief that this war can be won by dream ships which are not yet a reality." Howard Barnes, in his regular column in the New York *Herald Tribune*, urged readers to see the film but warned that its "ideological content" should be considered very carefully. The special pleading for air power, he wrote, easily made people forget that "there are other branches of the armed services than aviation which are contributing mightily to a certain victory."[21]

Victory Through Air Power had attempted a military formulation of Walt Disney's credo — an appeal to the virtuous American values of innovation and hard work that had produced progress in aviation, a reliance on efficiency in problem-solving that was almost magical, a vision of the future where technological progress would triumph over ideological divisions. But instead of inspiring and unifying, as Mickey Mouse and *Three Little Pigs* had done during the dark days of the Great Depression, this film tended to confuse and unsettle its audience.

Even with the failure of *Victory Through Air Power,* Disney publicly claimed that the war created new opportunities for his studio. As he told his employees, it had suggested a future where "the demand on us for the educational type of film will be as important as the demand for entertainment." This vision, he explained, demanded that "new and better types of educational motion pictures must give cohesion to this torn earth . . . Science, Economics, and Industry must be given a voice which all can understand."[22]

In private, however, he told a different tale. He complained long and bitterly about an array of wartime frustrations, most of which arose from his encounters with government red tape and bureaucrats. For instance, the government took over two years to pay for the enormous amount of gas, electricity, and other utilities the army used during its stay at the studio. At the war's onset, Disney and the studio board of directors agreed to make films at cost, but that patriotic decision proved to be very expensive. The flap in the House of Representatives over paying for *The New Spirit* caused him to burst out, "Here we broke our necks [to complete the film] and then . . . I get postcards calling me unpatriotic, a war profiteer." A similar pattern emerged with government contracts for movies. Military officials would initiate a project they described as vital to the war effort, but after it was well under way, bureaucrats would haggle over details, refuse to pay certain costs, and frequently withhold authorization. As Carl Nater affirmed, "We had a dickens of a time getting our money back from the government, just getting our costs back." Along the same lines, the government demanded that Disney form a separate production group for each project, thus forcing the studio to subsidize the group during slack periods in the production process. In addition, the studio was flooded by military advisers and consultants, some of whom were more concerned with asserting authority than with cooperating. "Some of those people, when they put a uniform on, it was like pinning a badge on somebody," Disney grumbled. "They couldn't hold it." Although he never articulated it quite so bluntly, he came to believe that the government was taking advantage of his patriotism. As he told Ben Sharpsteen when asking him to go to Washington for a contract talk, "I want you to go to that meeting with me, because I don't want you to let me give the studio away."[23]

Manpower shortages only compounded the studio's difficulties. On the one hand, the government continually pressed Disney to complete educational and training films quickly, and on the other hand, it kept drafting his artists into the service while they were in the middle of such projects. As a result, he had a series of run-ins with draft boards. He found it difficult to persuade them that his artists were needed for war work at a studio making cartoon films. Years later, he recalled a draft board member, proudly sporting an American Legion button, who reacted to his argument with particular disdain:

> Well, I had nothing against American Legion buttons, but I happened to notice that it was a silver one and not a gold, which meant that his service was in this country, not abroad. So he was actually what I would call a billboard American. He lit into me like I was some guy in there trying to save a no-good so-and-so from the draft . . . But when I went back the next time, you know what I did? I dug down in the bottom of my collar box and found my old Veterans of Foreign Wars button. So I got that out, and the next time I went to the draft board I sat and stared at him button to button.

Disney finally resolved many of his problems by inviting the draft board to the studio for a tour. They were impressed when even he could not get them security clearance to look at certain military film projects.[24]

Disney's associates saw a less evident problem at the wartime studio — their boss's growing creative boredom. Although some observers, like visiting screenwriter Eric Knight, found the studio chief to be "light, funny, and quick," to many animators, story men, and directors it seemed obvious that the ongoing problems had blunted his flair for creativity and experimentation. He chafed at the rigid requirements of the armed forces and their refusal to allow any humor or invention into their films. When he suggested such approaches at a training film meeting, according to one staffer, "You would have thought he had run a hot poker through the heart of the navy experts, because they just rose up and said, 'Well, Mr. Disney, you couldn't do a thing like that . . . This is a very serious subject here.'" Disney's annoyance only increased when, near the end of the war, military experts decided that their movies needed just these qualities. As one top member of the navy brass informed a Disney staffer in 1945, the earlier films had been honorable efforts, but they would have been more interesting if some humor had been injected into them![25]

Hamstrung by bureaucratic, financial, and creative constraints, Disney gradually withdrew emotionally from much of the wartime work. According to artist Bill Anderson, he would find out what was needed for a certain film, set up a crew to handle it, and then stand back. Unlike his earlier habits, the frustrated filmmaker "didn't get into the intricate day-to-day operation of each project."[26]

Reeling from wartime frustrations, Disney began to cast his old populist sensibility in a new mold. A darker, more defensive notion of the American way of life slowly moved to the fore as the joyous egalitarianism and inclusion of his Depression-era populism evaporated in the heat of pressing, disillusioning events. His old distrust of financial monopoly still flared on occasion. On August 22, 1944, for instance, he allied himself with Samuel Goldwyn in denouncing the major Hollywood studios that owned extensive theater chains that discriminated against the films of small, independent producers. In a statement of support for Goldwyn's crusade, Disney defined the central issue as "whether the motion picture industry should continue to exist under American competitive principles or be throttled by monopolistic restrictions and limitations." The small producer, he insisted, must be "permitted to operate without artificial obstacles being thrown in [his] path by selfish interests." But such espousals of opportunity and denunciations of privilege became less frequent. Instead, Disney increasingly articulated a more paranoid populism, which sought not the triumph of the little guy but the identification of the enemies of the American folk.[27]

A small signal of this shifting sensibility came with Disney's disparaging comments on the leftist political views of his boyhood idol, Charlie Chaplin. A reporter for the *New York Times Magazine* noted that "Walt wouldn't tell me about Mickey's politics, except to say that they do not resemble Chaplin's." Privately, the studio head expressed sadness that his former hero had become "all mixed up" by falling into extremist politics and going into exile. "He just got himself in a trap and I think that he's just too

stubborn to back down," Disney speculated. "I don't think he actually believes [radical doctrines]."[28]

On February 4, 1944, a number of Hollywood luminaries, with great
fanfare, founded the Motion Picture Alliance for the Preservation of American Ideals, or the MPA. Meeting at the Beverly Wilshire Hotel, this group of
producers, directors, executives, actors, and writers announced their opposition to leftist influences in the film industry. In a statement of principles
publicized a few days later, they made their agenda explicit. "We believe in,
and like, the American Way of Life; the liberty and freedom which generations before us have fought to create and preserve . . . the right to succeed or
fail as free men, according to the measure of our ability and our strength,"
the statement read. "Believing in these things, we find ourselves in sharp
revolt against a rising tide of Communism, Fascism and kindred beliefs, that
seek by subversive means to undermine and change this way of life." The
group worried that the film industry was falling under the sway of "Communists, radicals and crackpots," and it pledged to fight this subversive
influence and to depict in movies "the American scene, its standards and its
freedoms, its beliefs and its ideals, as we know them and believe in them."
Movie director Sam Wood, a fanatical anti-Communist with a penchant for
colorful outbursts against Hollywood subversives, was elected as the MPA's
leader. "I say Congress ought to make everybody stand up publicly and be
counted!" he told *The New Yorker*. "I say make every damn Communist
stand up and be counted. They're a danger and disgrace to the industry!"
Other prominent supporters included Gary Cooper, Barbara Stanwyck,
Adolphe Menjou, Ward Bond, King Vidor, Clark Gable, Irene Dunne,
Spencer Tracy, and later John Wayne. And the MPA's first vice president,
with his name listed right under Sam Wood's on the publicity releases, was
Walt Disney.[29]

The MPA began with a war of words. In early March 1944 it sent a long
letter to Senator Robert Reynolds of North Carolina, a sympathetic politician who entered the text into the *Congressional Record*. Denouncing the
"flagrant manner in which the motion-picture industrialists of Hollywood
have been coddling Communists," the missive promised spirited resistance
from "the decent, patriotic American element of the motion picture industry" the MPA represented. This bore political fruit, helping to inspire the
House Un-American Activities Committee investigation of Hollywood reds
in 1944 and state representative Jack Tenney's 1946 committee hearings on
Communist influences in education, labor, and filmmaking in Los Angeles.
The MPA also backed Roy Brewer and the IATSE in their successful crusade
to ruin labor leader Herb Sorrell, Disney's adversary during the studio
strike, and his leftist Conference of Studio Unions.[30]

Writer Ayn Rand, the primary intellectual spokesperson for the MPA, wrote the "Screen Guide for Americans" (1948) as the group's manifesto. Written for those who desired to "protect [their] pictures from being used for Communistic purposes," the pamphlet urged an initial, practical move upon loyal American filmmakers — "do not hire Reds to work on your pictures." Films supporting "Americanism," the author insisted, "don't smear" the free enterprise system, industrialists, the profit motive and wealth, the success ethic, American political institutions, or individualism. At the same time, Rand continued, such movies "don't glorify" failure, depravity, the common man, or the collective. As the "Screen Guide for Americans" concluded, while the Constitution guarantees freedom of speech, that "does not imply that it is our duty to provide a knife for the murderer who wants to cut our throat." Rand's vigorous formulations helped make the Motion Picture Alliance the bulwark of anticommunism in Hollywood well up into the 1950s.[31]

In fairness, it is difficult to gauge the extent of Disney's involvement with the MPA. He certainly was an early, high-ranking officer of the organization, and an article in *Time* on February 14, 1944, implied that he was an active participant. Focusing on political agitation in the film industry, it featured pictures of two Hollywood leftists on one side of the column and two conservatives — Sam Wood and Walt Disney — on the other. After the initial spate of publicity in the mid-1940s, however, Disney's name no longer appeared among the MPA's officers and leaders, although Gunther Lessing served on its executive board well into the next decade. Disney probably backed the group more in spirit than in terms of actual involvement. But while the extent of his support eludes precise measurement, the tenor of his emerging political sensibility could not be clearer.

By the late 1940s, Disney was claiming flatly that the studio strike in Burbank had involved "a Communist group trying to take over my artists." He named people involved in the dispute whom he believed to be Communists — the animator David Hilberman, who had studied at the Moscow Art Theater and, suspiciously, "had no religion"; the labor organizer Herbert Sorrell; union agents William Pomerance and Maurice Howard. In an earnest, folksy style, he warned that communism was a dangerous movement that threatened to taint "all of the good, free causes in this country, all the liberalisms that really are American . . . I feel if the thing can be proven un-American it ought to be outlawed." In Disney's new populist vision, communism had apparently replaced cultural elitism and economic restrictions as the deadliest danger to the American folk.[32]

After the soaring successes of the 1930s, the 1940s inaugurated a sustained crisis that severely tested Disney's sentimental populism. His experiences helped torpedo his democratic, egalitarian optimism, but like many Americans, he also came face to face with new, unfamiliar political pressures —

questions about distribution of economic power within a consolidating corporate order, uncertainties over the global responsibilities accompanying a new internationalism, fears of powerful ideologies such as fascism and communism. This "age of doubt," as one historian has termed the era, did not just color the political sensibility of this popular entertainer. It also inspired a growing aesthetic confusion at the heart of Walt Disney's films.[33]

13

Disney's Descent

AS POLITICAL STORMCLOUDS gathered and the creative atmosphere began to darken, the aesthetic mission of the Disney Studio became less clear. Disney entertainment films seemed unable to get off the ground. Audiences were puzzled, and arbiters of taste began to turn an increasingly skeptical eye toward the Burbank fantasy factory. The man who had been the darling of the critics only a short time before rapidly became their target.

In her 1945 essay "The Artlessness of Walt Disney," Barbara Deming suggested that Disney's growing confusion and aimlessness was a reflection of the times. His defining characteristic, Deming insisted, had always been his ability "to accept wholeheartedly the outlook of the hour, and to improvise with it, whatever it might be . . . he *is* uncritical of what he reflects. He is quite artless." Disney had now become a victim of his war-torn times, as reflected in the film *The Three Caballeros*. The movie presented a world that was falling apart. "Landscapes, objects, persons are shattered or blur, suffer translation, as if they were of no more body than reflections in water. Nothing holds its shape," Deming observed. "And [throughout] . . . runs the theme of a quest that, after nightmares suffered, attains its object only to have the moment emptied of all meaning." The result was a movie that dismayed the art critic but fascinated "the psychoanalyst, or the social analyst — the inquirer into the mythos, the ethos of the times." In a world immersed in warfare and just beginning to confront the horrors of the concentration camp and the awesome power of the atomic bomb, this chaotic movie showed more than it intended. For Deming, it was "a bad film, but it is a good nightmare. Like all good nightmares, its reference is wide." She perceived that Disney's troubles in the 1940s ran much deeper than labor strife and political disillusionment.[1]

Beset by political and financial pressures, Disney had wandered off creatively and lost his way. Several series of disappointing movies marked his meandering path. The uneven South American films of mid-decade gave way to a number of package films after 1945, which, using a watered-down *Fantasia* format, strung together disparate animated segments of popular and classical music. These films brought negligible financial gains while the critical reception became increasingly hostile. A jumble of themes, techniques, and styles produced a nervous experimentalism that showed flashes of innovation but ultimately degenerated into chaos or sentimentalism. Desperate for a lucrative new form, Disney dabbled for a time in educational and industrial movies before discovering their creative and economic limitations. To complete this dreary picture, his loss of creative focus only exacerbated a deepening financial crisis brought on by global economic forces.

To many observers, Walt Disney's steady decline was uncomfortably evident. The lingering aesthetic crisis, in concert with political and financial difficulties, seemed to mark the final stages of a remarkable career in popular entertainment. The halcyon days of the Disney Studio seemed to be over.

I. The Package Films

The beginning of Disney's artistic decline, perhaps appropriately, was marked by flight. As the strike dragged on through the summer of 1941, a frustrated Walt took advantage of an opportunity offered by the American government to leave his problems behind. The newly established Office of the Coordinator of Inter-American Affairs, under the direction of Nelson Rockefeller, was responsible for improving ties between the United States and South America because of fears of spreading Nazi influence in that region. It asked Walt to make a goodwill tour of the region, as Mickey Mouse, Donald Duck, and other Disney characters had achieved notable popularity there. He initially was reluctant but agreed to go when, first, the project was redefined as a trip to gather material for films, and second, the labor dispute had become bitterly deadlocked. Thus Disney, his wife, and fifteen artists, story men, and musicians left for South America in mid-August.

The Disney entourage, or El Groupo, as they came to be known, journeyed to Rio de Janeiro for a few days and then moved on to Buenos Aires for a more extended stay. Part of the group went to northern Argentina to study the rural life of the gaucho, some traveled to Bolivia, Peru, and the Lake Titicaca region, and still others headed for Santiago, Chile. A studio press release described their mission as an attempt "to utilize properly, in the medium of animation, some of the vast wealth of South American literature, music, and customs which has never failed to fascinate them." Accordingly, some Disney artists spent considerable time sketching people, clothing, buildings, animals, scenes, and landscapes while others collected folklore and music.[2]

The trip was decidedly casual. Animator Frank Thomas, for instance, reported that while everyone in the group talked to many people, collected stories, and sketched anything that smacked of local color, "mainly we were wined and dined all over the place . . . [and] it was real hard to do any work." Ken Anderson noted that at one stopover he and another member of the party commandeered a car on a whim and drove off into the back country to explore and sketch. When they returned, an angry supervisor assured him that Disney would be quite annoyed when he heard about this escapade. Anderson feared the worst when Disney asked to see the sketchbooks, but after a time Disney looked up and said, "Goddamnit, why can't anybody else around here do like Ken? Go out and see things and do things? This stuff is great."[3]

After several weeks of gathering material, El Groupo reconvened for a leisurely seventeen-day cruise to New York City and finally arrived back in California late in October. Disney had originally intended that the mass of drawings, impressions, and ideas from this trip would provide the basis for a series of animated shorts on regional themes. As he explained a few weeks after his return, the travelers had received so many impressions "that we came back with our heads swimming, and it wasn't until just recently that we were able to sort out all of our material, both mental and physical, and do some sort of production plan on our proposed South American shorts." As work on the project progressed, however, the blueprint changed. The proposed series was reconfigured into a pair of longer Disney movies. *Saludos Amigos,* released in 1943, was followed a year and a half later by *The Three Caballeros.* The nature of these films, and the reception accorded them, again demonstrated Disney's declining aesthetic fortunes.[4]

Saludos Amigos, with a running time of only forty-three minutes, presented the package structure that would become typical of Disney's 1940s movies. Four discrete animated sequences provided the basic framework, but they were interspersed with several other elements — humorously drawn relief maps of South America, carefully rendered musical scenes, and 16mm color footage of the Disney party as it boarded planes, observed picturesque scenes, and busily sketched colorful material. In the first animated section, Donald Duck visited Lake Titicaca; in the second, the movie moved southward to feature Little Pedro, a baby airplane who heroically masters the skill of flying the mail over the imposing mountains of Chile. The third section, "El Gaucho Goofy," was set in the pampas region and followed Goofy's comical struggles to acquire the skills of an Argentine cowboy. *Saludos Amigos* concluded at the Carnival in Rio, where a Brazilian parrot, José Carioca, took Donald Duck on a tour of South American art and music as a magical paintbrush brought various scenes to life and lively samba rhythms sounded in the background. The inclusion of the Argentine painter F. Molina Campos and the Brazilian musician Jose Oliveira added authentic regional color to the film.[5]

Saludos Amigos premiered in several South American nations before opening in the United States in early 1943. The critical response was positive, if somewhat muted. Gilbert Seldes, writing in *Esquire,* saw it as a happy departure from the filmmaker's recent "overblown masterpieces" and a return to "the Disney of the carefree early days; it is inventive, organized, funny, charming, dramatic, colorful." But James Agee, writing in *The Nation,* dismissed the movie as a depressing, embarrassing, overly cute attempt at cultural ingratiation, while John T. McManus, in *PM,* viewed it as poorer than Disney's earlier work and confessed "a mingled pride and sadness over the growing up of a beloved something we all foolishly hoped could stay young forever."[6]

Most reviewers preferred to see the film as an exercise in citizenship. They portrayed Disney as a patriotic filmmaker aiding his country and gave a generous evaluation of the film's merits by viewing it as a cultural arm of the war effort. Theodore Strauss, for instance, writing in the New York *Times,* praised Disney as "this country's No. 1 propagandist" and praised *Saludos Amigos* for allowing Donald Duck to become an "ambassador-at-large, a salesman of the American Way" who squawked "the perfect retort to Herr Doktor Goebbels." In the words of another reviewer, *Saludos Amigos* "should do more to cement friendly relations between North and South America than a dozen treaties or a score of diplomatic missions." Disney certainly encouraged this view. "While half the world is being forced to shout 'Heil Hitler,' our answer is to say 'Saludos Amigos,'" he said in a radio broadcast. The project, he explained with Disneyesque simplicity, was designed to encourage the American continents to "like one another better."[7]

This focus on "good neighborliness" and wartime solidarity, however, masked the less obvious but more far-reaching political implications of the film. While it certainly shored up a pan-American barrier against fascism, it also allowed Disney to recast the world subtly in the image of the United States. The Argentine gaucho was not so different from Goofy the Texas cowboy; José Carioca was a close cousin to Donald Duck; Pedro the baby airplane was a mirror image of the familiar "little engine that could." As Disney informed radio listeners in the United States, "our other American neighbors are gay and charming, but they know the meaning of hard work and achievement." There was evidence, he believed, that "a new and virile and unselfconscious American continental culture is on the way." But that culture, according to Disney, was clearly modeled on the values and practices of Americans. As *Saludos Amigos* reassured its audience, its neighbors could be counted on to pursue the same goals.[8]

The Three Caballeros, Disney's follow-up, proved to be a much more controversial effort in the same vein. A feature-length entertainment instead of transparent propaganda, it also drew on the material from the South American trip to create a package of divergent elements. Uniquely, it revived a technique Disney had not used since his Alice comedies from the 1920s — a combination of animation and live actors in the same scenes. Once again the film starred Donald Duck, who receives a huge gift-wrapped package full of surprises on his birthday. Inside he first discovers a projector and a home-movie reel that tells an all-animated story of Pablo the Penguin, who sails for the warmth of South America from his icy Antarctic home, and Little Gauchito, who wins a race with a magical flying donkey. Donald then removes a large pop-up book on Brazil, from which José Carioca bursts to lead a fast-paced, music-filled expedition to his native country. Donald meets the Brazilian actress and singer Aurora Miranda and falls in love, and their kiss becomes the signal for an elaborate musical scene. The final present in the birthday package begins the last segment, in which the Mexican rooster Panchito joins José and Donald and the trio heads off on a boisterous tour of Veracruz, Acapulco, and Mexico City. They cavort with bathing beauties on Caribbean beaches, join in with costumed folk dancers, and ride a magical serape through the country as Donald again falls in love, this time with the beautiful Mexican actresses Dora Luz and Carmen Molina. The movie ends on an appropriately rollicking note. As Donald engages in a bullfight, the mock bull explodes in a geyser of fireworks that light up the sky with "The End" in three languages.[9]

The most striking feature of Disney's second South American film was its frenetic experimentalism. The viewer faced not only a unique mingling of live people and animated characters but an escalating orgy of dazzling colors, outlandish humor, shifting perspectives, and nonstop action. While the opening sequence relies on gentle humor and fantasy, the last two segments veer away from Disney's sentimental modernism and crash headlong into surrealism as visually disorienting, frantically paced scenes pile one on top of another. As Donald shows one of the home movies, a character leaves the screen to walk up the projected beam of light and out of the picture; José uses his umbrella as a machine gun to shoot cascades of flower petals; characters leave a scene on one side of the frame and reenter from the top; Dora Luz steps out of the pages of an animated book and Carmen Molina turns into an animated cactus. At one point the torsos of the three caballeros are joined to three sets of real female legs, which walk off, leaving the characters without lower halves. Finally, Donald has a bizarre dream in which he is kissed by several disembodied lips, turns into a skyrocket, and is confronted by blindfolded women in bathing suits whose silhouettes chase him around.

The technological aspects of the film, particularly the use of live actors and animation within the same frame, elicited much wide-eyed amazement. Magazine articles explained the various ingenious techniques that lay behind this innovation and embroidered the old rhetorical question, "How on earth did he do that?" For a few critics, the technological razzle-dazzle of *The Three Caballeros*, in combination with its tone of fast-paced fun and its "good neighbor" sensibility, made it "a flashy fantasia of stunning tints and tabasco excitements."[10]

It is ironic, therefore, that this aesthetically daring film marked the beginning of the critical exodus. For the first time, a major Walt Disney production struck a long, sustained sour note with the movie press. The most frequent complaint was it displayed more flash than substance, more technique than artistry. "Dizzy Disney," a biting essay in the New York *Times* noted, "and his playmates have let their technical talents run wild . . . If Mr. Disney wants to make a cheap flea-circus out of cartoons he has found the way." Many felt keenly that the film's missing element was that old Disney staple, warmth. Others recoiled from its hodgepodge structure, explosive colors, and breakneck pace, believing that it culminated only in incoherence and confusion. The movie critic for the Baltimore *Sun* insisted that this movie "dazzles the senses, but it frequently arouses suspicions that it is never making any tangible sense."[11]

The sexual dynamics of *The Three Caballeros* caused particular concern. Watching an animated duck lustily chasing after curvaceous flesh-and-blood women in bathing suits — in a Disney film, no less — proved a discomfiting experience for many. The Philadelphia *Record* noted that "sex rears its pretty but definitely Freudian head . . . [as] our old friend Donald Duck becomes a very lusty drake as well as a girl-chaser to rival Harpo Marx." Struck by the phallic imagery of the film, *The New Yorker*'s critic commented that "a scene involving the duck, a young lady, and a long alley of animated cactus plants would probably be considered suggestive in a less innocent medium." Such libidinous shenanigans, in concert with the film's stylistic flash, caused many observers to fear that "if Disney continues to confuse creative artistry with technical development, and to rely on tricks rather than invention, I'm afraid he's had it, for every foot of this film shows up the sad change, shows how he is losing touch with all those individual qualities which made him great."[12]

When World War II finally ended and Disney found himself able to return full-time to entertainment films, he did not abandon the package genre. Instead, he continued to develop loosely glued-together animated segments based on short musical pieces or short tales. Described by Ben Sharpsteen as "vaudeville shows," they tried to lure an audience by combining various kinds of entertainment and offering something for everyone.[13]

Make Mine Music (1946), the first of this group, was a kind of poor man's *Fantasia*. It was composed of ten diverse musical segments, ranging from popular music (Benny Goodman, Dinah Shore, the Andrews Sisters) to more highbrow choices (Nelson Eddy, "tone poems," dancers from the Ballet Russe) to folklore ("The Martins and the Coys" and "Casey at the Bat") to a classical piece (Prokofiev's "Peter and the Wolf"). The animation style varied just as much. The segments "Blue Bayou" and "Two Silhouettes" followed a self-consciously arty format, seeking, with notable lack of success, to evoke beauty with lush drawings, swelling music, and images of cupids, flamingoes, and water reflections. At the other extreme, the delightful Benny Goodman segments, "All the Cats Join In" and "After You're Gone," utilized fast-paced, self-mocking, even surrealistic techniques to illustrate the bobby sox culture and the controlled frenzy of swing instrumentation. Somewhere in the middle, the folklore segments relied on the tried-and-true methods of Disney animated shorts — visual gags, personality animation, exaggerated humor. The high point of the film was "The Whale Who Wanted to Sing at the Met," a hilariously unlikely fantasy of a leviathan with an incredible operatic voice. Drawing on Disney's tradition of sentimental modernism, this segment created a fantasy world of magic and satire where a lovable creature sings his heart out as he towers over the Metropolitan Opera House, spouting water for tears (the audience protects itself with raincoats and umbrellas). And it offered a bittersweet ending. Shockingly, the whale is harpooned, after which he ascends to lead a huge heavenly choir as the Pearly Gates display a sign reading SOLD OUT.[14]

Films such as *Fun and Fancy Free* (1947), *Melody Time* (1948), and *The Adventures of Ichabod and Mr. Toad* (1949) followed a similar path, stringing together musical segments, creating a pastiche of short subjects, and blending animated characters with live actors. Even with popular entertainers such as ventriloquist Edgar Bergen, singer Bing Crosby, and movie cowboy Roy Rogers in their casts, these films never caught fire. Certain segments, such as *Melody Time*'s "Pecos Bill," recaptured some of the old magic, but ultimately these halfhearted films came across as exactly what they were — several animated shorts surrounded with considerable filler and stuffed into a concocted package. They were plagued by inconsistency, varying wildly in quality as episodes of inspired imagination gave way to insipid, stale, mediocre stretches of work.

In part, these problems stemmed from economic pressures, as Disney could not put together the financing he needed to spend the three years it took to do a feature. But they also flowed from his eroding artistic vision.

An all-over-the-field kind of experimentalism certainly displayed flashes of brilliance, but more often it suggested a desperate search for direction. Having beat a confused retreat from their earlier synthesis of sentimental modernism, Disney and his artists stumbled into a schizophrenic aesthetic that too often juxtaposed cloying emotion with bursts of frantic surrealism. The resulting pattern was alternately childish and jarring, and it satisfied few.[15]

The commentary on *Make Mine Music* typified the mixed critical reception to Disney's postwar films. Reviewers complained that the various segments were "not always in harmony with each other" and displayed an "absorption with technical razzle-dazzle for its own sake." Bosley Crowther, one of Disney's warmest supporters for many years, wrote that the film was "as disordered as the work of any artist can be . . . Some [of the segments] are delightful Disney fancies and some are elaborate junk. Watching it is an experience in precipitate ups and downs."[16]

In fact, in certain corners the critical reception turned into outright hostility. *Fun and Fancy Free*, for instance, brought a barrage of denunciation. *The New Yorker* wrote that "Walt Disney, who seems to have been determinedly aiming at mediocrity in his recent productions, has not even hit that mark" with this film, while *Newsweek* described it as "an uninspired Disney working on a strictly commercial basis." *Cue* said that Disney had become so "infantile . . . [and] smugly satisfied with the condescending, cute little tricks of his pastel-toned calendar art and drooling dialogue" that the film "will probably be as great a bore to worldly-wise children as to their naive elders."[17]

By the late 1940s, this backlash had gathered tremendous strength and become a huge problem for the Disney enterprise. Intellectuals abandoned Disney in droves, complaining that any semblance of genuine artistry had vanished as he had evolved into a formulaic, perhaps even a hack filmmaker. In the words of one critic, Disney "has been talking like a fool for so long now that most of us have almost forgotten the time when a new Disney film was an event." Even Gilbert Seldes, one of the entertainer's biggest boosters for two decades, reluctantly joined the chorus. "As the imaginative powers have dwindled, excitement has been pumped up; too often, when he is not exciting, Disney falls into a depressing area of sentimentality," he wrote. "What was once a unique bedazzlement of the senses has become routine and stale . . . and the sweetness and the lightness went out of his work."[18]

Disney's increasing penchant for cuteness usually topped the list of complaints. This trait had always been central to his work, of course, but in his earlier films it had been balanced by a mischievous, adventurous, occasionally dark quality that usually made it fresh and endearing. But gradually Disney's sweetness had become bloated, and by the mid-1940s, a growing reliance on cute characters and maudlin emotional situations struck many observers as merely manipulative and ingratiating. In a biting essay in the *New Republic,* for instance, Manny Farber described Disney films as "almost choked to death by a bad taste that combines callowness and syrupy sweetness." Characterized by "lollypop color," "prettiness," and an ambiance that was "happy, optimistic, and uncomplicated beyond belief," these movies were in "a bon-bon mode and will satisfy the people who do the printing on wedding cakes, those who invented Mother's Day, the people who write their names with a flourish and end them with flounces and curlicues." Another critic writing in the late 1940s mirrored this scornful evaluation: "Looking back on his career from the nadir which he has now reached, it is easy to discount his earlier success and claim that we always knew he was horribly sentimental and vulgar, completely devoid of taste, and a second- or even third-rate artist . . . He unfortunately shares with the great American public a deplorable taste for sentimentality and the worst clichés of June-moon love-dove mawkishness."[19]

Other critics were perturbed by Disney's use of American folklore as grist for his animation mill. James Agee argued that his appropriation of American myths and legends constituted a kind of fraud. He insisted that Disney had become a key carrier in a sweeping epidemic of cultural corruption wherein the American "folk tradition has become thoroughly bourgeoizified." But Hermine Rich Isaacs offered perhaps the most poignant assessment of Disney's aesthetic decline. In a 1946 essay in *Theatre Arts,* she argued that the filmmaker had fallen prey to cheap sentimentality. Isaacs spun out a sad analogy to describe Disney's decline:

> Suppose you go to visit a friend. You know that he has a warm heart and is kind to animals, that his sense of humor is infectious, his professional skill beyond compare. But when you enter his house you find to your dismay that his walls are festooned with second-rate art: romantic scenes of white doves against lush blue backgrounds; vapid landscapes; valentine motifs, complete with lace cutouts, tinsel stars and hearts of assorted sizes. You discover that his furniture is carelessly assembled with little regard for harmony or any other concern except to fill space. You would not therefore cease to love the man, to laugh at his jokes or admire his skill; but you would have to admit with regret that his taste is deplorable.[20]

Disney's earlier artistic triumphs seemed increasingly a dreamy memory as their creator now fought for audiences and respect. But in this desperate atmosphere, one animated character provided an intermittent ray of light.

II. Duck Tales

Facing a growing array of problems in the 1940s, Walt Disney found some solace in the escapades of Donald Duck. The squawking fowl had first appeared as a bit player in a Silly Symphony entitled *The Wise Little Hen* (1934), in which he spoke only a single line. Typically, he was resisting a task imposed on him: "Who? Me? Oh, no, I've got a bellyache." Later in the year he nabbed a key role in *Orphan's Benefit*, and followed in 1935 with prominent appearances in *The Band Concert* and *Mickey's Service Station*. For a time, along with Goofy, Pluto, and assorted other characters, he was part of a supporting ensemble in the Mickey Mouse films. Growing popularity, however, led to his own series of animated shorts in 1937. By the early 1940s, this foul-tempered duck had become not only the leading star at the Disney Studio but an American folk hero.[21]

Donald's abrasive personality, activated by the frustrations of everyday life, was his most distinctive feature. His outburst in *Orphan's Benefit* — an inept attempt to recite "Mary Had a Little Lamb" brings a string of abuse from heckling children and a response of helpless, sputtering rage — became the prototype for his legendary temper tantrums, each more outlandish than the last. For movie viewers, the duck's stamping feet, narrowed eyes, and antagonistic boxer pose promised to bring laughter, and critics vied with one another to describe the essential appeal of this rather unlovable character. Helen Thompson saw Donald as "an iconoclastic little fellow, bearing life's burdens and being one," while Gilbert Seldes described him as "a bad, wicked duck, a malicious and mischievous duck, a duck corresponding to all the maddening attractiveness of bad little boys and girls." In an essay entitled "Ya Wanna Fight?" J. P. McEvoy told his readers that this new screen star was "encouraged to be bad. The more obstreperous he acts, the more successful he becomes. The worse he is, the better he is liked."[22]

As usual at the Disney Studio, a careful and thoughtful process lay behind Donald's hilarious fulminations. A 1939 Story Department essay entitled "Character Analysis of Donald Duck," designed to help shape the plots and gags for his films, offered a series of shrewd observations on his personality:

> He is vain, cocky, and boastful; loves to impose on other people and to heckle them, but if the tables are turned he flies into a rage. In other words, he can dish it out, but he can't take it. It is his cockiness that gets him into most of his scrapes, because it is seasoned with a foolhardy recklessness.
>
> His most likeable trait is determination. In most of his pictures he has some goal to achieve, and he goes after it with a vim that brooks no interference. When an opposing factor rears its ugly head — and it always does — he loses his temper. The duck never compromises. Regardless of the odds against him, he comes back again and again to the fray, each time more determined than before, and rants and kicks and punches and yanks until either he or the opposition is in ruins . . .
>
> His well-known quick temper arises in most instances from frustra-

tions of his desires, but ridicule, petty annoyances, impatience, or ruthless destruction of some valued possession can make him turn the air blue. He doesn't stay angry for long periods; even in his wildest rages he can be completely and instantly mollified by a little gratification.

Always the characters that he beats up are menaces much larger than himself . . . [A] type of role that fits him well is the "little man vs. big menace" angle. In this medium he works excellently with the big bully, Pete.[23]

One key to Donald's striking screen impression, of course, was his voice. Few could forget his singular speaking style, a muddled, quacking assault on the English language that rose in pitch and intensity along with his bile as some indignity fell across his path. The mere sound of it was enough to raise a chuckle. It had to, because as the studio's character analysis admitted, "The duck's dialogue should be used sparingly, because it is funny only in sound; few people understand his words."[24]

The distinctive voice was the handiwork of Clarence "Ducky" Nash, a transplanted midwesterner who had traveled the Chautauqua circuit entertaining audiences with bird calls and animal noises. By the early 1930s he had drifted to Los Angeles, where he worked in publicity for the Adohr Milk Company. Nash drove a wagon pulled by six miniature horses — a painted message on the side proclaimed him "Whistling Clarence, the Adohr Bird Man" — and gave little shows to promote the sale of his company's products. Stories differ as to how he joined the Disney Studio. Nash remembered that he stopped by the Hyperion facility on impulse and got an impromptu audition, but Disney always claimed that he heard Nash on an amateur radio show and tracked him down. Whatever the case, Nash impressed Disney during his audition with his chicken, turkey, and cricket impressions. He really made a hit, however, with his baby goat voice, reciting "Mary Had a Little Lamb." When Disney heard it, he exclaimed, "That's our talking duck!" and signed the impersonator to a contract. Nash created the special voice by placing the left side of his tongue against his upper left molars, forming a pocket high in the left cheek, and forcing air through it. The result was a sustained, nasal sound somewhere between a snort and a screech, and it became the verbal signature of Donald Duck.[25]

Giving Nash's voice a physical presence and a personality, however, proved a complex process. Dick Huemer and Art Babbitt animated Donald Duck's first appearances, but Dick Lundy was most responsible for giving the early version his distinctive visual personality. In the mid-1930s, an angular Donald had a long beak, thin neck, small head, and skinny legs and knobby knees. Within a short time, however, he had a more rounded and pliable physique, a blunter beak and shorter neck, and a larger, more prominent head with big eyes and protruding eyebrows, all of which allowed him a much greater range of emotional expression. Throughout, of course, he was outfitted in his trademark sailor suit and ribboned cap. By about 1937, with the inauguration of a special series of Donald Duck cartoons, the famous studio team that produced the dozens of animated shorts that delighted audiences through the mid-1940s had taken shape. Supervised by director Jack King, the group included Jack Hannah and Carl Barks, whose innovative stories were the heart of the enterprise, and Fred Spencer, who became especially important in the actual animation of the character.[26]

Walt Disney also contributed to the duck's early success. As Nash admitted, the studio chief helped shape this character's personality by encouraging him to laugh and to express sadness or anger in Donald's voice, things Nash had never attempted but that expanded the emotional possibilities. Disney never liked Donald as much as Mickey Mouse, whose voice he himself had provided and whose mischievous but upright character seemed to mirror his own. In fact, he once disparaged Donald by comparing him to Harold Ickes, the curmudgeonly New Dealer in Franklin Roosevelt's cabinet. Nonetheless, Disney seemed to admire his pluck and did not hesitate to defend him when an irate visitor to the studio complained about Donald's consumption of hard liquor in a forthcoming cartoon. "What you apparently didn't learn was that we pointed a very definite moral against drinking when we showed his insides literally burned up by it; show him spitting fire; developing a violent case of hiccoughs and actually doing everything except vomiting," Disney responded testily. "Surely such a scene could hardly be construed, even by the widest stretch of imagination, as indicating Donald enjoyed the drink. Everything we do, in fact, indicates quite the reverse."[27]

Donald Duck had a spectacular ride to success by the late 1930s, and it continued well into the next decade. He starred in animated shorts such as *Don Donald* (1937), *Donald's Golf Game* (1938), *Officer Duck* (1939), and *Window Cleaners* (1940). With the outbreak of World War II, he moved to the center of activity in *Der Fuehrer's Face* and *The New Spirit*. In addition, he headlined a series of shorts that provided a humorous look at life in the armed forces, including *Donald Gets Drafted* (1942), *Sky Trooper* (1942), and *Commando Duck* (1944). By mid-decade Donald had climbed to the pinnacle of fame as the star of Disney's two South American features, *Saludos Amigos* and *The Three Caballeros*.[28]

Yet the Donald Duck phenomenon went far beyond a string of movie appearances. His image became a common one throughout American popular culture. Clarence Nash accompanied a two-foot-high model that could open its beak and wiggle its eyes and tail on several long promotional tours of the country. Donald also became a staple of playful pieces in the popular press. A 1938 story in *Family Circle* claimed that the cantankerous fowl had demanded a starring role in *Snow White,* and when that failed to materialize had begun agitating for the part of Rhett Butler in *Gone With the*

Wind. In a *Life* satire on art in 1945, Donald posed as Whistler's mother, Leonardo's madonna, Titian's Adonis, and Rembrandt's Noble Slav. He appeared in a rash of advertisements, such as a 1940 campaign for electric water heaters, in which he squawked out doggerel to his audience: "Oh, I'm tired of faucets trickling/and my H_2O icicling./Un-modern ways are just a lot of cheaters/So buy *electric* water heaters!" He even hosted a 1947 ABC radio show on the United States in 1960, for which he dutifully interpreted statistical trends on population growth and dispersement, economic development, transportation innovations, and resource allocation. Finally, in the best business tradition of the Disney Studio, licensed Donald Duck merchandise began to flood the country in 1935. Over the next decade and a half, these products came to include dolls, books, soap, games, cereal bowls, toothbrushes, a popular rail car for model trains from the Lionel Corporation, a Donald Duck watch from the Ingersoll-Waterbury Clock Company, and an array of food products, including popcorn and Donald Duck orange juice.[29]

Donald's skyrocketing success, however, could be attributed only in part to the well-oiled Disney star-making machinery. His contentious character and confrontational antics struck a genuine chord in his audience, as had Mickey Mouse some years earlier. In fact, the duck's eclipse of the mouse in the popular American imagination revealed broad cultural and historical forces at work. Essentially, one character type replaced another. Mickey's resilient, sweet-tempered perseverence made him more attractive to a Depression-era society plagued by doubts and insecurities. By the 1940s, however, the mouse's image as a pristine little hero had limited his comic possibilities. Donald's versatility made him more appealing, because, in the words of Jack Hannah, "He could be cute, mischievous, go from warm to cool at any moment . . . He'd start out looking like he just stepped out of Sunday school, and he'd try so hard to be good, but then he'd get tempted."[30]

At some fundamental level of American cultural perception, Donald Duck's appeal lay in historical change. Frank Nugent circled this issue in a 1947 *New York Times Magazine* essay on the Disney enterprise, when he noted that Mickey Mouse had become constrained by his do-gooder image. But Donald "has no such limitations, he can be diabolical," the author asserted. "The public's current preference for Donald over Mickey . . . is a vote for human fallibility." The foot-stamping, sailor-suited duck, whose attitude often skirted belligerence, confronted society face to face and resisted its affronts. Part of his appeal, it seems clear, lay in the fact that Americans had begun recovering from the painful ordeal of the Depression. With the gradual lifting of economic trauma and the return of confidence, Donald Duck offered a perfect expression of national rejuvenation.[31]

The duck gained our sympathy, one commentator asserted, "because he does all the things we'd like to do, only we dassen't." When frustrated by an assault on his well-being or an impediment to his happiness, he did not just sit back and take it. Instead, he tapped a large reservoir of repressed anger and struck back. Such scenes of "a rugged individualist in a regimented world" spoke to people who had suffered privation for years during the Depression, silently bottling up their anger. In the words of one observer,

> One night we go to the theater and a duck comes out on the screen and he does everything we have always wanted to do. He resents life and says so. He resents authority and refuses to submit meekly. He revolts. He storms. He rages. He breaks dishes, furniture, heads . . . All of us timid, repressed, downtrodden victims of a million tyrannies identify ourselves with this one free soul roaming the world. Vicariously through this one embattled duck we live in dark theaters for a few magic moments the brave, liberty-loving lives we would like to live in the bright world outside — if only we dared.[32]

Donald's character also symbolized a more complex, post-Depression era, in which economic recovery was still fragile and global pressures were mounting. His bombastic confidence masked a kind of insecurity as he desperately lashed out at impediments to his happiness. Quick to assert his prerogatives and delightfully ornery, he also became endearingly shame-faced after misplaced aggression ensnared him in various predicaments. He appeared mistake-prone as he raged at the world, but a constant striving for moral improvement proved his saving grace. In other words, Donald's contradictions made him a sympathetic character. With tantrums that were far more comical than dangerous, he ultimately seemed a bad-tempered, good-hearted figure battling life's injustices and petty annoyances. As Robert Feild wrote, viewers accepted Donald "as one of us because we recognize, particularly in his moments of despair, a gentle heroism that we would wish to emulate."[33]

The film *Self Control* (1938), for instance, beautifully illustrates Donald's compelling combination of characteristics. As he relaxes on a hammock during a summer afternoon, Smiling Uncle Smiley comes on the radio with his advice show. Urging listeners to control their tempers, he gently instructs them to laugh and count to ten when they start to become angry and to remember that "self-control should be your goal." Donald, impressed by the advice, squawks, "Good stuff! I'm gonna do it!" Typically, however, his practice falls short of his intentions. When a pesky bee and a hungry hen disturb his nap, he starts to get mad but, remembering the advice, counts to ten and laughs. After a bird takes a bath in his lemonade bowl and a woodpecker brings a torrent of apples down on his head, however, he grabs a shotgun. Failing to get the woodpecker with a burst of buckshot, he uses the gun as a club and beats the radio into a heap of splinters and wires when he hears Uncle Smiley's voice again.

In fact, Donald's unhappy encounter with self-help ideology recurred in a number of shorts. This therapeutic impulse followed a circuitous route, because the contentious fowl, as he once announced to the surprise of no one, had "never read *How to Win Friends and Influence People* and [wasn't] planning to." But that statement did not quite ring true. A closer examination reveals that Donald constantly sought ways to control his emotions. He was simply incapable of becoming a smooth, manipulative disciple of Dale Carnegie, since his volatile temper and overdeveloped sense of dignity always got in the way. In fact, many of Donald Duck's films revolved around his muddled attempts at therapeutic adjustment. *Donald's Better Self* (1938), for instance, actually depicted his "good self" and "bad self" engaged in an intense dialogue over the difference between right and wrong, with the former ultimately winning out. In *Cured Duck* (1945), he attempted to cure his nasty temper by taking a course on psychological techniques, although its effects did not last long. Such adventures reflected what historian Warren Susman has described as an age of adjustment psychology, when individuals traumatized by the Great Depression increasingly perceived success in terms of finding an acceptable social role and fitting into society. This culture of self-fulfillment had been growing, along with bureaucratic, consumer capitalism, throughout the twentieth century, and after being temporarily derailed by the Depression was regaining momentum. The gap between Donald Duck's striving for mental calm and his dramatic failure to do so had a broad historical resonance.[34]

Moreover, Donald's angry outbursts often resulted from the frustrations of the machine age and its alienating tendencies. As C.L.R. James once observed, "Donald Duck voiced a perpetual exasperation with the never-ending irritations of modern life." He did not just hunker down in the face of adversity to survive, as Mickey Mouse and company usually did in earlier films; he fought back and demanded recognition of his dignity and his rights, especially when confronting the forces of inhumane technology. In *Modern Inventions* (1937), for instance, Donald struggled against an array of machines that ranged from a robot butler who kept taking his hat to a mechanical barber chair that mistakenly provided a lovely haircut for his tail feathers while rubbing shoe polish all over his face. *The Riveters* (1940) presented him as a comically alienated industrial worker on a skyscraper. Put upon by an abusive, brutish foreman and a riveting gun with a mind of its own, the duck lashed out against his oppressors. Even *Der Fuehrer's Face*, the wartime propaganda film, reached its comic climax when Donald went berserk working on a speeded-up assembly line in a munitions factory. Melding images of authoritarianism and factory servitude, the film offered Donald as a figure of liberation.[35]

Yet while Donald Duck's popularity was rooted in the regenerative climate of the post-Depression United States, it also subtly reflected a gradual rethinking of America's global situation. By the late 1930s, a growing self-confidence at home was accompanied by a perception of the international arena as a crucial but threatening place. Mickey Mouse would never survive in this hostile environment. Film historian Lewis Jacobs argued in 1939 that the emergence of Donald Duck was related to the fact that authoritarian states had consolidated their hold on large parts of the globe and war loomed in Europe and East Asia. The declining popularity of the mouse and the ascendency of the duck's "inflammable temper and vicious tongue," he argued, reflected "the violent spirit of the times." Author Lloyd Morris advanced this theme. In *Not So Long Ago* (1949), a disillusioned account of massive social changes in the twentieth century, he argued that Donald's popularity mirrored the emergence of a violent, conflict-ridden, and brutal world. The fowl's explosive temper and violent rages, Morris asserted, depicted "a society in which aggression paid out, inhumanity was practical, and power, being right, was always admirable."[36]

By late 1941, the war had forced the United States to reject isolationism and embrace internationalism. Battling the Axis powers proved the first great step for American global involvement. With an aggressive posture well suited to the abandonment of isolationism, Donald's participation in American mobilization probably fit the temperament of his fellow citizens. At first he endorsed the war rather haltingly, even grudgingly, but then he offered his wholehearted support. In a series of war-service films, he was typically a rather cranky citizen-soldier who came to see the value of discipline and commitment and patriotism. In *Donald Gets Drafted*, for instance, his induction notice prompts dreams of curvaceous WACs eager for romance with a man in uniform — dreams that quickly give way to an ill-fitting uniform, a frightening drill sergeant, and exhausting marches. Later on, in films such as *Fall Out, Fall In* (1943), *Home Defense* (1943), and *Commando Duck,* he learns about military discipline, parachuting skills, alertness on the home front, and fighting behind enemy lines. Whether as a heroic hawker of democratic values or a trudging foot soldier, Donald symbolized the American fighting spirit and its new willingness to engage the world.[37]

Donald's representation of American internationalism gained an additional dimension when he strode forward as a goodwill ambassador to South America in the feature films *Saludos Amigos* and *The Three Caballeros.* This cultural diplomacy could not be separated from an expansion of American investment capital. As part of its South American sojourn, for instance, the Disney Studio produced *The Amazon Awakens* (1944), a commercial travel film that featured a visit to Henry Ford's gigantic rubber plantation, Fordlandia, on 17,000 acres of cleared jungle. As historian Emily S. Rosenberg has written, by 1940 American policymakers had concluded that "if American values were to uplift the world, then, so it seemed, so must its capital and its products." Donald Duck helped shoulder an important task in the country's new stance: to reassure Latin Americans of their importance to the United States, and to reassure U.S. citizens that the culture and values of their southern neighbors, while strange and interesting, were really not so different. As a pioneer in the exportation of American values in the early 1940s, Donald helped establish a trend that would become characteristic of the Cold War in a few years.[38]

Donald's popularity, however, proved unable to reverse the ebbing tide of Disney fortunes. His abrasive appeal shored up the studio's reputation to a certain extent, but he could do only so much. Theater managers had begun complaining that animated shorts — Donald's forte — were an extraneous and unprofitable part of the movie business, and Disney's feature films, of course, struck many as increasingly stale and uninspired. Popular audiences slowly drifted away, while the critics, like sharks, began circling for the kill. This painful situation soon took a toll on the Burbank fantasy factory.

III. *"We Must Be Prepared to Roll with the Economic Punches"*

Mounting political and aesthetic problems at the Disney Studio in the 1940s brought economic difficulties as well. As profit margins shrank, worry expanded, and Walt began relaying a sobering message to stockholders: "We must be prepared to roll with the economic punches." At the beginning of the decade, even before the strike and the war, the Disney brothers were forced to raise capital by putting up 150,000 shares of preferred stock for sale to the public. During the war, economic conditions forced Walt to put many film projects on hold. As he wrote to a friend on June 27, 1941, "Due to the present world market, we have suspended production, temporarily at least, on all such pictures as *Cinderella, Peter Pan, Alice in Wonderland* and others. The cost to properly produce these classics we do not feel is warranted under existing conditions, but instead we believe it is the better part of wisdom to turn out a type of production that can be brought to the screen for considerably less money."[39]

Things only worsened when the war came to a close. In 1946, the studio laid off nearly 450 employees, roughly one third of its staff. Rising salary schedules, escalating production costs, stagnant rental fees for films, and shrinking profits lay behind this drastic cost-saving measure, which prompted howls of protest from labor unions. But as *Time* noted, unless Disney made some adjustments to meet these problems, "Donald, along with his cartoon cousins, might soon be a stuffed duck." The following year Walt wrote to his employees, "It is imperative that some plan be agreed upon which will not only prevent the company from going further into debt, but which will make possible a reduction in bank loans." Laying out a series of steps for increased frugality and production efficiency, he demanded "on one hand, a constructive attitude toward every dollar which goes into developing, producing, and selling the scheduled pictures, and on the other hand, a hard-boiled attitude toward every dollar which isn't vital to these functions."[40]

The corporate annual reports from Walt Disney Productions throughout the 1940s provided a more accurate indicator of troublesome economic conditions. Such documents aim at reassuring stockholders, of course, so they describe conditions and trends in the best possible light and maintain a determinedly optimistic tone. Even so, the Disney reports during these years did not make for uplifting reading. From 1940 to 1945, thinly veiled warnings mentioned the wartime disruption to markets, personnel, and currency. The report for fiscal year 1941, for instance, noted that "the Company is operating with less than 50% of the personnel and payroll of May, 1941. Our capital position is strained because of the large amount of money tied up in feature negatives . . . In summary, we are still in an adjustment period brought about by world conditions and the consequent loss of markets, but we believe we have sustained the major shocks of this adjustment." Time would prove that belief wrong. The company struggled to break even but lost nearly $1 million in 1941 and 1942 before inching back into the black over the next three years.[41]

The report for fiscal year 1945 admitted that Walt Disney Productions faced a "vital reconversion problem which requires training personnel, readjusting production personnel through the absorption of returning veterans, and building up an inventory of entertainment products . . . As a result, next year will again be one of low earnings. We will be borrowing heavily from the bank in order to build inventories for future distributions." Reports over the next few years mentioned a "world-wide monetary crisis," a recapitalization plan that reconfigured the company's stock to bring a much-needed infusion of operating capital, and a massive layoff "to maintain a proper balance between rising labor costs and potential income." Once again the company was losing money.[42]

Walt's comments at the beginning of the 1949 report summarized the decade's downward spiral. After providing an upbeat assessment of current film projects, he offered these grim words:

In the light of world economic developments during the past year, some pretty clear thinking is needed in determining our future production policy. Devaluation in the important countries outside the United States, constricting domestic box office returns, and production costs, which have reached the saturation point, must be heavily weighed in our plans . . .

In this summary I have tried to weigh the difficulties confronting us against the brighter side of our ledger. It is the intangibles, the futility of looking into a crystal ball, which makes us take a realistic view of our future.

This same report also announced that Kay Kamen, the longtime merchandising wizard of Walt Disney Productions, had been killed in an airplane accident over the Azores. His unfortunate death seemed to symbolize the growing mood of dejection in Burbank.[43]

The financial wheel-spinning only exacerbated the Disney Studio's drift in direction throughout the 1940s. There was much brave talk about diversifying into industrial and educational films, and 1944 saw the establishment of an Educational and Industrial Film Division. Over the next several years the studio released eleven industrial films, such as *The Dawn of Better Living* for Westinghouse Electric Corporation and *Bathing Time for Baby* for Johnson and Johnson. But Disney quickly became frustrated by the limitations of this genre. The opportunity for creativity was restricted, the films brought in relatively little profit, and the companies that commissioned them owned them.[44]

Educational films proved to be another cinematic dead end. A spate of articles in the national press heralded this promising new direction for the studio, lavishly praising its wartime work and insisting that films about industrial techniques, disease prevention, and weapons operation presaged a bright new future. "Walt Disney's years as an entertainer have been invaluable preparation for his new career as a teacher," noted one. According to another, to say that his "picture language will revolutionize education would be no wild exaggeration."[45]

Walt himself was caught up in this wave of enthusiasm. In 1945, as the war was drawing to a close, he published several pieces in which he lauded motion pictures as a "valuable educational tool" in the rehabilitation of the postwar world and suggested that instructional films could make an important contribution to "the labor of enlightenment, civilization, and peace." But to his genuine sorrow — his enthusiasm for these projects was rooted in his uneasiness over his own lack of formal education, according to one associate — he discovered that educational films could not return enough profit even to meet their initial cost. This was simply not a viable activity for an organization with financial problems, and after some dabbling the Disney Studio quietly withdrew from the field.[46]

Critical attacks on his films, relentless economic woes, and constant worry began to take a heavy toll on Walt as the studio, in Roy Disney's words, emerged from the war "like a bear coming out of hibernation, having no fat on us." Demands on his time made for a harried, draining work schedule, while financial pressures tormented him. "My God, I wish we'd get this studio so [survival] doesn't hang on every picture," he once burst out to Ollie Johnston. His powerful faith in his own judgment, always a hallmark of his cinematic life, began to falter. In the blunt words of Frank Thomas, "Walt lost his confidence."[47]

14

The Search for Direction

BY THE MID-1940S, Walt Disney was ill-tempered to the point of
acrimony. This work-driven, temperamental man, operating under mounting stress, became increasingly cranky, even bitter, and
lashed out with greater frequency and intensity at his employees. Of course,
he had never been easy to work for, even in the flush days of the studio,
because of his high standards and volatile moods, but now his bad habits
worsened. Frank Thomas observed that he now made it a habit to neutralize
any compliment he might give out with some harsh remark. Moreover, as
many employees testified, their leader began to distance himself as he grew
increasingly preoccupied with studio problems. According to one, a grouchy
and unattentive Disney once concluded a story meeting by muttering half
apologetically, "You haven't got anything to worry about. It's me, I'm the one
that has to worry. Goddamn, I've got to stay up all night thinking about
things for you guys to do."[1]

I. The Wounded Bear

In the postwar era, some studio staffers began to call their boss "the
wounded bear" because of his increasingly cross temperament. Indeed,
some of Disney's professional relationships began to unravel under the
strain as he clashed openly with the artists. During the making of *Melody*

Time, for instance, when composer Ken Darby presented his music for the Johnny Appleseed segment during a staff meeting, Disney snarled contemptuously, "It sounds like New Deal music!" Bridling, Darby snapped back, "*That* is just a cross-section of one man's opinion!" While the others held their collective breath, Disney raised his eyebrow and glared, but he said nothing. Darby's comeback quickly made the rounds as an example of foolhardy courage, but after a couple of brief projects, he left the Disney Studio. Even T. Hee, one of Disney's favorites for many years, became a professional fatality of his boss's wrath. At a story meeting in the late 1940s, Hee argued that a movie's plot line needed to be altered. Disney initially disagreed, but as he mused out loud he began to adopt the ideas, which caused several sycophants to jump in and praise their boss's originality. In T. Hee's words, "I got a little upset and said, 'Walt, that's what I've been trying to tell you for the last half-hour.' And he looked at me and gave me the eyebrow, the elevated eyebrow. He didn't say anything, but he sure looked right into me. And after that I was put on a film that I didn't like and didn't want to do." A few months later, T. Hee was dismissed by the studio.[2]

In an extended 1956 interview, Walt gave his own account of the unhappy postwar years. It was, he admitted, "a big period of indecision, and you can't run an organization with indecision." Trying to pick up the pieces, he struggled to diversify the business in a context of economic privation. The package films, he remembered, were not very successful, but he didn't have enough money to venture into big feature films. Moreover, he admitted, he began to clash with Roy. More cautious than Walt, Roy worried even more about finances and tried to restrain his sibling's new projects. But when Roy tried to rein him in, Walt fought back, insisting that "we're going to either go forward, we're gonna get back in business, or let's liquidate and sell out." In this tense atmosphere, Roy browbeat Walt into attending a stockholders' meeting to see for himself the danger they were in. But when the moviemaker arrived and saw a room full of somber, dark-suited businessmen — he described the typical one as "some little character who just loves to attend stockholders' meetings like people do funerals" — his bile rose. So he stood up and read a letter from a small stockholder in Florida who praised Disney movies, told him to keep up the good work, and claimed not to care if the company ever paid dividends. Walt then said, "That's the kind of stockholder I like. It's been very nice to appear before you. Now if you don't mind, I'd like to get back and try to get this company on its feet!" He walked out.[3]

But such bravado flared only intermittently. More often, Disney was mired in a swamp of discouragement and depression. Not long after the end of World War II, he developed a hobby that soon became akin to an obsession. Ollie Johnston and Ward Kimball were devoted enthusiasts of miniature railroading and had built steam-powered units in their back yards. After seeing their operations, Disney began to develop his own plans, and by

1950 he had begun constructing a half-mile of track in his own back yard, complete with trestles and a tunnel, a one-eighth-scale steam-powered loco-motive, passenger cars, freight cars, cattle cars, and a caboose. Simple relaxation certainly held an allure, but so did escapism. Johnston noted that Disney simply needed "to get away from his work. The doctor told him he needed a hobby." Walt admitted that the railroad helped keep his mind off his problems and described it as a "lifesaver . . . I became so absorbed that the cares of the studio faded away, at least for a time." This impulse to withdraw had a tinge of desperation. Bosley Crowther, visiting the studio around this time, noted that Disney "seemed totally uninterested in movies and wholly, almost weirdly concerned with the building of a miniature railroad engine and a string of cars in the workshops of the studio. All of his zest for invention, for creative fantasies, seemed to be going into this plaything. I came away feeling sad."[4]

A subtler indicator of Disney's psychological uneasiness came in a 1948 radio broadcast for the University of the Air, "The Story of Mickey Mouse." Disney reflected on the history of the little character who had first carried his studio to fame. Filled with pride and whimsy, the piece also had a dark, introspective tone. Mickey's early career had brought Disney's first great success, he reminded listeners, as this character "enabled me to go ahead and do the things I had in mind, and the things I foresaw as a natural trend of film fantasy." But then, much like his creator, Mickey "reached a state where we had to be very careful about what we permitted him to do. He'd become a hero in the eyes of his audience." His popularity gradually waned. Disney's concluding assessment of his fading cartoon star suggested his own recent fate at the hands of the critics:

I often find myself surprised at what has been said about our redoubtable Mickey . . . The psychoanalysts have probed him. Wise men of critical inclination have pondered him. Columnists have kidded him. Admirers have saluted him in extravagant terms . . . But all we ever intended for him and expected of him was that he should continue to make people everywhere chuckle with him and at him. We didn't burden him with any social symbolism. We made him no mouthpiece for frustrations or harsh satire. Mickey was simply a little personality assigned to the purposes of laughter.

As if to underline the personal connection, Disney said that even though he had given up doing Mickey's voice, "He still speaks for me and I still speak for him."[5]

Perhaps the most telling signal of Disney's emotional turmoil during this period, however, came in the running of his organization. He had always played a vital role in the production of each and every animated film, but the late 1940s saw a gradual process of disengagement as he increasingly delegated authority to a group of trusted senior animators. Among this coterie of artists, one cut a particularly flamboyant figure. The studio bad boy for many years, he served as an outspoken analyst of the studio's operation and a shrewd observer of its troubled chief.

II. Ward Kimball and the Nine Old Men

In 1948, Ward Kimball received a rather peculiar phone call. "Goddamnit," the voice on the line said, "you have more fun than anybody I know. How would you like to go back to the Chicago Railroad Fair with me?" Disney, suffering from a chronic sore neck and nervous tension, had just come from a sobering checkup with his physician. Slow down, relax, and get away from work, or your body will break down, the doctor had warned him sternly. Exhausted and disillusioned, he made a rare decision — to go on a vacation completely divorced from the movie business and, even rarer, to go in the company of one of his staff members. Kimball, somewhat shocked, accepted the unexpected invitation, and the trip proved to be a very rich experience, producing several days of fun and a wealth of information about Walt Disney and the state of both his enterprise and his psyche in the late 1940s.[6]

The pair spent parts of three days and two nights on a train headed for Chicago. As they whiled away the hours, Kimball, always a keen observer of his boss's personality, encountered the domineering Disney temperament when Walt insisted on ordering for him at mealtimes and saw the familiar Disney obsession with work. As they sat gazing out the window at the passing countryside, Walt always seemed to turn the conversation to studio affairs, assuming a highly protective stance. One evening, for example, he pumped Kimball for information on what staffers said privately about the studio and its operation. When the animator reluctantly reported a couple of mild criticisms along with the obligatory praise, the studio chief quickly got a scowl on his face. He "got defensive," Kimball recalled, "took it as personal and explained it away."[7]

Kimball was surprised, however, at Disney's eagerness to talk about his own life as they headed east over the mountains and the Great Plains. And when they arrived in Chicago, Disney seemed eager to dispense with studio worries as the two attended the railroad fair and, in Kimball's words, "played like a couple of kids." Reveling in the collection of old trains, Disney revisited his boyhood and relived the romance of the rails. He visited the dozens of exhibitions mounted by the railroad companies, took the throttle on a couple of old steam engines, and delighted in donning a period costume to participate in a pageant. In the evenings, he insisted that he and Kimball spend hours riding the El around Chicago as he pointed out various stops and remarked on his memories of the city.[8]

Back in Los Angeles, Disney continued his gradual withdrawal from day-to-day involvement in film projects, letting his senior animators fill the void. Early in the 1940s, not long after the move to the Burbank studio, he had initiated this process by creating the Animation Board. Consisting of seasoned veterans, the board advised him on questions of hiring and firing, film assignments, training and promotion, and eventually development of film projects. By late in the decade, it had evolved into a permanent group of nine supervisors. Disney began to call them his "nine old men," a joking reference to Franklin Roosevelt's famous belittling of the hostile Supreme Court as "nine old men, all too aged to recognize a new idea." The name stuck, and this group began to assume a larger and larger role in the development of Disney animation.[9]

Extraordinarily gifted and experienced, the nine old men had grown up professionally within the Disney system, training under the likes of Fred Moore, Norm Ferguson, and Ham Luske. Now, some fifteen years later, they brought a healthy variety of personalities, styles, and strengths to Disney films. Les Clark, the senior member of the group, was a quiet and skilled draftsman who came to the studio in 1927. Woolie Reitherman, a man of enormous energy and determination, threw himself into every line he drew and revised his work endlessly. Eric Larson displayed great flexibility and sympathy as an artist, and his soothing demeanor and maturity made him a respected mediator among an opinionated group. Milt Kahl was an intense, blunt man whose brilliant clarity of drawing matched his irascible personality. Frank Thomas, an exacting animator given to research and careful thinking about his craft, brought an attention to detail and a concern with motivation that added complexity to his characters. Ollie Johnston's drawing possessed a natural appeal, focusing on acting, and he had a feel for emotion that practically defined personality animation. John Lounsbery, an introverted craftsman, developed a loose, energetic, and bold style in bringing to life a variety of characters. Marc Davis, the Renaissance man of the group, had a flair for the dramatic and animated characters, designed scenes, and worked in story development for many Disney movies over the years. Finally, Ward Kimball was a flamboyant and colorful artist whose tastes ran to unexpected and satirical humor, sharp mimicry, and surrealism.[10]

With Disney now seldom participating, the nine old men began to evolve new procedures and approaches to animation as they worked in a semiautonomous fashion. For instance, though artists had previously specialized in a single character, now they began to animate all the characters in a scene in order to enhance the emotional relationships among them. Moreover, they increasingly were encouraged to go beyond mere humor by delving into a broad range of emotions. Finally, the supervising animator gained the authority to alter scenes on storyboards or on rough film tests in order to strengthen plot points and make stronger cinematic statements. This system certainly kept new ideas flowing and fed the evolution of the Disney style. At the same time, granting authority to a handful of the studio's skilled artists was, according to one insider, "greatly resented by those not anointed by the master's wand."[11]

Among the nine old men, Kimball emerged as one of Disney's favorites. Not only did he share the hobby of miniature railroading, but his irreverent, mischievous personality seemed to hold a special appeal for his work-driven, straitlaced boss. Kimball was notorious for his antics, his salty temperament, and his wild sense of humor. His outspokenness on studio affairs — he was not afraid to publicly denounce its straw bosses, or "Disney despots," as he liked to call these meddling bureaucrats — caused studio politicians to give him a wide berth. Kimball also loved to mock Disney's saccharine reputation. He told anyone who cared to listen that "he did not animate cute little bunny rabbits"; he made pornographic drawings of Snow White and her seven consorts, and once created a minor scandal when he, along with Freddy Moore and Walt Kelly, gave an intoxicated demonstration of Disney characters to schoolchildren after an extended stop at the local bar. The animator carefully cultivated an outrageous image. At Hyperion studio volleyball games, for example, Art Babbitt consistently cheated by crashing over the top of the net to spike the ball, and one day Kimball decided to get even. During the game he waited until just the right moment, and when Babbitt went airborne over the net, he exploded a powerful torpedo firecracker under him. As Kimball recalled delightedly, "He had sand and everything else indented in his legs. Everybody thought I'd shot Art. It was a hell of a roar [from the explosion], and everybody said, 'Oh my God, Kimball's killed Art for coming over the net.' And it sort of cured him." Such an impish personality was literally just what the doctor ordered to help Disney escape the burden of his daily cares in 1948.[12]

Like the others on Disney's supreme court, Kimball had risen up through the system during the studio's golden age. He arrived in 1934 at age twenty-one with a portfolio of drawings from art school. Hired immediately, he soon became a full-fledged animator and cut his artistic teeth on Silly Symphonies such as *Elmer Elephant* (1936), *Toby Tortoise Returns* (1936), and *Ferdinand the Bull* (1938) and a pair of Hollywood satires, *Woodland Cafe* (1937) and *Mother Goose Goes Hollywood* (1938). In 1936 he began work on *Snow White and the Seven Dwarfs*, and he was heartbroken when Walt cut his two biggest scenes — a humorous soup-eating episode and another where the dwarfs construct a special bed for the visiting princess. His luck changed with the studio's next major production, *Pinocchio*, when he was handed the plum assignment of animating Jiminy Cricket. Over the next few years he drew the jolly, drunken Bacchus for the Pastoral Symphony in *Fantasia* and the famous black crow sequence in *Dumbo*. In *The Reluctant Dragon*, he even made a personal appearance onscreen to demonstrate for

Robert Benchley (and the movie audience) some of his drawing techniques.[13]

During the strike of 1941, Kimball evinced great sympathy for the strikers and their complaints about salaries and procedures. In fact, he gained something of a reputation for political radicalism, because his car carried a windshield sticker for Upton Sinclair. Nevertheless, Kimball remained loyal to Disney and the studio. He played a significant role in the World War II films, animating the humorous sections on the early history of aviation for *Victory Through Air Power* and working on a variety of sequences in the propaganda shorts. In *Education for Death* he drew the hilarious sequence in which Hitler romanced the portly princess Germania (a caricature of Goering) and himself served as a model for Emotion, the character who stole the show in *Reason and Emotion*. Kimball was especially proud of his work on *The Three Caballeros*, where he animated a wild, surrealistic dream scene with Donald Duck. This versatile artist went on to play a major role in the feature films *Cinderella*, *Peter Pan*, and *Alice in Wonderland*. Kimball, in the words of Ollie Johnston, was "a brilliant guy" whose talents lay in off-the-wall scenes where he could give his imagination free rein and come up with "unique ways of doing things."[14]

Much like Disney, Kimball was always in pursuit of something new, and he delved into many interesting projects through the years. His surrealistic bent in the 1940s gave way to an interest in limited animation in the early 1950s, a move that led to an animated short on the history of music entitled *Toot, Whistle, Plunk, and Boom* and a 1954 Academy Award. A few years later he became involved with Disney's television projects. Working with a team of rocket scientists headed by Wernher von Braun, he developed a series of popular Tomorrowland films with the titles *Man in Space, Man and the Moon*, and *Mars and Beyond*. Throughout this long course of artistic activity, Kimball also pursued a semi-professional music career. A trombonist and fervent jazz fan, he founded the famous Disney Studio band, which appeared regularly at Hollywood nightclubs, in films, on television shows, and later at Disneyland and cut several albums.[15]

Nonetheless, around the studio Kimball became almost as famous for his outrageous behavior as for his artistic achievements. Of medium height and stocky, with a broad face adorned by a shock of dark hair and a heavy five o'clock shadow, he was alternately gruff and mischievous. He often appeared in outlandish clothes calculated to shock — green pants, red shirt, and a yellow-striped tie were common attire. His personal reputation was mixed. His humor disarmed many, and his awesome artistic talent led Bill Cottrell to proclaim, "If anyone could run a studio on the creative side, it would be Ward Kimball." But others saw him as a smart aleck and a rather arrogant prima donna. In 1936, for instance, I. Klein joined the studio and encountered Kimball: "He came into my room about two or three days after my joining the staff. He said, 'I am Ward Kimball. You didn't think I was so young.' . . . He then turned and walked out. I had never heard his name before, I did not know what he was talking about. Nobody had told me he was one of the young geniuses of the new Disney animators."[16]

Much later, after years of dealing with him, Ben Sharpsteen exasperatedly described Kimball as "somebody that you never knew or ever thought you would know; he was entirely different . . . a loner. He was not always in sympathy with what we were producing." But Kimball's escapades earned him a prominent place in studio lore. He decorated a Christmas party with thirty Santas with nooses around their necks, and he wrote a book called *Art Afterpieces,* which poked fun at the masterpieces of Western art by altering *The Creation of Adam* to show Adam holding a cigarette and God a lighter, Mona Lisa with her hair in curlers, and Whistler's mother parked in front of a television set.[17]

Kimball's reputation for naughtiness probably peaked in early 1968, with a short animated film against the Vietnam War, produced at his own expense, that became an underground classic. Entitled *Escalation,* it depicted President Lyndon Johnson telling a pack of lies against the swelling background music of "The Battle Hymn of the Republic," his growing nose gradually transforming into an erect penis that exploded at the movie's end. Kimball cherished his wild reputation, asserting that "it's the people who are emotional and crazy who make the world progress, who think of the ideas . . . the crazies keep the world going." In the 1970s, one observer simply described him as "the world's first hippie — thirty years ago!"[18]

Disney had a special fondness for his bad boy, describing him in a 1956 publication as "one man who works for me I am willing to call a genius. He can do anything he wants to do." He appreciated Kimball's unvarnished honesty and seemed to take a secret delight in the animator's antics. He saw through the facade, as Frank Thomas noticed, and "always thought of Kimball as the kid who wrote on the back fence and enjoyed shocking people and made a show of being the tough guy and the dirty kid and everything, but really was a little sentimentalist at heart." Another longtime studio employee agreed that Disney really liked Kimball, but said that he "kept an eye on him" because he realized that Kimball's special talent for satire and bizarre humor could only work in certain situations. For his part, Kimball took pride in Disney's affection for him, noting that while his boss was a workaholic who tended to keep people at a distance, "I think I was as good a friend as he ever had." He recalled that in the 1950s, Disney even went so far, during a screening for a new film, as to "put his arm around me and call me 'son.' It was like if he ever wanted a son, I'd be it."[19]

At the same time, however, Kimball refused to see Disney as a saint. His analysis of his boss, expressed with characteristic candor, always disclosed the warts and all. On the one hand, Kimball fully realized the significance of Disney's emphasis on personality animation, noting its importance to fantasy ("If a tree was bashful, it had to act like it was bashful"), moral relationships ("If it was a villainous tree, it had to behave like a villain"), and humor ("The other studios' humor was based on episodical gags. Walt's gags came as a result of a situation or a personality development, which made them more valid and more funny"). He also appreciated Disney's instinctive reliance on the rhythms and emotion of music, and grasped that his humor, contrary to popular perception, was rooted in satire rather than sweetness. While often cute or disarming, he argued, Disney cartoons usually offered "an indictment of mankind." Kimball also appreciated his boss's disdain for corporate bureaucracy, describing how Disney would "walk down the halls in his shirtsleeves, come into your office and say, 'Ward, I've got an idea that might improve this sequence' . . . Walt came to see you without giving a second thought to protocol and pecking order." Kimball admired Disney's relentless prodding of his staff for innovation and improvement. "The thing that made Walt great was that he was creative himself and he recognized creativity in others," he reported. "He never repeated himself. He would say, 'We've done that. Let's do something new.' He'd frighten everybody half to death by challenging them that way. But then you'd get with it and new ideas would come."[20]

On the other hand, Kimball recognized that Disney was so absorbed in his work that he could be brutally insensitive to staff members' feelings. When he chewed people out in public and destroyed weeks of effort with a cruel comment, according to Kimball, he "didn't realize he was pissing people off and embarrassing them." This lack of awareness, or concern, drove some employees to double their efforts to earn praise, but it simply crushed other talented people, who left the studio. "I think the pressure of trying to please an egocentric man like Walt became an unbearable load for a lot of people here," Kimball observed.[21]

Kimball did not shy away from more personal issues. Seeing Disney light one cigarette from another while emitting a hacking cough, he confronted him: "I used to say to him, 'Walt, why don't you give up smoking?' He'd always answer, 'A guy has to have one vice, doesn't he?'" The animator also revealed the guarded secret that by the late 1940s Disney had begun drinking rather heavily after the workday had ended. At the studio, he reported, "Starting at five o'clock every day, a lot of people would say, 'I've got to get to Walt before he uncorks the bottle, because you can't really get the decision you want'" after that time. Nor did Kimball shy away from discussing topics that others would never have mentioned. While Disney's affinity for outhouse humor had never been a secret, Kimball noticed that this tendency seemed to come from a peculiar preoccupation with excrement and defecation. In typically unvarnished language, he said that Disney would "often talk about turds . . . He'd go on and on, and you kind of looked at him and wondered, when is he going to get to the punchline? There wasn't any punchline . . . Instead of considering defecation a normal biological function and a private matter better left undiscussed, he saw nothing wrong with talking about it for half an hour." Kimball was also fascinated by another notable Disney trait — an aversion to sexuality. He noticed that his boss always steered away from anything smacking of sex, whether it was dirty jokes, romantic scenarios in his films, or flirting. Both of these characteristics, Kimball concluded after many conversations and a good deal of thought, were psychological "hang-ups . . . [which were] a reaction to his strict upbringing." His interest in defecation represented a rebellion against the dominating moralism of his parents, while his aversion to sex represented its internalization. Moreover, Kimball believed, both were ways for Disney to keep people at a distance, the former through embarrassment and the latter through avoidance of any kind of intimate relationship.[22]

The Walt Disney who emerged from Kimball's descriptions was a bundle of contradictions, and the resulting tensions both drove him and ate away at his happiness. His insistence that everyone call him Walt, for example, certainly embodied a deeply ingrained dislike of pretense, but as Kimball pointed out, it also subtly reinforced "the paternal image he wanted" by cementing the image of a beloved nurturer and protector. Along the same lines, the animator argued, Disney's carefully cultivated persona of the self-effacing artist who lived in a world of fantasy masked a driving ambition and a tremendous ego. "Even though Walt played the role of the bashful tycoon who was embarrassed in public," noted Kimball, "he knew exactly what he was doing at all times." Finally, and perhaps at the deepest level of all, Disney's appearance of unwavering confidence in his own judgment and talents was a smokescreen for a carefully hidden secret. In fact, Kimball believed, "Walt was very insecure . . . He faced many situations where he would have to admit, 'I don't know the answer, but I won't let them know that I don't know the answer.' I think Walt never wanted to admit defeat because of this insecure feeling he had about himself."[23]

Disney's knot of internal tensions had been pulled tight by the late 1940s, as the trip to Chicago late in the decade demonstrated. Kimball knew that he was absorbed in his work, but conversation on this trip revealed how total that immersion was. "Sooner or later . . . no matter what you were talking about, he'd get back to this goddamn studio. He wanted to talk about it. This was HIM. This was his SEX! This was EVERYTHING! His sex wasn't with his wife. No. The orgasms were all here. Everything. This [the studio] was heaven."[24]

Kimball saw clear indicators of Walt's mounting unhappiness and tendency to withdraw. He was taken aback, for instance, when Walt appeared nearly every evening with a special traveling case, took out a cut-glass decanter and a set of glasses, and poured each of them three fingers of whiskey. No drinker, Kimball would struggle to finish one glass while his boss imbibed three or four before dinner. At the fair, an incident revealed Walt's determined avoidance of sexuality. As he and Kimball prepared to participate in the historical pageant, they had to push through a dressing room full of female dancers, all of them stripped down to their panties to deal with the steamy August heat, to get to the other side of the huge stage. A wide-eyed Kimball tried to walk very slowly and enjoy the scenery, calling out, "Not so fast, Walt, what's the hurry?" But Disney hurried through, calling out over his shoulder, "If you've seen one, Kimball, you've seen them all!" Kimball also observed close-up Disney's growing tendency to withdraw into his past. Walt "spent two nights telling me his entire history from the time he was a boy," he noted. "And he tells it just like a plot of one of his stories, where good will out and villains will be defeated." This tendency to mythologize his life story continued in Chicago, where Walt lost himself in memories of midwestern railroads and his long-gone adolescence.[25]

With an artist's insight, Ward Kimball uncovered the sources of what many others could only express in a vague way — that the guiding light of the Disney Studio had lost confidence in his ability, and maybe even his desire, to create the very special films for which he had become famous. This troubled situation also manifested itself in more concrete ways. Perhaps the most striking case came at the conclusion of World War II, when Disney poured his personal past and hopes for the future into a special movie project that he believed would triumphantly return the studio to its glory days. Instead, it became the victim of critical attacks, political controversy, and popular apathy. As one of the studio's biggest disappointments, it summarized many of Disney's larger problems as this dark decade drew to a close.

III. "A Bedraggled Magnolia Like Song of the South"

In a rash of interviews, articles, and press releases in 1946 and 1947, Disney explained the deep personal roots of his newest film. Saying that it "fulfills an ambition" and "realizes an ancient dream," he noted that this project brought to the screen a series of stories that had made a profound impression in his youth. These tales, he said at one point, were the "greatest American folk stuff there is. Came out in print when I was a kid, and I read every one . . . I was raised in Missouri and they were very popular there." Moreover, Disney stressed that animating these stories had demanded special innovations. As legends, they required a strong dimension of fantasy, which could be conveyed only with animation, but their narrator, in his opinion, needed to be a live actor. The Disney Studio was forced to develop new techniques for combining these two modes of cinematic expression "in a manner heretofore never undertaken on such a scale." In addition, Disney went on to say, the film presented a strong moral dimension, a pretty leading lady, two adorable child actors, and several catchy songs. This happy mix of ingredients resulted in *Song of the South*, a dramatization of Joel Chandler Harris's Uncle Remus tales from the turn of the century. Displaying just about everything in the Disney Studio repertoire, this film, Disney fervently hoped, would revive his enterprise in a period of hard times.[26]

Song of the South, released in November 1946, had a complex technological structure and a highly sentimental story line. Approximately two thirds of the movie consisted of live-action segments. The plot revolved around the travails of a little boy, Johnny, who goes with his mother to live on his grandmother's plantation when his parents separate. Unhappy and pining for his absent father, the child is about to run away when he encounters Uncle Remus, a grizzled black storyteller who becomes his friend and mentor. Uncle Remus explains how Brer Rabbit outwitted Brer Fox and Brer Bear, and his story soon lifts the boy's spirits. As the movie unfolds, Johnny becomes friends with Ginny, a poor white girl whose bullying brothers mistreat them, and again Uncle Remus tells several Brer Rabbit tales. The narrative culminates when the aged storyteller, castigated by Johnny's mother for detaining the boy with his nonsense, decides to leave the plantation. Johnny, heartbroken, chases after the old man and is mauled by a fierce bull as he cuts across a pasture. With the boy in a coma, his family gathers around — his absent father even returns to the fold — but Johnny responds only when Uncle Remus comes to his bed with his wise words and soothing manner. The film ends with Johnny's parents back together and the children reunited with the avuncular black sage. This live-action narrative is interspersed with animated versions of Uncle Remus's tales, which make up the remaining third of the film. They feature, of course, that clever rascal Brer Rabbit as he gains the upper hand over his powerful but slower-witted antagonists, Brer Fox and Brer Bear. These delightful cartoon segments — the most famous concerns Brer Rabbit's trickery in gaining his freedom after he has become stuck to the Tar Baby — provide humorous but wise moral instruction to the children in the story.[27]

Like many films from the golden age in the 1930s, *Song of the South* offered generous dollops of Disney's values and approach. Its populist political thrust reiterated the traditional Disney motif of the triumphant underdog. In this case it featured an alliance of outsiders — the elderly black sage, the white girl from an impoverished family, the alienated rich boy — that demonstrated the moral superiority of honest, plain, hardworking people. And the Brer Rabbit stories themselves stressed the triumph of someone who overcame his weakness by outwitting more powerful people. The wealthy white characters, almost without fail, were misguided or foolish figures, while Brer Fox and Brer Bear were strong but dumb. The film's sentimental modernism appeared in the enchantment of a rationalized world as live-action scenes periodically dissolved to disclose a hidden realm of animated fantasy. In the early sections of the film, Uncle Remus saunters through an animated wonderland of bright colors and friendly animals; at the movie's conclusion, the children conjure up a magical transformation as they summon forth the animated figures that Uncle Remus has seen only in his imagination before. The old man is left rubbing his eyes in delighted disbelief.

Song of the South, however, elicited only a lukewarm critical response. The animated segments garnered almost universal praise for their energy, humor, and whimsy, and the seamless technological blending of cartoons and live action prompted amazement. The musical score, especially the song "Zippadee Do Dah," ranked among the best Disney efforts. Many critics also praised the two child actors, Bobby Driscoll and Luana Patten, for their attractive screen presence, while James Baskett, a regular on *Amos 'n' Andy*, the radio show, before assuming his first movie role as Uncle Remus, received plaudits for his warm, natural portrayal of the legendary storyteller. Newspaper reviews observed that the film's "childlike simplicity gives it a universal appeal" and noted that it "is about Uncle Remus and his tales, and it is first-rate in the treatment of both." *Parents* magazine confirmed the film's appeal for children by awarding it a medal of merit for January 1947. But with few exceptions, even favorable reviews mirrored the conclusion of a small-town Georgia newspaper: "*Song of the South* is a pleasant picture, but not a great one."[28]

Many commentators were far less benevolent. The live-action segments became the focal point for a series of scathing denunciations. Critics contended that Disney "has sold his particular art down the river" in favor of a pedestrian, if not outright embarrassing, screenplay where uncompelling human characters "have virtually elbowed the cartoons off the screen." The Boston *Evening American*, for instance, complained that live actors "spoiled" the film and demanded, "We want Disney, Walt, and include out the humans." In the same vein, many critics found the live action to be smothered by syrupy emotion — the Philadelphia *Inquirer* blanched at the "soupily sentimental story" which framed the animation — and denounced its plot as contrived, awkward, and undeveloped. Newspapers complained about a story line that "isn't even clear in outline" and "colorless characters telling a drab tale," adding, "Apparently the Disney wonder workers are just a lot of conventional hacks when it comes to telling a story with actors instead of cartoons." As one reviewer put it bluntly, "*Song of the South* is an artistic failure."[29]

This aesthetic criticism, however, paled before the political controversy that erupted over the film's racial aspects. Immediately after its premiere in Atlanta and subsequent nationwide release, *Song of the South* became embroiled in an angry debate over its portrayal of southern blacks. Critics contended that it depicted servile, stupid, and shiftless black characters who bowed and scraped to the white characters. The black community was particularly incensed, and many black publications and essayists unleashed a storm of anti-Disney rhetoric. Richard B. Dier, writing in the *Afro-American*, insisted that *Song of the South* was "as vicious a piece of propaganda for white supremacy as Hollywood has ever produced." Ann Tanneyhill, speaking for the National Urban League, argued that the film offered "another repetition . . . of the stereotype casting of the Negro in the servant role, depicting him as indolent, one who handles the truth lightly." A bitter newspaper essay contended that the picture helped "perpetuate the idea that Negroes throughout American history have been illiterate, docile, and quite happy to be treated as children — without even the average child's ambition and without thought of tomorrow." A flyer handed out by the National Negro Congress cast this dissent in explicitly political terms. *Song of the South*, it asserted, "creates an impression of Negroes in the minds of their fellow Americans which makes them appear to be second-class citizens, childish in nature, who sing and dance and never shoulder the responsibilities of citizenship in this democracy."[30]

A firestorm of criticism erupted in the national, mainstream press as well. *Time*, for instance, offered a sobering preview when it warned that "ideologically, the picture is certain to land its maker in hot water," since the black characters, especially Uncle Remus, are "bound to enrage all educated Negroes, and a number of damyankees." *The New Yorker* chimed in with a biting declaration that the movie "consists of the purest sheepdip about happy days on the old plantation." An opinion column in *PM* denounced the film's contribution to the "race-hate neurosis" of the Jim Crow system, while the Los Angeles *Daily News* advised that its "portrait of Southern paternalism, with its emphasis on happy slaves and the crudities of poor whites," would certainly trigger resentment. The Los Angeles *B'nai B'rith Messenger*, viewing *Song of the South* from the vantage point of the Holocaust, simply observed that this movie "tallies with the reputation that Disney is making for himself as an arch-reactionary."[31]

This torrent of angry words prompted various actions against the film. The NAACP, led by executive secretary Walter White, sent a telegram to every major newspaper in the United States urging consumers to boycott the film. It also publicly denounced *Parents* for awarding *Song of the South* a medal and accused the picture of planting prejudice in the "unsuspecting minds of young people" and perpetuating "a dangerously glorified picture of slavery . . . [and] the impression of an idyllic master-slave relationship which is a distortion of the facts." Adam Clayton Powell, Jr., congressman from Harlem, urged the New York City commissioner of licenses to close down theaters showing the film, denouncing it as "not only an insult to

American minorities, but an insult to everything that America as a whole stands for." The National Negro Congress organized pickets at theaters in New York, Los Angeles, and San Francisco. Hundreds of patrons turned away as protesters waved signs reading "*Song of the South* is an insult to the Negro people" and chanted a parody to the tune of "Jingle Bells": "Disney tells, Disney tells/lies about the South./We've heard those lies before/right out of Bilbo's mouth."[32]

Such assaults on Disney's film quickly brought a counterattack on his behalf. Not surprisingly, most white newspapers below the Mason-Dixon line defended the film as a charming depiction of an era of American history, likable or not, and characterized adverse reactions to it as prejudice. Right-wing publications such as the Los Angeles *Criterion,* whose front-page banner proclaimed it to be "100% American, 100% Clean, 100% Free of Racial Prejudice," suggested that the ranks of anti-Disney picketers were filled with Communists. More moderate publications characterized the racial critiques as oversensitive and extremist. As denunciations of the film grew more intense, newspapers around the United States filled up with letters to the editor from resentful whites. Most insisted that the movie's use of caricature was not anti-Negro but aimed amiably at many groups. Typically employing sarcasm, they wrote to protest "Snuffy Smith, Li'l Abner, and Popeye as being a definite threat to the supremacy of the white race" and denounced the film *Sinbad the Sailor* as "an insult to our navy, our coast guard, our merchant marine . . . [and] every man who sails the seas and to the families of these brave lads." Interestingly, a portion of what was then called the colored press also mounted a defense of the film. Black critics such as George S. Schuyler and Herman Hill of the Pittsburgh *Courier* argued that the film would "prove of inestimable goodwill in the furthering of interracial relationships between the children of today who are the grownups of tomorrow." *Sepia Hollywood* also approved this "period piece," insisting that "they haven't distorted Uncle Tom at Walt Disney's Studio, they have glorified him." James Baskett, the actor who played Uncle Remus, offered the same view in a public interview. "I believe that certain groups are doing my race more harm in seeking to create dissension," he said, "than can ever possibly come out of the *Song of the South.*"[33]

With angry rhetoric flying in both directions, *Song of the South* became trapped in a political crossfire. This controversy set Disney back on his heels. Shortly after the film's premiere, a spokesman for the studio rushed to defend it, pointing out that its action took place *after* the Civil War and thus did not comment on slavery. Moreover, he insisted that the movie had only a benign intent, since it "was not trying to put across any message, but was making a sincere effort to depict American folklore." In fairness, surviving documents indicate that the Disney Studio did not intend the project to be a blatantly racist undertaking but rather one that would emerge from carefully considered folktales. As early as 1938, Disney staffers had begun examining not only the Joel Chandler Harris stories themselves but a great deal of supplementary material. Mary Goodrich, for instance, a researcher for the Story Department, combed through a wide variety of materials: writings of ethnologists and folklorists that talked about the origins of Harris's tales in African mythology; Zora Neale Hurston's novel *Moses*, with its use of authentic "Negro speech rhythms"; books dealing with "Negro superstitions" and "folk traditions," such as Julia Peterkin's *Roll, Jordan, Roll* and Orlando Kay Armstrong's *Old Massa's People*.[34]

At the same time, however, the studio could not claim total innocence. For months, and perhaps even years, preceding the movie's release, there had been considerable in-house debate over the film's racial aspects. Maurice Rapf, for instance, one of the authors of the screenplay, wrote a long memo to Disney and several of the directors addressing directly what was termed "the Negro question." He made a series of recommendations that were designed to avert trouble: don't refer to "Negro men" or "Negro women" but just men and women, avoid descriptions such as one that called for a boy to "run away like a black streak," and avoid "cheap, stereotyped humor" based on race. Rapf also suggested a wholesale revision of a minor black character who was "the eye-rolling, hysterical, easily frightened, stupid sort of Negro . . . That her type existed and still does (in all races) we can't doubt. But the Negroes don't like it." Moreover, Joseph I. Breen, an official with the Motion Picture Producers and Distributors of America, wrote to Walt Disney on August 1, 1944, about possible problems with the Production Code. Breen included a report from another member of the organization, Francis S. Harmon, who had read the entire script and offered this counsel regarding "the Negro question": "I would like to suggest that, before proceeding much further with the development of this story, you secure the services of a competent person to advise you concerning the over-all, as well as the detailed, acceptability of this story from the standpoint of the American Negroes. These good people in recent months have become most critical regarding the portrayal on the motion picture screen of the members of their race."[35]

The political atmosphere of the Disney Studio also played a role here. An unthinking and insidious disparagement of blacks prevailed throughout most of the United States in this era, and the Burbank compound was no different. The studio had a long tradition of crudely caricaturing blacks in its short films. *Cannibal Capers* (1930), for instance, portrayed a tribe of man-eating African natives whose lips were so outlandishly enormous that a fierce invading lion, fearing that *he* was about to be eaten, turned tail and ran off. *The Steeplechase* (1933) featured a pair of shuffling, dancing stableboys whose "yassir, boss" language was a focal point of the humor. *Mickey's*

Mellerdrammer (1933) presented a comic version of *Uncle Tom's Cabin* full of crude racial gags: Mickey Mouse and the gang in blackface, the characters singing "Dixie" and mouthing "I'z a-comin'," Goofy being pelted with a rotten vegetable that turns his face black. The black crows in *Dumbo,* of course, offered a complex case of racial construction. They caused some ill will, but Ward Kimball always insisted that they were designed as sympathetic, admirable characters rather than cheap stereotypes. In the Uncle Remus project, however, both racial insensitivity and crude caricature seemed to resurface. Surviving studio memos filled with references to "darkies" and "pickaninnies" — one describes Remus's reflections on "education and lazy niggers" — reveal that the film took shape in a typical American atmosphere of genteel racism.[36]

Walt Disney stood silently at the center of the controversy engulfing *Song of the South.* He revealed little about his own racial attitudes, and to this day they remain hard to pin down. He used casually racist language; in a letter to Roy and Ub in 1928, he noted with pride that the musicians and technicians "all worked like niggers," and in a letter written during the filming of *Song of the South* he reported that they "dug up a swell little pickaninny" to play the part of the young black child. On the other side of the ledger, however, he wrote a personal letter on January 30, 1948, to Jean Hersholt, president of the Academy of Motion Picture Arts and Sciences, suggesting that James Baskett be awarded a special Academy Award for his work in *Song of the South.* Baskett had not only brought to life the "immortal folklore character" of Uncle Remus, Disney argued, but was "a very understanding person and very much the gentleman." Such evidence suggests a mixed verdict: Walt Disney was neither a crusader for civil rights nor a virulent race-baiter, but a typical white American of his time who harbored a benign, genteel bias against blacks. But whatever the motivations or goals behind it, *Song of the South* clearly opened racial wounds at a time when the civil rights movement was about to engulf the United States in a great crisis.[37]

Billy Rose, film writer for the journal *PM,* expressed the misgivings of many when he chastised Disney in a long open letter. He argued that the aesthetic and political problems with *Song of the South* were emblematic of Disney's decline throughout the 1940s. In language that conveyed disappointment, perhaps even grief, rather than anger or contempt, he asked the filmmaker,

> What's got into you lately? Last night, I saw your latest movie, *Song of the South.* For a fellow with your talents, I thought it was a bum job . . . [and] I tried to figure out what had happened to you. You started some years ago with an inkwell and a head full of fire. Your stuff caught on and you made

money. Then some banking chap must have come around and sung you the Song of Big Business — big studio, big staff, big desk, lots of telephones. You stopped being Walt Disney and became Walt Disney, Inc. . . .

In *Saludos Amigos,* for the first time I got the feeling you were pumping . . . In *Three Caballeros* you had my boy Donald Duck ogling some live bathing beauties. Using this little hunk of dream stuff to get a cheap sex laugh was hitting below the national belt. It was like showing Snow White doing a striptease. I left the theater after *Make Mine Music* as I used to leave Yankee Stadium when the Babe struck out . . .

And now we come to the rough part of this piece — *Song of the South.* Take it from an old admirer, this "Uncle Tom" musical hasn't got it. Furthermore, we didn't like the way the picture was premiered in Atlanta. We felt embarrassed for you when we read that the colored actor who played Uncle Remus was not permitted to attend the gala opening.

As Rose concluded, Disney carried a heavy responsibility as an American artistic treasure. "When you waste your talents on a bedraggled magnolia like *Song of the South,*" Rose admonished, "it's like Shakespeare writing for Red Skelton."[38]

Wilting under such heated reactions, *Song of the South* was a devastating disappointment. Only modestly successful in financial terms, it left a bad taste in the mouths of many, and it seemed to confirm that as the 1940s drew to a close, Walt Disney was running out of gas as an important American cultural figure. He increasingly appeared a sour, retrograde political figure and a stale, stumbling artist bereft of new ideas. As he pulled back in disappointment and despair, a pall settled over the studio.

Yet miraculously, after years of spinning its wheels, the Disney Studio somehow seemed to catch firm ground and shoot forward in the early 1950s. Disney unexpectedly reached back and recaptured some of the magic of the golden age while moving courageously into several new entertainment forms. He refashioned himself as a symbol of prosperous postwar America. Few could have foreseen that within a few years, the Disney presence in American life would dwarf anything he had achieved previously.

Part IV

Disney and the American Century

15

Cold War Fantasies

I LIVE WITH A GENIUS," Lillian Disney's warm description of domestic life with her famous husband, was advertised on the cover of *McCall's* in February 1953. Right next to it sat another blaring headline, which created a neat ideological tableau. The dramatic title of the second article, "Stalin and His Three Wives: A Private-Life Exposé," promised a lurid account of the evil Communist dictator's private licentiousness. This vivid juxtaposition of the American icon of decency and the immoral Russian dictator highlighted the backdrop for Disney's revitalized cultural role — the long, intense confrontation with communism during the Cold War.[1]

Hints of this international atmosphere cropped up repeatedly in Disney Studio productions and activities during the 1950s. At the apocalyptic ending of *Twenty Thousand Leagues under the Sea* (1954), for example, a rolling mushroom cloud marked the mad Captain Nemo's explosive destruction of his island headquarters. In *The Shaggy Dog,* a goofy comedy released late in the decade, the plot revolved around the misadventures of atomic spies out to steal government missile plans. That same year, 1959, a circular movie theater developed by Walt Disney stood as an important part of an exhibition of American consumer goods in Moscow — the scene of the famous "kitchen debate" between Vice President Richard Nixon and Soviet Premier Nikita Khrushchev.[2]

Disney himself had provided clear evidence of a Cold War preoccupation some years earlier. In the autumn of 1947, the House Un-American Activities Committee went to Hollywood to hold hearings on Communist influence in moviemaking. This controversial maneuver was a culmination of the Hollywood red scare that had welled up in the aftermath of World War II, fully backed (perhaps even instigated) by the influential conservative group the Motion Picture Alliance for the Preservation of American Ideals. A parade of friendly witnesses — they included Sam Wood, Adolphe Menjou, Robert Montgomery, Gary Cooper, and Ronald Reagan — testified before HUAC about their knowledge of Communist influence in the production of movies. The last cooperative witness appeared on the afternoon of October 24. It was Walt Disney.[3]

His testimony proved revealing. Speaking as a producer and studio chief, he assured HUAC that although everyone in his organization was now "100 percent American," that had not always been the case. The 1941 strike at his studio had been inspired by Communists and supported by "Commie front organizations," while "throughout the world all of the Commie groups began smear campaigns against me and my pictures." Communism, he told HUAC, had proved to be "an un-American thing" whose unscrupulous agents infiltrated well-meaning groups of "100 percent Americans" and subverted them. As he concluded passionately, "I feel that they really ought to be smoked out and shown up for what they are."[4]

Thus the Cold War, with its powerful national and international pressures, provided a compelling context for Disney's 1950s productions. Early in the decade, a great revival saw animated movies, live-action films, nature documentaries, and amusement parks pour out of the Burbank studio to be embraced by an enthusiastic public. While the Cold War was not directly responsible for this, the Disney productions of this era, much like the studio's Depression-era films, which had smoothed many anxieties of the 1930s, resonated with contemporary American hopes and fears. In the highly charged political and cultural atmosphere, Walt Disney once again became an influential architect of mainstream values.

I. The Studio Resurgence

Early in the 1950s, Disney played a practical joke on his staff. Enthralled by his miniature trains, he had set up some track at the back of the Burbank lot for test runs, and now he was busy planning a permanent installation on the acre and a half behind his new house in Holmby Hills. One day he called up the prop department and said, with a twinkle in his eye but a deadly serious voice, "Boys, I want you to find me a few human beings, one-eighth scale, to ride the train. I need passengers to make it look right." The weary prop manager, used to his boss's outlandish requests, replied automatically,

"Okay, Walt, we'll try." Seconds later, of course, he did a giant double take as the preposterousness of the task sank in and he got the joke.[5]

Disney got a good chuckle out of this bit of tomfoolery, but the initial response to his joke was revealing. It suggested an instinctive, unthinking belief that the wizard of Burbank could do the impossible. In fact, this had become a growing conviction not only among Disney's staff but in the American public at large. It was based on a remarkable series of events that had begun to unfold early in the decade.

In 1950 Walt Disney Productions reasserted itself with a remarkable burst of activity, making bold moves in animation, live-action films, and the new medium of television. This trio of maneuvers, both psychologically revitalizing and financially profitable, marked a clear turning point in the history of the Disney enterprise.

Appropriately, this revival began with animation. With *Cinderella*, released in March 1950, the studio presented an animated feature squarely in the classic Disney style — a charming fairy-tale fantasy, lush drawing, personable characters, richly imagined settings, a compelling narrative full of humor and pathos, and a sympathetic heroine. The public bought tickets in droves and made the film a smashing box office success, while the critics applauded this return to Disney's animation roots. Almost without fail, writers noted that the film represented "Disney at his best stride in nearly a decade" and that it "filled the screen with a magical radiance which has been sadly missed" in his more recent efforts.[6]

Over the next decade the Disney Studio rolled out a series of animated features that also followed the fantasy format. Although only six full-length animated movies appeared between 1950 and 1961, these major productions once again made the release of a Disney animated film an event. *Alice in Wonderland* (1951), a project long considered to be a natural for the Disney touch, had bounced around the studio drawing boards since the late 1930s. After years of development, it finally emerged as a kind of surrealistic vaudeville show, replete with strong episodes of wild humor but weak in terms of warmth and cohesiveness. *Peter Pan* (1953), another longtime project, injected a healthy dose of adventure into the fantasy genre, and the result was a bright, delightful film. A little more than two years later, Disney presented *Lady and the Tramp*, the first animated movie to utilize the widescreen Cinemascope technique. This whimsical fable of canine romance featured a painstaking visual realism that lingered over every detail, a delightful musical score, and a sentimental story line of love lost and won. *Sleeping Beauty* (1959), an extravagant project that took shape in fits and starts over most of the decade, aimed to become the ultimate achievement of Disney animation. It was the most expensive animated movie ever made, and Disney artists labored for years to provide elaborately realistic detail, heavily stylized medieval images, and spectacular action episodes. The result was a technical tour de force that beckoned to adult sensibilities, but also an emotionally stiff film with limited appeal as fantasy. Finally, the more modest *One Hundred and One Dalmatians* (1961) offered a delightful return to the animal realm with its charming story of a married couple, their herd of lovable canines, and the heroic detective work that overcomes a nefarious plot to steal the dogs.[7]

Along with this impressive revival of animated features, Disney made an audacious move into live-action films. With the successful release of *Treasure Island* in 1950, the studio launched a series of movies that quickly affixed the Disney name to a fresh genre. Although originally the live-action films were something of a desperate move — they were produced in England to utilize funds that were frozen in that country during the postwar economic woes — the studio quickly caught its stride. While seldom blockbusters, these films provided modestly popular entertainment that pushed profits into the company's coffers. From 1950 through 1961, twenty-four live-action features appeared, spanning a number of genres. Historical adventures, such as a pair of movies compiled from television episodes, *Davy Crockett, King of the Wild Frontier* (1955) and *Davy Crockett and the River Pirates* (1956), were amply represented. Family dramas such as *Old Yeller* (1957) appeared regularly, while folklore and science inspired *Darby O'Gill and the Little People* (1959) and *Twenty Thousand Leagues under the Sea* (1954). The Disney Studio supplemented these films with the popular True-Life Adventures, a series of thirteen nature documentaries that appeared to great acclaim from 1948 through 1960.[8]

This flood of Disney movies ultimately set the stage for two more daring moves. First, after a successful Christmas special in 1950 called *One Hour in Wonderland,* followed by another the following year, Disney launched a twenty-nine-year run in television, beginning in 1954 with a weekly show on ABC entitled *Disneyland.* The following year he added a daily children's program, *The Mickey Mouse Club,* which also attracted a huge audience. After mounting difficulties with the ABC network, he switched affiliation to NBC in 1961 and offered *Walt Disney's Wonderful World of Color,* another long-running weekly show. Second, in the early 1950s Disney began to realize an old dream of building a fabulous amusement park. After maneuvering for years to gain financial backing, he finally purchased a 160-acre plot in Anaheim and began construction. Amid much fanfare, Disneyland opened in the summer of 1955 and became the linchpin of the entire Disney operation.

The breathtaking array of new projects in the 1950s and the popular reaction to them were in many ways a manifestation of Cold War pressures, reflecting both the anxieties and bravado of the time. It may not be immediately evident how fantasy films, television adventures, and amusement parks related to this international test of ideological wills, but in fact the connections were deep and complex.

II. Libertarian Populism

In the aftermath of World War II, a series of tense episodes became synonyms for international crisis — the Berlin airlift, the birth of Red China, the testing of nuclear weaponry, the descent of the iron curtain, the standoff between NATO and the Warsaw Pact in Europe, and the Korean War, to note but a few. Within the United States, the political implications of the Cold War radiated far and wide. Foreign policy became entangled in debates about strategies for containment, the deployment of nuclear weapons, and the merits of confrontation or negotiation with Communist countries. At a rhetorical level, American public leaders enshrined the free enterprise system as the emblem of a dynamic, expansive capitalism posed against the ravenous, restrictive Marxist authoritarianism of the Soviet Union. In terms of domestic politics, American fears of Communist conspiracy triggered a long string of red scares, investigations by the House Un-American Activities Committee, and eventually the paranoia of McCarthyism.[9]

With communism offering a dramatic rendering of social reform and historical evolution, Americans felt compelled to mount a countervailing crusade to identify a distinct vision of the good society. The Cold War inspired explicit attempts to explain the nature of the American people, American history, the American character, and the bedrock values that supported the whole. Walt Disney engaged his enterprise to grapple with these broad issues and emerged as a key figure in the process of national self-definition.

In particular, Disney played a crucial role as a mediator of American political principles. In the 1950s, ideological consensus gradually took shape around what many have termed "Cold War liberalism," shorthand for a political creed that combined anticommunism in foreign affairs with acceptance of the corporate welfare state in domestic life. This "vital center" mindset marginalized both leftist radicalism and free-market zealotry. Cold War liberals, with their dedication to controlled economic growth and stern opposition to Communist global expansion, dominated both the Democratic and Republican parties. They jettisoned ideological zealotry for pragmatism, proclaimed their belief in *pax americana,* and insisted that it was America's destiny to export the values, institutions, and politics of democracy and capitalism to achieve a peaceful dominion over the rest of the world.[10]

But the emergence of consensus was less inevitable than it may seem in hindsight. Corporate liberalism, with its ideal of a mosaic of negotiating interest groups in public life; corporate capitalism, with its Wall Street em-

phasis on the expansion of markets and investment; provincial conservatism, with its staunch defense of village values and small producers; and
urban technocracy, with its vision of a future directed by expertise and
scientific rationality — all flourished within the broader areas of agreement.
One of Disney's great achievements was to gather these strands, relax the
tensions among them, and braid them together emotionally into a resilient
political culture of Americanism. He acted half consciously, professing only
to seek entertainment and espouse patriotism, but in so doing he appealed
to deeper sources of inspiration. As he so often did, Disney instinctively
reached for the totems and aspirations at the core of the American way of
life and used them to construct an ideological code that audiences grasped
without need of interpretation.[11]

The unifying position that Disney forged, perhaps best described as "libertarian populism," stressed the autonomy of ordinary citizens in the face of
overweening authority. The remnants of the older, optimistic, inclusive
populism of the Depression era provided an important foundation for this
position, but Disney reshaped it to conform to the exigencies of the Cold
War. While offering a sentimental celebration of common American people,
he now proposed a narrower, more defensive rendition. His images of hardworking, God-fearing, community-building citizens increasingly were inspired by a homogenized vision of the WASP folk whose values he enshrined
and prospects he proclaimed.

The libertarian populism that pervaded Disney's films, television shows,
advertisements, and amusement park entertainment in the 1950s rested on
several basic principles. On the positive side, it offered faith in individual
autonomy, voluntarism, and a community of small producers while celebrating the work ethic, traditional Protestant morality, and a spirit of technological innovation. In negative terms, it encouraged a suspicion of big
bureaucratic institutions, be they governmental or financial, public or private. The entertainer added a strong sense of religious devotion and optimism about the United States as a model of modern progress. He infused
the whole, of course, with a large measure of sentiment and genuine, unabashed patriotism.

Against the threat of Communist collectivism and authoritarianism, Disney insisted on Americans' dedication to individualism and freedom. Yet at
the same time he carefully stressed his fellow citizens' instinct for community cohesion and their willingness to be team players in a larger cause.
Disney lauded Americans' rootedness in traditional village values but emphasized their modern yearning for innovation, better technology, and material abundance. He revered their respect for traditional religious morality
but praised their willingness to embrace the fantastic capabilities of American science. He honored the American past but encouraged his audience to
embrace the future. In the broadest sense of political culture, he helped

cement the Cold War American consensus by mediating a host of jarring impulses: individualism and conformity, corporate institutions and small-town values, science and fantasy, consumerism and producerism. In the political world of Walt Disney, Americans could unashamedly embrace "the people" without falling into the snare of leftist fellow-traveling. His expansive, optimistic outlook utilized ideas, words, and sentiments to which ordinary people were drawn, and the subtle power of this politics helped millions of Americans face a frightening external threat.

Disney's political agenda began to emerge most obviously in the wave of live-action history films that his studio began churning out early in the 1950s. British costume dramas, tales of the American frontier and the Wild West, and stories of the American Revolution and the Civil War tumbled out one after another throughout the decade. In a certain way, this turn to history was itself a clear product of the Cold War, since respect for the past had begun to emerge as a crucial article of faith in the anti-Communist creed. As historian Michael Kammen has pointed out, "Communism was feared for many reasons, but one of them had to do with its repudiation of and break with the past. Therefore, 'Americanism' came to connote a love of continuity and respect for the past." For Americans, history became an instrument of cultural nationalism in the struggle with an ideology of rootless radicalism.[12]

With his usual keen instincts, Disney seemed to sense this connection. His history movies were filled with nostalgic evocations of Americanism wherein a hardworking, God-fearing, freedom-loving people conquered a continent, carved out a life for themselves in the face of great challenges, and created the greatest society in human history. They painted American history as the story of progress animated by the triumph of ordinary citizens.

Disney himself helped lay the groundwork for these films in a number of public statements about his work. In the late 1940s, for instance, he began to stress the need to refurbish images of American folk heroes. Larger-than-life figures like Johnny Appleseed, John Henry, Pecos Bill, and Paul Bunyan, he insisted, were in fact "heroes made in our own likeness . . . [and] as good a reflection of our national traits as anything history can offer." As he told a newspaper columnist in 1948,

> I think this is a good time to get acquainted with, or renew acquaintance with, the American breed of robust, cheerful, energetic and representative folk heroes. One thing they all had in common, aside from their pride, their forgivable boastfulness and their invaluable championship of just causes and of the family in trouble or danger — they were all working men.
>
> The mighty man of American myth earned his keep riding herd, planting trees, felling timber, building railroads, pounding a steel drill, poling

keelboats, taming nature . . . They were just exaggerated portraits of the normal, busy, indomitable, toiling man of their day. And they are worth looking at — soberly and in fun — to re-educate our minds and our children's minds to the lusty new world called America.[13]

The prototype for Disney's emerging Cold War project was *So Dear to My Heart* (December 1948), the studio's first primarily live-action film. It celebrated the rural American folk at the turn of the century with a highly sentimental tale about a young boy, Jeremiah Kincaid, as he struggles to train his beloved but unruly black sheep, Danny, for show at the county fair. Presenting a gallery of memorable character sketches — the pious, stern, but gentle grandmother who reads her Bible and works hard to survive on her small farm; the hardworking, kindly blacksmith uncle who quietly dispenses wisdom; the cranky storekeeper with a heart of gold — the movie concluded with Jeremiah's triumph at the fair. He receives the Award of Special Merit because, in the judge's words, "It's what you do with what you got that counts."

This loving picture of village life a half-century before received critical praise for its invocations of the American way. One reviewer connected this "real American success story" with the recent political triumph of another midwesterner: "We don't know whether Harry Truman had a black sheep in his past, but he must have learned early that 'it's what you do with what you got' that counts." Senator Homer Capehart of Indiana, recommending this film on the floor of Congress, praised its creator as "a symbol of Americanism . . . [He] epitomizes the creative spirit which has made America great."[14]

A subsequent parade of Disney historical films displayed various aspects of the heroic American folk and their chronicle of progress and achievement. *Westward Ho the Wagons* (1956), for example, was an episodic tale of a wagon train heading across the Great Plains that focused on the family experience of this heroic travail. A much more compelling story came the following year with *Johnny Tremain,* which brought to life Esther Forbes's popular novel of a Boston boy whose involvement with revolutionary struggle in the 1770s made him a witness to the origins of the American Revolution. The first section of the film took place in 1773, as Johnny, a young apprentice silversmith, becomes drawn to the Sons of Liberty and makes the acquaintance of James Otis and Paul Revere. His involvement with that dissident organization culminates with the daring escapade of the Boston Tea Party. In the movie's second part, Johnny is swept up in the explosive events leading to American independence as angry Minutemen gather by the hundreds, the British army crumbles under the pressure, and a host of bonfires around Boston symbolize the growing flame of freedom.

Johnny Tremain elicited an overwhelmingly positive response both from popular audiences and the critics, who appreciated the film's brisk story line, dramatic episodes, and convincing characterizations. But a political subtext also quickly entered the discussion. Many critics correctly saw this production as a patriotic celebration of freedom and democracy, one with a direct application to the Cold War struggle. "*Johnny Tremain* is a very pertinent story," Disney noted in several interviews. "What we were fighting for then, we are fighting for now." A screening board representing national organizations such as the American Library Association, the National Council of Women, and the Protestant Motion Picture Council also weighed in on the film's behalf, proclaiming, "Since the fight for basic freedoms is as strong today as it was then, adults and young people alike may be reinvigorated by a picture with the spirit of '76." One reviewer saw *Johnny Tremain*'s stirring patriotism as a welcome antidote to the "scholarship" of those "bent on debunking history and attaching ignoble motives to heroic deeds." In her view, this movie was "history told with head high, chest up, heart bursting with pride . . . Walt Disney does a service to American youth in retelling the story of our nation's beginning with the accent on the high-minded principles, the soul-stirring ideas."[15]

Other history films from the 1950s expressed more directly Disney's antielitism and his intense suspicion of governmental power and the oppressions of wealth. In many ways, *The Story of Robin Hood* (1952) was representative. While the genesis of this film lay in a pragmatic desire to utilize studio funds held by the British government, this shot-in-England production did not skimp on political idealism. It told the tale of the famous folk hero who defied a corrupt monarchy in the name of the people, but Disney quickly shifted this theme into the American grain with a subsequent series of TV shows that portrayed heroic New World individualists who defended the people, battled privileged oppressors, and sought justice outside the parameters of government. Rapidly traversing the terrain of American history, the studio turned first to a guerrilla fighter in the southern colonies during the Revolution and then to the western frontier to identify a series of Robin Hood figures who were genuinely American.

One of the Disney Studio's most popular television offerings during this era was *The Swamp Fox*, a miniseries of eight one-hour shows broadcast on ABC's *Walt Disney Presents* from October 1959 through January 1961. It drew on the legendary exploits of Francis Marion, a heroic figure from South Carolina who was, in Disney's own words as he introduced the series, "a hero during the American Revolution second only to George Washington." Played by Leslie Nielsen, Marion appeared in the nation's living rooms as a populist hero who fought British oppressors by taking to the backcountry. He shunned the Continental Army and organized irregular troops — common farmers, frontiersmen, and tradesmen — who struck fiercely at redcoats headquartered in Charleston and then melted into the countryside. After his first experience with this cadre, the frustrated British commander complained bitterly that "even bloodhounds couldn't catch that swamp fox in terrain like this!" Thus a legend was born.

The *Swamp Fox* episodes illustrated various aspects of Disney's libertarian populist version of history. The opening segment, for instance, introduces the virtuous, patriotic Colonel Marion by contrasting him with American officers who cavort with the wealthy classes of Charleston while ignoring the impending threat of a British invasion. These foppish, inebriated men mock Marion's warnings, only to look like fools when he must rush in to save the governor and a group of captured patriots from disaster. As the Swamp Fox explains, patriotic self-sacrifice means that "sometimes what's good and right, matters of the soul, are more important than food or clothing." In another episode, a captain in the Continental Army joins Marion's force and tries to instill discipline by drilling these rough frontier farmers. Openly amused at such pretensions, they resist until their leader convinces the captain that formal military training is inappropriate for these citizen-soldiers. This popular television series, in other words, underlined Disney's creed of sturdy self-reliance, patriotic virtue, and community action outside the parameters of official power.[16]

Critical reaction to *The Swamp Fox* revealed an appreciation of the show's political subtext. The press widely reported the studio's original intent to cast Audie Murphy, a World War II hero, in the starring role. As the show began its run, writers emphasized the proud spirit of patriotism that infused this historical tale. Some reviews stressed the antielitist angle, flaunting headlines about the "Robin Hood of the South." As with Johnny Tremain, many stressed the Swamp Fox's resistance to political tyranny. This "freedom fighter," as he, too, was frequently described, "took to the swamps to organize a guerrilla force rather than to submit to the British yoke" and never hesitated to "strike a blow for freedom."[17]

Two other Disney television series portrayed historical figures who skirted established institutions and rules, when necessary, to achieve justice for common people. The first, *The Tales of Texas John Slaughter,* appeared in seventeen hour-long segments from October 1958 to April 1961. Its protagonist, played by Tom Tryon, was a cattleman and gunfighter who joins the Texas Rangers in the 1870s to combat gangs of cattle rustlers, horse thieves, and robbers who are preying on hardworking citizens. Slaughter, utterly fearless and a crack shot, ruthlessly guns down bad guys in the shoot-'em-up atmosphere of frontier Texas. But he also marries, settles down as a family man, and becomes a pillar of the community as a fearless sheriff who enforces law and order against an array of criminals and killers. As Tryon explained in an interview published nationally, Slaughter's violent defense of western ranchers stemmed from "a psychological hatred of those who don't respect private property."[18]

Around the same time, a similar western series ran on *Walt Disney Pre-*

sents. Named after its protagonist, Elfego Baca, the ten episodes followed the adventures of a flamboyant figure who lived in Socorro and Santa Fe, New Mexico, in the 1880s. A gunslinger like John Slaughter, Baca's strong sense of justice turns him toward the law. Deputized and then elected sheriff after his upright character and skill with a six-shooter help him stop a group of marauding cowboys, the lawman gains a reputation for having nine lives. Baca was clearly portrayed as a populist icon. In the series' initial segment, for instance, the newly elected sheriff releases from the local jail all prisoners being held for nonpayment of debt. In later episodes, after deciding that legal training might be more effective than bullets, he goes to Santa Fe for education and reemerges as an idealistic, crusading lawyer. Baca subsequently clashes with crooked judges, greedy land companies, corrupt bankers, and unscrupulous railroad companies. Moving from bloody clashes on the range to confrontations in the courtroom, he successfully defends the interests of an array of outsiders — ordinary citizens, small ranchers, reformed small-time crooks, harassed religious groups, and persecuted Spanish-American landowners.

Perhaps Disney's quintessential Robin Hood figure, however, appeared adorned with a black mask, swirling cape, and flashing rapier. The swashbuckling Zorro (the Spanish word means *fox*) became one of the studio's most popular figures in the 1950s. The historical morality tale of the same name was originally an ABC series of seventy-eight half-hour episodes running from October 1957 through July 1959. Over the next two years, the studio also produced four hour-long segments for inclusion on *Walt Disney Presents* and then spliced together several television presentations to create a feature-length movie. These productions proved enormously popular, and a Zorro craze swept the country. Guy Williams, the tall, dashing actor who portrayed the hero, became the subject of dozens of articles in movie and entertainment publications, and his string of publicity appearances at parades and rodeos brought out hordes of adoring fans. The Disney Studio's *Zorro Newsletter* gained thousands of subscribers, and as a spread in *Life* illustrated, black hats, capes, masks, and plastic swords became de rigueur for preadolescent boys, who flailed away at one another in backyard duels and pledged brotherhood in treehouse hideaways. The craze frequently reached the point of absurdity. Pediatricians accommodated their young patients by making allergy-test scratches in the shape of a *Z*, while the swank Colony Club in New York City added chicken à la Zorro to its menu. In 1958, families who were flooded out by torrential rains in Gulf Coast Texas gratefully fled to a Red Cross shelter in an elementary school, but the children proved to be a problem. According to one volunteer, "We can't put them to bed until after they see *Zorro.*"[19]

For all its adventure and romance, the show's political subtext held a subtle allure for Cold War Americans. The movie treatment of this caped crusader — the Disney Studio released *The Sign of Zorro* in May 1960 — recapitulated the essential elements of Disney's historical vision in the 1950s. A populist melodrama, it opens with a bleak picture of ranchers and farmers in Spanish California struggling against governmental tyranny in the early nineteenth century. When young Diego de la Vega, the son of local luminary Don Alejandro, returns home from Spain to *"pueblo de Los Angeles,"* he finds a corrupt, despotic military commander preying on local landowners with the aid of wealthy allies and dishonest judges. His father recounts a passionate litany of injustices: property owners taxed into poverty, citizens thrown into prison for debt, Indians forced into slave labor, and shrewd lawyers manipulating the law in the interest of Commandante Monastario. The people have fallen "under the heel of a dictator," Don Diego concludes, while Monastario pursues his goal of becoming "the richest man in California."[20]

Don Diego decides to pretend to be a foppish, timid scholar who shrinks before any sign of confrontation but to gather information secretly about Monastario and his machinations. At night he assumes the identity of Zorro, the masked scourge of evil oppressors. Aided by Bernardo, his mute, clever servant, and carried by his valiant steed, Tornado, he strikes suddenly and leaves his calling card with a quick slash with his rapier in the shape of a *Z*. As the *The Sign of Zorro* continues, he liberates political prisoners, frightens a corrupt judge into acquitting his unjustly accused father, and fights a duel with the pernicious Monastario. A number of populist declarations add political seasoning to this swashbuckling diet. In the introduction, a note knife-pinned to a wall reads, "My sword a flame to right every wrong. So heed well my name. Zorro," and after freeing an imprisoned landowner, the hero refuses to divulge his real identity, saying only that he is "a friend of the people, El Zorro." Throughout, the film takes pains to separate powerful figures like the commandant from ordinary people, who are terrorized into doing his bidding. Zorro, who stands out among Disney's heroic champions of the virtuous folk who fight against injustices foisted upon them by wealthy, powerful elites, was, as many newspaper stories proclaimed, "the Robin Hood of Old California."[21]

Many Disney productions put one final twist on their historical narratives. Numerous movies and television shows depicted Indians, Hispanics, and African-Americans valiantly struggling to become part of mainstream American culture. Far from being reactionary or exclusionary, the Disney Studio assumed an assimilationist, melting-pot stance that was rather progressive for the 1950s. For instance, *The Light in the Forest* (1958), set on the frontier of the American colonies in the 1760s, offered a sympathetic account of a young orphan whose fate swings between the Indians among whom he grew up and the white settlers whose blood he carries. He hates white society, but his conscience will not allow him to decoy innocent

settlers into an ambush. This tension is resolved wh.
ous settler who has killed one of his Indian friends, n.
tured servant with whom he has fallen in love, and
mediator between the two societies. *Tonka* (1958) was an.
which, in contrast to many other westerns of the time,
Americans in a positive light. Set on the Great Plains in the late
the tale of a young Indian named White Bull and his struggle to
his magnificent horse, Tonka, as his land is invaded by Colonel Cu
the Seventh Cavalry. His friendship with Miles Keogh, a kindly c
captain, is set against his relationship with Custer, whose demeanor a.
Indian-hating sociopath makes his demise at Little Bighorn well deserved.

Disney's television shows focused on other ethnic groups but tended to follow a similar pattern. *The Swamp Fox,* for instance, gave a prominent role to Oscar, a loyal black slave (played by Jordan Whitfield) who was treated as an equal by Francis Marion's patriots as they struggled together against the British. Although the irony of his slavery went unmentioned, his evident patriotism and pluck and the respect paid to him by others made for a very sympathetic character. Even more dramatically, Elfego Baca's defense of the rights of Spanish-American citizens was portrayed in such a positive, even stirring manner that viewers could not help but react sympathetically. And *Zorro* depicted Spanish settlers as rather transparent Americans who were vitally concerned with political freedom and fair treatment. While the extent of this integrationist impulse can be overstated — the fact remains that racial and ethnic minorities stood at the margins of the Disney vision of the good society — it nonetheless offered minorities entry into the ranks of the virtuous American people. Disney's populism may have been narrowly conceived, but it was undeniably assimilationist and inclusionary.

Although transfixed by the American folk, a host of Disney films in the 1950s simultaneously drew on the other great ingredient in libertarian populism — sturdy, self-reliant individualism. The Burbank entertainer paid homage to community cohesion in his historical productions, but he also included affirmations of personal character. American individualism became one of the most consistent, compelling themes in Disney's Cold War movies.

III. The Glad Game and the American Character

Throughout the 1950s, defining and exploring the national character was a central preoccupation of many American authors, artists, and intellectuals. Writers such as David Potter, Daniel Boorstin, William H. Whyte, and David Riesman tried to distill the essence of their countrymen's modern traits with meditations on the "people of plenty," "the organization man," "American destiny," and "the lonely crowd." In his own more modest and less self-conious way, Walt Disney engaged the same issues in the realm of popular culture. Having anchored the folk as a mainstay of the American way of life, he pursued his Cold War balancing act by dramatizing the possibilities of American individualism.

In numerous film and television productions, Disney enunciated a positive, optimistic sensibility regarding the single citizen and his efficacious social role. Perhaps the most striking example came in *Pollyanna* (1960), in which the cheerful young protagonist announced the wondrous capacities of the "glad game," her strategy for finding solutions to the most intractable problems. This determined young woman overcame pessimism and despair as she healed lives, solidified relationships, and brought moral and material improvements to the small town of Harrington. In a broad sense, this stress on the ability of individual integrity and willpower to change society became a hallmark of Disney's 1950s productions. He recognized tragedy, loss, and defeat, but saw them only as temporary barriers to be overcome by an army of sturdy individuals in the American march of progress.

The Disney Studio provided a taste of this preoccupation in a banquet of films released in the 1950s. A spate of British costume dramas, for instance, presented morality tales about individual freedom versus powerful social structures or governments. Filmed versions of English epics such as *The Sword and the Rose* (1953) and *Rob Roy, the Highland Rogue* (1954) depicted heroic individuals mustering their internal resources to overcome more powerful opponents. A series of Disney movies on nineteenth-century America also stressed the social impact of individual character. *The Great Locomotive Chase* (1956) told the exciting story of an attempt by Union army raiders to steal a train in the Civil War South and the herculean efforts of a single man, conductor William A. Fuller, to thwart the project. *Ten Who Dared* (1960) chronicled Major John Wesley Powell's expedition to explore the Colorado River, a scientific undertaking that he doggedly completed despite a host of obstacles and tragedies. But these productions only scratched the surface of the individualist theme, settling for displays of willfulness and heroism while seldom examining the character traits that lay beneath.[23]

One movie from the early 1950s underlined an aspect of character formation that became increasingly central to the Disney version of individualism — its explicitly male nature. *Treasure Island,* one of the postwar British productions and Disney's first all-live-action movie, was a rollicking adaptation of Robert Louis Stevenson's pirate novel, overflowing with red-blooded action and flamboyant characters. As the story begins, young Jim Hawkins accidentally comes into the possession of a secret map and ends up as a cabin boy on a Caribbean expedition to recover a stash of buried treasure. As events unfold, the ship's one-legged cook, Long John Silver, turns out to be the mastermind behind a pirate plot to grab the map and steal the riches. After an intriguing series of mysteries, a bloody mutiny, and a flurry of factional backstabbing, the treasure is finally found in a cave on Treasure Island. At the movie's climax, Jim helps Silver to escape with a boatload of coins and the old pirate waves his thanks as he floats out to sea.[24]

A strong thematic thread wove in and out of the brandished cutlasses, gleaming treasure, and bracing sea air of *Treasure Island*. For all its atmosphere of adventure, the film actually revolved around the character development of the youthful protagonist and his encounter with danger, struggle, achievement, and greed. Jim Hawkins experiences this series of trials and tribulations as part of becoming a man, and he learns the necessity of shaping a firm moral character. His foil throughout the film, of course, is Long John Silver, a charming, crusty rogue with a heart of gold who develops an affection for the boy. Unscrupulous and greedy but won over by the boy's virtue and courage, the pirate refuses to kill Hawkins even when his own life seems to depend on it.

Reactions to *Treasure Island* were predominantly positive, but many were struck by the maleness that saturated the movie. Not a single woman appeared in it, which led one critic to observe sarcastically that it could "be recommended as ideal entertainment for misogynists as for all men and women desiring an hour and thirty-five minutes of escapism." An impressive array of virile adjectives flavored the critical commentary — "lusty screen treatment," "a burly show," "blood and thunder adventure," and "buccaneer revel," to choose but a few. But perhaps most often evaluations focused on the film's direct connection to male fantasy life. For generations this familiar pirate story had thrilled every "small, hardened day-dreamer worthy of the proud name of 'Boy,'" as one writer put it, and it also resonated for adult males. *Parents* insisted that the film would appeal especially to "fathers and schoolboy sons," while the New York *Times* argued poignantly that it would set men "to daydreaming about excitements which are denied fulfillment by the inhibitions of advancing age." But it was not only adventure that generated a masculine appeal. The shaping of upright character — "Without ever being obnoxiously virtuous, young Jim is sturdier, braver, kinder, more honest and trustworthy than any lad you've ever met," observed one essayist — showed how "a few brave men and true" could triumph over evil.[25]

A few years later, one of Disney's most ambitious and popular movies from the entire decade probed more deeply into the sensibility of individualism. *Twenty Thousand Leagues under the Sea*, an adaptation of the Jules Verne novel, was an ambitious live-action movie that went far beyond anything Disney had attempted up to that point. With the Pacific Ocean providing a vast scope for the adventure, the film bubbled over with excitement — encounters with incredible submarines and gigantic squids, aquanauts and undersea farmers sustaining human life, fantastic special effects from a mythical underwater world, and a cast of big-name Hollywood stars. But undergirding the flashy structure was a more serious thematic concern: the problematic nature of individualism.

Once again, except for the two prostitutes on the arm of the protagonist as the film opens, no women appeared. Instead, this testosterone-saturated tale presented a series of male types for inspection. Kirk Douglas portrayed the boisterous sailor Ned Land, Paul Lukas played Professor Pierre Aronnax, the reflective French scientist, and Peter Lorre appeared as his assistant, the toady Conseil. But at the center of the story, of course, stood Captain Nemo, played by the elegant James Mason. This brilliant scientist and inventor, faced with an evil society that tolerates warfare, forced labor, injustice, and poverty, has withdrawn in horror and created a separate, blissful world under the ocean. Among his discoveries are a remarkable power source that propels the *Nautilus*, a fantastic submarine, and underwater diving suits that allow him and his fellow idealists to farm the ocean floor and hunt sea creatures for food during the day and retire in comfort in the evening to enjoy art, music, and reading. The *Nautilus*, however, also attacks and sinks any warships that wander into its path. Hearing tales of a monster that appears from the sea to destroy vessels, the American navy mounts an expedition to investigate. Aronnax, Conseil, and Land are on board the ship when it, too, is attacked. The warship goes down, but the three are rescued and become prisoners of Captain Nemo. The French scientist works quietly to bring Nemo's remarkable talents back to civilization, while Land chafes under the *Nautilus*'s restraints and plots escape. After a series of adventures, the movie comes to its apocalyptic ending when Nemo returns to his island headquarters to discover a waiting squadron of warships, whose powerful guns cripple his submarine. Driven over the edge by fury and despair, the mortally wounded captain scuttles his beloved *Nautilus* after detonating a huge explosion that incinerates the entire island. Land manages to escape with Aronnax and Conseil before the holocaust, and they frantically paddle to safety in a small skiff.[26]

Twenty Thousand Leagues under the Sea consistently intervened in its own adventure tale to chart the possibilities and parameters of individual action. Set in the nineteenth century, which framed the great era of individualism in American history, the story juxtaposed Ned Land, a common roughneck but a brave and decent person, and Captain Nemo and his brilliantly misguided, elitist, and sociopathic instincts. The uneducated, hard-drinking, aggressive harpooner scores no points for gentility, but ultimately he earns admiration as a pragmatic man of action with a streak of crude vitality and heroism. Before the others, he perceives that Nemo is a "mad dog." Land also displays strong principles, becoming outraged when the captain wantonly destroys ships full of common sailors like himself and, later, leaping into the battle with the giant squid to save Nemo's life even though he despises the man. Land's keen native wit and initiative also come to the fore when he breaks into Nemo's private quarters, calculates the latitude and longitude of the island, and secretly scatters messages in bottles to announce this position. When these missives bring warships to surround the *Nautilus,* he does not shrink from responsibility but declares, "Somebody had to strike a blow for freedom!" Thus Ned Land, the real hero of this film, fits the mold of Disney's 1950s individualist hero — the self-directed common man who rises up against oppressive power to defend the community.

Captain Nemo, in contrast, appears as a dark reflection of individualism, a kind of Nietzchean superman who lost his moral bearings when he rejected social obligation. Persecuted by a government that tried to capture his discoveries for evil purposes, he turned inward, fleeing to the bottom of the sea, where he sits in an environment of his own creation, compulsively playing emotional versions of grand Bach compositions on his great pipe organ. "I am not what is called a civilized man," he informs the trio of interlopers when they enter his submarine. "I have done with society for reasons which seem good to me. Therefore I do not obey its laws." In a sense, Nemo's desire to be free of an evil world has produced fantastic inventions and discoveries with great potential for enhancing the quality of human life. But at the same time he has been morally maimed. An isolated, flawed genius, he ultimately seems both pitiful and arrogant, a man whose complete severing of community ties leads to social devastation.

Twenty Thousand Leagues under the Sea taught the cultural lesson that while individualism is vital and pregnant with possibilities, it needs to be harnessed to the public good or disaster will ensue. In case viewers missed the obvious — throughout the film there are continuous, oblique references to Nemo's mysterious power source and its incredible potential — an enormous mushroom cloud accompanied the island's final destruction, a fiery reminder of the nuclear context of this film.

Disney steered his exploration of individualism directly into the American mainstream a couple of years later with *Old Yeller* (1957), the heartwrenching tale of a boy in 1869 Texas who learns some hard lessons over a summer when he is forced to grow up. When his father leaves the homestead on a cattle drive to Kansas, Travis Coates is left to shoulder the responsibility of supporting and protecting the family. As he works in the fields and hunts, he is accompanied by a big yellow mongrel who has strayed onto the farm. Old Yeller proves to be not only a wonderful hunter and herder of livestock but a fierce defender of the family as he attacks a mother bear, a herd of rampaging wild pigs, and finally a wolf that threatens their well-being. Unfortunately, the dog contracts rabies from the disease-crazed wolf and turns vicious. Travis, heartbroken by this turn of events, nonetheless sees what he must do and, though nearly blinded by tears, shoulders his rifle and destroys his beloved companion.

The forging of manly individualism lay at the heart of this sentimental narrative as the youth adopted the virtues of hard work, steadfast duty, and moral fortitude. When Jim Coates returns from the cattle range at the end of the story and hears about the travail with Old Yeller, he offers a little homily. Sitting on a log with his devastated son, he first expresses pride at how Travis has handled the ordeal "just like a grown man." Life, he admits, can give some pretty hard knocks, and all you can do is learn, persevere, and "go on being a man." The boy takes this fatherly advice, accepts the riding horse brought back for him from Kansas, and adopts one of Old Yeller's male pups as a way to ease his pain. As many noted, while the film presented an idyllic depiction of farm life and America's resilient pioneers — reviews typically noted the focus on "decent, sturdy, self-reliant folks" — it also, in the words of one review, "captured on film that most profound experience, the transformation of a boy into a man."[27]

Reinforcement of the theme of character formation also came from another quarter in the 1950s: the actors who portrayed Disney's populist heroes. With its usual energy and skill, the studio promoted a series of masculine, handsome leading men as figures of action and character. Tom Tryon, for instance, the star of *Texas John Slaughter,* was publicized as a diligent young man who had served his country in the navy for several years, studied art at Yale University and acting in New York, painted posters and scenery in a Massachusetts playhouse, and gradually struggled to success in the California film capital. In similar fashion, Leslie Nielsen, who portrayed the Swamp Fox, was described as a "ruggedly handsome" man with a "brawny physique," the son of a Canadian mounted policeman, a veteran of the Royal Canadian Air Force, and a determined actor whose years of study and training eventually earned him a successful Hollywood career. Guy Williams probably attracted the most attention as a masculine ideal; at the height of his show's popularity, dozens of articles with titles such as "At Home with Zorro" warmly portrayed him as a family man, with wife, child, and domestic chores, or stressed his years of frustration in Hollywood and the persistent work ethic that eventually brought him to deserved national fame. Thus amid the ideological tensions of the 1950s, a Disney pantheon of actors provided the public with role models for male individualism.[28]

At the end of this decade Disney released a film that neatly summarized the studio's Cold War vision. *The Swiss Family Robinson* (1960) came to the screen as a clear, charming case study of how self-reliant individualism and the virtues of the folk could converge to produce a utopian society. Based on the popular Johann Wyss novel, this film charted the adventures of a pious, hardworking, and clever family stranded on an uninhabited island. The Robinsons — a married couple and their three sons, Ernst, Fritz, and Francis — are emigrating to America when a storm destroys their ship and the cowardly crew abandons them, taking the only seaworthy boat. Foundered on a reef near an unknown island, they salvage material from the wreckage, float ashore on homemade rafts, and literally construct a life for themselves. Father and the three boys build a spectacular treehouse, complete with banistered stairs, separate bedrooms, skylights, a stove, and running water. They domesticate wild animals, cultivate crops, and prepare a fortification at the top of the largest hill in case they have to defend themselves. Once the family has created a blissful existence for itself, Fritz and Ernst head off in a small craft to circumnavigate the island, and they discover a young woman, Roberta, who has been captured and brought to the other side by pirates. After being rescued, she becomes a part of the family as well as an object of attention from the two jealous adolescents. At the movie's climax, the marauding pirates discover the Robinsons' enclave and launch a full-scale attack. Just as the family is heroically defending itself, Roberta's grandfather arrives with a warship and saves the day. Though pleased to reestablish contact with the outside world, most of the Robinsons decide to stay on their island paradise as the narrative draws to a close.[29]

The millions of moviegoers who flocked to see *The Swiss Family Robinson* saw, in the broadest sense, a parable of the American experience. On their way to the New World, the Robinsons are freed of governmental and institutional authority when the crew abandons ship, forcing them to fall back on their own resources for survival. The significance of this situation is made clear the first night on the island, when Father apologizes to Mother for bringing her into these harsh circumstances. She urges optimism, reminding him that they set out looking for "a chance to be free," and that this wilderness will provide opportunity because "there is no limit to what a man can do." And indeed, when the Robinsons put their shoulders to the wheel, the film lovingly dramatizes a cluster of small-producer values. Individual initiative and the work ethic move to the fore as the Robinson males, by the sweat of their brow, steadily secure shelter, food, and transportation. They also demonstrate considerable Yankee skill as their technological tinkering and innovation bring marvelous results. To bring the virtue of these endeavors home, the movie stresses the piety that lies behind them — the first thing the Robinsons do when they come ashore is kneel down in prayer.

The Cold War message of *The Swiss Family Robinson*, however, became most obvious in the film's climax, when the none-too-bright pirate gang intrudes on the island paradise, only to be routed by the clever family. The Robinsons have adopted a posture of preparedness that John Foster Dulles would have been hard-pressed to match. Determined to defend their freedom, they have wisely prepared a series of ruses and contraptions against a numerically superior enemy — a collapsible bridge, snares, rigged crossbows, disguised pits holding wild animals, crude land mines, rock slides, coconut hand grenades, and stockpiled logs to roll downhill. And the women as well as the men grab rifles to defend their tiny community. When the pirates actually attack, the resulting melee is presented in comic terms —

dozens of them are blown up or knocked flying but none is ever killed; unfortunate individuals fall into the tiger pit and come flying out like rockets; the chief pirate uncomprehendingly picks up a coconut with a burning fuse and throws it over his shoulder into the middle of his own followers. But beneath the patina of slapstick, this scene conveys a clear ideological code. The pirate rabble, as Asians, were a rather transparent rendering of the "yellow peril" which bedeviled the American imagination in the 1950s. As one essayist noted, using the starkest Cold War language,

> These pirates were oriental types, a collection of uglies with slant-eyes and bare bellies . . . Western ingenuity and charm paid off in full against all the perils a tropical isle could align against the indomitable Swiss. And I only hope Western civilization generally, when its time comes, can do half as well as the Swiss Family Robinson. Walt Disney, I suspect, could help Dean Rusk in some of his diplomatic problems with under-developed nations. We may need all of his ingenuity — and more — before it's finished.

In such fashion *The Swiss Family Robinson* encompassed every aspect of Disney's 1950s libertarian populism, weaving together individual character, the virtue of the folk, and preparedness against an external enemy into a seamless whole.[30]

Disney's depictions of the folk and individualism celebrated the merits of the American individual, as opposed to the image of the Soviet communal automaton. At the same time he stressed family loyalty and a willingness to join other small producers voluntarily as part of a virtuous community. And Disney infused this historical vision with basic optimism about such salutary American qualities as industriousness, competence, technological ingenuity, and religiosity. In subtle and entertaining fashion, he articulated a compelling American ideology for his fellow citizens which helped ground their opposition to their godless, collectivist foes in the international struggle. The influence of this message intensified as Disney carried it deeper into the recesses of American culture.

16

Disney and National Security

T HE POWERFUL INFLUENCE of the Cold War pervaded other innovative projects that poured out of the Disney Studio in the 1950s.
Disney's expansive Americanism, for instance, influenced new explorations of the natural world in an extremely popular series of documentaries. It colored a number of television productions and books that probed
the prospects of space travel and the secrets of atomic energy. It helped
shape the creation of a buckskin-clad hero who unexpectedly became a great
popular fad. Such endeavors eventually had a profound impact on Disney's
own public image. By the end of the decade, he and his work had become
synonymous with American virtue and creativity and its promise of triumph over communism in the world.

I. Americanizing Nature

The Disney Studio's nature films developed as something of an accident.
According to producers Winston Hibler and Ben Sharpsteen, Disney originally was interested in making a feature film on Alaska and sent a photographic team there to shoot some background footage. The results were
disappointing, but he was intrigued by film showing great herds of fur seals
on the Pribiloff Islands. The development of a story line, the addition of
clever narration, and some judicious editing produced a half-hour docu-

mentary. When Disney offered it to his usual distributors, however, they balked, because its awkward length fit neither the short-subject model nor the feature-length one. With typical stubborn conviction, Disney independently previewed the film to several audiences, who loved it, and then released it commercially. *Seal Island* (1948) garnered not only great popularity but critical acclaim, which culminated in an Academy Award.[1]

In such serendipitous fashion, Disney launched a series of True-Life Adventures, as he decided to call them, which proved to be among the most popular of the studio's productions in the 1950s. They included *Beaver Valley* (1950), *Nature's Half Acre* (1951), *The Olympic Elk* (1952), *Water Birds* (1952), and *Bear Country* (1953), thirty-minute short subjects shown in theaters in a package with full-length features. Their great popularity soon produced an expansion of this format. *The Living Desert* (1953), *The Vanishing Prairie* (1954), *The African Lion* (1955), *Secrets of Life* (1956), *White Wilderness* (1958), and *Jungle Cat* (1960) were all feature-length films. By the time they ran their course, the True-Life Adventures had received eight Academy Awards for documentary films.[2]

These nature films proved to be enormously attractive. Audiences flocked to see them, sending yet more profits pouring into the studio, and the critical reception was overwhelmingly favorable. One critic, writing in the Los Angeles *Times*, argued that "Walt Disney, having captivated the world as the Master of Fantasy, now has become, by the greatest contradiction of the age, the Master of Reality." Others saw these expeditions as a happy escape from "our incredibly troubled world . . . an enthralling reminder that despite the pettiness of mankind, our world has its immutable laws of change, growth, and wonder." A few observers expressed reservations about elements of anthropomorphism and morbidity in the movies — New York *Times* critic Bosley Crowther, for example, generally liked the films but complained about their "repetition of incidents of violence and death" and their "tendency to humanize the creatures" — but such misgivings largely were drowned out by a loud chorus of praise.[3]

The immediate appeal of the True-Life Adventures was not hard to locate. The footage of wild animals and majestic landscapes was usually spectacular, and often breathtaking. Moving at a brisk pace from episode to episode, these documentaries supplemented the impressive visuals with provocative mood music, an alluring voice-over narrative, and frequent touches of humor. Rare views of a bison giving birth to a spindly-legged calf whom she then gently nudges into walking, a fight to the death between a rattlesnake and a tarantula, wild ducks who upend comically and slide into one another as they attempt to land on a frozen lake, and a huge thunderstorm sending a flash flood rumbling through a desert canyon held audiences spellbound.

Smoothly blending education with entertainment, the True-Life Adventures were full of information about the natural world, and they carried a prescient message with their warnings about the environmental dangers of human invasion of the natural world. Yet sober admonishments always prefaced an optimistic conclusion. In *The Vanishing Prairie,* for instance, the somber title was belied by a final statement that nature always adapts to new challenges and humans are becoming more aware of the harm they have wrought. In other words, the dire subtext of these films always shrank in the face of Disney's reassurance that things were going to work out all right.

The True-Life Adventures also held a deeper kind of attraction. Reactions to the films suggested that nature did not really appear here on its own terms. Instead, it was a kind of cultural canvas upon which Disney and the American audience painted an array of Cold War concerns and values. Several themes consistently surfaced in the cinematic discourse surrounding these movies.

Perhaps the most frequent and powerful reaction triggered by them concerned nature and the struggle for survival. Al Milotte, one of Disney's nature cinematographers, for instance, described the scene in *The African Lion* where the camera caught one of its subjects taking down a victim. In his words, "The other animals just stand around and watch their friend being eaten. You can almost hear them say, 'There goes unlucky Pierre. Glad it ain't me!'" In fact, many observers focused on the harsh aspects of natural selection and interpreted these Disney films as depictions of inevitable natural processes. Articles and reviews typically noted "the deadly struggles the [animal] actors go through each day to survive." More significantly, however, this theme was projected onto Cold War issues. Most observers connected the survival-of-the-fittest motif to an implicitly American ethos of competition, adaptation, individual initiative, and industriousness. A review of *Beaver Valley,* for example, approvingly described its chronicle of "the hard-working life of the beaver . . . the construction of the dam to make the beaver pond, the building of the home, the gathering of the food supply, and the hazards of his life." Disney's True-Life Adventures seemed to affirm social competition as a natural process that enabled the best to emerge — an unspoken rejection of the hovering Communist specter of artificial government direction and centralized planning.[4]

At the same time, a subtle domestication of nature played at the edges of the narrative. However much these documentaries underscored the struggle for survival, they also depicted a taming of natural forces that appealed to an American audience becoming increasingly suburbanized and family-oriented. Morality was presented as a curious exponent in the survival-of-the-fittest equation, particularly a domestic morality that seemed to enlist wild creatures as loyal members of the suburban homeowners' association, the PTA, and the community improvement council. This came in part from Disney's public comments on his nature films, in which he stressed the striking parallels between human society and the animal kingdom, particularly with regard to a common commitment to "family devotion and parental care."[5]

Many reviewers and essayists also saw in these films, both positively and negatively, glimpses of a commentary on modern American life. A few complained about Disney's penchant for arranging certain scenes "so that it appears the wild life in them is behaving in human and civilized ways." But most observers found these qualities salutary. After seeing *Bear Country,* for example, one reviewer described a female bear with cubs as "a fine-type mother, a little of the old school in her demand for immediate obedience," and another praised a long segment on prairie dogs in *The Vanishing Prairie* for its warm treatment of "the family home . . . [and] the home life of the chubby inhabitants." An even more positive exposition of domestic morality appeared in a piece for children: "Mother Prairie Dog teaches her children well. First they learn about enemies, such as the swift-winged prairie hawk . . . Other lessons are important, too. It's good manners to kiss when one prairie dog meets another. Each puppy must do his share of the work . . . Homes have to be built with high-rimmed earth entrances to keep out prairie floods. Each lesson counts in the fight for life." "Desert creatures are forever falling in love," a reviewer of *The Living Desert* added. "All around the clock the seeming waste is alive with creatures building homes, gathering food and water, pitching woo, throwing parties, and generally behaving like humans." From such comments arose reassuring images of animals performing their duties as solid citizens and joining together in cooperative ventures. This blending of instinctive individualism with community obligation, of course, fit the larger mold of the 1950s American character.[6]

In a related fashion, Disney's nature films often came before the public with a multilayered patriotic veneer. Advertisements for *The Vanishing Prairie* showed a western butte and a solitary bison and stated that Walt Disney "reaches deep into the heart of America" to present this stirring entertainment. Reviewers praised the film for showing the grandeur of the Great Plains; in the words of one, it "skillfully penetrates the land where the buffalo roams, the deer and the antelope play, and the prairie dogs just about have the times of their life." Disney's intense appreciation of the beauty of the American landscape was a rather straightforward expression of nationalism in an era of ideological challenge. As a writer in the Indianapolis *Star* gushed, "Disney deserves a government medal for boosting national pride and wonder in the natural greatness of this land."[7]

A proud affirmation of American technological expertise added another layer. Incredible footage of mountain lions stalking their prey, hawks swooping down on happy-go-lucky prairie dogs, bighorn rams theatrically smashing heads during the rutting season, and gorgeous flowers blooming elicited a chorus of oohs and ahs from awestruck audiences, but it also triggered admiring commentary about the sophisticated technology and scientific knowledge that made these shots possible. Pieces in specialized magazines such as *American Cinematographer* and *Popular Mechanics* offered detailed looks at the array of magnifying and telephoto lenses, cold light generators, time-lapse cameras, and remote control devices wielded by Disney's "formidable corps of naturalist-scientist-cameramen." A kind of wonderstruck praise also came from more popular magazines. *Sports Afield* described the highly specialized, four-wheel-drive armored vehicle that allowed cinematographers to film rare shots of African wildlife on the savannah. *Woman's Day* detailed the complex facility used by photographer John Nash Ott to film segments of *Nature's Half Acre* and *The Living Desert:* "All the windows in his elaborate greenhouse are fitted with Venetian blinds. Inside, twenty-three time-lapse cameras are kept focused on an equal number of blossoming plants. Every fifteen minutes an electronic device snaps the blinds shut, turns on a battery of spotlights, and trips the camera shutters. A second later the lights go off and the blinds open. Presumably, all Mr. Ott has to do is water the plants and occasionally change the film." Sometimes the awe of technology prompted humor, as when Disney, responding to a critic who condemned *The Vanishing Prairie* for using staged shots, replied innocently, "Oh no! You're completely wrong. We took our most intelligent prairie dogs and gave them very small cameras and sent them down into the burrows." But in a larger and more serious way, Disney's technological wizardry brought reassurances that American ingenuity would prevail in an uncertain modern world.[8]

The True-Life Adventures' impressive displays of science and technology ultimately fell back before an even larger demonstration: in the best tradition of American religiosity during the 1950s, Disney's marvelous pictures of the natural world were seen as illuminations of God's divine order. As a host of reviews and essays made clear, the wondrous glimpses of flora and fauna, physical landscapes and forces of nature revealed the hand of the Almighty at work. Newspaper pieces from all over agreed. Disney's work proved that "the Creator has a plan for all, no matter how mighty or humble," claimed a New York publication, while the St. Paul *Sunday Pioneer Press* contended that the films transported viewers into "a sphere where God's master plan for the existence of this planet is dramatically enacted every second of the day." A Los Angeles newspaper claimed that one could not see these films "without thrilling to the wonders of creation and feeling a deeper sense of awareness of the Creator who made them all and ordered their lives." And in 1955, for the first time in its history, the *Christian Herald* selected for picture of the year two films that did not have a distinctly religious theme: *The Living Desert* and *The Vanishing Prairie*. According to the citation, the movies were chosen because of their "adherence to Christian concepts of morality and dramatic inspiration." Nature, in Disney's hands, became another denomination in an American federation of religious institutions.[9]

Disney added to the True-Life Adventures an adventurous but less popular series entitled People and Places, which presented half-hour-long looks at a variety of cultures around the world, including those of Eskimos, Swiss mountaineers, Thai farmers, and many more. Full of exotic shots and breathtaking scenery, these movies sought to expand the geographical and cultural horizons of their audience. At the same time, however, they promoted American values and standards as the modern ideal. As Disney explained in a book accompanying the series, "modern ways" were relentlessly overtaking the globe. Traditional societies should be preserved, but mainly as artifacts. Customs not yet overwhelmed by "the march of progress" needed to be captured and explained before they vanished entirely. In his words, while the series sought to preserve traditional customs, "it seems that the laws of progress dictate that, in all things, the old must steadily give way to the new . . . Our purpose has been to capture and preserve these stories before they become only dim memories." Much like the nature documentaries, the People and Places series presented informative and often beautiful glimpses of little-known areas of the world, but ultimately these fascinating vistas served to affirm the superiority of the American way of life. As Disney explained in a 1954 piece in *Woman's Home Companion*, foreign cultures might be different in some ways, "but all these people live, work, fear, love as we do. At bottom, the human family is one."[10]

Disney's expedition into the natural world also expanded beyond the confines of the globe, rocketing through the earth's atmosphere with a series of television programs that probed the possibilities of exploring outer space. Then it bored inward to look at nuclear science, also on the *Disneyland* show. These productions were yet another kind of cultural exercise in Cold War America. Part patriotism, part demonstration of technological superiority, and part pep talk about building a superior life through science, they encouraged their audience to contemplate a bright future.

II. Americanizing Science

The Disney Studio came to the theme of outer space through an interesting chain of circumstances. From 1952 through 1954, *Collier's* ran a series of articles on the possibility of space exploration. Written by a group of expatriate German rocket scientists — Wernher von Braun, Willy Ley, and Heinz Haber — these essays discussed the benefits of and barriers to journeys out of the earth's atmosphere and included illustrations of rockets and space stations. In fact, the series was part of von Braun's larger crusade in the 1950s to promote manned space travel. Ward Kimball, who had gravitated from animation to television production by the mid-1950s, read the articles and found them fascinating. Around the same time, in Kimball's words, "Walt came to me and said, 'You guys are the modern thinkers around here' — probably using the term in a snide way. 'Can you think of anything we can do on 'Tomorrowland' [on *Disneyland*]?'" Kimball mentioned the space articles, Disney expressed interest, and a team went to work on developing a television production based on them.[11]

Kimball became the producer of the project, and he worked closely with layout man Ken O'Connor and sketch artist and writer Bill Bosche. The group began to develop a story line, work up storyboards, and hold brainstorming conferences. In addition, they quickly contacted the authors of the articles, who arrived at the studio as consultants within a few months. Von Braun, a bureaucratic operator and salesman supreme, leaped at the chance to reach millions of people through television, and his prototype of a four-stage rocket to launch humans into space became the foundation of the show. He also made quite an impression with his humor, showmanship, and flair, as when he dramatically strode to the piano in the early morning hours after an exhausting staff meeting and launched into a dramatic rendering of a Bach piece. The other two authors also signed on, the academic Haber utilizing his expertise in space medicine and the cigar-smoking, encyclopedic Ley lending advice on the development of space stations.[12]

This collaboration eventually resulted in the *Man in Space* series, three one-hour shows on space exploration. The first segment, "Man in Space," aired on March 9, 1955, and used animation, mockups, graphics, and newsreel footage to explain how rockets would blast human beings into orbit around the Earth. With Ley, Haber, and von Braun alternating as narrators, it provided information on such newfangled issues as space suits, information-gathering satellites, and the effects of weightlessness. "Man and the Moon," the second episode, followed on December 28, 1955, with an analysis of what a manned space flight to the moon might look like. Von Braun first outlined how a rocket-fueled spaceship would be followed by construction of an orbiting, wheel-shaped space station. Then a long, suspenseful simulation of an actual moon flight — part animation, part live action — brought the show to its dramatic conclusion. The third installment, "Mars and Beyond," appeared much later, on December 4, 1957. The most speculative program, it veered near the realm of science fiction with its imaginative description of possible life forms on the planet, Martian weather conditions, and von Braun's vision of a fleet of atomic-powered spaceships. This series was received so enthusiastically that the programs were rebroadcast in the late 1950s and then released theatrically as part of Disney film packages.

Typical of Disney's postwar educational productions, the *Man in Space* series blended information and humor, pedagogy and entertainment. In an April 17, 1954, staff conference on the project, Disney set the agenda:

There are two sides to go on this — comedy interest and factual interest. Both of them are vital to keep the show from becoming dry. You need a good balance to keep it from becoming too dry or corny. We don't want to compete with Sid Caesar or do that type of thing. We want to do something new on our show . . .

We are trying to show man's dreams of the future and what he has learned from the past. The history might be a good way to work in a lot of your laughs. People laugh at inventions of the past . . . because with the inventions and the progress of science today, people feel superior . . . [But] we have to watch it so the material doesn't get corny . . . I think this parallels the "True-Life Adventures" — [presenting] facts, and opening up this world to people.

Along these lines, the space shows indeed mixed serious scientific treatments of topics such as medicine and physics with humorous depictions of what Martians might look like and legendary fantasies about the moon.[13]

Even more pronounced, however, was the aura of progress, achievement, and conquest that enveloped the *Man in Space* shows. In his introduction to the first installment, Disney told viewers that the human race was "now at the threshold of a new frontier." Wernher von Braun reinforced this with a cheerful claim that "if we were to start today on an organized and well-supported space program, I believe a practical passenger rocket could be built and tested within ten years." The narratives themselves conveyed steady confidence about the capacity of science and technology to carry off these interplanetary exercises, leaving little doubt that space stations could be built, ingenious space suits could be designed, and dangers from radiation, meteorites, and extreme temperatures could be overcome by technical expertise. As the narrator for one of the segments concluded confidently, "Man has taken his first great stride forward in the conquest of space. His next goal will be the exploration of the moon, then the planets and the infinite universe beyond!" Disney too placed this endeavor within the larger story of human progress. "Man's trip to the moon," he claimed, "would be only a beginning for tomorrow's adventures in space."[14]

But true to the imperatives of Cold War culture, these productions also confidently assumed that *American* scientific expertise would lead the human caravan into outer space. The series' opening section culminated with an admiring look at various projects of the U.S. government in New Mexico, and the entire discussion thereafter assumed an American context. When the crew heads off on a lunar expedition in the "Man and the Moon" segment, for instance, they are obviously American, eating, joking, reading, and playing cards on the long journey. While the drawings and descriptions of the orbiting space station depict teams of scientists studying the weather and conducting a variety of experiments, the station also clearly houses military personnel and sophisticated technology to observe critical points around the globe. Ironically, even though viewers heard much of the message expressed with a heavy German accent, they had no choice but to conclude that American science was clearing the path for this remarkable extension of human capability.

Because of his preoccupation with the building of Disneyland in the early 1950s, Disney was less directly engaged with *Man in Space* than with most past studio projects. He participated in the initial story conferences and reviewed some of the early storyboards, but then stepped aside to give the staff free rein. Both in private and in public, however, he expressed great enthusiasm for the undertaking. In fact, he was so impressed that at the conclusion of one of the early planning meetings, according to an astonished employee, he tore off a blank sheet of notepaper, handed it to Ward Kimball, and made the unprecedented statement, "Write your own ticket!" Many months later, when attending the first screening of the series for employees, he reacted very positively, turning to Kimball and exclaiming, "How in the hell do you guys think up all that stuff?" In the series itself, of course, Disney personally introduced each segment with an inspiring commentary about the prospects for space exploration, a theme on which he elaborated in many public statements. In an interview with columnist Hedda Hopper, for example, he promoted the studio's space shows not only for their "science-factual" dimension but for their use of an animated figure named "Homo Sapiens Extra Terrestrialis . . . very much like Mr. Average American, who tries to adapt his ordinary living habits to conditions in outer space." "Through many centuries, man has slowly and adventurously explored the planet earth," he summarized in a book accompanying the series. "Now science has given man the equipment to turn his eyes toward space, to explore it with the same curiosity and courage which led him across uncharted seas and unknown lands."[15]

The critical reaction to *Man in Space* was both enthusiastic and revealing. The shows garnered praise for their educational content, of course, but the political response proved even more striking. Newspaper and magazine articles quickly focused on their implications of competition with the Russians. As a columnist argued in the Los Angeles *Herald & Express,* "Walt Disney may be America's 'Secret Weapon' for the conquest of space! Apparently, and quite by accident, he has discovered the trigger that may blast loose his country's financial resources and place the Stars and Stripes of the United States aboard the first inhabited earth satellite . . . Half of the voting population of the USA has probably reached two impressive conclusions: 'It CAN be done!' and 'Let's get on with it!'" Some speculated that "Man in Space" had helped influence President Eisenhower to announce a program to build Earth-circling satellites in the summer of 1955. By late 1957, when the "Mars and Beyond" segment was broadcast, the political atmosphere had darkened because of the recent Russian launch of its Sputnik satellite. Believing that they had fallen behind in the space race, nervous Americans greeted the show with open arms. Reviewers suggested that "in some respects Disney is ahead of the government" and urged citizens who were worried about Sputnik to tune in for reassurance about American capabilities. In the words of one nationally syndicated columnist, "The Russians may have gotten the jump on the United States with their high-flying Sputnik, but they didn't beat Walt Disney." "Man in Space" became a featured presentation at at least one important conference on international relations, and "Mars and Beyond" was screened by a gathering of scientists from Cal Tech and the Mount Wilson observatory. As one of the professors told reporters, "After what I've seen, I suggest the government turn its guided missile program over to Disney."[16]

Around the same time, *Our Friend the Atom* appeared. Developed in mid-decade, this project was first a studio-sanctioned book written by Heinz Haber and then an episode of *Disneyland*, broadcast on January 23, 1957. The program utilized many familiar elements from the space series: Disney's uplifting introduction; the combination of animation, graphics, and live action; and the use of Haber as host, narrator, and intellectual authority. Both the book and the television show began with the old tale from *Arabian Nights* about the fisherman who discovers a genie in a bottle, which became the governing metaphor for how a liberated powerful force must be put to peaceful uses. Up to this point, of course, the atom had been used primarily by the military because of its "frightening power of destruction, more fearful and devastating than man ever thought possible." But just as the genie had granted the fisherman three wishes, the Disney program suggested, atomic energy had provided a trio of prospects to improve the lot of humankind. With great optimism and a torrent of scientific information, *Our Friend the Atom* argued that atomic energy could be used profitably as an energy source, a means of combating disease and improving biological and agricultural engineering, and an instrument of peace. As Haber summed up, "It lies in our hands to make wise use of the atomic treasures given to us. The magic power of atomic energy will soon begin to work for mankind throughout the world. It will grant the gifts of modern technology to even the most remote areas. It will give more food, better health — the many benefits of science — to everyone."[17]

With his ardent belief in progress and faith in technological solutions, Disney evinced a genuine zeal for this project. In an interview he stated proudly, "We are going to show the atom as it has never been shown before. When most people think of atoms, they think of bombs. We'll show the limitless peaceful uses of atomic energy." And though a few critics complained that the show ignored the military and political dangers of nuclear power, many more sang its praises. The device used to demonstrate a chain reaction — some two hundred mousetraps with Ping-Pong balls balanced on their springs were set in a room, and the host tossed a ball into their midst, triggering a progressive explosion as the little spheres were sent flying in every direction — earned nearly unanimous approval.[18]

On a more serious note, most critics embraced the show's theme of technological progress and acclaimed its picture of a "wonderful world of tomorrow, in which the mighty atom will play an increasingly vital part in the daily lives of everyone." They also endorsed *Our Friend the Atom* for easing stress regarding this powerful force in the modern world. War and destruction were not inevitable, Disney seemed to be saying, and humankind could make intelligent choices about the use of nuclear energy. As a long piece in the New York *Telegraph* summarized, "The Genii has not yet been put back into the bottle . . . [and] most of us are still afraid of the chaos it might wreak. But the hope remains, the path is clear, and it rests with us to decide what to do."[19]

Despite such successes, perhaps the most spectacular example of Disney's success in tapping into the Cold War ethos came from a historical segment developed for *Disneyland,* the story of a frontiersman whose exploits had made him a national hero in nineteenth-century America. Disney's modest treatment of his life, to the amazement of everyone involved with the project, ignited a craze that swept through the United States like a firestorm.

III. Fess Parker: "Be Sure You're Right, Then Go Ahead"

In April 1955, Fess Parker, clad in the buckskins and coonskin cap made famous in his recent television role, went to Washington for a dinner honoring a retiring assistant secretary of defense. The actor had been asked to present a special rifle to the guest of honor as a memento and the Disney Studio approved the stop as part of a promotional tour. Early in the day, he attended a private luncheon with Speaker of the House Sam Rayburn, presidential candidate Estes Kefauver, and Senate majority leader Lyndon Johnson. Parker found himself sitting at the head table in a hotel dining room, next to a number of prominent political leaders, admirals, and generals. Initially he felt awkward because the crowd was dressed formally while he was in frontier garb. Then, when various dignitaries began to speak, sheepish men in tuxedos and smiling women in formal gowns started lining up in front of him to get his autograph, completely ignoring the speakers. Later, the embarrassed Parker managed to maneuver the crowd to the side of the room with a whispered promise to stay afterward and sign programs, and indeed he did linger much of the evening. As he recalled with a chuckle many years later, this incident provided one of the first hints that he had become part of something very big in 1950s America.[20]

That something, of course, was the Davy Crockett series on *Disneyland.*

The studio broadcast a trio of segments about the legendary American frontiersman in the 1954–55 season, and they elicited a tremendous response. Public acclaim grew so loud that Disney ignored the uncomfortable fact that his hero had been killed in the third segment and followed with two more episodes in the 1955–56 season, "Davy Crockett's Keelboat Race" and "Davy Crockett and the River Pirates." The popularity of these shows was so enormous that Disney, never averse to turning a profit, decided to edit and combine the segments into a pair of movie productions. These cinematic releases, in summer 1955 and summer 1956, triggered yet another outpouring of public enthusiasm.

But the tremendous popularity of the TV shows and movies marked only the first stage of a remarkable event in American popular culture. The "Davy Crockett craze," as one observer termed it, built up incredible momentum as it took off into the stratosphere. In many ways it paralleled the *Three Little Pigs* fad of the early 1930s, but it occurred on an even larger scale. The Crockett phenomenon became the centerpiece of a huge marketing campaign focusing on records, books, and a cornucopia of consumer items. It also became key to the Disney operation's promotion of its new endeavors in television and the amusement park. And the show prompted a tidal wave of publicity, all the way from stories in major news publications all over the country to speeches on the floor of Congress. National photo magazines ran multipage spreads on Davy Crockett's invasion of American culture and Fess Parker's triumphant tour before thousands of fans throughout the United States. A whimsical *New Yorker* cartoon satirized the fad, showing a pair of hard-bitten talent agents quizzically observing a comely young woman clad in a buckskin bikini and coonskin cap and carrying a long rifle and a powder horn as she cavorted about their office singing, "Davy, Davy Crockett . . ." As *Time* summarized it succinctly in May 1955, "Davy Crockett is bigger even than Mickey Mouse."[21]

The fad also produced a flood of merchandise. By summer 1955, around two hundred separate items had produced some $100 million in retail sales, and the trajectory was still headed skyward. As a magazine piece noted, "Youngsters have swooped down on U.S. stores like marauding Indians, snapping up everything in sight that faintly resembles what Davy Crockett wore." But the hunger did not stop with buckskin jackets, moccasins, and blue jeans. As another essay observed, "Items being made in Davy's name included bathing suits, jigsaw puzzles, pajamas, school lunch boxes, guitars. There are also plastic powder horns which some children are filling with their mother's face powder." Department stores in big cities marked off special Davy Crockett sections where young shoppers could play with an array of items while a barrage of advertisements tried to grab the attention of their weary mothers: "Your bathtime struggles are over . . . They'll run to use Davy Crockett towels!" A seven-page photo layout in *Life* showed suburban kids whooping and hollering and wielding new cap-firing pistols and flintlock rifles, storming backyard stockades and treehouses as they ecstatically refought the battle of the Alamo.[22]

The coonskin cap, of course, became the signature item of the craze. Modeled on the one worn by the Disney character — a furry oval sitting on top of the head, with the ringed tail hanging down the back — these caps became almost a religious icon for American children in 1955 and 1956. The fur industry enjoyed a heyday as raccoon pelts, selling for twenty-five cents a pound only a short time earlier, shot up to nearly five dollars a pound. Disney merchandisers found a California warehouse full of decrepit raccoon skins, and almost magically it became the source for Disney-approved hats under the direction of a licensed company. Rather quickly, however, the demand became so overwhelming that the available stock was exhausted and producers frantically began using wolf, rabbit, squirrel, or any other available pelts to cash in on the action. As one storekeeper noted sardonically, "Anything with hair on it moved." Eventually, more than ten million "coonskin" caps were sold.[23]

"The Ballad of Davy Crockett," the song from the TV show, became another unlikely craze. According to producer Bill Walsh, after shooting for the series had stopped, the studio discovered it didn't have quite enough footage to fill three sixty-minute segments. Disney suggested that they gather some drawings and sketches of Crockett's life and back them up with a song to provide some filler. It seemed a good idea, so Tom Blackburn, who wrote the script, and George Bruns, the studio composer, huddled around a piano in an office and came back a couple of hours later with a song. Said Walsh, "I thought it was pretty awful, but we didn't have time for anything else." To everyone's amazement, the catchy little tune with lyrics about the Crockett legend quickly soared to the top of the charts. Pop singer Bill Hayes quickly recorded a version that sold over two million copies and became the number-one hit for five weeks. Some sixteen other versions followed — recorded by Tennessee Ernie Ford, Eddie Arnold, Burl Ives, the Sons of the Pioneers, Steve Allen, Mitch Miller, Fred Waring and the Pennsylvanians, and even Fess Parker himself — which eventually made for combined record sales of seven million in six months. As the song took the country by storm, curious musical offshoots such as the Davy Crockett mambo began to crop up. Weary parents cynically began adding their own verses to "The Ballad of Davy Crockett," muttering, "Kilt him a b'ar when he was only three/And lost his mother at the A & P." By the summer of 1955, the refrain "Daveeee, Davy Crockett, king of the wild frontier" was as familiar to American children as "Who's afraid of the big, bad wolf?" had been to their parents two decades earlier.[24]

In 1955 and 1956, magazines and newspapers overflowed with publicity about every conceivable aspect of the Crockett phenomenon, from the filming of the series to the marketing of merchandise to Fess Parker's love life. Bearing titles such as "Davy Crockett, Disney Style," "Davy Crockett Lives Again," and "Woodsman in Washington," these breathless stories scattered tidbits of minutiae to eager readers across the country. In a related vein, an array of books began pouring into the market. Two new editions of Crockett's autobiography were rushed into print; an essay in *The New Yorker* by E. J. Kahn, Jr., surveyed the appearance of nearly a dozen biographies written for both juveniles and adults; and in 1956 the University of North Carolina Press published a scholarly work — actually a revised doctoral dissertation completed at Vanderbilt University in 1948 — that drew on historical sources to disentangle the real David Crockett from the legend.[25]

The Disney Studio fanned the flames by arranging frenzied promotional tours featuring Fess Parker, who inspired mob scenes similar to those greeting Elvis Presley, only with entire families instead of teenagers. At the height of the craze, the star went on a tour of twenty-two cities, where he greeted crowds numbering in the thousands, shook countless hands and signed countless autographs, and dedicated playgrounds and ballparks. The effect could be exhilarating, and Parker proclaimed publicly, "I'm having nothing but fun." But often the pressure could be overwhelming, and occasionally it was scary. In New Orleans, cars and people lined a twenty-five-mile stretch of road from the airport, slowing Parker's procession to a crawl. At other stops the milling crowds accidentally pushed through plate-glass windows in department stores and chased him down public streets when he tried to retire. Publicity agents stuck a guitar in his hands and had him sing "The Ballad of Davy Crockett" in front of thousands of people with bands he had never even seen before, or walked him out to speak extemporaneously before huge crowds. Adding to the stress was an endless list of dignitaries seeking to cash in on the craze. When Parker visited Washington, for example, photographers snapped pictures of him lifting Julie and Tricia Nixon, the young daughters of the vice president, into the air, and when he visited Nashville, Governor Frank G. Clement whisked him off to the executive mansion for a private audience with his own children. While Parker enjoyed meeting his adoring fans, especially the children, the process took its toll. "I was uncomfortable a lot. In fact, I was terrorized a lot of times," he confessed later. "It was not possible to go to a restaurant and have dinner unaccosted. In fact, at the height of it I couldn't leave my room."[26]

The intensity of the craze prompted a simple question: what lay behind the incredible appeal of this homespun character from frontier America? No one had expected such an explosion of popularity, and when it happened the Disney Studio was as surprised as anyone. As Disney admitted later, "We had no idea what was going to happen to Crockett . . . It became one of the biggest overnight hits in TV history, and there we were with just three segments and a dead hero." In part, the craze reflected the powerful appeal of the new medium of television. In part, its roots lay in people's nostalgic yearning for an earlier, simpler age, before factories, bureaucracies, big government, labor unions, and other institutions of modern industrial society made it more difficult for individuals to confront and solve issues directly. As Dr. Evalyn Mills of the National Council on Family Relations argued, Davy Crockett's popularity was "due to the restiveness of our whole society, [as] children today . . . require tangible evidence of human beings able to battle the problems of their time." At a more basic level, however, Crockett symbolized the American character in the death struggle with the Communist foe. Walt Disney, with his instinctive feel for cultural pressure points, half consciously shaped an ideal, reassuring representative of the American way of life as it faced a daunting challenge from without.[27]

Initial evidence of the Cold War connection appeared in the productions themselves. *Davy Crockett, King of the Wild Frontier* (June 1955), the movie made from the first three episodes of the television show, offered a multidimensional ideological portrait. First, the frontiersman was presented as a sturdy American individualist who made his own way in the world with his charm, his honesty, and his skill with a rifle. This Crockett was a self-sacrificing volunteer who chafed at army discipline but fought hard when it counted and ultimately became a military hero. He defended American expansion into the hinterland, although he insisted that it be done legally and favored negotiations with the Indians, and he fearlessly faced the foreign hordes at the Alamo as he went down fighting. A homespun folk hero, he stood proudly as the embodiment of a virtuous, jocular, but tough American manhood. Here was a Cold War icon who gave his life defending freedom, as the famous ballad proclaimed at the movie's end: "Davy Crockett, fighting for liberty."

But *Davy Crockett, King of the Wild Frontier* also presented a populist hero. In the narrative, Crockett enters public life accidentally when he defends ordinary pioneers on the Tennessee frontier by routing a gang of bullies and their leader, Big Foot Mason. The grateful populace first makes him a law-and-order magistrate in the community, then sends him off to Nashville as a state representative, and finally selects him to go to Washington as a congressman. The plainspoken Crockett becomes a representative of the untutored but virtuous common man, a defender of the little guy, and an opponent of political machination. In an ironic development, this Indian-fighting hero reaches the high point in his political career by championing Native Americans when avaricious forces seek to crush them utterly after the declaration of peace. Crockett's fight with Big Foot Mason, for instance, comes after Mason has stolen the property of his Cherokee neighbor, Charlie Two Shirts, a nefarious act that causes Davy to exclaim, "Injuns got rights. They're folks like anyone else." After entering Congress, he defends Indian interests against greedy and unscrupulous land-grabbers led by the powerful President Andrew Jackson. In a highly emotional speech, an outraged Crockett denounces such policies and gives up his congressional seat rather than surrendering to political expediency.

Disney's second film, *Davy Crockett and the River Pirates* (July 1956), which combined two more television segments, took the frontiersman's story into the realm of national mythology. The first Crockett film had gestured in this direction, and the lyrics of "The Ballad of Davy Crockett" enhanced his legendary aura. But in *Davy Crockett and the River Pirates,* he was elevated to the same plane as Paul Bunyan, John Henry, Johnny Appleseed, and other heroes of American lore. In this film Crockett tangled with Mike Fink, a burly braggart who crowned himself "king of the river," won his friendship during a race to New Orleans, and then joined forces with him to defeat an unscrupulous gang of thieves who were impersonating Indians to rob river travelers.

In 1950s America, this larger-than-life portrait made for an inspirational icon. When Parker visited Washington, D.C., for instance, newspapers all over the country carried wire-service photos of the actor, Sam Rayburn, and Lyndon Johnson standing shoulder to shoulder holding Ol' Betsy, a replica of the frontiersman's prize rifle. In Pittsburgh, Davy Crockett received numerous write-in votes for a variety of city offices and actually was elected judge of elections in one ward. He became such a national hero that children visiting the congressional statuary hall in Washington immediately gravitated to a buckskinned figure with coonskin cap and rifle, proclaiming, "I know him, that's Davy Crockett!" They refused to believe adults who told them that the statue depicted Dr. Marcus Whitman, who helped open up the Pacific Northwest in the 1840s. On the floor of Congress in May 1955, Representative Martin Dies of Texas invoked Davy Crockett as a symbol of American fortitude. Quoting Crockett, who once said that he "went for the good of the country and for that only," Dies insisted that if those inspiring sentiments "are practiced by you and me, the security, the liberty and happiness of the Republic would be insured for all generations to come." Congressman Bass of Tennessee and Congressman Jonas of North Carolina quickly chimed in, agreeing that the Crockett dictum "Be sure you're right, then go ahead" was a galvanizing creed for national affairs; they argued only that the frontier hero was really a native of their respective states, not Texas![28]

Fess Parker himself was aware of the Cold War dimension of the Crockett phenomenon. He sensed, in at least a vague way, that the enormous appeal of his character was connected somehow to America's position in the world. He lauded Crockett as a "great American who stands a head above everyone else" and compared him to "Teddy Roosevelt, who said 'Walk softly and carry a big stick.'" He reinforced this image by describing his own military service in terms of "the pride a man has in playing only a very small part in upholding his country's traditions." Years later Parker observed that the

Crockett show had probably inspired in young Americans feelings of patriotism and a desire to fight for freedom. He reflected that the show had appeared in a certain "moral context" in which, after the pain of the Korean conflict and other international threats, "people were maybe looking for some reaffirmation and Disney gave it to 'em." The Crockett character, he suggested, helped Americans define who they were in this period.[29]

Of course, some critics were quick to point out the discrepancy between the historical Crockett and the television/movie version. John Haverstick, for instance, published an essay in the *Saturday Review* that contrasted Disney's Davy, the virtuous legend, with historian Vernon L. Parrington's Davy, who was "an assertive, likeable, hard-drinking fellow who liked to shoot and brag — first among the smart alecks of the canebreaks." Other writers, leaning toward the liberal side of the political spectrum and still traumatized by McCarthyism, denounced the "real" Crockett as an uneducated, drunken lout. John Fischer, editor of *Harper's*, wrote a vitriolic essay entitled "The Embarrassing Truth about Davy Crockett," in which he accused the frontiersman of being a juvenile delinquent who went on to abandon his family, hire a substitute to fight for him in the Creek War, and avoid work at all costs. In Fischer's words, "He was never king of anything except maybe the Tennessee Tall Tales and Bourbon Samplers Association. When he claimed that he had shot 105 bears in nine months, his fellow tipplers refused to believe a word of it, on the sensible grounds that Davy couldn't count that high." Worried that the frontiersman could be used by the Republican party in the 1956 elections, Brendan Sexton, education director for the United Auto Workers, characterized Crockett as "not at all an admirable character." Murray Kempton, a labor columnist for the liberal New York *Post*, reviled him as a hard-drinking buffoon, a corrupt politician, a ravager of natural resources, and an apologist for eastern industrialists. Crockett, he sneered, was a frontier brawler "who profited far less than other promoters from the fraudulent character of his legend, and who certainly, in life as he has in death, served American industry well."[30]

Political conservatives and moderates rushed to Crockett's defense, as did some unlikely supporters. William F. Buckley argued that recent debunkings of this popular hero were a case of "resentment by liberal publicists of Davy's neuroses-free approach to life. He'll survive the carpers." Kenneth S. Davis, writing in the *New York Times Magazine*, insisted that Disney's portrayal of Crockett as a populist icon was essentially correct. "In Washington, [Crockett] displayed remarkable good sense and such rare moral courage," wrote Davis, "as to make him an authentic spiritual as well as physical American hero." An editorial in *Collier's* contended that critics of Crockett had missed the point. "Children don't select their heroes on the basis of the exact historical record," it opined. "Furthermore, the child is sometimes wiser than the grownups. It is he who makes the hero real . . . [and] he knows that the real hero is not Davy Crockett or Galahad, it is himself. It is he who is searching for the Holy Grail, the cup of gold, the rainbow's pot." Even the *Communist Worker,* pursuing a popular-front strategy, enlisted among the Crockett enthusiasts, insisting that "it is all in the American democratic tradition, and who said tradition must be founded on 100 per cent verified fact?" Popular opinion sided with the defenders of Disney's frontier character. Letters poured into the *Saturday Review* exclaiming, "Damn you, Jack Fischer!" and insisting that Crockett "represented a frontiersman of the highest caliber and fighter for the good of our country." The San Antonio *News* carried a banner headline proclaiming "*Harper's* Doesn't Have a Chance Against the Coonskin Kids" and reported that a survey of readers showed strong disapproval of Fischer's essay. In New York City, youthful pickets gathered outside the New York *Post* carrying signs that read "What did Murray Kempton ever shoot — except the bull???" and "Who you gonna expose next — Santa Claus?"[31]

Additional support for Davy Crockett's status came from Fess Parker himself, who emerged as an inspirational representative of his country's values. Parker grew up in San Angelo, Texas, and went to Hollywood after serving in the navy during the war and obtaining a degree from the University of Texas. Quite by accident, his big break came when he appeared in a small role in the science fiction movie *Them.* Disney happened to screen the film because he was interested in James Arness, who played the lead, for Davy Crockett. When he saw Parker's six-foot-five-inch frame, rugged good looks, and sincere manner, he brought the unknown young man to Burbank for an audition and then hired him to play the frontier hero.[32]

Filming the TV series proved to be something of an adventure. Parker grew frustrated with what he saw as vague direction, and his inexperience often got in his way. But he received generous help from such veteran actors as Basil Ruysdael, who played Andrew Jackson, and Buddy Ebsen, who played Crockett's sidekick, George Russel. Working on location, he had to wear heavy split-leather buckskins day after day, which presented a significant olfactory challenge. Later, a bear clawed him, his horse tripped while crossing a river and sent him flying into the water, he missed a mattress during a fight scene and fell down an embankment into a bramble bush, and he was grazed on the head by an arrow. "I got more patches on me than an old inner tube," he ruefully told a reporter in 1954, and he confessed that the film crew called him "Painless Parker."[33]

As the Crockett craze gathered steam, however, Parker became more confident and emerged as a role model. Radiating the same combination of sincerity, humility, and homespun confidence as the character he played, the Texan made numerous public statements reinforcing several themes. First, he presented a "plain folks" image that valued hard work, friendship, and sincerity. A spate of articles described him as an "aw-shucks type hero" and praised his modest "country boy manner and way of thinking," while his humility, in the approving words of one writer, was "a refreshing thing in the midst of the oversized egos of Hollywood." As Parker always insisted, his success showed that "if young people work hard in their chosen ambitions, stay at it, and try to help the friends who help them, they will find their reward as I did."[34]

Second, Parker became a spokesman for religious faith and family values. After returning from a tour of American cities, for example, he told a reporter of his admiration for "all those wonderful young mothers" who brought their children to stand in line and see him. Not surprisingly, he was deluged with questions about his romantic plans, and his careful replies revealed a bedrock commitment to traditional gender and domestic formulations: he was on the lookout for a young woman who was a "lady," who could cook and raise children, and who would "be willing to make a career out of marriage." Men should be the head of the household, he told interviewers. "I want to be the one to bring home the bacon," he declared. "And I hope she'll be plenty busy just taking care of me and our youngsters. I'm not looking for a glamour girl. I'll settle for a girl with warmth and honesty and a real sincerity about the important things like integrity and ideals." At every opportunity, Parker also noted his commitment to religious faith. While no proselytizer for any denomination or creed, he insisted that it was "important that a person keeps on tryin' to develop and maintain a spiritual belief."[35]

Third, the young Texan proudly offered himself as an antidote to one of the great maladies haunting American society in the 1950s — juvenile delinquency. As he toured, Parker loved meeting and being photographed with children. Many years later, he admitted his great sense of personal responsibility about setting a moral example to the thousands of youngsters who idolized him. More specifically, he announced in the mid-1950s his belief that "through 'Davy Crockett' I can perhaps be doing some good to combat juvenile delinquency." In interviews, he talked about a gang of street kids who showed up in Central Park as some publicity photographs were being taken. Parker made a point of talking to them and signing a few autographs, and when he left, "the toughest of them wanted to know how he could start a fan club. So we're getting through to them, letting them know what kind of a person Davy Crockett was." Parker also contributed a piece to the New York *Herald Tribune*'s Sunday magazine entitled "Our Kids Are Hero Hungry." In modern America, he argued, "hero-hunger . . . [is] a children's ailment. It's like vitamin deficiency, only it affects the development of character rather than the body." Davy Crockett, happily, was part of "the rediscovery of national heroes" and served as a wonderful example of the "historical do-or-diers who stake their lives for ideals." Now it was the responsibility of adults, Parker concluded, to "let our kids know where our *own* values lie, and that we prize these men — and women — far above mere fictitious heroes of impossible exploits."[36]

Parker's position as a conservative spokesman also helped polish his reputation as an upright role model. In 1957, for instance, he appeared as a keynote speaker at a rally held by the Citizens' Committee for Fair Taxation, a coalition of conservative groups protesting high taxes and government wastefulness. He also publicly supported groups such as the National Rifle Association, which he lauded for "the high aims it has for the youth of this country, both in sport and in defense of the nation." At the height of the Davy Crockett craze, Parker bought his first home, and as he proudly informed columnist Louella O. Parsons, "Uncle Sam made it possible on the G.I. Bill of Rights. You see, I was attached to the Marine Corps Communication Unit No. 42 and saw duty aboard a mine sweeper in the Philippines." Such images enhanced his image as a hardy, self-reliant, patriotic person and clearly helped position him as a virtuous ideal in a tense Cold War context. It was no accident that publications such as *Hudson Family Magazine* praised him as "a vital moral leader to America's youngsters" and "a living example of the best in American manhood." *Time* magazine, in a story entitled "Davy's Time," explained the tremendous popularity of the Disney hero as part of a newfound self-confidence emerging in Cold War America. As one of the magazine's correspondents wrote, "Davy Crockett is the epitome of a man who can lick any problem with his wits and his own two hands." To drive the point home, the essay featured a picture of a grinning, confident Parker and placed beneath it the caption "Let Moscow do its worst." Next to it was planted a photograph of President Eisenhower and Secretary of State John Foster Dulles conferring about defense of the nation's vital security interests.[37]

A powerful Cold War atmosphere in 1950s America summoned forth a flurry of fringed leather, coonskin caps, and plastic Kentucky long rifles midway through the decade. Crockett's famous saying from the Disney episodes — "Be sure you're right, then go ahead" — became a rhetorical emblem of what Americans wanted to believe about themselves in their global contest with communism. But the influence of international ideological conflict also worked in a quieter fashion. The United States' struggle with the threat of communism did not restrict itself to troubling political issues. In addition to prompting worries about citizenship and ideology, the Cold War raised anxieties over family stability, child-rearing practices, and the social fabric of a democratic society. It forced Americans to ponder issues of domestic security, in the literal sense of that phrase, and Walt Disney stepped forward once again as a mediator.

17

Disney and
Domestic Security

THE COLD WAR, as it grew in intensity throughout the 1950s, compelled Americans to define their fundamental social and political values. As one historian has put it, "The search to define and affirm a way of life, the need to express and celebrate the meaning of 'Americanism,' was the flip side of stigmatizing Communism." Literature and pulp fiction, movies and radio, intellectual essays and popular magazine pieces all contributed to this search. From *Partisan Review*'s 1952 symposium on "Our Country and Our Culture" to the *Saturday Evening Post*'s string of Norman Rockwell covers depicting innocent village life, from the cinematic cult of the western to publisher Henry Luce's pronouncements on "the American Century" in the pages of *Life* and *Time,* a welter of images and words tried to articulate the meaning of America.[1]

In overarching fashion, numerous cultural commentators stressed the pragmatic, nonideological nature of the American political tradition. "The genius of American politics," historian Daniel J. Boorstin wrote in 1953, lay in its historical devotion to problem-solving and democracy and its aversion to theory. The contrast with communism could not have been clearer. Within a happily constituted civic life of utilitarianism and common sense, many observers argued, a cluster of characteristically American traits had flowered.[2]

Abundance and material prosperity appeared to many as an article of faith in 1950s America. Intellectuals such as David Potter, in *People of Plenty: Economic Abundance and the American Character* (1954), and John Kenneth Galbraith, in *The Affluent Society* (1958), offered powerful reflections on this theme, while Vice President Richard Nixon wielded statistics about American production of automobiles, televisions, radios, and washing machines as he slashed away at Soviet premier Nikita Khrushchev during the famous "kitchen debate" in Moscow in 1959. From the first credit card, offered by Diners' Club in 1950, to the debut of the Barbie doll in 1958, with her carefully packaged array of dresses, casual outfits, sports cars, wigs, and jewelry, consumption described an essential part of American life. It also promised a self-fulfilled personality. Advertising claimed that the purchase of consumer goods would boost status and romantic possibilities; child-rearing literature enjoined parents to cultivate their children's natural curiosity; success manuals such as Dale Carnegie's *How to Win Friends and Influence People* instructed eager readers to develop a winning style in interpersonal relationships. Cultural messages urged Americans to promote, in the words of one historian, "psychic and physical health defined in sweeping terms."[3]

A warm, comforting blanket of nondenominational spirituality was draped over the consensus of pragmatic politics, abundance, and personal fulfillment. Dwight Eisenhower proclaimed from the White House that American government must be "founded on a deeply felt religious faith, and I don't care what it is." Cecil B. DeMille released a popular string of biblical epics and FBI director J. Edgar Hoover urged Sunday school attendance in his best-selling book, *Masters of Deceit.* Urged on by immensely popular preachers such as Billy Graham and Norman Vincent Peale, pious Americans pictured themselves standing shoulder to shoulder against the forces of godless communism.[4]

Yet this powerful Cold War consensus masked an array of internal tensions. From Dwight Macdonald's warnings about "the tepid, flaccid middle-brow culture that threatens to engulf everything in its spreading ooze" to the critiques of crass, corporate commercialism offered by William H. Whyte and Vance Packard, to David Riesman's analysis of the corrosive effects of mass society on individual initiative and integrity, many intellectuals presented stinging criticisms of America's culture of abundance. The stirrings of the civil rights movement in the South and sporadic wildcat strikes in northern factories hinted at the racial and class fault lines beneath the imposing structure of material progress. A bohemian rejection of American consumerism flourished among urban Beats, while the growing popularity of country music, blues, and rock-and-roll suggested submerged alienation. Women's discontent over their tightly restricted roles slowly simmered in suburban subdivisions. Perhaps most pervasively, solid Middle Americans worried that the nation's social tranquillity was in danger from juvenile delinquency, rock-and-roll, manipulative advertisers, and beatniks. In a tense setting, such internal moral and social divisions posed no small threat.[5]

In the early 1950s, McCarthyism succeeded in silencing criticism and stifling debate over national values. Yet the very success of McCarthyism demanded a receptive populace. As one historian has put it, the hegemony of Americanism in this period required "not manipulation but legitimation." So a key question remains unanswered: how did commitments to pragmatic interest-group politics, a sentimental view of a homogenous American people, a nondenominational religiosity, a faith in technological expertise, and a belief in individual fulfillment attract widespread loyalty in 1950s America?[6]

One of the most important ways, especially at the level of popular culture, was through Walt Disney. The Burbank magician helped shape America's Cold War self-image, but the process was a complex, even ambivalent one. Disney moved deftly to preserve American individualism while embracing modern bureaucratic productivity, to preserve America's small-town virtues while promoting its role as a major world power, and to urge enjoyment of modern consumer goods while avoiding the dangers of conformity and moral dissolution. Using his cinematic niche as a base of operations, he engaged in a far-flung campaign to articulate the American way of life. Shrewdly, he focused on the American family. Relying on his instincts, he knew that domestic issues lay at the heart of his society's ideals and anxieties.[7]

I. The Disney Doctrine

In 1953, Walt Disney contributed an interesting essay to *American Magazine*. Entitled "What I've Learned from the Animals," it presented his thoughts on the True-Life Adventure series, dwelling on animals' incredible sense of "family devotion and parental care," especially among females:

> Take the care and raising of young birds, for example. Nowhere else do we find more hard-working and sympathetic mothers during the egg-hatching and forced-feeding period, nor more stern and unyielding ones when the time for independence has arrived . . . In spite of what I've said about the devotion of female birds to their young, I think that bears are the best mothers. Photographing in the wilds of Montana and Wyoming, we spied on Mrs. Black Bear, handsome in her fine fur coat, for the better part of two seasons. We saw her come out of her winter cave with two fat little cubs and begin their education. Father Bear had nothing to do with the rearing of his youngsters. But Mrs. Bear stayed with her kids two years, taught them where to find food, hugged them with affection, cuffed them

when they were unruly, and brought them up a credit to her name and to bear society.[8]

These musings suggest that like many Americans in the postwar era, Disney had become preoccupied by family issues in thinking about social cohesion. As a special 1954 issue of *McCall's* informed its readers, domestic togetherness was crucial to the new age of abundance. The most impressive feature of American consumption, education, and travel was that "men, women and children are achieving it *together*. They are creating this new and warmer way of life not as women *alone,* or men *alone,* isolated from one another, but as a *family* sharing a common experience." Behind this idealization of the family lay several concrete social influences — a drop in the average age at marriage, a decline in the divorce rate, and a rise in the birthrate, to its highest point in the twentieth century. The government had created unprecedented support for the family with the G.I. Bill of 1944, which made low-interest mortgage loans available to young families, and the Housing Act of 1949, which provided financial incentives to contractors to build single-family houses. Even more important was a powerful cultural movement to link domestic life to a set of compelling images — the suburban home as an emblem of abundance and locus of consumption, private life as the training ground for virtuous citizenship, the family as the mold for the individual's vibrant personality and self-fulfillment.[9]

Against this backdrop, Disney's persistent engagement with an array of domestic issues produced a powerful social resonance. It resulted in what might be called the Disney Doctrine: a notion that the nuclear family, with its attendant rituals of marriage, parenthood, emotional and spiritual instruction, and consumption, was the centerpiece of the American way of life. Illustrated through a long string of productions, this idea became a bulwark in America's defense against enemies, both foreign and domestic.

Interestingly, Disney's earlier, animated films had betrayed a pointed ambivalence about domestic security. Almost invariably, family units had been splintered, and those that appeared intact seldom existed in a state of tranquillity. For both Mickey and Minnie Mouse and Donald and Daisy Duck, for instance, an awkwardly defined relationship suggested cohabitation but explicitly rejected marriage, and children who appeared in these cartoons were orphans or distant relatives rather than real offspring. Moreover, the protagonists of feature films such as *Pinocchio, Dumbo,* and *Bambi* were typically orphans or children otherwise isolated from their families, desperately insecure and frantically searching for stability. But in the atmosphere of Cold War America, Disney modified his emphasis. His films continued to portray threats to family integrity, but the dangers were increasingly blunted or trivialized, and they appeared mainly as a pretext for the triumph of domestic stability at story's end.

Disney also began to develop a new, highly self-conscious emphasis on the *concept* of family entertainment. A special 1954 issue of the *Motion Picture Herald*, for example, informed readers that "Walt Disney believes the motion picture's first obligation to itself and its public is to be true to the American family without deviation." In public statements, Disney sprinkled his comments with allusions to the family focus of his entertainment vision. He described the evolution of movies in the twentieth century as a process wherein "mass entertainment began to take hold of American families" and announced that this genre, when developed by the right hands, "need never stale for the family taste." He asserted his dedication to enhancing "the sanctity of the home . . . [and] all that is good for the family and for our country." While other Hollywood studios aimed at more sophisticated or prurient tastes, Disney's famous sentiment that he never made a movie that he didn't want his family to see gradually became an article of faith among the American public.[10]

The studio's animated shorts, for instance, began to depict familiar Disney characters in new ways. These heretofore rural or urban sprites, often forced to scratch out a living, now were magically transformed into prosperous suburbanites with humorous stories rooted in domestic situations. Whereas movies such as *Window Cleaners* (1940), *The Riveter* (1940), and *Bellboy Donald* (1942) had portrayed Donald Duck as an urban worker, the 1950s saw the emergence of a domesticated, middle-class, fatherly fowl. The duck's short films increasingly revolved around his comic misadventures with his nephews Huey, Louie, and Dewey, as in *Spare the Rod* (1954), where Donald gets a lesson in child psychology. *Donald's Diary* (1954) displays a suburbanized Donald wrestling with the question of marriage to his sweetheart, Daisy Duck. Such short films as *Inferior Decorator* (1948), *The Greener Yard* (1949), and *The New Neighbor* (1953) took their humor from his encounters with the vexations of modern suburban life — home furnishing, lawn care, and neighborly relations.

Goofy became a suburban family man even more dramatically. His 1950s cartoon shorts presented him as a well-meaning but not too bright father confronting a series of family difficulties: in *Get Rich Quick* (1951), a scolding wife who confiscates all of his winnings from a poker game; in *Fathers Are People* (1951), a mischievous offspring who puts him through the wringer of parenthood; in *Two Weeks Vacation* (1952), the unexpected difficulties of finding genuine relaxation; and in *Father's Weekend* (1953), the pitfalls of spending a "restful" Sunday afternoon with the family. Fleeing the big city or streaming in from the countryside like thousands of their flesh-and-blood fellow Americans, Disney's animated characters settled into subdivisions to enjoy the fruits of American abundance. As suburban knights, Goofy and Donald ventured forth from their split-level castles to do battle with an array of new enemies — lawn pests and annoying neighbors, vacation vexations and family psychodramas, recalcitrant wallpaper and a rambling golf swing.

Disney's feature-length animated films in this period relied less on gags and suburban settings and offered a more complex picture of subversive forces facing the family. They focused on the fierce struggle often required to preserve its integrity and stability. In *Cinderella*, a cruel stepmother and scheming stepsisters torment the young heroine with degrading labor and emotional abuse, creating a hellish domestic scene which brightens only when a fairy godmother and a host of animal friends maneuver her toward marriage and family bliss. In like fashion, *Sleeping Beauty*'s trio of good fairies try to give Princess Aurora a semblance of normal family life while protecting her against the machinations of an evil fairy, and after many crises they eventually succeed in moving the young woman into a love match with her betrothed.

Another pair of Disney animated features from the 1950s were less mythic in form. Utilizing a format that substituted dogs for humans, these whimsical stories explored many of the disruptions of modern domestic life. *Lady and the Tramp* (1955) followed an upper-class female canine and her adventurous romance with a roguish male dog from the wrong side of town. Lady is evicted from the warmth of her family home when a mean aunt takes a dislike to her during her owners' absence, and the rakish Tramp valiantly saves her from a series of dangerous scrapes. The plot resolves itself when the two marry, settle down, and produce a quartet of puppies. *One Hundred and One Dalmatians* (1961) offered a defense of family virtue under threat from an evil, greedy villainess. Pongo and Perdita, two love-struck dalmatians, maneuver their single owners into a romance, and when the two humans marry, the dogs follow suit. A litter of puppies arrives in a short time, but this domestic felicity is destroyed when a scheming family friend, Cruella de Vil, kidnaps the puppies to make a spectacular fur coat. When the police are unable to help, the dogs take things into their own paws, and a canine network eventually locates the puppies in an abandoned country estate. After a hair-raising escape, the human and dog families are reunited.

The studio's live-action films from this period, contrary to the sugary Disney stereotype, also stressed the precarious nature of domestic well-being. These movies frequently pictured families as incomplete, harsh, occasionally abusive, and usually struggling to survive in one form or another. *So Dear to My Heart* (1948), for instance, concerned a young orphan who lived alone with his grandmother as they toiled on a small homestead. *The Littlest Outlaw* (1957) based its story on a ten-year-old who runs away from his cruel stepfather, while *Westward Ho the Wagons* (1956) showcased a wagon train of families who faced the onslaught of hostile Indians as they journeyed across the frontier. The protagonist of *The Light in the Forest* (1958), Johnny Butler, was a white youth who grew up among the Delaware Indians and found returning to his real parents an excruciating experience. In *Toby Tyler* (1959), yet another orphaned boy ran away to join the circus after being harshly treated by an abusive uncle. These tales of families under duress, however, always ended in reconciliation and healing as the characters found some semblance of domestic stability. And therein lay the great strength of Disney's domestic ideology in the 1950s: it resulted not so much from saccharine platitudes about togetherness as from a recurring dynamic of hard-fought achievement, where the family prospered only after struggling to overcome the most daunting challenges. Disney's Cold War audience seemed to be seeking, and finding, the gratifying message that while obstacles to family solidarity certainly loomed, they could be overcome by sustained, virtuous effort.

Disney's family ideology also gained considerable power from its gender formulations. In many of his 1950s films, the male characters carved out a domain within a consensus that was protective of family and hearth but clearly positioned outside it. The idealized female characters, however, were self-sacrificing moral instructors, skilled domestic managers, and compassionate caregivers. Yet, contrary to the stereotype, Disney did not offer a simple, saccharine female model characterized only by subordination, primness, and domestic imprisonment. His heroines, clearly dealing from a position of moral strength in the domestic realm, were not only physically attractive and even sexy in a subtle and wholesome way, but also frequently assertive and individualist as they defended and promoted their own interests. In Disney's films, women certainly presided over the family sphere, but they were not afraid to venture into the public realm when duty called.[11]

Idealized images of women as wives, mothers, and active moral agents were strewn throughout Disney's animated films in this era. In *Lady and the Tramp*, for example, a movie filled with appropriately stereotypical names, a demure wife named Darling cooks and cleans, sews, looks after her businessman husband, and generally appears "the epitome of the ideal American housewife of the 1950s," even though the story is set in 1910. She also dotes on her dog, Lady, who quickly becomes the canine guardian of the family's infant. After a series of harrowing adventures, Lady not only tames her rascally male suitor but becomes the proud mother of her own brood. Similarly, *One Hundred and One Dalmatians* presented the pretty and personable Anita as the owner of a female dog, Perdita, both of whom marry and settle into domestic harmony. While Perdita becomes a proud mother, she also proves unafraid to help with the heroic, dangerous rescue of her puppies after their kidnapping.[12]

In contrast with the girlish appearance and prepubescent sensibility of earlier protagonists such as Snow White, Disney's animated females in the 1950s also began to display a noticeable, if wholesome, sex appeal. *Peter Pan*'s Tinker Bell, for example, not only "throws off star dust in the proper tradition, but she is also a particularly endearing little vixen compounded of blond hair, feminine curves, and a pout," noted a *Newsweek* reporter, "and just a little too bosomy to squeeze through an oversized keyhole." Disney claimed in a newspaper article that Tinker Bell's full figure had been inspired by the popularity of the sexpot actress Marilyn Monroe.[13]

Perhaps the clearest animated image of the Disney female came early in the decade with *Cinderella,* the 1950 film that helped reestablish the studio's reputation. Its heroine was, quite simply, the ideal American woman of the period. Many articles described her as a young woman with a keen awareness that "matrimony was the object" of female endeavor. After observing how she appeared to be pursued by while actually pursuing Prince Charming, one writer suggested that "if Cinderella is honest — and she has all the noble virtues — she will, like all honest girls should, admit that at least she 'inspired' the proposal." As another piece observed, such feminine wiles were attractively packaged in an "athletic type" who was pretty without being a dazzling beauty. In interviews, Disney Studio artists admitted that certain characteristics had been drawn into this figure: "We didn't want to make her a 'sweater girl,' but her curves are obvious and correctly placed ... We want her to appeal to all women. Thus she can be neither too beautiful nor too homely. We want her to be a universal type, so any woman looking in a mirror will see something of Cinderella in herself . . . We gave her spunk. In the books, her fairy godmothers made things too easy for her. We made her problems tougher and gave her the guts to go after what she wanted." Cinderella, one critic concluded bluntly, was "the ideal American girl." The Disney Studio not only knew this but exploited it handsomely. The movie character inspired a whole line of clothing for young women: "With laced-up basque tops, puffed peplums that look like quaint overskirts, with ruffles and full skirts, this line of dresses hits a little girl just where her fairy tale heart is." Moreover, in early 1950, Disney officially sanctioned a series of contests in cities around the United States to find local Cinderellas. Publicity for the one held in Chicago stressed that the winning candidate "must have character, personality, charm. It is not just beauty. It can be a cheerful disposition, a friendly helpful nature or a particular talent for making others happy."[14]

Throughout the 1950s, the studio populated its movies with vivid countertypes to illustrate persistent threats to the feminine ideal. The animated features presented a gallery of villainous women whose baleful behavior explicitly violated every postwar standard of proper womanly conduct. They rejected domestic duty, and their public actions were selfish and corrupt. In *Cinderella,* for example, the haughty, cunning stepmother treats the young heroine as a slave, while the stepsisters are spoiled, selfish, shrill, and mean. Maleficent, from *Sleeping Beauty,* had a more striking impact. This tall, thin, black-clad evil fairy hates everything virtuous, commands a squadron of goons to do her dirty work, and literally transforms into a dragon to fight Prince Phillip. Cruella de Vil, with her wild shock of black-and-white hair and twirling cigarette holder, is a wealthy, sleazy sophisticate who kidnaps children, commits robbery, disrupts family peace, and generally destroys anything smacking of secure domestic life. These animated antiheroines not only frightened and disgusted but reinforced the idealized standard of female virtue. Once again, rather than simply displaying an ideal, Disney's films stressed that it must be the result of hard-fought achievement.

Disney's live-action films in this era offered similar portraits of female domestic virtue triumphing under duress. These films, however, almost always showcased strong male protagonists, so the female characters usually appeared in supporting roles. *So Dear to My Heart* and *Old Yeller,* for instance, both set in rural America in the late nineteenth century, presented warm maternal figures for whom family goals were uppermost. In the former movie, Granny Kincaid is a pious, widowed, motherly type overflowing with love for her energetic grandson. Her activities embody domestic endeavor — spinning, butter churning, doing housework, and issuing stern moral instructions to her young charge. At the same time, however, she determinedly confronts the workaday world, as in the movie's opening scene, where she plods along behind her mule, plowing the fields on her homestead. In *Old Yeller,* the frontier mother, Katie Coates, manages the family farm in Texas while her husband is away for several months. Not only does she feed and care for her two young sons, but she steps forward to manage the crisis that ensues when their beloved dog becomes rabid. Domestic moralists unafraid to venture into the public world, these hardy women struggle against daunting odds to fulfill expectations.

Perhaps the most fascinating portrayal of Disney's Cold War domestic ideology came from a young woman whom he elevated to stardom. Hayley Mills, the daughter of a prominent family of English thespians, was discovered by Disney when he saw her in a movie starring her famous father, John Mills. Her sparkling yet unspoiled personality and vibrant screen presence made a powerful impact on him, and he immediately envisioned her as the lead in *Pollyanna,* which was slated for production and release in 1960. Based on the 1911 Eleanor H. Porter novel, this live-action movie told the story of an orphan who arrives to live with her wealthy aunt in the small town of Harrington at the turn of the century. Pollyanna is determined to see the bright side of life — playing what she calls "the glad game" — and her engaging personality soon triggers a wholesale reform of this cramped Victorian village. A hypochondriac old woman is revitalized, a crotchety hermit adopts an orphan, the local minister exchanges his hellfire-and-damnation style for encomiums to the positive joy found in the Bible, and the icy spinster, Aunt Polly, moves toward reconciliation with her old beau, Dr. Chilton. At the movie's conclusion, a banner hung from the local train station reads "Harrington — The Glad Town."

While studio spokesmen stressed *Pollyanna*'s appeal for people of all ages, newspaper stories and reviews placed it at the cutting edge of a happy trend in Hollywood. One described it as "a family entertainment of rare wholesomeness," while another asserted bluntly, "Everyone keeps talking about the need for 'family' pictures. Well, here it is." This appeal framed the film's broadest cultural theme — a rejection of old-fashioned, rigid Victorian morality in the name of openness, optimism, fun, and personal happiness. With its invocations of the "glad game," this Disney film pushed a version of positive thinking, the popular socioreligious philosophy associated with one of the great moral icons of Cold War America, Norman Vincent Peale.[15]

Moreover, even though set at the turn of the century, the movie painted a compelling portrait of the modern female ideal. Pollyanna, an explicitly post-Victorian heroine, is a domestic moralist who bravely ventures out to become an active agent in society. She is, as one reviewer wrote, no pristine moral scold but "a less cloying type . . . who is naive but strangely discerning about problems besetting her elders." In fact, the movie's director, David Swift, confirmed that the Disney Studio explicitly updated the moral tone of the novel. The original book, he explained, had been so sentimentally optimistic that "your stomach turns over a little . . . The day when women would sit around at night, reading and crying, is finished. Pollyanna has to be made more palatable." He added, "We've simmered her cheerfulness down to merely emphasize the things-could-be-worse attitude." Pollyanna's modern cast was most apparent, of course, in the ongoing juxtaposition of her with her aunt, who eventually succumbs to her charms and embraces a vision of marriage and domestic happiness.[16]

Appropriately, Hayley Mills emerged from this cinematic exercise as "America's sweetheart," in the language of one admiring journalist. During the making of *Pollyanna*, Disney contributed no small amount to creating an idealized image of the actress. In a widely publicized statement, he proclaimed, "In my opinion, that little lady is the finest young talent to come into the motion picture industry in the past twenty-five years." A torrent of popular newspaper and magazine stories portrayed Mills as an earnest, pretty, unspoiled, and personable young woman who was full of didactic moralism but also an active "modern" girl. Journalists reassured readers that Mills's mother always purchased clothes for her, that she had never been on a date alone, that she avoided excessive makeup, and that she considered herself cute but not beautiful. This image of upright, modest character was leavened by disclosures that she had fallen in love with rock-and-roll, particularly Elvis Presley, and that her mother had talked to her "about the dangers of premarital sex and left it at that — with complete confidence in her daughter's intelligence and sense of morality." In interviews, young Mills opined that the original Pollyanna was "too sickeningly sweet. If you met any girl like that today, you'd want to kick her in the pants." In contrast, her movie character was optimistic but "a real girl, too. She can stick out her tongue when she is angry. She is much more believable." As one movie magazine summarized approvingly, Mills "still wanted to be 'a mother' when she grew up, but she also wanted to be an actress." With this combination of domestic zeal and worldly engagement, Hayley Mills emerged as an ideal woman-in-training for postwar America.[17]

Appropriately, this young actress went on to play the leading role in Walt Disney's ultimate expression of domestic ideology, *The Parent Trap* (1961). Instead of the usual historical setting, it was situated squarely in the contemporary American scene. Hayley Mills plays Sharon and Susan, two girls who meet at summer camp, bicker with one another even while noticing that they look remarkably alike, and finally discover they are identical twins who were separated when their parents divorced. Yearning to see both parents and eager to facilitate a reconciliation, they hatch a plot to switch places at the end of the summer. After several weeks, the twins finally confess their subterfuge, and the mother is forced to bring her charge to California to sort things out. With their father on the verge of remarrying a younger woman, the girls' matchmaking focuses on a family camping trip, where they succeed in driving away their father's fiancée. At this point the parents finally realize how much they still love each other, and a joyful reconciliation of the whole family brings the film to a happy close.

Although a comedy, *The Parent Trap*, more than any other Disney film, explored explicitly and seriously the threat to the Cold War American family. Drawing on broad fears of social and cultural decay, the backdrop for its amusing action was in fact rather grim — divorced parents, unhappy children, domestic disarray. This splintering of the family became the dramatic raison d'être of *The Parent Trap* and a premise for preaching Disney's domestic gospel.

The opening titles, even with their light touch, clearly established an atmosphere of domestic trauma. Two animated cupids hold up a framed sampler that reads "Bless Our (Broken) Home." This theme recurs time and again. Early in the movie, after the twins have discovered their sisterhood and are talking about their parents, one opines, "It's scary the way nobody stays together anymore these days. Pretty soon there's going to be more divorces than marriages." The other replies, "Isn't that the truth!" After the twins' ruse has been discovered, a poignant scene features Susan ruefully telling her newfound mom the social facts of life. Probably the best she can hope for, she confesses, is a "six-month split. A lot of the kids at camp have that problem — six months with one parent and six with another. Like a yo-yo."

As part of its valiant effort to rescue the Cold War family, *The Parent Trap* reinforced gender expectations. True to form, Mitch, the father, conforms to the postwar male image of hardworking provider and family man. A rough-hewn, honest outdoorsman who falls short on social graces, this successful California rancher adores his children and eventually discovers his repressed love for his wife. Vicky, Mitch's fiancée, is a kind of female villain. A gold-digger on the prowl, she dresses in flashy clothing, dyes her hair, and smokes cigarettes. Maggie, Mitch's ex-wife, could not be more different. She is naturally beautiful but modest, so much so that she must be persuaded to shop for new clothes and to get a new hairstyle before the trip to California. Genteel and domestic, she spends a great deal of time with her daughter and charity work. Maggie, however, does not lack assertiveness. After getting into a shouting match with her ex-husband soon after her arrival in California, she actually punches Mitch so hard that he spends the rest of the film with a black eye. To highlight the contrast, Maggie makes clear her loathing for Vicky. In public, she artfully undermines the young woman's base motives for marriage, while in private she scathingly describes her as "the child bride with the electric hips."

In the end, of course, the twin daughters are the key figures in *The Parent Trap*. They light up the screen as energetic young women determined to regain domestic security. They represent a social ideal — polite but assertive, respectful of parental authority but willing to circumvent it in the larger interests of saving the family, highly moral but thoroughly modern (one comic scene has Sharon gently explaining to her flustered father that she already knows about sex). Significantly, these attractive teenagers model themselves on their mother and hate their prospective stepmother. In the final analysis, they work hard and shrewdly to surmount a variety of daunting challenges and maneuver their parents into reconciliation and family reunion.

The Parent Trap's happy ending underlined the key elements in Disney's persistent rendering of 1950s family life: threat, vigorous defense, and revitalized stability. With its moral lesson that even the most divided families can regain stability and create happiness for all, *The Parent Trap* embodied Disney's domestic doctrine in the postwar era. The movie's final image ties the ideological package together quite neatly — the animated cupids hover over the original sampler and change its message to read "Bless Our Happy Home."

Throughout the postwar era, Walt Disney's films stood as a beacon of domestic security, sending out gentle warnings and encouragements to guide their audience. As part of his cultural labors in support of the American family, however, the filmmaker took special pains to address children. In explicit and self-conscious ways, he moved to become an educator and moral guide for America's youth. This became a central part of his family

Walt tinkering with his beloved miniature steam train in the back yard of his Holmby Hills residence in the late 1940s. The passengers are Mrs. Ward Kimball, Ward Kimball, and Roger Broggie.

Lillian, Walt, Diane, and Sharon on their return from a trip to Europe, 1949.

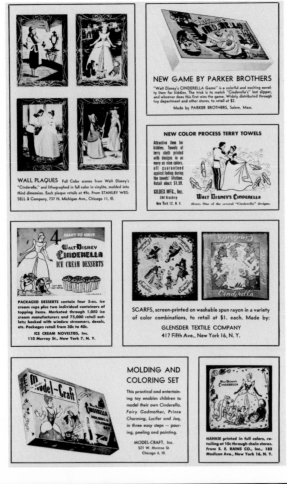

As this advertisement demonstrates, all kinds of licensed merchandise increasingly accompanied the release of a Disney film — in this case, Cinderella, *in 1950.*

In the early 1950s, Walt began exploring opportunities in the new field of television. He was accompanied by CBS vice president Adrian Murphy when he toured the CBS studios in New York in 1951.

Walt playfully holding up a stagecoach full of children at the Burbank studio while Disneyland was under construction, 1954.

An aerial view of Disneyland in the summer of 1955, when it opened. The vast amusement park was created on 160 acres in Anaheim, California.

Walt testified before the House Un-American Activities Committee in 1947.

Our purposes are to uphold the American way of life, on the screen and among screen workers; to educate, not to smear.

We seek to make a rallying place for the vast, silent majority of our fellow workers; to give voice to their unwavering loyalty to democratic forms and so to drown out the highly vocal, lunatic fringe of dissidents; to present to our fellow countrymen the vision of a great American industry united in upholding the American faith.

These are our purposes. We have no others.

MOTION PICTURE ALLIANCE FOR THE PRESERVATION OF AMERICAN IDEALS

OFFICERS
SAM WOOD, President

WALT DISNEY, First Vice-President	LOUIS D. LIGHTON, Secretary
CEDRIC GIBBONS, Second Vice-President	CLARENCE BROWN, Treasurer
NORMAN TAUROG, Third Vice-President	GEORGE BRUCE, Executive Secretary

EXECUTIVE COMMITTEE
JAMES K. McGUINNESS, Chairman

GORDON CHASE	FRED NIBLO, JR.	HARRY RUSKIN
CARL COOPER	OSCAR S. OLDKNOW	MORRIE RYSKIND
VICTOR FLEMING	CLIFF REID	JOSEPH P. TUOHY
ARNOLD GILLESPIE	WALTER A. REDMOND	KING VIDOR
FRANK GRUBER	CASEY ROBINSON	ROBERT M. W. VOGEL
RUPERT HUGHES	HOWARD EMMETT ROGERS	GEORGE WAGGNER
BERT KALMAR	LELA E. ROGERS	

In the late 1940s, the Motion Picture Alliance for the Preservation of American Ideals explained its goals with this announcement, which listed Walt Disney as its first vice president.

Fess Parker, dressed in his Davy Crockett buckskins, talking to two young admirers in coonskin hats, 1956.

Producer Bill Walsh admiring the view in Paris in 1961, during the filming of Bon Voyage.

Among the many famous visitors to Disneyland were the shah of Iran and the empress Farah, here enjoying the Matterhorn ride with Walt and a park hostess in 1962.

The cover story in the December 31, 1962, Newsweek surveyed the rapidly expanding scope of the Disney enterprise.

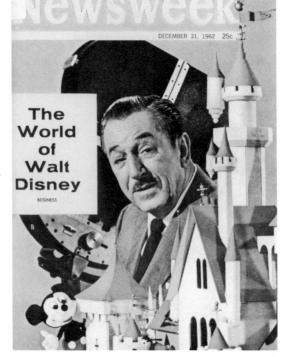

Walt and WED staff members experimenting with balloons from "It's a Small World, After All," the Disney-built attraction for Pepsi-UNICEF at the 1964 World's Fair.

Walt working with WED engineers on the Audio-Animatronic figure of Abraham Lincoln, 1964.

John Hench, in dark suit and tie, strolling beside an automobile on the WEDway system test track at the studio in 1961. This system was featured at the Ford Pavilion during the World's Fair.

Walt a few weeks before his death, in 1966, standing beside a large wall map of the EPCOT project in Florida.

ideology, and it appeared most clearly in a remarkable television show for children that appeared in the mid-1950s.

II. "Why? Because We Like You"

In late summer 1957, a startling assessment of Walt Disney's newest television project appeared. The studio's afternoon program for kids, according to a journalistic analysis, inspired such extraordinary devotion that it could only be described in religious terms. The author began with a rhetorical question:

> Have you worshiped with your children lately? No, I don't mean have you been to church with them, at eleven o'clock Sunday morning, but right at home in front of your television set, every weekday at five p.m. . . .
>
> Religious educators who worry about the fragile "attention span" of children, who use every gimmick and teaching aid that we can lay our hands on to hold their attention, may find some food for thought in this program and in the children's reaction to it . . . Just try tapping them on the shoulder! You'd better use a sledgehammer if you expect to be noticed. As for a whispered suggestion to quiet down, you will have to shout and you still won't get through. For the children are off, gone, inhabiting another world, held in enraptured ecstasy for the next solid hour.[18]

Twenty-five years later, such devotion had not faded. A former cast member reported that during her tour of Vietnam with a rock-and-roll band in the late 1960s, without fail a soldier in the audience would stand and request that she lead them in singing the show's theme song. Thousands of battle-hardened American troops would voluntarily rise to their feet and raise their voices in unison, bellowing out the lyrics.[19]

Such scenes point to the enduring social impact of *The Mickey Mouse Club*, a runaway hit for Disney in the mid-1950s. This television show, beamed out to a national audience on a daily basis, was the studio's most noteworthy contribution to the raising of America's children during the Cold War.

The Mickey Mouse Club made its debut on Monday, October 3, 1955, running from 5 to 6 P.M. on the ABC television network. It ran for four seasons, the final segment airing in September 1959, before going into syndication as a half-hour program from 1962 to 1965. After just one month of broadcasts, the Nielsen report noted that it was "completely dominating regular daytime television," while by its second season it was drawing an audience of 12 million children and 7 million adults, statistics that simply overwhelmed the competition. This show testified once again to Disney's gift for entertainment innovation. With a cast composed almost entirely of children and a format of wide-ranging forays into amusement, education, and socialization, it was unlike anything that had ever appeared before. Since families were central to American social stability, and well-adjusted and educated children were central to the family, the proper training of youngsters was a bedrock component of the American way of life. *The Mickey Mouse Club* became a key link in this chain of logic.[20]

In 1954, the Disney Studio began shaping plans for the show. Flush with the immediate success of *Disneyland*, the weekly television program begun in that year, Disney quickly began to formulate plans for a follow-up project aimed specifically at a juvenile audience. After months of brainstorming over various formats, casts, and themes, *The Mickey Mouse Club* began to come together under producer Bill Walsh, personnel manager Bill Justice, director Sidney Miller, and publicist Leonard Shannon. This brain trust first plucked a red-haired, personable man from the studio music department, Jimmie Dodd, to become the adult leader of the club. For Dodd's on-air assistant and show mascot, Disney himself picked Roy Williams, a corpulent, gruff, but kindly old studio artist and gagman. As Williams recalled, Disney was in his office one day when suddenly "he looked up at me and said, 'Say, you're fat and funny-looking. I'm going to put you on [the show] and call you the Big Mooseketeer.' The next thing I knew I was acting." Perhaps most important, after weeks of thinking and rethinking the cast structure, Disney and his producers decided to create the Mouseketeers, a group of children who, as club members, would shoulder the bulk of the show's efforts. After extensive auditions in early 1955, they cast a collection of talented, precocious youngsters who eschewed Hollywood slickness for kid-next-door energy, sparkling personalities, and casual charm. Wearing black felt Mickey Mouse hats with prominent ears and simple pullover shirts with their names emblazoned in block letters across the front, these youthful performers became idols to an awestruck audience of American children as they proudly chirped their names into the camera at the start of each segment: "Sharon! Bobby! Lonnie! Tommy! Annette! Darlene! Cubby! Karen! Doreen!"[21]

Beaming out to millions of viewers, the hour-long program opened with the circular Mickey Mouse Club logo as animated Disney characters paraded along to blood-pumping march music with its famous spelled-out lyrics: "Who's the leader of the club that's made for you and me?/M-I-C-K-E-Y M-O-U-S-E./Hey there, hi there, ho there, you're as welcome as can be./M-I-C-K-E-Y M-O-U-S-E." After some welcoming remarks from Mickey himself, the show settled into song-and-dance routines, comedy skits, newsreels, inspirational stories, travelogues, and cartoons. The very first segment, for example, featured a boat ride into the Florida Everglades, a filmed performance by a children's orchestra in Rome, news stories from Europe and Japan, a visit to the Disney Studio, a pair of singing-and-dancing numbers by the Mouseketeers, a presentation of "What I Want to

Be," which focused on airline careers as a pilot and a stewardess, and finally the "Cartoon of the Day," which brought one of the Disney animated shorts out of the studio vault.

Children, and often their parents, were enthralled by such fare, and the show, like a television version of the hula hoop, became one of the great fads of 1950s American popular culture. Tongue-in-cheek newspaper stories joked that kids' constant repetition of the singsongy phrase "M-I-C-K-E-Y M-O-U-S-E" had begun driving perfectly responsible adults crazy, while cartoons in the *Saturday Evening Post* depicted mouse-eared youngsters being chased around the living room by the family cat, or perched happily in front of the television munching on a piece of cheese as parents looked on muttering, "I'm worried." When the Mouseketeers went on national tours to promote the show, their appearances often caused scenes of bedlam as children grew excited to the point of hysteria. In February 1958, for instance, a crowd in Bridgeport, Connecticut, became so enthusiastic after a twenty-five-minute performance by the Mouseketeers that they refused to leave the theater and demanded an encore. When this did not happen, an ugly scene developed. Policemen had to be called to clear the theater, at which point the unruly children swarmed to the outside stage door and pelted the performers' bus with snowballs as it left the area, protected by a chain of police. As with any good fad, of course, a bizarre rumor eventually became attached to the club — a ghoulish story began to circulate in 1957 that the Mouseketeers had been killed or seriously injured in a transportation accident. This rumor persisted with such intensity that the Disney Studio, deluged with letters from worried fans, was forced to issue a public denial.[22]

While *The Mickey Mouse Club* carved out its public image, the show privately displayed its share of intriguing personalities. The adult cast members, for example, offered a study in contrasts. Jimmie Dodd, the boyish forty-year-old leader, was a genuinely saintly figure whose warmth and sincerity melted even the coldest-hearted cynic. The Mouseketeers adored him as a gentle father figure who encouraged and nurtured them. Bobby Burgess's description was typical: "He was a good Christian man . . . He liked working with kids. He and his wife could not have children, so we were his children. So it was real special." Second banana Roy Williams was a lovable curmudgeon who told off-color stories to the boys off-camera, served as a bearlike protector to the girls, and presided over pool parties held at his house. One of the show's staffers sniffed that he was "a very vulgar man . . . he wasn't the kind of fellow you would associate with the Disney image." But the children loved him. He liked to take an afternoon nip during extended rehearsals or on long train rides during promotion tours, and Mouseketeer Doreen Tracy claimed that she actually helped him hide his bottles so he could drink undiscovered. Director Sidney Miller was another important presence on the set. A stern taskmaster with a long history in show business, he demanded professional conduct from his young cast and occasionally made them cry by berating them for mistakes. The Mouseketeers both respected and feared Miller.[23]

As for the bright, personable kids who wore the funny hats and charmed their way into American households every afternoon, in many ways they were nothing so much as typical budding teenagers. Rambunctious, talented, delightful, and occasionally trying, they combined long stretches of intense work with episodes of fun and games. Since studio policy kept mothers and fathers off the set, the cast members did not fall into the Hollywood brat syndrome of parent-driven professional ambition. Instead, the Mouseketeers grew up more normally. Like most young teens, for instance, they developed crushes on one another and embarked on romantic explorations. Sharon Baird reported that she and Tommy Cole "went steady" for a couple of weeks during the show's second season, an innocent attachment that mainly consisted of him leaving presents of vending-machine candy on her desk, while Lonnie Burr admitted that some members of the group once had a fumbling makeout party after a performance at Disneyland. Tommy Cole laughingly confessed much later that he occasionally had peeked through the dressing room keyhole "to look at the girls undressing. All of us were going through puberty, and the girls were all developing. Of course, we knew this right away!" The Mouseketeers also nurtured cliques and, less frequently, petty rivalries. Like talented people of any age, competition sometimes spilled over into jealousy — Tommy Cole and Darlene Gillespie, for instance, two of the most gifted members of the group, developed a kind of love-hate relationship — and in some cases personalities meshed and offstage friendships became intense. The two youngest Mouseketeers, Cubby O'Brien and Karen Pendleton, became nearly inseparable; Tommy Cole and Lonnie Burr hung out together; Annette Funicello, Sharon Baird, and Doreen Tracy became pals.[24]

The heart of *The Mickey Mouse Club*'s appeal, it seems clear, was its powerful connection to American family life in the postwar era, particularly with regard to the nurturing of children. In a very practical way, the show attracted baby-boom families by providing a welcome daily baby sitter, giving busy mothers a much-needed break by entertaining and instructing their children. Women wrote letters of thanks to the studio. In Virginia, when a local television channel replaced *The Mickey Mouse Club* with another program in early 1957, angry women flooded the station with complaints. Replying in a full-page ad in the local newspaper, the station admitted ruefully that the letters and calls had demonstrated the program to be "the most popular and efficient baby sitter of all time — that it brings children in off the playgrounds on time and keeps them happy and contented while mother goes about her household tasks." They further pointed out the educational and character building values of the program. *The*

Mickey Mouse Club also provided a reassuring picture of what ordinary Americans *wanted* their families and children to look like. As a rash of newspaper stories proclaimed, the Mouseketeers "epitomize all that's healthy, normal, and happy in the country's youth" and were "a symbol of all American youth."[25]

More directly, however, the show fit snugly within a child-rearing paradigm growing increasingly popular. With the baby boom producing millions of new families and an ideology of family security announced from every cultural streetcorner, expert advice on raising children was a central feature of postwar domestic life. Dr. Benjamin Spock's *Baby and Child Care* was a bible for millions of anxious young parents. Crammed with practical information on sickness, diet, behavioral problems, and stages of juvenile development, the text also presented parents with broad guidelines for rearing happy, healthy children. It rejected the moralistic style of Victorianism — stern discipline, character formation, "bending the will" of the child — in favor of an approach advocated by, in the author's words, modern "educators, psychoanalysts, and pediatricians." In his reassuring, conversational style, Dr. Spock presented anxious young parents with a set of interlocking principles. First, he advocated a general ethic of what one contemporary called "fun morality," arguing that "play is serious business . . . [where] children are hard at work learning about the world." Second, he argued for parental indulgence of children's exploratory impulses and desires, because spontaneity and inquisitiveness were the mainsprings of human achievement. Finally, this popular author insisted that positive reinforcement was the best instrument of genuine learning and healthy development. Punishment, he insisted, "is *never* the main element in discipline" but only an occasional tool, because "the main source of good discipline is growing up in a loving family — being loved and learning to love in return." Youngsters' problems in school, for instance, stemmed mostly from "rigid teaching methods, when the attitude toward the children is regimenting and harsh."[26]

In fact, *Baby and Child Care* synthesized several broad intellectual influences in mid-twentieth-century America. In part it reflected a strain of social theory which held that authoritarian personalities emerged from excessive strictness and parental coercion, a concern that had arisen in response to fascism in the 1930s but now easily switched its aim to communism. In part it relied on a strain of psychological theory particularly associated with Erik Erikson, which focused on proper identity formation as the key to happy and harmonious human development. Finally, Spock drew on progressive theories of education, most of them rooted in the work of John Dewey, which advocated a group-oriented process of learning and placed the child in the center of things as an active participant. Moreover, Dr. Spock's wildly popular book had a much broader cultural resonance. Its ideal of a personable, popular, fully socialized, and interpersonally skilled child converged with the rapid development of a bureaucratic, corporate social order in postwar America and its demands for "team players." As Dr. Spock said outright, "How happily a person gets along as an adult in his job, in his family and social life, depends a great deal on how he got along with other children when he was young." Thus parents should never forget their responsibility for "bringing up a child to be sociable and popular."[27]

The creators of *The Mickey Mouse Club*, of course, did not formally draw on Dr. Spock's text or on any child-rearing literature or theories of education. But the program's basic agenda of fun, discovery, participation, and social cooperation as the basis of learning promoted a scheme very similar to that of *Baby and Child Care* and its many imitators. As one journalist described it, *The Mickey Mouse Club* attempted to "meet a child's need to explore the world around him and gain a sense of his own importance."[28]

Walt Disney himself, evincing decided opinions about modern families and the proper way to bring up children, pointed the way. In many of his general statements about education in this period, he underscored the necessity of hands-on experience, positive reinforcement, and fun. In a statement made ten days before the debut of *The Mickey Mouse Club*, he formally summarized the thinking that lay behind his new show:

> At our studio, we regard the child as a highly intelligent human being. He is characteristically sensitive, humorous, open-minded, eager to learn, and has a strong sense of excitement, energy, and healthy curiosity about the world in which he lives.
>
> Lucky indeed is the grownup who manages to carry these same characteristics over into his adult life. It usually makes for a happy and successful individual. Essentially, the real difference between a child and an adult is experience. We conceive it to be our job on the 'Mickey Mouse Club' show to provide some of that experience . . . happy, factual, constructive experience, whenever possible.

In an interview a few months later, he described the show in simpler terms as an attempt to show that children "can accomplish things, can do things . . . I don't believe in talking down to children. Children are always reaching." Mirroring the sentiments of *Baby and Child Care*, Disney steered the show down the mainstream of contemporary American thinking about child nurturing.[29]

Many segments of *The Mickey Mouse Club* served as direct conduits for these notions. Jiminy Cricket, for example, hosted recurring features entitled "Encyclopedia," "I'm No Fool," "The Nature of Things," and "You," which combined cartoons and live-action footage to teach kids about everything from spelling to milk production, Navajo jewelry to the steel industry. The theme of education-through-entertainment gained reinforcement from words to the song that accompanied the show's special Wednesday segment:

"Yes, we Mouseketeers think you're gonna have some thrills/And it's true that a laugh can cure your ills/And so if you're pleasure bent/We are glad to present/the Mouseketeers' 'Anything Can Happen Day.'" Similarly, the "Newsreel Specials" took young viewers around the United States and all over the world, making a wide variety of cultures, landscapes, and people visually exciting. Disney's paradigm of learning gained force from an array of Mouseketeer skits stressing cooperative, harmonious efforts. The "Fun with Music" segment, for example, not only had the whole group performing synchronized song-and-dance routines but introduced them with a theme song whose lyrics underlined group interaction and interpersonal relations. As a magazine for juveniles stressed, the Mouseketeers "work as a team, and every one of the children is just as anxious to see their fellow actors get ahead as they themselves."[30]

The Mickey Mouse Club articulated clear role models for boys and girls. The show conveyed a host of messages for young men, tutoring them on success, personality development, and future careers. The image of the male Mouseketeers reinforced day after day a subtle sense of what mattered — well-groomed appearance, inquisitiveness and willingness to learn, politeness and good manners, a friendly personality, and respect for authority. A special report, "Inside the FBI," hosted by two scrubbed Mouseketeers in suits and ties, suggested any number of exciting career possibilities for bright, dedicated boys. In the "What I Want to Be" series, the show took young viewers through every phase of the modern airline industry, gently pointing out a wide variety of attractive jobs. As Disney noted in the inaugural issue of *The Mickey Mouse Club Magazine,* the show aimed to shape "the leaders of the twenty-first century, some of whom are among you Mouseketeers of today. The skills and arts and sciences which you are developing will help fashion a better world for tomorrow. Every one of us has some talent, and talent is developed by doing." Mouseketeer Bobby Burgess delivered a similar message about competition in the song "Words to Grow By": "The race is won by running/There is no other way/And if you keep on running/You will win one day." For boys, Disney's show pointed out the path for becoming responsible adults in a free, opportunity-filled American society.[31]

Role models for girls also flourished on *The Mickey Mouse Club,* and Darlene, Doreen, Karen, and Sharon became national idols. In tune with the domestic ideology of the postwar era, their image combined moral restraint and assertive displays of talent, a yen for the home and an eagerness to embrace the world. As one journalist put it after interviewing one of the bright but modest young female Mouseketeers, Americans "have no reason to worry about our own teenagers." The show's 1957 newsreel story on midget-car racing focused on the girl among a group of boys who surprised everyone by winning the big race. Her father, the mechanic for her speedster, beamed proudly as the second-place finisher offered congratulations with an awkward kiss on the cheek. Another episode featured an earnest song, appropriately sung by a female trio of Mouseketeers, which addressed girls on the subject of beauty. The lyrics suggested a feminine model that combined physical attractiveness with intellect: "Beauty is as beauty does, that's what wise men say/Now if you would be beautiful, do this every day/Listen to your teacher, because she is well trained/This is what she has to say: 'A beauty needs a brain.'"[32]

For many young viewers in the mid-1950s, however, Annette Funicello was the embodiment of the Disney female ideal. Much to the surprise of the staff, who had chosen her as the last member of the cast and then only on a trial basis, this shy, attractive Italian-American girl generated an extraordinary popular reaction, receiving hundreds of fan letters every week from admiring girls and loads of candy, perfume, and puppy-love missives from boys. Part of the appeal was physical; Annette, in the admiring words of a magazine article, offered "the classic Latin features — a creamy velvet complexion, lustrous eyes, naturally wavy hair." Moreover, by the second and third seasons of the show, her obvious physical development had become a national preoccupation for young boys, who fell in love by the thousands. With newspaper pieces increasingly describing her as "full-busted," the show's staff found itself in the strange position of being sure their young star was strapped down tightly under her sweaters and pullovers to deemphasize her physical allure. Nonetheless, in the words of the show's director, Sidney Miller, Annette "sparks. She's magnetic. She's sexy, even at that age." This innocent sensuality was reinforced by stories about her attractions and ambitions. In typical teenage fashion, Annette confessed her love for rock-and-roll and 1950s male heartthrobs — in her bedroom, it was reported, were pinups of Elvis Presley, Tommy Sands, Pat Boone, Tab Hunter, James Dean, and the dashing star of Disney's *Zorro* series, Guy Williams — while in interviews she talked about her aspirations as an actress and playfully claimed that "kids are taking over" the entertainment industry.[33]

With the help of Disney Studio publicists, Annette enhanced her appeal as a modern, energetic teenager, appearing in public print as intensely religious, a devoted student, and a conscientious young woman dedicated to hospital and charity appearances. Moreover, she dutifully considered herself to be a "second mother" to her baby brother, and her mother described her as being comfortable in the kitchen, where "she can boil spaghetti, broil a steak, bake a potato, and prepare hotcakes. She's learned to cook all the things she loves to eat." Publicity releases stressed her ethic of hard work, noting that "Annette works at a pace which would discourage most people — young or old." Tying all of this together, of course, was the claim that her virtues flowed from a simple source, "the love and affection in the Funicello family." This charming, dark-haired young Mouseketeer offered another version of Disney's idealized 1950s female: both beauty and brains, both energetic ambition and demure domesticity.[34]

The Mickey Mouse Club melded its newfangled notions of progressive child-rearing with more conservative cultural influences, an instinctive tactic that eased its popular acceptance. The theme of American democracy and its virtuous struggle against communism, while never expressed explicitly or heavy-handedly, lurked in the wings and occasionally moved center-stage. Newsreel segments, for example, took children on a filmed tour of the White House, followed a typical day in the life of a U.S. congressman, and praised the process by which a free American press gathered and disseminated the news. Once, a few days before the national election in 1956, Disney himself presented a special message on American democracy, urging young viewers to "remind your mothers and fathers, respectfully, that a full vote on Tuesday means a true majority will select the government we will have for the next four years. Now it doesn't matter to which party your family belongs. What does matter is that every grownup in your family votes." Support for American political institutions also emerged in special stories such as the 1957 "Inside the FBI," which not only provided information on activities such as fingerprinting but dramatized the agency's efforts to ferret out domestic spies.[35]

Even more prominent was a steady diet of traditional moral instruction. *The Mickey Mouse Club* was chock full of reminders — presented lightly, of course, or with a humorous twist — that good Mouseketeers always respected the authority of teachers, policemen, and parents. Not surprisingly, subtle invocations of family stability also appeared constantly, with filmed segments showing parents and children participating together in activities ranging from sports to farm chores, vacations to home projects. As Tommy Cole recalled years later, "The show had something important to say at the time about family values . . . It was such a wonderful show for parents to watch with their kids." *The Mickey Mouse Club* also infused its proceedings with a powerful sense of religiosity. Periodic references to the lessons of "the good book" and the power of prayer often took place in front of the club-house, over the door of which hung a sign saying GOD BLESS THE MICKEY MOUSE CLUB.[36]

Jimmie Dodd played a conspicuous role in establishing the show's moral stance. A deeply religious man who was president of the Hollywood Christian Group, he never appeared self-righteous and preachy. Instead, he gently advocated his Christian principles by combining them with an attitude of positive reinforcement. As Doreen Tracy described, "He always gave us the feeling we could do it, whatever it was. If we said, 'Can we do this or can we do that?' his response was always the same. With a big smile, he'd say, 'Sure you can!'" That same feeling of encouragement and understanding came through on the television screen. With his daily homily, or "Doddism," which appeared near the end of the show, he offered a brief, gentle lesson on moral values. Typically combining traditional values with positive thinking, these sincere little talks, for which he often strummed on his guitar under soft lights, covered proverbs, human relations, beauty, and philosophy. Dodd's kindly, virtuous television stance was reinforced by a spate of public statements and interviews throughout *The Mickey Mouse Club*'s four-year run. Speaking all over the country, Dodd proudly noted the show's attempt to "set a good example for the youth who watch it." He juxtaposed it with rock-and-roll, which he described as a bad influence for children because its lively rhythm could not compensate for lyrics that were "very suggestive and bad for the kids." The head Mouseketeer also talked openly, but in an understated style, about his own religious conversion in the early 1950s, when "I decided to turn my whole life over to Him," and discussed how his Doddisms placed "particular emphasis on the power of prayer."[37]

Dodd's most heartfelt observations, however, focused on the American family and its child-rearing responsibilities. In many interviews, for example, he stressed that *The Mickey Mouse Club* had chosen its cast with such concerns in mind. During interviews and auditions, he reported, staff members spoke with parents to insure that the final selections had a "normal, stable, wholesome family life." "Let me tell you right now," he told one reporter, "not one of these children comes from a broken home. Not that it's the child's fault if such trouble develops. But the trouble nonetheless is bound to be reflected in the child." In fact, as Dodd noted pointedly, responsibility for a problem child usually could be placed on the doorstep of negligent parents, too many of whom "are more interested in having a ball for themselves rather than spending time with their children. I think you'll find if there's real love in the home you won't find delinquent children."[38]

Thus *The Mickey Mouse Club*'s basic recipe of enlightened child-rearing and progressive education, sweetened with spoonfuls of traditional morality, ultimately aimed to enhance children's self-esteem. Ending every show with a slow reprise of its theme song, Jimmie Dodd interrupted the Mouseketeers' last refrain to say, "See you real soon. Why? Because *we like you*." This statement, as a magazine article insisted in 1957, was crucial because

> every one of the millions of watching children feels warm and good inside. For how many other adults, mothers, fathers, teachers, ministers, anyone, bother to tell our children once every day, 'I like you'?
>
> This program is affording countless children a warm and satisfying experience. Day after day children, especially between six and twelve, are finding a great deal in this hour that encourages healthy growth. It is helping many of them to feel all right about some of their growing-up problems and reassured about their own developing sense of values.[39]

Disney's reassuring messages about family security issued not just from the small green screen flickering in American living rooms nor from the large silver one in theaters throughout the country. They also appeared in a growing flood of publicity about his personal life. Dozens of stories utilized a palette of Cold War colors to paint a compelling portrait of the entertainer at home and of his private character. Here, the family man and the patriot converged to create another powerful Disney image.

18

Citizen Disney

B Y THE MID-1950S, Walt Disney had become once again a fixture in American popular journalism. His burst of activity in movies, television, and documentaries early in the decade made him an attractive topic, and an explosion of articles followed. The broad and kindly face with its pencil mustache, combed-back hair, and twinkling eyes began to look out at readers of the nation's largest-circulation periodicals on a regular basis. In about a year and a half, from late 1953 to mid-1955, Disney appeared on the covers of *Look, Newsweek, Saturday Evening Post, Time,* and *TV Guide.*

These articles analyzed the nature of the Disney appeal and provided colorful descriptions of the studio's increasingly vast undertakings. But increasingly they also focused on Walt's personal life and values, exploring the relationship between the public figure and the private man. One theme consistently wove in and out of them: this entertainer was no longer Walt Disney, film producer, or Walt Disney, studio head, but instead Walt Disney, symbol of postwar America and its values. Somehow, as his celebrity status rose, Disney came to embody the tenets defined in his work: democracy and patriotism, domestic stability and family loyalty, citizenship and creativity. In the Cold War era, Disney became a kind of screen for the projection of national self-definition.

I. Walt Disney, American

As Disney's new parade of films and television shows wound their way down the avenues of popular culture, a swelling volume of commentary transformed the studio head into something more than a moviemaker or even an artist. He increasingly appeared as a spokesman for American ideals of democracy and freedom.

As the decade unfolded, a barrage of essays and articles bombarded the public with images of Disney as an invaluable asset in the Cold War ideological struggle. Many of these described him as a thorn in the side of international communism. The Russians, commentators noted in the early 1950s, once had swooned over Mickey Mouse as a proletarian symbol but now denounced him as a warmonger and tried to keep Disney productions from being seen. Communist "overlords look upon them as frivolous emanations of a decayed culture and unfit for the eyes and ears of their subjects," one essayist claimed, but then pointed out gleefully the fact that private citizens behind the iron curtain took "awful chances" to procure bootlegged copies of these movies. Disney's *Man in Space* shows elicited another outburst of patriotic fervor; one newspaper proclaimed that "Russian scientists next week will be beaten hands down by one Walt Disney. He'll be the first man to send a rocket to Mars." These public pronouncements were mirrored by private expressions of support, such as a letter to Disney praising one of the studio's recent television shows on mathematics. "I wish it would be translated into Russian to be shown to the Russian people," the writer said, "especially to inspire the atheistic Communists that there is truly an Intelligent being who created our universe in such mathematical perfection."[1]

This picture of the genial and creative but tenacious foe of communism was enhanced by Walt's own steady flow of comments on the history, values, and virtue of the United States and his unabashed patriotism, which became a dependable feature of Cold War discourse. He loved to hold forth on American history, enthusing about the inspiring heroes "who helped make this country great" and reassuring his fellow citizens that progress continued to mark the nation's path. "The age we're living in is the most extraordinary the world has ever seen. There are whole new concepts of things, and we now have the tools to change these concepts into realities. We're moving forward," he insisted in 1959. He consistently paid homage to his fellow Americans as "folks I trade with, go to church with, vote with, compete in business with, help build and preserve a nation with." On occasion, Walt even commented directly on the Cold War. "With Wernher von Braun as our scientific consultant, we were two years ahead of the Russians and their sputniks," he told the Chicago *Tribune* in 1958. "If our military experts had listened to von Braun, perhaps we would have kept better pace with the Soviets."[2]

Walt's religiosity made for another important component of his growing reputation. He insisted that religious freedom was central to the American way of life and a key issue in the contest with communism. "In our troubled time, the right of men to think and worship as their conscience dictates is being sorely pressed," he warned in an article. "We can retain these privileges only by being constantly on guard and fighting off any encroachments on these principles."[3]

Walt's unwavering patriotism, religious faith, and sentimental regard for the American people were not just platitudes for public consumption. These values were consistent in his private life. Diane Disney Miller reported that her father's sense of American history and his ardent patriotism inspired many conversations at home and were extremely important to him. In numerous private discussions, Walt would ruminate on the inspiration offered by the Founding Fathers, the Constitution, and the conquest of the wilderness and the western plains. He remained convinced that American technological expertise would triumph over all problems, telling friends, for instance, that the constructive use of atomic energy could "unite the world." He also confided to friends his great thankfulness for his religious upbringing and encouraged his daughters to practice religious toleration, because on essential matters, "there is no difference" among Christian denominations. According to Lillian, her husband was no Bible thumper and occasionally got angry at pious ministers, but his demeanor and comments made it clear that "he was very religious."[4]

The filmmaker's advocacy of American self-reliance, voluntarism, and producerism revealed the libertarian cast of his Cold War populism. At a local gathering of the Big Brothers Association, for example, he said that joining together to address social problems "is what makes this country great. It's not the government doing it, it's the people themselves. It's a voluntary thing, a spontaneous thing." In informal discussions, he reinforced this by insisting that "you have to be very careful giving people anything. I feel that people must earn it." He complained to associates about government regulations and confessed how a string of personal experiences — his gift of seat cushions to employees at the early studio, who then started agitating for *two* cushions; the traumatic studio strike; his gift of company stock to employees who then sold it at the first opportunity — gradually had caused him to drift away from his father's socialism until "I became a Republican." Yet in the words of his daughter, Walt never was an ultra-conservative. He fully endorsed Social Security, and his passionate commitment to individual freedom caused him to tell his family, "You know, I consider myself a true liberal."[5]

Without question, however, Walt remained a committed anti-Communist. His testimony as a friendly witness before HUAC in 1947 was no aberration, and midway through the 1950s he still complained about how the "Commie element" had infiltrated Hollywood and the newspapers after World War II. In private conversations, he approved of the policy of deterrence, describing the nuclear stalemate between the Americans and the Russians as a "Mexican stand-off . . . and [as a result] maybe we'll get some peace." According to studio associate Donn Tatum, Walt saw the Sputnik episode as an opportunity for boosting American interest in science education and prompting the country to "catch up to the Russians." In general, he was proud of his stance as an upstanding conservative citizen. In a 1957 speech in Burbank, he noted that after receiving several minor traffic tickets for improper left turns, he had been advised by the local police chief to make only right turns. Joked Walt, "Well, I do go to the right most of the time. I sort of lean that way."[6]

Disney's conservative, anti-Communist stance was reflected in another aspect of his private life. In the 1950s, he developed a cordial, if distant, relationship with the Federal Bureau of Investigation and its director, J. Edgar Hoover. Hoover, eager to pursue his red-hunting expeditions, cultivated many figures in Hollywood. In 1954, according to a memo in Disney's FBI file, the entertainer offered the agency "complete access to the facilities of Disneyland for use in connection with official matters and for recreational purposes." For its part, the FBI approved Disney as a "SAC contact," a largely honorary designation given to friendly community leaders who were willing to talk with the agency's special agent in charge for their region. Hoover sent Disney a formal letter of congratulations in 1956 after he received the Milestone Award from the Screen Producers Guild, and Disney replied with a note of thanks. There was little additional contact until 1961, when the agent in charge of the FBI's Los Angeles office presented Disney with a copy of Hoover's book, *Masters of Deceit*. The filmmaker posted a brief letter of appreciation to Hoover, in which he expressed his "appreciation as a citizen for what you have done and the fight which you are continually waging for the protection of our way of life." But Disney's sympathy for Hoover's anticommunism did not keep the FBI from circulating in-house memos casting a suspicious eye on his attendance at two gatherings hosted by leftist groups under surveillance in the 1940s. Nor did it keep Disney from satirizing the agency as bureaucratic bunglers in his films *That Darn Cat* and *Moon Pilot* in the early 1960s. Walt Disney, contrary to some overheated accusations, did not serve as a spy for the FBI. Like a great many others in the political mainstream, he simply endorsed the agency's broader agenda of anticommunism during the tense days of the Cold War.[7]

Public accolades for Walt Disney, American, began to pile up in many different forms. As early as 1949, Disney was praised on the floor of the U.S. Senate as a man who "epitomizes the creative spirit which has made America great." Essayists and columnists called him a "powerful social force," "this nation's best salesman abroad," and a person who was "essentially American." *Time* placed Disney on the cover of its December 27, 1954, issue and followed with a long article analyzing his growing influence around the world and his intuitive identification with common people, concluding that "Walt Disney is a genuine hand-hewn American original . . . a grassroots genius in the native tradition of Thomas A. Edison and Henry Ford." Special awards arrived from the American Legion, for dramatizing "to old and young alike the unique heritage of America," and from the Freedom Foundation, for his "patriotic dedication in advancing the concept of Freedom under God." In 1957, a columnist wrote, with tongue only slightly in cheek, that if the Democrats and Republicans could unite on a presidential candidate who somehow combined the virtues of Franklin Roosevelt, Abraham Lincoln, Woodrow Wilson, and Dwight Eisenhower, "this still would not be enough to beat Disney should he choose to form a Disneyland party."[8]

Perhaps the most revealing evidence of Disney's stature, however, came in the hundreds of letters from ordinary citizens that poured into Burbank every year. The overwhelming proportion lauded the studio chief for his productions, and many described him as a great American. A typical example arrived at the end of the decade from a self-described wife and mother in Jacksonville, Florida. It thanked Disney for his stimulating television productions and "the entertainment you gave to our family." Then, in tones resonant of the ideological pressures of the age, it concluded with this poignant declaration:

> I must concede we are a confused people, with the clouds of war all around us. We're sick, and we're an anxious people, who desire with all our might to leave a good world for our children and their children. Thank you so much, Mr. Disney, for working so diligently . . . Your talent has always been so well directed, you are the perfect example of the Bible parable when God gave out the talents. Your efforts have borne *good* fruit! . . . Thank you from the hearts of all of us. We love you so. And if all the children, young and old, love you, what greater reward could any man ask?[9]

With issues of domestic security also coming into play in the 1950s, Disney received much praise as a personal symbol of family virtue as well. This image was bolstered by many stories and essays, but one in particular stood out, written by someone who knew the famous entertainer better than anyone.

II. Lillian Disney: "A Practical Family to Watch Over Him"

In February 1953, *McCall's* carried an article entitled "I Live with a Genius," by Lillian Disney, who had been a rather mysterious figure up to this point. The wife of the famous filmmaker had never been fond of publicity — in the article she admitted to having made a career out of avoiding the press — but as her husband's popularity surged, she stepped forward with a fascinating account of their private life together. Writing as Mrs. Walt Disney, she described her famous mate's everyday, self-effacing manner and chuckled about his quirks — the miniature train hobby, which the family tolerated because it helped relieve his nervous stress, his obsession with work, his good-natured grumbling about female domination. Lillian admitted that Walt's willfulness and dizzying flights of imagination frequently overwhelmed her; instinctively a more cautious person, she confessed to getting the jitters about some of his more daring schemes. She also stressed their common determination to have a normal family life free of the glare of publicity. As she reassured readers, although her husband was "one of the busiest men in Hollywood, he has never neglected his family for business."[10]

This article provided the American public with its first glimpse of a woman who quietly had been near the center of her husband's remarkable career for nearly thirty years. It was a reassuring portrait. In many ways Lillian Disney's narrative dovetailed nicely with the larger ideology of the American family in postwar America — the stay-at-home mom, the hard-working dad whom she succored and counseled, the suburban setting, the home as a haven of security for children. At the same time, the article illuminated only a tiny sliver of Disney family life and the marriage that served as its foundation. Lillian had a long, complex, and fascinating relationship with Walt, which reveals a great deal about the doctrine of domestic security that became such a central part of the Disney enterprise in the 1950s.

Lillian Marie Bounds was born and raised in Lewiston, Idaho, the youngest of ten children and the product of sturdy forebears who had homesteaded in the late nineteenth century. In later years she told her daughters stories about her father's blacksmith shop that were full of love for small-town life. In 1923, after completing high school and two years of business school, she trekked down to Los Angeles to live with her married sister and look for work. After meeting a girl who worked at the fledgling Disney Brothers Studio, she applied for and got a job as an inker and painter. Paid $15 a week, she proved to be an efficient and dedicated worker and eventually caught the eye of the young studio chief. Walt especially appreciated the way she agreed not to cash her paychecks until sufficient funds were available. He began calling on her, and then one day when they were working overtime, he leaned over the desk as she was taking dictation and kissed her. In April 1925 she served as the maid of honor for Edna Francis when she wed Roy Disney, and a few months later, on July 13, she and Walt were married at her brother's house in Lewiston. Their marriage proved to be a long, comfortable one that was still going strong three decades later.[11]

As surviving photographs demonstrate, Lillian was a pretty girl who matured into a handsome woman. Slightly below medium height and with a pleasant and open face, she had a shy smile and was unfailingly neat and poised. With little interest in intellectual affairs and no passion for movies or the Hollywood social whirl, she was content with household management and providing support for her ambitious husband. As Walt's studio began to flourish, she developed a taste for stylish but not flashy clothes, antiques, and home decoration. Collecting jewelry and antique gold seals became favorite hobbies, and her everyday life was a comfortable routine of genteel lunches with friends, trips to the hairdresser, and redecorating projects. Motherhood came first in 1933, with the birth of Diane, and again in 1936, with the adoption of Sharon. As a household manager eager to keep herself and her children out of the public eye, Lillian Disney could have been the wife of any upwardly mobile American businessman in this period.[12]

But this typical American housewife also displayed a surprising streak of independence. Unlike the dozens of Disney Studio employees who were cowed by her husband's volatile moods and iron will for many years, she refused to be overwhelmed by his powerful personality. In fact, Lillian's stubborn defense of her position sometimes spilled over into intractability, and even resentment. She gained something of a reputation among family acquaintances for yanking her husband back to earth when he got bigheaded. She would chide Walt about being a "big shot . . . she used to deflate him," Roy Disney observed, and Ward Kimball noted how she would affect an "I could care less" attitude when she appeared with her husband at the studio. Stories about Lillian's gruffness made the rounds. Once, on a trip to San Francisco in the late 1940s, after years of complaining about the old, dirty porkpie hat that Walt wore on such journeys, she reached over, grabbed it, and threw it out the window. After the initial shock wore off, Walt decided that her action was pretty funny. When an employee gave the family a baby goat, Walt had to give it away, reporting ruefully that "Lillie told me it was me or the goat." For many years she refused to have a dog at home, insisting that they were dirty, smelled bad, and got hair on everything. Walt finally broke through one Christmas when he found an adorable chow puppy and presented it to her in a hatbox with a ribbon. When the puppy pushed up the lid and looked out with its big eyes, she fell in love at first sight, and the dog seldom left her side thereafter.[13]

Lillian's prickly mindset flowed from a kind of possessiveness about her husband. In the words of her daughter Diane, "He was the most important thing in the world to her, and she demanded equal time." She wanted to be at the center of his world, when in fact Walt was totally immersed in his work most of the time. According to Diane, "She was very possessive of him and I think at times jealous of other people who were fond of him — of the world, almost, for making such a fuss over him." This could lead to a certain coldness on her part toward those who worked at the studio. Animator Marc Davis, for instance, observed that he met Mrs. Disney probably thirty times over the years but always had to be reintroduced. Ben Sharpsteen related a story of running into Walt and Lillian at a restaurant; when the exuberant studio head stopped to tell him about a new idea for an animated short film, complete with mimicry and gestures, his wife noted gruffly, "Hmmph, I don't think I want to see that picture." At times, Lillian's defensiveness flared into an intense resentment about being pushed to the margins of her famous husband's life, a fact to which family members again testified. On the South American trip in 1941, Diane said, a mob of well-wishers converged on Walt and shoved Lillian so far out of the way that she ended up wedged into the men's bathroom! According to Roy, whenever the couple went out in public, people would be "really interested in Walt Disney, and pretty soon she'd find herself all alone while they surrounded Walt . . . So she used to get provoked at being left alone like that . . . Walt was always wonderful with the public and that's what used to aggravate Lilly . . . as Lilly says, he thought more of the public and the press than he did of her. He would keep her waiting. But that was the pleasant jibing that went on continually [between the two]."[14]

Lillian's strong personality, in combination with her husband's notorious willfulness, combined to create a durable, if sometimes difficult, relationship. By the 1950s, like many long-married couples, Lillian and Walt played down the romantic element in their marriage. Their banter — he claimed he married her to get a new roommate, while she joked that he proposed because he was so far in debt to her — suggested a comfortable but not passionate relationship. A few surviving letters from the late 1920s, however, tell another story. While in New York City trying to save his studio, Walt wrote a number of long letters to his "Dear Little Sweetheart," and they overflowed with love. Describing a recent phone call home, for example, he exclaimed, "I was so excited I could hardly talk . . . Gosh, honey, I sure was thrilled. I almost cried after I hung up." Over the years, of course, such intensity moderated into affection, respect, and comfort. Confirmed homebodies, Walt and Lillian occasionally got together with a small circle of friends — the Art Linkletters, the Edgar Bergens, the Kay Kysers, Dinah Shore and George Montgomery, and a few others — while avoiding the nightclubs-and-parties scene. Walt traveled fairly frequently, and often he took Lillian with him, combining business and pleasure. In other words, the Disneys had a solid, old-fashioned marriage where expectations were clear, minimal, and met. As Lillian stated emphatically almost seventy years after her wedding day, she wouldn't trade one minute of "our wonderful life together. [He was] just the sweetest thing. I adored him."[15]

Yet the affection occasionally gave way to friction. Walt would grow cross, for example, over his perception that Lillian had become spoiled. In a 1954 magazine piece, he complained with mock dismay that his wife was ruining him financially by landscaping their property: "Last year it was the trees. Every tree she saw she wanted. I told her I was broke . . . Now she wants to put in new flagstones all over the place. Says the old ones are chipped." His private crack that he wanted to name a new puppy Madame Queen after his wife was a bit more barbed. Intensely inquisitive, he grew frustrated with Lillian's disregard for history, public affairs, and books. One morning at the breakfast table in the mid-1950s, Walt was reading the preamble of the Constitution to his family and exclaiming, "Now, aren't these glorious words! Just imagine the command of words and the ability of the man who wrote this. It's just beautiful prose." To which Lillian responded, "Yes, and wasn't it wonderful that Lincoln wrote that all by himself." Walt, according to a family member, just "looked at her with this sad expression." At the same time, however, he expressed great pride in her sense of fashion and design. According to Diane, "He thought no woman in the world could dress as well as my mother. And he was proud of what she did with decorating their homes." Another sign of high regard was Walt's willingness to help put at least one of Lillian's relatives through college and to welcome two of her sisters and her mother into the household for several years. Above all, perhaps, Walt valued his wife's frankness. Lillian said with some pride that the reason Walt always confided in her was "I was the only person he could count on never to 'yes' him."[16]

For her part, Lillian sometimes bristled at her husband's imperious manner and cranky temperament. According to her, Walt had a terrific (if short-lived) temper, just like his father, and he got "angry if he wanted to do something and I didn't like it." But she would stand her ground. Once when the two were having a spat, Diane recalled, her mother threw a cup of coffee at Walt because "she wouldn't let herself be put upon. She stood up for her rights, and I think that Dad always respected her for it." More than once Lillian locked Walt out of the house when they were having an argument, and he would have to spend the night at his studio office, a two-room suite with a small bed and spacious bathroom. Lillian also fretted about financial security because of her husband's constant risk-taking with new and ever bigger projects.[17]

This old-fashioned woman, however, demonstrated enormous patience with her dynamic husband. Lillian listened for hours as Walt talked about his film projects, studio problems, and script ideas, because he needed someone to listen (although later she confessed to her daughter that "it went in one ear and out the other, most of it"). And she clearly felt enormous respect and admiration for her husband. "It was an exciting thing to live with Walt," she once told an interviewer. "He was never bored." She admired his restless quest to learn through constant reading, his eagerness to talk to anyone with interesting ideas or fresh information, his "groping for new things," and his prodigious memory, which kept it all in. While his work ethic could be relentless and demanding, his innocence, eagerness, and curiosity worked to moderate it. As Lillian fondly recollected, Walt "was enthusiastic about everything. He never thought anything would turn out badly. He met people easily and had no inhibitions. He was completely natural."[18]

Lillian and Walt's relationship with their children proved to be a more complex matter. In most matters the Disney family mirrored the values of the age, but a kind of role reversal colored this endeavor. Mothers in postwar America were expected to focus their emotional energy on rearing children, and Lillian certainly met her responsibilities on this count. At the same time, however, she seems to have been much more distant, even cold, than mothers were supposed to be. Lacking a nurturing temperament, she was something of a domineering figure at home. Moreover, her relationship with her daughters could become strained. Lillian seldom went with Walt, Diane, and Sharon on their many weekend outings to local parks, the studio, or sights around Los Angeles. At Diane's wedding in 1954, she remained remarkably poised, while Walt cried abundantly. A few years later, in fact, Walt complained to a colleague that Diane had come to him and explained that she was "scared to death to say anything to Mother" about being pregnant with another child. Walt was delegated to break the news to her. When he did so one morning over coffee, "she didn't say a word, went back into her bedroom, closed the door, and didn't come out until four o'clock." Lillian's attitude may have been rooted in emotional pain; during the late 1920s and early 1930s she had lost several babies during a protracted, frustrating effort to have children. This problem gnawed at Walt, who desperately wanted a son, and according to Roy's wife, Edna, Lillian always remained "very quiet about it."[19]

Walt, in contrast, was a doting parent whose emotional involvement with his children ran very deep. He adored his daughters and reveled in domestic life, feelings that transcended the father-as-breadwinner model of male behavior. He immersed himself in child-rearing, which he genuinely enjoyed, and he strove to create an atmosphere of encouragement, enthusiasm, and learning for his daughters. He urged Diane to look up new words in the dictionary, for example, and always expressed genuine delight when she told him about new things she had learned. "He was interested in everything, and he stimulated your interest. He would have been a marvelous teacher," she remembered. When building a new house in Holmby Hills, Walt made sure to include a soda fountain where he would make ice cream treats for his children and their friends. He spent hours teaching Diane and Sharon to swim and to ride horses, and he took them on outings nearly every weekend. When they were young, the Disney girls were driven to school by their father, and he never missed a "fathers' function" when they were older. At home, he was fond of joking with them, often with the same earthy, barnyard sense of humor he exhibited at work. According to Diane, one evening he developed a deliberately absurd running gag prompted by some recent reading about outer space and a big bowl of radishes on the dinner table. With a straight face, he observed that he would be in bad shape if he ever went to the moon and ate radishes, because without the force of gravity, "if he broke wind, it would just come up around him and envelop him" and he would never escape the smell. His daughters gasped and giggled, of course, which encouraged him to keep bringing up the scenario in new and absurd contexts that had the whole family in stitches. Yet his playfulness did not hide his deep devotion. In 1947, Sharon accompanied him on a several-day trip to Alaska, and in rather primitive conditions he looked after her with the greatest attention, braiding her hair and washing out her clothes every day. When Diane reached puberty, one evening she burst in, both angry and scared, to confront her parents with the news of her first menstrual period. Walt handled the situation with great aplomb, gently explaining that this natural function meant she was becoming a woman and there was nothing to be frightened of. His soothing, empathetic manner, Lillian remembered fondly, completely defused their daughter's anxiety.[20]

Comfortably ensconced in a solid, old-fashioned marriage, Walt sometimes halfheartedly bemoaned living in a household dominated by women. In a 1956 interview, for instance, he talked wryly about having to "fight for recognition around the house with the wife and the daughters and the aunties and the nurse and everything else." He groused to his daughters that "I can't even have a male dog. I've got nothing but females around here." Such complaints usually were voiced in a joking tone, but they had a serious undertone. When he blew up over some minor incident, according to Sharon, "he'd go on about the women in the house and he would usually digress quite a bit." In part, this emotional trigger seems to have been related to a nagging unhappiness over the lack of a son. In Ward Kimball's view, "one of the great disappointments of Walt's life was that he never had a son," and Sharon agreed that this issue preoccupied him.[21]

Yet Walt's complaints about female domination also reflected a very old-fashioned view of women. Not surprisingly for a man of his age and time, he held to a set of traditional, genteel attitudes — men did not curse around ladies, a woman's natural place was in the home as a wife and mother, women should take a supportive role toward their husbands' career. Although there were rare exceptions — Mary Blair, for example, was a favorite artist involved in many projects from the 1940s through the 1960s — Walt generally assumed that women at the Disney Studio were best suited to clerical work and assembly-line tasks such as inking and painting. In general, he remained skeptical about ambitious females.[22]

Much more unusual for someone in the Hollywood spotlight, however, was Walt's extremely straitlaced attitude about sexuality. With his usual bluntness, Ward Kimball expressed the studio's common wisdom: "It's a well-known fact you could never tell Walt a dirty story. You might just as well forget it, because you knew he'd look the other way." Animator Frank Thomas recalled how during the making of one film the artists got carried away drawing a female character in a very sexy manner. When Thomas warned the studio chief that she was starting to look like a whore, Walt looked at him and replied, "Gee, Frank, I wouldn't know what one looks like." Everyone who knew Walt also swore that he never played around. Kimball declared flatly, "One thing I'm sure about Walt — he had no extra-marital affairs. He had a wife, and that was it." Ken Anderson concurred, noting that during the construction of Disneyland in the mid-1950s, Walt once referred to how many of the male staffers were womanizing in the evenings down in Anaheim. "Boy, I just can't understand that, Ken," he said. "It's like women are their hobby." Infidelity seems to have been an alien concept to him. In Walt's own words, he was a "one-woman man" comfortably wrapped up with his family "just like an old dog."[23]

Occasionally, though, his comments hinted at a deep suspicion, perhaps even a resentment, of women. With a touch of sourness, Walt would muse out loud that successful moviemakers should aim their productions at women, because "the female is the influential human all the way through, anywhere. They influence the world." Clearly, this ambitious and creative man was most comfortable in a male world of competition and achievement. With a powerful work ethic standing at the center of his life, he put women on the periphery, and in the words of one colleague, "I don't think Walt was that much interested in the female sex." Lillian herself recognized this. As she mentioned to Kimball at the opening of Disneyland, she approved of her husband's total immersion in his work because he had no time for "playing around with other women." Walt, for his part, appreciated his wife's emotional support but did not particularly value her advice. As he snapped to an artist who had requested a raise at his wife's prodding, "I hate to tell you where I'd be if I had listened to my wife." Moreover, as Kimball recalled, "Walt once said to me, 'I love Mickey Mouse more than any woman I've ever known.'" For this transplanted midwesterner, the home was a domain to be honored and respected, but it was clearly a realm where men, however reluctantly, had to submit to female authority.[24]

As Lillian Disney told the American public in *McCall's*, she tried to insure that her famous husband always had "a practical family to watch over him." But the private life of the Disney family, of course, was part of a much bigger story. With the image of a supportive wife and loving daughters clustered around him, this genial family man was a personal representative of domestic virtue, becoming an avuncular figure in the larger American family.

III. Uncle Walt

Not surprisingly, the very qualities that made highbrow critics increasingly suspicious of Disney's postwar work — an emphasis on sentimentalism, wholesomeness, innocence, and virtue — made him a beloved figure in millions of middle-class households. He may have drifted away from the adventurous modernism and insurgent populism of the 1930s, but if ticket sales were any indicator, his domestic doctrine received widespread sympathy and support. As *Newsweek* reported in a 1955 cover story, during Disney's Wednesday evening television show "American families . . . have begun serving their children's evening meals on trays or moving their TV sets into dining rooms and kitchens" while the other networks were "hunting desperately for family-oriented programs" to put up against him. A cover article in *Look* that same year described Disney's magnetic pull on "Mr. and Mrs. America and children." *Redbook* described *Disneyland* as "entertainment for all the family," and Jack Gould, critic for the New York *Times,* concurred, writing that "to hear all members of a family laugh out loud is not something that happens very often in watching TV. But it must have occurred in millions of homes on Wednesday night."[25]

Public reaction to *The Mickey Mouse Club,* for example, highlighted Disney's role as domestic idealogue. Newspaper stories described this show as one of two worthy television productions for children (the other was *The Captain Kangaroo Show*) and denounced its competitors as "undiluted trash." According to one report, the show served as a model to help parents "discern what is good or evil in the programs their children view so often." Walt's public comments fanned these fires. His television shows, as he put it in a 1954 press release, created "a place for people to find happiness and knowledge, for parents and children to share pleasant times in one another's company."[26]

Publicity about the Disney family reinforced an image of domestic virtue. Readers around the nation became familiar with the entertainer as a "hardworking family man" and saw numerous pictures and admiring descriptions of his loyal wife and loving daughters. Walt and Lillian were presented as devoted parents, nurturing "a wonderful family life." As Louella Parsons wrote, the Disneys were "two of the really happily married people in our town." The photographs accompanying her text — the whole family look-

ing out over the yard behind their sprawling, ranch-style home — embodied the suburban ideal.[27]

Walt's public pronouncements defined the rearing and teaching of children as a key task facing the United States. As we have seen, he recommended a model of learning based on practical work, fun, morality, and the
wise counsel of parents and teachers. In an essay entitled "Deeds Rather
Than Words," he reminded readers of his own upbringing in a religious
family and reiterated his belief in "the sanctity of the home." Pledging
support for "all that is good for the family and for our country," Disney
offered these thoughts on child-rearing:

> I don't believe in playing down to children, either in life or in motion
> pictures. I didn't treat my own youngsters like fragile flowers, and I think
> no parent should. Children are people, and they should have to reach to
> learn about things, to understand things, just as adults have to reach if
> they want to grow in mental stature . . . The American child is a highly
> intelligent human being — characteristically sensitive, humorous, open-
> minded, eager to learn, and has a strong sense of excitement, energy and
> healthy curiosity about the world in which he lives. Lucky indeed is the
> grown-up who manages to carry these same characteristics over into
> adult life.

The best teachers from his own childhood, he said, had not scolded or
shamed but encouraged individual interests and made learning interesting
for their students. *His* educational scheme mixed abstract learning with
practical application, thus giving youngsters ideas and goals, meeting their
curiosity, and shaping their work ethic. In other words, his progressive ideas
were made more palatable by the comforting, traditional moral guidelines
in which he placed them. His efforts were largely successful. In 1954, the
National Education Association gave him the American Education Award
for his "outstanding contributions to education."[28]

Walt Disney gained even more credibility by directly addressing an issue
that haunted middle-class families in the postwar United States — juvenile
delinquency. Estes Kefauver's Senate hearings on juvenile delinquency, the
rise of rock-and-roll, such films as *The Blackboard Jungle* (1955), and books
such as Frederic Wertheim's *Seduction of the Innocent* (1953), among other
things, highlighted what seemed a growing trend toward youthful misbe-
havior and lawbreaking. This development posed a serious challenge to
American values, according to one scholar, because it "coincided with other,
larger fears about the reliability of traditional American institutions such as
the family and the tensile strength of American society under the duress of
the Cold War."[29]

In 1957, the Hearst newspapers carried an exclusive story about Disney's enrollment in "the nationwide campaign against juvenile delinquency." He fingered several culprits. Sensationalistic movies and television helped corrupt morality among young people, while social conditions in crowded urban areas created a situation where "people are lonesome. They want to be a part of something. And kids are restless and uncertain." But most often, he contended, it was "the parents who are delinquent, not the children." "We cannot coddle juveniles," he asserted. "But I don't think we can get anyplace by lecturing them, either. We have to show them, set examples for them, give them leadership." In particular, he concluded, youngsters should be set on the right track in the home, where "programs of parent education along practical lines" could be joined with activities to "stimulate children's interest in the right direction." He did not shirk his own responsibility, but pledged to make movies that showed the good side of teenagers. In his final assessment, "Preaching won't help kids out of trouble. But keeping their minds occupied will."[30]

It was no accident that Disney gained the moniker "Uncle Walt" in the 1950s. In a very real way, he became a beloved avuncular presence in millions of ordinary American homes, hovering in the cultural background as he offered uplifting amusement to inquisitive children and sage advice to anxious parents, dispensing reassurance, wholesomeness, and inspiration with his special touch. His productions, as one commentator put it, aimed "to be true to the American family without deviation." Millions of parents and children responded with devotion.[31]

This staunch defender of national and domestic security became a source of strength in an era of tremendous ideological pressures. Yet Disney's powerful evocation of Americanism during the Cold War included another important element of modern life. Consumerism, the buoyant cultural outgrowth of a dynamic capitalist economy, became increasingly critical to the postwar American economy of abundance. It also became central to Walt Disney's appeal.

19

Disney and the Culture Industry

N 1959, *Life* published a special double issue that explored at length a striking shift in American society over the past decade. It analyzed the prosperity and comfort growing out of the automation of manufacturing, the growth of a consumer economy, and a new national emphasis on leisure. In its words, "For the first time a civilization has reached a point where most people are no longer preoccupied exclusively with providing food and shelter . . . There was a time when only the rich had much leisure. Then came mass production and automation — and suddenly what used to be the small leisured classes became the big leisured masses." The stubborn persistence of prudent, work-obsessed habits and the pursuit of happiness by improving the physical and social environment often caused consumers to misuse or misunderstand leisure, but progress now dictated that "leisure could mean a better civilization," as the editors concluded. Americans needed to reorient their values and "discover the internal quest for happiness, which is the highest use to which leisure can be put."[1]

Around the same time, the *Wall Street Journal* analyzed how the modern Disney operation had smoothly, almost imperceptibly, connected itself to this leisure ethic. The article probed the management, financing, marketing, and organizational techniques that had fueled Disney's spectacular growth over the previous few years and reduced it to a formula: "Dream, diversify, and never miss an angle." Disney had climbed to a pinnacle of success by "diversifying into a wide variety of activities, then by dovetailing them so all work to exploit one another." Using an elaborate flow chart, the article showed how Disney's efforts in filmmaking, television, commercials, music, merchandising and licensing, publications, comic strips, reissues and distribution, and the amusement park continuously reinforced one another to get the company's products before consumers. Struggling businesses, the *Wall Street Journal* concluded admiringly, "may find some profit-making pointers by elbowing the kids aside and taking a look at the integrated doings in the wondrous world of Walt Disney Productions."[2]

It was a revealing moment. A leading organ of the American business community took a long, close look at the operation of the Burbank entertainer and came away rather awestruck at the sight. The Disney company's successful marketing of a vast array of entertainment commodities, and the simultaneous creation of a wide-ranging, tightly integrated organization to oversee this effort, reflected an integral involvement in the explosive growth of consumer capitalism after World War II. Additionally, it suggested Disney's important role in defining the cultural dimension of this process.

After the serious economic dislocations forced by the Great Depression and World War II, Americans rushed to enjoy a vast array of goods — automobiles and home appliances, toiletries and televisions, processed foods and sporting goods, barbecue grills and children's toys. Expanding abundance in this era reflected economic growth and fed the fires of anti-communism. But at a deeper level, it represented the shaping of a broad consumer culture that linked happiness to material goods and, as one historian has put it, a notion of "psychic and physical health defined in sweeping terms."[3]

Not surprisingly, one crucial consequence of the new consumerism of the 1950s was an intense commercialization of leisure. An interlocking structure of Hollywood movies, radio and television networks, advertising agencies, newspaper chains, record companies, and magazine publishers which had slowly built up in earlier decades now flowered. The "culture industry" swiftly came to dominate the dispersal of entertainment and information in postwar America. Large corporations mass-produced cultural commodities by industrial techniques and then marketed, advertised, and sold them to an enormous national audience.[4]

Disney was a key player in this process. For many years, in fact, he had been serving as an enthusiastic salesman for the new consumerism. In a 1942 radio speech, he had insisted that the modern proliferation of home appliances, electrical gadgets, and automobiles should make every citizen "stand up and cheer for the American way of life." By the following decade, like many others, he was going much further in connecting consumption to leisure and happiness. Many forms of recreation had become central to the country's well-being, and mass entertainment stood high on the list. In fact, it had become, in his words, "a vital public necessity — as important as food, shelter, and a job." Thriving in this climate of opinion, Disney created the prototype of a culture industry juggernaut in the postwar years.[5]

His ascendency in these terms was due to several factors — the company's successful marketing forays in the past; the economic travail of the 1940s, which demanded diversification or destruction; his instinctive grasp of the postwar social and economic milieu; and his restless creativity, which naturally led into various areas. But in a more practical sense, the springboard for Disney's launch of a cultural invasion came with a daring venture in television, a new form of entertainment. While definitely a gamble financially, this move promised a great return.

I. Television: Broadcasting the Disney Product

Walt Disney took the plunge into television in 1950. For many years he had been intrigued by the possibilities of this new medium. As early as 1938, the official handbook of the studio had observed that television, "although in its infancy, opens up a vast field of entertainment," and in 1944 the studio had briefly undertaken an educational project about this medium called "The World in Your Living Room." A few years later, Walt told a visiting reporter that television "is here to stay and here now. What is more, it will go further than any of us can dream at this moment." Then, in 1950, after much deliberation, the studio prepared a Christmas special for NBC entitled *One Hour in Wonderland*. Sponsored by Coca-Cola at a cost of $125,000, this trial run took the form of a party in Walt's studio office, with Edgar Bergen, the popular ventriloquist, and his dummy, Charlie McCarthy, as cohosts. They were attended by a crowd of children, including Disney's daughters and two child actors from studio films, Kathryn Beaumont and Bobby Driscoll. The variety format featured animated scenes from *Snow White* and *Song of the South*, a series of short cartoons of Donald Duck, Pluto, and Mickey Mouse, and a brief performance of Dixieland jazz by the studio band, the raucous Firehouse Five Plus Two. The climax was a five-minute preview of the forthcoming film *Alice in Wonderland*.[6]

Heartened by a torrent of critical praise for this show, Disney followed a year later with another special, *The Walt Disney Christmas Show*. Sponsored by Johnson and Johnson at a record cost of $250,000, this show appeared on CBS and once again took the form of a Christmas party at the Disney Studio. This time Walt hosted the program alone, surrounded by children of ten different nationalities, and he presided genially over a variety format very similar to the first Christmas special — several short cartoons starring the Mickey Mouse gang, animated segments from *Bambi* and *Song of the South*, an appearance by radio and television star Hans Conried, and the promotion of Disney films, in this case a clip from the just rereleased *Snow*

White and the Seven Dwarfs and a preview of *Peter Pan*. Once more, favorable reviews poured in from every corner. In the words of one critic, "The show lighted up Christmas Day as pure magic. Television can use much, much more of Disney."[7]

In this way Disney became a pioneering figure in television. Its commercial potential beckoned clearly. Tailor-made for private enjoyment by mothers, fathers, and children, this "window on the world" also emerged as a cornerstone of the suburban family ideal of this era, with its values of security and stability. Moreover, the purchase of television sets, the nightly watching of their presentations, and the steady encounters with a dazzling array of goods promoted by the sponsors reflected the renewed emphasis on leisure and consumption in the dynamic postwar economy.[8]

Most movie studios, of course, were terrified that this new medium would entice away film audiences and denounced it at every opportunity. But Disney, with his usual shrewdness, saw clearly that television could complement moviemaking as part of a larger campaign for leisure and recreation. In 1950, he solicited a research firm, C. J. LaRoche and Company, to prepare a study of the television prospects for his studio. Their report examined costs and sponsorship, the merits of various formats, and the connections to be made with the studio's theatrical releases. LaRoche urged the studio to enter the field but advocated two special initiatives. First, it argued that Disney should maintain production quality and flexibility by putting all television shows completely on film rather than utilizing the low-grade kinescopes then in use, which were good only for broadcasts. Second, in a far-reaching recommendation, it suggested that Disney retain ownership of its product rather than surrender it to a network or sponsors.[9]

Beginning early in the 1950s, Disney was regularly approached by the major networks about a television series. He resisted, and in late 1951 even turned down a reported $8 million from a network that wanted to buy his films for broadcasting. As he told a UPI reporter, "I'm not selling. Why should I? They're still good for movie theaters, and because they're timeless they always will be." A brief negotiation ensued with General Foods, which was interested in long-term corporate sponsorship of a series, but things fell through when the chairman of General Foods asked for a pilot. An angry Walt replied, "We don't do samples!" and stalked out of the room. The momentum for a television commitment was gathering force, however, and by summer 1953 the studio had begun preparing formal outlines and formats for a weekly series entitled *The Walt Disney Show*. A report of September 30 carried outlines for several other prospective series: *Mickey Mouse Club TV Show*, *The True-Life TV Show*, *The World of Tomorrow*. A few weeks later, the Grant Advertising Agency turned in a feasibility study of the proposed *Walt Disney Show*, which strongly recommended the series, providing that the entire Disney library be made available for television use and that Walt himself serve as the host of the program, in order to establish "key *personality* contact with the audience."[10]

But the move into television, it turned out, pivoted on Walt Disney Productions' determination to integrate its business and entertainment operations. As the studio maneuvered to cut a television deal, its central demand was badly needed financial backing for Walt's new pet project — the Disneyland amusement park. When Disney emissaries, led by Walt's brother Roy, went to New York for meetings with all three major networks in the autumn of 1953, they made it clear that funding for the park would be part of any deal. They even toted along a large, fold-out painting hurriedly produced by artist Herb Ryman which provided a visual overview of the proposed park. CBS expressed some interest but resisted investing in an amusement park, an undertaking they saw as very risky. NBC and its parent company, the electronics giant RCA, entered more seriously into negotiations, which lasted for several months. But they kept delaying a final decision, and a frustrated Disney finally turned to the third network, ABC, and its head, Leonard Goldenson. Walt provided a handwritten outline of his proposed series, and ABC, which saw this association as a strong boost for its stature, eagerly entered into negotiations.[11]

After several weeks of hard bargaining, Walt Disney Productions and ABC signed a seven-year contract in April 1954. The studio agreed to provide a weekly TV program entitled *Disneyland,* while the network consented to help finance the amusement park. Disney stock immediately soared in value, and news of this pioneering agreement hit the entertainment community like a bomb. The New York *Times* described the alliance as "the most important development to date in relations between the old and the new entertainment form." The *Motion Picture Herald* saw it as a "historic agreement," while *Film Bulletin,* reflecting opinion among moviemakers, spoke somberly of "the Disney Revolution." In its words, "Nothing in years has produced the soul-searching among executives and important stockholders as the cartoon genius' compact with ABC television interests. The issues at bay are so fundamental as to unmistakably alter the entire mode of industry conduct."[12]

Disneyland launched its tremendously popular run on October 27, 1954, becoming over the next few years a mainstay of American television. It presented a mélange of original productions, ran segments from the studio's large library of animated shorts and feature-length films, and offered enticing glimpses of upcoming movies. In its inaugural season, for instance, the series featured a battery of shows on the studio's animated stars: "Story of Mickey Mouse," "Story of Donald Duck," "Story of Pluto," and "The Goofy Story." It also presented a number of condensed True-Life Adventures, including *Nature's Half Acre, The Vanishing Prairie, Beaver Valley, Water Birds,* and the upcoming *African Lion.* Segments from or serializations of Disney feature films — *Alice in Wonderland, So Dear to My Heart, The Three Caballeros, Treasure Island,* and the upcoming *Lady and the Tramp* — also appeared. The initial season included special productions of two very popular series, *Davy Crockett* and *Man in Space.* Finally, *Disneyland* seasoned its first-year offerings by taking viewers on guided tours of the Disney Studio.

But even as it presented this array of entertainment, *Disneyland* sailed out as the flagship in the studio's larger campaign for business integration. From the very beginning, the show was carefully designed to provide maximum publicity for the Disney Studio's rapidly expanding activities. Clips from new movies, for instance, were larded regularly into the mix to gain priceless publicity and whet the appetites of theatergoers. A more obvious promotion lay in the television show's organization, which mirrored the structure of the Disneyland amusement park, presenting its offerings under a quartet of headings: a "Fantasyland," devoted to animation and fairy tales; a "Frontierland," devoted to American folklore and history; an "Adventureland," featuring wildlife documentaries and live-action tales; and a "Tomorrowland," offering space and science shows.

To draw the connection even tighter, *Disneyland* drew on a playful, shrewd operational aesthetic which dated back at least to the ploys of that nineteenth-century master showman P. T. Barnum. This engaged the curiosity of audiences by inviting them to examine the very entertainment structures and operations that beguiled them, "to learn how they worked." Put simply, Disney broadcast documentary-style segments that gave viewers an insider's look at studio activities. The show's premiere, for instance, offered a tour of the studio which included a stop at a soundstage to witness the filming of *Twenty Thousand Leagues under the Sea* and a layover at the animation building, where artists were observed hard at work on *Sleeping Beauty.* It also included discussions with directors Norman Foster, about upcoming "Frontierland" features, and Ward Kimball, about upcoming "Tomorrowland" segments, as well as film clips and screen tests from the television projects already under way. Perhaps most important, the show regularly featured extensive discussions and tours of Disneyland. As a studio executive enthused to *TV Guide* on the eve of the series' premiere, within a few months "there will be hardly a living soul in the United States who won't have heard about the Disneyland amusement park and who won't be dying to come see it. Yessir, television is a wonderful thing."[13]

Disneyland's web of corporate sponsorship revealed another side of the Disney enterprise's integrative impulse in the 1950s. In its first season, the show was supported by American Motors Corporation, Derby Foods, and the American Dairy Association. These corporate giants secured the services of three prominent advertising agencies — Geyer Advertising in New York, and McCann-Erickson, Inc., and Campbell-Mithun, Inc., in Chicago — to develop their marketing strategies. The result was not only promotions of company products per se but more extensive tie-ins with the Disney name. American Motors, for example, promoted its Hudson and Nash Rambler automobiles by securing Fess Parker and Buddy Ebsen to go on a national tour on behalf of these products. In similar fashion, Derby Foods struck a deal to advertise its Peter Pan peanut butter with animated characters from the Disney movie *Peter Pan*. As for ABC, it saturated the press with advertisements linking the network both to Disney and the show's sponsors.[14]

After *Disneyland*'s first episode, congratulatory telegrams from ABC president Robert Kintner and American Motors president George Romney arrived at the Burbank studio, and they raved about the quality of the show and its public appeal. Indeed, soaring Trendex ratings lent substance to such enthusiasm. They indicated that in a nine-city survey, *Disneyland*'s premiere had cornered 52 percent of the viewing audience (compared to CBS's 26.5 percent and NBC's 14 percent). The show vaulted immediately into the "Top 10 Nielsens," one of television's most popular shows, a position it continued to occupy for many years. In addition, awards began to pile up. After only a month and a half on the air, for example, *Disneyland* won the coveted Sylvania TV Award for the best television series. The next spring it pulled down two Emmy Awards and received *Redbook*'s award for "Year's Best TV Show." The critics proved equally enthusiastic. A flood of newspaper and magazine stories stressed the public's delighted reaction to the show, especially among children. Commentators competed with one another for words of praise. One suggested that ABC "has receipted for a genius"; another dubbed Walt a "human dynamo"; and Hedda Hopper simply bestowed on him the title Disney the Great. Arthur Godfrey, long the kingpin of Wednesday evening viewing, saw his hit show on CBS plummet to thirty-fourth in the ratings after several weeks of head-to-head competition with *Disneyland,* and he could only admit ruefully, "I love Disney. I wish I didn't have to work Wednesday night and could stay home to watch his show."[15]

Disney became a public cheerleader for the new medium of television. In a 1951 interview, he had described it as the "greatest sales medium of the age" and marveled that, because of its ability to reach millions of viewers instantaneously, "it doesn't matter in the slightest whether you are selling toothpaste, cereals, or motion pictures." In other public statements, he insisted to the entertainment industry that "television today should command our utmost respect as a medium for exploiting our wares." At that point, Disney was most concerned with promoting his movies, and he had learned an important lesson when one of his Christmas specials had previewed a scene from *Alice in Wonderland*. The studio was swamped with inquiries about its release. As he mused to a studio associate around this time, "I am a great believer in the TV medium to sell pictures and what we are doing here with ALICE is sort of proving it. Gallup found that our Christmas show sent the [audience] penetration way up. We plan to use TV for point of sale."[16]

In a more idealistic vein, Disney also waxed eloquent on the educational possibilities of this new medium. In 1957, he argued that his studio had always relied on animation as a special tool for opening new worlds to viewers, but now, he insisted, it had become apparent that

> television, too, can be such a boon . . . It will become the great illimitable medium for imparting knowledge, as well as bringing pleasure to the millions, regardless of their previous educational background. This I firmly believe and enthusiastically state.
>
> Television is playing a major role in informatively entertaining the masses. It appeals to people of all ages and all classes. It is the most intimate medium of communication yet developed. This 20th century miracle can wield a tremendous influence in self-education or the augmentation of formal schooling.[17]

Even more important, Disney emphasized how television, by diversifying studio activities, had rejuvenated his entire operation. It provided "a new lease on life," he told one reporter. "I haven't had so much fun since my early days in the business when I had the latitude to experiment," he exclaimed in *TV Guide*. "With TV, it's like a cage has been opened — I can fly again." Moreover, this medium helped him shape the way his entertainment product was presented to the public. In his own words, "Now when television came, I said, 'There's a way that we can get the public . . . Television is going to be my way of going direct to the public, bypassing the other men who can sit there and be the judge . . . When we get a television show, we've got to get it so we can control it." And indeed, that is precisely what happened with *Disneyland*. Finally, in his usual instinctive fashion, Disney grasped television's potential for promoting the operational aesthetic. Most people, he was convinced, were fascinated by what the studio was creating and how it was doing it, and television allowed him to open a window on that. "Why would a magazine like the *Saturday Evening Post* or *Life* devote space at all to Hollywood's backstage if there wasn't reader interest, you see?" he explained to an interviewer at mid-decade. "So I say that people want to know what I'm doing. And I'm telling 'em."[18]

In the 1958–59 season, *Disneyland* underwent a cosmetic change. The studio revised the show's name to *Walt Disney Presents* and moved it to Friday evenings. In addition, with the Anaheim park now in operation for several years, the old link between the television episodes and the park's "lands" was growing strained, so such references were downplayed. ABC began to pressure the studio to develop a cache of western stories to stay competitive with hit shows such as *Wagon Train*, *The Rifleman*, *Wyatt Earp*, and *Gunsmoke*. Disney resisted strenuously, claiming that this genre made for an awkward fit with his studio's style and hampered his creativity, but he finally gave in. According to Donn Tatum, he burst into a top-level meeting with ABC executives wearing a cowboy outfit and a gunbelt, threw the guns down on the table, and exclaimed, "Okay, you want westerns, you're gonna have westerns!" The new *Walt Disney Presents* featured Walt, often attired in semiwestern garb, introducing the episodes from a western set. The show premiered two new serial stories in the first season, *Texas John Slaughter* and *Elfego Baca,* and the following season it offered the Swamp Fox tales.[19]

But *Walt Disney Presents* continued to offer segments focusing on fantasy, nature, science, and adventure. In 1958, for example, it offered "Magic High-way, U.S.A.," which examined the future of mass transportation. After consulting traffic engineers and highway planners, the Disney Studio's creative staff came up with an intriguing vision of future innovations — superhighways for nuclear-powered submarines transporting passengers to Europe, automobiles powered by efficient gas-turbine engines, moving sidewalks suspended above the crowded flow of city vehicles, air-conditioned highway tubes crossing the desert. In the 1959–60 season, after the wave of shoot-'em-up cowboy shows had crested, Disney vowed to soft-pedal "violence merely for the sake of violence" and padded his series with more shows appropriate to family viewing. He led off the season with a two-part serial entitled *Moochie of the Little League,* starring Kevin Corcoran, a child actor who went on to become a Disney Studio film star.

The enormous success of Disney's weekly variety show proved to be only the cutting edge of the studio's larger television effort. *Disneyland*'s great popularity prompted the development of other series with ABC. Disney hit his second jackpot, of course, with *The Mickey Mouse Club,* from 1955 to 1959. Then a third hit series came with *Zorro,* the weekly adventure serial, which ran from 1957 to 1959. These shows not only enhanced Disney's prestige among viewers but boosted ABC's popularity. By late in the decade, when the ratings and advertising revenue of this youngest, smallest network finally rivaled that of NBC and CBS, its president, Leonard Goldenson, admitted that the Disney connection had been "the turning point."[20]

By that time, however, Disney's relationship with ABC had begun to sour. Walt was unhappy over ABC's constant pressure to jump on the western bandwagon, and he resented the fact that ABC overloaded the early *Mickey Mouse Club* with commercials (some twelve minutes out of sixty), a fact that caused the National Association for Better Radio and Television to complain that many parents "feel that the high standards of the program are appreciably lowered by the preponderance of commercials." Then ABC claimed that it couldn't find enough sponsors interested in appealing to the show's audience and cut it back to a half-hour format. Around the same time, the network also declined to renew *Zorro,* contending that programs that it owned would be more profitable than those it bought from independent producers such as Disney. At this point Walt "nearly blew his top with ABC," according to a Disney executive, and moved to offer these shows to other networks. But ABC warned that the studio could not do so legally.[21]

As a result of this friction, in July 1959 Walt Disney Productions filed suit against ABC to dissolve their contract under provisions of federal antitrust laws. In a statement to company stockholders, Roy Disney claimed that ABC had "announced publicly that they would not televise *Zorro* or *The Mickey Mouse Club* over their network next season, and at the same time they told us we could not offer these programs to any other television outlet . . . Although we do not dispute ABC's right to discontinue these, or any other programs on their own network, we will certainly fight ABC's maneuvers to suppress these programs from public exhibition over other television stations." Publicly, Disney and ABC agreed to keep *Walt Disney Presents* out of this dispute, a move that kept the show on the air while the litigants worked through the courts. But privately, both Walt and Roy were visibly angry about ABC's position, describing it to associates as "a breach of faith" and "high-handed."[22]

In 1960, the two parties finally negotiated a settlement, which allowed the studio to take *Walt Disney Presents* to another network and to purchase ABC's one-third interest in Disneyland for around $7.5 million. Walt immediately began dealing with the largest television network, NBC, because of its cutting-edge development of technology for color broadcasting. The studio chief, surrounded by color mockups of various show segments, personally made a pitch to NBC executives in New York City, and in a cab on the way to the airport told his associates Donn Tatum and Card Walker, "Fellas, I want this deal. If necessary I'll stand on my head in Macy's window." NBC was delighted to accommodate him, and an agreement was reached quickly. A weekly program entitled *Walt Disney's Wonderful World of Color* appeared on NBC in September 1961, and this long-running show became a Sunday evening tradition for millions of American families. As Walt confidently told stockholders in the 1960 annual report, the new association opened up "an exciting new world of color, which we pioneered in the motion picture field. Color adds an all-important dimension for which we are thoroughly equipped."[23]

Disney's move into television in the 1950s prompted a rapprochement between moviemakers and this dynamic new medium. "The very same film executives who, just a year ago, kept assuring everyone that they would have nothing to do with TV are now engaged in feverish activity to serve and exploit it," noted a 1955 essay. "The sudden removal of Hollywood's mental block on TV can be traced almost directly to the success of Walt Disney's 'Disneyland' show." While the ABC alliance did not in itself generate much direct profit for the studio, it cemented Disney as a household name by bringing his entertainment product into the homes of American consumers on a weekly basis. It dramatically popularized other studio activities by advertising both Disney films and the new amusement park. It served as a mechanism for displaying and selling a cornucopia of Disney merchandise. Last of all, television made Walt Disney a national celebrity by making his face instantly recognizable to tens of millions of Americans.[24]

In a profound way, television dramatically connected the various fiefdoms in the growing Disney empire. It was, however, only the most obvious manifestation of the much larger principle that fueled expansion of the postwar Disney enterprise. "Integration," a sacred word in the Disney lexicon, became the heart and soul of this culture-industry behemoth in the 1950s.

II. Integration: Selling the Disney Product

In 1953, *Life* helped celebrate the twenty-fifth anniversary of Mickey Mouse's appearance with a long text-and-photo story on the prospering Disney enterprise. It surveyed the studio's many entertainment projects but made special note of the hundreds of licensees who were manufacturing Disney products around the world and the millions of dollars flowing into the studio's coffers. The Disney name, the article noted, was fanning out all over the globe. A story that recently had reached the Burbank facility really drove the point home. According to this tale, wrote *Life*, when explorers hacked their way through the most remote jungles of Brazil, "the first little boy to greet them was wearing a Mickey Mouse sweater!"[25]

A firm business reality lay behind such legends. By the mid-1950s, public attention and press coverage had moved from Disney-as-entertainer to Disney-as-businessman, and interest increasingly focused on the intricate profitmaking connections between his various entertainment endeavors. The 1954 release of *Twenty Thousand Leagues under the Sea* demonstrated his surehanded grasp of the culture industry. First, a massive marketing campaign promoted the film with a self-styled "publicity and exploitation barrage" of print advertisements, radio spots, and theater trailers which described an exciting adventure tale full of unique special effects. Second, *Disneyland* broadcast the Emmy-winning "Operation Undersea," an hourlong segment that took viewers on a backstage (and underwater) tour of the making of the movie. Third, Disney merchandising developed a line of mechanical toys and clothing items. Fourth, the studio contracted for books, comic books, and records related to the movie. Finally, Walt tied up the package by enshrining *Twenty Thousand Leagues* in his Anaheim amusement park, first with a lavish display of the interior of the *Nautilus* and later with the more elaborate Submarine Voyage, an underwater ride. As this promotional sequence unfolded, it became clear that the integrative capacity and selling power of the Disney enterprise had evolved to a very sophisticated level.[26]

As Roy Disney explained to the *Wall Street Journal* in 1958, "Integration is the key word around here: we don't do anything in one line without giving a thought to its likely profitability in our other lines." This notion was no postwar flash in the pan, but rather the result of long development in the studio. In the 1930s and 1940s, Kay Kamen had orchestrated a variety of energetic marketing efforts that linked movies like *Snow White* to merchandising in clothing and toys. Even earlier, the Mickey Mouse Clubs at movie theaters all over the country had offered games, prizes, and activities for children in an attempt to cement their loyalty to Disney cartoons. By the early 1950s, however, such activities were reaching an unprecedented level of consolidation.[27]

In the marketing operation, O. B. Johnston and Vince Jefferds were key figures in Disney's Character Merchandising Division by the early 1950s, and they helped develop the integrated promotional blitz into a commercial art form. A steady progression of marketing campaigns appeared throughout this decade, harnessing the various abilities of Disney production. Probably the most spectacular example came in 1955–56 with the Davy Crockett craze, which not only involved a convergence of television, movies, and music but prompted a flood of studio-licensed consumer products ranging from coonskin hats to bedsheets. Smaller campaigns surrounded other popular television shows. *The Mickey Mouse Club* became the inspiration for millions of Mickey Mouse hats (black felt beanies adorned with large mouse ears) and dozens of other children's products, and *Zorro* triggered a stampede for capes and toy swords. The release of animated features such as *Cinderella* and *Sleeping Beauty* continued, in the traditional Disney way, to be linked with advertisements for related lines of toys and clothing. By later in the decade, even individual segments of *Disneyland* became part of a larger integration effort. Disney marketers linked the broadcasting of "Our Friend the Atom," for instance, to the publication of a studio-created Dell paperback book of the same name, which sold some 200,000 copies in its first edition.

Occasionally, such marketing maneuvers went to rather extreme lengths. In late 1957, the opening of *Old Yeller* prompted a nationwide promotion that admitted dog owners and their pets (as long as they were on a leash) to a special preview of the film. At theaters throughout the United States, special doggie delicacies — Grow-Pup dog food, Milkbone dog biscuits, a solid rubber fire hydrant — were distributed to each canine visitor while dogcatchers and veterinarians stood at the ready and wary theater owners welcomed visits to temporarily modified bathroom facilities. The dogs then viewed the film from regular theater seats as their owners sat proudly behind them. Journalists, of course, milked the episode for every drop of absurd humor. The Chicago *American* featured a large photo of a ribboned, carefully coifed female Yorkshire champion, Star Twilight, seated demurely next to a muscular Italian greyhound named Ulysses in the front row of a prominent city theater. A reviewer for the New York *World Telegram and Sun* complained with mock bitterness, "Nothing worse than being a human outcast at a movie about a dog where all the seats in the house are held down by dogs." Stories groaned under pun-laden titles such as "Dog Gone Good Show!" and one analyst concluded, "Very few of the special guests had biting comments about the film."[28]

Movie production also reflected the studio's integrated structure. For years Disney had relied on RKO to distribute its movies, but at the prodding of Roy Disney and because of the unique selling strategy required for the innovative True-Life Adventures, it established the Buena Vista Film Distribution Company in 1953. Leo F. Samuels, president of the new entity and worldwide sales manager for Walt Disney Productions, told the *Motion Picture Herald* in 1954, "In succeeding steps we have taken over the handling of our own music, merchandise, and accessories. It was only natural that we should one day take over the selling of our own pictures." Buena Vista gradually assumed control of distribution for all studio films and became crucial to the actions by which Disney gained nearly complete control over its vast entertainment process, from production to consumption.[29]

The studio generally used television to promote its movies. In January 1959, for example, *Disneyland* featured "The Peter Tchaikovsky Story," a biographical treatment that concentrated on the composition of the ballet *Sleeping Beauty* and culminated with takes from the studio's forthcoming animated movie of the same name. Stars also moved easily between these genres. Fess Parker made his mark both in the televised *Davy Crockett* series and a progression of historical films. Child star Kevin Corcoran debuted on television as Moochie on *The Mickey Mouse Club* and starred in *Moochie of the Little League,* the premier *Disneyland* segments of 1959–60, crossed into films with starring roles in *Old Yeller, The Swiss Family Robinson, Toby Tyler,* and *The Shaggy Dog,* and then reappeared on Disney's television show in episodes of *Johnny Shiloh* and *Daniel Boone.* Probably the clearest example was Annette Funicello, who became a star on television, moved into movies with roles in *The Shaggy Dog, Babes in Toyland, The Misadventures of Merlin Jones,* and *The Monkey's Uncle,* and finally became a popular singer with Disney-created hits such as "Tall Paul" and "Pineapple Princess." Such integration created a model akin to the interchangeable parts of modern American industry, only this time with actors and media forms working smoothly within the Disney machine.[30]

As it maneuvered to tie together its expanding entertainment forays, the Disney enterprise also moved decisively to establish sweeping connections with corporate America. It struck lucrative deals with Coca-Cola and Sears, Roebuck, which used millions of plastic figurines of Disney characters in special promotions. Joint ventures were also established with DuPont, the American Automobile Association, and Sealy Mattress, for which a series of animated shorts starring Goofy and Jiminy Cricket — *Motor Mania, I'm No Fool on a Bicycle,* and *How to Sleep* — were shaped into commercials. Not surprisingly, the television projects offered particularly fruitful areas for corporate cultivation. For *Disneyland,* the studio participated in advertising campaigns boosting such economic giants as Derby Foods, the American Dairy Association, Reynolds Metals, and Hills Brothers Coffee. A long alliance with American Motors proved especially dynamic; an array of advertisements featured Snow White, Donald Duck, and other Disney characters pointing joyfully to shining new cars and proclaiming "You'll Be Years Ahead with Nash" (while reminding readers, "Hey folks — tune in to *Disneyland* TV program, Wednesday at 6:30"). Individual episodes of *Disneyland* attracted specific corporate backers, as when "Magic Highway, U.S.A." gained significant funding from a grateful Portland Cement Association.[31]

Disney's ballyhooed move to NBC in 1961 mined another rich vein of corporate support. This important shift of studio resources involved not only a tie-in with the new technology of color television but explicit support for RCA Victor, the leading manufacturer of television sets. Not coincidentally, RCA was the parent company of NBC, and it shared sponsorship of *Walt Disney's Wonderful World of Color* with Eastman Kodak. On the first episode of the new show, Walt and Ludwig Von Drake, a new animated character created especially for the venture, spent considerable time praising the virtues of color television to viewers. As the studio chief confessed to journalists, "The show is being planned to give the big push to color TV . . . If people have things they want to see in color, they'll find a way to buy sets." As for RCA, it embraced the Disney alliance wholeheartedly. Full-color newspaper advertisements paraded a cast of animated characters and urged readers to "step into Walt Disney's Wonderful World of Color!" The company put together special promotions, such as a large exhibition in New York that displayed an array of Disney production "secrets" — the multiplane camera, colored animation cels, sound-effects mechanisms, an actual studio artist doing sketches — alongside the entire new line of RCA television sets. Such efforts bore fruit. In the spring of 1962, a few months after the debut of the show, RCA announced a 166 percent rise in sales of color TV sets and its best quarterly earnings since the initial television boom in 1951.[32]

Ultimately, such marketing, media, and manufacturing efforts depended on the value system promoted by Disney in the 1950s. A leisure ethic that eschewed the older standard of Victorian self-control in favor of a modern notion of self-fulfillment through material acquisition and recreation had gathered force since early in the twentieth century, but it reached a new level of intensity in 1950s America. According to Ernest Dichter, a prominent advertiser and corporate analyst of consumer habits during this era, modern prosperity demanded that "we abandon the idea that a comfortable life is automatically an immoral one . . . What has become imperative for us is to revise our morality. Hedonism, as defined by the old Greeks, has to be brought to the surface again." While Disney certainly shrank from advocating hedonism, throughout the 1950s he did endorse self-fulfillment and leisure enjoyment, which helped ease the transport of consumer products to a rapidly growing middle-class audience. "In my opinion, entertainment in its broadest sense has become a necessity rather than a luxury in the life of the American public," he told readers in 1957, and it had a central position within "today's standard of living, levels of culture, and the national economy."[33]

The Disney company's yearly financial reports in the 1950s charted a dramatically rising profit curve. In the fiscal year ending in September 1950, the report showed a gross income of $7.3 million and net profits of $720,000 (the company had lost money only the year before). After climbing steadily over the next several years, income exploded in 1955, more than doubling the previous year's totals to reach $24.6 million (net profits were $1.3 million). By the end of the decade, another quantum leap had occurred, with gross income soaring to $58.4 million and net profits to $3.4 million. Walt told shareholders, "We end this year with confidence and the expectancy of an equally busy year ahead."[34]

Disney's increasingly gaudy reputation within the American business community provided another yardstick of success. Articles in such publications as the *Wall Street Journal, Forbes, Business Week, Barron's,* and *Tide: The Newsmagazine for Advertising Executives* scrambled to heap praise on the Burbank entertainer and his operation. As one summarized a bit too cutely, studio diversification had brought stunning financial success: "After more than a quarter-century of paw-to-mouth existence, Mickey Mouse is finally piloting his creator, Walt Disney, to the pot of cheese at the foot of the rainbow."[35]

But Disney's integration was not without its critics. Some observers were unimpressed with this culture industry machine. When the studio entered the television arena, some critics deeply resented the way it used the medium relentlessly to promote other undertakings. A reviewer in the Newark *Evening News* complained that *Disneyland*'s premiere "amounted to little more than an hour-long commercial for Walt Disney — with intervening commercials by paying clients yet." It was, he concluded, "a bit hard to take." Over the next few years, others joined in condemning the studio for using television to plug every Disney project in sight. The New York *Mirror* said that Walt was following "a policy of self-promotion . . . and apparently nobody at ABC has the courage to tell him when and where to stop." One writer denounced his "pure unadulterated gold-making brass" as reflecting "contempt for the viewing public," while another noted that "he is the only guy in the business who can get away with a solid hour of huckstering for himself and make it come out like entertainment." Even a laudatory cover article in *Newsweek* had to admit that for some cynical observers, Disney's television show was little more than "a long, long trailer."[36]

Some critics were especially livid over Disney's heavy-handed promotion of color television on his NBC show. Some believed it to be in bad taste, a case of taking advantage of a loyal audience with a "devious," "brazen," "insulting," and "hard-sell approach." A class dimension also entered the discussion. In the bitter words of one writer, Walt's unstinting praise for color would not "compensate in the long run for the stinging he gave the feelings of the poor, pathetic millions of peasants who are making do with black-and-white sets." Apparently at least some viewers shared such harsh views. As an angry letter to the Los Angeles *Examiner* complained, "I have never seen anything to equal the outright gall of trying to sell color sets for an entire program! I will now watch TV in glorious black and white for a long time to come." *Variety* suggested that for many modestly middle-class viewers, "this seemingly interminable hard sell of the virtues of living color probably registered as the last word in aggravation and frustration . . . The first 25 minutes of the premiere amounted to one continuous sales pitch, complete with models, splashes of paint, kaleidoscopic images, nature scenes, and Uncle Walt addressing the elite few with remarks such as 'color does brighten things up, doesn't it?'" But even these negative reactions eloquently, if ironically, testified to the success of the studio's campaign for integration in the postwar years.[37]

The many-headed Disney organization became the nerve center of a rapidly expanding cultural empire in the 1950s. This involved a striking personnel shift as many new young employees whose talents were not necessarily in animation gained prominence. Artists such as Peter Ellenshaw, for example, became well known by providing background matte paintings and special effects for Disney's live-action movies. But most of the new leadership was drawn not from the art world at all but from the world of business bureaucracy.

Donn Tatum went to the studio in 1955 after serving as head of ABC's West Coast operation. He joined the studio, in his words, because Disney "wanted to get someone with experience in the [television] production department." Over the next decade Tatum rose to become executive vice president for administration. Card Walker, the quintessential Disney success story, had started at the studio in 1938, right out of college, working as a messenger boy; he moved up to become a cameraman, unit manager for production of animated shorts, an executive in advertising and publicity, and eventually director of marketing. By 1960, Walker and Tatum occupied a powerful niche just beneath Walt and his brother Roy, and they embodied the new trend. Coming from fields such as finance, public relations, advertising, and television, their skills lay in deftly weaving together the varied strands of an increasingly vast entertainment tapestry.[38]

III. Bill Walsh: "Make Sure People Go to See It"

Among the new figures at the Disney Studio, none rose more meteorically than Bill Walsh, a portly, energetic, multitalented publicist who began his studio career in the mid-1940s. Walsh became the ultimate organization loyalist during the 1950s, and it seemed that whenever and wherever a new idea appeared — whether live-action movies, popular television projects, or the amusement park — he had a finger in it. Within a few years of his arrival, his remarkable abilities had carried him to great heights as a writer, movie and television producer, and, eventually, to Walt's side as creative right-hand man.

Raised in the Midwest, Walsh had worked as a magazine writer, public relations man, and joke writer for Edgar Bergen and the team of George Burns and Gracie Allen. He drifted to Hollywood in 1945 with Bergen to work on *Fun and Fancy Free,* one of the Disney Studio's postwar pastiche films. Bergen and his dummies, Charlie McCarthy and Mortimer Snerd, starred in the live-action segments of the movie, narrating and introducing the animation, and Walsh not only contributed jokes but cowrote one of the songs, "My Favorite Dream." He ended up staying on at the Disney Studio, writing jokes for the Mickey Mouse comic strip (something he continued to do until 1968, well after he became a famous producer) and managing publicity projects. A few years later, Walt asked him to accompany him to England, where the studio was filming *Robin Hood.* When the befuddled young man inquired as to his duties on the trip, Walt told him, "There's a funny little magic word called 'initiative,' and that will tell you what to do." Once in England, Walsh conceived the idea of doing a backstage film about the shooting of *Robin Hood.* With the publicist's instinctive grasp of the principle of integration, he saw the promotional possibilities of a movie *about* the filming of this exciting legend. *The Riddle of Robin Hood,* the title of this fifteen-minute documentary, was planted with TV stations and schools all over the country. His boss was delighted, because, in Walsh's words, "we were getting a lot of mileage out of this goofy little film, and Walt was sort of enchanted by all that free space promoting the film."[39]

Walsh's emergence as a key player at Walt Disney Productions came with the move into television, yet this important step resulted from happenstance rather than planning. In 1950, Walsh wrote a long, impassioned memorandum urging Walt to keep the studio out of television, because it was unlikely to succeed: "something like going to the moon . . . it consisted of the roller derby and a lot of wrestling." But Walt, intrigued by the possibilities of this new medium and notoriously perverse about staffing projects, saw Walsh in the hall the next day, pointed his finger, and said, "You. You be the producer of my TV show." When the startled writer replied, "But I don't have any experience as a television producer," Walt had the perfect rejoinder: "Who does?" Walsh had to agree with him. He produced the studio's Christmas specials in 1950 and 1951. These shows, Walsh later said, were "kind of stuck together with glue and chicken wire, very cheaply," but their impressive audience ratings "somehow gave Walt the idea maybe I was a producer."[40]

When Walt decided to take the plunge with *Disneyland*, Walsh played a major role in the conception of the series. In June 1953, even before the ABC deal was struck, he composed a nine-page memorandum outlining the architecture for a weekly show. This report sketched out what became central elements of Disney's television projects: an "appeal to the collective family taste," the showcasing of both established and new Disney characters, routines that could "be tied into the sponsor's merchandising plans," an element of education "carefully concealed by the chlorophyll of entertainment," and a physical setting of Disneyland, whether the actual amusement park or an imaginary "palace of Prince Charming, the deck of the *Nautilus* or the *Hispaniola*, Sherwood Forest, a fairgrounds, a jungle, or a glade in Never Land."[41]

Typically, Walsh's report also demonstrated a special Disney sensitivity to popular taste. The public, he argued forcefully, was not impressed with the "big, expensive, clambake type of show" with big orchestras, glittering stars, literary dignitaries, and other "pretentious trappings." Instead, they loved characters — "homely, brave, ignorant, cowardly, two-headed, *anything*, as long as they are definite characters." He insisted that the studio had an advantage in that "the public has been conditioned to the Disney imagination," and he urged that Walt himself act as host to help identify and reinforce that predisposition. *Disneyland* should strive to maintain, in his words, "a distinctive, easy-going personality that invites both fact and imagination — that leaves a clean, pleasant taste in the mouth — that bespeaks a friendly relationship between the show and the viewer — and establishes a contact between every member of the family as they sit before the viewing screen." Within a few short weeks, Walsh was busy trying to realize these principles by writing sample scripts that were "typical Disney with heart appeal and a surefire story." Walt chose him as producer of the new series.[42]

Walsh's success stemmed from the fact that he came to share his boss's shrewd perception of television as a key tool for studio integration. The Christmas specials, he believed, were "the first time Walt saw TV in proper relationship to us — as a promotional device for theatrical film," and the studio chief went on to see television as a way to "promote everything. Everything that moved around here he promoted [on television]." Walsh's sensitivity to this strategy became evident in his adept development of "Operation Undersea," the Emmy-winning television show about the making of *Twenty Thousand Leagues under the Sea.*[43]

As *Disneyland*'s producer during its first season, Walsh played a key role in shaping the show's great popularity. Among his triumphs, of course, were the *Davy Crockett* segments, although the fabulous success of that series seemed inexplicable to him. He was stunned when, after the first broadcast, "the whole country came unglued" and a craze was born. "It was just a story about some guy shooting at Indians, but all hell broke loose. I just can't understand it," he confessed.[44]

After *Disneyland*'s initial season, Walt called Walsh in to announce, "I'm taking you off the evening show." The grateful producer thanked him and asked for a vacation, admitting that "doing an hour show every week was murder." Then Walt smiled and told him that he was being shifted to a new show that was "an hour every *day.*" When Walt added, "with children," the dumbfounded Walsh could only mutter, "Oh boy." Thus he became the producer of the wildly popular *Mickey Mouse Club,* a post he held for all four seasons of the show's run. As with *Disneyland,* he played a crucial role by taking some of Walt's ideas and developing a basic architecture for the program. In a long memorandum to the studio chief in January 1955, he sketched out a variety show broken into fifteen-minute segments, with a strong emphasis on cartoon entertainment, different themes for each day of the week, the regular appearance of guest stars appealing to children, and an atmosphere of spontaneity, imagination, and fun. Ever the publicist, Walsh also added this special note: "As in the parent 'Disneyland' show, proper exploitation of Disney films and merchandise becomes a basic part of our structure."[45]

Walsh stood at the center of things with *The Mickey Mouse Club.* He helped audition the dozens of youngsters who wanted to become Mouseketeers, shaped and refined the show's segments, wrote songs, and supervised much of the script writing. "It was kind of hysterical, it was like a Chinese fire drill," he said. "But it was fun because we'd have meetings in the mornings with the kids, then we'd have the writers, then we'd have the guys who did the sets and costumes . . . and about three o'clock that afternoon we'd shoot it." Walsh recalled stopping into a bar at the height of the show's popularity and shaking his head as "at five o'clock, all the drunks would stand up with their hand over their heart and sing the Mickey Mouse Club theme song."[46]

In spite of his pressing duties with these television hits, Walsh found time for brief forays into the studio's live-action movie projects. He produced the Davy Crockett movies and *Westward Ho the Wagons,* wrote the screenplay for *The Littlest Outlaw,* and produced *Twenty Thousand Leagues under the Sea.* With these achievements under his belt and *The Mickey Mouse Club* having run its course, at the end of the decade Walsh finally called in a promise from Walt. The studio head had agreed that by staying on for a third and fourth season with the children's show, Walsh had finally "paid his dues" and that he was not going to be stuck with any more television.[47]

So at the end of the 1950s, Walsh turned to movies full-time and began to amass a record that became the envy of many in the film industry. A talented, highly productive man, he served as the screenwriter and producer for many of the Disney Studio's most popular and profitable films from this era: *The Shaggy Dog* (1959), *The Absent-Minded Professor* (1960), *Son of Flubber* (1963), *Mary Poppins* (1964), *That Darn Cat* (1965), and *Lt. Robinson Crusoe, U.S.N.* (1966). He also wrote the screenplay for *Toby Tyler* (1959) and *Bon Voyage* (1962) and the story that became the basis for *The Misadventures of Merlin Jones* (1964). Throughout these years, he worked particularly closely with director Robert Stevenson, scriptwriter Don DaGradi, and songwriters Richard M. and Robert B. Sherman as part of a talented team whose movies were among the highest-grossing of the era. A high point of his film career came with *Mary Poppins,* the studio's popular, award-winning 1964 film, when he was nominated for two Oscars as the coproducer (along with Walt) and coscreenwriter (along with DaGradi).[48]

As Walsh's successes mounted, he became a highly regarded figure on the Burbank lot. A balding, heavyset, "lovable bear of a man," in Peter Ellenshaw's words, with a pencil mustache and a soft-spoken demeanor, he was rarely seen without a cigarette hanging from the corner of his mouth. He often dressed rather haphazardly, plodding around the studio in a pair of old shoes with a piece of rope holding up his trousers and a scarf tied around his neck. Somewhat reserved and self-effacing, yet witty and warm around friends, he earned great affection from his colleagues. But his increasingly lofty stature rested on more than charm. Walsh's unique strength as a producer, much like Walt's, lay in his instinctive empathy for the values and reactions of a mass American audience. One day, at his boss's urging, he went to a little theater in Long Beach to watch one of his own movies and observe the audience response. The experience, he observed, was a revelation:

They were playing *Shaggy Dog.* And there was a guy sitting next to me and he was a truck driver, apparently. Sleeves rolled up. He's got a baby with him and the two are watching the picture together. Daddy's stuck with watching the baby while the wife goes shopping . . . And then this wonderful thing happened. The kid started to laugh along with the father and there were the two of them laughing at the screen together. And I thought that was better than [a review in] the New York *Times.* And I said, "Boy, if I can do that, then I know what it is that I want to do."[49]

By the early 1960s, many believed that Bill Walsh was the logical candidate to take over from Walt if the studio chief ever decided to step down. Ub Iwerks, Walt's collaborator since the early 1920s, was overheard commenting that Walsh was "the most creative man at the studio." Even Ward Kimball, a biting critic of many of the new Disney executives, made an exception. "Only one guy over there I admire, I respect as far as creativity is concerned," he declared, "[and that] is Bill Walsh."[50]

Perhaps the key to Walsh's successful career at the studio, however, lay in his relationship with Walt Disney. By all accounts, the two men grew very close professionally, and to a certain extent personally. In Fess Parker's assessment, Walsh served as "Walt Disney's right arm as far as production was concerned," and the two were "creative twins." It became clear to many that Walt held a very high opinion of Walsh's talent and had great confidence in his judgment. He allowed Walsh to push him into being the emcee for the 1950 Christmas show, and over the next decade and a half he relied on Walsh for a variety of important tasks.[51]

For his part, Walsh developed an admiration for Walt so intense that it bordered on hero worship. The producer believed his boss to be a genius and was astounded by his myriad talents. In one sense, Walt's ability to see "the whole package" — deciding what elements would make a story right for a Disney audience, thinking about promotion, covering possible angles with television, considering audience response — impressed Walsh mightily. At the same time, however, Walt demonstrated a keen grasp of the more mundane but equally crucial cinematic elements of pacing, visual interest, dialogue, and basic believability. But for Walsh, the studio chief's two most impressive traits lay elsewhere. First, he devoted enormous amounts of time and energy to developing projects correctly from the very beginning of the process. "Walt would go through a script page by page and line by line," the producer remembered. "You would never hear 'I don't like this' or 'I don't know what's wrong.' Walt would work with you to solve the problems. This is the hardest kind of work on a picture." Second, Walt simply had an unerring, even eerie instinct for what would work visually or the right touch to put on a character or a plot line. He was right so often that Walsh would think, as he put it, "My God, he's really in touch with something in outer space . . . The guy was just haunted. He knew something that no one else knew in this town."[52]

Yet for all his tremendous respect for Walt, Walsh displayed a remarkable willingness to stand up to his boss on creative matters. He revered the studio chief as a father figure, and his wife, Nolie, believed this stemmed from the fact that Walsh had lacked a father when he was growing up. In fact, when Walsh died, in January 1975, he was buried not far from Walt's final resting place. But Walsh was no sycophant. He engaged in some legendary arguments with Walt, a fact that enhanced his reputation at the studio. According to Kimball, Walsh "had the greatest arguments with Walt of anybody. They were always at each other because they were both creative." Sidney Miller, the director of *The Mickey Mouse Club*, remembered a clash after Walsh had submitted a filmscript draft to Walt. The studio head took it with him on vacation and upon returning called the producer to his office. "Bill came out white," Miller said. "I said, 'Tell me what happened!' Bill replied, 'Walt threw the script at the wall!'"[53]

Yet Walsh was shrewd enough to use honey rather than vinegar most of the time, and he handled his boss the way few others at the studio could. He not only tried to amuse Walt with his writing and his presentations but used a secret trick to gain approval for his scripts. "I always stuck a little bit of Walt in the main character, so he could recognize himself," Walsh confessed later. "He would say, 'Now this kid's got it here. It's true, real, the character is real.' If I'd make the father in *The Shaggy Dog* or the professor in *The Absent-Minded Professor*, I'd give him some of Walt's own personal characteristics."[54]

As longtime colleague Card Walker once put it, Walsh became an outstanding producer at the Disney Studio because he could take a project and "think of it at the end. In other words, if he has a story idea, he's thinking in terms, *now*, of the newspaper ad or a trailer or a radio spot for the public. [He would say], 'I've made the picture, now what am I going to say? Is it exciting? Is it a good title?' [He'd] work from the back forward." And his ultimate goal was clear: "to make sure people go to see it." Walsh took a special creativity consisting of gentle wit, vivid characterization, brisk storytelling, and a sentimental desire to please ordinary people and combined it with the publicist's feel for promotion and audience reaction. Understanding integration and embracing the Disney image, he mirrored perfectly the impulses of the postwar entertainment company.[55]

As Bill Walsh's career illustrates, Disney's rise as an architect of the culture industry was no simple tale of naked corporate domination. For Americans vaguely troubled by the drudgery inherent in rationalized work life, spiritual emptiness amid material plenty, and vanishing individualism with the cocoon of organizational security, Disney provided a cultural balm. His enterprise seemed to be a seedbed of fantasy, where consumption of images and commodities produced a joyful, dreams-come-true world. By far the most elaborate, and seductive, realization of the Disney vision occurred in a former orange grove some thirty miles south of Burbank. It was Walt's most remarkable undertaking in the 1950s.

20

The Happiest Place on Earth

O N THE AFTERNOON of July 17, 1955, the grand opening of Disneyland held the rapt attention of millions of Americans. The construction of this fantastic amusement park had been the subject of feverish press speculation for over a year, and when the gates swung open, the event was broadcast live on ABC in a two-hour spectacle hosted by Art Linkletter, Bob Cummings, and Ronald Reagan. Entitled *Dateline Disneyland,* the show offered a series of striking images: a jovial Walt running his beloved steam-powered locomotive around the edge of the park, a host of political dignitaries and Hollywood celebrities proclaiming their impressions, Fess Parker and Buddy Ebsen dashing in on horseback. These scenes and many more were captured by television cameras whose jerking and occasional malfunctioning only enhanced the sense of drama. Meanwhile, media reports from Los Angeles detailed the huge crowds descending on Anaheim and the monstrous traffic jams resulting from thousands of cars on the freeways.

Amid such fanfare, Disneyland burst onto the postwar American scene. This outpouring of public enthusiasm may have seemed outlandish, but it was not misplaced, because the significance of the park was genuine. As a creative amusement center, its likes had never been seen before. Moreover, from its very inception, Disneyland functioned as a kind of command center linking together (and publicizing) the studio's myriad projects in television, movies, music, and merchandising. But in a larger sense, Disneyland was a unique embodiment of prosperous, middle-class, postwar America. As nothing else quite did, it stood, literally, as a monument to the American way of life. Millions of citizens journeyed there to pay homage to the idealized image of themselves created by a master cultural mediator.[1]

I. Disneyland: Consolidating the Disney Enterprise

Disneyland's origins had deep, tangled roots in Walt's own past. He always told inquirers that he had the idea when he took his two young daughters out for fun on weekends and found that existing kids' parks and fairs were often dirty, sleazy, money-grubbing places. Actually, the notion seems to have been percolating in his mind from a much earlier date. His sister, Ruth Disney Beecher, remembered his utter fascination when, as children, they peered through the fence at Fairmont Park in Kansas City, a "fairyland" they couldn't afford to enter. Wilfred Jackson noted that at the 1937 premiere of *Snow White*, as he and Walt strolled by a small-scale replica of the dwarfs' cottage built outside Cathay Circle Theater, Walt observed that someday he would "make a park for kids, a place scaled down to kids' size." On a 1940 trip to New York, Walt told Ben Sharpsteen at some length about his plan to display "Disney characters in their fantasy surroundings" at a park near his Burbank headquarters, a scheme that would give studio visitors a place to experience something more than "just seeing people at work."[2]

In the late 1940s, Walt began tinkering with a traveling, small-scale exhibit of scenes from American history that featured miniature mechanical people moved by tiny pulleys and gears, which he envisioned presenting in department stores around the country. He assigned artist Harper Goff to work on this project, which he called Disneylandia or Walt Disney's America. He also began toying with the idea of presenting steam-powered trains to the public. In 1948, he outlined a modest amusement park that incorporated these ideas and added more expansive elements. This blueprint began with a Main Village containing a small park, town hall, railroad station, opera house, movie theater, post office, and drugstore. A variety of "little stores" around the park would offer toys, old-fashioned candy, music and books, hobby materials, and artwork by studio artists. A "horse car" would transport visitors around the park, while a livery stable would rent ponies and buckboards. A carnival area would offer "roller coaster, merry-go-rounds, and typical midway stuff." A special Western Village would present a general store, a cowboy museum, a corral full of horses for riding, a stagecoach, and a donkey pack train. Over the next few years, this plan gradually expanded to include spaceship and submarine rides, a Mississippi steamboat, a zoo of miniature animals, and various exhibit halls. In 1952, Walt actually petitioned the Burbank city government to begin developing this facility on land adjacent to the studio.[3]

As the idea began to expand, Walt found little enthusiasm for the project within his own company. His brother Roy, the financial director of the studio, stoutly opposed it, believing that this fanciful, expensive amusement park would lead to financial ruin. Most bankers and investors agreed. But Walt, supremely confident of his own vision, simply sidestepped the studio and began to gather funds by borrowing on his life insurance and selling some vacation property in southern California. He began to assemble a staff of designers, planners, and artists and formed WED Enterprises — the letters were his initials — as a personal corporation to house them. Operating out of a small building on the Burbank lot, the WED group began a long process of creative brainstorming. Its members conceptualized, designed, and reworked Walt's broad ideas and visited other amusement attractions around the country to gather data and impressions.

By 1953, two large hurdles — financing and securing an actual location — still blocked the launching of the park. In July of that year, Walt solicited a pair of marketing studies from the Stanford Research Institute, one of which would examine the economic prospects of Disneyland and the other its ideal location. After determining that such a facility could be profitable, the Stanford group closely examined a host of factors — demographic statistics, urban growth trends, population concentrations, traffic patterns, freeway construction, weather conditions — before recommending a sight in Anaheim, a rapidly growing town just southeast of Los Angeles. This study eventually led to the purchase of a 160-acre orange grove at the juncture of Harbor Boulevard and the new Santa Ana freeway. A few months later, the financial breakthrough came with the Disney-ABC deal, which brought the television network in as a major investor. Disneyland Incorporated became the corporate overseer of the park project, with a complex partnership structure: Walt Disney Productions owned 34.48 percent, ABC-Paramount 34.48 percent, Walter E. Disney (through WED) 16.56 percent, Western Printing and Lithographing 13.80 percent, and a number of minor investors made up the rest. ABC put up $500,000 immediately and guaranteed loans for another $4.5 million. The partnership contract also stipulated that Disney could buy out the other major investors after two years.

As Disneyland began to move closer to reality, Walt's development team slowly emerged from the shadows. Centered in WED, this updated version of the nine old men included artists and designers such as Harper Goff, Marvin Davis, John Hench, Ken Anderson, and Marc Davis; Roger Broggie, head of the studio machine shop, who played a leading role in the construction of the rides; general manager C. V. Wood, from the Stanford Research

Institute; and landscaping supervisor Bill Evans. Most important, the group was under the leadership of Joe Fowler, an engineer and retired navy admiral who became construction supervisor and later park manager for ten years, and Dick Irvine, an old hand at the studio who had left for a brief stint at Twentieth Century-Fox before returning as art director for Disneyland. This duo worked together closely and served directly under Walt, who oversaw every detail of the park's construction.

With financing in place and a location secured, Walt's team broke ground and began supervising the building of this remarkable facility in late summer 1954. Aiming for an opening date in midsummer 1955, the Disneyland group began a steady routine of long work weeks with habitual Saturday sessions. By late spring, various delays and roadblocks were creating enormous pressures and prompting round-the-clock labor.

In the first days of construction, the engineers were startled to find that all of the existing orange trees had been bulldozed out, including a large number that had been carefully flagged for saving with bright strips of cloth. The equipment operator, it turned out, was colorblind. After the buildings had begun to go up, Walt and Ken Anderson proudly escorted the fastidious, white-suited set designer Emile Kuri on an inspection of the half-completed Sleeping Beauty Castle, only to gaze in amazement as Kuri picked up a gunny sack from a pile of lumber, turned pale, and began jumping around like a madman, swatting at his body. The sack, it turned out, was infested with fleas from the large number of cats let loose in the park to control mice. When the pair hurried over to help, they also became covered with fleas, and the trio went running through the park to the crude wardrobe facility to be fumigated. Some weeks later, after weeks of work, Walt and his engineers' delight at seeing the Rivers of America filled with water turned to horror when it nearly dried up in only a few days. The substance they had used to seal the river bottom, a synthetic compound widely used in earth dams, proved unable to sustain the river, and they solved the problem only when they located a source of clay.[4]

As the opening date drew near, panic set in. A thousand tasks remained, money was running short, and last-minute strikes by plumbers and at local asphalt plants created havoc. Fearing disaster, many of the WED staff began advocating pushing back the park's opening until early fall. But Admiral Joe Fowler, with Walt's full support, refused to hear of it. Used to meeting deadlines during World War II, he determinedly pushed things along. He negotiated a deal with the plumbers' union, hauled asphalt in from San Diego, and encouraged everyone to make herculean efforts. Finally, a few days before the televised opening, the park was near enough to completion for a birthday party for Walt and several hundred guests. After dinner and drinks at the Golden Horseshoe Revue, the guests were scheduled to take a jaunt on the Mark Twain steamboat. When Fowler went down early to check out the boat, he was met by a distinguished-looking woman on the gangplank, who handed him a broom and said, "Let's get this place cleaned up. It's terrible." As they swept wood shavings and other construction debris off the decks, the admiral was happy to make the acquaintance of Lillian Disney.[5]

Nearly a year of frenzied construction finally produced the gala opening on July 17, 1955. While ABC cameras conveyed scenes of bustling joy and announcers pontificated about the historical significance of the event, the behind-the-scenes situation veered dangerously close to total collapse. Construction went on throughout the night until just moments before the ceremonies began, and Tomorrowland remained muffled in banners and balloons to hide its half-completed state. Near chaos ensued as traffic jams tangled up the Santa Ana freeway and the festivities prompted one disaster after another. A gas leak forced a temporary shutdown of Fantasyland, the park restaurants ran out of food, a paucity of bathrooms and drinking fountains made many guests grumpy, and the blazing heat melted freshly laid asphalt into sticky black goo that caught and broke many a lady's high heel. Jack Kinney, the studio animator and director, remembered that staff members and their families had been assigned to populate certain areas, and they did their duty by smiling and waving when the television cameras turned on them. The sweating, thirsty group on the steamboat, where Kinney was stationed, "pushed and shoved to reach dry land, drank warm colas at the Frontierland Saloon, and escaped to our cars and the nearest bars . . . Later we traded stories with other employees and found that some were locked in cattle cars on the Disneyland railroad, marooned on Tom Sawyer's Island, restricted to the crowded theater, and jammed into rocket rides and other 'fun' places. But at least we could all say we were there."[6]

After the staff recovered from the opening-day frenzy, worked out the park's kinks, and settled down to business, the seductiveness of the place became clear. Enthusiastic crowds began streaming through the gates day after day, and very quickly attendance far exceeded everyone's expectations. Within six months a million customers had entered the park, and by 1960 the annual number of visitors numbered around 5 million. A decade later it had grown to 10 million. The number of employees at Disneyland rose correspondingly, climbing from around 1300 in 1955 to 6200 fifteen years later. These impressive statistics indicated a tremendous public approval of Walt's dream park and made it one of the biggest tourist attractions in the United States.[7]

Daily life at Disneyland produced numerous incidents, many amusing and some memorable. Visiting Russian journalists in 1957, for instance, returned to Moscow to report that Disney was keeping a tribe of American Indians captive in Frontierland to entertain attendees. When told about this, Chief Riley Sunrise replied indignantly, "Captivity my eye! How many Russians make 125 bucks a week?" Another story concerned a four-year-old boy who emerged from an encounter with Maleficent in the dark, gloomy corridors of Sleeping Beauty Castle and tugged the skirt of a young park attendant. "Lady, you better not go in there," he warned. "Why not?" she asked. "Because," the boy replied, "it'll scare hell out of you." Occasional glitches also provided grist for the story mill. For example, Walt nurtured a misplaced faith in the educational possibilities of the Autopia ride, believing that children would drive these miniature cars on a mock freeway and learn respect for one another and for the rules of the road. After a couple of weeks, however, only six cars survived of the original thirty-six, and the staff had to report that the children loved the ride mainly for the excitement and hilarity of smashing into one another. Autopia was altered. The western stagecoach in Frontierland had to be dropped because of its tendency to become top-heavy and turn over when more than a few passengers climbed aboard. Another of Walt's pet ideas, a live circus, was quietly phased out as problems mounted. Once a herd of llamas escaped from confinement to go stampeding through the park before being recaptured, and during the old-fashioned circus parade down Main Street, USA, a tiger and a panther broke through the partition separating them and began grappling in a furious death struggle. Horrified onlookers witnessed a bloodbath before attendants could bludgeon and separate the big cats.[8]

But such snafus rarely disrupted the Disneyland experience, and ordinary guests were joined by a long list of famous visitors. Shortly after the park opened, Vice President Richard Nixon made a much-publicized visit with his family and announced, "This is a paradise for children and grown-ups, too. My children have been after me for weeks to bring them here." He returned in 1959 to cut the ribbon at the grand opening of Disneyland's Monorail system. In 1957, Moroccan king Mohammed V was so enchanted by his formal visit to Disneyland that he sneaked out of his hotel the next day to make an incognito return visit. That same year former president Harry Truman went to the park and wisecracked to reporters that he took his wife on all the rides except Dumbo the Flying Elephant, because of its Republican symbolism. And in September 1960 Soviet premier Nikita S. Khrushchev became the center of an international incident when his request to visit Disneyland was turned down by the State Department for security reasons. The angry Soviet leader denounced this example of American capitalist oppression, and for good measure announced his country's intent to build an even grander amusement park in Moscow called Miracle Land.[9]

What exactly made Disneyland so incredibly appealing to millions of people? The query, while simple, demands a complex answer, because like so many Disney films and television shows, the park's seductive appeal operated at several levels.

Most obvious, Disneyland was a place where customers, from step one, found themselves immersed in a fantasy world where unique images and experiences evoked laughter, wonder, curiosity, and emotional warmth. All visitors entered Disneyland by walking down Main Street, USA, a sentimental recreation of turn-of-the-century, small-town life, complete with Victorian storefronts, city hall, silent-film theater, and horse-drawn streetcar. They were next funneled to Sleeping Beauty Castle, the looming attraction at the heart of the park, from which a quintet of theme areas radiated outward. Visitors could go into Adventureland, where lush vegetation and attractions such as the Jungle Cruise evoked the studio's True-Life Adventures. Frontierland, with its triple-deck steamboat cruising the Rivers of America and Fort Wilderness protecting against Indian attack, presented a rendition of nineteenth-century American pioneer history. Fantasyland, entered through Sleeping Beauty Castle and the area of the park most closely linked to the animated films, transported guests through rides embodying fantastic scenes from movies such as *Peter Pan, Alice in Wonderland,* and *Snow White and the Seven Dwarfs,* or sent them hurtling down Matterhorn Mountain on bobsled rides, or floated them on a peaceful excursion through the miniaturized Storybook Land. Tomorrowland, a reflection of the Disney interest in science and technology, offered a peek into the future with its monorail system, 360-degree Circle Vision theater, and Rocket to the Moon ride. Each of these areas shaped an elaborate multimedia experience that combined striking visual images, a complementary musical atmosphere, and active participation. The result was not a fast-paced, brassy, carnivalesque encounter in the Coney Island mode, but a gentle, reassuring, enchanted environment. From the Davy Crockett canoes to the Dumbo ride, the Swiss Family Robinson Treehouse to the plastic House of the Future, Disneyland's array of elaborate attractions converged around a simple formula: a large dose of pure fun.

At a deeper level, this mélange of fun and fantasy was enhanced by the profoundly optimistic psychology of the park. A shrewd design and engineering scheme, for example, manipulated both the movements and emotions of the huge crowds. One essential principle emphasized what Walt liked to call "weenies," which were the large visual attractions in each "land" which caught the eye and drew people along preordained routes so that crowds flowed smoothly. This was augmented by another clever design ploy, which muted the frustration of waiting in long lines for the park's attractions. Disney planners came up with a unique system: first, a snakelike pattern masked the length of a line by running it back and forth in parallel lines; then a variety of visual and audio images kept those in line entertained; and finally, a cleverly engineered schedule kept visitors steadily embarking on the ride so the line would always appear to be moving forward. From yet another direction, the small-scale dimension of Disneyland — the railroad running around the perimeter was built on a five-eighths scale, for instance, while the buildings on Main Street shrank from nine-tenths on the first floor to eight-tenths at the second — subtly contributed to a childlike, intimate, fairyland atmosphere.[10]

Moreover, Walt and his creative staff took his unique brand of sentimental modernism, developed over many years in the studio's fantasy movies, and expanded it in a more sophisticated form. They drew on the studio's traditional juxtaposition of imagination and reality, free-flowing fantasy and technology, folklore and rationalized production to create a three-dimensional wonderland in Anaheim that totally enveloped the consumer. Marc Davis described Disneyland's attractions as "a new medium of entertainment . . . You could not tell a story, but you can give an experience, and when we do it well, a very unique experience. An experience you can't get any other place." In other words, the park did not tell a story in traditional cinematic fashion but instead made the visitor an active participant in a kind of three-dimensional movie. The creative team tried to blur the line between fantasy and reality by completely immersing visitors in a totally controlled environment. A writer for *McCall's* argued that at Disneyland, "Walt Disney's cartoon world materializes bigger than life and twice as real," while an admiring article in *Popular Science Monthly* described the park as Disney's "real-life dream world." A *Woman's Home Companion* editorial saw Disneyland as "probably the closest yet to life-as-we-wish-it-were combined with life-as-it-is." British cultural critic Aubrey Menen, surprised by his fascination with the park, concluded similarly that he "spent the morning riding through the dreams that lay somewhere at the bottom of my mind. We all have them: they lie there from our childhood, gathering dust. It is one of the functions of artists to blow away the dust and make them fresh again for a little while. It is a delicate operation that must be done with the sureness of a mature master who can still retain the vision of a child."[11]

Disneyland's optimistic, sentimental, fantasy-infused psychology depended on two additional elements. First, Walt insisted on a genuine commitment to quality. The notion of visitors' getting their money's worth became a kind of gospel at Disneyland. Park designers and managers appreciated Walt's avid commitment to "plussing," the term he employed to describe a continuous search for new ideas, new angles, and new additions to make Disneyland more attractive. Marc Davis recalled a revealing experience during a staff meeting when he proposed to rework a park ride, noting that there was a cheap way and an expensive way to accomplish it. Walt, he remembered, got up and walked around the table to lay a hand on his shoulder. "Marc, you and I do not worry whether anything is cheap or expensive. We only worry whether it's good," he said. "I have a theory that if it's good enough, the public will pay you back for it."[12]

A carefully sculpted Disneyland philosophy toward visitors added the final dimension to the psychological profile of the park. Employee handbooks with titles such as *Your Disneyland: A Guide for Hosts and Hostesses* (1955) and *You're on Stage at Disneyland* (1962) made it clear that customers were to be treated as guests while park workers were to view themselves as actors and actresses who were onstage and committed to enhancing the experience of the throngs they encountered. "Every guest receives the VIP treatment," these handbooks instructed. "We roll out the red carpet for the Jones family from Joliet just as we would (with a few embellishments) for the Eisenhowers from Palm Springs." In addition to courtesy and perkiness, Disneyland demanded that its hosts and hostesses possess the natural look of the "kid next door" — no jewelry or heavy perfume and modest hairstyles for women, short hair and shined shoes for men, neatness and good grooming for both. To guarantee these standards, the company established Disneyland University, under the direction of Van Arsdale France, as a training institution for park employees.[13]

Disneyland can also be seen as the quintessential expression of the Disney culture industry machine in the postwar era. Its vital link to television was clear from the outset, since it had the same name as the ABC show. Bill Walsh's earliest blueprint for the television series in June 1953 stressed the need for televised progress reports on the Anaheim facility. They would encourage the viewing audience, he argued, to remain interested as the park was "transformed from the world of the imagination into physical reality from week to week." The show's regular segments on construction in the mid-1950s successfully wooed an audience. As one visiting parent testified, "To my kids it is the Taj Mahal, Niagara Falls, Sherwood Forest, and Davy Crockett all rolled into one. After years of sitting in front of a television set, the youngsters are sure it's a fairyland before they even get here." Walt himself provided a simple summary for an interviewer: "I saw that if I was ever going to have my park, here, at last, was a way to tell millions of people about it — with TV."[14]

Inside the high dirt berm of Disneyland, of course, all of the rides and attractions used an array of Disney motifs. From *Snow White* to *Peter Pan*, *Twenty Thousand Leagues under the Sea* to *Davy Crockett*, the True-Life Adventures to *The Swiss Family Robinson*, they brought to life an incredible array of characters, themes, and settings from the long history of movie productions. The plethora of stores intensified this atmosphere by offering a cornucopia of Disney merchandise — records, clothing, keepsakes, souvenirs, and others. This saturation strategy took millions of visitors and immersed them in an enchanted, Disney-created world while softly selling an array of Disney products. Its success quickly became evident. In 1955, Walt Disney Productions' gross income more than doubled from the year before, and it continued to grow by leaps and bounds, going from $11.6 million in 1954 to $58.4 million in 1959.[15]

In all of these ways, Walt's Anaheim wonderland encapsulated the Disney appeal. It joined the aesthetic elements of the company's creations — fun, fantasy, sentiment, optimism — in a compelling three-dimensional form. Disneyland also consolidated the various wings of the vast entertainment enterprise that had been taking shape since the early 1950s. Ultimately, however, the park cut an even wider cultural swath.

II. Disneyland: Animating the American Vision

Perhaps the most subtle seduction of Walt's grand theme park came from its evocation of national values. In myriad ways that visitors encountered consistently but perceived only half consciously, the park offered a remarkable distillation and reaffirmation of postwar American culture. The hordes of middle-class families who streamed into Anaheim in the decade after 1955 found themselves completely submerged in a fantasized but nearly pitch-perfect representation of their deepest commitments and beliefs.

This cultural influence appeared, for instance, in Disneyland's subtle yet pervasive political ambiance. Steeped in the patriotic sensibility of the Cold War, the park continually served up powerful images of Disney's 1950s-style sentimental populism. The ceremonies on opening day set the tone. On a warm July afternoon, Walt and the assembled dignitaries launched this unique undertaking by reciting the pledge of allegiance, raising the American flag, leading the crowd in singing the national anthem, and bowing their heads as a Protestant minister invoked the Almighty's blessing. In his prepared remarks, Walt explicitly dedicated the park to "the ideals, the dreams, and the hard facts which have created America." In his speech, Goodwin Knight, the governor of California, informed listeners that it had been "all built by American labor and American capital, under the belief that this is a God-fearing and God-loving country." After this display of patriotic rhetoric, air force jet fighters flew overhead as a Marine Corps contingent led a joyful parade down Main Street, USA. The following year, a promotional film informed viewers that the park "could happen only in a country where freedom is a heritage and the pursuit of happiness a basic human right."[16]

As visitors moved through Disneyland in the years that followed, they encountered a series of populist political emblems that further reinforced an American way of life. The park promoted an unproblematic celebration of the American people and their experience: Main Street, USA with its nostalgic images of turn-of-the-century small-town life, the heroic conquest of the West represented in Frontierland, the sturdiness of the heartland reflected in the Rivers of America, the Jungle Cruise in Adventureland with its playful pacification of the Third World, the promise of continued technological progress with Monsanto's House of the Future in Tomorrowland. The showcasing of sophisticated robot technology in the early 1960s — Audio-Animatronics, in Disney parlance — enhanced Disneyland's celebration of the American people. The Enchanted Tiki Room, which initiated this technology at the park in 1963, created a jovial melting-pot atmosphere as its brightly colored electronic birds comically represented French, German, Irish, and other stereotypes. But Great Moments with Mr. Lincoln was probably the culmination of the park's roboticized version of American values. In this attraction, an electronically controlled replica of the sixteenth president rose to his feet against a swelling backdrop of patriotic music and solemnly paid homage to the tradition of democratic constitutionalism in the United States.

For many, Disney's Anaheim park provided a particularly impressive display of American technical achievement and free enterprise. Articles in a variety of journals described Disneyland as a marvel of city planning, municipal construction, landscaping, architectural design, interior and exterior lighting, air compression, hydraulic mechanics, and the innovative use of materials such as plastics. Awestruck writers praised this "mechanical wonderland" for its development of innovative, state-of-the-art engineering techniques, construction materials, and technical expertise. In 1963, the chairman of a conference on urban planning at Harvard University described Disneyland as "the greatest piece of urban design in the United States."[17]

In a 1957 interview with Hedda Hopper, Walt clearly summarized Disneyland's patriotic dimension. "There's an American theme behind the whole park," he told readers. "I believe in emphasizing the story of what made America great and what will keep it great." Private conversation supported such public utterances. During construction, for instance, Walt stressed a democratic political rationale for Disneyland's scale when he told artist and designer Ken Anderson, "You know, tyrants in the past have built these huge buildings [that would say] look how big and powerful I am. And they towered over the people just to impress them."[18]

Disneyland's strong family appeal clearly linked it to yet another powerful 1950s trend. Official descriptions of the park placed a heavy emphasis on its family function. A full-color, twelve-page newspaper section entitled "Welcome to Disneyland" was printed all over the country in midsummer 1955, and it opened with Walt's personal assurance that the park was "a magic place where every family can find and share happy hours and experiences together." Magazine and newspaper stories cooperated by flooding readers with images of Disneyland's wholesome family appeal. *Life* trumpeted a message about the "new park with the stuff children's dreams are made on," and *Woman's Day* described the park as "*the* family enchantment center." *Better Homes and Gardens* elaborated on this theme, noting that "parents entering Disneyland with their children are due for the same surprise they got from other Walt Disney creations. What is planned as a dutiful pilgrimage for the sake of the children turns out to be an eye-opening day of adult entertainment and education." To prove "Disneyland's appeal for families," the magazine sent a photographer to accompany a family to the park to record their delighted experiences.[19]

From its very inception, the Anaheim playground took shape as a vacation mecca for an America on wheels, promoting the gospel of leisure. *Disneyland Holiday,* a special company publication for tourists, captured this impulse, describing the facility as "America's favorite vacationland" and offering information on the park's many attractions, the unique appeal of southern California, travel games and puzzles for children, and maps of the Los Angeles freeway system. From the mid-1950s on, travel sections in dozens of newspapers all over the United States promoted trips to Anaheim, extolling the park's pleasures for "people who are seeking release from the cares and concerns of today's tense times." Once inside Disneyland, of course, visitors luxuriated in a large number of unique shops and stores. The park even inspired a California firm to design a special line of clothing for women and little girls called "Fashions in Fantasy."[20]

Disneyland became a showcase for thriving corporate capitalism as well, proudly featuring an imposing array of big-business entities that underwrote its consumer paradise. The corporate sponsorship of many stores and attractions was clearly visible, tying images of modern capitalist dynamism, productivity, and organizational stability to the park's warm evocations of American values. As a report in the *Wall Street Journal* noted, some sixty-five companies were involved in the park, and Disney's own publicity proudly promoted these affiliations. It assured potential visitors that they could expect (to choose just a few examples) the finest food products from Carnation, Swift, and Frito; quality clothing from Pendleton Woolen Mills; and efficient services from Gibson Greeting Cards, the Bank of America, and Eastman Kodak. Corporate sponsorship of various attractions also enjoyed heavy promotion. Trans-World Airline's presentation of the Rocket to the Moon ride, Richfield Oil's fueling of miniature autos in the Autopia ride, Kaiser Aluminum's giant telescope, Monsanto's all-plastic House of the Future, and the Golden Horseshoe dance hall, sponsored by Pepsi-Cola, all earned space in Disney publicity. Moreover, business journals such as *Advertising Requirements, Printer's Ink,* and *The Westerner* jumped on the bandwagon, stressing the shrewdness of Walt Disney Productions' integrated, saturation-style advertising strategy and the huge profit potential of what one described as "a wonderland of brand names with a captive viewing audience of 5,000,000 a year." Disneyland successfully identified large corporations with fantasy fulfillment and populist virtue.[21]

Booming attendance made the Anaheim playground the leading tourist attraction in the western United States. Moreover, market surveys solicited by the company showed visitor satisfaction to be extremely high: by 1959, 98.6 percent of customers surveyed said they received their money's worth at the park and 83 percent planned to return. A torrent of admiring news stories also appeared in publications from all over the United States. Gladwyn Hill, writing in the New York *Times*, suggested that the key to Disneyland's success lay in its skillful encouragement of a "suspension of disbelief" among patrons, just as the theater had for ages, and its creation of a "let's pretend" mentality which encouraged a childlike sense of fun. Arthur Gordon told readers of *Look* that "Mr. and Mrs. America and children," upon arriving in Anaheim, would encounter a fantastic facility full of delightful paradoxes:

> Nostalgia jammed up against the needle-pointed promises of the future. The relentless urge to reduce reality, somehow, to smaller, more graspable terms . . . The small-boy fascination with explorers, big-game animals, outlaws, Indians. The delight in pure fantasy, balanced by a ferocious attention to detail. The profusion of imaginative ideas so wild and luxuriant as to give the startled observer an impression of carefree chaos — but timed to the last split second and planned down to the last glint in the spun-glass elephant's eye.[22]

Not surprisingly, many intellectual observers deplored Disney's amusement park, though others rushed to its defense. Aubrey Menen, for instance, disliked certain parts of Disneyland but found himself amazed at encountering "the private world of a genius . . . a masterpiece of its age," built not for the enjoyment of kings and queens but "for my pleasure and everyone else's." Kevin Wallace, writing in *The New Yorker*, confessed to experiencing an "uncritical euphoria" while in the park, but he attributed it to a more mundane factor: an atmosphere where "the engineering of ease" had inspired the Disney staff to "figure out what could worry anybody, and then remove it."[23]

Perhaps the most famous critical controversy over the park, however, took place in the pages of *The Nation*. In June 1958 Julian Halevy wrote an article entitled "Disneyland and Las Vegas," wherein he viciously denounced the park as "a collection of midway rides, concessions, hot-dog stands and soft drink counters, peep-shows and advertising stunts for big corporations . . . a sickening blend of cheap formulas packaged to sell." It was filled, he argued, with pathetic throngs whose empty lives allowed them to respond to such fake escape and adventure. Like Las Vegas, Halevy concluded, Disneyland could only exist in a conformist, rigid society "for the relief of tension and boredom, as tranquilizers for social anxiety . . . [providing] fantasy experiences in which not-so-secret longings are pseudo-satisfied." Ray Bradbury, the science-fiction writer and novelist, replied with an outraged letter to the editor in which he defended Disneyland as "an experience of true delight and wonder" and described Halevy as typical of a certain class of people "who, for intellectual reasons, steadfastly refuse to let go and enjoy themselves. I feel sorry for him. He will never travel in space, he will never touch the stars." In an analysis published a few years later, Bradbury insisted that Disneyland "liberates men to their better selves" and thus had a genuine historical force. The park's array of visual delights and sensory surprises, he argued, culminated in its robotics project, which, by instilling human qualities in machines, promised to enhance human life greatly in terms of education, service, and imaginative possibilities.[24]

But regardless of the critical response, there was no doubt that Disneyland was a wonder of postwar America. Its powerful cultural brew — a smooth blend of sentimental modernism, sentimental populism, nostalgia, consumerism, family virtue, and corporate abundance — proved an intoxicating experience for the millions of Americans who passed through its gates. It allowed visitors to revel in the fantasy life of their culture during the halcyon days of the American century and ritually reaffirm an idealistic view of themselves. By realizing Walt Disney's greatest postwar dream, Disneyland also took its creator's personal image, already towering, to the point of apotheosis.

III. The Magician and the Manager

In 1954, Walt Disney confronted a watershed in his personal life. After he agreed to become the master of ceremonies on *Disneyland,* things were never quite the same. "What movies couldn't do in many years, television has done in less than twelve months," wrote one reporter. "It has made Walt Disney famous on his own." Bill Walsh recalled with a chuckle that when Walt first began to host the show he was terrified, but "once he began performing every week, he kinda liked it. He uncovered a streak of ham in him that he didn't know existed."[25]

His new role as a celebrity pushed him squarely into the limelight in unfamiliar ways. Stories and photos began to pile up, of course, and popular television shows such as *Toast of the Town* and *The Jack Benny Show* featured him. Such exposure, while it strengthened his sense of close connection to ordinary citizens and offered reassurance "that he was doing something big" with his work, also brought less felicitous results. A few years after the Disneyland park opened, for example, a chagrined Walt wrote a letter of apology to a visitor who complained when he overlooked her daughter's request for an autograph. "It isn't that I object to giving my autograph to fans while in the Park, but I have found that if I stop to sign autograph books for the youngsters, I usually get inundated with them and never get to where I was going nor accomplish what I had set out to do," he explained. To help mend hurt feelings, he sent along an autographed photo of himself and his pet poodle, Lady.[26]

Part of Disney's newfound celebrity involved his image as a family man and patriot. In addition, he took on qualities associated with his role as a culture-industry impresario. On the one hand, he appeared in the public eye as a kind of beloved magician who amazed, amused, inspired, and reassured the millions of fellow citizens who flocked to his creations. On the other hand, he managed a corporate behemoth, performing a host of tasks which daily grew more complicated and daunting. This juxtaposition of the manager and the magician helped unlock the myriad meanings of the name Disney as it evolved in this era.

By the mid-1950s, news stories regularly portrayed Walt Disney as a creative figure whose wondrous powers indeed bordered on the magical. *National Geographic*'s cover story explored "The Magic Worlds of Walt Disney," *Reader's Digest* saluted "Walt Disney's Magic Kingdom," and *Life* acclaimed a man who dealt in "the stuff children's dreams are made on." The New York *Daily News* simply dubbed him "the modern Merlin." The man with magical powers who dabbled in dream life and conjured up wish fulfillment became a familiar image.[27]

But attempts at definition always returned to the reality of his work life. Disney himself always pointed in this direction by substituting labor for genius in explaining creativity. "Everybody can make their dreams come true," he told an interviewer in 1955. "It takes . . . a dream — faith in it — and hard work. But that's not quite true because it's so much fun you hardly realize it's work."[28]

By this time, however, the parameters of his work had shifted in subtle but significant ways. Increasingly he functioned as a kind of corporate manager in a large-scale economic setting. Instead of the old micromanagement style he used in the prewar period, actively involving himself in every animated project coming out of his studio, he now supervised more generally a vast array of undertakings in several different media. He still played an important role in defining projects, but seldom did he become completely involved in any one undertaking. Walt's task increasingly was to keep his machine running smoothly by overseeing skilled personnel and lubricating its array of moving parts with creative ideas.

At Walt's insistence, for example, teamwork became a watchword in the organization. This concept, as he announced, constituted a "way of life" for himself and his staff: "It seems to be shallow and arrogant for anyone in these times to claim he is completely self-made and that he owes all his success to his own unaided efforts. While it is true that it is basic Americanism that a man's standing is, in part, due to his personal enterprise and capacity, it is equally true that many hands and hearts and minds generally contribute to anyone's notable achievements." In a 1961 interview, he described his function as the head of such a team: setting up projects at "the formative stage," then turning day-to-day production over to talented artists and trusted supervisors, helping out when "we hit a snag," and making decisions on the final project as "a good editor."[29]

Visitors to the Burbank lot confirmed the tremendous scope of the demands facing the studio chief, which involved a host of close, intense conversations with artists, master mechanics, gag men, and producers as he supervised "half a hundred projects." In this context, Walt's mature management style depended less on demands than on suggestions. Although he could, and often did, assert his authority with a vengeance or angrily express his disapproval, he increasingly utilized his famous raised eyebrow to indicate dissatisfaction, used informal talks as a way to communicate his desires, and strove to make everyone on his far-flung staff feel that he or she was an important part of the Disney team. In fact, in the early 1960s, when a business executive tried to offer a compliment by suggesting that the studio's energy and achievements came directly from Walt, the entertainer became angry. According to observers, he replied testily, "I have an organization here. I don't do everything myself, it's all a bunch of decisions that come from everybody. We're a big team."[30]

Yet for all his increasing reliance on organization, Walt did not become an absentee landlord in the creative process. He still worked intensely with his greatest love, scripts and story. Movie producer Bill Anderson, who collaborated closely with him on several projects, was amazed at the hours that Walt put into shaping a story line and revising dialogue. On the television side, producer Winston Hibler participated in numerous story meetings in Walt's office and often received scripts filled with his boss's notorious "slashing blue pencil lines." According to Joe Fowler, Walt was a superb boss who explained his fascinating ideas, made his desires clear without screaming or yelling, delegated authority, and supported his staff in their endeavors. Moreover, he insisted on using first names throughout his organization and encouraged participation by forming management committees to help shape movie production or develop the Anaheim park. While he recognized the need for a large, rationalized business structure in the modern corporate age, he struggled hard to humanize it and instill vitality.[31]

Behind the skilled manager and the dexterous magician admired throughout America, however, stood a private man whom very few knew well. Part of the mystery lay in the fact that Walt was simply too devoted to his work, and too private, to make many close friends. His fame had changed the context of his life but not its essence. He remained a homebody who was, in the words of his wife, "too busy for social life. He didn't go to nightclubs or parties. We ate at home nearly all the time." Walt hated to waste time, and when visitors came to his home, he found it difficult to sit and visit with them. He didn't like holidays because he couldn't work, Lillian noted, and even at Christmas, "when he got through with the festivities, he went to his room and read." Although Walt and Lillian often went together on trips, most were work-related; Sharon recalled that "he never went anyplace that wasn't on business." People often could not believe that this unassuming man, immersed in work and content with family activity in his free moments, was the source of so much creativity and influence. Thus they found him enigmatic when, ironically, he was exactly what he appeared to be.[32]

For all his growing celebrity status, Walt seemed to go out of his way to be ordinary. By the late 1950s, in late middle age, he had rounded off many of the edges of his appearance and personality. Dropping the flashy look of earlier years, when he had sported colorful clothes and fashionably long hair, he adopted a more somber, conservative wardrobe consisting of dark suits or jackets and slacks and sweaters. The famous pencil mustache remained, but he cut his thick, graying hair more closely. According to Diane, "He was a very clean man, physically, and he expected it in others." To complete the avuncular image, he had gradually put on weight over the years, which made his angular features more distinguished. Walt's personality, after the stormy 1940s, underwent a similar softening. To be sure, he still displayed his characteristic flare-ups of temper followed by equally quick apologies — Lillian and Edna, Roy's wife, laughingly commiserated about the "Disney disposition" — but much of his emotional intensity had subsided. He also displayed some personal quirks. Diane noticed that when her father read, as he often did at home, he moved his lips. While he was an easy conversationalist, he could become curiously inarticulate, especially about ideas that fascinated him. The thought process seemed to outrace the capacity for speech, prompting him to use his hands to shape pictures behind the searching words.[33]

Walt's personal schedule settled into a familiar, if often hectic, pattern in the 1950s. His day-to-day activities took him between the poles of the Burbank studio and his home in Holmby Hills, although he spent increasing amounts of time at Disneyland after its opening, maintaining a comfortably furnished apartment over the firehouse on Main Street, USA. This busy itinerary was punctuated by occasional business trips and family holidays at Smoke Tree Ranch, a development of vacation houses in Palm Springs. Walt had a hashhouse appetite — chili and hamburgers were among his favorite foods — and actually complained at home when fancy dishes were served. Lillian recalled with a laugh that once, when he began carping about an elaborate cake, she became so exasperated that she flung a piece of it at him, splattering him in the face with whipped cream. He retaliated in kind, and a full-blown food fight ensued.[34]

When he wasn't working, Walt relaxed at home with simple diversions such as badminton and lawn bowling. He loved to tinker with mechanical projects in his shop in the barn behind the house, and after his grandchildren were born, he supervised their swimming in the backyard pool. A physically affectionate man, he constantly draped an arm around his wife, daughters, and grandchildren or reached to hold their hands. In a fumbling fashion that was endearing, he strove to fulfill family obligations. Frank Thomas recalled how Walt took dancing lessons at his wife's insistence, so they could go dancing with friends. He would manfully trudge around the dance floor with Lillian, and "his lips would be going 'one, two, three.' Never could get the hang of it." Similarly, he faithfully took his daughters to the opera and the symphony, even though he later admitted to hating it. As a longtime associate concluded, "We always had the feeling that Walt was basically a good Middle American."[35]

By the late 1950s, Walt radiated a commanding, inspiring presence that could leave his colleagues awestruck. One of them noted the sense of "magic about him that caught you up, a charisma," while another struggled to describe his aura as "an actual physical feeling. It reaches out, it touches you like electricity. We could feel him coming down the hall; figuratively our hair would stand on end, the backs of our necks would tingle." Walt enhanced this personal aura with a dynamic sense of salesmanship. He was, as Card Walker said, a "great convincer" who could make you believe absolutely in a project's potential. His sense of humor, especially in its self-deprecating mode, also added to his personal charm, as when he quipped to some particularly fawning admirers, "I already tried walking on water, and it doesn't work." But without question, he still could be extremely demanding with his subordinates, and outright acerbic when they failed to meet his expectations. Bill Anderson, for example, actually feared for his job when Walt exploded over cost overruns on *The Swiss Family Robinson*. At the same time, however, this powerful corporate manager returned easily to his working-class roots. In the early 1950s, he went to Ken Anderson for advice on designing and building a traveling show of miniature figures and scenes from American history, saying, "Hey, Ken, you know, I want to do something with my own hands. You guys are always drawing and everything. I want to do something myself."[36]

The personal sentimentality that always had influenced his work, both aesthetically and politically, reached a high point in the postwar era. As Walt made clear to both associates and family, he made no apologies for the optimistic emotion of creations such as *Pollyanna*, *The Mickey Mouse Club*, or Main Street, USA. When the adolescent Diane, embarrassed about the sentiment of Disney movies, complained to her father, he became angry and defensive about what he liked to call "corn." As studio head, he preached the same message to his associates, frequently saying, "There's nothing wrong with good schmaltz, nothing wrong with good heart . . . The critics think I'm kind of corny. Well, I am corny. As long as people respond to it, I'm okay." This strong sentimental streak, in his mind, was one of the identifying marks of a Disney creation.[37]

As Walt's public persona swelled to gigantic proportions, he increasingly reflected on the public context of his work. Pondering his relationship with and obligations to a vast popular audience led to several significant judgments. In the broadest sense, he came to view his company's productions explicitly in terms of a stewardship of Middle American values. "Good, wholesome entertainment for all ages" became the Disney Studio motto, and public opinion its guide. Walt delighted in telling interviewers, "I just kind of put my cards with the masses. All right, I am corny. But I think there's just about a hundred and forty million people in this country that are just as corny as I am." After decades in the business, Walt now perceived his audience as old friends who knew and trusted him. Unashamed, he cultivated the approval of these ordinary citizens and felt a great sense of responsibility to them. At mid-decade, for instance, nervous about serving as host for *Disneyland* and anxious about his limited education, he hired a special assistant whose sole job was to check his diction. As he explained, "I would like to have proper pronunciation of words because children are looking."[38]

Walt's reverence for the values and expectations of his vast popular audience also had a flip side. By the mid-1950s, he could not hide his growing contempt for critics, who increasingly dismissed Disney productions as sentimental drivel. In both private interviews and public statements, Walt expressed his disdain for "the intelligentsia," "geniuses," and "wizards" who panned his work while the public acclaimed it. His critique of the critics, replete with class and moral resentments, was in full flower when he angrily told an interviewer that his films

> go straight out for the honest adult, not the sophisticate, not these characters who think they know everything and you can't thrill them anymore. I go to the people who retain that, no matter how old they are, that little spirit of adventure, that appreciation of the world of fantasy. I go for them, I play to them . . . These sort of lost souls, sophisticates, who are so bored and turn their nose up at everything, they say it's childish. Well, what the hell's wrong with something being childish, you know? You can't have everything profound . . . It's the equivalent of not getting so stuffy that you can't laugh.

The critics had turned on him at the same time his popularity with the public had soared to new heights. Thus his conclusion was not surprising: "The hell with the critics. It's the audience we're making the picture for."[39]

In a practical sense, Walt ultimately placed responsibility for reaching that audience squarely on his own shoulders. He came to view himself as a yardstick of popular values and would tell directors, story men, and animators that if he liked a production, everybody would like it. He would simply say, "I play it to my own taste." This rule of thumb was nearly chiseled in stone at the Disney Studio, but it did not reflect Walt's ego so much as a confidence in his empathy for everyday Americans and their lives. Walt, characteristically unskilled with the spoken word, could not always articulate his requirements and standards and drove artists and writers to distraction by stumbling through an explanation of what he was looking for and then concluding, "Just do something that everybody will like." But then he would stun them by dramatically improving scenes with acute, shrewd recommendations for revision when he was able to see and hear what they had done.[40]

Perhaps one activity more than any other stitched together the various fragments of Walt's public and private life in the postwar period — his total creative involvement with Disneyland. The park not only galvanized his inventive and commercial talents but seemed to muster his emotional commitment as well. Ward Kimball, who often accompanied him to the park to consult on various projects, noted that Walt personally walked every inch of Disneyland and supervised every detail. "Every damn thing that you see at Disneyland, Walt checked on," Kimball wrote. "He said, 'My fun is working on a project and solving the problems. If I just sit in the office and okay drawings and what we're doing in Anaheim, what fun is that? Why let other people have all the fun doing all the work?'" His devotion was complete. The night before the park opened, for instance, he put on a protective mask and stayed up all night in a miserably hot, enclosed area helping to spray-paint the backdrop for the *Twenty Thousand Leagues under the Sea* exhibit. He preached to the park staff about the need for absolute cleanliness and warm public relations. The park actually became his artistic medium of choice, because, as he once told Dick Irvine, "If there's something I don't like at Disneyland, I can correct it. I can always change it [here], but not in the films." In the early 1960s, he ordered the already half-completed New Orleans Square to be torn up and redesigned because it wasn't working right. As he once explained, the park was an entity "that will never be finished. Something that I can keep developing, keep plussing and adding to. It's alive."[41]

Like a shiny, challenging new toy presented to a precocious kid, Disneyland became a wonderful outlet for Walt's enthusiasm, sense of wonder, and intense work ethic. "Dammit, I love it here," he once remarked to Marc Davis. "WED is just like the Hyperion studio used to be in the days when we were always working on something new." In spite of the yeoman's work he usually did there, Walt found the park to be a source of relaxation and fulfillment. Escaping the production demands of the Burbank studio, he loved to roam through Disneyland, checking out the attractions and watching the visitors. As he once remarked to Joe Fowler when they were riding on the top deck of the steamboat, "You know, when we get too old to work, we can just sit up here on the *Mark Twain* and see all the people and the enjoyment they're having." The park seemed to epitomize everything that he was after in his life's work. He clearly communicated this feeling in 1960 during the national elections. He and Lillian were visiting Herb Ryman's house for dinner one evening when someone quipped that Walt could be elected president if he wanted to. He got a quizzical look on his face and replied, "Why would I want to be president of the United States? I'm the king of Disneyland."[42]

Disneyland, "the happiest place on earth," served as a showcase for its creator's warm, resilient, virtuous rendering of the American way of life in the postwar period. For millions of his fellow citizens, the park embodied the marvelous creative capacities of American free enterprise to meet the deepest kinds of human wishes. This symbolism also attached itself to the man himself. By the early 1960s, Walt Disney had been canonized as an American institution. As events soon demonstrated, however, the construction of the Disney culture-industry machine in the 1950s was only the foundation for a much greater vision.

21

Pax Disneyana

BY THE EARLY 1960s, grand honors and outlandish acclaim had become the rule rather than the exception for Walt Disney. In 1963, he received one of his greatest honors when the Freedom Foundation presented him with its coveted George Washington Award for promoting the American way of life. Former president Dwight D. Eisenhower, who read the citation in a ceremony, praised the entertainer as an artist who excelled in "communicating the hope and aspirations of our free society to the far corners of the planet." The following year, a group of admirers campaigned to award Disney the Nobel Peace Prize, while others agitated to make him the director of the Los Angeles rapid transit system. President Lyndon Johnson bestowed on him the Presidential Medal of Freedom, the highest civilian award of the American government. As one observer noted, the master of a sprawling entertainment empire not only enjoyed colossal popularity but was widely considered to be "an authentic genius of our time."[1]

The Disney entertainment enterprise was flourishing financially, firing on all cylinders as it sped along the highways of American popular culture. In addition to Disneyland and *Walt Disney's Wonderful World of Color*, the moviemaking division maintained its vitality. A string of live-action films fell into several niches — adventures such as *In Search of the Castaways* (1962), musical fantasies such as *Babes in Toyland* (1961), mysteries such as

The Moonspinners (1964), dramas such as *Those Calloways* (1964), historical tales such as *Greyfriars Bobby* (1961), animal films such as *Savage Sam* (1963) — and they usually proved to be profitable and popular, if not particularly distinguished. The studio's oldest endeavor, animation, continued to produce pleasant, occasionally impressive movies such as *One Hundred and One Dalmatians* (1961), *The Sword in the Stone* (1963), and *The Jungle Book* (1967).

The situation seemed ripe for corporate complacency. But as events proved, nothing could have been further from the truth. The early 1960s saw the launching of an enormous expansion and fresh initiatives that promised to overwhelm even the grand diversification of the previous decade. Walt Disney had become a social, cultural, and even political force to reckon with, and his plans gradually encompassed not only the amusement or inspiration of a mass audience but a larger and more substantive reshaping of their everyday lives. Nothing less than the reformation of modern America became the object of his vision. Disney's magic kingdom, increasingly vast in scope, incorporated several undertakings before finding its ultimate expression in the swampy landscape of central Florida.

I. "Disney Stands for Something to the Public"

By the early 1960s, Walt had come to terms with the curious fact that his name was no longer his own. As he told Marty Sklar, a young employee then rising through the ranks of the studio's upper echelon, "You see, I'm not Disney anymore. I used to be Disney, but now Disney is something we've built up in the public mind over the years. It stands for something, and you don't have to explain what it is to the public." Walt understood clearly that "Disney" now symbolized an amalgamation of qualities and that he personally had evolved into a many-sided image: a revered national moralist, an example of American achievement, a trusted guardian of the nation's children, and a representative of average citizens and their values, tastes, and desires. For the millions of people enthralled by his creations, he had become Will Rogers, Dale Carnegie, Thomas Edison, and Abraham Lincoln, all rolled into one.[2]

Two cinematic case studies dramatically illustrated Disney's extraordinary hold over his audience. Hardly anyone pegged a humble black-and-white movie entitled *The Shaggy Dog* (1959) to be much of a hit. The Disney Studio's first venture into live-action comedy, its script had been adapted by Bill Walsh from *The Hound of Florence*, a novel by Felix Salten, the author of *Bambi*. In many ways, the screenplay simply took an animal fantasy that probably would have been an animated project in the studio's earlier years and translated it into a new format. The plot concerned the comic adventures of Wilby Daniels, a teenager who leaves a museum unaware that a magic ring has fallen into the cuff of his trousers. Accidentally invoking an ancient spell, he is transformed by the ring into a large sheepdog identical to the one owned by his neighbor. As he endures one of his periodic shifts into a dog, he overhears the neighbor's conversation and realizes he is part of a spy ring trying to steal secret missile plans from the American government. The bulk of the movie then follows the boy's on-again, off-again canine transformation as he convinces his father of the plot's existence, is discovered and pursued by the spies, and ends up a hero by saving the neighbor's beautiful daughter as the evil interlopers are captured. The movie's comedy comes from its images of a large sheepdog wearing pajamas, brushing his teeth, and driving a car.

The Shaggy Dog proved to be one of the most important films in the entire history of the Disney operation. It grossed an amazing $8 million in its initial release and became a roaring box office success. More important, it altered the evolution of the studio's films, inspiring a whole host of medium-budget live-action comedies: *The Absent-Minded Professor* (1961), *Moon Pilot* (1962), *Bon Voyage* (1962), *Son of Flubber* (1963), *The Misadventures of Merlin Jones* (1964), *That Darn Cat* (1965), *The Monkey's Uncle* (1965). Many of these films starred Fred MacMurray and Tommy Kirk, the featured actors in *The Shaggy Dog,* who became two of the studio's biggest stars. Filled with sight gags, broad slapstick humor, and cute characters, these gentle comedic fantasies were hits with the moviegoing public, although they were usually dismissed by the critics.[3]

The Shaggy Dog also solidly reinforced several social themes that characteristically endeared Disney to his vast audience. The film's "Boy-Pooch Tackles Atomic Spies" plot, as one newspaper described it, gently appropriated Cold War tensions and rendered them humorous and harmless. The movie's family orientation and wholesome moralism, by now expected Disney traits, elicited praise from cold warriors who saw this film as a defensive weapon against "our arch enemies, the comintern, who have long held the opinion that they . . . can ruin us from within by breaking down our economic and educational system, morals, and physical and mental health."[4]

A few years later, Walt pulled out all the stops to make a dazzling film that became his greatest entertainment achievement of the 1960s. *Mary Poppins* (1964) flashed onto screens as a brilliant musical fantasy that blended live action and animation, technological expertise and family entertainment, appealing characters and striking settings, comedy and dance. P. L. Travers's series of stories about a magical British nanny, published during the 1930s, provided the basis of the screenplay, and Walt took great pains to secure the author's cooperation, even granting her the right of approval of the screenplay. In the early 1960s, the studio chief, along with Richard and Robert Sherman, the songwriting team of brothers, and writer Don DaGradi, began preliminary work, choosing seven of Travers's most visual, dynamic chapters as a basis for the movie and transferring the time period to colorful, turn-of-the-century Edwardian London. After song sketches and a story line had been developed, Bill Walsh formalized the screenplay and wrote most of the dialogue. The result was a broad adaptation of the original stories that emphasized fantasy, sentiment, and humor. Spicing the whole with a number of lovely songs, energetic dance routines, and delightful animated special effects, the Disney Studio laid out a visually stunning, emotionally delectable feast.[5]

Mary Poppins's central theme, in true Disney form, involved family regeneration. Mr. Banks, an aloof, work-obsessed banker, and his wife, a flighty figure preoccupied with the suffragette movement, preside over a household in disarray. Their two young children, Jane and Michael, have just driven off yet another nanny with their incorrigible behavior. A newspaper ad draws a line of applicants, but they are blown away by a blast of wind as Mary Poppins floats down from her cloud perch, using her umbrella as a parachute. Taking over as nanny, she promptly proves to be a "practically perfect" woman with powers to create magical adventures. She helps the children clean their rooms by snapping her fingers and causing the toys and clothes to fall into order. When the trio meets Bert, a local artist drawing on the sidewalk, all four jump into his drawing and are transported into an animated fantasy would where penguins serve as waiters at outdoor cafés and merry-go-round horses break free to race through the countryside. In another episode they visit Mary's Uncle Albert, whose exuberant laughter causes him (and eventually them) to float to the ceiling. In perhaps the movie's most spectacular scene, Mary and the children are escorted to the rooftops of London by Bert, who is also a chimney sweep, where they witness a song-and-dance routine performed by a sooty cohort of chimney cleaners. The climax comes when Mr. Banks is fired from his job at the bank and realizes that his attempts to arrange his family life in ledger-book style have failed. After castigating the directors of the bank, he returns home to repair an old kite and then takes his family to the park for an outing. Seeing Mr. Banks emotionally reconnected to his children, Mary Poppins knows her work is done and floats off into the sky to face new challenges.

The film's magnificent cast, featuring Julie Andrews and Dick Van Dyke, lit up the screen. For many moviegoers, however, the most memorable aspect of *Mary Poppins* was its music. The Sherman brothers composed perhaps the best musical score ever to grace a Disney movie, including the melodious "A Spoonful of Sugar," the rollicking "Supercalifragilisticexpialidocious," and the Academy Award–winning ballad "Chim-Chim-Cheree." The Disney Studio's considerable technical expertise also was evident, but never intrusive, especially in the scenes mixing actors and animation.

Audiences were enthralled. The film's old-fashioned premiere at Grauman's Chinese Theater set a glamorous tone, launching one of the largest publicity campaigns ever held by the Disney Studio, including a special "Spoonful of Sugar" promotion coordinated with the National Sugar Company and the licensing of forty-six companies to churn out merchandise. The movie brought in an astonishing $31 million in domestic ticket sales during its initial release. Untold millions more were generated by the sales of a vast assortment of music, records, clothing, toys, and household items. When the dust settled, the film had received thirteen Academy Award nominations, including the studio's first for best picture, and it ended up winning five, including best actress and best musical score. Other awards and citations, from the Golden Globe to movie-of-the-year from various publications and groups, came pouring into the Burbank lot by the truckload.[6]

While nearly all reviews of *Mary Poppins* praised its songs, dancing, acting, and visual flair — many critics proclaimed it "Walt Disney's masterpiece" — some observers also insisted that it made an important social statement. They pointedly contrasted its innocent charm with a modern formula holding that "sex and sensationalism are generally regarded as necessary for show-business success." *Mary Poppins's* family theme, innocent comedy, and enchanting fantasy prompted the reviewer for the Atlanta *Journal* to note sarcastically that its lack of sex, violence, and profanity dictated that it "couldn't possibly be worth the price of admission." This movie, according to another essayist, made "false prophets" of those moviemakers who "magnified and gave example to all the harshness, the dark, morbid, seamy sickness, the violence, lusts, and greeds" of the world. The portrait of *Mary Poppins* as a virtuous moral exercise gained added luster from the publicity accorded its two biggest stars. Both Julie Andrews, portrayed as a devoted mother who demurely confessed that "I suspect my best talent is being a housewife," and Dick Van Dyke, pictured as an ardent churchgoer and family man, were presented in national publications as paragons of wholesome values. As the *Ladies' Home Journal* pointed out, Walt Disney first had become interested in casting Van Dyke when he spotted an interview in which the actor had vowed never to make a movie he couldn't take his kids to see.[7]

The favorable moral critique of *Mary Poppins,* however, triggered a skirmish in a larger cultural war. On one side stood ordinary Americans, who generally adored the innocent fun, fantasy, moral uplift, and sentimental emotion of Disney's productions. On the other stood many critics, who increasingly loathed his work as morally naive, socially conservative, and artistically appalling. Advocates for *Mary Poppins* sensed a wonderful opportunity to slam snobbish intellectuals who had mocked Disney for years while tolerating, and even encouraging, what many saw as the depraved morality of many modern films. An editorialist in the Kansas City *Star,* for instance, wrote a sarcastic essay entitled "Here's a Movie to Waste an Evening With." After a mock denunciation of *Mary Poppins* for eschewing nudity, grim tragedy, sardonic social satire, and all other marks of "the cinema that is Really Worthwhile," the author concluded that actual enjoyment of the film's whimsy, laughter, wonderful music, and cute children would "get you drummed out of every intellectual circle you ever dreamed of being involved with." The Hollywood *Reporter,* an influential industry organ, praised *Mary Poppins* as one of the four or five best movies ever made and then offered a biting commentary in the same vein:

> It is a strange fact that the entertainment public . . . has for some years now recognized Disney's artistic talents, while many of his cohorts in Hollywood seem somehow embarrassed by his presence — like they wish he'd go away. When an occasion arises, as it does from time to time, that the name Disney comes up in certain Hollywood circles, a rather odd disease seems to strike the conversationalists. They shuffle their feet and stare off into space like some virus-carrying bug has infected them with a loss of their powers of speech.

Even Judith Crist, the reputable critic for the New York *Herald Tribune,* confessed herself uneasy that a "breathtaking" film like *Mary Poppins* was automatically ignored by "sophisticates" because of their premise that "anything that is popular or even potentially popular cannot be good." This cinematic triumph thus revealed a widening split over Disney between popular audiences and intellectual critics. The situation was ironic — in fact, nearly every critic in the country recommended the film — but that seemed only to affirm the old aphorism of the exception proving the rule.[8]

There was little irony, however, in the explosion of outright hostility the following year between defenders and detractors of Disney. In the spring of 1965, Dr. Max Rafferty, superintendent of public instruction in California, wrote a piece in the Los Angeles *Times* lauding the entertainer for his educational achievements. The essay, entitled "The Greatest Pedagogue of Them All," argued that Disney animation, by reviving a collection of folklore classics that a cynical society had allowed to languish, had provided "compensatory education for a whole generation of America's children." It went on to praise his live-action movies as "lone sanctuaries of decency and health in the jungle of sex and sadism created by Hollywood producers." Overall, Rafferty concluded, this man with limited formal learning and no academic credentials had become "the greatest educator of this century — greater than John Dewey or James Conant or all the rest of us put together."[9]

Rafferty's opinion did not go unchallenged. A few days later, Dr. Frances Clark Sayers, a senior lecturer in library science and English at UCLA and an academic expert on children's literature, fired off a letter to the same newspaper. In a stinging rebuke, she not only dismissed Rafferty's "absurd appraisal of Walt Disney as a pedagogue" but went on to assail the entire Disney corpus of work. In fact, she insisted, the entertainer was a "shameless nature faker," a thoughtless mutilator of folklore and children's stories, a garish artist, and a creator of cliché-ridden texts and scripts. She accused him of transforming the unpredictable, occasionally acerbic Mary Poppins stories into "one great marshmallow-covered cream-puff." Where Rafferty saw educational genius, Sayers perceived "genuine feeling ignored, the imagination of children bludgeoned with mediocrity, and much of it overcast by vulgarity."[10]

This nasty exchange quickly triggered a larger debate over Disney's merits. Over the next year, Sayers took to the hustings to publicize and expand her attack. In magazines such as the *National Observer* and *FM and Fine Arts*, she broadened the assault, stating flatly, "I find almost everything [in Disney's films] objectionable." To previous criticism of his approach to folklore, art, and writing, she added denunciations of his sentimentality — he "falsifies life by pretending that everything is so sweet, so saccharine, so without any conflict except the obvious conflict of violence" — and his tawdry commercial instincts. She described the Mickey Mouse Club as "that terrible organization of children . . . which makes me cringe." Finally, she took a swipe at Disney's audience, commenting haughtily, "There is no reason why good books should be lowered or lessened to meet the demands of people who are not ready or not interested enough to make the effort to read."[11]

Other intellectual critics rallied to Sayers's side. In *The New Yorker*, Whitney Balliett sputtered that Disney was "the most assiduous anthropomorphist since Beatrix Potter" and argued that his animation was full of "sadism, violence, stupidity, greed and fear" while his live-action work was characterized by a too-easy morality demonstrated by "pale, witless characters." In the pages of the *New York Times Book Review* and *Book Week*, experts on children's literature accused him of "blurring the difference between corporate fancy and true imagination," of fostering "a fantastic outpouring of literary junk," of foisting on audiences and readers productions that "mongrelized the classics." Such outrages were unlikely to cease, one noted contemptuously, because "money and gimmickry have always exerted a spell over Walt Disney."[12]

In the ensuing uproar, legions of admirers from Disney's America joined the fray by flooding the Los Angeles *Times* with letters to the editor. While a few respondents sided with Sayers, the majority vented their anger over her remarks. Some writers addressed the issues, arguing that Disney in fact had saved many a literary classic by giving it new artistic form, or questioning what was so sacred about a venerable story that it could not be intelligently updated for modern tastes. But many others simply attacked Sayers for "being too long at the vinegar jar." They claimed that Walt Disney stood for "Decency, U.S.A.," and praised his efforts to create uplifting, moral entertainment "in this day of misguided educators, lecturers, and peddlers of smut and obscenity." Summarizing this climate of opinion, one writer insisted that Sayers's blast "deserves a simple evaluation — NUTS."[13]

Disney's reaction to the Sayers affair was both predictable and revealing. He shrugged his shoulders, refused to comment publicly, and proudly admitted to producing corn. Confident of his stature with the public, he realized that academic critiques, whatever their nature, could only work to his advantage with a mass audience. If positive, such commentary reinforced the opinion of the few who cared, and if negative, it only fueled the resentments of many more who were predisposed to suspect intellectual elites. If Disney's reputation had shrunk in artistic circles, where he was widely considered to be a commercial hack, his beloved status had soared among ordinary Americans who shared his moral principles and entertainment values. As Sayers admitted ruefully in an interview, "It's like attacking motherhood to attack Walt Disney . . . [People] think I'm tearing down an American institution." Rebukes like hers mattered little in the face of the breathtaking expansion of the Disney enterprise, which had begun gathering force on several fronts by the mid-1960s.[14]

II. The Empire Expands

With the onset of a new decade, an ever-restless Walt Disney began venturing beyond the borders of filmmaking, television production, and amusement parks. In many ways, the energy behind this drive had arisen with the development of Disneyland, when WED had established a new creative nerve center for his enterprise. By the 1960s, a number of fascinating technical and aesthetic initiatives had begun to emerge from this organization and ripple outward. A more definite organizational structure had evolved, and the staff had grown from around 100 in 1961 to 300 in 1965. Bill Cottrell, longtime studio functionary and Disney's brother-in-law, served as WED's president for a number of years. Key personnel included designer and artist John Hench, animator Marc Davis, sculptor Blaine Gibson, engineer Don Edgren, background painter Claude Coats, artist Herb Ryman, writer Marty Sklar, designers Jack Gladish and Wathel Rogers, machinists Bob Gurr and Roger Broggie, art directors Dick Irvine and Marvin Davis, landscaper Bill Evans, and model builders Harriet Burns, Fred Joerger, and Jack Ferges. This array of diverse talents eventually gave rise to the word "Imagineers," a Disneyspeak term that tried to describe WED's hard-to-label endeavors.

These artist/technicians developed new transportation systems such as the Disneyland-Alweg Monorail, which in 1959 became the first daily operating monorail in the United States, and the WEDway People Mover, a continuous-flow system that transported vehicles with a series of wheels recessed beneath a hard-surface track. They developed new "ride-through" attractions at Disneyland, such as the Haunted Mansion and the Pirates of the Caribbean, for which spectators sat in moving carts and were taken into the middle of the action, where they received a pleasant barrage of sensory experiences. They spent years developing a sophisticated electronics and hydraulics system for the creation of mechanical but amazingly lifelike animal and human figures.[15]

As these endeavors unfolded, Walt developed a special fondness for WED. He spent many hours roaming its premises, inspecting mockups in the model room, tossing around ideas, and brainstorming with the staff about potential projects. The pressures that attended the Disney Studio's extensive production schedule of movies and television shows had become overwhelming, and Walt found a kind of respite by escaping to this smaller, more innovative group. A sign of his esteem came in 1953 when he granted this personal company the commercial rights to use and license his name. WED, of course, quickly entered into an agreement with Walt Disney Productions and the Disney Studio to employ Walt's name, but it gained a hefty percentage of the leasing profits.[16]

Perhaps the most interesting of WED's endeavors was its venture into robotics. Back in the 1940s, while traveling in France, Walt had stumbled across a mechanical bird that moved in its cage and warbled a tune by means of a clever but simple system of small levers and cams. Roger Broggie and other studio mechanics disassembled the toy to see how it worked, and several years later it became the starting point for Walt's miniature Americana project. This collection of scenes from the past included a design for an opera house, and the studio chief came up with the idea of a tiny mechanical figure who would sing and dance on its stage. Project Little Man was born. Buddy Ebsen was hired to come in and tap-dance in front of a grid pattern, which provided the graphic model for a nine-inch dancing figure that moved by means of cams and cables controlled by a console beneath the stage. This particular display of miniatures never reached the public, but WED continued to develop more sophisticated versions of this technology for Disneyland. For instance, much larger but fairly crude versions of mechanical hippopotamuses, elephants, zebras, and crocodiles appeared in the popular Jungle Cruise ride.[17]

WED designers eventually coined the name Audio-Animatronics to describe a more sophisticated robotics system from their workshops. Utilizing an electronic tape system, pneumatic valves, and hydraulic pressure rather than cams and cables, this new system featured a complex combination of movements and sounds. It made its debut in the Enchanted Tiki Room at Disneyland, which opened in June 1963. This attraction surrounded a seated audience with a boisterous seventeen-minute show of over two hundred moving, talking birds, flowers, and tiki gods. But more striking developments came with the creation of a human figure. A few years earlier, a plan for a Chinese restaurant in Disneyland had included a mechanical

"Confucius-type character" who was to entertain patrons in the lobby by moving and reciting wise sayings. WED engineers and artists had come up with a prototype head with skin made from latex and solenoid coils that powered both voice and movement. By the early 1960s, however, work on such figures was utilizing the advances made with hydraulic air cylinders, electronic tape for more sophisticated programming, and a hot-melt vinyl plastisol called Duraflex for skin, which didn't crack as latex did. The dramatic culmination of this technology came with the famous Abraham Lincoln project, which one wag described as the "winkin' blinkin' Lincoln." Enshrined in a permanent exhibit in Disneyland by 1965, this strikingly accurate figure rose to his feet and exhorted his listeners, complete with gestures and mouth movements, to honor the traditions of American democracy.[18]

A WED press release somewhat overheatedly described this robot technology as "the grand combination of all the arts. This technique includes the three-dimensional realism of fine sculpture, the vitality of a great painting, the drama and personal rapport of the theater, and the artistic versatility and consistency of the motion picture." Despite such hyperbole, Audio-Animatronics remained genuinely significant. In one sense, as Walt explained in numerous public statements, the robotics project capped a long process of evolution within the Disney Studio. He told an interviewer from the Canadian Broadcasting Corporation in 1964, "It's sort of another door that's opened for us. You see, our whole forty-some-odd years here have been in the world of making things move. Inanimate things move, from a drawing through all kinds of little props and things. Now we're making these three-dimensional human figures move, making animals move, making anything move, through the use of electronics. It's all programmed, predetermined . . . It's just another dimension in the animation we have been doing all our lives."[19]

But the development of Disney robotics also involved larger issues. It enhanced the participatory mode of entertainment pioneered in Disneyland, as new rides such as the Haunted Mansion and the Pirates of the Caribbean transported visitors into scenes where they were surrounded by a spectacular array of robotic figures and immersed in the images and sounds of a ghost-ridden New Orleans mansion or the fiery ransacking of a town by pirates. It also nourished the growing instinct for control in Disney entertainment. Going back to the 1920s and 1930s, animation always had been a compulsive's delight, because of the artist's ability to regulate even the most minuscule action on the screen. But Audio-Animatronics allowed Disney's Imagineers not only to expand control over the multidimensional sensory experience but to regulate completely the three-dimensional, robotic "actors" that conveyed those experiences. Walt headed off any suggestion of dehumanization. He offered reassurances that his robots had been developed only for their durability and their capacity to deliver a quality show over and over. "We're not going to replace the human being, believe me on that," he said. "[They are] just for show purposes, because in Disneyland down there we operate fifteen hours a day and these shows have to go on." Nonetheless, Audio-Animatronics seemed to symbolize a growing Disney desire to govern human nature, even while taking it into new realms of fantasy and leisure.[20]

The 1964–65 World's Fair in New York City provided the clearest demonstration of Audio-Animatronics' scope. It also revealed WED's central role in the new Disney initiatives. This giant exposition, under the management of Robert Moses, the powerful New York urban planner and builder, had been designed as a showcase for the American way of life, particularly with regard to material and technological progress. In 1960, as large American companies began scrambling to develop exhibits, Walt shocked the WED staff with a rather abrupt announcement of his intention to become involved. "All the big corporations in the country are going to be spending a helluva lot of money building exhibits there. They won't know what they want to do," he insisted. "Now, they're all going to want something that will stand out from the others, and that's the kind of service we can offer them." According to Walt's shrewd assessment, such companies would finance the development of new attractions — and the innovative technology that went with them — which eventually could be used at Disneyland.[21]

After discussions with many large corporations, WED contracted to develop exhibits for General Electric, Ford, Pepsi-Cola, and the state of Illinois. Matters moved quickly with General Electric, since Walt had been talking seriously with the company for years about a sponsored attraction in Disneyland to be called Edison Square, which would celebrate Thomas A. Edison's invention of the incandescent lamp as an instrument of profound progress in twentieth-century America. While this project never got off the ground, it became the basis for the undertaking at the World's Fair. In 1959, when General Electric asked Disney to develop a show that would present "the role electricity has played in bettering man's living conditions," WED designers dusted off the Edison Square plans and used them as the foundation for an expanded project.[22]

The General Electric pavilion featured a novel design — a revolving theater on which a segmented stage remained stationary as the audience moved around it in their seats. This enormous revolving "doughnut," as it came to be known, rested on railroad wheels and allowed customers to view a series of six shows. Labeled the Carousel of Progress, this attraction was introduced to audiences with an elaborate constellation of lights through a transparent screen, a burst of stereophonic music, and a narration on the theme of progress:

Now, most carousels just go round and round without getting anyplace. But on this one we're really going places — and that's progress! Yes, and it's a great deal more than that. Progress is the fulfillment of man's hopes and dreams for a better way of life. It is measured by our ability to harness electric energy for the betterment of mankind. Progress is the sound of a motor [sound of a motor], the hum of a turbine [electric turbine humming], the heartbeat of a factory [machinery running], the sound of a symphony [musical strings], the roar of a rocket [rocket taking off]. And because of man's dreams, tomorrow will find us further than today.

Audiences then saw, in succession, four household scenes, set in the late 1800s, the 1920s, the 1940s, and the 1960s. Each set was inhabited by a family of Audio-Animatronic figures dressed in period costume, while the atmosphere was enhanced by period renditions of the show's theme song, "There's a Great Big Beautiful Tomorrow," composed by the Sherman brothers. The Carousel of Progress eased visitors out with a brief stop at the Gateway to Future Progress, which pointed people to "the doorway to the future" as a colorful light display created abstract moving patterns. After exiting, visitors encountered the Skydome Spectacular, a visual story of the harnessing of energy which projected complex images on the underside of the huge dome that covered the pavilion. Beginning with the crudest uses of fire, the story ended with fabulous predictions about the potential uses of nuclear energy. Appropriately, visitors then experienced the nuclear fusion demonstration, a sight-and-sound model showing how thermonuclear fusion soon would be churning out energy, and Medallion City, a walk-through exhibit of General Electric's latest products, ranging from household appliances to satellites.[23]

Although involved in all the World's Fair projects, Walt took a special interest in the General Electric exhibit. As Joe Fowler observed, "There was more of Walt in the Carousel of Progress show than in anything else we've done." Combining nostalgia with rosy predictions of progress, the attraction seemed to capture his special sensibility. He worked to impart a midwestern flavor to the show, personally choosing the robot voices for their flat midwestern sound, and fussed over every detail as he included his own childhood memories in the historical depictions. Early mockups left him dissatisfied with the lack of a "weenie" to hook the audiences, and after some thought he designed an Audio-Animatronic family dog, which left viewers chuckling as he appeared in every segment and mugged for the audience. The WED director, in a playful mood, even came up with an effective publicity stunt for General Electric. Always fascinated with the lifelike qualities of the Audio-Animatronic figures, he decided one day to send Granny, the matriarch of the Carousel family, to New York by airplane. Aided by an attendant who pushed her around in a wheelchair and helped her get settled in her first-class seat, Granny ended up going on a one-hundred-city tour on the way to the East Coast, fooling observers, generating newspaper stories, and drawing considerable attention to the latest Disney marvel.[24]

The Ford Company's Magic Skyway attraction also embroidered the theme of progress, but in even more cosmic proportions. Disney designers began with the idea of transporting guests through the attraction in actual automobiles, something that caused Ford executives' eyes to light up. Walt had the idea of standardizing and controlling the movement of the cars rather than having people drive them, a notion that WED engineers then picked up and developed. The result was an early version of the WEDway People Mover system, a series of motorized wheels buried beneath a grooved track which moved especially adapted automobiles. These Ford, Lincoln, and Mercury convertibles took their occupants into a prehistoric environment. A series of primordial vignettes loomed up, the first replete with immense Audio-Animatronic dinosaurs. An exploding volcano led to several scenes from the lives of prehistoric cave people who struggled to tame fire, fight gigantic mastodons and bears, and derive the wheel from the crude practice of rolling logs. The Magic Skyway then whisked visitors through a time tunnel for a quick glimpse of a utopian Space City full of futuristic spires, gleaming domes, and whirring transportation systems. The whole exhibit was housed in a huge building dubbed the Ford Wonder Rotunda, the largest structure at the fair, of some 275,000 square feet. This impressive structure, with large glass tunnels circling its wedding-cake exterior, beckoned to fairgoers with a ten-story domed entrance.[25]

Perhaps the most beloved Disney exhibit at the World's Fair was funded by Pepsi-Cola. The giant soft drink company was collaborating with UNICEF, the United Nations children's agency, and approached Disney only a year before the fair to ask him to create an attraction saluting "all the world's children." To the shock of his already stressed Imagineers, Walt agreed, proposing a vague idea for "a little boat ride." Within a few weeks, the blueprint for a large L-shaped building had been drafted, a plan for a system of moving boats was being engineered, and artist Mary Blair had been designated to design the exhibit. The choice of Blair, who had worked on various projects at the Disney Studio in the 1940s before turning to illustrations for children's books, turned out to be a masterful one. Her powerful visual style, which combined festive colors, a childlike innocence, the use of collage backgrounds, and toylike images, proved perfect for this project. Her efforts, aided by those of Marc Davis and Claude Coats, produced It's a Small World, a lovely attraction that took boatloads of visitors on a leisurely trip through the regions of the world, each represented by dozens of childlike dolls garbed in the vivid costumes of their native lands. These representations offered a common face, modified a little for skin color and racial characteristics, and they moved, sang, and played with an assortment of toys. Blair's compelling color schemes underlined regional differences, with brilliant yellow shades for the Middle East, cool blues and greens for Africa, hot pinks and oranges for South America, and shimmering white for the Grand Finale combining all the world's children. An addictive ditty called "It's a Small World (After All)," sung as a round by children's voices in many different languages, provided a unifying theme. The Pepsi-Cola Pavilion, presenting a child's view of the world with its assortment of colorful dancing dolls and striking visual images, proved to be a great favorite.[26]

Perhaps the most memorable Disney exhibit at the New York fair, however, was the special historical show prepared for Illinois. Beginning in the late 1950s, Walt's longtime love of American history had inspired plans for a Disneyland attraction called One Nation Under God, which would present a cinematic narration of early American history leading up to the crisis of the Civil War, followed by entry into the Hall of the Presidents, featuring Audio-Animatronic figures of perhaps a half-dozen of the most prominent presidents. When the 1964 World's Fair was announced, however, Walt saw this as a golden opportunity to find a sponsor for a limited version of the attraction. He decided to focus on a figure of Abraham Lincoln, one of his personal heroes, and the WED staff shifted into high gear to develop an Audio-Animatronics version of the Great Emancipator.

What emerged was the most sophisticated expression of this technology yet developed. Lincoln's head was modeled after a life mask made in 1860; his facial movements came from solenoid coils located inside the head, his body motions were controlled by hydraulic and pneumatic valves, and a special Duraflex skin allowed for remarkable flexibility. Project engineers encountered many mechanical difficulties as they struggled to program the figure to rise to its feet and present a speech, complete with gestures, a swiveling head, and mouth and eye movements. Sometimes the robot would malfunction and go into electronic convulsions, smashing its chair and sending technicians scurrying for cover. Robert Moses was astounded when he witnessed the prototype Lincoln, however, and helped solicit sponsorship from Illinois, which was seeking to advertise itself as the "Land of Lincoln." Thus Great Moments with Mr. Lincoln became the star attraction of the Illinois pavilion. Audiences watched an uncannily lifelike sixteenth president solemnly get up from his armchair and, with a clear, high voice and emphatic gestures, eloquently explain the meaning of American liberty and the virtues of representative government. Most were held spellbound during the show and reacted with wild cheering, applause, and even tears at its conclusion. As the New York *Daily News* reported, "Those who have seen Lincoln 'come to life' are stricken with something akin to awe."[27]

The great New York World's Fair ended under a dark cloud of financial scandal, but for Walt Disney and his enterprise, the results were spectacular. Throughout the run of the fair, Disney's quartet of exhibits garnered gushing praise from every direction. *Time* announced that "the perennial Walt Disney is the fair's presiding genius," and scores of journalists declared that the "Magician of Disneyland has outdone himself" or reported that "as a matter of fact, the whole fair seems to have a Disneyesque air" or insisted that "everywhere was evidence of the great talent of Walt Disney." Informal surveys among visitors revealed that the four Disney shows consistently ranked among the most popular seven or eight attractions. A sour note sounded only occasionally. Not everyone was fond of Audio-Animatronics; for example, one critic described the blinking, head-shaking robots in the Carousel of Progress as presenting "the general effect of a family under the influence of drugs." Another difficulty emerged when it came to light that Robert Moses secretly had loaned $250,000 to Illinois to fund the Lincoln exhibit. Given the insolvency of the Fair Corporation, the fact that this money ended up in the pockets of Disney and WED left a bad taste in the mouths of some observers.[28]

In a larger sense, however, the 1964–65 World's Fair proved to be a critical step for Walt Disney and his creative empire. In a practical sense, he had reached beyond southern California to prove that a "Disneyland experience" appealed to an eastern audience. Along the same lines, he and WED reaped long-term financial benefits by developing innovative, exciting attractions paid for by corporate and civic sponsors and then transporting them wholesale for display at Disneyland. Moreover, the fair tightened connections between Disney and corporate America, since, as Walt insisted to anyone who would listen, "through entertainment and showmanship, [American] industry could reach the public." The resulting vision of technological progress, growing material comfort, and continued improvement in the quality of life linked the captains of American industry with Disney's naturally optimistic sensibility. Even more important, though no one realized it at the time except Disney himself, the New York exposition planted a clear signpost to the future path of the Disney enterprise. Disney's fair attractions served as a seedbed for Walt's ideas about entertainment, leisure, and social reform. Thus the 1964–65 World's Fair, a self-conscious display of the United States's confidence and might at the high tide of the American century, gave Walt Disney and WED a springboard into the creation of a bold new project in Florida.[29]

Yet the World's Fair work, for all its importance, was only one among a herd of projects that came thundering out of WED. Beginning in the early 1960s, for instance, Walt began pushing another idea far removed from the traditional Disney entertainment arena — the development of a vast ski resort, to be built halfway between San Francisco and Los Angeles in the Sierra Nevadas. The blueprint for the Mineral King project, as it came to be known, sketched out an expansive facility consisting of ten square miles of skiing area, fourteen lifts, ten restaurants, abundant lodging, convenience shops, a conference center, an ice-skating rink, a ski school, and a WED-designed replication of an Alpine village, the whole designed to handle between five and seven thousand visitors a day and costing $35 million. This huge project, however, ended unhappily, as a series of lawsuits by environmentalists scuttled the plans.[30]

Also in the early 1960s, Walt became quite enthusiastic about building a California Institute of the Arts, an idea that had its genesis in his long association with the Chouinard Art Institute. By 1955 the school was teetering on the brink of collapse because of lax financial practices, an embezzling employee, and mismanagement. The elderly Mrs. Chouinard turned to Walt for help, and over the next five years he provided operating funds, management reform, and repair of the facilities. Mrs. Chouinard, grateful for the help, retired to her home in Pasadena, and Walt took over the operation completely. But true to form, he began to envision a grander scheme, seeing Chouinard as the centerpiece of a great "city of the arts" where teaching and learning in all of the fine arts would combine artistic training with practical experience and produce graduates who could move into the entertainment industry.[31]

By coincidence, around the same time the Los Angeles Conservatory of Music, which had also fallen on hard financial times, came under the temporary protection of several wealthy benefactors. These patrons were brought into contact with Walt, and after extensive discussions, all interested parties agreed to a plan whereby Chouinard and the conservatory formally merged in 1961 under a single administration and financial structure. This new entity, the California Institute of the Arts, was modeled on the California Institute of Technology, and it was a pet project of Walt's throughout the 1960s. He donated a thirty-eight-acre parcel from the studio-owned Golden Oak Ranch, a filming location just north of the San Fernando Valley, and plans for construction of a campus and development of a curriculum began.

In terms of the pedagogical mission of Cal Arts, Walt planned to incorporate some of his utilitarian ideas about education. He did not want, as he often phrased it, an "ivory tower" school turning out dilettantes who knew a great deal about esoteric topics but could do nothing with their knowledge. Instead, he sought a more practical institution that would be staffed by practicing artists, who would transmit some of their knowledge and experience by working closely with students. Walt believed strongly that training in principles and techniques needed to be combined with actual application of those ideas in a commercial context, since that was the arena in which graphic and performing artists would have to survive. He pushed for a flexible curriculum that would include internships, interdisciplinary projects ranging widely through the arts, classwork combined with fieldwork, regular public performances, and marketing of students' work to the public. The result, he hoped, would be "multiple opportunities for the arts to interact, to influence and enhance one another, to coalesce, to merge, to be transformed, even to evolve new and as yet undreamed of art forms." In press interviews, Walt described Cal Arts as a collection of "workshops" or as a "lyceum in the Greek tradition, where artists and musicians live and train together." But the upshot, as he made clear to T. Hee in 1965, would be to produce students who could work effectively in the real world. "Hell, I've hired theorists, and they don't have any knowledge that I can use," he burst out. "I want to have everyone in that school come out capable of going right in and doing a job. These dilettantes who come out with pseudo-knowledge, they give me a pain."[32]

Walt's disdain for formally schooled artists who floundered in the real world of commercial art pointed to another important aspect of the undertaking. He foresaw a definite commercial dimension to his city of the arts. On one side, of course, was the educational institution, but right alongside it lay the blueprint for a commercial complex consisting of theaters, galleries, shopping centers, and restaurants. The cross-fertilization between these two sectors, Walt insisted, would provide financial support for education "from within the profit-making framework of commercial enterprise." It would make this city of the arts, he concluded, the "internationally known tourist and entertainment attraction and educational center which it must be to be successful."[33]

Part of the impetus for creating Cal Arts came from Walt's uneasy relationship with the contemporary art world. For many years he quietly had nurtured a growing disenchantment with modern abstract art. Suspicious of what he saw as its elitism, avant-garde arrogance, and cavalier techniques, he sought to return skilled draftsmanship and popular appeal to the artistic process. In conversations and interviews, he regularly denounced the unskilled artist who dissembled with "a beatnik pose" and the abstractionists "who don't know how to paint; they splash some colors on and think they're doing something. It's a cover-up for poor draftsmanship." An illustrative incident occurred around 1960, when Walt went to San Francisco to receive an award from a civic organization that had commissioned a young sculptor to make an abstract bronze statue in honor of him. But when it was presented, Walt's reply was unexpected: "I don't mean to be offensive. It is interesting, but what is it? To me it looks like a burnt turkey. You know, it's just my own ignorance. I'm really only a cartoonist. I don't know anything about art. I'd appreciate it if the artist, if he's here, would explain this sculpture to me." The sculptor came forward and explained that as a longtime admirer of Walt's creativity, he had tried to symbolize it with an abstract rendering of a sprouting seed. But, he admitted, "it does look like a burnt turkey!" The crowd shared a laugh, and any tension quickly dissipated.[34]

Yet Walt was no simpleminded neanderthal who denounced all modern abstractions but a genuine admirer of artists with drawing skill and emotional appeal. A visitor to his studio office, for example, was startled to see two original paintings by artists he admired, one by Norman Rockwell and one by Salvador Dali. In many ways, like the millions of ordinary Americans whose tastes he represented, Walt simply had become suspicious that the term "art" was being "tossed recklessly at anything around that appears avant-garde or iconoclastic." He hoped that by infusing talented students with drawing fundamentals, creative spirit, and a sense of appealing values, Cal Arts would help return graphic arts to the stylistic mainstream.[35]

By the mid-1960s, Walt began putting his plan into motion with a fundraising and publicity blitz. This project, as he once noted, had become "the principal thing I hope to leave when I move on to greener pastures. If I can provide a place to develop talent for the future, I think I will have accomplished something." In fact, he felt so strongly that he left 45 percent of his personal fortune to Cal Arts upon his death, a bequest reportedly totaling nearly $28 million. When ground was broken in 1969 and the new campus officially opened in 1971, with a student body of around 1200, the entertainer's vision of a special institution for the arts finally came true.[36]

In the early 1960s, Disney's new ventures into technological development, resorts, world's fair exhibits, and art schools, along with the more traditional projects in movie and television production, seemed to represent a kind of scattershot approach to entertainment. To most observers, even at the highest level of management in Walt Disney Productions and WED, the relationship among these varied endeavors was either obscure or nonexistent. But there was a connection, one that had been gradually formulated and nourished by Walt alone. Eventually its enormous scope became clear, with the announcement of an entertainment complex to be built far from the golden coast of southern California.

III. The Florida Project

On November 15, 1965, Governor Haydon Burns of Florida called a press conference at the Cherry Plaza Hotel in Orlando. When an army of television, radio, and newspaper reporters crowded into the room, they saw him seated behind a table flanked by Walt Disney, Roy Disney, and Card Walker. Burns rose to his feet, greeted the press, and introduced the famous figure next to him as the man "who will bring a new world of entertainment, pleasure, and economic development to the state of Florida." With this, Walt began to speak about his hopes for developing in the Orlando area "something more than just an entertainment enterprise." When the press conference ended, reporters rushed out with the story of a truly enormous project that would consist of a theme park, a cluster of resorts and hotels, and a planned city, all to be erected on a gigantic tract of land. This announcement finally squelched the rumors that had been sweeping through central Florida for months about mysterious purchases of large chunks of land around Orlando. But when the Florida Project, as it was known within the Disney organization, came to light publicly, it also had a much more extensive impact. This initiative not only dwarfed anything ever undertaken in the long, illustrious history of the Disney enterprise, but it had profound significance for the cultural and social evolution of modern America.[37]

As early as 1959, Walt offhandedly had asked John Hench, "How would you like to work on the city of the future?" He never mentioned it again, although in succeeding years he dropped tantalizing hints about building another Disneyland. The eastern United States provided the logical choice, because the great majority of visitors to Anaheim came from west of the Mississippi, so a great portion of the American audience remained untapped. By the early 1960s, the Disney organization took its first steps on Project X, as it was called in this embryo stage, by exploring a number of potential sites. For example, Walt checked out areas around New York while working on the World's Fair. A site near Niagara Falls, possibly in Canada, also received brief attention. St. Louis came under serious consideration when civic leaders and locally based corporations such as Monsanto asked Disney to consider building a riverfront theme park as part of the rebuilding of the downtown area. After several months of planning, however, this deal fell through when Walt made a presentation at a dinner gathering in St. Louis and noted in passing that liquor would not be allowed on the premises. August A. Busch, the local brewery magnate, rejoined in a loud stage whisper, "Anybody who doesn't believe in selling beer and drinking beer is a [expletive]." An embarrassed silence followed, and Disney interest in the undertaking quietly evaporated.[38]

The real groundwork for Project X came from a series of studies conducted by Harrison Price and his Economics Research Associates, the same organization that surveyed the feasibility of most Disney projects. From 1958 through 1963, Price and his researchers quietly conducted four separate surveys on the question of an eastern Disneyland, and where, if anywhere, to build it. Florida emerged as the top choice because of its warm climate and prospects for year-round operation, although conclusions differed as to whether Palm Beach, Ocala, or Orlando would provide the best site. Calculation of interstate highway construction eventually determined the latter site to be the best, and over the next few years Price made nine more studies, on the size of the park, seasonal patterns in Florida tourism, peripheral land use, housing and lodging requirements, and the need for special legislation to facilitate construction.[39]

Plans for the Florida Project began to come together as the World's Fair ground to a halt in the fall of 1965. Walt set up a "secret room" at WED's Glendale headquarters where he, Marvin Davis, and Joe Potter grappled with defining and designing this enormous, multifaceted undertaking. As work progressed and more Imagineers entered the picture, it became evident that Walt's vision encompassed much more than anyone had anticipated. The blueprint included not only a theme park based on the Disneyland model, which everyone had assumed from the beginning, but clusters of hotels and resorts and recreation facilities. Most striking, however, was a planned city that included commercial and residential areas, a thousand-acre industrial park, and a highly sophisticated transportation system.

As WED designers moved forward on the planning front, Walt and Roy put into motion a scheme for secretly buying land in central Florida. Since the price of acreage would skyrocket if landowners knew of the Disney presence, the company designated Robert Foster, the general counsel for Disneyland, to buy land around Orlando beginning in 1964. Without divulging the identity of his employer, Foster began to negotiate with an array of real estate agents, lawyers, and landowners. When Walt and high-ranking Disney officials traveled to Florida to monitor the operation, they concealed their identity and used fake names. By fall 1965, over 27,000 acres had been purchased, an area twice the size of Manhattan Island. As rumors about the buyer circulated wildly — speculation centered on Ford, McDonnell Douglas, and Boeing — Florida newspapers began to investigate, and the Orlando *Sentinel* finally broke the story. At this point, Walt Disney Productions, in concert with the governor's office, decided to hold the press conference that announced the project to the world.[40]

This undertaking flowed out of Walt's frustrations with Disneyland, which he had begun to express within a few years of the Anaheim opening. As the park's popularity boomed, commercial opportunity beckoned, and dozens of motels, bars, and eateries mushroomed along Harbor Boulevard and other nearby streets. Often cheap and tawdry, these establishments detracted from Disneyland's atmosphere while cashing in on its crowds of visitors. Walt grumbled about this for years, and associates such as John Hench reported that "he would shake his head and say that we should have more land." Thus, in one sense the Florida Project represented an opportunity to redo Disneyland and insulate it from the sprawling eyesores of commercial interlopers. The result — more complete control of the environment by Walt and his Imagineers — would allow them to enhance their presentations, amplify the experience of visitors, and refine the leisure ethic that they had been pioneering since the 1950s.[41]

But the project involved much more than an enlarged, enhanced Disneyland East, as some commentators promptly (and inaccurately) labeled it. EPCOT, the "Experimental Prototype Community of Tomorrow," provided a truly startling revision of the Anaheim blueprint. Walt announced publicly that this urban experiment was "the most exciting and by far the most important part of our Florida Project, in fact the heart of everything we'll be doing in Disney World." As Joe Fowler explained, Walt conceived that "the amusement park would be the 'weenie' and that EPCOT would be the real big construction." His enthusiasm was so intense that it bordered on obsession. In the earliest stage of this project, he would become so excited when arising in the morning that he would scribble ideas and sketches on his breakfast napkin and then drop it off for Marvin Davis to amplify or clarify. As plans developed, one old-time Disney hand claimed he had not seen his boss so zealous since the days of *Snow White*.[42]

Although still in an embryonic state, Walt's plans appeared clearly in a promotional movie produced by the company in late autumn 1966. This twenty-five-minute film presented Walt as guide of a cinematic tour of the urban utopia he envisioned. With the aid of giant wall maps, footage of WED Imagineers at work, artists' sketches, and animation, he explained that the EPCOT master plan included several key features. First, it was based on the utilization of state-of-the-art industrial technology, district planning, and a spirit of experimentation to create a livable urban space free from crime, congestion, and slums. Second, its physical layout followed the radial plan, with a central hub from which highways and mass transit radiated outward like spokes of a wheel, and around which carefully delineated areas (business and commercial districts, apartment complexes, greenbelt lands, residential areas) were stacked in concentric rings. Third, a tightly controlled environment made the pedestrian king of the city by arranging transport in a sophisticated three-layer system: electric mass transit on the surface level, automobile traffic on a submerged network of roads, and a truck route buried even deeper and linked to commercial docks. Fourth, EPCOT's thousand-acre industrial park, located away from the central city and residential areas, would provide employment for many of the city's residents. Reached by mass transit and constructed in a parklike setting, it would consist of "experimental prototype plants, research and development laboratories, and computer centers for major corporations." EPCOT, with its twenty thousand inhabitants and its safe, efficient, fulfilling environment, Walt concluded hopefully, would "influence the future of city living for generations to come."[43]

The Florida Project promised to weave together the many threads of the great Disney expansion of the 1960s. On a scope unimaginable even a few years before, it promised to transcend entertainment by entering directly into the social and political realm. Disney's magic kingdom, it seemed, was about to become a concrete reality as well as a state of mind.

22

It's a Small World, After All

OVER THE SWEEP of his long entertainment career, one of Walt
Disney's greatest strengths was his ability to attract talented, loyal
artists, managers, and operatives. With the dramatic expansion
of the Disney entertainment empire in Florida, this ability became crucial.
The demands of this project made two things clear. First, it seemed obvious
that the undertaking would require a corporate structure unprecedented in
the experience of the Disney Studio, and perhaps in the history of American
entertainment. Second, this undertaking demanded an expansive, even daring aesthetic vision which would elevate Disney thinking about leisure and
recreation to a new plane.

In both of these areas, dozens and eventually hundreds of talented people
devoted themselves to bringing their leader's creative fancy to life. But two
proved particularly important: the quiet brother who had been at Walt's side
throughout his life, and a multitalented artist and intellectual who, more
than anyone in the Disney empire, grappled with the significance of its
efforts.

I. Roy Disney: "Walt Never Cared about Business"

Throughout the late 1930s and 1940s, a story made the rounds at the Disney
Studio so many times that it became something of a legend. At a work-in-

progress preview of *Snow White*, the staff filled out audience-survey cards detailing their reactions to the film and making suggestions. Nearly all the responses were extremely positive, but someone had the temerity to jot down a brief, rather surly recommendation: "Walt, stick to shorts!" The studio head was shocked, of course, and the anonymity of the comment drove him crazy. At first he fretted. "I've got to find this guy and talk to him," but no one ever came forward. The incident became a running joke at the studio, and for years afterward, whenever Walt wanted to throw one of his artists off balance, he would whirl around, point at him, and laughingly say, "It's you! You're the one who told me to stick to shorts!" In fact, however, a few of the top Disney artists knew who had written the note. They kept their mouths shut, because the author of the quip was none other than Roy Disney, Walt's brother and the studio's business manager.[1]

From the beginning, Roy had questioned the wisdom of embarking on *Snow White*, pleading with Walt to consider the dangers of going heavily into debt to finance this experimental project. Such a genre had no demonstrated audience appeal, he argued, and its failure would drive the studio into bankruptcy. In long, occasionally acrimonious debates with his creative brother, he argued for staying with the proven moneymakers — the Mickey Mouse and Silly Symphony shorts. Thus Roy's anonymous response on the questionnaire was but a playful shot in a much longer skirmish. In a larger sense, this episode symbolized the working relationship between the two brothers over four decades as they struggled to the summit of the Hollywood entertainment industry. As everyone who worked with them knew, the juxtaposition of the quiet, prudent, security-minded steward of studio finances and the gambling, mercurial, and highly creative showman explained much about the flourishing of the Disney Studio.

Roy Oliver Disney was born in Chicago in 1893, the third of four boys and some eight years before Walt. He often was delegated to care for his infant sibling, pushing him around the neighborhood in a stroller and amusing him. The two brothers became close, even sleeping together in the crowded Disney household. This arrangement proved difficult because as a very young boy, Walt had a problem with wetting the bed. In later years this was a source of much amusement, as the famous producer would grin and inform acquaintances that he had peed on Roy's legs for years as a kid and he had been doing it ever since! Roy played a key role during the family stint at the Marceline farm, taking over most of the work and management duties when Elias was struck down with typhoid in 1909. After the family lost the farm and left for Kansas City, Roy worked for a time with Walt and their younger sister, Ruth, in Elias's newspaper distribution business. He went to Kansas to help his uncle with the harvest in 1912 and 1913 and then left the family nest for good to take a position as a bank teller. World War I brought service in the U.S. Navy until 1919, when Roy returned to Kansas City, where he once again worked as a teller at the First National Bank. At this point the young man encountered health problems and entered the gloomiest period of his life. Two serious bouts of influenza in 1920 led to a serious throat infection, and x-rays subsequently disclosed that he was suffering from tuberculosis. He was placed in a VA hospital in New Mexico for a couple of years, then transferred to a facility in Tucson, Arizona, and finally to a hospital near Los Angeles.[2]

Throughout this period, Roy periodically sent money to Walt to help sustain his struggling cartoon business in Kansas City. When Walt's Laugh-O-Gram Films finally went under, Roy urged him to come to southern California. More or less by accident, Roy ended up as Walt's associate in 1923 when the younger brother took his advice. After many heart-to-heart talks, Roy loaned Walt more money and agreed to handle the finances for a new filmmaking venture.

In the mid-1920s, Roy worked as a jack-of-all-trades at the Disney Brothers Studio office on Kingswell Avenue. As his brother launched the Alice cartoons and then the Oswald the Lucky Rabbit series, he kept the books and managed the accounts, of course, but he also spelled the cameraman, washed cels for reuse, and punched holes in the cels and animation paper for the artists. With a swelling production schedule and the rather unexpected craze for Mickey Mouse talkies late in the decade, Roy moved exclusively into the financial arena. His money management assumed a crucial role as loans, bills, and accounts took on ever greater importance in the studio's growth.

Over the next several decades, Roy navigated the twists and turns of market fortune and guided Walt Disney Productions in its career of steady financial growth. Throughout the 1930s and 1940s, he negotiated a series of deals with the Bank of America and secured desperately needed loans to sustain Walt's pathbreaking animation projects. He arranged the financing for the new Burbank facility, completed in 1940, and during that same year managed the company's first offering of public stock. He kept the studio afloat financially during the dark days of the labor strike, the shrinking market during World War II, and the postwar economic recession. With renewed prosperity in the early 1950s, he arranged the complex business deal among Walt Disney Productions, the American Broadcasting Company–Paramount Theaters, and Western Printing and Lithographing, which not only led Disney into television production but provided the much-needed financing for Disneyland.

All along, Roy's relationship with Walt provided perhaps the central dynamic in the evolution of the studio. The two brothers maintained a close, if occasionally stormy, working relationship that endured for more than four decades. The elder Disney stood firm as a steady emotional rock while the more explosive, imaginative, and moody younger brother ebbed and flowed around him. The general pattern of their interaction established itself early in the studio's history: Walt would come up with an expansive, innovative new project; Roy would question the costs and financial implications and counsel caution; Walt would persist, arguing and charming and maneuvering for all he was worth, and finally win his brother's grudging consent; Roy then would climb on board and find the financial wherewithal for the undertaking.

As nearly everyone at the Disney Studio knew, Roy and Walt waged some fierce battles over the years. Roy may have barricaded himself behind facts and figures and displayed little creative flair, but he was no unimaginative cipher, nor a mere punching bag for Walt. With a shrewd feel for business and an intimate knowledge of his brother's gambling temperament, he did not hesitate to apply the brakes to projects he believed dangerous to the studio's financial health. Unlike Walt, who had a fervent, almost childlike belief in the popular appeal of his ideas, Roy faced more practical pressures and could not rely on faith alone.

In the early 1930s, for instance, Roy and Walt clashed over the dangers and expenses of going into color animation, and a few years later over betting the studio's future on *Snow White*. As usual, Walt's charm and creative impulses carried the day, and color cartoons and animated feature films became Disney hallmarks. Roy found himself in the familiar position of reluctantly financing expansion, all the while praying that disaster was not around the next corner. By the late 1930s and early 1940s, acute growing pains at the studio seemed to be proving his apprehensions correct. Even many years later, Roy's description of this period still conveyed his frustration: "Walt had moved with his own creative talent on his own bent. Business was a damn nuisance to him. After *Snow White*, he wanted to make two animated features a year. We couldn't sustain it. We grew like a mushroom and operated uneconomically. The war, plus overloading and a failure to study the market, put us down. Every creative fellow is so concentrated, he doesn't like to think through the market. Walt was that kind of guy until he learned his lesson."[3]

After surviving the dark days of the 1940s, Roy and Walt found new bones of contention. They clashed over *Seal Island*, the first of the True-Life Adventures, Roy arguing that distributors would find no appeal in a thirty-minute nature documentary. Then they had a huge fight over the production of *Alice in Wonderland* and *Peter Pan*, two animated films that Roy opposed because of their terrific expense. A short time later, however, he enthusiastically supported *Twenty Thousand Leagues under the Sea*, a big-budget, live-action project. A shocked Walt quipped, "I thought something was wrong with him."[4]

The Disney brothers spent much of the early 1950s in a long, protracted struggle over plans for the Anaheim amusement park. The usual pattern appeared: Walt brimmed over with enthusiasm while Roy, reflecting the judgment of every financial expert and banker he knew, worried that it was a dangerous gamble. As early as 1951, in a letter to a business acquaintance that seemed more designed to convince himself, Roy wrote that Walt was "more interested, I think, in ideas that would be good in an amusement park than in running one himself." Such was not the case, of course, and the brothers' disagreement did not abate: when Roy resisted sinking company funds into the project, Walt reacted by forming his own company. He also needled his brother by asking Hazel George, the studio nurse, to go around the Burbank lot and gather ten-dollar pledges from the staff to back the park. As usual, Roy finally came around, against his better judgment, and negotiated the deal that financed the construction of Disneyland. It was only on opening day that his skepticism began to abate. Headed down to Anaheim from Burbank, he encountered highways jammed with people headed to the park, and upon his arrival a harried parking lot attendant told him that so many people were stalled on the freeways and backed up into the parking areas that "children are peeing all over the lot." Simply relieved to see hordes of paying customers, Roy exclaimed, "God bless 'em! Let 'em pee!"[5]

Then came the bitterest confrontation in Roy and Walt's relationship. Their rifts had reached the boiling point before; for instance, the dispute over *Alice in Wonderland* and *Peter Pan* had produced an argument of several hours in Walt's office. Walt became so angry that Roy responded, "Look, you're letting this place drive you nuts, and that's one place I'm not going with you," and walked out. After both spent a sleepless night, Walt appeared at his brother's office, so emotional that he could hardly talk, and confessed, "Isn't it amazing what a horse's ass a fella can be sometimes?" But in the late 1950s, a much more serious division occurred, although details are scarce because studio insiders would not and will not talk much about it. Apparently it stemmed from Walt's formation of a pair of private companies earlier in the decade: WED, the design group, and Retlaw (Walter spelled backward), another family company. The crucial issue concerned the use of Walt's name. The entertainer granted exclusive name use to these private companies and then presented Walt Disney Productions and his brother with an ultimatum, demanding certain conditions for leasing the name. Roy felt betrayed, and a feud ensued. According to Roy's son, Roy E. Disney, during this "terrible fight" the two brothers avoided each other and barely spoke for a couple of years. Another longtime studio employee claimed that certain photographs of the Disney brothers released to the public during this era had to be pasted together and airbrushed because of their reluctance to appear alongside each other. The matter was resolved only in 1961, when

Walt wrote an emotional letter to Roy on his birthday and sent along a peace pipe as a symbol of his desire to heal the rift. The brothers reconciled and resumed a close working relationship, which lasted throughout the 1960s.[6]

Through all of these cycles, two sturdy threads held the Disney brothers together. As many observers noted over the years, their complementary talents created checks and balances that consistently promoted the health of the studio. One Disney artist, for instance, described how "one brother was a safety valve for the other," while another contended that Walt's creative instincts and Roy's business judgment formed a "complement of talents . . . unique in the history of motion pictures." In addition, the two Disneys, for all of their contention, colorfully illustrated the old saying that blood is thicker than water. Like many brothers from traditional family back-grounds, these two strong-minded figures felt free to say harsh things about each other. In fact, Roy E. Disney recalled cutthroat croquet games between all four Disney brothers, during which the children had to leave the area because the brutal competition threatened to deteriorate into fistfights. But woe to anyone who tried to disparage one within earshot of the other. As Lillian Disney related, Walt and Roy always closed ranks against outsiders, and "nobody could say an unkind word about either of them in the presence of the other."[7]

A complex blend of love, admiration, and frustration thus flavored the long, productive relationship of Roy and Walt Disney. In a 1957 speech to the Big Brothers organization, Walt said of Roy, "I sometimes think he's the stubbornest so-and-so I ever met in my life. But I don't know what the hell I'd do without him . . . If it hadn't been for my big brother, I swear, I'd have been in jail several times for check bouncing." A long series of private interviews with journalist Pete Martin in the mid-1950s disclosed the same feelings. In one breath, and with evident emotion, Walt would praise his older sibling for looking after him and having faith in his vision, admitting that most of their arguments came because "Roy has felt that he had to protect me." Then, in the next breath, he would disparage his brother as "mule-headed," a mere banker, a "figures man" who could only look back-ward in his obsession to recover costs. But ultimately, and true to form, Walt asserted that he and Roy always supported each other in any crisis: "We were together on it, and we would never make a maneuver that was false . . . And we licked 'em all!"[8]

For his part, Roy deeply loved his brother and had immense admiration for his talents. In interviews, he expressed amazement at Walt's relentless perfectionism, which for decades drove him and others to new heights of achievement. Every Disney film ever made, Roy claimed, bore Walt's "stamp of creativity . . . He was the motivating, congealing force in it." And the studio chief's "single-mindedness," noted the older Disney, was something to behold: "When he decides he wants to do something, or do something a certain way, nothing stops him, literally nothing." But Roy's great respect for Walt contained little fear or awe. In the 1930s, for instance, he sat in on some animators' meetings when Walt was out of town and eventually grew exasperated when the artists refused to deviate at all from Walt's instructions. "What in the hell!" he burst out. "Is Walt some ogre? Is he some tough prizefighter you are afraid of? Are you a lot of dogs who stick your tails between your legs because you're scared of Walt?" Over the years, he would comment to staffers, "Walt's not a genius. He's just my brother." Roy also grew annoyed over what he saw as Walt's penchant for exaggerating parts of his family history, particularly his tales about how their father beat him or took his money. The older brother would sigh, shake his head, note certain people's talents for embellishing stories, and say exasperatedly, "That's Walt." But just like Walt, Roy had a sense of family connection that always won out in the end. As he liked to say of his loyalty to Walt, "My brother made me a millionaire. Why shouldn't I be?"[9]

Roy's physical presence and personality reflected his preference for working behind the scenes. He shared the Disney dark eyes and angular features but was slightly smaller than Walt, with a blander, less expressive face and a slightly bucktoothed grin. As a young man, he was usually seen in a neat three-piece suit with white shirt and tie, exhibiting none of Walt's debonair taste for flashy sport jackets and sweaters. In the postwar period Roy slowly put on weight; his hair thinned drastically, and he took to wearing dark horn-rimmed glasses. Throughout his life he displayed a quiet, calm, unpretentious quality that earned him a reputation for kindliness and sweet temper. His understated disposition could flare into anger but just as quickly subside, while his placid, serious demeanor occasionally veered toward dourness. While not a gregarious man, Roy talked and kidded with studio employees in his own gentle fashion and treated them well, probably better than Walt did.

Like Walt, Roy evolved politically into a staunchly conservative Republican, but he was more pragmatic and less emotional than his brother. His attitude toward the strike of 1941 was illustrative. With typical frankness, he opined that Hollywood Communists were behind this disruptive episode, but unlike Walt, he did not take it personally. Roy saw the strike as an unfortunate but probably inevitable clash between labor and management in a growing business, and he became the central figure in negotiating its settlement when Walt left the country. In broader terms, he was much more concerned than Walt with the interests and concerns of stockholders in Walt Disney Productions, and his interactions with company investors were tinged with respect and humor. When he presented a glowing profit report on *Mary Poppins* at a stockholders' meeting in the mid-1960s, for instance, he concluded with the sly comment, "Don't expect this every year."[10]

Roy was a down-to-earth man who elicited respect and affection from nearly everyone who knew him. He came across, as one studio insider put it, just like a small-town banker. But as many learned to their surprise, and occasionally at their peril, his agreeable appearance masked an inner toughness. He approached business with an honest, old-fashioned, no-nonsense attitude. He cared deeply about his brother and the studio they had built together, and its interests remained uppermost in his mind as he drove hard bargains, proving a tenacious negotiator regarding salaries and contracts. In the 1920s, animator Hugh Harman envied Walt because "he had Roy paving the way for him. A guy of such honesty and such toughness . . . but such a gentle and gently spoken man." During the following decade, another studio artist described how Roy's image as a tightfisted manager was enhanced by "an ominous-looking, four-foot-long row of books entitled *Management vs. Labor* [that] occupied the shelf behind his desk." But however genial this businessman appeared to be in social encounters or how tough he proved in business dealings, there was no doubt of his integrity. Roy made it clear that he abhorred commercial chicanery and practiced a brand of straightforward, honest business dealings rooted in an old-fashioned ethic according to which you negotiated in good faith, your loyalty to your institution never wavered, and your handshake was your word. As he once said, "If I contributed anything, I contributed honest management for Walt."[11]

Roy's traditional values and traits were reflected in his personal life. Its centerpiece was his forty-six-year marriage to the former Edna Francis of Kansas City, a woman who shared his down-to-earth temperament. The couple's domestic existence was even less "Hollywood" than Walt and Lillian's. Their only child, Roy E. Disney, was born in 1930, and the little family's life was quite ordinary. Roy kept fairly routine business hours, came home every night for dinner, and puttered around his yard as an amateur gardener. When they wanted to relax, he and Edna would go for drives into the countryside around Los Angeles. They liked to host traditional midwestern dinners of fried chicken, mashed potatoes, and corn on the cob on Sunday afternoons, especially for foreign employees of the Disney company, after which everyone would sit around the kitchen table and talk. Much like Roy, Edna was loyal, plainspoken, and tough. As her son once quipped, if the Disney brothers had been pioneers coming across the country and their mule had died, Edna and Lillian would have "jumped off and pulled the goddamn covered wagon the rest of the way themselves." Edna was fiercely loyal to her husband and apparently resented that he did not get enough credit for the studio's success. As a family friend noted, she was a dear, caring person, "but if she didn't like you, God help you!" One time, for instance, when she and Roy were in Paris consulting with the Disney office there, Edna became suspicious that whispering French employees were making fun of her husband in their native language. Furious, she went home and learned basic French from a Berlitz tape course. When they returned to Paris, she sat quietly, listened closely, and had her suspicions confirmed. As a result, several employees were chastised for their impertinence. Like Roy, Edna had no fear of Walt, and she occasionally deflated him by treating him like the tag-along kid she and her husband had known back in Kansas City. Even in late life, Roy and his wife maintained a close relationship and an unpretentious manner. Roy often picked up the dinner check when studio executives, along with their wives, had flown east to work on the Florida Project. The pair would often hold hands when they were out together, and whenever they landed in an airplane, Roy would habitually turn to Edna and say, "Well, we cheated death again, didn't we, darlin'?"[12]

Early articles on the Disney Studio always focused on the celebrity brother, granting Roy a kind of footnote status if they noted him at all, but insiders never doubted that the older, quieter brother was a serious, influential, and talented man in his own right. In fact, many described Roy as a financial genius who could take credit for much of the Disney Studio's progress. While relentlessly pruning production costs and keeping an eye on the details — when employees returned from abroad, for example, they were surprised to learn that he always knew the latest exchange rates for currency — he also moved surefootedly over much larger and more treacherous economic terrain. He not only negotiated a series of loans in the early years but promoted several shrewd initiatives that kept the company's economic lifeblood pumping. For instance, he was the key figure in plotting the studio's merchandising moves, which began in the 1930s and expanded steadily thereafter, not only in the United States but in many foreign markets. Roy also made the suggestion to produce live-action films in England to free up studio funds that had been frozen there during World War II. In the early 1950s, it was his idea to found the Buena Vista Film Distribution Company to take over distribution of Disney Studio films, a move that proved enormously profitable. One of his greatest business achievements came as the key architect of postwar integration, the strategy that deployed films, television, music, books, and a variety of merchandise to publicize one another. As Roy told *Newsweek* in 1962, with characteristic simplicity, "Everything we do helps something else."[13]

Gradually, the breadth and depth of Roy's contribution to Disney's spectacular success began to sink in. Analysts of the company eventually stumbled across the crucial role he played, and by the 1950s and 1960s a spate of stories in the national media, many of them in business journals, began to grant him increasing credit. Stories in the *Wall Street Journal, Financial World,* and *Forbes* analyzed his role at some length, while *Business Week* approvingly quoted a Disney employee: "I think Roy's even more of a genius in his way than Walt is in his."[14]

Roy's greatest challenge came in the mid-1960s with the advent of the gigantic Florida Project. Typically, the two brothers were at odds over how to get the project off the ground. The business manager insisted on building the theme park first to establish a profit flow to support the other projects, while the entertainer wanted to jump in and begin construction of the urban area. But the brothers, determined not to disrupt their reconciliation, muted this disagreement and kept it behind the scenes. In fact, when Walt publicly announced this venture, he went out of his way to pay tribute to Roy. His brother's financial skill and personal loyalty, he told reporters, had always provided "proper balance" in the Disney enterprise and been crucial to its success. Throughout their history, Walt said, he had depended on Roy to gauge his wild ideas and "either straighten me out and put me on the right path or . . . I'd work on it for years until I got him to agree with me." But with the Florida Project, he continued, his brother "was with me from the start."[15]

Roy's brilliant plan for financing this tremendously expensive undertaking proved Walt's words to be no exaggeration. According to an admiring assessment in *Forbes*, "The financial story behind Walt Disney World is almost as fantastic as the physical development itself." Roy's bold scheme involved selling several convertible debenture issues — bonds that can be converted to stock — to investors, which raised nearly $100 million. They were then retired quickly when the price of Disney stock, stimulated by expectations of great profit, soared above the conversion price. Under Roy's direction, Disney then marketed a $72 million common stock issue, part of which went to retire debt on a $50 million credit line with the Bank of America, the company's longtime financial backer. By passing on to investors most inflationary costs, the company was able to save itself millions of dollars. Moreover, using rising stock value to beat the conversion rate on the bonds meant that new Disney stockholders "contributed half of the company's current equity and yet ended up with only 25 percent of the company." Finally, and perhaps most important, Roy's financial plan allowed Walt Disney Productions to own the entire Florida facility, spending some $230 million while remaining debt-free. As *Forbes* concluded, "that lovely, clean balance sheet . . . will be Roy Disney's legacy just as the cartoon characters and the fantasy were Walt's."[16]

Unfortunately, a good part of Roy's financial plan for the Florida Project unfolded after Walt's death. But the demise of the younger, more famous Disney brother probably spurred the older one to even greater achievement. Not only did Roy announce that the Florida park would be called *Walt Disney World*, as a sign of respect for his brother, but he joked to studio employees that he had to get the project open because "when I see Walt again, I don't want to have to explain to him why I failed." The Florida Project revealed one thing clearly: the imposing corporate structure that allowed Walt to extend his entertainment grasp in the postwar period was

Roy's creation. The big brother with the small ego provided the financial foundation for Disney's flights of fantasy.[17]

II. John Hench: "Something about Life and Survival"

Walt Disney was notoriously tightlipped when it came to compliments for his staff. Thus people took note when, throughout the 1950s and 1960s, he would comment to associates and family members, "Johnny has never let me down." This rare bit of praise offered tribute to John Hench, one of the most intensely creative figures in the history of the Disney enterprise. Along with Marc Davis and Ward Kimball, whose activities also covered many fields, Hench was one of the true Renaissance men of the Disney Studio. His name became synonymous with Disney "imagineering."[18]

When Walt launched WED in the early 1950s, he turned to Hench, a versatile, elegant, and highly intelligent man. Plucked from the studio ranks and installed in Walt's personal company, Hench was central to every major project from the Anaheim theme park through the World's Fair exhibits to the Florida Project. He designed buildings, developed transportation systems, worked out color schemes, and created rides, all with a special feel for the Disney touch. Eventually he became chief project designer, and later executive vice president and chief operating officer of WED. But in the Disney operation, where titles meant little and achievements everything, Hench's true stature was marked by the fact that he became one of Walt's most trusted creative advisers.[19]

After a boyhood in southern California and extensive artistic training in Los Angeles and New York, Hench took a position at the Disney Studio, in 1939. He began work in the story development unit and then moved into layout and background painting. During his first years at the studio, his background paintings adorned *Fantasia* and *Dumbo,* while his layout paintings appeared in *The Three Caballeros* and *Fun and Fancy Free.* As his career progressed, he served as an art supervisor on *Make Mine Music,* worked on the animated sections of *So Dear to My Heart,* and provided color and styling for *The Adventures of Ichabod and Mr. Toad, Cinderella,* and *Peter Pan.* A high point came with *Twenty Thousand Leagues under the Sea,* where Hench's work led to an Academy Award for special effects.

Hench really came into his own, however, with the formation of WED and its involvement with Disneyland. He was sitting at his desk one day when Walt came by, stated rather brusquely, "I want you to work on Disneyland, and you're going to like it," and kept walking. Hench was a bit unnerved by this switch to a project about which he knew little, but he quickly found it fascinating. He became one of the key proponents of "imagineering," the unique WED combination of imagination and engineering.[20]

Hench's growing influence in part stemmed from an imposing personal presence. With an expressive, forceful face, penetrating eyes, and a trim mustache, he looked a little like a balding version of Walt and was occasionally mistaken for his boss by people on the street. An impeccable dresser, he wore well-cut dark suits and restrained ties in middle age and sported ascots with jackets and sweaters as he got older. A suave, erudite man, he enjoyed holding forth as an intellectual, spinning out grand theories at the drop of a hat as he conversed with his colleagues. He radiated confidence and intelligence. His casual elegance also earned him a reputation as a ladies' man, and his favorite method for charming a young woman was to cradle her hand in his and read her palm.

Hench also displayed serious artistic concerns. From the very beginning of his training, he was curious about how art worked as communication. When he questioned exactly how forms and images conveyed emotions, his art teachers simply told him to follow established aesthetic laws and forget about underlying processes. Dissatisfaction with this response led him first to the movie industry, because of its focus on communicating with images, and eventually to the Disney Studio, where, in his words, "I discovered very quickly what I was looking for." Hench's versatile array of talents did not fit neatly into the usual categories at a movie studio, but they flourished in the more eclectic field of Disney entertainment. When he first came to the studio, for example, he spent a solid week observing a ballet production in Los Angeles as research for his background paintings for "The Nutcracker Suite" section of *Fantasia*. Somewhat later he encountered problems with integrating food service into the overall design for Disneyland, a difficulty he overcame by taking a course in restaurant management at UCLA. His natural sense of color led to his role as supervisor of color styling for *Cinderella*, *Peter Pan*, and a host of projects at WED; his bent for conveying emotional impact through design prompted his work on Disneyland's Rocket to the Moon attraction; his feel for shape and form inspired his architectural design of the Carousel of Progress and the Sky Dome Spectacular at the New York World's Fair. As a result of such varied talents, Hench cut a wide swath through the Disney enterprise, ranging from working closely for several months with Salvador Dali on the short film *Destino* (never released) to serving as the official portrait artist for Mickey Mouse.[21]

It was Hench's intellectual bent, however, that made him a fascinating figure in the Disney operation. Here was someone who not only created fantastic entertainment forms and leisure environments but thought about their larger significance. Hench struggled to come to terms with the meaning of Disney's work in modern American society, and his reflections dripped with allusions to Freud and Jung, theories of communication, mythology, and architectural principles. Articulated with great verve and bursts of insight, his thoughts revealed much about the aesthetics of Disney's work.

For example, he noted that Disneyland drew on several communication devices from films. Much like designers of movie sets, park planners proceeded in sequential fashion by taking a series of spaces and creating a special reality within each. They used the old theatrical tricks of false perspective and fading colors on upper stories of buildings to create spatial illusions. They even came up with a version of the cinematic "cross-dissolve," where subtle changes of setting, music, imagery, even paving stones encouraged a shift of emotional response as visitors moved from one "land" to another in the park. But WED Imagineers went a step beyond film by encouraging active participation. The result of this hybrid model, Hench argued, was a kind of aesthetic logic that led visitors through Disneyland and encouraged certain reactions. Functioning as a kind of three-dimensional movie, the park offered guests an ordered sequence of environments that began with the optimistic, nostalgic warmth of Main Street, USA, progressed to the innocent thrills of Adventureland, the patriotic history of Frontierland, the childlike sense of wonder in Fantasyland, and the confident futurism of Tomorrowland. Subtle psychological touches — a carousel where all of the horses are painted white, a haunted house where death is funny, a miniaturized automobile ride where order and safety prevail — combined to encourage feelings of security, harmony, and well-being.[22]

In fact, Hench's reading of the aesthetic structure of the Anaheim park concerned several themes, which, over many years, he gradually elaborated into a shrewd interpretation of the Disney appeal. First of all, he became convinced that one key was Disney's total control of an environment to create an experience for the visitor. And experience — "not watching someone else do something, but doing it yourself" — was a basic component of the human condition. As Hench explained to an interviewer,

> The only thing we really keep in this world are experiences. We have to give up everything else. We can't keep our favorite shirt or car. Everything we have finally wears out or we have to throw it away, or it loses its usefulness or its zest. But our experiences we keep. They're not only what we are, but they're added to that great big bundle we carry around with us — the experiences of our ancestors . . . Walt was trying to . . . really give people a kind of package experience that they wouldn't be capable of having on their own.

The Imagineers grasped this and made experience the central feature of Disneyland and the World's Fair attractions, where, "through images and through color and through sound . . . [we were able] to evoke an idea in somebody else's head so that they understand."[23]

Infusing this controlled environment, Hench continued, was a powerful maneuver he described as "removing the contradictions." Another offshoot of the theatrical and moviemaking world, this tactic involved strengthening a visual statement by removing extraneous elements that might cloud its essential meaning. As Hench noted, in designing a stage set for a stage show or a film, "you have to know what kind of action is going to take place in it, because you want to support that action. You don't want to deny it or oppose it or contradict it." This same principle was applied to Disneyland, where a more complex kind of communication with visitors demanded the same purification of aesthetic statements. Adopting this tactic, WED Imagineers created Main Street, USA, an idealized village center unlike any that ever existed in real life. The key, Hench insisted, lay in the fact that this purified image embodied people's *image* of small-town life, and therefore it generated an unconscious appeal that stirred certain emotions. A similar dynamic informed Sleeping Beauty Castle, another idealized structure; standing at the hub of the park, it conveyed, in Hench's words, "the old image of a secured point, a strong place." This essence of the *image* of a medieval fortress strengthened the visitor's sense of security.[24]

The removal of contradictions, Hench argued, had appeared over and over again in the history of the Disney Studio. The early animation, for instance, had presented stripped-down aesthetic statements with its delightful depictions of Mickey Mouse and his friends cavorting through a minimalist world. This purifying impulse received additional support from the studio's reliance on themes and images drawn from the animal world. Animals, as Hench noted, have always attracted human sentiment, because they lack guile and "have no ambiguities." The development of Audio-Animatronics offered a new way to remove the contradictions. This robotic technology was maligned in many quarters as a kind of cheap fraud that diminished the humans or animals it replicated, but Hench saw it in an entirely different light. He insisted that Audio-Animatronics helped achieve Disney's controlled environment by repeating the same quality performance time and time again to shape a dependable experience for viewers. "It's like saying music should never be recorded," he insisted. "That it should always be played live, regardless of who [does it] — a high school group or a symphony orchestra. You don't really get the best performance every time." But even more important for Hench, Disney's sophisticated robots, like the ancient Greeks' masks of comedy and tragedy to help actors rid themselves of ambiguities, were "visually explicit, they say one thing."[25]

Nourishment of the Disney aesthetic, Hench believed, ultimately came from a much deeper source. Beneath the fantasy and the sentimentality, and supporting the environmental controls and the purified expressions of Disneyland, surged a profound, primordial impulse to regenerate life. This primitive urge to reaffirm one's existence permeates human consciousness, Hench believed. "I think our pleasure comes from survival. The first thing we strive for as an infant is this kind of life experience, and it's the last thing we want to give up," he observed. "We strive for . . . the experience of being alive." Hench argued that people carry around various inherited survival patterns that have been shaped over millions of years of human experience. These patterns in some way involve a feeling of overcoming adversity. "Pleasure is sweetest when we are triumphant, when we have survived," he noted. "The implication is that we have one struggle behind, and we are that much stronger for the next one." This survival instinct is embedded in the myths of every civilization and even in cultural rituals such as the Christmas tree, which symbolizes the regeneration of life. What few people realize, however, is the crucial connection between survival and visual perception and hence images and aesthetics. "The better you use your eyes, the further away you can size up a situation and relate it to survival or its opposite, the better off you are," Hench argued. "So those of us who are here today, whose ancestors survived, are very good at relating images together." Naturally, imagery-as-survival bleeds into aesthetics as people are drawn to visual representations such as "the colonnade at the Vatican; it's a pair of arms. It's anthropomorphic and that's why it works."[26]

Disney, Hench argued, had succeeded in tapping this survival impulse and making it the basis of the studio's aesthetic endeavors. For instance, Mickey Mouse's basic shape consisted of a set of circles, and his beloved status around the world stemmed from the fact that round shapes are universally associated with breasts, babies, fruit, and other signs of fecundity, nurture, and the regeneration of life. In parallel fashion, the early Disney Studio told fairy tales, which embodied the survival script: a protagonist, often innocent and defenseless, falls prey to a severe challenge, perseveres, and finally emerges triumphant. In Disneyland, Hench contended, park planners created rides, haunted houses, jungle adventures, and fantasy excursions that "throw a challenge at you — not a real menace, but a pseudo-menace, a theatricalized menace — and we allow you to win . . . People win, and they feel good about it." When enhanced by a harmoniously designed environment of architectural forms, pictorial images, verbal expressions, and musical themes carefully arranged to dispel anxiety and encourage optimism, the resulting emotional impact is profound. "There's something beyond an amusement park here. It *obviously* works on people."[27]

Thus for Hench, the Disney aesthetic gained its power from expressing a basic optimism about life. Rooted in a survival ethos stretching back to the dawn of humankind, it underscored regeneration and rejected cynicism and despair. Continuously whispering to visitors "You're going to be okay" and "Life doesn't need to be bad," Disneyland's essential message was a simple one: "There is nothing to fear." So while Walt Disney was certainly in the entertainment business, his product did not meet the usual definition of "an escape from problems, an escape from responsibility . . . What we are selling is not escapism but reassurance."[28]

For all of these reflections, Hench insisted on one simple fact — that Walt himself must be given credit as the great facilitator of this extraordinary mode of communication. As he acknowledged frankly, Walt made no pretense of being an intellectual and never expressed interest in defining or explaining the aesthetic tendencies at work in Disney creations. But what Walt lacked in analytical rigor, he made up for by being "extraordinarily intuitive" and committed to reaching a popular audience. Hench recalled an incident during construction of some project at Disneyland, when he complained, "I'm wasting my time, because people are never going to get this." Walt went up to him, thumped him on the chest with his large forefinger, and said passionately, "If they don't get it, it's because you're a poor communicator! If you can reach out and touch people, they'll get it." As Hench once observed of Walt, "I think actually, underneath it all, he wanted to make people believe about themselves the way he felt about them."[29]

Ultimately, in Hench's view, Walt was "a genuine mystic." In some instinctive fashion, he envisioned his company's evolutionary path, though ideas came to him in whole packages which he then found it difficult to explain in "a logical, step-by-step" way. The move from short cartoons to full-length animated films, then into television, and then into theme parks, the World's Fair, and resorts seemed to be enormous gambles at the time but made perfect sense in hindsight. While others wondered where he was going, Walt "held all of this in his head like a road map, the relationship of one concept to another." They were parts of a larger, instinctive Disney vision. In Hench's view, entertainment involves much more than mere amusement, diversion, or thrills. It is an activity rooted in primitive stages of society, where in caves or forest glens a shaman put on animal skins and horns, painted his face, and through rituals and symbols taught others how to survive. As a modern shaman, Walt helped people affirm their humanity and achieve a sense of security. In the assessment of this studio intellectual, audiences responded to Disney's ideas about life because "we *must* believe in them too."[30]

John Hench became the theorist of the magic kingdom. In the postwar Disney enterprise, he served as the supreme example of the new-style studio operative, whose grounding in art, aesthetics, psychology, architecture, communications, and design took him far beyond the old Disney reliance on animation. This wide-ranging Imagineer, full of shrewd insights and fascinating ideas, helped Walt in one of his most important accomplishments: teaching his audience "something about life and survival."[31]

III. "A Showcase to the World of American Free Enterprise"

The Florida experiment in urban reform seemed a particularly curious departure from traditional Disney entertainment and its fare of fantasy, nature, and sentiment. What lay behind this daring move into the realm of social, economic, and even political affairs? The answer, it seemed, lay in a complex intermingling of political and aesthetic impulses that had developed in the postwar evolution of the Disney enterprise.

As usual, Walt's explanation was simplicity itself: his observation of urban blight in modern America. As he said in an October 1966 interview, "When I see things I don't like, I start thinking why do they have to be like this, and how can I improve them? City governments, for example. We pay a lot of taxes and still have streets that aren't paved or are full of holes. And city street cleaners and garbage collectors who don't do their jobs. And property owners who let dirt accumulate and help create slums. Why?" This concern with a decline in the quality of urban life was reinforced by his experience as a longtime resident of Los Angeles who had witnessed the congestion accompanying growing numbers of cars. "I'm not against the automobile," he told a large group of journalists in 1965, "but I just feel that the automobile has moved into communities too much. I feel that you can design [cities] so that the automobile is there, but still put people back as pedestrians again."[32]

Some of Disney's film comedies in the 1960s provide another clue to the genesis of EPCOT. These lighthearted productions, while nearly devoid of serious content, embroidered a theme of government ineptitude and bureaucratic bungling. Both *The Absent-Minded Professor* and its sequel, *Son of Flubber,* depicted the national government as a collection of mean-spirited buffoons who underestimate and harass the eccentric inventor Professor Ned Brainerd. *Moon Pilot* (1962) offered a variation on this theme as Disney took satirical swipes at the air force, the FBI, the Secret Service, the U.S. Senate, and the space program, which fall over one another in trying to control an astronaut who has fallen in love with a mysterious female alien. *That Darn Cat* (1965) unflatteringly portrayed the FBI as a group of bumbling incompetents who botch several attempts to trace a feline lead and capture a pair of bank robbers who are holding a hostage. In other words, throughout these slapstick comedies ran a strong thread of suspicion about the capabilities of modern government.[33]

This cinematic theme provided a hint of Walt's own ideological evolution. From the early 1940s through the 1950s, of course, he had changed from a Democratic populist into a conservative Republican whose intense patriotism, loyalty to the work ethic, suspicion of regulatory government, and support for American individualism had grown steadily more intense. By the early 1960s, however, he had gone a step further, becoming an enthusiastic advocate of American industry and its capacity for solving social problems. The free enterprise system, which Walt saw as a collection of individual producers rather than a corporate bureaucracy, had created a vast constellation of companies and businesses whose creative capacities, technological innovations, and efficient production of goods and services were the envy of the world. He became convinced that industrial expertise and creativity, under private initiatives rather than government directions, could be harnessed to help ordinary people lead better lives.

Thus Walt, although he expressed disdain for politics, in fact embraced a kind of "technocratic populism" by the 1960s. This ideology, which sought to harness the creative, technological, and productive capacities of modern industry and use them for the benefit of ordinary people, was the inspiration for EPCOT. As Walt explained to the public, his utopian city would "take its cue from the new ideas and new technologies" being developed by a host of private companies and "bring together the technical know-how of American industry and the creative imagination of the Disney organization." As one WED associate noted, he "believed in the free enterprise system" and he wanted to show how "you could take virgin land and develop it properly without government subsidy." This enthusiasm was fired by a round of visits to industrial labs in the early 1960s. During visits to research facilities at Westinghouse, IBM, Allied Chemical, RCA, Bell Telephone, Rockwell, Union Carbide, General Electric, AT&T, and many other companies, Walt and WED staffers such as Joe Potter and Jack Sayers explored technological advances being made in transportation, housing, communication, and many other areas. But at the same time, Walt made it clear that his search for technological solutions to social problems remained firmly wedded to a populist rationale. EPCOT, he insisted publicly, stemmed from a belief that "people still want to live like human beings" and was "dedicated to the happiness of the people who live and work and play here." Privately, he expressed frustration over the fact that American companies felt proprietary about their technological discoveries and were reluctant to share them because they feared losing profit. As he stressed to associates at WED, his "primary interest was in people" and the ways their lives could be improved by creating at EPCOT a "vast living laboratory for the great advances that were being made in medicine, in science, in metallurgy, in health, in sociology."[34]

Disney's technocratic populism had significant political and social implications. At first glance, his agenda for urban reform seemed to swim against the national political current of effervescent, 1960s-style liberalism, which marshaled an array of government programs to combat social ills. With Lyndon Johnson and the Great Society at high tide, the federal government, not private industry, was the primary engine of social reform. But Disney's Florida Project expressed the spirit of the times equally. Like urban renewal and federal housing projects, it represented an idealistic experiment in social engineering that relied on the expertise of technocrats. Moreover, much like Johnson and his liberal cohorts, Disney and his collaborators shared a towering confidence in America's capacity to solve any problem. While liberals thought in terms of government programs that would eliminate any socioeconomic plight, Disney thought in terms of a business activism that would promote reform, prosperity, and happiness. In many ways, Walt Disney and Lyndon Johnson offered two varieties of the overweening hubris of the American Century.

In a longer trajectory, however, EPCOT hewed to a strong tradition of social engineering in modern America wherein technocrats, social scientists, and planners sought to tame, regulate, and rationalize corporate capitalism in the interests of the public. As early as the 1880s, Edward Bellamy's *Looking Backward*, an enormously popular and influential utopian novel, envisioned an American society of the twenty-first century where peace and plenty had been created through rational organization, technological advance, and bureaucratic control. In the early twentieth century, order-minded Progressives such as Herbert Croly, John Dewey, and Walter Lippmann, disgusted with the petty partisanship of traditional politics, promoted a new public sphere dominated by disinterested professionals, economic planners, and technocratic experts. By the 1930s, influential intellectuals and social scientists had pushed this agenda even further. Sociologist Robert Lynd advocated a rational social order shaped by scientific managers, while theorist Lewis Mumford dreamed of utilizing urban planning to create efficient "greenbelt communities" and a group of "technocratic progressives" shaped New Deal policy with designs for a planned economy of abundance. This reforming tradition played a key role in shaping a larger ideology of corporate liberalism, the dominant political creed of modern America, which enshrined the modern regulatory state with its negotiation between organized interest groups, its protection of economic abundance, and its use of government assistance to guarantee social stability. Having established the parameters of political discourse in the United States from early-century Progressivism through Franklin Roosevelt's welfare state, corporate liberals floated comfortably in the mainstream before triumphing completely with the Great Society.[35]

The EPCOT project fell squarely within this technocratic tradition, yet attempted to join it to a populist sensibility rooted deep in Walt's own past. For example, the rhetoric of free enterprise that enveloped the project in fact relied on business-government cooperation. The Disney company moved forward on its plans in Orlando only after assurances that the state government would grant it tax breaks and cede control over all municipal, zoning, and environmental affairs within its domain. According to Joe Fowler, Disney representatives (including Walt and Roy) held a series of private meetings with Governor Burns and other high-ranking state officials to get guarantees about legislation along these lines. As the governor informed the public during the Orlando press conference, "I pledged today, on behalf of all of the [state government] officials, we would cooperate to the fullest degree to meet the requirements of Disney Productions in this development." Joe Potter, one of Walt's right-hand men on the Florida Project, detailed how the state legislature created the Reedy Creek Improvement District, which granted Disney dominion over land use and development, utility and sewer systems, roadways, drainage, police and fire protection.[36]

After securing government concessions, Walt placed a special burden on the private sector by demanding energy, creativity, and public-mindedness in addition to profit-seeking. As John Hench observed, Walt envisioned EPCOT as transcending the normal business ethic of competition, which tended to produce a "chaotic situation." Instead, he sought to create a "system city" that would use business to foster cooperation, technological invention, and planning. As Hench quickly added, however, Walt was "smart enough to know that he had to be very careful with this kind of concept, because it's very easy to relate it to communism or fascism." As with many corporate liberals, the Disney vision of technocratic planning pursued a middle course — systemic control, reliance on the expertise of social engineers, the careful nurture of stability and abundance — which twisted its way between chaotic private competition on the one hand and governmental domination on the other.[37]

EPCOT's promise of urban reform, however, even with its admirable prospects for using mass transit, intelligent zoning and planning, and technological discoveries to improve the nastier aspects of modern urban life, carried an equal portion of danger. It amplified one of the more troubling impulses of modern corporate liberalism — to diminish, if not outright destroy, democracy. Disney's obsession with controlling an urban environment removed not only political dispute but political participation entirely and substituted for it benevolent control from above. In EPCOT, as he bluntly told an interviewer in 1966, "there will be no slum areas because we won't let them develop. There will be no landowners, and therefore no voting control." Thus his blueprint for engineering happiness, with the best of intentions, seemed to shove American traditions of representative government completely out of the picture. The ghost of authoritarianism, even if it emerged from Cinderella Castle and appeared benignly adorned with Mickey Mouse ears, hovered in the background. In jettisoning democracy for technocratic engineering and exchanging the pleasures of citizenship for the rewards of material comfort, EPCOT charted a dangerous course. Rather than realizing the benevolent technocratic populism that Walt genuinely intended, this utopian city might, or even would, give rise to a kind of authoritarian corporate order.[38]

But the Florida Project involved more than politics. Its amusement attractions, resorts, hotels, restaurants, and cornucopia of Disney products were part of a strictly controlled environment that advanced a powerful leisure ethic in this fantasyland. The holistic experience of Disney World offered consumption as the pathway to happiness and, as John Hench argued, strove to make visitors feel good about themselves by promoting feelings of security and life enhancement. As much as any other single creation, Disney World demonstrated the powerful, interlocking appeal of consumer capitalism, leisure, and self-fulfillment in modern America.

Ultimately, however, the leisure attractions of Disney World and the political/social model of EPCOT were two sides of the same coin. In many ways, Disney's planned city sought to institutionalize the images and impulses of the theme park. The controlled environment, the engineering of happiness, and the technological ethos of abundance were shared by the WEDway People Mover and the Abraham Lincoln robot, the pristine industrial park and the Jungle Cruise, the monorail and Mr. Toad's Wild Ride, the greenbelt areas and New Orleans Square. Designer Dick Irvine asserted that "EPCOT is an extension of Disneyland ideas and philosophies toward people," while art director Marvin Davis observed shrewdly that Walt focused "the showmanship he used on everything to make this thing not only a place to live comfortably, but an exciting and entertaining place to live."[39]

Ultimately, Walt envisioned his urban community, in the best American tradition, as a city on a hill, a shining example and inspiration to people all over the globe who were wrestling with the problems of modern life. In his proud words, EPCOT would be "a showcase to the world of the American free enterprise system." Arising from the swamps of central Florida, this utopian expression of the postwar American way of life promised to provide ordinary people with a monument to material progress, security, and wish fulfillment beyond their wildest fantasies. This was Walt Disney's greatest dream by the mid-1960s, one that he pursued with enormous energy. Sadly, however, he never saw it realized.[40]

Epilogue

I T ALL HAPPENED SO quickly. When news of Walt Disney's death on December 15, 1966, swept through the Burbank studio and Disneyland like a shock wave, his associates reacted with surprise, grief, and anxiety for the future. Stricken, some cried out "No!" while others wept quietly. Hardly anyone, even in Walt's family, had expected his death. On New Year's Day 1966 he had served as grand marshal of the Tournament of Roses Parade in Pasadena. Throughout the spring and summer he had flown all over the United States to inspect shopping centers, rapid transit systems, or giant trash-composting equipment that might be adapted for the fledgling Florida Project. In fact, he had spent several draining days in late October shooting a half-hour promotional film that explained that undertaking to the public. But now the man who had built a leisure empire and directed its every move was gone.

Walt had been complaining for years about a series of nagging health problems. By the mid-1960s, his notorious cough had grown worse, becoming more persistent and hacking. He also complained of intense, intermittent neck pains which streaked down into his back and leg, a condition that doctors attributed to an old polo injury. A sinus condition flared up regularly, colds became a steady affliction, and bouts of mysterious, intense facial pain seemed to come out of nowhere. The legendary Disney energy also waned, and the studio chief began showing signs of wear and tear — a slower gait, graying hair, a raspy voice, and a deeply lined face. In search of relief from pain some years before, he had begun late-afternoon therapy sessions with Hazel George, the studio nurse, who joked irreverently with him while applying hot packs and administering soothing shoulder and neck treatments. He always had been an enthusiastic social drinker, but now he began upping his late-afternoon intake of scotch to blunt the physical discomfort. A few colleagues suspected a more serious health problem when, at a mid-September press conference in the Sierra Nevadas, he grew pale and exhausted and nearly collapsed.[1]

But few expected the rapid sequence of events that unfolded at the end of 1966. In July, pain had led Walt to the UCLA medical center, where tests and x-rays revealed calcification in the neck area. He agreed to an operation sometime after the end of the year. In early November he entered St. Joseph's Hospital, where more tests revealed a growth on one of his lungs. He underwent exploratory surgery on November 7, during which his left, cancerous lung was removed. The situation was diagnosed as very grim. Doctors informed his stunned family that he had six months to two years to live. He seemed to recover from the operation, however, and a couple of weeks later returned to the studio, where he assured colleagues that he would soon be back at the helm. After Thanksgiving he grew weaker, though, and he returned to St. Joseph's on November 30. On the evening of December 14, he reassured Lillian about his prospects by hugging her with renewed strength, and then discussed the Florida Project with Roy, using the foot-square ceiling tiles above his bed to plot his plans for the various amusement rides, industrial parks, and housing complexes. In the early morning hours, his physical condition deteriorated rapidly, and he died around 9:30 A.M. from acute circulatory collapse.[2]

The studio, concerned about the financial impact, withheld announcement of the death until the next day, at which point his body already had been cremated and interred at Forest Lawn Cemetery during a secret family ceremony. In an official statement, Roy Disney, the company's president and chairman of the board, assured stockholders and the public that Walt had "built an organization with the creative talents to carry on as he had established and directed it through the years. Today this organization has been built and we will carry out this wish." But the secrecy and quickness of the burial, along with the delayed announcement, gave birth to a wild rumor. Walt's supposed interest in cryogenesis prompted speculation that his body had been frozen and stored in a lab somewhere to be revived later. There was no truth to this story. Much more striking was the enormous outpouring of grief and love that came from every corner of the United States, and indeed from all over the globe.[3]

Over the next few days and weeks, hundreds of obituaries and essays paid homage to this beloved entertainer. Eric Sevareid spoke poignantly of Walt on the NBC evening news, describing him as "not just an American original, but an original, period . . . To a child this weary world is brand-new, gift-wrapped; Disney tried to keep it that way for adults . . . People are saying we'll never see his like again." In special interviews with a Los Angeles radio station, outgoing California governor Pat Brown, a Democrat, noted that Walt had "contributed tremendous pleasure to millions and millions of people," while incoming governor Ronald Reagan, a Republican, confessed "a very deep sense of personal grief, and I think the world is poorer for his having gone. He's brought a great many bright dreams to all of us." *Variety* eulogized him as "a truly creative force," while the *Christian Science Monitor* insisted that "Walt Disney always looked at himself as an entertainer. But history may measure him as a social force." A few weeks later, former president Dwight D. Eisenhower spoke for many when he said,

> To many tens of millions, Walt Disney brought good cheer and happy hours with entertainment that lightened their hearts and refreshed their minds. To Americans of all ages and all walks of life, he was unique. Children loved his characters and his portrayal of them. Parents honored him and were obligated to him for his far-reaching aid in the sensible upbringing of families. Grandparents saluted him as a genius with films that were messages of fun and education and character building . . . His work will endure so long as men and women and children retain a sense of wonder, a need for bright laughter, a love of the clean and decent. Consequently, Walt Disney's name and his creations will endure through generations. In honoring him, we salute an American who belongs to all the world.[4]

Nonetheless, Walt Disney's reputation did not stand completely triumphant. Nearly everyone mourned his passing, but not everyone honored his influence. That important fact could be traced to an overarching but subtle aspect of the Disney legacy. The long trajectory of Disney Studio productions had altered significantly in mid-arc, a development that inspired some and disgusted others. In the early days, Walt and his artists had spiced their fantasy-laden productions with playful critiques of the social order. While thoroughly in the American grain, films such as *Three Little Pigs* and *Dumbo* and characters such as Pinocchio and the seven dwarfs had slyly criticized modern mass society by evoking images of populism, producerism, egalitarian individualism, and village virtue. Even Mickey Mouse, with his generous spirit and scamplike subversiveness, and Donald Duck, with his determination to do good and his legendary temper tantrums, had helped position early Disney films both inside and outside the mainstream culture, expressing fundamental American values while gently and humorously censuring attendant social injustices. This provocative political sensibility had been accompanied by an adventurous aesthetic impulse that explored new ground with its hybrid sentimental modernism.

After 1941, however, Disney's work shifted noticeably. In the aftermath of the studio strike and the struggles during World War II, and increasingly influenced by the growing pressures of the Cold War, Disney productions began to display a new cast. From *So Dear to My Heart* to Disneyland, *The Mickey Mouse Club* to *Pollyanna*, they evidenced a new instinct to identify and uphold American values rather than playfully to probe or lampoon them. Individual achievement, consumer prosperity, family togetherness, celebratory nationalism, and technological promise became the beacons of the new Disney corpus. An aesthetic retrenchment accompanied this move toward social and political consolidation. The confident, occasionally breathtaking artistic experimentalism of works such as *Pinocchio* and *Fantasia* settled into an enjoyable, predictable "Disney style" of animation in films such as *The Jungle Book* or gave way entirely in pleasant, undistinguished live-action films such as *The Shaggy Dog*. In other words, the internal juxtaposition of elements, once a source of vitality in Disney films, collapsed as populist dissent was folded into Cold War patriotism, satirical energy subsided in the face of corporate social engineering, and modernism retreated before the advance of sentimental realism. The spirit of Disney creativity now flowed into the creation of multidimensional leisure experiences at Disneyland, the World's Fair, and the Florida Project.

This shift, simultaneously ideological, aesthetic, social, and psychological, caused a rift in Walt Disney's audience. The embrace of convention further endeared him to the mass public, for whom social stability, patriotism, consumption, middle-class morality, and sentimental fantasy served as a compelling formula. The solid-citizen Disney of the 1950s secured an even larger place in the hearts of millions of ordinary Americans than had the more rambunctious Disney of the 1930s. At the same time, however, the postwar reorientation of Disney's oeuvre indelibly tainted his reputation among a growing oppositional culture. Intellectuals growing unhappy with stifling bourgeois standards, emerging leftist critics of America's Cold War politics, and racial minorities demanding inclusion and justice decried Disney as emblematic of everything wrong with the United States.

By the 1960s, these growing tensions had become palpable. They finally exploded in the uproar accompanying the appearance of Richard Schickel's *The Disney Version: The Life, Times, Art, and Commerce of Walt Disney* (1968). This book, written by a noted film critic and reviewer for *Time* and *Life* magazines, had been started at mid-decade. Schickel, who originally had access to the studio, its records, and its staff, was banished from the Burbank compound by Walt himself after the critical nature of his study began to emerge. According to one studio artist, the annoyed studio chief exclaimed, "I don't want that s.o.b. on my lot!" The author persevered, however, and his book's publication immediately galvanized defenders and denouncers of Disney and ignited a firestorm of controversy.[5]

Schickel presented a comprehensive, razor-sharp version of the leftist intellectual critique of Disney's creative decline. With sparkling prose and searching questions about cultural values, he insisted that Walt Disney represented modern American society gone sour. A close look at Disney's work revealed a disquieting "microcosm embodying a good deal of the spirit of our times . . . [and] what is most childish and therefore most dangerous in all of us who were his fellow Americans." This stinging attack focused on the midwestern, middle-class values of Disney and his audience, whom Schickel described as juvenile, addicted to cuteness, steeped in nostalgia, and given to political conservatism and a mindless "go-getter" sensibility. Like most ambitious American businessmen, Schickel contended, Disney was obsessed with creating order and building an organization, as the commerce in his makeup consistently shoved aside the art. For the author, the Audio-Animatronic Lincoln marked the nadir. In his scathing words, "Disney, caught in the grip of his technical mania and protected by his awesome innocence about aesthetic and philosophical matters, had brought forth a monster of wretched taste . . . Are we really supposed to revere this ridiculous contraption, this weird agglomeration of wires and plastic? . . . Here is the dehumanization of art in its final extremity."[6]

Schickel's condemnation emerged clearly from the widening cultural and ideological divisions of the 1960s. It was revealing, he noted, that while intellectuals had disdained Disney's work for the past quarter-century, that same period had seen the entertainer achieve his "greatest economic success, his greatest personal power." And now, when the middle class and its traditional values were coming under sustained attack, Disney had become, "in the minds of his public, something more than a purveyor of entertainment. He became a kind of rallying point for the subliterates of our society."

> His statements were often vulgar. They were often tasteless, and they often exalted the merely technological over the sensitively humane. They were often crassly commercial, sickeningly sentimental, crudely comic. They were easy ones to criticize, and, overall, they had little appeal to anyone of even rudimentary cultivation. But the flaws in the Disney version of the American vision were hardly unique to him. They are flaws that have crept into it over decades, and they are flaws almost universally shared by the masses of the nation's citizens.

Schickel judged Walt Disney to be no artist but a representative of "the industrial and entrepreneurial tradition," the only one that really counted in America. Of the Mickey Mouse empire, he concluded, "As capitalism, it is a work of genius; as culture, it is mostly a horror."[7]

Schickel's pull-no-punches analysis rallied many supporters, and intellectuals, academics, writers, and leftist critics of modern America gleefully joined in the bashing. An assessment in the *New York Times Book Review* praised the book for exposing Disney as "a hustler from Kansas City" and accurately capturing him "in all his two dimensions." Other reviewers reveled in the book's depiction of Disney's "philistinism" and snidely suggested that "it might be best to think of him as the head of the nation's largest pharmaceutical firm — until his death, America's foremost dispenser of placebos." But more significantly, many commentators went on to denounce the mass audience who loved Disney's work. They lauded *The Disney Version* for courageously bringing to light "some ugly things about our so-called popular culture" and assured readers that the entertainer had attracted a vast audience because "his juvenile nature was theirs." Peter Michelson, in an eloquent essay in the *New Republic*, joined Schickel in denouncing Disney as the leader of "the international happiness conspiracy" and a man who "made images for the mind on vacation." But, he warned, one also had to recognize that the entertainer's faults were "fundamentally American." Disney was "largely what his culture made him; he did what it wanted him to do. And it paid top dollar, so there was a fair bargain. But he was diminished by such trafficking, and so, I fear, was the culture that bade him do it."[8]

Others, however, were outraged by this assault on an American icon. As one Disney defender noted, reading the book was "a bit like seeing a drawing of Whistler's mother with a mustache." More to the point, others complained that Schickel's adversarial approach had produced a "bitter and basically unfair portrait of a man." John Allen, writing in the *Christian Science Monitor*, granted that while the book probed the artistic and ideological qualities of Disney's work, ultimately it made the entertainer a "scapegoat" for a larger "diatribe against middle-class values." Angrier reactions also appeared. *Film Fan Monthly* featured a cover sketch of Mickey Mouse collapsed against a book entitled *The Schickel Version*, with a stake driven through his heart. Inside appeared heated denunciations of "the evil volume" as "a study in propaganda." According to one essayist, the book's innuendoes and distortions created "the purest example of McCarthyism since the late Senator's demise. Coupled with the character assassination of Walt Disney is a political diatribe revealing a viciousness I had always attributed to the opposite end of the political spectrum."[9]

The Disney Version was published when the Tet Offensive, waves of student demonstrations, the assassinations of Martin Luther King, Jr., and Robert Kennedy, and the melee at the Democratic National Convention were bringing controversy over Vietnam and civil rights to a boiling point, and it reflected the increasingly bitter divisions of that era. In fact, it became something of a litmus test for choosing sides in the late 1960s. A growing oppositional culture of leftist intellectuals and students held up Disney's work as illustrative of the barriers that impeded the wholesale reform of American values — unquestioning patriotism, bourgeois moral nostrums, gauche middle-class taste, racist exclusion, corporate profitmongering, bland standards of social conformity. A silent majority of more conservative citizens, however, closed ranks around the Disney legacy as part of a defense of traditional American opportunity, entrepreneurialism, patriotism, middle-class decency, and moral uplift.

The imbroglio over *The Disney Version* and the fallout from it have continued to cloud a clear view of Disney and the impact of his work. The intense divisions of the late 1960s have persisted, in more muted form, in the "culture wars" besetting the United States for the last quarter-century. Both admirers and detractors of Walt Disney continue to simplify a complicated man and flatten his creations. It is still possible, however, to step carefully through this emotional and ideological minefield and arrive at a more complex, nuanced view of Disney's legacy.[10]

To begin with, Walt Disney, as all sides agree, appealed to and reflected the values of a mass audience of middle-class Americans. But neither a patronizing, elitist view of this audience as a collection of "subliterate," "inhuman," "uncultivated" dupes nor an equally deluded view of common people as the ultimate standard of all creative worth provides much insight into the American culture that gave rise to this popular figure. Instead, it is more useful to note that from Mickey Mouse to the True-Life Adventures, *Fantasia* to Davy Crockett, *Snow White and the Seven Dwarfs* to Disneyland, *Three Little Pigs* to *Mary Poppins,* Disney demonstrated a remarkable capacity to grasp the essence of American attitudes about work, family, social life, and success and yet to interpret them in light of evolving historical circumstances. Largely unintentionally, he achieved this by melding emerging values and institutions, which were attractive yet frightening, with soothing, residual images and commitments from an earlier age. From the trauma of the Great Depression to the dislocations of World War II, from the anxious confrontations of the Cold War to the confident social engineering of the 1960s, Disney helped ordinary Americans define themselves.

Moreover, a scan of the Disney landscape reveals a patchwork of alluring and repugnant features. At their best, as the studio's productions took shape over four decades, they combined whimsical fantasy, aesthetic daring, and a vibrant mixing of high and low cultural forms. They featured a genuine respect for ordinary people, a willingness to prick the pretensions and injustices of the powerful, and a sensibility of kindness and optimism. Bursts of satire were moderated by gentle humor. Perhaps above all, stretching from *Steamboat Willie* to EPCOT, Walt's insistence on always moving into new creative territory made Disney's work consistently interesting and often challenging. At their worst, however, Disney creations degenerated into a cultural ritual of mindless consumerism, corporate shilling, saccharine sentimentalism, and embarrassing naiveté. Moreover, an obsession with control and social conformity veered too closely toward authoritarianism, while a determinedly Panglossian posture indulged a form of anti-intellectualism in the Disney worldview.

These same conflicts and contradictions, of course, characterize modern America itself. Walt Disney did nothing if not embody the tenor of his times. In a stream of memorable work over several generations, he shaped into a synthetic, compelling form the diverse bundle of images, values, and sensibilities that many twentieth-century Americans struggled with — individualism and community, fantasy and technology, populism and corporate authority, modernism and sentimentalism, consumerism and producerism, progress and nostalgia. Similarly, he somehow melded together a series of conflicting images — populist Walt and corporate Walt, Walt the artist and Walt the entrepreneur, producer Walt and consumer Walt — into a compelling personal image of American success.

This legendary entertainer may have spoken for his society most clearly when he expressed an overweening confidence that the world, and life itself, can be shaped as we wish it to be. Disney's enormous creative energy, having exhausted its potential in films, cut a bold, new, late-career channel that sought to actualize the fantastic reality depicted in earlier cinematic productions. His magic kingdom, in typical "American Century" style, expressed a mythical, idealized version of the values and aspirations of the modern United States. As a close associate once put it, Disney unfolded for his audience "a dream of the way the world ought to be." This impulse both touches and chills. When expressed as imaginative statements, in films or the three-dimensional experiences of particular Disneyland attractions, images of an idealized reality leave room for reception, contemplation, and decision-making by the viewer or the visitor. With the rigidly controlled aspects of the amusement parks and the EPCOT experiment, however, the Disney vision is subtly imposed on the subject. Here the genuine utopianism of the magic kingdom, much like that of the United States, too easily becomes a kind of paternalism and manipulation.[11]

In the middle of *Snow White and the Seven Dwarfs*, Dopey, whose inability to talk only enhances his expressive powers, picks up a large diamond from the underground mine and stares into it. He reacts with childlike wonder as his face, reflected on the jewel's brilliant planes, fragments into a dozen facets. This image suggests the difficulty of coming to terms with Walt Disney: when you hold him up for observation, many things appear, depending on the angle of sight. But regardless of where you stand, ultimately this legendary figure must be seen as a major architect of modern American culture. As the United States ascended to great power and prominence in the middle decades of the twentieth century, a sparsely educated but highly imaginative midwesterner emerged as perhaps the preeminent interpreter of its fantasy life. The result — an idealized version of America rendered in Walt Disney's magic kingdom — may be deemed simply silly or contemptible, as some have done, or enchanting and reassuring, as many more have decided. Like most dreams, however, it is probably best described as simultaneously delightful and distressing, evocative and unsettling.

Notes

Most of the following notes refer to documents held at the Disney Archives, located at the Walt Disney Studio in Burbank, California, where the bulk of the research for this book was conducted. This facility is an enormous repository of materials on the history of Walt Disney and his enterprise. The dozens of Disney films analyzed in the text are on file there, as are thousands of letters, story meeting notes, publicity packets, studio handbooks, staff memos, artworks, and so on. Unless otherwise noted, all cited material other than books can be found in the archives (DA).

Three sources require special explanation. First, the archives hold hundreds of interviews with Disney staffers, the great majority of which have been transcribed. The page numbers in the notes refer to the transcriptions; second and subsequent references give the names of the participants and the page numbers only. References with only the interviewee's name were conducted by the author.

Second, dozens of publicity scrapbooks for Disney films released since the early 1930s can also be found in the archives. These contain hundreds of newspaper and magazine clippings: reviews, publicity releases, stories about characters and artists, and other relevant material. In the notes, each scrapbook is denoted by the letters PS accompanied by a letter and a number.

Finally, many citations refer to a series of interviews of Walt Disney (WD) conducted in 1956 by journalist Peter Martin and Diane Disney Miller. Recorded on twelve reels of tape, they are on file at the archives, as are transcriptions organized by reel number. These are cited as "Martin/Miller interview" followed by reel number and page number.

My analysis has been bolstered by an enormous scholarly literature on such topics as mass culture, populism, modernism, and the Cold War. In the interests of brevity, the notes indicate only the most salient secondary sources I have consulted. The reader will have to trust me on the rest.

1. Disney and the Rural Romance

1. WD, "Speech at Marceline, Missouri, 1956," DA. See *Marceline, Missouri, the Magic City: Diamond Jubilee, 1888–1963* (Marceline, Mo.: 1963), 14–15, for a brief account of Disney's visit.

2. *Marceline, the Magic City.*

3. Bob Thomas, *Walt Disney: An American Original* (New York, 1976), 32.

4. Lillian Disney, interview by Bob Thomas, Apr. 19, 1973, 1; T. Hee, interview by Richard Hubler, July 2, 1968, 18–19.

5. Jack Kinney, *Walt Disney and Other Assorted Characters: An Unauthorized Account of the Early Years at Disney* (New York, 1988), 158; WD, Marceline speech.

6. David Swift, quoted in Leonard Mosely, *Disney's World* (Chelsea, Mich., 1990), 260; Winston Hibler, interview by Bob Thomas, May 22, 1973, 27; WD, quoted in Leonard Maltin, *The Disney Films* (New York, 1984), 89.

7. The relevant literature on this watershed era is enormous. Among the many insightful treatments of American cultural history during this period, see John F. Kasson, *Amusing the Millions: Coney Island at the Turn of the Century* (New York, 1978), 17–28; James Gilbert, *Perfect Cities: Chicago's Utopias of 1893* (Chicago, 1991); Alan Trachtenberg, *The Incorporation of America: Culture and Society in the Gilded Age* (New York, 1982); T. J. Jackson Lears, *No Place of Grace: Antimodernism and the Transformation of American Culture, 1880–1920* (New York, 1981); Simon J. Bronner, ed., *Consuming Visions: Accumulation and Display of Goods in America, 1880–1920* (New York, 1989).

8. Kinney, *Walt Disney and Other Characters,* 149; Ward Kimball, interview by Richard Hubler, June 4, 1968, 40–41; Ward Kimball, "The Wonderful World of Walt Disney," in Walter Wanger, ed., *You Must Remember This* (New York, 1975), 274.

9. See Diane Disney Miller, *The Story of Walt Disney* (New York, 1956), and Thomas, *Walt Disney,* for accurate biographical details on Walt's youth.

10. Ruth Disney Beecher interview, Nov. 4, 1974, 28; Walt Pfeiffer, interview by Bob Thomas, Apr. 26, 1973, 6; Roy Disney, interview by Richard Hubler, Nov. 17, 1967, 16–18.

11. WD, "I'll Always Remember a Country Doctor," *Parade,* Sept. 23, 1956, 2; Ruth Disney Beecher interview, 36, 4–5, 10; Walt Pfeiffer interview, 8; Roy Disney, Hubler interview, Nov. 17, 1967; Martin/Miller interview.

12. Ruth Disney Beecher interview, 16.

13. Martin/Miller interview, Reel 11, 22–23, Reel 3, 48, Reel 11, 52.

14. Diane Disney Miller, interview by Richard Hubler, June 11, 1968, 3–5.

15. Martin/Miller interview, Reel 3, 55–56; Kimball, Hubler interview, 24; Kimball, "Wonderful World," 274.

16. Martin/Miller interview, Reel 5, 34–35.

17. Walt Pfeiffer interview, 11, 21; Diane Disney Miller interview, 6; Ruth Disney, quoted by Diane Disney Miller, Aug. 18, 1993.

18. Martin/Miller interview, Reel 11, 14–15; WD to Miss Daisy Beck, Sept. 27, 1940; Ruth Disney Beecher interview, 3.

19. Martin/Miller interview, Reel 3, 65–66, 67–68.

20. Ibid., Reel 4, 11, Reel 5, 31; Walt Pfeiffer interview, 9.

21. Diane Disney Miller, Hubler interview, 7.

22. Don Taylor, interview by David R. Smith, Aug. 6, 1971, 3; WD to "Cousin Lena," Aug. 6, 1931; WD, Marceline speech; Martin/Miller interview, Reel 3, 20, 24, 29–31, 34–35; Roy Disney, Hubler interview, 11.

23. Audiotape of golden anniversary celebration.

24. Roy Disney, Hubler interview, 2. See Thomas, *Walt Disney*, and the Martin/Miller interview for the facts of Elias Disney's life.

25. Taylor, Smith interview, 3–4; Lillian Disney, Thomas interview, 1; WD, quoted in Lawrence E. Watkin, "Walt Disney," unpublished ms., 384–85.

26. Martin/Miller interview, Reel 3, 45–46.

27. Ibid., Reel 3, 21–22; Pfeiffer, Thomas interview, 2.

28. Taylor, Smith interview, 2; Watkin, "Disney," 384–85.

29. Martin/Miller interview, Reel 5, 41; Thomas interview, 2; Alice Disney Allen, interview by David R. Smith, Oct. 5, 1972, notes.

30. Ruth Disney Beecher interview, 12; Watkin, "Disney," 384; Martin/Miller interview, Reel 11, 9–10.

31. Martin/Miller interview, Reel 11, 22; Kimball, Hubler interview, 5; Diane Disney Miller, Hubler interview, 5.

32. Martin/Miller interview, Reel 3, 61–62, 57.

33. Ibid., Reel 3, 43, 59–60, Reel 11, 14.

34. Ibid., Reel 3, 46–47, Reel 11, 18.

35. Dudley L. McLure, "The Real Lowdown on Mickey Mouse," *New Movie Magazine*, Feb. 1932, 11; WD, quoted in Watkin, "Disney," 388.

36. Martin/Miller interview, Reel 11, 15; William Cottrell, interview with the author, Aug. 19, 1993.

37. "Walt Disney Issue," *Wisdom* 32 (1959), 72.

38. Richard Schickel, *The Disney Version* (New York, 1968), 323.

39. Ibid.

2. Young Man Disney and Mickey Mouse

1. These photographs, as well as many others, can be found at the Disney Archives.

2. The information in this section comes from the Martin/Miller interview; Thomas, *Walt Disney*; Christopher Finch, *The Art of Walt Disney: From Mickey Mouse to the Magic Kingdom* (New York, 1973); Russell Merritt and J. B. Kaufman, *Walt in Wonderland: The Silent Films of Walt Disney* (Rome, 1992).

3. WD to Margaret Winkler, quoted in Thomas, *Walt Disney*, 71.

4. David R. Smith, "Disney Before Burbank: The Kingswell and Hyperion Studios," *Funnyworld* (Summer 1974), 32–38.

5. David R. Smith, interview by the author, Aug. 14, 1992.

6. See Lary May, *Screening Out the Past: The Birth of Mass Culture and the Motion Picture Industry* (Chicago, 1983), 167–99, which offers a brilliant analysis of Hollywood as the new frontier.

7. On the studio system in this period, see Tino Balio, ed., *The American Film Industry* (Madison, Wis., 1976), 103–252, and David Bordwell et al., *The Classical Hollywood Cinema: Film Style and Mode of Production to 1960* (New York, 1985), 85–154.

8. Among many works on the emergence of mass culture in early twentieth-cen-

tury America, see May, *Screening Out the Past;* John Kasson, *Amusing the Million: Coney Island at the Turn of the Century* (New York, 1978); Lewis A. Erenberg, *Steppin' Out: New York Nightlife and the Transformation of American Culture, 1890–1930* (Chicago, 1981); T. J. Jackson Lears, "From Salvation to Self-Realization: Advertising and the Therapeutic Roots of the Consumer Culture, 1880–1930," in Jackson Lears and Richard Fox, eds., *The Culture of Consumption: Critical Essays in American History, 1880–1980* (New York, 1983).

9. Merritt and Kaufman, *Walt in Wonderland,* 86; "Mickey the Mouse and Ziegfeld," *The Film Spectator,* Oct. 11, 1931; Harry Carr, "The Only Unpaid Movie Star," *American Magazine* (1931), 55–56; James William Fitzpatrick, "Catering to the American Amusement Diet," New York *Motion Picture Herald,* Mar. 4, 1931.

10. Carr, "Unpaid Movie Star," 123.

11. Martin/Miller interview, Reel 11, 3–4.

12. Atlantic City, N.J., *Press,* Jan. 21, 1931, PS M14.

13. WD, "The Cartoon's Contribution to Children," *Overland Monthly,* Oct. 1933, 138.

14. "Mickey Mouse Steps into Print," *Publishers Weekly,* Mar. 28, 1931, PS M14.

15. *Life,* Mar. 20, 1931; "The Nation's Honor Roll for 1930," *Nation,* Jan. 7, 1931, PS M14.

16. May, *Screening Out the Past,* 165–66, 190–97, 232–36. See also Charles J. Maland, *Chaplin and American Culture: The Evolution of a Star Image* (Princeton, 1989).

17. Henry Pringle, "Mickey Mouse's Father," *McCall's,* Aug. 1932, 28; unspecified 1931 newspaper clippings, PS M14 and PS M17.

18. Mike Barrier, "An Interview with Carl Stalling," *Funnyworld* 13 (Spring 1971), 22.

19. Martin/Miller interview, Reel 2, 32–33; Eric Larson, interview with Christopher Finch and Linda Rosenkrantz, July 25, 1972, 3.

20. Gilbert Seldes, "Mickey Mouse Maker," *New Yorker,* Dec. 1931, 26–27; Richard Watts, Jr., "Thoughts on Cinema Optimism," New York *Herald Tribune,* Oct. 26, 1930. A host of similar articles can be found in PS M17.

21. 1930 Columbia Pictures press sheet, PS M17.

22. J. B. Kaufman, "The Shadow of the Mouse," *Film Comment,* Sept.–Oct. 1992, 71; WD, "Give Me the Movies," Norfolk, Va., *Pilot-Landmark,* Sept. 2, 1938, PS M39; Martin/Miller interview, Reel 10, 52.

23. Harold W. Cohen, "An Appreciation of the Disney Works," Pittsburgh *Post Gazette,* Nov. 15, 1930, PS M17.

24. 1930 Columbia Pictures press sheets, PS M17; Seldes, "Mickey Mouse Maker," 25.

3. The Entertainer as Success Icon

1. Newman Laugh-O-Grams, 1920 sample reel, DA.

2. On success ideology, see John G. Cawelti, *Apostles of the Self-Made Man* (Chicago, 1965); Donald Meyer, *The Positive Thinkers: A Study of the American Quest for Health, Wealth, and Power from Mary Baker Eddy to Norman Vincent Peale* (New York, 1965); Carol V. R. George, *God's Salesman: Norman Vincent Peale and the Power of Positive Thinking* (New York, 1993).

3. Edna Disney, interview by Richard Hubler, Aug. 20, 1968, 10; Carmen Maxwell,

quoted in Burbank, Calif., *Daily Review,* May 25, 1972; Friz Freleng, "I'll Never Get Home: An Oral History of Friz Freleng," interview by Joseph Adamson, July 28, 1968, and June 26, 1969, 10.

4. Roy E. Disney, interview by the author, Dec. 27, 1993. Disney noted his father's annoyance at the name change, but David Smith, Disney archivist, said that Roy O. Disney once told him that it was *his* decision to change the studio name because of Walt's dominant creative role.

5. Alice L. Tildesley, "A Silly Symphony Becomes America's Slogan," Nov. 4, 1933, PS M8; Martin/Miller interview, Reel 2, 41–42.

6. Martin/Miller interview, Reel 11, 3, Reel 5, 47, Reel 2, 36; Friz Freleng, quoted in Donald Crafton, *Before Mickey: The Animated Film, 1898–1928* (Cambridge, Mass., 1984), 208, 363. See also Merritt and Kaufman, *Walt in Wonderland,* 66.

7. Martin/Miller interview, Reel 2, 27–28; Ben Sharpsteen, interviews by Don Peri, Apr. 24, 1974, 2–3, and Feb. 6, 1974, 3.

8. Merritt and Kaufman, *Walt in Wonderland,* 62, 108, 112–14; Carmen Maxwell, Rudolf Ising, and Walt Pfeiffer, quoted in the Burbank, Calif., *Daily Review,* May 25, 1972; Bob Thomas, "Laugh-O-Grams Film Co.," 1972 ms., file box, DA.

9. Will Friedwald, "Hugh Harman, 1903–1982," *Graffiti* (Spring 1984), 3; Freleng, "I'll Never Get Home," 46. According to Merritt and Kaufman, *Walt in Wonderland,* 134, 120, "Ham" Hamilton also left in 1926 because he "couldn't stand being abused by Disney."

10. Freleng, "I'll Never Get Home," 5–6, 25; "Friz Freleng," in Jeff Lenburg, *The Great Cartoon Directors* (New York, 1993), 3–4; Jami Bernard, "Looney Tunes and Friz Freleng," *Comics Scene* 7 (1989), 18–19, Freleng clippings file, American Film Institute, Los Angeles.

11. See Freleng's comments in Lenburg, *Cartoon Directors,* 4, and in Mike Barrier, "The Careers of Hugh Harman and Rudolf Ising," *Millimeter,* Feb. 1976, 46–47.

12. Martin/Miller interview, Reel 11, 5–6.

13. Edna Disney, Hubler interview, 22–23; Roy Disney, Hubler interview, 24; Merritt and Kaufman, *Walt in Wonderland,* 58; Barrier, "Carl Stalling," 23.

14. Adolph Kloepper, quoted in David R. Smith, "Up to Date in Kansas City," *Funnyworld* (Fall 1978), 33; Roy Disney, Hubler interview, 28; Martin/Miller interview, Reel 6, 9–11, 22–23.

15. Lillian Disney, Thomas interview, 4; WD, "Mickey Mouse: How He Was Born," *Windsor* (1931), 642; Martin/Miller interview, Reel 5, 41–74, Reel 6, 1–8, 17–19, Reel 11, 76–77.

16. Hamilton, "Life Story of Mickey Mouse," 100–101, 127; Carr, "Only Unpaid Movie Star," 56–57; Douglas Churchill, "Now Mickey Mouse Enters Art's Temple," *New York Times Magazine,* June 3, 1934, 1; "The Big Bad Wolf," *Fortune,* Nov. 1934, 146.

17. Shamus Culhane, *Talking Animals and Other People* (New York, 1986), 36; John Canemaker, "Grim Natwick," *Film Comment,* Jan.–Feb. 1975, 59; Les Clark, interview by John Canemaker, July 1973, 4.

18. Richard Hubler, "Walt Disney," unpublished ms., 99–100, 106; Watkin, "Walt Disney," 110; Rudolf Ising, quoted in Merritt and Kaufman, *Walt in Wonderland,* 64. See also David R. Smith, "Ub Iwerks, 1901–1971," *Funnyworld* (Spring 1972),

33–37, 47; Peter Adamakos, "Ub Iwerks," *Mindrot*, June 15, 1977, 20–24; Jeff Lenburg, "Ub Iwerks," *Blackhawk Film Digest*, Mar.–Apr. 1979, 76–78; Lenburg, "Ub Iwerks," in *Great Cartoon Directors*, 25–41.

19. Watkin, "Disney," 261–62; Martin/Miller interview, Reel 11, 54; David Iwerks, interview by the author, Aug. 20, 1993. Leonard Mosely writes in *Disney's World* that Disney constantly tormented Iwerks during their stay in Kansas City and that Iwerks deeply resented it. I have uncovered no evidence to support this, although David Iwerks told me that "the chances are pretty good" that the dating story is correct.

20. WD to Ubbe Iwerks, June 1, 1924. See also WD to Dr. Thomas McCrum, Aug. 4, 1924.

21. Ub Iwerks, interview by George Sherman, July 30, 1970; Ub Iwerks, 1956 interview notes.

22. Friz Freleng, "I'll Never Get Home," 24, 50; Merritt and Kaufman, *Walt in Wonderland*, 108–10, 120–22.

23. Smith, "Ub Iwerks," 34.

24. Thomas, *Walt Disney*, 85.

25. Ibid., 88; David Smith interview; Diane Disney Miller, conversation with the author, Aug. 18, 1993.

26. Ub Iwerks, 1956 interview notes; Ub Iwerks interview, July 30, 1970; Donald Iwerks, interview by the author, Aug. 17, 1993; David Iwerks interview.

27. Ub Iwerks, 1956 interview notes; Smith, "Ub Iwerks," 35–36; WD to Lillian Disney, Feb. 1929, DA; Ben Sharpsteen, Peri interview, Feb. 6, 1974, 33. Thanks to David Smith for pointing out the Disney-Iwerks screen credits on the early Mickey Mouse shorts.

28. Ub Iwerks interview, July 30, 1970, 2–3; David Iwerks interview; Les Clark and Jack Cutting, quoted in Frank Thomas and Ollie Johnston, *Disney Animation: The Illusion of Life* (New York, 1981), 538.

29. Martin/Miller interview, Reel 2, 37–38; Iwerks, 1956 interview notes, 1, 3; Thomas, *Walt Disney*, 100–103.

30. Iwerks, 1956 interview notes, 1, 3.

31. Watkin, "Disney," 262–64; Hubler, "Walt Disney," 177; David Iwerks interview.

32. Martin/Miller interview, Reel 5, 54.

33. Watkin, "Disney," 269; David Iwerks interview; Ub Iwerks interview, 3.

34. WD to Ub Iwerks and Roy Disney, Oct. 6, 1928, 1, 3, 4; Dave Hand, quoted in Thomas and Johnston, Disney Animation, 538.

35. Martin/Miller interview, Reel 2, 37; WD telegram to Roy Disney, Feb. 9, 1930; WD telegram to Roy Disney, Jan. 21, 1930; Ben Sharpsteen, interview by David Smith and Larry Watkins, May 19, 1971, 3; Ben Sharpsteen, Peri interview, Feb. 6, 1974, 34; Roy Disney to WD, Jan. 25, 1930, 3–4.

36. Lenburg, *Great Cartoon Directors*, 31–40.

37. Culhane, *Talking Animals*, 71–72, 79–80; Grim Natwick, interview by David Smith, Oct. 28, 1971, 1; Ben Sharpsteen, Peri interview, Feb. 6, 1974, 34–35.

38. David R. Smith, "The Kingswell and Hyperion Studios," 34, 36; Culhane, *Talking Animals*, 76–77; David Iwerks interview.

39. Ben Sharpsteen, Peri interview, Feb. 6, 1974, 35–36.

40. Smith, "Ub Iwerks," 37, 47; Thomas and Johnston, *Disney Animation*, 538; Donald Iwerks interview; David Iwerks interview.

41. Watkin, "Disney," 269, 267, 264–65; Ub Iwerks, 1956 interview notes, 4; David Iwerks interview.

42. Watkin, "Disney," 261–62; Dave Hand, in Thomas and Johnston, *Disney Animation,* 538.

43. Kinney, *Walt Disney and Other Characters,* 149; Hubler, "Walt Disney," 99; Martin/Miller interview, Reel 11, 54.

44. Dale Carnegie, "Walt Disney Made a Fortune Out of a Mouse and Three Little Pigs," 1938, and "Talent for Showmanship," 1938, PS M39; Dale Carnegie, "Little Known Facts About Well-Known People — Walt Disney," *Caravan* 3 (1937), 19; Norman Vincent Peale, "The American Dream Still Bursts Forth," Spokane, Wash., *Spokesman Review Sunday Magazine,* July 2, 1972.

45. WD, "There's Always a Solution," *Guideposts,* June 1949, 1–2, 23–24; "Walt Disney Issue," *Wisdom* 32 (1959), 46.

46. WD, "Walt Disney Issue," 80, 79.

47. Ibid., 78, 79.

48. Ibid., 76, 80, 76, 77, 78. See also "Walt Disney," *The Magazine of Success,* May–June 1964, 2–7; Larry Wolters, "The Wonderful World of Walt Disney," *Today's Health,* April 1962, 26–31.

4. Disney and the Depression: Sentimental Populism

1. Roy E. Disney interview; Marc Davis, interview by Bob Thomas, May 25, 1973, 1–2; Ken Anderson, interview by Bob Thomas, May 15, 1973, 7.

2. On Disney finances in this period, see Schickel, *The Disney Version,* 150–51, 214.

3. WD, "The Cartoon's Contribution to Children," 138.

4. "Mouse and Man," *Time,* Dec. 27, 1937, 21.

5. Richard Hofstadter, *The Age of Reform: From Bryan to F.D.R.* (New York, 1959), 4–5, 11–12. On populism, see also Christopher Lasch, *The True and Only Heaven: Progress and Its Critics* (New York, 1991), 223, 531, and James Turner, "Understanding the Populists," *Journal of American History* 67 (1980), 354–73.

6. Christopher Lasch, "Foreword," in Richard Hofstadter, *The American Political Tradition* (New York, 1973), vii–xxiv. On 1930s populism, see also Warren Susman, *Culture as History: The Transformation of American Society in the Twentieth Century* (New York, 1984), 150–83, 184–210; Alan Brinkley, *Voices of Protest: Huey Long, Father Coughlin, and the Great Depression* (New York, 1982); Erika Doss, *Benton, Pollock, and the Politics of Modernism: From Regionalism to Abstract Expressionism* (Chicago, 1991).

7. Martin/Miller interview, Reel 11, 9–10, Reel 12, 26, 28.

8. Ben Sharpsteen, interview by Richard Hubler, Oct. 29, 1968; WD to Roy Disney, Sept. 25, 1928; WD to Lillian Disney, Oct. 20, 1928.

9. Kimball, Hubler interview; Ollie Johnston, interview by Bob Thomas, 1973; Shelley Ford, "He Wanted a Little Fellow," *Hollywood Quarterly,* June 1930; Alice T. Tildesley, "A Silly Symphony Becomes America's Slogan," Lincoln, Neb., *Star-Journal,* Dec. 24, 1933. On Walt and FDR, see Martin/Miller interview, Reel 12, 28–29.

10. Richard L. Tobin, "Mickey Mouse as Heroic Slapstick," New York *Herald Tribune,* Aug. 25, 1935; Terry Ramsaye, "Mickey Mouse: He Stays on the Job," *Motion*

Picture Herald, Oct. 1, 1932; L. H. Robbins, "Mickey Mouse Emerges as Economist," *New York Times Magazine,* Mar. 10, 1935, 8.

11. Robert D. Feild, *The Art of Walt Disney* (New York, 1942), 282–83; Gilbert Seldes, *The Movies Come from America* (New York, 1937), 47. See similar commentary in Gilbert Seldes, "Disney and Others," *New Republic,* June 8, 1932, 171; "Who's Afraid of the Big, Bad Wolf," *Scholastic: The National High School Weekly,* Oct. 28, 1933.

12. Richard L. Plant, "Of Disney," *Decision,* July 1941, 84; Edward G. Smith, "St. Francis of the Silver Screen," *Progress Today,* Jan.–Mar. 1935, 43.

13. "Mickey Mouse, the Children's Friend," Evanston, Ill., *Union Signal,* Mar. 9, 1935; "Who's Afraid," Albany *News,* Oct. 24, 1933; Jay Leyda, ed., *Eisenstein on Disney* (Calcutta, 1986), 7–8; Jay Franklin, "Hope for the World in 'Snow White,'" Des Moines *Register,* Feb. 22, 1938.

14. B.K.H., "The Sideshow," Providence *Journal,* Oct. 30, 1933; "Who's Afraid of the Big, Bad Wolf," *Scholastic;* Gleason Pease, "Rambling On," Anoka County, Minn., *Union,* Oct. 18, 1933.

15. New York *Motion Picture Herald,* Nov. 4, 1933; WD, "Three Little Pigs," *Christian Science Monitor,* Jan. 1934, 6; Dallas *Times-Herald,* Nov. 1, 1933; Peoria, Ill., *American Hampshire Herdsman,* Feb. 3, 1934.

16. On the making of this film, see J. B. Kaufman, "Three Little Pigs — Big Little Picture," *American Cinematographer,* Nov. 1988, 38–44.

17. Don O'Malley, "New York Inside Out," Auburn, N.Y., *Citizen-Advertiser,* Oct. 9, 1933; Frank Sullivan, "Who's Afraid of Walt Disney?" *New Yorker,* Oct. 28, 1933, 15–16.

18. Sidney Solsky, "Tintypes," Boston *Traveler,* Nov. 4, 1933; B.K.H., "The Sideshow"; "Three Little Pigs," Hollywood *Spectator,* Nov. 11, 1933. See also Warren Stokes, "From Me to You," *Box Office,* Oct. 19, 1933; "On the Screen," *Literary Digest,* Oct. 14, 1933, 29.

19. "We Huff and We Puff," Cedar Rapids, Ia., *Gazette,* Nov. 4, 1933; Florence Fisher Parry, "Who's Afraid," Pittsburgh *Press,* Oct. 16, 1933; Richard Watts, Jr., "Sight and Sound: What Disney Did," Philadelphia *Record,* Oct. 15, 1933.

20. Pease, "Ramblin' On"; Kaspar Monahan, "The Show Shops," Pittsburgh *Press,* Oct. 15, 1933.

21. Schickel, *Disney Version,* 154–55, believes that *Three Little Pigs* articulates Hoover's perspective, but Robert Sklar, *Movie-Made America: A Cultural History of the Movies* (New York, 1975), 204, sees in the film the "confident, purposeful spirit of the New Deal."

22. Leyda, *Eisenstein on Disney,* 4; "Who's Afraid," Albany, N.Y., *News,* Oct. 24, 1933. See also Robert G. Rau, "Letter to the Editor," *Literary Digest,* Nov. 4, 1933.

23. "The Power to Laugh," Houghton, Mich., *Mining Gazette,* Oct. 19, 1933; G. J. Badura, "Three Little Pigs," *California Parent Teacher,* Oct. 1934; "The Big Bad Wolf," High Point, N.C., *Enterprise,* Nov. 28, 1933.

24. "Letter to the Editor," Dayton, Ohio, *News,* Oct. 22, 1933; "United Artists Kills 'Big Bad Wolf' of Depression," *Canadian Moving Picture Digest,* Dec. 23, 1933. See also an academic analysis by Dean Ray Immel, in Mark Dowling, "Three Little Pigs Bring Home the Bacon," PS M8.

25. "Who's Afraid," Warren, Pa., *Times-Mirror,* Oct. 11, 1933; "Who's Afraid of the

Big Bad Wolf?" New York *Times,* Oct. 13, 1933, 7; "Who's Afraid of the B.B.W.?" New Haven *Journal-Courier,* Oct. 15, 1933.

26. Dowling, "Three Little Pigs Bring Home the Bacon"; "Mouse and Man," *Time,* Dec. 27, 1937, 21. Disney also denied any "social message" in his films in "Profit Nothing to Walt Disney," New York *Post,* Nov. 11, 1940.

27. WD, "Cartoon's Contribution to Children," 138; WD, "Three Little Pigs," 6.

5. Disney and the Depression: Populist Parables

1. Transcripts of *Snow White* story conferences, Oct. 2, 1936, 1, 3, 5, 6, and Oct. 28, 1936, 4, 5, 6, 10, 11.

2. Gilbert Kanour, "For Film Fans," Baltimore *Evening Sun,* Nov. 23, 1938; James Dugan, "Snow White and Seven Dwarfs New High for Entertainment," *Daily Worker,* Jan. 15, 1938; Robert Gregory Gifford, letter to the editor, Springfield, Mass., *Republican,* Jan. 18, 1938; Frank S. Nugent, "One Touch of Disney," New York *Times,* Jan. 23, 1938.

3. Transcripts of *Pinocchio* story conferences, Sept. 27, 1938, 3–4; July 7, 1938, 1; Dec. 8, 1938, 13; Sept. 13, 1938, 9.

4. "The New Pictures," *Time,* Feb. 26, 1940; "Disney Curbs Pinocchio's Reform School Tendencies," Houston *Chronicle,* June 4, 1939. See also "'Pinocchio' New Movie Milestone for Disney," Los Angeles *Times,* Jan. 30, 1940.

5. "'Pinocchio' Screen Triumph," Hollywood *Reporter,* Jan. 30, 1940. See also "It's a Disney," *New Republic,* Mar. 11, 1940, 11; "Preview: Pinocchio," *Variety,* Jan. 30, 1940; Harriet Parsons, "Disney's Bad Boy," *Woman's Day,* Feb. 1940, 6–7.

6. Bosley Crowther, "Yes, But Is It Art?" New York *Times,* Nov. 17, 1940; John Martin, "The Dance: Chorecinema," New York *Times,* Nov. 24, 1940.

7. John Culhane, *Walt Disney's Fantasia* (New York, 1983), 10; "Profit Nothing to Walt Disney," New York *Post,* Nov. 11, 1940; Ollie Johnston, interview by Howard Green, 1990, 21; *Fantasia* theater program. See also WD to Mrs. Walter Connolly, Nov. 29, 1940; Irene Thirer, "Deems Taylor, Movie M.C.," New York *Post,* Oct. 29, 1940; B. H. Haggin, "Music," *Nation,* Jan. 11, 1941, 54.

8. "Films on Ideals of Youth Proposed," New York *Times,* Nov. 17, 1940; Ed Sullivan, "The Reviewing Stand," New York *Citizen News,* Nov. 22, 1940.

9. Howard Barnes, "The Screen: Follow-Ups on Disney," New York *Herald Tribune,* Nov. 17, 1940; Herbert Cohn, "The Sound Track," Brooklyn *Eagle,* Nov. 17, 1940; Crowther, "Is It Art?"; William Boehnel, "Fantasia's Episode 9 — The Frantic Critics," New York *World Telegram,* Nov. 16, 1940; Richard Griffith, "Critics of 'Fantasia' at Loggerheads," Los Angeles *Times,* Nov. 26, 1940.

10. Griffith, "Critics at Loggerheads"; Cohn, "The Sound Track"; Pare Lorenz, *Lorenz on Film: Movies 1927 to 1940* (New York, 1975), 207–8. Barnes, "The Screen," described Disney as a "simple democratic artist."

11. Bosley Crowther, "The Screen in Review," New York *Times,* Oct. 24, 1941; Howard Barnes, "The Screen in Review," New York *Herald Tribune,* Oct. 24, 1941; Archer Winsten, "Movie Talk," New York *Post,* Oct. 24, 1941; Herbert Cohn, "'Dumbo,' Disney Charmer, Bows in at Broadway," Brooklyn *Eagle,* Oct. 24, 1941; "Movies," *Newsweek,* Oct. 22, 1941.

12. "Walt Disney's 'Dumbo,'" RKO campaign book, PS D14.

13. Evon Nollette, "A Gossip Column," Minneapolis *Evening Times*, Nov. 5, 1941; Cecelia Ager, "Disney's 'Dumbo' Is a Darling," *PM*, Oct. 24, 1941.

14. Frank Thomas, interview by Bob Thomas, May 17, 1973, 18–19.

15. This biographical sketch draws on John Canemaker, "Vladimir William Tytla (1904–1968): Animation's Michelangelo," *Cinefantastique* (Winter 1976), 9–19; John Canemaker, "Vladimir Tytla: Master Animator," exhibition catalogue, 1–33; I. Klein, "Golden Age Animator Vladimir (Bill) Tytla," *Cartoonist Profiles* 1, Aug. 1970, 6–14; Grim Natwick, "Animation," *Cartoonist Profiles* 40, Dec. 1978, 42–49; Thomas and Johnston, *Disney Animation*, 130–39; Dick Huemer, "Thumbnail Sketches," *Funnyworld* 21 (Fall 1979), 38–43.

16. Canemaker, "Michelangelo," 10–12; Klein, "Tytla," 6, 7, 12; Thomas and Johnston, *Disney Animation*, 134–35; Leonard Maltin, *Of Mice and Magic: A History of American Animated Cartoons* (New York, 1987), 13, 130–33.

17. Canemaker, "Michelangelo," 12.

18. Ibid.; Thomas and Johnston, *Disney Animation*, 239. Christopher Finch, *The Art of Walt Disney: From Mickey Mouse to the Magic Kingdom* (New York, 1973), 117, analyzes Tytla's early work at the Disney Studio.

19. The quote comes from a source who prefers to remain anonymous. See Canemaker, "Michelangelo," 14–16; Culhane, *Talking Animals*, 172–73; Klein, "Tytla," 8, 11.

20. Thomas, Thomas interview, 25–26; Culhane, *Talking Animals*, 172; Maltin, *Of Mice and Magic*, 45. See also Woolie Reitherman, interview by Christopher Finch and Linda Rosenkrantz, May 9, 1972, 6.

21. Canemaker, "Michelangelo," 12; Thomas, Thomas interview, 25–26; Natwick, "Animation," 42.

22. Thomas and Johnston, *Disney Animation*, 63, 131–33, 138, 358–59; Huemer, "Thumbnail Sketches," 42; Canemaker, "Michelangelo," 9.

23. Finch, *Art of Walt Disney*, 256; Thomas and Johnston, *Disney Animation*, 133, 499; Canemaker, "Michelangelo," 16, 14.

24. Natwick, "Animation," 42, 43, 49; Klein, "Tytla," 7, 8–9; Culhane, *Talking Animals*, 171–73, 177; Canemaker, "Michelangelo," 12, 16; Thomas and Johnston, *Disney Animation*, 13, 93, 130.

25. Finch, *Art of Walt Disney*, 210–14; Canemaker, "Michelangelo," 14; Culhane, *Talking Animals*, 221.

26. Culhane, *Fantasia*, 81, 104; David R. Smith, "'The Sorcerer's Apprentice,' Birthplace of *Fantasia*," *Millimeter*, Feb. 1976, 64–65.

27. Culhane, *Fantasia*, 182, 185–86; Thomas and Johnston, *Disney Animation*, 139, 133–34. See also Tytla, interview by George Sherman, May 13, 1968, 13, and Tytla, quoted in Culhane, *Fantasia*, 194.

28. Bill Tytla, "Action Analysis Class on Snow White 'Dwarfs'," Dec. 10, 1936, 1, 4–5, 7. See also Bill Tytla, "Class on Action Analysis," June 8, 1937, in Thomas and Johnston, *Disney Animation*, 548–49.

29. Tytla, "1936 Action Analysis Class," 4, 6, 1–2; Tytla, "1937 Action Analysis Class," 548, 549.

30. Canemaker, "Michelangelo," 14–15; Culhane, *Talking Animals*, 174–75.

31. Tytla, Sherman interview, 12–13, 14; Canemaker, "Michelangelo," 16.

32. Tytla, Sherman interview, 14; Culhane, *Talking Animals*, 225; Klaus Strzyz, "Art Babbitt," *Comics Journal*, March 1988, 83.

33. Canemaker, "Michelangelo," 16.

34. Ibid., 16–18; Culhane, *Talking Animals*, 238; Klein, "Tytla," 10–11; Ward Kimball, interview by Klaus Strzyz, *Comics Journal*, Mar. 1988, 95.

35. Paul Hollister, "Walt Disney: Genius at Work," *Atlantic Monthly*, Dec. 1940, 701. John Culhane, *Fantasia*, 20, identifies the speaker as Tytla.

36. Culhane, *Talking Animals*, 171.

37. Westbrook Pegler, "Fair Enough," Washington *Post*, Dec. 5, 1941.

38. Culhane, *Talking Animals*, 184; Barnet G. Braver-Mann, "Mickey Mouse and his Playmates," *Theater Guild Magazine*, Mar. 1931, 14; Harry Alan Potamkin, "Film Cults," *Modern Thinker and Author's Review*, Nov. 1932, 547, 549, 550; Herbert Russell, "L'Affaire Mickey Mouse," *New York Times Magazine*, Dec. 26, 1937, 4–5.

6. The Entertainer as Artist: Sentimental Modernism

1. Feild, *Art of Walt Disney*, 53, 56, 62.

2. *Time*, Aug. 17, 1942, 49–50; Boston *Evening Globe*, Feb. 7, 1939; *Christian Science Monitor*, Feb. 10, 1939. Reviews of Feild's book can be found in *Saturday Review of Literature*, June 6, 1942, 5; *Time*, June 8, 1942, 58–60.

3. David Low, "Leonardo da Disney," *New Republic*, Jan. 5, 1942, 18; "Walt Disney and Hogarth," *Art Digest*, Oct. 1, 1934, 8; Dorothy Grafly, "America's Youngest Art," *American Magazine of Art*, July 1933, 337.

4. Muriel Babcock, "Soft Soap and Sandpaper," *Picture Play*, Sept. 1938.

5. The huge body of interpretive literature on modernism includes Malcolm Bradbury and James McFarlane, ed., *Modernism, 1890–1930* (New York, 1976); Robert Kiely, ed., *Modernism Reconsidered* (Cambridge, Mass., 1983); Irving Howe, ed., *The Idea of the Modern in Literature and the Arts* (New York, 1967); David Harvey, "Modernity and Modernism," in his *The Condition of Postmodernity: An Enquiry into the Origins of Cultural Change* (Oxford, 1990), 24.

6. This synthesis relies on Daniel Joseph Singal, "Towards a Definition of American Modernism," *American Quarterly* 39 (Spring 1987), 7–26; Morton White, *Social Thought in America: The Revolt Against Formalism* (New York, 1976); Cecelia Tichi, *Shifting Gears: Technology, Literature, Culture in Modernist America* (Chapel Hill, 1987); and Marshall Berman, "Why Modernism Still Matters," *Tikkun*, Jan.–Feb. 1989, 11–15.

7. Northrop Frye, *The Modern Century* (Toronto, 1967), 26. On the sunny Victorian cultural tradition, see William Dean Howells, *Criticism and Fiction* (New York, 1891), 128; Sarah Burns, *Pastoral Inventions: Rural Life in Nineteenth-Century Art and Culture* (Philadelphia, 1989).

8. On the training of Disney artists, see Thomas, *Walt Disney*, 115–16, 123–24; Finch, *Art of Walt Disney*, 137–39; Thomas and Johnston, *Disney Animation*, 71–79.

9. Frank Thomas, interview by the author, Aug. 19, 1993. See also Marc Davis, interview by the author, Aug. 16, 1993; Ollie Johnston, interview by the author, Aug. 17, 1993.

10. Davis interview; Sharpsteen, Peri interview, Apr. 26, 1974.

11. Sharpsteen, Peri interview, Feb. 6, 1974, 15; Thomas, Thomas interview, 10; Marc Davis, interview by Richard Hubler, May 28, 1968, 14; Ken Anderson, interview by Steve Hulett, May 4, 1978, 1.

12. "The Story of Pinocchio," *Canadian Home Journal*, Feb. 1940, 10.

13. H. H. Gerth and C. Wright Mills, eds., *From Max Weber: Essays in Sociology* (New York, 1974), 51, 139, 282, 352. Weber borrowed the phrase "disenchantment of the world" from Friedrich Schiller.

14. WD, studio memo to Don Graham, Dec. 23, 1935, 2–3.

15. Ibid., 3–4, 6.

16. Ibid., 2, 3, 7.

17. See "Studio Animation Handbook," 1936, especially Ham Luske, "General Outline of Animation Theory and Practice."

18. Friz Freleng, "I'll Never Get Home," interview by Joseph Adamson, July 28, 1968–June 26, 1969, 24, 33–34; WD to Knowles Blair, May 13, 1937. See also Ollie Johnston, interview by Christopher Finch and Linda Rosenkrantz, June 2, 1972, 10; Milt Kahl, interview by Richard Hubler, February 27, 1968, 15; Culhane, *Talking Animals*, 136–38.

19. Ham Luske, "Character Handling," Oct. 6, 1938, 3; Larson, Finch and Rosenkrantz interview, 1–2; Davis, Thomas interview, 6.

20. WD, "Mickey in Color," New York *World Telegram*, July 13, 1935.

21. WD, interoffice memo, Nov. 16, 1937; Ben Sharpsteen, interview by David Smith, Oct. 21, 1974, 10–11. Culhane, *Fantasia*, offers the best account of the making of the film.

22. Disney Studio, Story Department memorandum, Nov. 15, 1937, DA; WD, interoffice memo, Nov. 16, 1937, DA; Ollie Johnston, interview by Howard Green for 1990 reissue of *Fantasia*, 20; Bill Garity, in "Tricks of Sound in Disney Films Told by Expert," New York *Herald Tribune*, Oct. 27, 1940.

23. Dick Huemer, interview by Christopher Finch and Linda Rosenkrantz, May 5, 1972, 18–20; Dick Huemer, "Thumbnail Sketches," *Funnyworld* (Fall 1979), 41.

24. Huemer, "Thumbnail Sketches," 41. On visitors to the Disney Studio during filming, see Culhane, *Fantasia*, 22–23.

25. Theater program for *Fantasia*, 1940.

26. Thomas R. Dash, "Disney's 'Fantasia,'" *Women's Wear Daily*, Nov. 14, 1940; "Mr. Disney and 'Fantasia,'" New York *Times*, Nov. 15, 1940; Peyton Boswell, "Wonder of Fantasia," *Art Digest*, Dec. 1, 1940, 3; Hermine Rich Isaacs, "New Horizons: Fantasia and Fantasound," *Theatre Arts*, Jan. 1941, 59; Emily Genauer, "Walt Disney's Music Pictures Range from Beautiful to Banal," New York *World-Telegram*, Nov. 16, 1940.

27. "Films on Ideals of Youth Proposed," New York *Times*, Nov. 17, 1940; Culhane, *Fantasia*, 36–37; Martin/Miller interview, Reel 11, 42–44. See also William Moritz, "Fischinger at Disney," *Millimeter*, Feb. 1977, 25–28, 65–66.

28. Pare Lorenz, "Fantasia," *McCall's*, Feb. 1941, reprinted in Lorenz, *Lorenz on Film*, 207; Crowther, "Is It Art?"; Genauer, "Walt Disney's Music Pictures."

29. Sam Robins, "Disney Again Tries Trailblazing," *New York Times Magazine*, Nov. 3, 1940, 6–7, 19; "Disney Revolutionizes Movies Again," *Look*, Dec. 3, 1940, 31; "Disney's Cinesymphony," *Time*, Nov. 18, 1940, 52, 55; "Review Board Hails 'Fantasia,'" New York *Morning Telegraph*, Oct. 30, 1940.

30. Olin Downes, "Disney's Experiment: Second Thoughts on 'Fantasia' and Its Visualization of Music," New York *Times*, Nov. 17, 1940; Franz Hoellering, "Films," *Nation*, Nov. 23, 1940, 513–14. See also Richard Griffith, "Critics of 'Fantasia' at Loggerheads," Los Angeles *Times*, Nov. 26, 1940, and Crowther, "Is It Art?" Among a host of reviews describing the film as a new art form, see Robert

Gessner, "Class in 'Fantasia,'" *Nation*, Nov. 30, 1940, 543–44; Philip T. Hartung, "Once in a Lifetime," *Commonweal*, Nov. 29, 1940, 152–53.

31. B. H. Haggin, "Music," *Nation*, Jan. 11, 1941, 53–54; Oscar Thompson, "Music's Role in 'Fantasia,'" New York *Sun*, Nov. 16, 1940; Benjamin DeCasseres, "The March of Events," New York *Journal and American*, Dec. 3, 1940. See also Horace B. English, "'Fantasia' and the Psychology of Music," *Journal of Aesthetics and Art Criticism* (Winter 1942), 27–28.

32. Dorothy Thompson, "On the Record: Minority Report," New York *Herald Tribune*, Nov. 25, 1940, 13.

33. Howard Barnes, "The Screen," New York *Herald Tribune*, Dec. 1, 1940; Carl E. Lindstrom, "Music," Hartford *Times*, Dec. 2, 1940.

7. Of Mice and Men: Art Critics and Animators

1. Mortimer Franklin, "The Art of Mickey Mouse," *Screenland*, Sept. 1933, 26–27.

2. "The Pie in Art," *Nation*, Nov. 7, 1934; C.A.L., untitled column, Boston *Transcript*, Nov. 15, 1930; Morton Thompson, "North Northwest," Hollywood *Citizen News*, Feb. 19, 1940; "A New Art in the Making," *Art Digest*, Jan. 7, 1933, 8; untitled column, *Art Digest*, Feb. 15, 1940, 13.

3. William R. Weaver, "Walt Disney, Artist," *Chicagoan*, May 10, 1930, 38; Mark Van Doren, "Fairy Tale," *Nation*, Jan. 22, 1938, 108–9; Low, "Leonardo da Disney," 16–18; Mel Scott, "Mickey Mouse and Michelangelo," Hollywood *Citizen-News*, Feb. 28, 1938.

4. Dorothy Grafly, "America's Youngest Art," *American Magazine of Art*, July 1933, 336, 337, 338, 342. See also a long quotation from Grafly in "Dopey, Grumpy, and Co.," *Art Digest*, Sept. 1, 1938.

5. Fenn Sherie, "Poetry in Celluloid," *Pearson's Magazine*, July 1933, 73, 75; unattributed newspaper article from 1930, PS M17; Susan Breul, "Words and Music," Bridgeport, Conn., *Post*, May 29, 1938. See also Creighton Peet, "Miraculous Mickey," *Outlook and Independent*, July 23, 1930, 472; "Distinct Contribution to Modern Art and Culture," Montreal *Daily Star*, Apr. 6, 1940.

6. Barnet G. Braver-Mann, "Mickey Mouse and His Playmates," *Theater Guild Magazine*, Mar. 1931, 14, 17–18; Jean Charlot, "But Is It Art? A Disney Disquisition," *American Scholar* (Summer 1939), 262; Claude Bragdon, "Mickey Mouse and What He Means," *Scribner's*, July 1934, 43.

7. "Walt Disney Hailed for His Music," New York *Evening Journal*, May 25, 1936, 13; "Disney's Mickey Wins Toscanini," New York *Telegraph*, June 13, 1935; Marcia Davenport, "Not So Silly," *Stage*, July 1936, 51.

8. Maltin, *Disney Films*, 14–15; Richard R. Plant, "Movies: Of Disney," *Decision*, July 1941, 83–85. See also Ralph M. Pearson, "The Artist's Point of View," *Forum and Century*, Nov. 1937, 271.

9. Christopher La Farge, "Walt Disney and the Art Form," *Theatre Arts*, Sept. 1941, 673, 678–79, 680, 677.

10. "Immortality for Mickey and Dopey," Norfolk *Pilot*, Jan. 27, 1939; "Walt Disney at the Metropolitan," New York *Post*, Jan. 25, 1939; "Disney Cartoon Originals Become New Art," *Screen and Radio Weekly*, Feb. 4, 1940. See also "Mickey Mouse Finds Niche at Chicago Art Institute," Chicago *Tribune*, Dec. 14, 1933; Dorothy Adlow, "Walt Disney's Art Seen in Backstage Exhibits," *Christian*

Science Monitor, Mar. 1, 1939; "Disney Museumized," *Art Digest,* Dec. 15, 1940, 11; "Walt Disney at the Metropolitan," New York *Post,* Jan. 25, 1939, and similar articles in PS S28.

11. "Mickey Mouse Invades Gallery," *Art Digest,* May 1, 1933, 12; "Walt Disney, M.A., M.S.," *Newsweek,* July 4, 1938, 18–19; "Come Home, Mickey Mouse," Baton Rouge *State Times,* Nov. 16, 1938.

12. Philippe Lamour, "The New Art: Mickey Mouse; A Note on the Talking Film," *New Hope,* Sept. 15, 1934, 9; "Europe's Highbrows Hail 'Mickey Mouse,'" *Literary Digest,* Aug. 8, 1931, 19.

13. James Thurber, "The 'Odyssey' of Disney," *Nation,* Mar. 28, 1934; Helen G. Thompson, "Madame Cluck, Prima Donna," *Stage,* May 1936, 60.

14. Kaspar Monahan, "The Show Shops," Pittsburgh *Press,* Oct. 15, 1953; Quintus Quiz, "That Awful Word 'Art,'" *Christian Century,* Jan. 22, 1936, 137–38; "Studio and Screen," Brooklyn *Eagle,* Mar. 21, 1931.

15. Alva Johnston, "Mickey Mouse," *Women's Home Companion,* July 1934, 12; "Mickey Mouse and Art," Pawtucket *Times,* Dec. 18, 1933; Johnston, "Mickey Mouse," 13.

16. "Recognition for an Artist," Schenectady *Gazette,* Jan. 30, 1939; Arthur Millier, "The Art Thrill of the Week — by the Art Critic," Los Angeles *Times,* Feb. 4, 1940.

17. Ken O'Connor, "Designing Fantasia," undated lecture.

18. Harry Alan Potamkin, "Film Cults," *Modern Thinker and Author's Review,* Nov. 1932, 550; Bragdon, "Mickey Mouse and What He Means," 40, 42.

19. Quinn Martin, "How Animated Cartoons Are Made," *New York World Sunday Magazine,* Sept. 28, 1930, 8, 14; "Disney's Popularity," unnamed Winnipeg, Manitoba, newspaper, Oct. 21, 1933, PS M8; Kenneth White, "Mickey Mouse, A Chronicle," *Hound and Horn,* Oct.–Dec. 1931, 103; Lawrence Gould, "America Comes of Age — Age 2?" Philadelphia *Record,* June 12, 1938.

20. Leyda, *Eisenstein on Disney,* 2–3, 54–55, 43, 44, 10.

21. Ibid., 42, 3–4.

22. Ibid., 9, 23, 33, 1.

23. See Myron O. Lounsbury, *The Origins of American Film Criticism, 1909–1939* (New York, 1973), 141–48, 169–75, 211–17, 410–20; Michael G. Kammen, *The Lively Arts: Gilbert Seldes and the Transformation of Cultural Criticism in the United States* (New York, 1996).

24. Seldes, "Mickey Mouse Maker," 27; "Disney and Others," *New Republic,* June 8, 1932, 171; "No Art, Mr. Disney?" *Esquire,* Sept. 1937, 91, 172. See also Seldes, *Movies Come from America,* 45–47.

25. Gilbert Seldes, "Motion Pictures," *Scribner's,* Mar. 1, 1938, 65, 66, 68.

26. Lewis Jacobs, *The Rise of American Film: A Critical History* (New York, 1939), vii, 3, 496, 499. On Jacobs, see Lounsbury, *American Film Criticism,* 464–77.

27. Ibid., 499–500.

28. Ibid., 502, 503–4, 505.

29. Seldes, "Disney and Others," 172; Grafly, "America's Youngest Art," 337; Lamour, "The New Art," 9; Jacobs, *Rise of American Film,* 503–4; "Pinocchio," *Art Digest,* Feb. 15, 1940, 13.

30. See Thomas and Johnston, *Disney Animation,* 98–99; Culhane, *Talking Animals,* 151–52, 188.

31. Thomas and Johnston, *Disney Animation,* 99, 50, 79; Culhane, *Talking Animals,* 151–52.

32. Huemer, "Thumbnail Sketches," 38. See also Thomas and Johnston, *Disney Animation,* 105–7; J. B. Kaufman, "Norm Ferguson and the Latin American Films of Walt Disney," unpublished ms., 1, 3.

33. Huemer, "Thumbnail Sketches," 38; Culhane, *Talking Animals,* 155–56.

34. Kinney, *Walt Disney and Other Characters,* 42; Thomas and Johnston, *Disney Animation,* 105; Culhane, *Talking Animals,* 169.

35. Thomas and Johnston, *Disney Animation,* 99.

36. Ibid., 99, 104; Ward Kimball, interview by Richard Shale, 1976, 10.

37. Huemer, "Thumbnail Sketches," 38.

38. Thomas and Johnston, *Disney Animation,* 99, 104. On Ferguson's artistic influences, see also Culhane, *Talking Animals,* 176, 156, 191–92.

39. Kaufman, "Latin American Trip," 1; Culhane, *Fantasia,* 170; Huemer, "Thumbnail Sketches," 38; Norman Ferguson, "Analysis of Pluto," Jan. 4, 1936, 1–4.

40. Cottrell interview; Thomas and Johnston, *Disney Animation,* 98–99, 105; Culhane, *Talking Animals,* 129.

41. Culhane, *Talking Animals,* 351. See also I. Klein, "The Disney Studio in the 1930s," *Cartoonist Profiles,* 1974, 15; Ward Kimball, interview with Klaus Strzyz, *Comics Journal,* 1988, 92.

42. WD, "Interview at the Time of Snow White," n.d. (probably 1959), 1.

43. Thomas and Johnston, *Disney Animation,* 125–26, 119, 126; Culhane, *Talking Animals,* 170.

44. Thomas and Johnston, *Disney Animation,* 128, 119–20; Anderson, Thomas interview, 9–10.

45. Thomas and Johnston, *Disney Animation,* 120, 123, 129; Johnston, Thomas interview, 6; Huemer, "Thumbnail Sketches," 42; Art Babbitt, interview by David R. Smith, May 23, 1978, 1.

46. Thomas, Thomas interview, 8; Thomas and Johnston, *Disney Animation,* 122–23, 127, 128, 129; Finch, *Art of Walt Disney,* 215, 214.

47. Johnston, Thomas interview, 5–7.

48. Thomas and Johnston, *Disney Animation,* 122.

49. Kinney, *Walt Disney and Other Characters,* 47; Johnston, Thomas interview, 8–9; Thomas and Johnston, *Illusion,* 120, 122; Huemer, "Thumbnail Sketches," 41, 42. On Moore's technique, see also Anderson, Thomas interview, 10; Kimball, Hulett interview, 5.

50. Thomas and Johnston, *Disney Animation,* 125.

51. Ibid., 128.

52. Ibid., 551–53.

53. Kinney, *Disney and Other Characters,* 155; Kimball, Shale interview, 10–11. See also Thomas and Johnston, *Disney Animation,* 105; Culhane, *Talking Animals,* 351–52; Cottrell interview.

54. Thomas and Johnston, *Disney Animation,* 129; Johnston, Thomas interview, 6–7; Kimball, Shale interview, 14; Kimball, Hulett interview, 5–7.

55. Glen Keane and Eric Larson, interview by Mike Bonifer, press kit for 1983 release of *Snow White.*

56. S. J. Woolf, "Walt Disney Tells Us What Makes Him Happy," *New York Times Magazine,* July 10, 1938, 5.

57. Ibid.; Frank S. Nugent, "Disney Is Now Art — But He Wonders," *New York Times Magazine*, Feb. 26, 1939, 4–5.

58. Ibid.

59. Ibid.

60. Woolf, "What Makes Disney Happy," 5; WD, "Mickey Mouse Presents," in Nancy Naumberg, ed., *We Make the Movies* (New York, 1937), 269, 271; Frank Daugherty, "Mickey Mouse Comes of Age," *Christian Science Monitor*, Feb. 2, 1938, 8.

61. Nugent, "Disney Now Art," 5, 4.

8. Disney and American Culture

1. Dowling, "Three Little Pigs Bring Home the Bacon," PS M8; Alva Johnston, "Mickey Mouse," *Women's Home Companion*, July 1934, 12–13; Lorenz, *Lorenz on Film*, 150.

2. WD, "Temperamental Dwarfs Held Up Snow White," New York *World Telegram*, Jan. 8, 1938.

3. "Mouse and Man," *Time*, Dec. 27, 1937, 19–21.

4. "Pollen Man," *New Yorker*, Nov. 1, 1941, 14; Richard Watts, Jr., "The Theater," New York *Herald Tribune*, July 16, 1939. See also Daugherty, "Mickey Mouse Comes of Age," 9.

5. Gene Fowler, "The Cosmopolite of the Month: Walt Disney," *Cosmopolitan*, Aug. 1937, 8; Garrett D. Byrnes, "Looking at Hollywood," *Evening Bulletin*, Dec. 27, 1935.

6. Edward G. Smith, "St. Francis of the Silver Screen," *Progress Today*, Jan.–Mar. 1935, 44; Charles W. Brahares, "Walt Disney as Theologian," *Christian Century*, Aug. 10, 1938, 968–69.

7. Dale Carnegie, "Comments On," New York *Mirror*, Nov. 19, 1937; Fowler, "Cosmopolite of the Month," 8; Seldes, "Mickey Mouse Maker," 24; Pringle, "Mickey Mouse's Father," 28; Dan Thomas, "Movieland's Most Popular Star," Columbus, Ohio, *State Journal*, Mar. 8, 1931. A host of 1930s articles on Disney's populist image can be found in PS M14 and PS S26.

8. Ernie Pyle, "Disney Is Plain People," Indianapolis *Times*, Feb. 28, 1938.

9. On the early Mickey Mouse Clubs, see Richard Holliss and Brian Sibley, *The Disney Studio Story* (New York, 1988), 20, and Cecil Munsey, *Disneyana: Walt Disney Collectibles* (New York, 1974).

10. Mickey Mouse Idea publicity announcement, PS M12; Columbia Pictures advertisement for Mickey Mouse Club for Boys and Girls, 1931, PS M14; *Official Bulletin of the Mickey Mouse Club*, Oct. 1, 1931, PS M14.

11. Pringle, "Mickey Mouse's Father," 28; "Mickey Mouse's Fourth Birthday Finds Organization Worldwide," *Motion Picture Herald*, Oct. 1, 1932, 42; *Official Bulletin of the Mickey Mouse Club*, PS M14; "Kiddies to Have Own Mickey Mouse Club," Wharton, Texas, *Spectator*, Mar. 4, 1932.

12. Merritt and Kaufman, *Walt in Wonderland*, 144; 1931 Columbia Pictures press sheets, PS M14; WD, "Mickey Mouse: How He Was Born," 643; Seldes, "Mickey Mouse Maker," 25.

13. Frank Nugent, "That Million Dollar Mouse," *New York Times Magazine*, Sept. 21, 1947, 61–62. See also "Mickey Mouse, Salesman," *Advertising and Selling*, Aug. 30,

1934; "Mickey Mouse — Merchant," *California: Magazine of Pacific Business*, Mar. 1937, 17.

14. L. H. Robbins, "Mickey Mouse Emerges as Economist," *New York Times Magazine*, Mar. 10, 1935, 8. See also "Mickey Mouse Steps In and Bankrupt Firm Recovers," *Advertising and Selling*, Jan. 21, 1935; "Mickey Mouse and New Trains Help Lionel Out of Bad Business Bog," *Sales Management*, Feb. 1, 1935.

15. See Robbins, "Mickey Mouse as Economist"; M. J. Hirsch, "Mouse Minter," *Advertising and Selling*, July 18, 1935, 61–62; Holliss and Sibley, *Disney Studio Story*, 20–21.

16. Clippings of these advertisements are in PS P18.

17. "Mickey Mouse, Financier," *Literary Digest*, Oct. 21, 1933; "Mickey Mouse Goes into Business," *System and Business Management*, Feb. 1934, 68; "Mickey Mouse and the Bankers," *Fortune*, Nov. 1934, 94; Arthur Mann, "Mickey Mouse's Financial Career," *Harper's*, May 1934, 714–21; Robbins, "Mickey as Economist," 8.

18. Earnest Elmo Calkins, untitled article, *Advertising and Selling*, Feb. 1, 1934, PS M8.

19. Kinney, *Walt Disney and Other Characters*, 149.

20. Martin/Miller interview, Reel 2, 43–44. See also Thomas, Thomas interview, 9–10; Roy Disney, quoted in Hubler, "Walt Disney," 203.

21. Pyle, "Disney Is Plain People." See also Martin/Miller interview, Reel 2, 43–44; Hubler, "Walt Disney," 201.

22. WD to Roy Disney and Ubbe Iwerks, Feb. 9, 1929.

23. Ibid., Mar. 7, 1928; Sept. 7, 1928; Sept. 11, 1928, 3.

24. Ibid., Sept. 23, 1928, 3; Oct. 27, 1928, 3; Sept. 21, 1928; Sept. 14, 1928, 2; Oct. 6, 1928, 3–4.

25. Ibid., Sept. 11, 1928, 3; Sept. 23, 1928, 2; Sept. 20, 1928, 1; Oct. 6, 1928, 5.

26. Edna Disney, Hubler interview, 11; Sharpsteen, Peri interviews, Apr. 26, 1974, 11, Feb. 6, 1974, 17, and Feb. 7, 1975, 10; Sharpsteen, Hubler interview, 27–28.

27. Thomas, Thomas interview, 14–15, 21; Sharpsteen, Peri interview, Feb. 6, 1974, 8–9; Bill Cottrell, interview by Bob Thomas, June 6, 1973, 7–8; Pfieffer, Thomas interview, 17–18; Kinney, *Walt Disney and Other Characters*, 148.

28. Roy Disney, Hubler interview, 33, 16; Hugh Harman, quoted in Mike Barrier, "Silly Stuff: An Interview with Hugh Harman," *Graffiti* (Spring 1984), 6; Ward Kimball, "The Wonderful World of Walt Disney," in Walter Wagner, ed., *You Must Remember This* (New York, 1975), 266.

29. Kinney, *Walt Disney and Other Characters*, 198; Anderson, Thomas interview, 7.

30. Sharpsteen, Peri interview, Feb. 6, 1974, 6–7; Kahl, Hubler interview, 3, 5; Kimball, Hubler interview, 36–37; I. Klein, "Some Close-up Shots of Walt Disney During the 'Golden Years,'" *Funnyworld* (Spring 1983), 48.

31. Jack Cutting, interview by Christopher Finch and Linda Rosenkrantz, May 4, 1972, 6; Kimball, Hubler interview, 27–28, 19.

32. Thomas, Thomas interview, 7–8, 21–22.

33. Kimball, "World of Walt Disney," 271; Don Peri, "Roy Williams: An Interview," *Funnyworld* (Fall 1977), 34, 33.

34. Sharpsteen, Peri interview, 7–8; Davis, Hubler interview, 2–3; Kinney, *Walt Disney and Other Characters*, 157; Cutting, Finch and Rosenkrantz interview, 5–6.

35. WD to Alice Howell, July 2, 1934; Martin/Miller interview, Reel 2, 45–46; Kimball, Hubler interview, 45; Sharpsteen, Hubler interview, 29–30.

36. Kimball, "World of Walt Disney," 268–69; Sharpsteen, Hubler interview, 9; Martin/Miller interview, Reel 12, 23, 24–25, 26.
37. WD to Lillian Disney, Oct. 20, 1928, 3; WD to the "studio gang," Oct. 2, 1928, 1; WD to Roy Disney, Sept. 28, 1928, 1; WD to Roy Disney, Sept. 25, 1928, 3; WD to Roy Disney and Ub Iwerks, Sept. 14, 1928, 4.
38. Sharpsteen, Peri interview, Feb. 6, 1974, 38, 39, 40; Sharpsteen, Hubler interview, 10–11; Roy Disney, Hubler interview, 2, 3–4, 21.
39. Martin/Miller interview, Reel 10, 11, 54.
40. Sharpsteen, Peri interview, Feb. 6, 1974, 5; Cutting, Finch and Rosenkrantz interview, 4; WD, "The Cartoon's Contribution to Children," 138.
41. Kahl, Hubler interview, 16; Sharpsteen, Hubler interview, 26; Hibler, Thomas interview, 4; WD, Lux Radio Theater, interview by Cecil B. DeMille, Dec. 26, 1938.
42. Daugherty, "Mickey Mouse Comes of Age," 9; Don Peri, "Roy Williams: An Interview," *Funnyworld* (Fall 1977), 34; Kahl, Hubler interview, 12; Hibler, Hubler interview, 28.
43. Irving Hoffman, "Review Points," *Hollywood Reporter*, Jan. 18, 1938; Clark Wales, "Reviews of New Films," *Screen and Radio Weekly*, Jan. 9, 1938. See also Westbrook Pegler, "Fair Enough," Knoxville, Tenn., *News-Sentinel*, Jan. 15, 1938; Pare Lorenz, "Snow White," in Lorenz, *Lorenz on Film*, 148–50; W. Ward Marsh, "Snow White . . . One of the Greatest Films of All Time," Cleveland *Plain Dealer*, Feb. 13, 1938. See PS S19, S25, S26, S28, and S38 for dozens of outlandishly favorable reviews of this film.
44. M.F.L., "Walt Disney Scores Again," *Wall Street Journal*, Jan. 14, 1938; "Brainy People Flock to See Snow White," Boston *Evening Globe*, Feb. 26, 1938; "Snow White and Escape from Reality," *Christian Century*, July 20, 1938; Edith Johnson, "Is 'Snow White' Escape from Reality?" Oklahoma City *Oklahoman*, Aug. 23, 1938.
45. "Walt Disney Puts Soap in the Movies," *Soap*, Dec. 1, 1937, 34–35, 45; "And Now the 'Dwarf Hat'," Philadelphia *Bulletin*, Jan. 19, 1938; *Women's Wear Daily*, Feb. 9, 1938, 1–20; George T. Bristol, "Snow White: Inanimate Characters Become a New Force in Merchandising," *Dun's Review*, Apr. 1938, 13, 15.
46. WD, "Our American Culture," Mar. 1, 1942, 1–2, 2–3, 3.
47. Ibid., 2, 3.
48. Ibid., 2, 4.

9. The Fantasy Factory

1. Paul Hollister, "Walt Disney: Genius at Work," *Atlantic Monthly*, Dec. 1940, 689, 691–97.
2. See Thomas, *Walt Disney*, 123, and Eric Larson, interview with Steve Hulett, Apr. 19, 1978, 3.
3. See David R. Smith, "Disney Before Burbank: The Kingswell and Hyperion Studios," *Funnyworld* (Summer 1979), 32–38.
4. George Nagel, "Mickey Mouse's Home Is Like College," Birmingham, Ala., *News-Age Herald*, Dec. 4, 1938, 6; WD, "Growing Pains," unpublished ms., 7; Harry Carr, "Hollywood's Only Unpaid Movie Star," *American Magazine*, Mar.

1931, 123; Arthur Millier, "Walter in Wonderland," *Los Angeles Times Sunday Magazine*, Sept. 4, 1938.

5. Ada Hanifin, "Mickey Mouse and His Father Found at Work," San Francisco *Examiner*, Oct. 26, 1930; Edwin C. Parsons, "Adventures with Mickey Mouse," PS M17; William Stull, "Three Hundred Men and Walt Disney," *American Cinematographer*, Feb. 1938, 48; "The Big Bad Wolf," *Fortune*, Nov. 1934, 88.

6. Thomas and Johnston, *Disney Animation*, 188; Mark W. Schwab, "The Communalistic Art of Walt Disney," *Cinema Quarterly* (Spring 1934), 150–53; Richard Watts, Jr., "The Theater," New York *Herald Tribune*, Jan. 16, 1939; Millier, "Walter in Wonderland"; Sam Robins, "Disney Again Tries Trailblazing," *New York Times Magazine*, Nov. 3, 1940. For articles praising Walt's role, see Otis Ferguson, "Walt Disney's Grimm Reality," *New Republic*, Jan. 26, 1938, 340, and Ernie Pyle, "$50 Hotel Room Nearly Ruined Disney's Trip," Indianapolis *Times*, Mar. 1, 1938.

7. *Organizational Manual*, May 16, 1938, 1.

8. *An Introduction to the Walt Disney Studio* (Walt Disney Productions, 1938), 5, 16, 22; *The Ropes at Disney* (1943), n.p.

9. George Drake, "Disney-Chouinard Series," May 26, 1937, 14–15.

10. WD, interoffice communication, May 20, 1935; WD, "Mickey Mouse Presents," in Nancy Naumberg, ed., *We Make the Movies* (New York, 1937), 266.

11. WD to Roy Disney and Ub Iwerks, Oct. 1 and Oct. 6, 1928.

12. "The Big, Bad Wolf and Why It May Never Huff nor Puff at Walt Disney's Door," *Fortune*, May 1934, 93; WD, "Growing Pains" ms., 9–12; Millier, "Walter in Wonderland."

13. Kinney, *Walt Disney and Other Characters*, 28; Culhane, *Talking Animals*, 111; Dick Huemer, "Interview," *Funnyworld* (1977), 40; Nancy Massie, quoted in John Canemaker, *Raggedy Ann and Andy* (1977), 258, 262. See Thomas and Johnston, *Disney Animation*, especially 154–55, for a more detailed description of the bureaucracy.

14. Hamilton Luske, "General Outline of Animation Theory and Practice," *Studio Animation Handbook*, 1936, n.p. See also Ham Luske, "Character Handling," Oct. 6, 1938, 1.

15. Frank S. Nugent, "Disney Is Now Art — But He Wonders," *New York Times Magazine*, Feb. 26, 1939, 5. See also Culhane, *Talking Animals*, 113, 149–50; I. Klein, "At the Disney Studio in the 1930s," *Cartoonist Profiles*, Sept. 1974, 15–16; Kinney, *Walt Disney and Other Characters*, 44, 63, 148.

16. Fenn Sherie, "Poetry in Celluloid," *Pearson's Magazine*, July 1933, 77; "The Ropes at Disney," [1].

17. Klein, "Disney Studio in the 1930s," 18; Stull, "Three Hundred Men," 48; Culhane, *Talking Animals*, 113–14.

18. Thomas and Johnston, *Disney Animation*, 140–45; Kinney, *Walt Disney and Other Characters*, 39.

19. Kinney, *Walt Disney and Other Characters*, 20–21, 49–51, 96–103; Bill Peet, *An Autobiography* (Boston, 1989), 99.

20. *An Introduction to the Walt Disney Studio*, 19.

21. Huemer, "Thumbnail Sketches," 38; David Hand, *Memoirs* (Cambria, Calif., 1986), 72.

22. Thomas, Thomas interview, 13, 37–38; Huemer, "Thumbnail Sketches," 42; Davis, Hubler interview, 4, 18.

23. Sharpsteen, Hubler interview, 32; Culhane, *Talking Animals,* 147. See "Disney's Philosophy," *New York Times Magazine,* Mar. 6, 1938, 23, on the studio's combination of individual latitude and organizational demands.

24. Nugent, "Disney Is Now Art," 5.

25. Hand, *Memoirs,* 79; Tebb, quoted in Thomas and Johnston, *Disney Animation,* 146; Robert Weinstein, interview by the author, Oct. 27, 1993. See also Don Peri, "Roy Williams: An Interview," *Funnyworld* (Fall 1977), 34–35; Cutting, Finch and Rosenkrantz interview, 2–4.

26. Huemer, "Thumbnail Sketches," 38–39; John D. Ford, "An Interview with John and Faith Hubley," in Danny Peary and Gerald Peary, eds., *The American Animated Cartoon* (New York, 1980), 183.

27. Diane Disney Miller, Hubler interview, 43.

28. Kinney, *Walt Disney and Other Characters,* 20–21, 96; Cutting, Finch and Rosenkrantz interview, 7.

29. Kinney, *Walt Disney and Other Characters,* 22–23, 160, 170, 74–75; Thomas and Johnston, *Disney Animation,* 42; Robert Weinstein interview.

30. Ward Kimball, interview by Christopher Finch and Linda Rosenkrantz, May 10, 1972, 7; Kinney, *Walt Disney and Other Characters,* 89.

31. Culhane, *Talking Animals,* 180–81; Ward Kimball, "The Wonderful World of Walt Disney," in Walter Wagner, ed., *You Must Remember This* (New York, 1975), 269–70.

32. Kinney, *Walt Disney and Other Characters,* 114.

33. Ibid., 128–29; Thomas and Johnston, *Disney Animation,* 339–41.

34. Kinney, *Walt Disney and Other Characters,* 65.

35. Anderson, Thomas interview, 16–20; Thomas, Thomas interview, 31–32.

36. Kinney, *Walt Disney and Other Characters,* 94; Thomas, Thomas interview, 19–20, 4–5.

37. Culhane, *Talking Animals,* 127, 132, 157; Art Babbitt, interview by John Canemaker, Feb. 21, 1979, 2–3; Kinney, *Walt Disney and Other Characters,* 33; Klein, "Disney Studio in the 1930s," 15–16; Ward Kimball, interview by Steve Hulett, April 1978, 15.

38. Thomas and Johnston, *Disney Animation,* 85–86, 81, 155; Ollie Johnston and Frank Thomas, *Bambi: The Story and the Film* (New York, 1990), 110–12; Kinney, *Walt Disney and Other Characters,* 28–29; Hand, *Memoirs,* 71–83.

39. Huemer, "Thumbnail Sketches," 41. See also Kinney, *Walt Disney and Other Characters,* 73; Larson, Finch and Rosenkrantz interview, 16; Larson, Hulett interview, 1–2; Watkin, "Walt Disney," 323–24; Ted Sears, ed., *He Drew as He Pleased: A Sketchbook* (New York, 1948), 1–6.

40. Sears, *He Drew as He Pleased,* 3.

41. Hee, Hubler interview, 7–8, 30–31; Culhane, *Fantasia,* 164–71, 176–78; Thomas and Johnston, *Disney Animation,* 268–69.

42. Thomas and Johnston, *Disney Animation,* 87, 90; John Grant, *Encyclopedia of Walt Disney's Animated Characters* (New York, 1993), 62–63; Kinney, *Walt Disney and Other Characters,* 201, 205.

43. Kinney, *Walt Disney and Other Characters,* 30–33, 68–69, 79–83.

44. Kimball, Hubler interview, 25–26; Kimball, Hulett interview, 8; Kimball, Cane-maker interview, 10; Anderson, Thomas interview, 10–11; Thomas and Johnston, *Disney Animation*, 376–79; Bill Cottrell, Ollie Johnston, Frank Thomas, and Marc Davis, interviews by the author, August 1993. See Peet's own account in *An Autobiography*, 70–185.

10. The Engineering of Enchantment

1. Culhane, *Talking Animals*, 113.
2. Ward Kimball, interview by Christopher Finch and Linda Rosenkrantz, May 10, 1972, 5–7.
3. Peet, *Autobiography*, 110; Thomas, *Walt Disney*, 157–60.
4. WD, "Mickey Mouse Presents," 253–71.
5. Canemaker, *Raggedy Ann and Andy*, 20, 30–33, 36, 50–54, 58–60; John Cane-maker, *Before the Animation Begins: The Art and Lives of Disney Inspirational Sketch Artists* (New York, 1996), 51–63.
6. Canemaker, "Grim Natwick," 59; Hee, Hubler interview, 40–41; Anderson, Finch and Rosenkrantz interview, 4–5; Huemer, "Thumbnail Sketches," 43; Davis, Thomas interview, 14.
7. Martin/Miller interview, Reel 6, 52; Thomas, *Walt Disney*, 130; Ollie Johnston, interview by John Canemaker, July 1973, 3–4; Canemaker, "Grim Natwick," 59–60; Culhane, *Talking Animals*, 159.
8. Thomas, Thomas interview, 12–13.
9. Transcript of Bambi meeting, Apr. 5, 1939, 6, 14, 2–3, 17–18, 21–22.
10. "Overall Showing — Audience Reactions," "Bambi Questionnaire," "Com-ments," Oct. 24, 1940, in *Bambi* file, DA. On the making of this film, see Johnston and Thomas, *Bambi*.
11. Sharpsteen, Peri interview, Feb. 6, 1974, 10.
12. Thomas, Thomas interview, 1.
13. Johnston, Thomas interview, 2–3; Sharpsteen, Hubler interview, 25–26; Klein, "The Golden Years," 49; Anderson, Hulett interview, 1; Wilfred Jackson, inter-view by Steve Hulett, July 25, 1978, 2.
14. Kinney, *Walt Disney and Other Characters*, 150–51.
15. Culhane, *Talking Animals*, 150–51; Sharpsteen, Peri interview, Apr. 24, 1974, 1; Larson, Hulett interview, 4.
16. Johnston, Thomas interview, 13–14; Larson, Hulett interview, 4; Thomas, Thomas interview, 6; Hibler, Thomas interview, 21–22; Ken Anderson, interview by Christopher Finch and Linda Rosenkrantz, Apr. 21, 1972, 5.
17. Thomas, Thomas interview, 12; Huemer, "Thumbnail Sketches," 38; Culhane, *Talking Animals*, 163; Lillian Disney, Hubler interview, 14; Thomas, Thomas interview, 25.
18. Sharpsteen, Smith interview, 14; Sharpsteen, Smith and Watkins interview, 3; Hee, Hubler interview, 9; Jackson, Hulett interview, 3.
19. Davis, Hubler interview, 14–15; Huemer, "Thumbnail Sketches," 39; Cutting, Finch and Rosenkrantz interview, 18; Milt Kahl, interview by Bob Thomas, May 14, 1973, 19; Kahl, Hubler interview, 10, 7.
20. WD, "Mickey Mouse Presents," 259–60.

21. Cutting, Finch and Rosenkrantz interview, 19–20; Ollie Johnston, "Remembering Walt," 1986, 1; Huemer, "Thumbnail Sketches," 38.
22. Kimball, Finch and Rosenkrantz interview, 13; Davis, Hubler interview, 13–15; WD, quoted in Canemaker, *Raggedy Ann and Andy,* 45.
23. Sharpsteen, Peri interview, Apr. 26, 1974, 5; Thomas, Thomas interviews, May 17, 1973, 34–35, and May 10, 1973, 24; John Hench and Dick Irvine, interview by Richard Hubler, Sept. 24, 1968, 2; Cutting, Finch and Rosenkrantz interview, 1.
24. Kahl, Hubler interview, 8; Sharpsteen, Hubler interview, 35–36; Sharpsteen, Peri interview, Apr. 26, 1974, 4.
25. Kinney, *Walt Disney and Other Characters,* 152; Kimball, quoted in Hubler, "Walt Disney," 326; Johnston, Thomas interview, 18.
26. Martin/Miller interview, Reel 10, 17; Kahl, Hubler interview, 23; Kimball, Hubler interview, 32.
27. Thomas, Thomas interview, 11; Johnston, Thomas interview, 16; Cutting, Finch and Rosenkrantz interview, 7.
28. Jackson, Smith interview, 10; Jackson, Hulett interview, 2; Huemer, "Thumbnail Sketches," 37; Kimball, Finch and Rosenkrantz interview, 10; Sharpsteen, Smith and Watkin interview, 5.
29. Kimball, Hulett interview, 8; Johnston, Finch and Rosenkrantz interview, 49; Thomas, Thomas interview, 11–12; Kahl, Finch and Rosenkrantz interview, 5; Johnston, Canemaker interview, 3.
30. Kinney, *Walt Disney and Other Characters,* 9, 148; Johnston, Thomas interview, 1; Anderson, Thomas interview, 14–16.
31. Sharpsteen, Peri interview, Feb. 6, 1974, 22–23.
32. This section relies heavily on Sharpsteen's extensive battery of interviews at the Disney Archives, as well as the comments about him scattered throughout other archival records. The only published piece is David R. Smith, "Ben Sharpsteen: 33 Years with Disney," *Millimeter,* Apr. 1975, 38–40.
33. Smith, "Sharpsteen," 39–45; Culhane, *Talking Animals,* 161–62; Larson, Finch and Rosenkrantz interview, 20; Watkin, "Walt Disney," 270.
34. Sharpsteen, Peri interview, Feb. 6, 1974, 12–13, 11; Sharpsteen, interview by Mike Barrier, Sept. 1974, 19–20.
35. Sharpsteen: Smith interview, 16, 13; Peri interview, Apr. 24, 1974, 6–7; Barrier interview, 2–3, 4–5; Peri interview, Feb. 6, 1974, 4–6; quoted in Watkin, "Walt Disney," 282, 284; Peri interviews, Feb. 7, 1975, 6–8, and May 2, 1974, 1–3; Smith interview, Oct. 21, 1974, 8; Smith and Watkin interview, 4.
36. Smith, "Sharpsteen," 42.
37. Johnston interview; Cottrell interview.
38. Kinney, *Walt Disney and Other Characters,* 37.
39. Sharpsteen, Smith interview, 14; Sharpsteen, Barrier interview, 6; Kimball, Finch and Rosenkrantz interview, 8.
40. Culhane, *Talking Animals,* 162, 164–67, 196–97; Kinney, *Walt Disney and Other Characters,* 109; William Tytla, interview by George Sherman, May 13, 1968, 12.
41. Anderson, Thomas interview, 13–14; Kahl, Finch and Rosenkrantz interview, 6; Natwick, Smith interview, 1; Hubler, "Walt Disney," 327.
42. Hubler, "Walt Disney," 327; Watkin, "Walt Disney," 285.

43. Kimball, Hubler interview, 29–32.
44. Kimball, Finch and Rosenkrantz interview, 8–9.
45. Kinney, *Walt Disney and Other Characters,* 154; Hubler, "Walt Disney," 327; Sharpsteen, Peri interview, Feb. 6, 1974, 41.
46. Sharpsteen, Peri interview, Feb. 6, 1974, 41.
47. Ibid., 22–23.
48. Watkin, "Walt Disney," 286.
49. Sharpsteen, Hubler interview, 3–4.

11. Animation and Its Discontents

1. Holly Allen and Michael Denning, "The Cartoonists' Front," *South Atlantic Quarterly* (Winter 1993), 90–91, 96–97; Lary May, ed., *Recasting America: Culture and Politics in the Age of the Cold War* (Chicago, 1989), 129, 150; Larry Ceplair and Steven Englund, *The Inquisition in Hollywood: Politics in the Film Community, 1930–1960* (Garden City, N.Y., 1980), 216–17.
2. Kinney, *Walt Disney and Other Characters,* 137; Sharpsteen, Peri interview, Feb. 6, 1974, 22; Kimball, Hubler interview, 33–34; Kimball, Canemaker interview, 10–11.
3. Sharpsteen, Peri interview, Feb. 6, 1974, 20–22; Kimball, Finch and Rosenkrantz interview, 9; Culhane, *Talking Animals,* 185–86; Klein, "The Disney Studio in the 1930s," 18.
4. Culhane, *Talking Animals,* 141; Allen and Denning, "The Cartoonists' Front," 104–6; Hurtz, quoted in Maltin, *Of Mice and Magic,* 23.
5. Kimball, Hubler interview, 30; Larson, Hulett interview, 3; Johnston, Thomas interview, 12–13; Johnston interview.
6. Kinney, *Walt Disney and Other Characters,* 137; Mosely, *Disney's World,* 188–91; Allen and Denning, "Cartoonists' Front," 93. As Disney archivists point out, most movie credits before the 1950s were minimal compared to those of today.
7. Hollywood *Daily Variety,* Feb. 4, 1941, Disney strike file, DA.
8. Allen and Denning, "The Cartoonists' Front," 89–118; Carol Cook, unpublished seminar paper, 1–27, DA.
9. For general descriptions of the strike, see Allen and Denning, "The Cartoonists' Front," 97–98; Thomas, *Walt Disney,* 168–69; Kinney, *Walt Disney and Other Characters,* 137–38.
10. Herbert Sorrell, testimony on March 3 and 4, 1948, *Hearings Before Special Subcommittee, 80th Congress* (Washington, D.C., 1948), Vol. 3, 1907–8; Arthur Babbitt, tape recording of 1978 ASIFA meeting, DA.
11. Johnston interview; Jack Hannah, interview by David R. Smith, July 8, 1975, note to p. 29; Kinney, *Walt Disney and Other Characters,* 137–38.
12. Sorrell, House testimony, 1908; "Police Quell Fistic Battle of Disney Labor Factions," Hollywood *Citizen News,* July 1941, Disney strike file, DA.
13. In Disney strike file, DA: *The Animator: Bulletin of the Screen Cartoon Guild,* March and May 1941; "The Artists at the Walt Disney Studio Are Out on Strike," late May 1941?; "Help Us Put a Union Button on Mickey Mouse," early June 1941?; "Why We Are on Strike," June 2, 1941; "This Is Your Fight," early July 1941?; SCG broadside, untitled, July 21, 1941.
14. SCG broadside, July 28, 1941, Disney strike file, DA.

15. Committee of Twenty-One, "Exposé No. 1," Disney strike file, DA.
16. Committee of Twenty-One, "Exposé No. 2" and untitled exposé, Disney strike file, DA.
17. Sorrell, House testimony, 1875–76, 1905, 1906, 1917.
18. Allen and Denning, "The Cartoonists' Front," 101–2; John Canemaker, "David Hilberman," *Cartoonist Profiles* 48, Dec. 1980, 18; Culhane, *Talking Animals,* 225–26.
19. Sharpsteen, Peri interview, Feb. 6, 1974, 23; Sharpsteen, Smith interview, 8–9; Roy Williams, interview by Don Peri, *Funnyworld* (1977), 35; Davis, Thomas interview, 13; Dick Huemer, interview in *Funnyworld* (1977), 39; Roy Disney, Hubler interview, 13–14.
20. In Disney strike file, DA: ad in *Variety,* July 3, 1941; "To All Disney Artists," July 9, 1941; "Technicolor Will Not Process Disney Film," July 11, 1941; "Disney Rejects Federal Mediation Offer with Blast at Labor Board," July 18, 1941.
21. In Disney strike file, DA: "AF of L Quits Disney Strike," *Variety,* July 9, 1941; "Nine AFL Unions Report to Disney," *Box Office,* July 12, 1941; W. R. Wilkinson, "Trade Views," *Hollywood Reporter,* July 7, 1941.
22. In Disney strike file, DA: "Disney Strike Spread Threat," *Variety,* May 28, 1941; "Walt Disney Cartoonists Strike in Bargaining Dispute," Los Angeles *Times,* May 29, 1941; "Disney Strikers Picket 'Dragon,'" Hollywood *Reporter,* July 7, 1941; "U.S. Enters Disney Walkout, Willie Bioff Shoved Out of Picture," *Variety,* July 7, 1941; "Bioff Botches, Cartoonists Like Disney Terms, But Ban Willie As Boss," *Screen Actor,* July 9, 1941; "Disney Strike Offer Spurned," Los Angeles *Examiner,* July 3, 1941; "Police Quell Fistic Battle."
23. Charles Glen, "Exploding Some Myths about Mr. Walt Disney," *Daily Worker,* Feb. 17, 1941, 7; "Labor Fantasia," *Business Week,* May 17, 1941, 48–50; "Disney Developments," *Business Week,* June 14, 1941, 46; Anthony Bower, "Snow White and the 1,200 Dwarfs," *Nation,* May 10, 1941, 565; "Speaking of Disney," *Art Digest,* Mar. 1, 1941, 3; Philip T. Hartung, "The Screen: Stars, Strikes, and Dragons," *Commonweal,* Aug. 8, 1941, 377.
24. Tape recording of 1978 ASIFA meeting, DA.
25. On Babbitt's life and career, see John Canemaker, "Art Babbitt: The Animator as Firebrand," *Millimeter,* Sept. 1975, 9–10; John Canemaker, "Art Babbitt," *Cartoonist Profiles,* Dec. 1979, 8–13; Klaus Strzyz, "Art Babbitt Interview," *Comics Journal,* Mar. 1988, 77–87; Joseph McBride, "Animator Arthur Babbitt, 85, Dies," *Variety,* Mar. 6, 1992, 8.
26. Strzyz, "Babbitt," 77–78; Canemaker, "Firebrand," 11, 42–43; Richard Williams, "Character Analysis of the Animator — January 1974," *Sight and Sound* (Spring 1974), 95; Huemer, "Thumbnail Sketches," 42.
27. Canemaker, "Art Babbitt," 9–10; Art Babbitt, "Character Analysis of the Goof — June 1934," *Sight and Sound* (Spring 1974), 94–95.
28. Art Babbitt, "Fairest of Them All," n.d., 38–39, Babbitt file, DA.
29. Canemaker, "Firebrand," 42; Strzyz, "Art Babbitt," 78.
30. Canemaker, "Firebrand," 10, 42; I. Klein, "Walt Disney and the Golden Years," *Funnyworld* (1983), 48.
31. Canemaker, "Firebrand," 42, 43, 11.
32. Babbitt, Canemaker interview, 1–2; "Animator Arthur Babbitt," 8; Watkin, "Walt Disney," 443.

33. Strzyz, "Babbitt," 78.
34. Babbitt, Smith interview, 1; Strzyz, "Babbitt," 78.
35. "Disneyites Elect Officers," *The Animator: Bulletin of the Screen Cartoon Guild,* Mar. 1941, 1; Strzyz, "Babbitt," 78–79; 1978 ASIFA tape.
36. Strzyz, "Babbitt," 79–80.
37. Ibid., 81; 1978 ASIFA tape.
38. Strzyz, "Babbitt," 80, 81–82; "Animator Arthur Babbitt," 8.
39. Strzyz, "Babbitt," 82–85; Canemaker, "Firebrand," 43–44; Kinney, *Walt Disney and Other Characters,* 139; "Animator Arthur Babbitt," 8.
40. Strzyz, "Babbitt," 81–82.
41. WD to Roy Disney and Ubbe Iwerks, Sept. 20, 1928; Culhane, *Talking Animals,* 186–87.
42. "Walt Disney's Speech to His Staff," transcript, Feb. 10–11, 1941, 1, 2.
43. Ibid., 1, 2–3, 8–9.
44. Ibid., 10–11, 9, 3–8, 22–24.
45. Ibid., 19–20, 16, 18–19.
46. Ibid., 24–26.
47. WD, speech to staff, May 27, 1941, transcript, 1; Walter P. Spreckels, open letter to Disney Studio employees, May 5, 1941, Disney strike folder, DA.
48. Johnston, Thomas interview, 20; Davis, Thomas interview, 12; Kinney, *Walt Disney and Other Characters,* 137.
49. Kimball, quoted in Mosely, *Disney's World,* 186–87; Culhane, *Talking Animals,* 186–87, 224–25; Thomas, Thomas interview, 25; Kimball, 1978 ASIFA tape.
50. WD, "To My Employees on Strike," July 2, 1941, Disney strike file, DA.
51. In Disney strike file, DA: "Disney Strikers Back Today," *Variety,* July 29, 1941; "Disney Strike Ends as Gov't Mediator Sends Men to Work," Hollywood *Reporter,* July 29, 1941; "U.S. Steps Back into Cartoonist Arbitration," *Variety,* Aug. 13, 1941; "Disney Studio Closed for Two Weeks in Layoff Beef," *Variety,* Aug. 18, 1941; "Disney Shutdown to Be Continued," Los Angeles *Examiner,* Aug. 28, 1941; "Disney Rehiring Formula Drawn," Los Angeles *Times,* Sept. 10, 1941; "Work Resumed at Disney Plant," Hollywood *Citizen News,* Sept. 15, 1941; "Walt Disney Studios Resume Production," Los Angeles *Times,* Sept. 15, 1941.
52. WD to Westbrook Pegler, Aug. 11, 1941, 1–3.
53. Ibid.
54. Davis, Thomas interview, 12; Thomas, Thomas interview, 25–26. See also Johnston, Thomas interview, 21–23, 13; Ham Luske, 1956 interview, notes, 2.
55. Martin/Miller interview, Reel 7, 46, 32–34, 36, 40, 45; Kinney, *Walt Disney and Other Characters,* 139; Culhane, *Talking Animals,* 236.
56. "Letter to the Editor," Los Angeles *Times,* Sept. 11, 1941, Disney strike file, DA.
57. Martin/Miller interview, Reel 7, 46.

12. Disney and the Good War

1. Martin/Miller interview, Reel 7, 47–48.
2. Carl Nater, transcript of comments recorded for David Smith, Oct. 7, 1972, 5; Sharpsteen, Peri interview, Feb. 6, 1974, 29; Carl Nater, "Walt Disney Studio — A War Plant," *Journal of the Society of Motion Picture Engineers,* Mar. 1944, 171, 173.
3. For a complete listing of Disney-produced training films, see Richard Shale,

Donald Duck Joins Up: The Walt Disney Studio During World War II (Ann Arbor, Mich.: UMI Research Press, 1982), 163–70. See also Nater transcript, 3.

4. Shale, *Donald Duck Joins Up,* 21–26, 51–61; Martin/Miller interview, Reel 8, 9.

5. Shale, *Donald Duck Joins Up,* 89–96.

6. Ibid., 61–65.

7. Martin/Miller interview, Reel 7, 51–52, 54–56; Wilfred Jackson, "Letter on 'The New Spirit,'" *Funnyworld* (Fall 1978), 4–5; WD to Sheridan Downey, Mar. 19, 1942; Dick Huemer, "The Battle of Washington," *Funnyworld* (Spring 1981), 22–23.

8. Shale, *Donald Duck Joins Up,* 27–28; Marcia Blitz, *Donald Duck* (New York, 1979), 125–26; Eric Smoodin, *Animating Culture: Hollywood Cartoons from the Sound Era* (New Brunswick, N.J., 1993), 172–74; "Teacher Disney," *Time,* Aug. 17, 1942, 49; "The New Spirit: Disney's Tax Film," *Life,* Mar. 16, 1942, 48–50; "D. Duck Joins Up," *New York Times Magazine,* Feb. 22, 1942, 20–21; J. P. McEvoy, "Disney Goes to War," *This Week Magazine,* July 5, 1942, 8–10.

9. Johnston, Thomas interview, 24; Bill Anderson, interview by Bob Thomas, May 17, 1973, 1–2; Lou Debney, interview by David R. Smith, Dec. 4, 1975, 11, 15; Kinney, *Walt Disney and Other Characters,* 140.

10. Kimball, Shale interview, 4; Erwin Verity, interview by Rick Shale and Dave Smith, Jan. 19, 1976, 18; Nater transcript, 10; Debney, Smith interview, 2.

11. *Dispatch from Disney,* 1943, and call sheets for Disney camp show, Nov. 2, 1944, and Jan. 11, 1945, World War II Miscellany file, DA.

12. "Mickey Mouse and Donald Duck Work for Victory," *Popular Science Monthly,* Sept. 1942, 98–99; "Walt Disney Goes to War," *Life,* Aug. 31, 1942, 61–69; "New Disney Film Shows How Nazis Educate Youth in Brutality," *PM's Daily Picture Magazine,* Nov. 8, 1942, 8–9. On Disney's wartime productions, see also J. P. McEvoy, "Of Mouse and Man," *Reader's Digest,* Oct. 1942, 85–88; "Disney's Troupe Goes to War," *New York Times Magazine,* Nov. 5, 1942, 20–21; and clippings in PS S29, DA.

13. Thornton Delehanty, "The Disney Studio at War," *Theatre Arts,* Jan. 1943, 31; McEvoy, "Disney Goes to War," 8.

14. WD to Leo Samuels, May 4, 1942, DA.

15. Shale, *Donald Duck Joins Up,* 71–74; Maltin, *The Disney Films,* 61–63; Audience Research Institute report, Sept. 2, 1942.

16. Verity, Shale and Smith interview, 1; Hee, Hubler interview, July 2, 1968, 37; Kinney, *Walt Disney and Other Characters,* 141. On Seversky's achievements and personality, see John Gunther, *Taken at the Flood* (New York, 1960), 281–86, and Betsy Luce, "Walt Disney's Highest Flier," New York *Post,* July 7, 1943.

17. WD, transcript of interview by "March of Time," 1943; WD and Alexander P. de Seversky, "A Joint Statement About the Motion Picture 'Victory Through Air Power,'" New York *Herald Tribune,* July 29, 1943; WD to Upton Close, July 9, 1943; WD to H. Alice Howell, May 11, 1943; Martin/Miller interview, Reel 29, 29–33.

18. Thomas, *Walt Disney,* 186; Carl Nater, 1968 memo to Marty Sklar, 2.

19. "'Victory Through Air Power' Misses Bus," *Daily Worker,* July 21, 1943; James Agee, "Films," *Nation,* July 17, 1943, 82; "Air Power Film Lacks Power," *PM,* July 19, 1943; Waverley Root, "Raps Film Version of 'Victory Through Air Power,'" Boston *Daily Globe,* July 21, 1943; George E. Sokolsky, "These Days," New York *Sun,* July 22, 1943.

20. Walter Wanger, "Mickey Icarus, 1943: Fusing Ideas with the Art of the Animated

Cartoon," *Saturday Review of Literature*, Sept. 4, 1943, 18–19; "Air Power on the Screen," New York *Times*, July 26, 1943; "New Films in Review," *Cue*, July 17, 1943; "Reviews," *Motion Picture Daily*, July 7, 1943; Lee Mortimer, "'Air Power' Disney's Greatest Film," New York *Mirror*, July 19, 1943. See also "Victory Through Air Power," *Christian Science Monitor*, July 19, 1943; "Serious Disney," *Wall Street Journal*, July 20, 1943.

21. Kate Cameron, "Victory by Air Power On Screen at Globe," New York *News*, July 18, 1943; Archer Winsten, "Movie Talk," New York *Post*, July 19, 1943; "Victory Through Air Power," *Life*, July 19, 1943; Howard Barnes, "On the Screen," New York *Herald Tribune*, July 19, 1943. See also Thomas Pryor, "The Screen," New York *Times*, July 19, 1943; "Sascha's Show," *Time*, July 12, 1943.

22. WD, introduction to untitled manual on technical procedures, World War II Miscellany file, DA; WD to employees, *Dispatch from Disney's*, n.p.

23. Martin/Miller interview, Reel 7, 48–49, 58–59, Reel 8, 17–18, 14–15, 10; Nater transcript, 1, 12; Sharpsteen, Peri interview, Apr. 26, 1974, 12–13.

24. Martin/Miller interview, Reel 9, 26–27.

25. David Culbert, "'A Quick, Delightful Gink': Eric Knight at the Walt Disney Studio," *Funnyworld* (Fall 1978), 15–16; Nater transcript, 4; Johnston, Green interview, 26.

26. Bill Anderson, Thomas interview, 3–4.

27. A brief explanation of Disney's support for Goldwyn appears in WD's FBI file; see A. Rosen, "Office Memorandum to the Director," Nov. 4, 1944, and WD's telegram in report no. SU 60-86, Oct. 19, 1944, 1–4.

28. Frank Nugent, "That Million Dollar Mouse," *New York Times Magazine*, Sept. 21, 1947, 61; Martin/Miller interview, Reel 7, 7–9.

29. "Memorandum for the Director," WD's FBI file, June 8, 1944; MPA's "Statement of Principles," Motion Picture Alliance file, Margaret Herrick Library, Motion Picture Academy of Arts and Sciences; Lillian Ross, "Come In, Lassie!" *New Yorker*, Feb. 21, 1948, 32; Nancy Lynn Schwartz, *The Hollywood Writers' War* (New York, 1982), 204–11.

30. Hon. Robert R. Reynolds, "Our Own First," *Congressional Record, Appendix* [Mar. 7, 1944], A1120; Schwartz, *Hollywood Writers' War*, 208–11, 221, 233, 243, 250–51, 253–68; Ceplair and Englund, *Inquisition in Hollywood*, 209–15, 258–61.

31. Ayn Rand, "Screen Guide for Americans," MPA (Beverly Hills, Calif., 1948), 1–12.

32. U.S. House of Representatives, Committee on Un-American Activities, *Hearings Regarding the Communist Infiltration of the Motion Picture Industry*, 80th Cong. 1st Sess., Oct. 20–24 and 27–30, 1947, 280–86.

33. William Graebner, *The Age of Doubt: American Thought and Culture in the 1940s* (Boston, 1991). See also May, *Recasting America*, 1–13, and David Noble, *The End of American History: Democracy, Capitalism, and the Metaphor of Two Worlds in Anglo-American Historical Writing, 1880–1980* (Minneapolis, 1985), 8.

13. Disney's Descent

1. Barbara Deming, "The Artlessness of Walt Disney," *Partisan Review* (Spring 1945), 226–31.

2. Thomas, *Walt Disney*, 171–74; Shale, *Donald Duck Joins Up*, 41–44; press release, n.d., South American Stories file, DA.

3. Thomas, Thomas interview, 29–31; Ken Anderson, Thomas interview, 24–26.

4. WD, draft of an article for Dec. 1941 *Variety,* South American Stories file, DA.

5. Maltin, *The Disney Films,* 57–59; Shale, *Donald Duck Joins Up,* 44–47.

6. Gilbert Seldes, "Eight 21-Gun Salutes," *Esquire,* Apr. 1943; James Agee, "Films," *Nation,* Feb. 20, 1943; John T. McManus, "'Saludos' Is Disney Plus," *PM,* Feb. 14, 1943. See also PS S29 for many clippings on the production of *Saludos Amigos.*

7. Theodore Strauss, "Donald Duck's Disney," New York *Times,* Feb. 7, 1943; Howard Barnes, "Saludos Amigos," New York *Herald Tribune,* Feb. 21, 1943; WD, transcript of radio show, Dec. 12, 1942. See also Leo Mishkin, "New Disney Film S.A. Policy Boon," Brooklyn *Eagle,* Feb. 13, 1943; "Yanqui Donald Duck," *Newsweek,* Jan. 25, 1943; "Disney's Ambassador Duck," *Pan American,* Jan. 1943.

8. WD, transcript, World Broadcasting System, 1943; untitled ms., n.d., South American Stories-Personnel file, DA.

9. Maltin, *Disney Films,* 65–67; Shale, *Donald Duck Joins Up,* 99–106.

10. "How Disney Combines Living Actors with His Cartoon Characters," *Popular Science,* Sept. 1944, 106–11; "Donald Duck and Pals Now Making Love to Real, Live Actresses," San Francisco *News,* Nov. 4, 1944; "Donald Duck Mingles with Real People," Washington *Star,* Oct. 8, 1944; Harold V. Cohen, "The New Film," Pittsburgh *Post-Gazette,* May 4, 1945. Other favorable reviews include "Donald Duck, Revolutionista!" *Cue,* Jan. 6, 1945; Edwin Schallert, "Disney Magic Expands in 'Three Caballeros,'" Los Angeles *Times,* Mar. 22, 1945; John T. McManus, "The Three Caballeros," *PM,* Feb. 5, 1945.

11. Bosley Crowther, "Dizzy Disney," New York *Times,* Feb. 11, 1945; Gilbert Kanour, "For Film Fans," Baltimore *Evening Sun,* Feb. 26, 1945. Other critical reviews include Otis L. Guernsey, "On the Screen," New York *Herald Tribune,* Feb. 5, 1945; David Platt, "'The Three Caballeros' Is Short on Content, Long on Technique," *Daily Worker,* Feb. 7, 1945; Eileen Creelman, "'The Three Caballeros,' a Disappointing Walt Disney Cartoon Feature," New York *Sun,* Feb. 5, 1945.

12. Elise Finn, "'The Three Caballeros' Is Bright, Gaudy, Gay," Philadelphia *Record,* June 3, 1945; W. G., "What Hath Walt Wrought," *New Yorker,* Feb. 10, 1945, 36; Lesley Blanch, "Flesh or Fantasy? Walt Disney's New Picture Proves That These Two Don't Mix," *News Leader,* June 16, 1945.

13. Sharpsteen, Peri interview, Feb. 6, 1974, 30.

14. *Make Mine Music* has never been rereleased commercially in its entirety. Along with the other package films from this era, it was raided for segments aired on Disney television shows in the 1950s and 1960s.

15. Film historian Robin Allan, in "Make Mine Music, or the Forgotten Years at Disney," *Animator* (Spring 1978), 28–32, and "Time for Melody: A Reappraisal of 'Melody Time,'" *Animator* (Spring 1990), 9–13, argues that Disney should be given more credit for his courageous experimentation with new forms and styles in the late 1940s.

16. Archer Winsten, "Disney's 'Make Mine Music' Is Ten Separate Shorts," New York *Post,* Apr. 21, 1946; John Maynard, "'Make Mine Music' Opens at the Globe," New York *Journal American,* Apr. 22, 1946; Bosley Crowther, "Making Music," New York *Times,* Apr. 28, 1946. See PS M1 for many more reviews.

17. See "Disney with No Improvements," *New Yorker,* Oct. 4, 1947; "More Fancy Than Fun," *Newsweek,* Oct. 13, 1947; "Fun and Fancy Free," *Cue,* Sept. 27, 1947.

See PS F1 for many more reviews. Negative reviews of *Melody Time* can be found in PS M38 and of *The Adventures of Ichabod and Mr. Toad* in PS I1.

18. D. Mosdell, "Film Review," *Canadian Forum*, Dec. 1949, 206; Gilbert Seldes, *The Great Audience* (New York, 1950), 283–84.

19. Manny Farber, "Make Mine Muzak," *New Republic*, May 27, 1946, 769; Mosdell, "Film Review," 206.

20. James Agee, *Agee on Film* (New York, 1958), vol. 1, 18, 404–10; Hermine Rich Isaacs, "The Films in Review," *Theatre Arts*, June 1946, 343–45. For a similarly devastating review, see John Mason Brown, "Mr. Disney's Caballeros," *Saturday Review*, Feb. 24, 1945, 22–24.

21. For general information on Donald Duck, see Marcia Blitz, *Donald Duck* (New York, 1979); *Walt Disney's Donald Duck: 50 Years of Happy Frustration* (Tucson, 1984); and John Grant, *Encyclopedia of Walt Disney's Animated Characters* (New York, 1993), 61–71.

22. Helen G. Thompson, "Wanna Fight?" *Stage*, July 1935, 21; Gilbert Seldes, quoted in Jim Korkis, "A Brief Look at the Films of Donald Duck," *Blast/Commicollector*, Sept. 1979, 26; J. P. McEvoy, "Ya Wanna Fight?" *Country Gentleman*, July 1937, 20.

23. "Character Analysis of Donald Duck," Story Department Reference Material, June 20, 1939, 1–2.

24. Ibid.

25. Tony Hiss and David McClelland, "The Quack and Disney," *New Yorker*, Dec. 29, 1975, 33–43; Martin/Miller interview, Reel 7, 67–69.

26. *Walt Disney's Donald Duck*, 14; Grant, *Encyclopedia*, 63–66; Korkis, "Brief Look at Donald Duck," 27–28; Mike Barrier, "Screenwriter for a Duck: Carl Barks at the Disney Studio," *Funnyworld* (Fall 1979), 9–14.

27. Hess and McClelland, "The Quack and Disney," 40; Martin/Miller interview, Reel 7, 69; WD to Everett W. Harding, August 12, 1942.

28. For a complete filmography, see Blitz, *Donald Duck*, 230–50.

29. "Starring Snow White and the Seven Dwarfs," *Family Guide*, Feb. 2, 1938; "Speaking of Pictures . . . Disney's Donald Duck Poses for the Old Masters," *Life*, Apr. 16, 1945; ad, Portsmouth, Va., *Star*, Mar. 10, 1940; Harriet Van Horne, "Donald Duck Reports on the State of the Nation," New York *World Telegram*, Sept. 10, 1947; Jack Gould, "Prognostic Fantasy," New York *Times*, Sept. 14, 1947; *Walt Disney's Donald Duck*, 84–86, 90.

30. Hannah, quoted in Korkis, "Brief Look at the Films of Donald Duck," 26–27. See also Sharpsteen, Smith interview, 11–12; Hannah, Smith interview, 20–21.

31. Nugent, "That Million Dollar Mouse," 61.

32. John Stanley, "Introducing D. Duck — Fighting Professor," Toledo, Ohio, *Times*, Oct. 20, 1937; McEvoy, "Ya Wanna Fight?" 20, 72.

33. Feild, *Art of Walt Disney*, 41.

34. *Cue*, Aug. 14, 1937; Warren Susman, *Culture as History: The Transformation of American Society in the Twentieth Century* (New York, 1984), 200–201.

35. C.L.R. James, *American Civilization* (Cambridge, Mass., 1993).

36. Lewis Jacobs, *The Rise of the American Film: A Critical History* (New York, 1939), 499; Lloyd Morris, *Not So Long Ago* (New York, 1949), 208–9.

37. Shale, *Donald Duck Gets Drafted*, 90–95. See also Kate Holliday, "Donald Duck Goes to War," *Coronet*, Sept. 1942.

38. Emily S. Rosenberg, *Spreading the American Dream: American Economic and Cultural Expansion, 1890–1945* (New York, 1982), 202–28. Ariel Dorfman and Armand Mattelart, in *How to Read Donald Duck: Imperialist Ideology in the Disney Comic* (New York, 1975), offer a stinging critique of Donald Duck as a purveyor of cultural imperialism.

39. Walt Disney Productions Annual Report, 1949, 2–3; WD to Dorothy Ann Blank, June 27, 1941. See also "Mickey on Wall Street," New York *Times*, Mar. 17, 1940.

40. "Stuffed Duck?" *Time*, Aug. 12, 1946, 86; WD, studio memorandum, Jan. 1, 1947, to Sept. 30, 1948, in Kinney, *Walt Disney and Other Characters*, 144–45. See also "But Is It Art?" *Business Week*, Feb. 10, 1945, 72–76; "The Mighty Mouse," *Time*, Oct. 25, 1948, 96–98.

41. Walt Disney Productions Annual Report, 1941, 7. See also annual reports for FY 1940, 1942, 1943, and 1944, and Walt Disney Productions Annual Report for Employees for FY 1944.

42. Ibid., 1945, 5; 1946, 9; 1947, 1.

43. Ibid., 1949, 2–3, 4.

44. Shale, *Donald Duck Joins Up*, 111–12, 157; Nater transcript, 14–15.

45. "Walt Disney, Great Teacher," *Fortune*, Aug. 1942, 95; "Walt Disney, Teacher of Tomorrow," *Look*, Apr. 17, 1945, 24. See also "Teacher Disney," *Time*, Aug. 17, 1942, 49–50; Thomas M. Pryor, "Disney the Teacher," New York *Times*, Aug. 4, 1943.

46. WD, "Motion Pictures as Medium for Rehabilitation," Philadelphia *Inquirer*, Feb. 11, 1945, 1, 9; WD, "Mickey as Professor," *Public Opinion Quarterly* (Summer 1945), 119–25; Nater transcript, 17–19.

47. Roy Disney, Hubler interview, 33; Johnston, Thomas interview, 17; Thomas, Thomas interview, 26–27.

14. The Search for Direction

1. Thomas, Thomas interview, 22, 36; Davis, Hubler interview, 1–2; Hee, Hubler interview, 38.

2. Kinney, *Walt Disney and Other Characters*, 156; Hee, Hubler interview, 16–17.

3. Martin/Miller interview, Reel 8, 20–21, Reel 9, 23, 36–37, 40, 44, 41–42.

4. Johnston, Thomas interview, 1–2; WD, quoted in "The Story of Walt Disney's Private Collection," *Small Talk*, Feb. 1978, 8; Bosley Crowther, "The Dream Merchant," New York *Times*, Dec. 16, 1966, 40. On Disney's miniature railroading, see also WD, "I Have Always Loved Trains," *Railroad*, Oct. 1965, 16; Roger Broggie, "Walt Disney's Carolwood-Pacific Railroad," *Miniature Locomotive*, May–June 1952, 14–16.

5. WD, "The Story of Mickey Mouse," transcript, 1–5.

6. Ward Kimball, "The Wonderful World of Walt Disney," in Wagner, *You Must Remember This*, 272; Kimball, Hubler interview, 39–40.

7. Kimball, Hubler interview, 40–42.

8. Ibid., 40–43. See also "An Interview with Ward Kimball," *Storyboard: The Journal of Animation Art*, Oct./Nov. 1991, 6–19, 34. Leonard Mosely, *Disney's World*, 216–17, discusses the 1948 train trip based on his own interviews with Ward Kimball.

9. Thomas and Johnston, *Disney Animation*, 159–68; Frank Thomas and Ollie

Johnston, *The Disney Villain* (New York, 1993), 105; John Culhane, "The Last of the Nine Old Men," *American Film*, June 1977, 10–16.

10. Thomas and Johnston, *Disney Animation*, 168–77; Culhane, "Last of the Nine Old Men," 10–16.

11. Kinney, *Walt Disney and Other Characters*, 146; Culhane, *Talking Animals*, 244.

12. Kimball, Finch and Rosenkrantz interview, 7–8; Sharpsteen, Barrier interview, 18; Ward Kimball, interview by Klaus Strzyz, *Comics Journal*, Mar. 1988, 96; Kimball, "Wonderful World of Disney," 269; Kimball, Green interview, 1.

13. Ross Care, "Ward Kimball: Animated Versatility," *Millimeter*, July/August 1976, 18–22, 62–65; Kimball, "Wonderful World of Disney," 264–65; Kimball, Strzyz interview, 89–91; John Canemaker, "Ward Kimball," 1973, 1–3.

14. "Interview with Ward Kimball," 18; Johnston interview.

15. Kimball, Shale interview, 5, 27–28, 34; Kimball, Strzyz interview, 90–94; Care, "Kimball," 22, 62–65.

16. Cottrell interview; Klein, "The Disney Studio in the 1930s," 15.

17. Sharpsteen, Barrier interview, 17–18; David Iwerks interview; Davis interview; Ward Kimball, *Art Afterpieces* (New York, 1964).

18. Kimball, Shale interview, 32, 28; David R. Smith, quoted in Canemaker, "Kimball," 3.

19. WD, quoted in Diane Disney Miller, *The Story of Walt Disney* (New York, 1956), 173; Thomas, Thomas interview, 16; David Iwerks interview; Kimball, "Wonderful World of Disney," 264, 280.

20. Kimball, Finch and Rosenkrantz interview, 13, 15; Canemaker, "Kimball," 8; Kimball, "Wonderful World of Disney," 275, 271, 281.

21. Kimball, "Wonderful World of Disney," 268; Kimball, Hubler interview, 27–28, 36.

22. Kimball, "Wonderful World of Disney," 278, 270; Kimball, Hubler interview, 24–25, 41, 9–13.

23. Kimball, Hubler interview, 15, 35–36, 19.

24. Ibid., 40–43.

25. Kimball, quoted in Mosely, *Disney's World*, 218; Kimball, "Wonderful World of Disney," 282.

26. WD, "Walt Disney Realizes an Ancient Dream," New York *Herald Tribune*, Jan. 12, 1947; "Disney Fulfills an Ambition," publicity release, PS S22; WD, radio interview by Henry Dupree, 1946, DA; WD, radio interview by Paul Hochuli, 1946, DA.

27. Maltin, *The Disney Films*, 73–78.

28. Latimer Watson, "'Song of the South' Is Pleasant Picture, But Not a Great One," Columbus, Ga., *Ledger*, Nov. 21, 1946. Favorable reviews can be found in PS S21.

29. Peggy Doyle, "Live Actors Spoil This Disney Film," Boston *Evening American*, Dec. 23, 1946; "Disney's 'Song of the South' Opens at Aldine Theater," Philadelphia *Inquirer*, Dec. 26, 1946; Claude La Belle, "A Sorrowful Letter to Mr. Walt Disney," San Francisco *News*, Jan. 10, 1947; Tom Donnelly, "Massa Disney's Spading Cold, Cold Ground," Washington *Daily News*, Dec. 25, 1946; "Song of the South," Philadelphia *News*, Dec. 26, 1946. Many more negative reviews can be found in PS S21.

30. Richard B. Dier, "'Song of the South' Called White Supremacy Propaganda," *Afro-American*, Nov. 30, 1946; Tanneyhill, quoted in Betty Moorsteen, "'Song of

the South' Assailed for Racial Stereotyping," *PM*, Nov. 28, 1946; Leon Hardwick, "Hollywood Broadcast," Los Angeles *Sentinel*, Aug. 24, 1944; Fredi Washington, "Fredi Says," *People's Voice*, Nov. 30, 1946; "Why We Picket," National Negro Congress flyer, PS S21.

31. "The New Pictures," *Time*, Nov. 18, 1946; John McCarten, "Song of the South," *New Yorker*, Nov. 30, 1946; Albert Deutsch, "How Jim Crow Picks the Pocket of Impoverished Southland," *PM*, Nov. 29, 1946; Virginia Wright, "Song of the South," Los Angeles *Daily News*, Jan. 31, 1947; Phineas J. Biron, "Strictly Confidential," Los Angeles *B'nai B'rith Messenger*, Jan. 3, 1947.

32. "White Regrets Film," New York *Times*, Nov. 28, 1946; "Parents Magazine Rapped for Award to 'Song of South' Pic," *Afro-American*, Jan. 18, 1947; "Rep. Powell Asks N.Y. City to Ban 'Song of the South,'" California *Eagle*, Jan. 9, 1947; "'Song of the South' Picketed," New York *Times*, Dec. 14, 1946; "Brooklyn Movie Chain Ban Sought on 'Song of South,'" *Afro-American*, Feb. 8, 1947; "Theater Pickets," San Francisco *People's World*, Feb. 1, 1947.

33. "Alleged Communist Inspired Pickets Haunt 'Uncle Remus,'" Los Angeles *Criterion*, Feb. 10, 1947; Arthur T. Sullivan, letter to the editor, Washington *Post*, Jan. 8, 1947; Nina C. Kyle, letter to the editor, Palo Alto *Times*, April 8, 1947; Herman Hill, "Baskett Looms as Hit in New Disney Picture," Pittsburgh *Courier*, Nov. 9, 1946; George S. Schuyler, "Views and Reviews," Pittsburgh *Courier*, Feb. 22, 1947; "Walt Disney Presents 'Song of the South,'" *Sepia Hollywood*, Dec. 1946; James Baskett, quoted in Los Angeles *Criterion*, Feb. 10, 1947. Southern defenses of the film include "Dixie Reviewers Have Praise for 'Song of the South,'" Atlanta *Journal*, Nov. 13, 1946; "Silly Censorship," Atlanta *Journal*, Dec. 30, 1946; "'Song of South,' Disney Film, Is Rated Super," Birmingham *News*, Oct. 31, 1946. See PS S21 for many more such articles.

34. Moorsteen, "'Song of the South' Assailed"; Mary Goodrich, reports, Uncle Remus Story Research Folder, DA: "Research Memorandum," Apr. 8, 1938; "Negro Speech Rhythms," Nov. 30, 1939; Story research report, Mar. 1, 1940; "Negro Superstitions," May 27, 1940.

35. In Uncle Remus Story Research Folder, DA: Maurice Rapf, "Notes on Uncle Remus," n.d.; Joseph I. Breen to WD, Aug. 1, 1944; Francis S. Harmon, memo on Uncle Remus script, July 31, 1944.

36. Dick Creedon, "Remus Outline," June 21, 1940; Goodrich, Story research report, Uncle Remus Story Research Folder, DA; Kimball, quoted in Maltin, *Disney Films*, 52.

37. WD to Roy Disney and Ubbe Iwerks, Sept. 14, 1928; WD to C. W. May, Apr. 19, 1945; WD to Jean Hersholt, Jan. 30, 1948.

38. Billy Rose, "Pitching Horseshoes," *PM*, Dec. 17, 1946. See also Bosley Crowther, "Spanking Disney," New York *Times*, Dec. 8, 1946.

15. Cold War Fantasies

1. Lillian Disney, "I Live with a Genius," *McCall's*, Feb. 1953, 38–41.

2. Karal Ann Marling, *As Seen on TV: The Visual Culture of Everyday Life in the 1950s* (Cambridge, Mass., 1994), 249.

3. On the HUAC hearings and the red scare, see Ceplair and Englund, *Inquisition*

in Hollywood, 254–98; Schwartz, *The Hollywood Writers' War*, 266–69; and May, *Recasting America*, 143–48.

4. U.S. House of Representatives, *Hearings Regarding the Communist Infiltration of the Motion Picture Industry*, 280–86.

5. Lillian Disney, "I Live with a Genius," 42.

6. W. Ward Marsh, "'Cinderella' Is Made Rare Screen Delight," Cleveland *Plain Dealer*, Mar. 30, 1950; Helen Eager, "Walt Disney's 'Cinderella' Enchanting New Film," Boston *Traveler*, Feb. 10, 1950. For a host of favorable reviews, see PS C1.

7. See Maltin, *The Disney Films*, 101–4, 107–10, 124–28, 152–57.

8. Ibid., 97–180.

9. On the politics of anticommunism, see Richard M. Fried, *Nightmare in Red: The McCarthy Era in Perspective* (New York, 1990).

10. Among a vast literature, see Stephen J. Whitfield, *The Culture of the Cold War* (Baltimore, 1991); Richard H. Pells, *The Liberal Mind in a Conservative Age: American Intellectuals in the 1940s & 1950s* (New York, 1985), 96–107, 130–162.

11. See Peter Biskin, *Seeing Is Believing: How Hollywood Taught Us to Stop Worrying and Love the Fifties* (New York, 1983), 14–19, for an insightful discussion of the ideological variations within American political culture in the 1950s.

12. Michael Kammen, *Mystic Chords of Memory: The Transformation of Tradition in American Culture* (New York, 1991), 657. Disney's turn to history in the 1950s also can be seen as a compensatory gesture of nostalgia by a modernizing entrepreneur who was at the forefront of destroying tradition.

13. WD, quoted in Hedda Hopper, Chicago *Tribune*, May 9, 1948.

14. "Following the Films," *World Week: A Scholastic Magazine*, Dec. 8, 1948; Capehart, quoted in RKO "Information Guide: World Area Premiere" for *So Dear to My Heart*, and in RKO publicity release "Ned Depinet Drive," Jan. 22, 1949, PS S2 and S3. For dozens of favorable reviews of the film, see PS S2 and S3.

15. WD, quoted in "Johnny Tremain, Teen-Age Patriot in the American Revolution," *Senior Scholastic*, May 17, 1957; "Johnny Tremain," *The Film Estimate Board of National Organizations*, May 15, 1957; Ann Barzel, "Disney's 'Tremain' Is U.S. History With Heads High," Chicago *Tribune*, July 8, 1957. See PS J1 for many similar comments.

16. "The Birth of the Swamp Fox," Oct. 23, 1959; "Horses for Greene," Jan. 15, 1961.

17. Norman Shavin, "Ex-Canadian to Portray 'Robin Hood of the South,'" Atlanta *Journal*, Sept. 1, 1959; "Freedom Fighter," Buffalo *Evening News*, Oct. 17, 1959; "New Disney Series Begins Friday," Provo, Utah, *Daily Herald*, Oct. 19, 1959; "Swamp Fox," Los Angeles *Times*, Oct. 25, 1959. For many similar articles, see PS S15.

18. Steven H. Scheuer, "Tom Tryon Latest Disney Discovery," Hackensack, N.J., *Evening Record*, Dec. 13, 1958. For many additional articles on Texas John Slaughter, see PS T14.

19. "Hundreds Displaced by Texas Floods," Nashua, N.H., *Telegraph*, Jan. 7, 1958. See also "Guy Williams, Faces of Love," *Movie Star Parade*, Sept. 1958; "Zorro Foiled His Rivals," *TV Guide*, Apr. 26, 1958, 24–26; *The Zorro Newsletter*, June 1958 and Dec. 1958; "The Marks of Zorro," *New York Times Sunday Magazine*, July 13, 1958; "The Mark of Zorro," *Life*, n.d. See PS Z1 for many more articles.

20. Maltin, *Disney Films*, 179–80.

21. Charles Maher, "Zorro, 'Robin Hood of Old California,'" Palo Alto *Times*, July 20, 1957.
22. Maltin, *Disney Films*, 146–48, 150–52.
23. Ibid., 110–12, 115–17, 132–34, 174–75.
24. Ibid., 97–100.
25. See Clifford M. Sage, "Curtain Going Up," Dallas *Times Herald*, Aug. 4, 1950; "Treasure Island," *Look*, May 18, 1950; "Walt Disney's Answer to the Psychologists," New York *Sunday Mirror Magazine*, June 11, 1950; "Treasure Island Is Buccaneer Revel," Los Angeles *Times*, Aug. 11, 1950; B. R. Crisler, "Hispaniola, Ahoy!" *Christian Science Monitor Magazine*, July 29, 1950; "Treasure Island," *Parents Magazine*, Aug. 1950; "The Screen," New York *Times*, Aug. 16, 1950; Doris Arden, "Treasure Island," Chicago *Sun Times*, Aug. 3, 1950. For many more reviews, see PS T3.
26. Maltin, *Disney Films*, 119–22.
27. Ibid., 145–46; Ben S. Parker, "New Movie at the Malco Tells Story of Loyal Dog," Memphis *Commercial Appeal*, Jan. 19, 1958; "Disney's 'Old Yeller' Tells Boy-to-Man Transformation," *Independent*, Sept. 24, 1957, PS O1. For many other reviews, see PS O1.
28. Hedda Hopper, "Tom Tryon: Has Gun and Now He Travels!" Chicago *Sunday Tribune Magazine*, Nov. 2, 1958; Scheuer, "Tom Tryon Latest Disney Discovery"; Reba and Bonnie Churchill, "Tom Tryon Becomes Another Disney Hero," Williamsport, Pa., Nov. 16, 1958; "Swamp Fox Rides Again," Chicago *Daily Tribune TV Week* (Oct. 24, 1959); J. Kontowicz, "At Home with Zorro," New York *Sunday News*, Apr. 13, 1958; Erskine Johnson, "From Door Hanger to Star in One Swashbuckle," *NEA Pictures, Maps, and Charts*, Oct. 18, 1957.
29. Maltin, *Disney Films*, 176–79.
30. W.D.S., "Indominable Swiss," Greensboro, N.C., *Daily News*, Jan. 3, 1961. For many other pieces on the movie, see PS S14.

16. Disney and National Security

1. Hibler, Thomas interview, 7–8; Sharpsteen, Peri interview, Feb. 6, 1974, 31–32. For Walt's thoughts on the series, see WD, "The Lurking Camera," *Atlantic Monthly*, Aug. 1954, 23–27; WD, "What I've Learned from the Animals," *American Magazine*, Feb. 1953, 22–23, 106–9; Martin/Miller interview, Reel 8, 24–42.
2. J. P. McEvoy, "McEvoy in Disneyland," *Reader's Digest*, Feb. 1955, 19–26, presents a general survey of this series. See also Maltin, *The Disney Films*, 113–15, 117–19, 128–30, 137–38, 142–44, 148–49, 172–74.
3. Ed Ainsworth, "Disney Creating New Era of Realism," Los Angeles *Times*, Nov. 29, 1954; Richard Cox, "DuPont's Got Disney's Best," Washington *Post*, Nov. 5, 1956; Bosley Crowther, "The Screen," New York *Times*, Nov. 10, 1953; Bosley Crowther, "Disney's Nature Film 'The Vanishing Prairie' Has Animals Like Those in Familiar Cartoons," New York *Times*, Aug. 22, 1954.
4. McEvoy, "McEvoy in Disneyland," 22; Jack Alexander, "The Amazing Story of Walt Disney," *Saturday Evening Post*, Nov. 7, 1953, 99; Richard L. Coe, "Disney's Nature Seems Certain of a Long Life," Washington *Post*, April 13, 1952; "The Living Desert," *Newsweek*, Nov. 23, 1953; Will Shuster, "Eager Beaver Shuster Salutes," Santa Fe *New Mexican*, Sept. 24, 1950. Only one review among those I

surveyed suggested that the law of the jungle reflected "atheistic Communism," Rev. James M. Gillis, "No Need to Fight, Just Wait," *Catholic Transcript,* June 30, 1949. See also clippings in PS T5, T6, T12, T22.

5. WD, "What I've Learned from the Animals," 23.

6. Al Hine, "Bears and Banditry," *Movie,* June 1953; "Picture Windows for Prairie Dogs," *Good Housekeeping,* Oct. 1954; "Prairie Dogs," *Child Life,* Nov. 1954; "The Light Side, by Henry McLemore," Los Angeles *Times,* Oct. 7, 1953. See Bosley Crowther, "The Screen," New York *Times,* Nov. 10, 1953, and "'The Vanishing Prairie' Has Animals" for criticism of Disney's anthropomorphism.

7. Advertisement, New York *Times,* Aug. 15, 1954; Edwin Schallert, "Historic Prairie Lives on Screen," Los Angeles *Times,* Aug. 2, 1954; "The Vanishing Prairie," *Newsweek,* Aug. 9, 1954; Polly Cochran, "2nd Lesson in Natural Life Offered by Disney," Indianapolis *Star,* Oct. 23, 1954.

8. Hollis Alpert, "Curious Cameras," *Woman's Day,* May 1954; Hibler, Thomas interview, 14. See also "Time-Lapse and Telephotos Probe Nature's Secrets," *American Cinematographer,* Oct. 1956; Tom McHugh, "Animals Are Like Other People," *Popular Mechanics,* Sept. 1954; Frederick Foster, "Walt Disney's Naturalist-Cinematographers," *American Cinematographer,* Feb. 1954; Ormal I. Sprungman, "Disney Films Nature," *Sports Afield,* Aug. 1953.

9. Justin Gilbert, "Disney's 'The African Lion' Teaches, Thrills, Fascinates," New York *Daily Mirror,* Sept. 15, 1955; Bill Diehl, "Walt Disney Series Unmasks Nature," St. Paul *Sunday Pioneer Press,* Aug. 10, 1952; William H. Mooring, "Disney's Contribution to Genuine Cinema Art," Los Angeles *Tidings,* June 20, 1952; "1954 Picture of the Year," *Christian Herald,* March 1955.

10. WD, "Foreword," in Jane Werner Watson et al., *Walt Disney's People and Places* (New York, 1959); WD, "Why I Like Making Nature Films," *Women's Home Companion,* May 1954, 39.

11. Kimball, quoted in David R. Smith, "They're Following Our Script: Walt Disney's Trip to Tomorrowland," *Future,* May 1978, 54.

12. See Smith, "Following Our Script," and Mike Wright, "The Disney–Von Braun Collaboration and Its Influence on Space Exploration," 1993, 1–10, DA.

13. WD, "Television Meeting," May 14, 1954, in Man in Space/Moon Picture folder, DA.

14. WD, *Tomorrow the Moon: A Tomorrowland Adventure* (Syracuse, N.Y., 1959).

15. Ward Kimball, interview by John Canemaker, July 7, 1973, 6; Bill Bosche, quoted in Smith, "Following Our Script," 56; WD, quoted in Hedda Hopper, "Genius of Walt Disney into Different Fields," clipping, 1955, PS W21; WD, *Man in Space: A Tomorrowland Adventure* (Syracuse, N.Y., 1959).

16. Scholer Bangs, quoted in Smith, "Following Our Script," 59; James Abbe, "Top U.S. Missiles Expert Bows in 'Mars and Beyond,'" Oakland *Tribune,* Dec. 4, 1957; Bob Thomas, "Hollywood," Grants Pass, Ore., *Courier,* Oct. 15, 1957; "Disney's 'Mars and Beyond' Impressed Space Scientists," Portland, Me., *Independent Republican,* Dec. 4, 1957. See also "Rocket Men Impressed by Disney," Niagara Falls *Gazette,* Dec. 4, 1957; "Institute at Reed College to Deal with Nuclear Weapons Policy," Portland *Oregon Journal,* June 14, 1957; many other clippings in PS D12, D13, and D16.

17. Heinz Haber, *The Walt Disney Story of Our Friend the Atom* (New York, 1956), 13, 160.

18. WD, quoted in Jack Quigg, "Disney Flouts Movie Tradition by Specializing in Versatility," clipping, PS W21. See also Martin/Miller interview, Reel 10, 26.

19. "World of Tomorrow Told in Disneyland Presentation, 'Our Friend the Atom,'" Reno *Independent,* Jan. 21, 1957; Leo Mishkin, "Sight and Sound: Disney Project Superbly Done," New York *Telegraph,* Jan. 25, 1957; "Kudos and Choler," *Time,* Feb. 4, 1957. Many more favorable reviews can be found in PS D12.

20. Fess Parker, interview by the author, July 1995, 14–16.

21. "U.S. Again Is Subdued by Davy," *Life,* Apr. 25, 1955, 27–33; "Meet Davy Crockett," *Look,* July 26, 1955, 36–37; cartoon by J. B. Modell, *New Yorker,* May 21, 1955; "The Wild Frontier," *Time,* May 23, 1955, 92. Many more clippings can be found in PS D9, D10, and D11. For two excellent surveys of this fad, see Margaret J. King, "The Davy Crockett Craze: A Case Study in Popular Culture," Ph.D. dissertation, University of Hawaii, 1976, and Paul F. Anderson, *The Davy Crockett Craze: A Look at the 1950s Phenomenon and Davy Crockett Collectibles* (Hillside, Ill., 1996).

22. "The Wild Frontier," *Time;* "U.S. Again Subdued," *Life;* "Mr. Crockett Is Dead Shot as a Salesman," New York *Times,* June 1, 1955, 38; Peter White, "Ex-King of the Wild Frontier," *New York Times Magazine,* Dec. 11, 1955, 27.

23. White, "Ex-King of the Wild Frontier," 27.

24. Bill Walsh, quoted in Frank Thompson, *Alamo Movies* (East Berlin, Pa., 1991); "Davy Crockett's Songsmith," Portland *Sunday Oregonian Magazine,* Dec. 4, 1955; "U.S. Again Subdued," *Life,* 27. See also David Tietyen, *The Musical World of Walt Disney* (Milwaukee, 1990), 111–14.

25. "Davy Crockett, Disney Style," *Nashville Tennessean Magazine,* Oct. 3, 1954; "Davy Crockett Lives Again," *Parade,* Dec. 5, 1954; "Woodsman in Washington," *TV Program Week,* Jan. 22–28, 1955; E. J. Kahn Jr., "Be Sure You're Right, Then Go Ahead," *New Yorker,* Sept. 13, 1955, 71–77; Walter Blair, "R.I.P.: King of the Wild Frontier," *Saturday Review,* July 21, 1956, 26.

26. "Meet Davy Crockett," *Look,* 37; Hedda Hopper, "Fess Wins Europe for Davy," clipping, PS D11; "Julie Meets Davy," Washington *Daily News,* Apr. 1, 1955; Parker interview, 16–21.

27. WD, quoted in Maltin, *Disney Films,* 122; Dr. Evalyn Mills, quoted in "Crockett Is Dead Shot," *Newsweek,* 38.

28. "Davy Crockett and Old Betsy," Santa Ana, Calif., *Register,* Apr. 1, 1955; "Davy Crockett 'Elected,'" New York *Times,* May 19, 1955; "Hero Stands in for Davy Crockett," New York *Times,* June 20, 1955, 12; Dies, quoted in James Reston, "Even Davy Crockett Can't Do Everything," New York *Times,* May 22, 1955, 8.

29. Fess Parker, "My Life as Davy Crockett," in Carl Schroeder, *The Real Life Story of Fess Parker* (New York, 1955), 4, 20; Jonathan King, "The Crockett Craze," Los Angeles *Times,* Feb. 27, 1995, E1–E2; Parker interview, 27–28.

30. John Haverstick, "The Two Davy Crocketts," *Saturday Review,* July 9, 1955, 19, 30; John Fischer, "The Embarrassing Truth about Davy Crockett," *Harper's,* July 1955, 16; Brendan Sexton, quoted in "Davy: Row and a Riddle," *Newsweek,* July 4, 1955, 56; Murray Kempton, "The Real Davy," New York *Post,* June 21, 1955.

31. Magazines quoted in "Davy: Row and a Riddle," 56; Kenneth S. Davis, "Coonskin Superman," *New York Times Magazine,* Apr. 24, 1955, 20; "Decline of a Hero," *Collier's,* Nov. 25, 1955, 102; "Letters," *Harper's,* Sept. 1955, 4; "Crockett and Circulation," *Newsweek,* July 18, 1955, 60–61.

32. Schroeder, *Fess Parker,* 9–32; Parker interview, 1–4.

33. Parker interview, 37–38; Thompson, *Alamo Movies,* 53–54; John Parris, "Star of Disney TV Saga Finds Work with Cherokees Realistic," Asheville, N.C., *Citizen,* Sept. 17, 1954.

34. Charles Berkeley, "Davy Crockett Is Going to the Movies," *TV,* July 1955, 62–63; Bill Martin, "$650,000 Baby," *TV Fan,* July 1955, 41, 60–61; "Fess Parker," *Movie Stars Parade,* August 1955; Jon Bruce, "What Davy Crockett Did to Fess Parker," *TV-Radio Life,* July 8, 1955, 4–5.

35. Fess Parker, quoted in "Date Bait for a Guy Like Me," *Photoplay,* Jan. 1956, 53, 72–73; Jack Holland, "At Home with Davy Crockett," *TV-Radio Life,* July 8, 1955, 5–6.

36. Isobel K. Silden, "Davy Lives Again: Fess Parker Feels He Can Help Combat Juvenile Delinquency," Boston *Independent Democrat,* June 12, 1955; Fess Parker, "Our Kids Are Hero Hungry," New York *Herald Tribune's This Week Magazine,* Oct. 9, 1955; Parker interview, 30–34.

37. "6,000 Cheer Attacks on High Taxes," Hollywood *Citizen-News,* Dec. 7, 1957; Schroeder, *Fess Parker,* 8; Louella O. Parsons, "Davy Settlin' but Won't 'Fess Up' on Marriage," *Los Angeles Examiner Pictorial Living,* July 24, 1955, 8; *Hudson Family Magazine,* n.d., clipping, PS D11; "Davy's Time," *Time,* May 30, 1955, 9–10.

17. Disney and Domestic Security

1. Stephen J. Whitfield, *The Culture of the Cold War* (Baltimore, 1991), 53. See also Jackson Lears, "A Matter of Taste: Corporate Cultural Hegemony in a Mass-Consumption Society" in May, *Recasting America,* 38–43.

2. Daniel Boorstin, *The Genius of American Politics* (Chicago, 1953). See also Daniel Bell, *The End of Ideology: On the Exhaustion of Political Ideas in the 1950s* (New York, 1960), 402–5; Whitfield, *Culture of the Cold War,* ix, 53–58.

3. T. J. Jackson Lears, "From Salvation to Self-Realization: Advertising and the Therapeutic Roots of the Consumer Culture, 1880–1930," in Richard Fox and T. J. Jackson Lears, eds., *The Culture of Consumption: Critical Essays in American History 1880–1980* (New York, 1983), 4. On the culture of abundance, see also Stuart Ewen, *Captains of Consciousness: Advertising and the Social Roots of the Consumer Culture* (New York, 1976), 205–14; Marling, *As Seen on TV,* 150–56; Warren Susman, *Culture as History: The Transformation of American Society in the Twentieth Century* (New York, 1984), 271–85.

4. Whitfield, *Culture of the Cold War,* 77–100.

5. Lears, "A Matter of Taste," 41–42; George Lipsitz, *Class and Culture in Cold War America* (South Hadley, Mass., 1982), 135–225; Elaine Tyler May, *Homeward Bound: American Families in the Cold War Era* (New York, 1988); W. T. Lhamon, *Deliberate Speed: The Origins of a Cultural Style in the American 1950s* (Washington, D.C., 1990).

6. Lears, "A Matter of Taste," 49–51.

7. I am indebted to Peter Biskind, whose *Seeing Is Believing* shows brilliantly how U.S. cinema in the 1950s expressed and mediated a range of social and ideological impulses.

8. WD, "What I've Learned from the Animals," 23, 106–8.

9. "Live the Life of McCall's," "A Man's Place Is in the Home," "Ed and His Family

Live Together and Love It," and "The Importance of Being Father," *McCall's*, May 1954, 27–35, 61. See also Lynn Spigel, *Make Room for TV: Television and the Family Ideal in Postwar America* (Chicago, 1992), 33–34, 37; May, *Homeward Bound*, 11, 16–36, 162–82.

10. William R. Weaver, "Walt Disney, Artist and Storyteller," *Motion Picture Herald*, Nov. 20, 1954, 42; WD, "Film Entertainment and Community Life," *Journal of the American Medical Association*, July 12, 1958, 1344; WD, "The Future of Fantasy," *Catholic Preview of Entertainment*, April 1959, 36.

11. In a certain sense, Disney's domestic ideology revived traditional Victorian categories of female and male "separate spheres." But as Joanne Meyerowitz has noted, in mainstream 1950s ideology, "domestic ideals coexisted in ongoing tension with an ethos of individual achievement that celebrated nondomestic activity, individual striving, public service, and public success." See "Beyond the Feminine Mystique: A Reassessment of Postwar Mass Culture, 1946–1958," in Meyerowitz, *Not June Cleaver: Women and Gender in Postwar America, 1945–1960* (Philadelphia, 1994), 23.

12. John Grant, *Walt Disney's Animated Characters: From Mickey Mouse to Aladdin* (New York, 1993), 248.

13. "Peter Pan: Real Disney Magic," *Newsweek*, Feb. 16, 1953; Maltin, *The Disney Films*, 109.

14. See "Disney's 'Cinderella': Of Mice and Girls," *Newsweek*, Feb. 13. 1950, 84–88; "'Cinderella' Poses Moot Question about Courting," Columbus, Ohio, *State Journal*, Feb. 22, 1950; Jack Quigg, "Cinderella, Tough Girl to Cast, Emerges as Athletic, Curvy Type by Disney," Washington, D.C., *Star*, Sept. 4, 1949; Cynthia Cabot, "Fairyland Glamour," *Philadelphia Inquirer Magazine*, Jan. 29, 1950, 24–25; "A Thrilling Search for the Girl Who Is Chicago Area's Modern Cinderella," Chicago *Herald-American*, Jan. 29, 1950.

15. John C. Waugh, "Hollywood Remembers Family," *Christian Science Monitor*, Apr. 24, 1960; John Beaufort, "Pollyanna Freshened Up as Evocative Period Piece from Disney," *Christian Science Monitor*, May 24, 1960. See also "Star Hails 'Pollyanna' as Family Film," Philadelphia *Inquirer*, June 12, 1960; Kate Cameron, "Disney's 'Pollyanna' an Endearing Film," New York *Daily News*, May 20, 1960. For many more clippings on the film, see PS P9.

16. Al H. Weiler, "The Screen: 'Pollyanna,'" New York *Times*, May 20, 1960; David Swift, quoted in Marray Schumach, "New Pollyanna Will Be Subtle," New York *Times*, June 9, 1959; Paine Knickerbocker, "Out West with New England's 'Pollyanna,'" New York *Times*, Aug. 30, 1959.

17. John C. Waugh, "Hayley Mills: New America's Sweetheart?" *Christian Science Monitor*, Oct. 11, 1960; WD, quoted in Santa Ana *Register*, Sept. 29, 1959, clipping, PS P9; Bob Thomas, "New Pollyanna Is Elvis Fan," Los Angeles *Mirror-News*, Oct. 9, 1959; "Pollyanna Gives Tips on Beauty," Chicago *Daily Tribune*, Sept. 12, 1960; "Hayley," *Modern Screen*, Dec. 1960, 28, 73–74.

18. Edith F. Hunter, "Because We Like You," *Children's Religion*, Aug. 1957, 23.

19. Doreen Tracy, interview by Lorraine Santoli, 1994, 21–22.

20. Lorraine Santoli, *The Official Mickey Mouse Club Book* (New York, 1995), 58, 150.

21. Roy Williams, interview by Don Peri, *Funnyworld* (1977), 35. See also Santoli, *Mickey Mouse Club*, 15–42. Through the show's four seasons, thirty-nine differ-

ent Mouseketeers appeared, but a core group of nine persisted: Sharon Baird, Bobby Burgess, Lonnie Burr, Tommy Cole, Annette Funicello, Darlene Gillespie, Cubby O'Brien, Karen Pendleton, and Doreen Tracy.

22. "Has Mouse Turned to Monster?" clipping, n.d., PS M6; cartoon, *Saturday Evening Post,* clipping, n.d., PS M6; "Fickle Fans Pelt Mouseketeers After Stratford Performance," Bridgeport, Conn., *Independent,* Feb. 21, 1958; Gene Hansaker, "Mysterious 'Accident' Rumors Plague Mouseketeers on Coast-to-Coast Tour," San Jose, Calif., *Mercury News,* Sept. 22, 1957.

23. Bobby Burgess, interview by Lorraine Santoli, 1993, 6–7. See also Leonard Shannon, interview by Lorraine Santoli, 1993, 5–6; Lonnie Burr, interview by Lorraine Santoli, 1993, 9–10; Tracy, Santoli interview, 19, 23.

24. Burr, Santoli interview, 14–15; Tommy Cole, interview by Lorraine Santoli, 1993, 18; Tracy, Santoli interview, 15–16.

25. "The Case of the Missing Baby Sitter," Bayside, Va., *Pilot,* Feb. 24, 1957; "Jimmie Baby-Sits for Millions," Miami *News,* Feb. 16, 1959; William Howard, "Mickey Mouse: Refreshing Entertainment for Youth," Boston *Post,* Apr. 22, 1956.

26. Dr. Benjamin Spock, *Baby and Child Care* (New York, 1963), 2, 304, 332, 404. For the term "fun morality," see Martha Wolfenstein, "Fun Morality: An Analysis of Recent American Child-Rearing Literature," in Margaret Mead and Martha Wolfenstein, eds., *Childhood in Contemporary Cultures* (Chicago, 1955), 169–78.

27. Spock, *Baby and Child Care,* 388. On Spock's thought and influence, see William Graebner, "The Unstable World of Benjamin Spock: Social Engineering in a Democratic Culture, 1917–1950," *Journal of American History* 67 (Dec. 1980), 612–29; Michael Zuckerman, "Dr. Spock: The Confidence Man," in Charles E. Rosenberg, ed., *The Family in History* (Philadelphia, 1975), 179–207.

28. "Mickey Mouse Club," n.d., PS M5.

29. Santoli, *Mickey Mouse Club,* 26; Martin/Miller interview, Reel 10, 31.

30. Santoli, *Mickey Mouse Club,* 135–37, 130, 125–26; "Calling All Mouseketeers," *Calling All Girls,* Jan. 1958, 93.

31. *Mickey Mouse Club Magazine,* 1956, 1.

32. Rose Mann, "Mouseketeer Doreen Tracy Poses No Teenage Problem," Jan. 8, 1958, PS M6; Santoli, *Mickey Mouse Club,* 146.

33. Gaspard St. Onge, "Stars of the Mouseketeers," *Young Catholic Messenger,* Feb. 28, 1958, 8; Gordon Budge, "The Dolly Princess," *TV Radio Mirror,* July 1958; Sidney Miller, interview by Lorraine Santoli, 1993, 11; John Crosby, "All the Kids Are Singing," New York *Herald Tribune,* July 7, 1958.

34. Budge, "Dolly Princess"; Fairfax Nisbet, "Funicello," Dallas *Morning News,* Aug. 4, 1957; "Calling All Mouseketeers," 91; Santoli, *Mickey Mouse Club,* 152; "An Interview with Annette Funicello and Darlene Gillespie," n.d., PS M6.

35. Santoli, *Mickey Mouse Club,* 138–40.

36. Cole, Santoli interview, 13–14; Santoli, *Mickey Mouse Club,* 219.

37. Santoli, *Mickey Mouse Club,* 144–47; Ray Hoffman, "Youth Shows Must Set Good Examples," *Pittsburgh Press,* July 21, 1958; Jack Holland, "The Mouseketeers Hit the Road," *TV-Radio Life,* Aug. 24, 1956; Billie O'Day, "Jimmie Baby-Sits for Millions," Miami *News,* Feb. 16, 1959; George Groobert, "Television Entertainer Comments on Rock 'n Roll, Youth Highjinks," Meriden, Conn., *Independent Republican,* Feb. 20, 1958.

38. See "Interview with Funicello and Gillespie"; St. Onge, "Stars of the Mouseketeers"; Groobert, "Television Entertainer Comments."

39. Hunter, "Because We Like You," 23.

18. Citizen Disney

1. "Father Goose," *Time*, Dec. 27, 1954, 45; Jack Alexander, "The Amazing Story of Walt Disney," *Saturday Evening Post*, Oct. 31, 1953, 84; Bob Foster, "Last Week Was Filled with Entertainment and TV's Best," San Mateo, Calif., *Times and News Leader*, Nov. 30, 1957; Jane Zegarski to WD, Sept. 25, 1961, PS W11.

2. WD, quoted in Hedda Hopper, "Genius of Walt Disney into Different Fields," n.d. [1955], PS W21; "Walt Disney Issue," *Wisdom*, 78, 79; Larry Wolters, "Disney Off to the West with a Bang," Chicago *Tribune*, Oct. 3, 1958.

3. WD, "There's Always a Solution," *Guideposts*, June 1949. See also "Walt Disney Issue," *Wisdom*, 77.

4. Martin/Miller interview, Reel 12, 47–48, 55, Reel 9, 71, Reel 10, 26; WD to Mrs. Fred Rensch, Oct. 18, 1950; WD to Ruth Beecher, Jan. 22, 1943; Lillian Disney, Thomas interview, 6.

5. WD, speech at Big Brothers Annual Award of Merit, Mar. 14, 1957, 4; Martin/Miller interview, Reel 12, 26–28, Reel 9, 49–50.

6. Roger Broggie, interview by Jay Horan, Nov. 22, 1983, 162; Harper Goff, interview by Jay Horan, Sept. 21, 1982, 107; Donn Tatum, interview by Bob Thomas, May 24, 1973, 18; WD, Big Brothers speech.

7. WD's FBI file: see document 94-4-4667-2 (Dec. 16, 1954) for information on Disney's designation as an SAC contact; 94-4-4667-6 (Nov. 9, 1956) and 94-4-4667-7 (Nov. 26, 1954) for Hoover and Disney's exchange of letters on the Milestone Award; 62-60527-25 (July 26, 1951), 62-68527-42803 (May 10, 1955), 62-102561-58 (Dec. 14, 1956) for the FBI's concern about Disney's attendance at leftist gatherings in the 1940s; 94-4-4667-3 (Mar. 16, 1956), 94-4-4667-13 (Apr. 17, 1957), 94-4-4667-20 (Oct. 22, 1957) on the FBI's reluctant cooperation with the filming of the Mickey Mouse Club Newsreel; 94-4-4667-49 (Aug. 14, 1963), 94-4-4667-37 (Mar. 13, 1961), 94-4-4667-39 (Mar. 27, 1961) for the FBI's annoyance with *That Darn Cat* and *Moon Pilot*. Marc Eliot, *Walt Disney: Hollywood's Dark Prince* (1993), makes outlandish claims about Disney and his FBI connection amid a barrage of accusations about his supposed immoral private life, illegitimate birth, and alcoholism. The vast majority of these charges are preposterous and are not supported by the evidence.

8. Homer Capehart, quoted in "Ned Depinet Drive," RKO press release on *So Dear to My Heart*, Jan. 22, 1949, PS S2; "Small Fry World Fires Up Disney," Los Angeles *Mirror-News*, Apr. 29, 1954; Louis Berg, "Happy New Year, Hollywood," San Francisco *Chronicle*, Dec. 31, 1950; Allen M. Widem, "Disney Responsible for Trailblazing," Hartford *Times*, Mar. 5, 1958; "Father Goose," 43–44; "Legion Honors Show Greats," Los Angeles *Examiner*, Sept. 21, 1961; "Geo. Washington Award Given Walt Disney," *Daily Variety*, Feb. 25, 1963; Bill Sumner, "Reporter's Diary," Pasadena *Independent*, Feb. 18, 1957.

9. Dorothy Mealy to WD, Sept. 23, 1961, PS W11.

10. Lillian Disney, "I Live with a Genius," 38–41.

11. See Thomas, *Walt Disney*, 77–78; Diane Miller and Lillian Disney, Martin/Miller

interview, Reel 8, 44–49, 50–52, 65–67; Lillian Disney, interview by the author, Aug. 18, 1993.

12. See Theodore Strauss, "Donald Duck's Disney," New York *Times*, Feb. 7, 1943; Watkin, "Walt Disney," 155–56, DA; Diane Miller, Martin/Miller interview, Reel 2, 2.

13. Roy Disney, Hubler interview, 11; Kimball, Hubler interview, 6; Hee, Hubler interview, 18–19; Martin/Miller interview, Reel 11, 55–56, 52–55.

14. Diane Miller, Hubler interview, 26–27, 19; Marc Davis, interview by Richard Hubler, May 21, 1968, 1–2; Sharpsteen, Peri interview, Feb. 6, 1974, 9; Diane Miller, Martin/Miller interview, Reel 4, 41–42; Roy Disney, Hubler interview, 5, 12, 29.

15. WD to Lillian Disney, Oct. 19, 26, and 27, 1928; Watkin, "Disney," 157–58; Lillian Disney interview.

16. John Grover, "Small Fry World Fires Up Disney," *Mirror-News*, Apr. 29, 1954; Diane Miller, Hubler interview, 18, 20; Diane Miller, Martin/Miller interview, Reel 2, 1; WD to Bill and Grace Papineau, Aug. 8, 1933; Lillian Disney, interview by Richard Hubler, Apr. 16, 1968, 4, 6.

17. Lillian Disney, Hubler interview, 4; Roy Disney, Hubler interview, 4a; Diane Miller, Martin/Miller interview, Reel 8, 54, 57, 78–79, 84. See also Davis, Hubler interview, 3; Lillian Disney, Thomas interview, 5.

18. Diane Miller, Martin/Miller interview, Reel 2, 56; Lillian Disney, Thomas interview, 5, 9–10; Lillian Disney, Hubler interview, 8, 1–2, 3–4.

19. Diane Miller, Martin/Miller interview, Reel 2, 56, Reel 12, 52–54; Davis, Hubler interview, 1; Edna Disney, Hubler interview, 17–18.

20. Diane Miller, Hubler interview, 38, 3–4; Diane Miller, Martin/Miller interview, Reel 2, 60–61, Reel 5, 24, 12–14, 1–7, Reel 12, 32–33, 39–40, 44, Reel 4, 77–79; WD to Jessie Perkins, Nov. 16, 1949; Lillian Disney interview.

21. Martin/Miller interview Reel 11, 51; Sharon Disney Lund, interview by Richard Hubler, July 9, 1968, 28–29, 38; Kimball, "The Wonderful World of Walt Disney," 280.

22. For comments on WD's view of women, see Thomas, Thomas interview, 2; Culhane, *Talking Animals*, 142.

23. Thomas, Thomas interview, 2–3; Kimball, Hubler interview, 12; Ken Anderson, Thomas interview, 30; Diane Miller, Hubler interview, 18.

24. Martin/Miller interview, Reel 10, 32–33; Ken Anderson, Hubler interview, 5; Kimball, Hubler interview, 7–8; I. Klein, "Some Close-up Shots of Walt Disney During the 'Golden Years,'" *Funnyworld*, Spring 1983, 48; Kimball, "Wonderful World of Walt Disney," 281.

25. "Growing Impact of the Disney Art," *Newsweek*, Apr. 18, 1955, 62; Arthur Gordon, "Walt Disney," *Look*, July 26, 1955, 29; "Year's Best TV Show," *Redbook*, June 1955; Jack Gould, "Television in Review," New York *Times*, Oct. 29, 1954.

26. Marie Torre, "Parents Hit Lack of Children's Shows," New York *Herald Tribune*, Mar. 13, 1958; "Walt Disney's Talented Youngsters," West Virginia *Register*, c. 1955; WD, quoted in "Introducing Disneyland," *TV Radio Mirror*, Dec. 1954, 62. See also Frank Hanifen, "St. Francis Would Have Loved Walt Disney," *Padre*, Feb. 1955, 80.

27. Louella O. Parsons, "Walt Disney, the Loveable Genius Who Never Grew Up," *Los Angeles Examiner's Pictorial Living*, Jan. 9, 1955. For an earlier idealized

depiction of the Disney family, see Elmer T. Peterson, "At Home with Walt Disney," *Better Homes and Gardens,* Jan. 1940, 13–15. Among many admiring stories in the 1950s, see Cameron Shipp, "Meet the New Walt Disney," *Today's Woman,* Jan. 1953; "The Wonderful World of Walt Disney," *Catholic Preview of Entertainment,* June 1957, 4–10; Will Jones, "Great Man with a Toy," Minneapolis *Sunday Tribune,* June 12, 1955.

28. WD, "Deeds Rather Than Words," c. 1962, 2–3, in "There's Always a Solution" file, DA. See also "Walt Disney, Showman and Educator, Remembers Daisy" and "Disney, M.S., M.A.," *California Teachers Association Journal,* Dec. 1955, 4–6; WD, "Schoolday Tips from Walt Disney," Washington *Star Sunday Magazine,* Aug. 25, 1957, 32–33; WD, "The Storyteller and the Educator," *Television Quarterly* (Spring 1955), 3–5.

29. James B. Gilbert, *A Cycle of Outrage: America's Reaction to the Juvenile Delinquent in the 1950s* (New York, 1986), 71.

30. WD, quoted in Frank Purcell, "Youth Crime Link Seen," Los Angeles *Examiner,* Mar. 1, 1957; "Walt Disney Issue," *Wisdom,* 79; Disney, "Deeds Rather Than Words," 3; Bob Thomas, "Disney Says Kids Must Have Something to Do," Coeur d'Alene, Id., *Press,* Dec. 2, 1957. For an appreciative analysis of Disney's attempts to reform "our rising crop of potential young thugs," see Robert C. Ruark, "Decency Dividend," New York *Herald Tribune,* Sept. 2, 1954.

31. William R. Weaver, "Walt Disney — Artist and Storyteller," *Motion Picture Herald,* Nov. 20, 1954, 42. For WD's comments on his family orientation, see WD, "Film Entertainment and Community Life," *Journal of the American Medical Association,* July 12, 1958, 1345; WD, "The Future of Fantasy," *Catholic Preview of Entertainment,* Apr. 1959, 37.

19. Disney and the Culture Industry

1. "Special Issue: The Good Life," *Life,* Dec. 28, 1959, 13–14, 62–63. See also "Cause of Breakthrough toward a Life of Plenty," 36–40; "A $40 Billion Bill Just for Fun," 69–74; Sloan Wilson, "Happy Idle Hours Become a Rat Race," 118–20.

2. Mitchell Gordon, "Walt's Profit Formula: Dream, Diversify, and Never Miss an Angle," *Wall Street Journal,* Feb. 4, 1958, 1, 12.

3. T. J. Jackson Lears, "From Salvation to Self-Realization," in Lears and Fox, *The Culture of Consumption,* 4.

4. For the formulation of the "culture industry" concept, see Theodor Adorno and Max Horkheimer, *Dialectic of Enlightenment* (New York, 1972 [1944]). See also the scholarly debate in *American Historical Review* 97, Dec. 1992, especially Lawrence W. Levine, "The Folklore of Industrial Society: Popular Culture and Its Audience," 1369–99, and, much more convincing, Jackson Lears, "Making Fun of Popular Culture," 1417–26. Among the vast literature on consumerism and culture, see Jean-Christophe Agnew, "Coming Up for Air: Consumer Culture in Historical Perspective," *Intellectual History Newsletter* 12 (1990), 3–21.

5. WD, "Our American Culture," transcript, Mar. 1, 1942, DA, 3–4; WD, "Film Entertainment and Community Life," 1342. See also WD, "The Future of Fantasy," 35.

6. *An Introduction to the Walt Disney Studio,* 1938. See also Winston Hibler, proposal on "The World in Your Living Room," Jan. 4, 1945; W. Ward Marsh, "Dis-

ney Studio Now Humming with Feature Film Activity," Cleveland *Plain Dealer,*
May 16, 1948.

7. Larry Wolters, "Walt Disney's First TV Show Is Big Success," Chicago *Tribune,*
Dec. 26, 1950. Other favorable reviews include Roger Swift, "On Television:
Disney's First Venture a Success," Boston *Herald,* Dec. 27, 1950; Jack Gould,
"Television in Review," New York *Times,* Dec. 26, 1950; "Disney Debut,"
Newsweek, Jan. 1, 1951. See PS C2 and PS C3 for clippings on the Christmas
specials.

8. See Lynn Spigel, *Make Room for TV: Television and the Family Ideal in Postwar
America* (Chicago, 1992); Cecelia Tichi, *Electronic Hearth: Creating an American
Television Culture* (New York, 1991).

9. C. J. LaRoche and Company, "Television for Walt Disney Productions," 1950,
DA.

10. Virginia MacPherson, "TV Millions Don't Tempt Walt Disney," Brooklyn *Eagle,*
Dec. 24, 1951; Walt Disney Productions, "Report on Television," Sept. 30, 1953;
Grant Advertising Agency, "Preliminary Analysis for the Walt Disney Show,"
Oct. 26, 1953.

11. Donn Tatum, interview by Richard Hubler, June 18, 1968, 1–4; Card Walker,
interview by Bob Thomas, May 23, 1973, 2–5. The story of Ryman's preparation
of the painting (with Walt's help) can be found in his interview by Jay Horan,
Nov. 9, 1992, 30–38. The most complete account of Walt Disney Productions'
move into television can be found in Christopher Anderson, *Hollywood TV: The
Studio System in the Fifties* (Austin, Tex., 1994), 133–55.

12. Thomas M. Pryor, "Disney to Enter TV Field in Fall," New York *Times,* Mar. 30,
1954; "Walt Disney Goes to Television," *Motion Picture Herald,* Apr. 10, 1954;
"The Disney Revolution," *Film Bulletin,* May 3, 1954. See also "Disney Stock
Soars," *Daily Variety,* Mar. 30, 1954. Many clippings on the Disney-ABC deal and
the studio's early television operation can be found in PS D20.

13. Unnamed Disney aide quoted in "Disney in TVland," *TV Guide,* Oct. 23–29, 6.
For a very smart discussion of the operational aesthetic, see Neil Harris, *Hum-
bug: The Art of P. T. Barnum* (Chicago, 1973), 56–57, 72–79. See PS D10 for
clippings on the *Disneyland* premiere.

14. Marjorie Thomas, "Walt Disney's Plans for TV," *Broadcasting-Telecasting,* Oct.
11, 1954, 97; ABC advertisement, *Variety,* Oct. 27, 1954, 37, 33. Many advertisement
clippings are in PS D20.

15. Bob Kinter to WD, Oct. 28, 1954, and George Romney to WD, Oct. 28, 1954, PS
D10; "ABC's Chest-Thumping as Trendex on 'Disneyland' Stirs Hope Anew,"
Variety, Nov. 3, 1954; "'Disneyland' Cops Sylvania TV Award," clipping, PS D20;
"Disney, Danny Thomas Each Cop Two Emmys," New York *World-Telegram and
Sun,* Mar. 8, 1955; "Year's Best TV Show," *Redbook,* June 1955; John Maynard, "TV
Gets the Disney Treatment," Los Angeles *Examiner,* Sept. 5, 1954; Bob Thomas,
"Great Future Show Business Plans Told by Human Dynamo," Los Angeles
Herald Express, Mar. 15, 1955; Hedda Hopper, "Disney the Great," Chicago *Trib-
une Magazine,* Jan. 30, 1955; Arthur Godfrey, quoted in "Growing Impact of the
Disney Art," *Newsweek,* Apr. 18, 1955, 62.

16. WD, quoted in "Televiewing and Listening In," New York *Daily News,* Dec. 13,
1951; Harold Heffernan, "Disney Use of TV Proves He's a Shrewd Producer,"
Long Island *Star and Journal,* Dec. 21, 1951; WD to Perce Pearce, April 19, 1951.

17. WD, "The Story Teller and the Educator," *Television Quarterly*, Spring 1957, 5.
18. WD, quoted in "Extraordinary Man in Extraordinary Age," *TV Guide*, Dec. 1957, 19; Martin/Miller interview, Reel 11, 36–37, Reel 9, 51–52, 58–62; WD, interview by Pete Martin, 1961, 36–37.
19. Tatum, Thomas interview, 14–15. On Disney's turn to westerns, see Anderson, *Hollywood TV*, 279–80; clippings in PS W7.
20. Anderson, *Hollywood TV*, 141.
21. Bill Davidson, "The Latter-Day Aesop," *TV Guide*, May 20, 1961, 9–11; NABRT, quoted in Lorraine Santoli, *The Official Mickey Mouse Club Book* (New York, 1995), 180.
22. Roy Disney, Walt Disney Productions Annual Report 1959, 5; Tatum, Thomas interview, 13–14.
23. Tatum, Thomas interview, 15–18; Walt Disney Productions Annual Report 1960, 2.
24. Walter Lowe, "Hollywood Follows Disney into TV," New York *Herald Tribune*, June 5, 1955.
25. "A Silver Anniversary for Walt and Mickey," *Life*, Nov. 2, 1953, 90.
26. On the diversifying Disney operation, see "The Disney Story: From Mickey Mouse to Buena Vista," *Motion Picture Herald*, Nov. 20, 1954, especially p. 34; "The Mouse That Turned to Gold," *Business Week*, July 9, 1955, 72–76; and "Growing Impact of the Disney Art," *Newsweek*, Apr. 18, 1955, 60–64. On *Twenty Thousand Leagues* campaign, see two-page advertisement, *Motion Picture Herald*, Nov. 20, 1954.
27. Roy Disney, quoted in Gordon, "Walt's Profit Formula," 1.
28. Gladys Erickson, "Dogs Have Their Day — Elite Greet Old Yeller," Chicago *American*, Dec. 17, 1957; William Michelfelder, "Dogs and Press Agents All Yell for Best, Noblest, Etc. Old Yeller," New York *World Telegram and Sun*, Nov. 20, 1957; Paul Rosenfeld, "Dogs Wag about Viewing Movie," Dallas *Times Herald*, Jan. 12, 1958.
29. Samuels, quoted in Vincent Canby, "Buena Vista — A Distributor with Built-In Exploitation," *Motion Picture Herald*, Nov. 20, 1954, 43. See also Card Walker, interview by Richard Hubler, July 2, 1968, 27–28.
30. See John Crosby, "Music Is Saving Virtue of Disney's 'Tchaikovsky Story,'" Seattle *Times*, Feb. 5, 1959; Jack Gould, "TV: 'Sleeping Beauty,'" New York *Times*, Jan. 31, 1959; Maltin, *Disney Films*, 293–94; John G. West, *Disney Live-Action Productions* (Milton, Wash., 1994), 101–4, 207–9, 116–17, 164–66; Tietyen, *Musical Worlds of Walt Disney*, 124.
31. "Walt's Profit Formula," 12. For stories on Disney's forging of corporate links through television, see "Disneyland," *Automotive News*, Oct. 18, 1954; "How ABC-TV Promotes a Promotion Natural," *Tide*, Oct. 23, 1954; "Commercials by Disney," *Tide*, Nov. 20, 1954; "Reynolds Metals Making $7 Million Splurge on ABC-TV," *Hollywood Reporter*, Sept. 5, 1958; many other clippings in PS D17, D16, and W7.
32. WD, quoted in Bob Thomas, "Burst of Color: Disney Enthusiastic about TV," Pratt, Kan., *Daily Tribune*, Jan. 21, 1961. See also Joseph Kaselow, "Disney Bares Secrets to Tout Color," New York *Herald Tribune*, Sept. 9, 1961; "RCA Color TV Sales Up 166 Pct.," *Hollywood Reporter*, Apr. 12, 1962; many other clippings in PS W10.

33. Ernest Dichter, *The Strategy of Desire* (Garden City, N.Y., 1960), 263; WD, "Can TV Save the Movies?" 17; WD, "Industry Is Prepared to Provide Better Shows," Yuma, Ariz., *Sun and Sentinel,* Dec. 27, 1957.

34. Walt Disney Productions Annual Reports, FY 1950 to FY 1959.

35. "The Mouse That Turned to Gold," 72. See also "Less Animation," *Forbes,* Aug. 1, 1959, 20–21; "How Walt Disney Sells Fairy Tales," *Tide,* Mar. 2, 1951, 40–43; "He'll Double as a Top-Notch Salesman," *Business Week,* Mar. 21, 1953, 43–44; "Another Bright Showing in Earnings in View for Walt Disney Productions," *Barron's,* May 19, 1958, 23–24.

36. Roland E. Lindbloom, "Disney TV Premiere Hard to Take," Newark *Evening News,* Oct. 28, 1954; "TV Last Night: Free Commercials Mar Disney's Show," New York *Mirror,* Apr. 4, 1957; Harry Harris, "Disney Spiels, Critic Squeals," Philadelphia *Inquirer,* Sept. 13, 1957; Bob Williams, "Around the Dials: Mouseketeers 'Persuade' Walt Disney," Philadelphia *Bulletin,* Sept. 12, 1957; "Growing Impact of the Disney Art," *Newsweek,* Apr. 18, 1955, 62–63.

37. Hal Humphrey, "Disney in Hard Sell for Color," Los Angeles *Mirror,* Sept. 23, 1961; "Disney Sells Color Sets," *Hollywood Reporter,* Sept. 25, 1961; Fred Danzig, "Disney 'World of Color' Had Raucous, Hard-Sell Format," Beverly Hills *Citizen,* Sept. 25, 1961; Mrs. Verna Jayka, letter to the editor, Los Angeles *Examiner,* Oct. 1, 1961; "Walt Disney's Wonderful World of Color," *Variety,* Sept. 26, 1961.

38. Tatum, Thomas interview, 6. See also Walker, Hubler interview, and Thomas interview. On Peter Ellenshaw's emergence at the studio, see his American Film Institute lecture, Nov. 12, 1979, DA; Paul M. Sammon, "Peter Ellenshaw: An Effects Legend Crowns His Brilliant Career," *Cinefantastique* (Spring 1980), 84–93.

39. Bill Walsh, interview by Bob Thomas, May 23, 1973, 1–2, 4–5. Information on Walsh's career also comes from Nolie Walsh Fishman, interview by the author, July 2, 1996; Bill Walsh, interview by Richard Hubler, Apr. 30, 1968; Bill Walsh, interview by Christopher Finch and Linda Rosenkrantz, June 27, 1972, 1–2; Bill Walsh, interview by Leonard Shannon, Apr. 9, 1974; "Bill Walsh — A Moviemaker Who Believes in Teamwork," *Motion Picture Herald,* Apr. 3, 1968, 2.

40. Walsh, Hubler interview, 2; Walsh, Thomas interview, 8–9; Walsh, Finch and Rosenkrantz interview, 3; Walsh, Shannon interview, 3–4.

41. Bill Walsh, "Disney TV Show" memorandum, June 17, 1953, 1–9.

42. Ibid., 1, 3–4, 6; Bill Walsh to WD, Aug. 6, 1953, 1–2.

43. Walsh, Hubler interview, 2; Walsh, Finch and Rosenkrantz interview, 3–4.

44. Walsh, Thomas interview, 9–10; Walsh, Shannon interview, 7–8.

45. Walsh, Thomas interview, 15–16; Walsh, Finch and Rosenkrantz interview, 5–6; Walsh, Hubler interview, 5; Walsh, "The Mickey Mouse Club Children's TV Show: General Format Notes and Preliminary Structure," in *The Mickey Mouse Club Scrapbook,* Keith Keller, comp. (New York, 1975), 20–25.

46. Walsh, Thomas interview, 17–18; Walsh, Shannon interview, 10. On Walsh's role in *The Mickey Mouse Club,* see Sidney Miller, interview by Lorraine Santoli, 1993, 6.

47. Walsh, Thomas interview, 6–7.

48. See "Bill Walsh — A Moviemaker," 2, and David Iwerks interview.

49. Ellenshaw interview; Walsh, Thomas interview, 19–20. See also author's interviews with Fess Parker, David Iwerks, John Hench, and Nolie Walsh Fishman.

50. David Iwerks interview; Kimball, Canemaker interview, 7–8.
51. Parker interview. On WD's high regard for Walsh, see Ellenshaw interview; Martin/Miller interview, Reel 10, 21; WD to Robert Stevenson, Nov. 28, 1961.
52. Walsh, Hubler interview, 9–11; Walsh, Thomas interview, 14, 16.
53. Fishman interview; Kimball, Canemaker interview, 7–8; Miller, Santoli interview, 17–18.
54. Walsh, Thomas interview, 18–19.
55. Walker, Thomas interview, 22–23.

20. The Happiest Place on Earth

1. I am indebted to the following works: Warren Susman, "Did Success Spoil the United States?" in May, Recasting America, 19–37; Karal Ann Marling, "Disneyland 1955," American Art 5 (Winter/Spring 1991), 169–201; Marling, "Disneyland, 1955" in As Seen on TV: The Visual Culture of Everyday Life in the 1950s (Cambridge, Mass., 1994), 87–126; George Lipsitz, "The Making of Disneyland," in William Graebner, ed., True Stories from the American Past (New York, 1993), 179–96; Judith A. Adams, "The Disney Transformation," in The American Amusement Park Industry (Boston, 1991), 87–105; Margaret J. King, "Disneyland and Walt Disney World," Journal of Popular Culture (Summer 1981), 116–40; John Findlay, "Disneyland," in Magic Lands: Western Cityscapes and American Culture after 1940 (Berkeley, 1992), 52–116.
2. Martin/Miller interview, Reel 9, 67–70; Ruth Disney Beecher, interview by Bob Thomas, Nov. 4, 1974, 30; Wilfred Jackson, interview by David R. Smith, May 14, 1971, 9–10; Ben Sharpsteen, interview by Don Peri, Feb. 7, 1975, 4–6.
3. See WD to W. L. Stensgaard, Nov. 29, 1951; Harper Goff, interview by Jay Horan, Sept. 21, 1982, 27–34; WD, memo for Dick Kelsey, Aug. 31, 1948, 1–3; "Studio Seeks Permit for Amusement Center," Hollywood Citizen-News, Mar. 28, 1952.
4. See Joe Fowler, interview by Bob Thomas, March 20, 1973, 7; Ken Anderson, Bill Cottrell, and Herb Ryman, interview by Jay Horan, Sept. 15, 1983, 65–66; Dick Irvine, interview by Bob Thomas, April 24, 1973, 11–12, 18–19.
5. Fowler, Thomas interview, 18–21.
6. Kinney, Walt Disney and Other Characters, 176. See also Fowler, Thomas interview, 18; Irvine, Thomas interview, 20–21.
7. Findlay, Magic Lands, 62.
8. Ray Parker, "Disneyland, a Fabulous Giant at 2 Years," Los Angeles Herald Express, July 17, 1957; Robert Cahn, "The Intrepid Kids of Disneyland," Saturday Evening Post, June 28, 1958, 118. See also Roger Broggie, interview by Jay Horan, 188–89; Joe Fowler, interview by Jay Horan, Mar. 12, 1984, 25–26.
9. "Nixon in Disneyland," Los Angeles Herald Express, Aug. 11, 1955; "King Visits Disneyland, Sneaks Back Incognito," Eugene, Ore., Register Guard, Dec. 4, 1957; "Trumans Join Disneyland Fun," Los Angeles Examiner, Nov. 3, 1957; Martin A. Sklar, Walt Disney's Disneyland (New York, 1974).
10. On the "weenie" concept, see Irvine, Thomas interview, 2–6. On the Main Street architecture, see Anderson, Cottrell, and Ryman, Horan interview, 64.
11. Davis, Thomas interview, 21; "Disneyland," McCall's, Jan. 1955, 8; "Kid's Dream World Comes True," Popular Science Monthly, Aug. 1955, 92; Woodrow Wirsig, "Disneyland," Women's Home Companion, June 1954, 12; Aubrey Menen, "Daz-

zled in Disneyland," in Leo Hamalian, ed., *In Search of Eden* (New York, 1965), 317.

12. Davis, Thomas interview, 23. See also Dick Irvine, interview by Richard Hubler, May 14, 1968, 26.

13. *Your Disneyland: A Guide for Hosts and Hostesses* (1955) and *You're on Stage at Disneyland* (1962). On Disneyland University, see Van Arsdale France, *Window on Main Street: Thirty-five Years of Creating Happiness at Disneyland Park* (Nashua, N.H., 1991).

14. Bill Walsh, "Disney TV Show Memo," 3; "How to Make a Buck," *Time*, July 29, 1957, 76; WD, quoted in Schickel, *The Disney Version*, 313.

15. Walt Disney Productions Annual Report 1959, 12–13.

16. "Dateline Disneyland," July 17, 1955, ABC; Findlay, *Magic Lands*, 92.

17. James W. Rouse, "The Regional Shopping Center: Its Role in the Community It Serves," Apr. 26, 1963, 2. See also J. S. Hamel, "Disneyland: Engineering for Amusement," *Consulting Engineer*, Feb. 1956, n.p.; Tom McHugh, "Walt Disney's Mechanical Wonderland," *Popular Mechanics*, Nov. 1957, 138–43; Ernst Behrendt, "Plastic House," *Popular Science*, Apr. 1956, 144–46, 262.

18. WD, quoted in Hedda Hopper, "Dream of Disneyland Still Being Realized," Los Angeles *Times*, July 9, 1957; WD, quoted in Anderson, Cottrell, and Ryman, Horan interview, 64.

19. WD, quoted in "Welcome to Disneyland," Los Angeles *Times*, July 15, 1955; "Disneyland," *Life*, Aug. 15, 1955, 42; "What Goes on Here," *Woman's Day*, June 1957, 5; "The Land That Does Away with Time," *Better Homes and Gardens*, Feb. 1956, 62–63.

20. *Disneyland Holiday* (Spring 1957), 1–16; "Fashions in Fantasy," *Los Angeles Examiner's Pictorial Living*, Oct. 30, 1955. Dozens of travel articles on Disneyland can be found in PS D4, D5, and D6.

21. Gordon, "Walt's Formula," *Wall Street Journal*, 3. See also Phil Seitz, "Disneyland," *Advertising Requirements*, Jan. 1956, 31–34; "For Big Advertisers: New Wonderland," *Printer's Ink*, July 1955, 24–27; "Disneyland Issue," *The Westerner*, Aug. 1955.

22. "Disneyland Inc. . . . It Is a Small World at Disneyland: A Report to Exhibitors and Lessees, June 1, 1959, 9; Gladwyn Hill, "Disneyland Reports on Its First Ten Million," New York *Times*, Feb. 2, 1958; Gladwyn Hill, "The Never-Never Land Khrushchev Never Saw," New York *Times*, Oct. 4, 1959; Arthur Gordon, "Walt Disney," *Look*, July 26, 1955, 29.

23. Menen, "Dazzled in Disneyland," 314, 320; Kevin Wallace, "The Engineering of Ease," *New Yorker*, Sept. 7, 1963, 129.

24. Julian Halevy, "Disneyland and Las Vegas," *Nation*, June 7, 1958, 510–13; Ray Bradbury, "Not Child Enough," *Nation*, June 28, 1958, 570; Ray Bradbury, "The Machine-Tooled Happyland," *Holiday*, Oct. 1965, 100–104.

25. Rolly Charest, "Disney Made Fortune Out of Hobby," Boston *Traveler*, July 4, 1955; Walsh, Thomas interview, 13–14.

26. Kimball, Hubler interview, 21; WD to Mrs. Max Hill, Dec. 1, 1961.

27. Robert De Roos, "The Magic Worlds of Walt Disney," *National Geographic*, Aug. 1963, 158–207; Ira Wolfert, "Walt Disney's Magic Kingdom," *Reader's Digest*, Apr. 1960, 144–47; "Disneyland," *Life*, Aug. 15, 1955; Phil Santora, "Disney: Modern Merlin," New York *Daily News*, Sept. 29 and 30, Oct. 1 and 2, 1964.

28. WD, quoted in Adela Rogers St. John, "Walt Disney Gambles," *American Weekly*, May 1, 1955, 18.

29. WD, "Teamwork: A Way of Life in Disneyland," *Little Leaguer*, Mar. 1955, 9; WD, interview by Pete Martin, 1961, 38–39.

30. J. P. McEvoy, "McEvoy in Disneyland," *Reader's Digest*, Feb. 1955, 25; Claude Coats, interview by Jay Horan, Dec. 14, 1982, 42.

31. Bill Anderson, Thomas interview, 32–33; Hibler, Thomas interview, 22; Fowler, Horan interview, 10, 23–24.

32. Lillian Disney, Hubler interview, 12; Lillian Disney, Thomas interview, 10–11; Sharon Lund, interview by Richard Hubler, July 9, 1968, 15.

33. Diane Miller, Hubler interview, 38, 15; Edna Disney, Hubler interview, 16–17; "Small Fry World Fires Up Disney," *Mirror News*, Apr. 29, 1954, clipping, PS D11.

34. Lillian Disney, Thomas interview, 10–11; Diane Miller, Hubler interview, 40, 20, 41; Lillian Disney and Diane Miller, Martin/Miller interview, Reel 9, 6–10.

35. Diane Miller, Martin/Miller interview, Reel 13, 4–5; Thomas, Thomas interview, 9; Ken Anderson, Thomas interview, 22.

36. David Iwerks interview; Huemer, "Thumbnail Sketches," 39; Walker, Hubler interview, 7; Tatum, Hubler interview, 25–26; Bill Anderson, Thomas interview, 20; Ken Anderson, Thomas interview, 26–27.

37. Diane Miller, Hubler interview, 16; Harry Tytle, interview by Richard Hubler, Mar. 5, 1968, 31; John Hench, interview by the author, July 2, 1996.

38. WD, quoted in Harry Harris, "Walt Disney Helps Santa the Year Around," *Philadelphia Inquirer's TV Programs*, Dec. 22, 1957, 2; Martin/Miller interview, Reel 10, 23–24.

39. Martin/Miller interview, Reel 11, 42, Reel 9, 65, Reel 10, 18–19; WD, interview by Pete Martin, 1961, Reel 1, 18–19.

40. Martin/Miller interview, Reel 10, 32; Ryman, Horan interview, 61–62; Hibler, Hubler interview, 11.

41. Kimball, "Wonderful World of Walt Disney," 272; Anderson, Cottrell, and Ryman, Horan interview, 26; Irvine, Thomas interview, 42; Martin/Miller interview, Reel 10, 405, Reel 9, 69–70.

42. Marc Davis, quoted in Thomas, *Walt Disney*, 305; Fowler, Thomas interview, 30; Ryman, Horan interview, 68.

21. Pax Disneyana

1. "Freedom Foundation Award," *The Disney World*, Apr. 1963, n.p.; "President Says Walt Is Creator of Folk Lore at Medal Presentation," *The Disney World*, Oct.–Nov. 1964, n.p.; Bill Davidson, "The Fantastic Walt Disney," *Saturday Evening Post*, Nov. 7, 1964, 71. Among a host of 1960s articles on Disney and his growing influence, see Ira Wolfert, "Walt Disney's Magic Kingdom," *Reader's Digest*, Apr. 1960, 144–52; "Wide World of Walt Disney," *Newsweek*, Dec. 31, 1962, 48–51; Stephen Birmingham, "Greatest One-Man Show on Earth," *McCall's*, July 1964, 98–101, 121.

2. Thomas, *Walt Disney*, 279.

3. See Maltin, *The Disney Films*, 157–59, for a shrewd assessment of *The Shaggy Dog*'s impact on subsequent Disney films.

4. Clyde Gilmour, "Boy-Pooch Tackles Atomic Spies," Toronto *Telegram*, Mar. 26,

1959; Hazel Flynn, "Destroyers of America," Beverly Hills *Citizen*, Sept. 23, 1958. For many more reviews of the movie, see PS S9.

5. For the best account of the making of *Mary Poppins*, see John G. West, Jr., *The Disney Live-Action Productions* (Milton, Wash., 1994), 139–55.

6. On the promotional campaign for *Mary Poppins*, see Leonard Sloane, "Advertising: Mary Poppins Fad Designed," New York *Times*, July 24, 1964; "Big Products Tieup for 'Mary Poppins,'" *Box Office*, Aug. 17, 1964; clippings in PS M24.

7. Mae Tinee, "Disney Has Formula for 'Family' Movies," Chicago *Tribune*, June 28, 1964; Ernest Rogers, "It Lacks Everything, But It's a Delight," Atlanta *Journal*, Oct. 28, 1964; "MP Review — Walt Disney's 'Mary Poppins.'" *Hollywood Close-Up*, Sept. 24, 1964; "Walt Disney's Magic Formula," New York *Times*, Nov. 4, 1964; "Julie Andrews Goes to Hollywood," *Look*, Nov. 19, 1963, 123–25; C. Robert Jennings, "The Star Who Thinks He Isn't," *Ladies' Home Journal*, Oct. 1963, 78. For a host of favorable reviews, see PS M22, M24, M25, and M26.

8. Bill Vaughan, "Here's a Movie to Waste an Evening With," Kansas City *Star*, Nov. 29, 1964; Mac St. Johns, "Editorial," Hollywood *Reporter*, Sept. 11, 1964; Judith Crist, "Mary Poppins: Magic Casements," New York *Herald Tribune*, Sept. 9, 1964.

9. Dr. Max Rafferty, "The Greatest Pedagogue of Them All," Los Angeles *Times*, Apr. 19, 1965.

10. Frances Clark Sayers, letter, Los Angeles *Times*, Apr. 25, 1965.

11. "Walt Disney Accused: An Interview with Frances Clark Sayers Conducted by Charles M. Weisenberg," *FM and Fine Arts*, Aug. 1965, 4–11.

12. Whitney Balliett, quoted in John E. Fitzgerald, "The Controversial Kingdom of Walt Disney," *U.S. Catholic*, Aug. 1964, 17–18; Donald Barr, "The Winnowing of Pooh," *Book Week*, Oct. 31, 1965, 2, 42; Peter and Dorothy Bart, "As Told and Sold by Disney," *New York Times Book Review*, May 9, 1965, 2, 32–34.

13. Letters to the editor, Los Angeles *Times*, May 1, 1965.

14. Sayers, "Walt Disney Accused," 11.

15. For useful information on the birth and evolution of WED, see Walt Disney Imagineering: Historical File, DA, and Walt Disney Productions Proxy Statement, Feb. 2, 1965, 5–9, DA.

16. On WD's attention to WED and the important issue of licensing his name, see Walker, Thomas interview, 24; Cottrell, Horan interview, 67, 73; 1965 Proxy Statement, 6.

17. Roger Broggie, interview by Jay Horan, Nov. 22, 1983, 113–14; Ken Anderson, Thomas interview, 26–29. See also "Imagineering: Audio-Animatronics at the Fair," *Compressed Air Magazine*, June 1964, 7.

18. See Bob McGrath, "From Dream to Reality," Walt Disney Imagineering: Historical File, 3–4, DA; Randy Bright, *Disneyland: The Inside Story* (New York, 1987), 171–73.

19. WED press release, quoted in Schickel, *The Disney Version*, 335; WD, interview by Fletcher Markle, Sept. 25, 1963, reprinted in Kathy M. Jackson, *Walt Disney: A Bio-Bibliography* (Westport, Conn., 1993), 130–34.

20. WD, Markle interview, 133–34.

21. WD, quoted in Paul F. Anderson, "A Great Big Beautiful Tomorrow," *Persistence of Vision* 6–7 (1995), 30–31. My account of Disney's involvement in the World's Fair relies heavily on Anderson's impeccably researched and incredibly detailed

work, which is based on dozens of interviews with Disney personnel and on extensive research.

22. "Edison Square: Disneyland, U.S.A.," WED Proposal to General Electric, 1958, 4–26, DA.

23. Anderson, "Great Big Beautiful Tomorrow," 63. See also "Imagineering: General Electric Company," *Compressed Air Magazine*, July 1964, 16–18; "General Electric," *Cue*, May 8 and May 22, 1965; James L. Hicks, Jr., "The Hit of the Fair: GE's Progressland '65," New York *Amsterdam News*, June 5, 1965. See also WED's World's Fair Scrapbooks 1A, 2A, 3A, and 4A, DA.

24. Anderson, "Great Big Beautiful Tomorrow," 68–69, 80–82.

25. Ibid., 32–58; "Imagineering: Ford Motor Company," *Compressed Air Magazine*, Sept. 1964, 20–22.

26. Anderson, "Great Big Beautiful Tomorrow," 99–108; "Imagineering: Pepsi-Cola Company," *Compressed Air Magazine*, Aug. 1964, 10–11. On Mary Blair's career at the Disney Studio, see Canemaker, *Before the Animation Begins*, 115–42.

27. Anderson, "Great Big Beautiful Tomorrow," 98.

28. "Fun in New York," *Time*, May 1, 1964, 40–41; Vernon Scott, "Magician of Disneyland Has Outdone Himself," clipping, WED Scrapbook A1, DA; Charles Goodman, "It's a Big, Beautiful Fair in New York," San Jose *Times*, Sept. 2, 1964; "Exhibits at Fair Praised by YW Viewers," Newburyport, Mass., *News*, Aug. 31, 1964; Robert Alden, "Illinois Received Payment from Fair," New York *Times*, Sept. 3, 1965.

29. WD, quoted by Irvine, Hubler interview.

30. "Mineral King Diary," n.d. [1967], Mineral King file, 1–15, DA.

31. For background information on the Cal Arts project, see Harrison A. Price, "A Historical Summary of California Institute of the Arts," July 13, 1967, Cal Arts box, 1–3, DA; Hubler, "Walt Disney," 743–53; Watkin, "Walt Disney," 652–64; Thomas, *Walt Disney*, 329–32.

32. WD, quoted in California Institute of the Arts statement, Jan. 5, 1977, Cal Arts box, DA; WD, quoted in Hubler, "Walt Disney," 745–46; WD, quoted in Thomas, *Walt Disney*, 331–32; WD, "The Valuator Interviews: Walt Disney," *Valuator*, Summer 1966, 12; T. Hee, paraphrase of WD's comments in Hubler, "Walt Disney," 749.

33. WD to William L. Pereira, May 13, 1960, Chouinard-City of the Arts file, DA.

34. Martin/Miller interview, Reel 12, 1; "Valuator Interviews," 12; WD, quoted in Anderson, Cottrell, and Ryman, Horan interview 28.

35. W. Ward Marsh, "Disney Studio Now Humming with Feature Film Activity," Cleveland *Plain Dealer*, May 16, 1948; Martin/Miller interview, Reel 12, 1.

36. WD, quoted in Roy Disney to L. W. Hills, Jan. 11, 1967, in Cal Arts box, DA. Diane Miller, Hubler interview, relates her father's bequest to Cal Arts. On the publicity blitz for Cal Arts, see Christy Fox, "Disney Spirit Animates L.A. Culture Project," Los Angeles *Times*, Aug. 2, 1964.

37. Florida press conference transcript, Nov. 15, 1965, DA.

38. John Hench, interview by Randy Bright and Beth Black, Dec. 19, 1974, 1–2; Fowler, Thomas interview, 42.

39. On these feasibility studies, see Harrison A. Price, "The Theme Park Comes of Age," Nov. 15, 1971, 3–4, DA.

40. See Joe Fowler, interview by Jay Horan, Mar. 12, 1984, 43–46; Walker, Thomas

interview, 29–36; Marvin Davis, "Disney Planned a City," *SM: Sales Meeting Magazine,* July 1969, 84–85; Thomas, *Walt Disney,* 334–38.

41. Hench, Bright and Black interview, 2.
42. WD, "Walt's EPCOT Film," 1966, DA; Fowler, Thomas interview, 54; Marvin Davis, interview by Richard Hubler, May 28, 1968, 27–28, 25.
43. "Walt's EPCOT Film."

22. *It's a Small World, After All*

1. John Hench, interview by the author, July 2, 1996, 31–32. Another long-time studio insider, who wishes to remain anonymous, confirmed this story.
2. For biographical details, see Roy Disney, interviews by Richard Hubler on Feb. 20 and June 18, 1968; Roy E. Disney interview; Steve Fiott, "A Sincere Tribute to Roy Oliver Disney," *Storyboard: The Journal of Animation Art,* Sept.–Oct. 1994, 6–17.
3. Quoted in John McDonald, "Walt Disney: Turning a Career of Art and Business Around an Imaginary Game," in John McDonald, *The Game of Business* (Garden City, N.Y., 1977), 235. On the brothers' clashes, see Bill Cottrell, interview by Jay Horan, Aug. 10, 1983, 40; Martin/Miller interview, Reel 10, 36; Roy Disney, Hubler interview, 24–25; Roy Disney to Arthur McKeogh, Apr. 2, 1935.
4. Martin/Miller interview, Reel 9, 55–56. See also J. P. McEvoy, "McEvoy in Disneyland," *Reader's Digest,* Feb. 1955, 23; Roy Disney, Hubler interview, 32–33.
5. Roy Disney to Arnold Stoltz, June 21, 1951; Roy Disney, quoted in France, *Window on Main Street,* 31. See also Walker, Thomas interview, 9, 18–20; Fowler, Thomas interview, 57; Tatum, Thomas interview, 6.
6. Roy Disney, Hubler interview, 32–33; Roy E. Disney interview, 17–18; Steve Fiott, "Tribute to Roy Disney," 14.
7. Kimball, Hubler interview, 36; Roy E. Disney interview, 3; Lillian Disney, Thomas interview, 2. See also Culhane, *Talking Animals,* 140; David Iwerks interview; Hench interview, 31–33.
8. Walt Disney, Big Brothers speech, 1957, 6; Martin/Miller interview, Reel 11, 24, Reel 10, 9–10, Reel 6, 49, Reel 1, 55–57, Reel 9, 43; WD, quoted in "The Wonderful World of Walt Disney," *Catholic Preview of Entertainment,* June 1957, 6.
9. Roy Disney, Hubler interview, 16, 21–22, 25, 21; Roy Disney, quoted by Sharpsteen, Peri interview, Feb. 6, 1974, 15–16; Roy Disney, quoted in Arthur Gordon, "Walt Disney," *Look,* July 26, 1955, 34; Roy Disney, quoted in Cottrell, Horan interview, 40. For a distillation of his attitude toward Walt, see Roy Disney, "Unforgettable Walt Disney," *Reader's Digest,* Feb. 1969, 212–18.
10. Roy Disney, quoted in "Disney's Live-Action Profits," *Business Week,* July 24, 1965, 82. On his politics, see Roy Disney, Hubler interview, 14–15; Roy E. Disney interview, 25; Marc and Alice Davis interview, 34; Parker interview, 12.
11. Mike Barrier, "Silly Stuff: An Interview with Hugh Harman," *Graffiti,* Spring 1984, 11; Culhane, *Talking Animals,* 140–41; Roy E. Disney interview, 12–13; Roy Disney, Hubler interview, 33–34.
12. Marc and Alice Davis interview, 37–41; Roy E. Disney interview 16, 21–22.
13. Roy Disney, quoted in "The Wide World of Walt Disney," *Newsweek,* Dec. 31, 1962, 49. See also descriptions of Roy's role in "Mickey Mouse and the Bankers," *Fortune,* Nov. 1934, 94; "TV Show Called Disney Film Aide," *Independent Film*

Journal, Jan. 22, 1955; Murray Horowitz, "Roy Disney Says: Integration of TV, Theatrical Films Logical," *Motion Picture Daily*, Mar. 8, 1955.

14. "Disney's Live-Action Profits," *Business Week*, July 24, 1965, 78–82. See also Gordon, "Walt's Profit Formula," 1, 3; Louis J. Rolland, "The World of Disney," *Financial World*, Apr. 27, 1966, 24; "The Brothers Un-Grim," *Forbes*, Feb. 15, 1964, 38–39.

15. WD, Florida press conference transcript, 2. On the disagreement over how to proceed with the Florida Project, see Roy E. Disney interview, 18–19.

16. "Disney Dollars," *Forbes*, May 1, 1971, 20–21. See also Joe Potter, interview by Jay Horan, Mar. 7, 1984, 54; Hench interview, 32–33.

17. Roy Disney, quoted in Hench interview, 32.

18. Hench interview, 24.

19. For biographical details, see Hench, Hubler interview; Hench, Thomas interview, n.d., n.p.; Hench, Horan interview; Hench, Bright and Black interview; John Hench, interview by Gabe Essoe, Apr. 13, 1972; "'Another Kind of Reality': An Interview with John Hench," *The "E" Ticket*, Winter 1993–94, 16–25; Charlie Haas, "Disneyland Is Good for You," *New West*, Dec. 4, 1978, 13–19; A. Eisen, "Two Disney Artists," *Crimmer's*, Winter 1975, 35–44.

20. Hench interview, 4.

21. Hench interview, 25–26; "Another Kind of Reality," 16–23.

22. See Haas, "Disneyland Is Good for You," 16–19; "Another Kind of Reality," 17, 20–24; Hench interview, 5–10.

23. Hench, Essoe interview, 6; Hench, Horan interview, 20. See also "Another Kind of Reality," 17, 19, 23–24; Haas, "Disneyland Is Good for You," 18–19.

24. Hench, Essoe interview, 1; Hench, Thomas interview; "Another Kind of Reality," 18–19; Hench and Irvine, Hubler interview, 2–3.

25. Hench, quoted in "Two Disney Artists," 37; Hench, Hubler interview, 21; Hench, Horan interview, 61, 71.

26. Hench interview, 11; Hench, quoted in "Two Disney Artists," 36–37; Hench, Horan interview, 64, 62, 57–59; Haas, "Disneyland Is Good for You," 17.

27. Hench, quoted in "Two Disney Artists," 37; Haas, "Disneyland Is Good for You," 16–17; Hench interview, 11–12.

28. Haas, "Disneyland Is Good for You," 18–19, 16; Hench, Horan interview, 57–58, 64, 40.

29. Hench, quoted in "Two Disney Artists," 36; Hench, Hubler interview, 22; Hench interview, 14–15; Hench, Horan interview, 17.

30. Hench, Bright and Black interview, 5–6; Hench, Hubler interview, 15; Hench interview, 30.

31. Hench interview, 30.

32. WD, quoted in Norma Lee Browning, "Disney's Future World Is Soon to Come," Chicago *Tribune*, Oct. 25, 1966; WD, Florida press conference, 19–20.

33. See Maltin, *The Disney Films*, 185–87, 196–98, 206–8, 238–39. Disney's satirization of the FBI caused an uproar at the agency; see Richard L. Trethewey, *Walt Disney: The FBI Files* (Pacifica, Calif., 1994), 172–223.

34. WD, "Walt's EPCOT Film"; Dick Nunis, quoted in "Walt Disney — The Real Man," *Storyboard*, Aug.–Sept. 1993, 16; WD, Florida press conference, 19; Potter, Horan interview, 30–32; Fowler, Horan interview, 62.

35. Among a vast literature, see Terence Ball, "The Politics of Social Science in

Postwar America," in May, *Recasting America*, 76–92; Barry Karl, *The Uneasy State: The United States from 1915 to 1945* (Chicago, 1983); Thomas P. and Agatha C. Hughes, eds., *Lewis Mumford: Public Intellectual* (New York, 1990); Ellis W. Hawley, "The Discovery and Study of 'Corporate Liberalism,'" *Business History Review* (Autumn 1978), 309–20.

36. Gov. Haydon Burns, Florida press conference, 22; Potter, Horan interview, 33–35.

37. Hench, Bright and Black interview, 7, 10. See also Fowler, Thomas interview, 48; Alan Bryman, *Disney and His Worlds* (London, 1995), 115–17.

38. WD, quoted in "Disney's Future World." For an eloquent warning about the political threat of the Florida Project, see Michael Harrington, "To the Disney Station: Corporate Socialism in the Magic Kingdom," *Harper's*, Jan. 1979, 35–44, 86.

39. Hench and Irvine, Hubler interview, 5; Marvin Davis, Hubler interview, 25.

40. WD, "Walt's EPCOT Film." See also Hench, Bright and Black interview, 6. The EPCOT eventually constructed bore little resemblance to Walt's original plan; see John Pastier, "The Incredible Shrinking Dream," *New West*, Dec. 4, 1978, 24–30.

Epilogue

1. On WD's treatments by Hazel George, see Thomas, Thomas interview, 30; Kahl, Thomas interview, 1. Walt's drinking did not veer into alcoholism, as biographers Leonard Mosely and Marc Eliot have argued. Although he often drank with enthusiasm, he did not allow it to interfere with his demanding work schedule. See Diane Disney Miller, Martin/Miller interview, Reel 13, 19–23, Reel 5, 1–3; Robert Perine, *Chouinard: An Art Vision Betrayed* (Encinitas, Calif., 1985), 165; Roland Crump, interview by John Canemaker, Jan. 5, 1995.

2. On Walt's deteriorating health, see Diane Disney Miller, Hubler interview; Johnston, Thomas interview, 13–15; Hibler, Thomas interview, 19–20; Tommie Wilck, interview by David R. Smith, Aug. 27, 1971.

3. Roy O. Disney, statement, Dec. 16, 1966, DA.

4. Eric Sevareid, "A Tribute to Walt Disney," broadcast Dec. 15, 1966, DA; KLAC Radio 570 interviews, Walt Disney Tribute, KLAC file, Dec. 15, 1966, DA; "End of a Torch Bearer," *Variety*, Dec. 21, 1966; John C. Waugh, "Walt Disney's World: Impact Etched Deeply," *Christian Science Monitor*, Dec. 17, 1966; Dwight D. Eisenhower, "Tribute to Walt," April 26, 1967, DA. See *Walt Disney: Showman to the World*, a twenty-volume series of scrapbooks, DA, for commentaries on Disney's death from all over the world.

5. Ken Anderson, interview by Paul Anderson, June 21, 1992. The story inside the Disney company is that when Schickel met with Walt in the early stages of his research, Walt was put off by his questions and refused to cooperate.

6. Schickel, *The Disney Version*, 12, 335. See also pp. 72–75, 84–86.

7. Ibid., 12–13, 339, 361–62, 18. On Schickel's coming of age in the radical atmosphere of the University of Wisconsin in the 1950s, see his "A Journalist Among Historians," in Paul Buhle, ed., *History and the New Left: Madison, Wisconsin, 1950–1970* (Philadelphia, 1990), 85–98.

8. Edmund Carpenter, "Very, Very Happy," *New York Times Book Review*, May 5, 1968, 5, 24; Katherine Gaus Jackson, "Books in Brief," *Harper's*, June 1968, 94–95;

Joseph Epstein, "Fantasia," *Commentary,* Sept. 1968, 102; Jane Gibson, "The Disney Version," *Commonweal,* July 12, 1968, 474; Peter Michelson, "What Disney Teaches," *New Republic* (July 6, 1968), 31–33.

9. "The Disney Version," *Saturday Review,* Sept. 6, 1969, 35; Henry Halpern, "The Disney Version," *Library Journal,* Apr. 15, 1968, 1650; John Allen, "Pop-Artist as King," *Christian Science Monitor,* May 23, 1968, 7; *Film Fan Monthly,* Sept. 1968, cover, 2, 3. I should note that the left/right division over Disney was often more complicated. Plenty of pot-smoking, antiwar hippies could be found flocking to showings of *Fantasia* in this era, while many cultural conservatives who defended high culture against the inroads of popular culture certainly expressed no fondness for Walt Disney.

10. In the 1990s, a steady stream of leftist academic analysts have deconstructed and denounced Disney for its treatment of race, class, and gender and its commercialism. See, for example, Eric Smoodin, ed., *Disney Discourse: Producing the Magic Kingdom* (New York, 1994); Elizabeth Bell, Lynda Haas, and Laura Sells, eds., *From Mouse to Mermaid: The Politics of Film, Gender, and Culture* (Bloomington, Ind., 1995); and Susan Willis, ed., "The World According to Disney," special issue of the *South Atlantic Quarterly* (Winter 1993).

11. Hibler, Hubler interview, 28.

Bibliographic Essay

The literature, both scholarly and popular, on Walt Disney and his enterprise is simply enormous. The notes for this text cite hundreds of primary source materials on various aspects of Disney's history, from his birth to the late 1960s. The general reader interested in pursuing particular topics, however, can turn to a number of useful publications.

Perhaps the best place to begin is with Kathy Merlock Jackson's *Walt Disney: A Bio-Bibliography* (Westport, Conn., 1993). This compilation offers a brief biography of the filmmaker, a reasonably complete listing of hundreds of articles, scholarly essays, and books on Disney that have appeared over the last six decades, a survey of Disney's impact on various aspects of media and popular culture, and extracts from a number of Walt's statements and interviews over the years. *Persistence of Vision,* a journal devoted to the history of Walt Disney and his enterprise, is edited by Paul F. Anderson in Salt Lake City, Utah, and offers an array of fascinating articles on every aspect of Disney's evolution from the 1920s to the present.

Those in search of biographies should begin with Bob Thomas's *Walt Disney: An American Original* (New York, 1976), a studio-sanctioned portrait by a veteran journalist. It is clearly written, factually accurate, and full of detail, if unquestioning in its favorable analysis. Leonard Mosely's *Disney's World: A Biography* (New York, 1985), while well written and decently, if unevenly, researched, suffers from a reliance on psychobabble and a tendency to embellish the facts in the interests of scandalmongering. Marc Eliot's *Walt Disney: Hollywood's Dark Prince* (New York, 1993) travels much farther down the road of tabloid-style biography. This unrelentingly hateful treatment is full of far-fetched accusations — Walt Disney is presented as, among other things, a raging alcoholic and abuser of drugs, a Nazi sympathizer, and a dabbler in incest — and offers little of value. Richard Schickel's *The Disney Version: The Life, Times, Art and Commerce of Walt Disney* (New York, 1968) in many ways remains the most thoughtful and provocative critique of Walt Disney's life and his enterprise. This brilliant, biting analysis reveals a great deal about Disney's relationship to modern American culture, but it displays an annoying condescension and overlooks many crucial artistic and political connections in its scathing indictment of Disney and his audience.

Richard L. Trethewey's *Walt Disney: The FBI Files* (Pacifica, Calif., 1994) presents a thorough, balanced analysis of Disney's much-ballyhooed FBI file, which has recently come to light under the Freedom of Information Act. It sensibly notes the largely honorary, superficial relationship between Walt and the Bureau over several decades. It also details the FBI's investigation of Disney and the tension between the two over the 1960s films *Moon Pilot* and *That Darn Cat.*

A number of books present useful surveys of Disney's artistic production over the decades. Leonard Maltin's *The Disney Films* (New York, 1973) is an indispensable guide to the subject, providing brief synopses of every Disney feature film made up to the date of publication, as well as sections on the studio's animated shorts and television productions. Robert Feild's *The Art of Walt Disney* (New York, 1942) offers one of the earliest evaluations of the Mickey Mouse factory, its production techniques, and its impact on modern art. Christopher Finch's *The Art of Walt Disney: From Mickey Mouse to the Magic Kingdom* (New York, 1973), a highly informative and lavishly illustrated volume, relies on archival research and a host of interviews with Disney staffers to trace the development of the studio's artistic output over many decades. Bob Thomas's *Disney's Art of Animation: From Mickey Mouse to Beauty and the Beast* (New York, 1991) leads the reader on a brief jaunt through the development of animation at the studio. John Canemaker and Robert E. Abrams's *Treasures of Disney Animation Art* (New York, 1982) brings to light dozens of the sketches, drawings, and watercolors from the Disney Archives that helped inspire the studio's animated movies for over fifty years. David Tietyen's *The Musical World of Walt Disney* (Milwaukee, 1990) surveys the hundreds of songs that constituted a crucial dimension of Disney films from the early shorts through *Fantasia* and *Mary Poppins* to the present.

The structure, workings, and production techniques of the Disney Studio have prompted several explorations of its evolution. Richard Holliss and Brian Sibley's *The Disney Studio Story* (New York, 1988) offers the most comprehensive treatment of the studio's history. Russell Merritt and J. B. Kaufman's *Walt in Wonderland: The Silent Films of Walt Disney* (Baltimore, 1993) provide a highly informative analysis of the making of the pre–Mickey Mouse animated films in Kansas City and Los Angeles in the 1920s. A well-researched, nicely written, and beautifully illustrated examination of the studio's inspirational artists over several decades — which is also full of revealing information about the workings of the fantasy factory — is John Canemaker's *Before the Animation Begins: The Art and Lives of Disney Inspirational Sketch Artists* (New York, 1996). Charles Solomon's *The Disney That Never Was: The Stories and Art from Five Decades of Unproduced Animation* (New York, 1995) opens another revealing window on studio life by examining a host of film projects that were developed but never finished or released.

Revealing "inside" views of the Disney Studio from longtime employees have appeared over the past couple of decades. Frank Thomas and Ollie Johnston's *Disney Animation: The Illusion of Life* (New York, 1981) is a huge book by two of Walt's nine old men that presents a comprehensive, fascinating explanation of the evolving techniques of Disney animation. This technical exposition, however, is interlaced with numerous sketches of the studio's key personnel and many fascinating stories of its everyday life. Jack Kinney's *Walt Disney and Assorted Other Characters: An Unauthorized Account of the Early Years at Disney* (New York, 1988) presents an irreverent, occasionally hilarious account of daily life at the studio from the 1930s through the 1950s, and is enhanced by the author's numerous caricatures and line drawings. Shamus Culhane's *Talking Animals and Other People* (New York, 1986) includes several informative vignettes about the Disney Studio in the 1930s. Dave Hand's *Memoirs* (Cambria, Calif., 1986), an account by Walt's production manager during the studio's golden age, and Bill Peet's *Autobiography* (Boston, 1989), a reminiscence by perhaps the most talented story man in the studio's history, provide firsthand descriptions of studio operations and personalities.

A number of interesting books focus on particular Disney productions and characters. Richard Holliss and Brian Sibley's *Snow White and the Seven Dwarfs and the Making of the Classic Film* (New York, 1987) and Martin Krause and Linda Witkowski's *Walt Disney's Snow White and the Seven Dwarfs: An Art in the Making* (New York, 1994) examine the creative process that produced this groundbreaking movie. John Culhane's *Walt Disney's Fantasia* (New York, 1983) draws on archival sources, both written and visual, to examine the making of Disney's most experimental film, while Ollie Johnston and Frank Thomas's *Walt Disney's Bambi: The Story and the Film* (New York, 1990) does the same for one of the studio's most beloved efforts. Johnston and Thomas also wrote *The Disney Villain* (New York, 1993), an illustrated look at the series of delightfully scary characters who have populated Disney films over the years.

A few Disney characters have come in for biographical treatments. The most famous inspired Richard Holliss and Brian Sibley's *Mickey Mouse: His Life and Times* (New York, 1986) and David Bain's *Mickey Mouse: Fifty Happy Years* (New York, 1977), two books that chart Mickey's career and explore the nature of his appeal. Flora O'Brien's *Walt Disney's Donald Duck: Fifty Years of Happy Frustration* (Tucson, 1984) and Marcia Blitz's *Donald Duck* (New York, 1979) look at the films and personality of the Disney Studio's most cantankerous star, while Flora O'Brien's *Walt Disney's Goofy* (Tucson, 1984) does the same for its most hilariously inept one. John Grant's *Encyclopedia of Walt Disney's Animated Characters* (New York, 1993) is a treasure for the Disney historian, with a description, analysis, and illustration of every character who has appeared in Disney animated films from the 1920s up to the present. Extended descriptions of the feature-length films are included, as are brief descriptions of the animated shorts.

Only a few books have explored the diversifying activities of Walt Disney and his studio after the end of the golden age. In *Donald Duck Joins Up: The Walt Disney Studio During World War II* (Ann Arbor, 1982), Richard Shale takes a close look at a neglected era of Disney history: the studio's mobilization to produce wartime training and propaganda films. One of the studio's biggest hits during the following decade has prompted extended treatments from Paul F. Anderson, in *The Davy Crockett Craze: A Look at the 1950's Phenomenon and Davy Crockett Collectibles* (Hillside, Ill., 1996) and Margaret King, in the unpublished dissertation "The Davy Crockett Craze: A Case Study in Popular Culture" (University of Hawaii, 1976). There is no book-length study of the Disney Studio's groundbreaking move into television in the 1950s, although most of the essential points of this important development can be found in Christopher Anderson's *Hollywood TV: The Studio System in the Fifties* (Austin, Texas, 1994). The fullest treatment of Disney's role in television over many years promises to be William Cotter's forthcoming *The Television World of Disney* (New York). Lorraine Santoli's *The Official Mickey Mouse Club Book* (New York, 1995), a book based on a host of interviews with the Mouseketeers and archival research, gives a thorough and delightful account of this popular children's show in the 1950s. While Leonard Maltin offers synopses and brief evaluations of the Disney Studio's live-action films of the 1950s and 1960s as part of *The Disney Films,* the only extended treatment of these movies, their making, and the key personnel involved is John G. West, Jr.'s *The Disney Live-Action Productions* (Milton, Wash., 1994).

Books on Disneyland are surprisingly rare, and they tend to come from company insiders. Martin A. Sklar, a longtime employee and close associate of Walt's, briefly outlines the process by which this fabulous amusement park was made and surveys its various "lands" in his *Walt Disney's Disneyland* (New York, 1966). Van Arsdale France's *Window on Main Street: Thirty-five Years of Creating Happiness at Disneyland Park* (Nashua, N.H., 1991) offers a charming memoir by the founder and head of Disneyland University, the training program for this fabulous amusement park. Randy Bright, who worked up through the ranks from college-student employee to high-ranking manager in the Disney organization, presents a lengthy chronicle of the park's history spiced with abundant photographs and numerous anecdotes in *Disneyland: Inside Story* (New York, 1987). More analytical treatments of this unique facility can be found in several articles and book chapters. The interested reader should consult the following: Karal Ann Marling, "Disneyland 1955," *American Art* 5 (Winter/Spring 1991), 169–201, and *As Seen on TV: The Visual Culture of Everyday Life in the 1950s* (Cambridge, Mass., 1994), 87–126; George Lipsitz, "The Making of Disneyland," in William Graebner, ed., *True Stories from the American Past* (New York, 1993), 179–96; Judith A. Adams, "The Disney Transformation," in *The American Amusement Park Industry* (Boston, 1991), 87–105; and John Findlay, *Magic Lands: Western Cityscapes and American Culture After 1940* (Berkeley, 1992), 52–116.

Disney's visionary expansion during the early to mid-1960s has inspired little in the way of lengthy treatments. A special double issue of the journal *Persistence of Vision* entitled "A Great Big Beautiful Tomorrow" (Salt Lake City, Utah, 1995), written by Paul F. Anderson, gives a wonderfully detailed account of the process by which Walt Disney and the WED staff created the many Disney attractions at the New York World's Fair. Richard Beard's *Walt Disney's Epcot Center: Creating the New Myth of Tomorrow* (New York, 1982) provides a lavishly illustrated, mythical, and uncritically favorable description that argues (rather unconvincingly) that the final version of EPCOT realized Walt's original vision. On the other side of the ledger, sharply critical evaluations of the Florida theme park can be found in Michael Wallace's "Mickey Mouse History: Portraying the Past at Disney World," in Warren Leon and Roy Rosensweig, eds., *History of Museums in the United States* (Urbana, Ill., 1989), and Michael Harrington's "To the Disney Station: Corporate Socialism in the Magic Kingdom," *Harper's* (January 1979), 35–44. For more analytical treatments, consult Judith Adams's "Walt Disney World Resort," in *The American Amusement Park Industry* (Boston, 1991), 137–61, and Margaret J. King's "Disneyland and Walt Disney World: Traditional Values in Futuristic Form," *Journal of Popular Culture* (Summer 1981), 116–40. Stephen M. Fjellman's *Vinyl Leaves: Walt Disney World and America* (Boulder, Col., 1992) presents a difficult, highly theoretical treatment of the Florida park. A forthcoming issue of *Persistence of Vision* titled "The Florida Project," based on an extensive battery of interviews and a great deal of archival digging by editor Paul F. Anderson, promises a more complete picture than we have ever had of Walt's plans for this project and the first stages of its creation.

Index